KAUTILYA'S ARTHASHASTRA

'Rare indeed is a study of political science and political theory that can reset how we understand politics. Mitra and Liebig have written such a remarkable book. Their brilliant analysis will most deservedly resurrect Kautilya and his stupendous *Arthashastra*. Kautilya is convincingly analysed as probably the first political economist and, along with Plato and Aristotle, among the first serious students of politics.... The *Arthashastra* should gain a central place in all political science.'
Bruce Bueno de Mesquita,
Julius Silver Professor and Professor of Politics, NYU

'Any discourse on politics and statecraft in India is incomplete without a reference to Kautilya. Generations of scholars around the world have constructed and in fact, deconstructed his foundational text on statecraft and found that across time and regions, the principles continue to be relevant. In this stellar contribution, Subrata Mitra and Michael Liebig add to the emerging thoughts among political scientists and practitioners in contemporary India and thinkers around the world. Mitra's concept of "re-use of the past" is in fact gaining greater relevance as the underlying relevance of modern day statecraft—be it in internal politics or diplomatic relations. The book is a must read for any person even remotely associated with contemporary politics.'
Vinod Rai, Head, panel of administrators,
Board of Control for Cricket in India (BCCI), and
former Comptroller and Auditor General of India

'In many ways India remains an inscrutable bundle of economic, social and political contradictions; yet, it embodies a fusion of "modern politics" and ancient "tradition" combining to make for the unique model that we know as "Indian democracy." Subrata Mitra and Michael Liebig bring to bear in this volume their deep insights, mastery over theory, and powerful analytical skills to explain the reasons why, in an admirably lucid fashion.... *Kautilya's* Arthashastra is a "must read" for anyone interested in the understanding of contemporary India.'
Iftekhar Ahmed Chowdhury, former Foreign Minister of Bangladesh

'Kautilya's *Arthashastra* is an amazing monument of ancient political science. "Artha" encompasses politics and economics. Kautilya deals not only with foreign policy in terms of his famous "circle of kings" (*rajamandala*), but also with public administration and jurisprudence. He is not interested in metaphysics but is a thorough realist. This present contemporary study highlights his importance for Indian political tradition.'
Dietmar Rothermund, Emeritus Professor of History, Heidelberg University

'India must understand its past ... in order to become modern. New research on India's globalization and citizen well-being demonstrates the significance of the ideational roots of Indian modernity. India assimilates from the West but internalizes the normative structure of governance in its own way. Kautilya is a critical source for understanding the Indian way. This book is pioneering work that will inspire further research on the re-discovery of India.'
Rahul Mukherji, Professor and Head, Department of Political Science, South Asia Institute, Heidelberg University

'Kautilya's relevance has been under-appreciated in the study of Indian politics. Mitra and Liebig's *tour de force* will set that right. In a volume of unprecedented scale and depth encompassing India's intellectual and strategic history, they bring out the profound contemporary impact of one of India's truly great political thinkers.'
Rajesh Basrur, Professor of International Relations, S. Rajaratnam School of International Studies, Nanyang Technological University, Singapore

'Mitra and Liebig explain how Kautilya's ancient wisdom influenced the evolution of political thought and governmental system of India far more than the world cares to acknowledge. A work of deep and passionate scholarship that takes you up the intellectual ladder.'
Duvvuri Subbarao, former Governor, Reserve Bank of India

'Subrata Mitra and Michael Liebig have made a signal contribution to the emergent discourse on Kautilya in the subcontinent and beyond. As India reconnects to its past, Mitra and Liebig steer away from romanticism and condescension towards the ancient sources of modern India to offer a compelling analysis of the relevance of Kautilya's *Arthashastra* in understanding contemporary India's politics and strategic culture. For anyone interested in a deeper appreciation of the internal and external orientation of a rising India, this book is a good place to start from.'
C. Raja Mohan, Director, Carnegie India, New Delhi

'This is an attempt on the part of two scholars of comparative politics to resurrect an ancient and venerable text from India on statecraft, and demonstrate its relevance for the contemporary politics of India and South Asia. The authors demonstrate a supple grasp of the subject, a keen awareness of historical context and an acute sensitivity to local political realities. This work should command a wide and diverse audience.'
Sumit Ganguly, Professor of Political Science and Rabindranath Tagore Chair in Indian Cultures and Civilizations, Indiana University, Bloomington

KAUTILYA'S ARTHASHASTRA
An Intellectual Portrait

The Classical Roots of Modern Politics in India

SUBRATA K. MITRA & MICHAEL LIEBIG

RUPA

Published by
Rupa Publications India Pvt. Ltd 2017
7/16, Ansari Road, Daryaganj
New Delhi 110002

Sales centres:
Bengaluru Chennai
Hyderabad Jaipur Kathmandu
Kolkata Mumbai Prayagraj

Copyright © Nomos Verlagsgesellschaft mbH & Co. KG

This edition published by arrangement with the original publisher.

The views and opinions expressed in this book are the author's own and the facts are as reported by them been verified to the extent possible, and the publishers are not in any way liable for the same.

All rights reserved.

No part of this publication may be reproduced, transmitted, or stored in a retrieval system, in any form or by any means, electronic, mechanical, photocopying, recording or otherwise, without the prior permission of the publisher.

P-ISBN: 978-81-291-4865-0
E-ISBN: 978-81-291-5153-7

Twelfth impression 2024

15 14 13 12

The moral right of the author has been asserted.

This edition is for sale in Indian Subcontinent only.

Printed in India

This book is sold subject to the condition that it shall not, by way of trade or otherwise, be lent, resold, hired out, or otherwise circulated, without the publisher's prior consent, in any form of binding or cover other than that in which it is published.

CONTENTS

Foreword — ix
A Note for Readers on Reading Kautilya's Arthashastra — xiii
Preface — xix
Introduction — xxiii

SECTION A
AN INTERPRETIVE EXPOSITION OF KAUTILYA'S *ARTHASHASTRA*

1. The Work and Its Author — 3
2. The *Arthashastra*'s Oral and Written Transmission — 9
3. A Methodological Approach to Kautilya's *Arthashastra* — 13
4. Kautilya's *Arthashastra* in the Context of Comparative Political Theory — 23
5. The Key Features of Kautilya's *Arthashastra* — 38
6. Paraphrase of Book I of the *Arthashastra*: The Ideal Ruler — 45
7. The Concept Cluster *Saptanga*: The Seven State Factors (*Prakriti*) — 74
8. The Seven *Prakriti* Constitutive of State Power — 98
9. The Concept Cluster *Shadgunya*: The Six Methods of Foreign Policy — 104
10. The Kautilyan Idea of Raison D'état — 116
11. The Concept Cluster *Upayas*: The Four Basic Methods of Politics — 127
12. Kautilya's Political Anthropology — 133
13. Kautilya's Assumption About Politics and the Theory of Political Realism — 142

SECTION B
KAUTILYA AND MODERN INDIA
A COMPLEX RESONANCE

1. Kautilya and Modern India: Methodological and Theoretical Approaches — 153
2. The Kautilyan Legacy Embedded in Longue Durée Cultural Continuity — 158
3. Kautilya's *Arthashastra* as an Endogenous Politico-Cultural Resource — 184
4. Nehru and Kautilya — 197
5. The Manifest Presence of Kautilyan Thought in Modern India — 236
6. The Latent Presence of Kautilyan Thought in Modern India — 252
7. Kautilya and the Strategic Culture of India — 296
8. A Distant Relationship: Kautilya and the Social and Political Sciences in India — 331
9. Trend Reversal: A 'Comeback' of Kautilya? — 363

SECTION C
KAUTILYA REDUX?
RE-USE OF THE PAST AND THE MAKING OF THE MODERN POLITICS OF INDIA

1. Hybridity and the Postcolonial State — 396
2. Core Features of the Kautilyan State — 401
3. Kautilyan Thought, 'Re-use of the Past' and 'Political Habitus' — 409
4. The Postcolonial Condition: The Hybridity of the 'Modern' State in Transitional Societies — 412
5. Hybridization as a Political Strategy of Dominance and Resistance — 418

6. Satyagraha: The Gandhian Conflation
   of Modernity and Tradition 421
7. The Hybrid Postcolonial State as
   Both Structure and Agency 424
8. A Dialectic of the 'Pure' and the 'Hybrid':
   Implications of the Indian Case for a General
   Theory of State Formation in Transitional Societies 435

SECTION D
KAUTILYA, INDIA AND GLOBAL POLITICAL THEORY
DEMOCRATIC ASPIRATIONS AND INSTITUTIONAL EVOLUTION IN THE NON-WESTERN WORLD

1. Culture, Structure or Political Capital?: Some General
   Lessons of India's Counterfactual Democracy 447
2. The Impact of Path Dependence on Transition to
   Democracy and Its Consolidation 450
3. Making Democracy Work: India's Political Capital 452
4. Democracy in General and in the Non-Western Context 458

SECTION E
THE 'KAUTILYAN MOMENT', THE POWER-KNOWLEDGE MATRIX AND THE GENEALOGY OF GLOBAL POLITICAL THEORY

Conclusion: The Emergent 'Kautilyan Discourse' in India 462

Endnotes 472
Glossary of Sanskrit/Hindi Terms 507
Bibliography 511
Index of Names 533
Index of Subjects 540

FOREWORD

I am delighted to contribute the Foreword to this unique interpretive account of Kautilya's contribution to the evolution of modern Indian political thought by Subrata Mitra and Michael Liebig. Kautilya's *Arthashastra* is the world's oldest comprehensive treatise on the science of statecraft. It is also a practical, hands-on manual on how to run the affairs of the state and assure the welfare of its citizenry. Not only does it provide instructive guidance for conducting *rajadharma*, including the administration of justice and the management of internal and external security, but it also provides strategies for protecting the state and expanding its frontiers.

Of the same vintage as Aristotle's *Politics*, the *Arthashastra* is, however, broader in its approach. Unlike in the discourses of Plato and Aristotle, founders of the Western political tradition, the *Arthashastra* embraces all aspects of political, military, social, economic, and cultural life, and the diverse components of power that are the constitutive elements of the state.

Mitra and Liebig's work is neither a history book, nor is it a fresh rendering of the tenets of *Arthashastra*. What is new in it is the effort by its authors to demonstrate how the inheritance of Kautilya's philosophy is embedded in the Indian political praxis right through history. They explain how this ancient text is connected to contemporary India, and how the 'hybridity of pre-modern political thought and modern political practice' came about.

This work traces the imprint of *Arthashastra* on the psyche of key Indian leaders including Mahatma Gandhi, Jawaharlal Nehru and Sardar Patel. In this context, there appears a quote from Nehru's letter to his thirteen-year-old daughter, Indira, written from prison. It relates to how, for Kautilya, the right of kingship was derived from legitimacy of actions, not divine dispensation. Kautilya plotted the overthrow of a despotic king, Dhana Nanda, to place Chandragupta Maurya on the throne. Nehru explained how Kautilya spoke of war and peace, and of laws and law courts, as also about 'social customs, of the rights of women, of the maintenance of the old and helpless, of marriage and divorce, of taxation ... of agriculture, of spinning and weaving, of artisans', and even of passports and prisons.

The authors also make a seminal contribution in recalling the connection between Kautilyan thought and Gandhi. On the basis of a detailed enumeration of Gandhi's political acts, they contend that as the master strategist of India's struggle for freedom, as also the undisputed leader of the Congress party for much of the period after his arrival in India from South Africa in 1915 until India's independence (quite astonishingly, without holding formal office), 'Gandhi not only knew the four *upayas*', but as 'his political conduct reveals [...] he applied the first three *upayas*—*saman, dana* and *bheda*—and was not dogmatic with respect to *danda*'.

Had Antonio Gramsci, incarcerated in prison, got access to *Arthashastra*, he might have agreed with the foregoing proposition. The third of his Prison Notebooks reflects a comprehension of Gandhi's tactics—ever responsive to the changing dynamic of colonial repression and the mobilization of the masses against it. In his own way, Gandhi fought a battle of attrition against the British. In 1930, about the same time as the launch of the salt satyagraha, Gramsci wrote: 'Gandhi's passive resistance is a war of position, which at certain moments becomes a war of movement, and at others underground warfare.' Doctrinally, for Gandhi, the congruence between ends and means, and the primacy of non-violence were important. Contrarily, for Kautilya, these were non-issues, since for him, desirable outcomes came first. In practice, however, Gandhi was supportive of mobilization during the First World War. And when his 'Quit India' call gained strength in 1942, resulting in revolts and violent acts, he refrained from issuing any injunctions against them.

The *Arthashastra* advocates the use of measured violence to preserve the state and promote its interests, mindful of nurturing both internal and external security. It reflects, nevertheless, a broader conception of security, beyond deterrence, dissimulation, defence, and diplomacy. The success of statecraft depends on the quality of its leader, advisors, peoples, defences, finances, armed forces, and allies. The sovereign needs foresight to avert *vyasana* (calamity): prevent it before it appears, and overcome it when it occurs. Productive economic activity is key to state building. 'Hence,' wrote Kautilya, 'the king shall be ever active in the management of the economy,' without which 'both current prosperity and future growth will be destroyed.' These are precepts that resonate to this day.

When Michael Liebig first came to India before turning to academic pursuits, his acquaintance with Kautilya began while interviewing retired Brigadier Dr Vijai Nair, better known as Magoo Nair. 'Kautilya, who?' was Michael's response when Magoo asked him to read Kautilya's *Arthashastra*. Since then, both Subrata Mitra and Michael Liebig have been part of a core group of distinguished scholars from the Institute of South Asian Studies of the University of Singapore, the South Asia Institute of the University of Heidelberg, and the Institute for Defence Studies and Analyses (IDSA), New Delhi, which have been engaged in a collaborative study of the *Arthashastra*, and its contemporary relevance to strategic thinking and its practices.

This has been a journey of discovery for both scholars, as much as for the three institutions, located in different geographies, and for the informed public in India and the world. Their book is a significant step forward in creating a wider understanding of how the *Arthashastra* has been applied in modern times.

Jayant Prasad
Director General
Institute for Defence Studies and Analyses (IDSA)
New Delhi, India

A NOTE FOR READERS ON READING KAUTILYA'S *ARTHASHASTRA*

This book is divided into three parts. The first part presents an exposition of key sections and ideas from the original text of Kautilya's *Arthashastra* focusing primarily on statecraft. The second part traces the connectivity of core principles of the Kautilyan state with contemporary politics. The analysis, also offering a view of everyday life in Indian politics, draws from interviews conducted with well-known politicians and academics. The third part focuses on the linkage between India's constitution and institutional arrangement with the fundamental ideas of Kautilya's *Arthashastra*. A brief summary, provided at the beginning of each part, is intended to help guide the reader through the detailed arguments made in that section.

The first part features paraphrases of the twenty-one chapters of Book I of the *Arthashastra*. They include Kautilya's treatment of the necessary intellectual and moral qualities of the ruler, the principle of secularism, internal security policy, and the role of diplomacy and intelligence in foreign affairs. Next, Kautilya's *saptanga* concept cluster—'the seven state factors' (*prakriti*)—is presented and analysed. The aggregate of seven *prakriti* constitutes the state and state power. The *saptanga* theory is also the basis for Kautilya's *shadgunya* concept cluster: 'the six methods of foreign policy'. The correlation of forces between states—measured by their respective *prakriti*—is the key factor in deciding which of the six policy options—in between peace and war—should be adopted. In this section, the *mandala* scheme is analysed as well. Following that, Kautilya's political anthropology is investigated which underpins his 'four principles of politics' (*upayas*). Yet, in spite of Kautilya's political realism, Kautilyan policy-making is norm-based.

In the first part, we also dispute the assertion that Kautilya's *Arthashastra* was lost for more than two thousand years to be rediscovered only in 1904. We argue that there has been a continuous oral and written transmission of the *Arthashastra* across time, as well as a lasting influence of Kautilyan thought on the polities in South Asia throughout the pre-modern longue durée. It is important to note here that Max Weber, who is broadly featured here and who is generally recognized as one of the foundational thinkers of modern social sciences, was the first Western social scientist to recognize the significance of Kautilya.

The second part deals with the relevance of Kautilyan thought for contemporary India. We present Kautilyan thought as an 'endogenous politico-cultural resource' and draw on a range of interviews with India's politico-strategic and academic elite on how they see the latent and manifest influences Kautilyan ideas have had in contemporary India. In this context, we look at Kautilya's relevance to Jawaharlal Nehru, who thoroughly studied the *Arthashastra* while imprisoned by the British during 1930–31. We find that in today's India, one finds not only multiple conscious and explicit references to Kautilya in both 'high' politics and popular politicizing. Equally significant is the subconscious use of Kautilyan ideas and norms. That applies not only to India's political culture, but also its strategic culture.

Some readers may not be overly interested in the question as to why Kautilya has been marginalized among India's social scientists. However, this sad fact is one of the main reasons for our writing this book. Probably, more readers, particularly younger scholars, will be interested to read what we write about the 'comeback' of Kautilyan thought in India's politico-strategic and academic community.

The third part of the book explores the significance of Kautilya's teachings in the context of contemporary political life, and their implicit presence in the institutional arrangements of India. The main argument of this section suggests that the resilience of the Indian state—whose durability is an exception in the ephemeral world of postcolonial states—arises from the ability of the designers of modern Indian institutions to tap into the endogenous reservoir of stateness. The analysis in this section draws on the earlier parts of the book and suggests that the state and politics in India today are the results of a seamless evolution from the pre-modern past. Modern India's institutions are the result of the strategic adaption of some imported institutions in order to make them compatible with its deep-rooted traditions in the political sphere. Such hybridization of exogenous institutions and practices with their endogenous homologues is the consequence of two complementary processes: the conscious strategies of political actors to 're-use the past' in addressing contemporary problems; and, the semi-conscious attitudes and thought-patterns that can be described as the 'habitus' in the field of Indian politics. Based on Pierre Bourdieu's sociological concept, 'habitus' is understood here as the repository of past ideas, patterns of thought and practices that subconsciously influence present thinking and acting in the political field. Thus, the habitus enables the 'flow' of ideas and attitudes across time—independent of their conscious transmission in discursive contexts.

The general reader, seeking to get a sense of Kautilya's teachings might wish to focus on the following chapters:

Section A, Chapter 1: The Work and Its Author
Section A, Chapter 2: The *Arthashastra's* Oral and Written Transmission
Section A, Chapter 5: The Key Features of Kautilya's *Arthashastra*
Section A, Chapter 6: Paraphrase of Book I of the *Arthashastra*: The Ideal Ruler
Section A, Chapter 7: The Concept Cluster *Saptanga*: The Seven State Factors (*Prakriti*)
Section A, Chapter 8: The Seven *Prakriti* Constitutive of State Power
Section A, Chapter 9: The Concept Cluster *Shadgunya*: The Six Methods of Foreign Policy
Section A, Chapter 10: The Kautilyan Idea of Raison D'état
Section A, Chapter 11: The Concept Cluster *Upayas*: The Four Basic Methods of Politics
Section A, Chapter 12: Kautilya's Political Anthropology
Section A, Chapter 13: Kautilya's Assumption About Politics and the Theory of Political Realism
Section B, Chapter 4: Nehru and Kautilya

Section C, Chapter 7: The Hybrid Postcolonial State as Both Structure and Agency

Students of comparative politics and area studies will benefit from the following chapters:

Section B, Chapter 3: Kautilya's *Arthashastra* as an Endogenous Politico-Cultural Resource
Section B, Chapter 4: Nehru and Kautilya
Section B, Chapter 5: The Manifest Presence of Kautilyan Thought in Modern India
Section B, Chapter 6: The Latent Presence of Kautilyan Thought in Modern India
Section B, Chapter 7: Kautilya and the Strategic Culture of India
Section C (Chapters 1–8): Kautilya Redux? Re-use of the Past, and the Making of the Modern Politics in India
Section D (Chapters 1–4): Kautilya, India and Global Political Theory: Democratic Aspirations and Institutional Evolution in the Non-western World

Those specializing in international relations might wish to focus on the following chapters:

Section A, Chapter 9: The Concept Cluster *Shadgunya*: The Six Methods of Foreign Policy
Section A, Chapter 13: Kautilya's Assumption About Politics and the Theory of Political Realism
Section B, Chapter 4: Nehru and Kautilya
4.4.2 *Nehru: A political realist in the Kautilyan tradition*
4.4.3 *Nehru as 'political idealist'*
4.4.4 *'Nehruvianism' as synthesis of realism and idealism*
Section B, Chapter 6: The Latent Presence of Kautilyan Thought in Modern India
6.6 The latent presence of Kautilyan thought-figures in the strategic document 'NonAlignment 2.0'
6.6.1 *Grand strategy and 'hard' realism*

6.6.2 Strategic autonomy
Section B, Chapter 7: Kautilya and the Strategic Culture of India
Section B, Chapter 8: A Distant Relationship: Kautilya and the Social and Political Sciences in India
8.1 Kautilya's absence in Indian Academia
8.2 The Anglo-American influence in Indian universities
8.4.3 Kautilya and International Relations theory in India
8.4.4 Social constructivism
8.4.5 Postcolonial theory
Section B, Chapter 9: Trend Reversal: A 'Comeback' of Kautilya?

The indices at the end of the book are intended to guide all readers to their chosen queries.

PREFACE

Kautilya's *Arthashastra* is one of the world's earliest examples of scholarly analysis of political and strategic affairs. Despite the significance of this classical work of ancient India, its mention in current academic discourse at most places outside India is likely to raise a question of mild curiosity: 'Kautilya, who?'. In India itself, Kautilya is mentioned for reasons that are more sentimental and patriotic than analytical and comparative. Even as we celebrate Kautilya in the audio-visual media, and name public buildings and diplomatic enclaves after him, the significance of his theoretical contributions to statecraft is rarely given the importance it deserves. In academic circles, Kautilya is given less importance than his European equivalent. He is often labeled as the 'Indian Machiavelli'—despite the fact that the *Arthashastra* was written some eighteen hundred years prior to Machiavelli's *Discorsi* and *Principe* and is much broader in scope.

This book is intended to fill this void, and to give the *Arthashastra* its rightful place in the canon of political science, and contemporary political discourse. The project is most timely. With the modern state in India locked in battle against social segments that reject the secular tenets of modernity, Kautilya's ruler—the ideal-type—the firm centre of the community who holds conflicting social segments together, acquires an added significance. For a country like India that has already become one of the main strategic actors in the twenty-first-century multipolar world, his ideas are of enormous importance amid political and strategic thinkers.

The living legacy of Kautilya's ideas constitute a vital link between India's modern institutions with the classical past. It is a marker of the 'modernity of tradition' in contemporary India, a key factor for the 'hybridity' of India's political institutions and processes. Understanding Kautilya is to come to grips with the resilience of India's political system.

The biographical data on Kautilya—often named Chanakya in India—are scarce. He lived at the turn of the fourth- to third-century BC and was thus a near-contemporary of Aristotle and Alexander the Great. Kautilya was no 'ivory tower' scholar. His writings reflect his experience as a political actor who played a key role in the establishment of the Maurya Empire (ca. 320–180 BC)—the first pan-Indian state extending over most of the Indian subcontinent. Yet, Kautilya's opus magnum, the *Arthashastra*, should not be seen essentially as a historiographical work of the Maurya Empire. Its Sanskrit title, *Arthashastra*, can be translated as 'Textbook on Statecraft'. Therein, Kautilya addresses governance, public administration, economics, law, foreign policy/diplomacy, military affairs and intelligence. The text of the authoritative English translation extends over 511 pages.

This book is the first dedicated research effort to explore the relevance of Kautilyan thought in contemporary India, based on a systematic analysis of conversations with a select group of scholars, statesmen, political leaders and civil servants. We draw on the vast research done on the *Arthashastra* by Indologists to whom we owe the work's translation from Sanskrit into English (and German). Yet, by its very nature, the Indologists' approach to Kautilya is one of Sanskrit philology and historiography. The place of the *Arthashastra* in political science and the relevance of its core concepts to the understanding of contemporary Indian and comparative politics are theoretical, comparative and heuristic. As such, the implications of Kautilya's thought as a tool for understanding political life raises questions beyond the scope of Indology. That is the raison d'être of our book.

The collaboration between us which led to this book, started in 2012. However, our individual encounters with Kautilyan scholarship started even earlier. Michael Liebig was first introduced to the *Arthashastra* in 2002 in course of his fieldwork in India, and has, since then, followed up on that early encounter with advanced research on India's intelligence culture, inspired by Kautilyan ideas. Subrata Mitra, who grew up with *Chanakya-Niti* like many in his generation, introduced Kautilya as part of the curriculum in political theory when he was named to the Chair in Political Science at the South Asia Institute of Heidelberg University in

1994. However, Kautilya gained a special significance for his research in comparative politics and area studies of South Asia when he developed hybridity and 're-use of the past' as analytical tools for the analysis of institutional evolution and political culture of contemporary India. The seamless connectivity between India's classical political tradition and contemporary politics with Kautilya's teaching as a template thus became a major tool of analysis of citizenship, governance and the resilience of Indian democracy.

Bringing Kautilya 'home' to India and making the significance of his teachings accessible to the general reader have been one of our prime objectives. We are most grateful to Rupa and its visionary leader Shri Kapish Mehra for making this possible. The encouragement and support that we have received from Shri Vinod Rai, former Comptroller and Auditor General of India, has been a vital source of inspiration for us. Several colleagues, including, in particular Sekhar Bandyopadhyay, Rajesh Basrur, Bruce Bueno de Mesquita, Iftekhar Ahmed Chowdhury, Sumit Ganguly, Arvind Gupta, Pradeep Kumar Gautam, Gyanesh Kudaisya, Saurabh Mishra, Rahul Mukherji, Jayant Prasad, Jivanta Schoettli, Duvvuri Subbarao and Seyed Hossein Zarhani have been generous with comments and suggestions. Dr Sandra Frey at NOMOS, and Rudra Sharma and Elina Majumdar at Rupa have helped expedite the process of publication. The administrative support of the Institute of South Asian Studies (ISAS, NUS) of Singapore, particularly that of its Chairman Ambassador Shri Gopinath Pillai, Senior Associate Director Hernaikh Singh, and Peggy Tan, Management Assistant Officer, has been most valuable. We are grateful to all these friends.

The book is aimed at multiple audiences. It draws substantially on its earlier publication under the same title by NOMOS (Baden-Baden, Germany, 2016). It was originally written for an academic audience of specialists. The general reader might find some sections dealing with methodology and detailed results of fieldwork, onerous. As such, we have signposted the sections likely to be most helpful to the general reader to get a sense of Kautilya's teachings and their relevance to contemporary politics in the 'Readers' Guide'. If the tools of enquiry that we develop, drawing on the teachings of Kautilya help our readers see the strategic intentions that underpin everyday politics, and thus, help them cope with the challenges of everyday life, that would be the best reward for having undertaken the project in the first place.

Subrata K. Mitra
Institute of South Asian Studies,
National University of Singapore

Michael Liebig
South Asia Institute,
Heidelberg University

INTRODUCTION

Politics in contemporary India stretches across an extraordinary range of themes. The role of religion in public affairs and the limits of secular authority jostle for space in competition against the threat to public order. The classical heritage of modern India and the seamless connectivity of the pre-modern with the modern, both explain the capacity of the political system to sustain the coexistence of apparent contradictions. Kautilya's *Arthashastra*, along with a few other iconic sources of India's political tradition, account for the ability of India's political culture to integrate these different strands and to generate a coherent political process. India's classical political heritage, of which *Arthashastra* is a crucial part, constitutes the normative reservoir that underpins modern India's political identity.

Since the publication of the first edition of this book, there has certainly been advancement in bringing the Kautilyan discourse onto the pages devoted to meticulous examination of the same in the academia. However, the few articles that have been published in academic journals since 2014 on Kautilya and his contemporary relevance, suffer from a limited understanding of the *Arthashastra*, because, these are based not on genuine text analysis, but assessment of mostly secondary literature. Further, one finds in them neither attempts to understand the text and its author, nor efforts to trace the connectivity of the distant past of the *Arthashastra* to the structure and process of modern politics. In fact, the usage of phrases like Indian Machiavelli (without ironic quotation marks) in some of the studies, indicates conceptual problems of locating Kautilyan knowledge in its own context rather than presenting it as a derivative of a western referent. Further, a synergy between the Indological analysis of Kautilya and the interpretations of his teaching in terms of the core concepts of Political Science is yet to emerge, in India and internationally. Therein lies the relevance of our study of Kautilya's *Arthashastra*.

Though slim in volume, there has nevertheless been a steady stream of scholarly endeavour to locate Kautilya in the space of contemporary statecraft and international relations. Following the 'Fourth Global International Studies Conference' held at the Goethe University, in Frankfurt, Germany in August 2014, three more conferences have been held between 2014 and 2017 in Delhi, Heidelberg and Singapore, in collaboration between the IDSA, the South Asia Institute of Heidelberg University, and the Institute of South Asian Studies, NUS, Singapore. A comprehensive volume titled *The Arthashastra in a Transcultural Perspective* edited by Michael Liebig and Saurabh Mishra emerged from these deliberations. Encouragingly, the world of practical politics has kept pace with advancement of the theoretical knowledge of the deep structure of Indian politics. The trends in contemporary Indian politics, with its solicitude to conflate political order and general welfare, also project an implicit reflection of Kautilyan statecraft. The power of Indian democracy in holding the state accountable to the people in myriad consultations at all levels of the system, as we argue in this book, ultimately results from the combination of the longue durée that connects the present to the classical past, and the evolution of the habitus that bound the *raja* and the *praja* in an implicit social contract, both spiritual and material, based on justice and order.

India is an important part of the multipolar world system that has been in the process of consolidation since the beginning of the twenty-first century. India's political resilience and economic rise—slow, incremental and steady—is mostly seen as an adaption to the liberal democratic paradigm of the West. India has a democratic system, semi-liberal capitalism, a growing consumerist middle-class, a competitive IT sector and nuclear weapons. India's emergence as a rising power is partly due to its successful adaptation of its traditional society to modernization but also to its capacity to draw on its classical past. That past is present in modern India, but in ways that are confusing for 'outsiders' who tend to think of it merely in terms of stagnation and backwardness.

We are glad to note that some political scientists have begun to address India's pre-modern politico-cultural resources and their relevance for modern India. In their study *Bargaining with Rising India: Lessons from the Mahabharata*, Amrita Narlikar and Aruna Narlikar (2014) have examined negotiating strategies in the epic *Mahabharata* and put them in correlation to those of twenty-first century India. In the study, they address the question 'to what extent does India's bargaining behaviour, as a rising power, reflect cultural continuities' (2). They emphasize the importance of the engagement between India's classical political theories and current problems of statehood and statecraft.

Though little understood in these terms—both at home in India and abroad—the twenty-first century multipolar system marks the prospects of India's return to its 'normal' status in world politics and the world economy. In the fourth and third centuries BC, the Indian Maurya Empire under Chandragupta and Ashoka was the greatest political and economic power on the globe, along with China. Between the third and sixth century AD, the Gupta Empire in India could measure up to Rome, Byzantium, the Persian Sassanid Empire and China. In the sixteenth century, the Indian Mughal Empire under Akbar belonged to the handful of genuine great powers: China, the Spain of Charles V, the Ottoman Empire and emerging England. Until about 1750, India held—roughly at par with China—the leading position in the world economy (cf. Maddison 2006). It was only afterwards that India was economically and politically marginalized for two centuries under British colonial rule.

The absorption and hybridization of Western political and economic categories notwithstanding, the elites as well as the people of post-independence India have been drawing on endogenous politico-cultural resources. These mostly pre-modern resources—some going back three or four thousand years—are not tapped for reasons of romantic or even reactionary nostalgia, but serve as catalysts for India's rise towards great power status. The strategic 're-use' of endogenous politico-cultural resources for tackling problems and challenges of the present is a key factor that explains the resilience of India's political system, and also a theoretical puzzle for postcolonial state-building in general. The 'conservative dynamism' of India resulting from the confluence of India's classical heritage and the modern imports is little understood in these terms. The same applies to the endogenous politico-cultural resources in which India's contemporary politics is rooted. One such endogenous resource is Kautilya's *Arthashastra*, written in the fourth century BC.[1]

In the *Arthashastra*, Kautilya theorizes state structures, statecraft and political economy as entangled concepts and devotes one chapter exclusively to issues of methodology to underline the analytical character of the work. The *Arthashastra* is a theoretical and normative work, not a historical description of ancient Indian polities. The 'Kautilyan state' is an ideal-type conception (in Max Weber's sense) but no utopia of an 'ideal' state. Kautilya's theorizations in the *Arthashastra* are both empirically referenced and draws critically on antecedent texts of political theory.

The *Arthashastra*'s significance for the evolution of Political Science, notably International Relations (IR) theory, would be obvious to anyone who is familiar with the book. The ideas and concepts that the work contains remain intellectually stimulating for both disciplines. They also constitute a significant factor of influence for contemporary India's political and strategic culture. In our study, we argue that the influence of Kautilyan thought in modern India can be seen in the 're-use' of the past by actors in the political sphere and among the Indian strategic community (cf. Mitra 2011a; 2012a). Equally important is the latent influence of Kautilyan thought upon the attitudes, thought patterns, and modes of behaviour of political and strategic actors in contemporary India. When re-using Kautilyan thought, they may not explicitly refer to Kautilya and the *Arthashastra* since these ideas have become part of the political culture in political and strategic contexts. The practical, pragmatic and efficient actors in Indian politics are 'Kautilyans'—not 'Hobbesians'[2] or 'Machiavellians'. The lasting efficacy of Kautilyan thought is a case in point of the 'modernity of tradition' in India. Actually, the 'modernity of tradition' has been a tradition in Indian politics since antiquity.

Yet, irrespective of its intrinsic theoretical value, Kautilya and the *Arthashastra* have mostly been ignored, marginalized or 'orientalized' in Political Science and IR theory. That a foundational text of the discipline would be treated so casually even in the country of its origin is indeed puzzling. Moreover, Kautilya can be considered as the pre-modern 'founding father' of the theory of Political Realism typified by Niccolo

Machiavelli in early modernity or Hans J. Morgenthau in the twentieth century. Remarkably enough, Morgenthau grounds his theory on ancient Indian political philosophy among other sources and refers explicitly to Kautilya (Morgenthau 1978, 4; 1958, 36, 48, 56, 67). Despite that, if known at all among political scientists, Kautilya is usually labeled the 'Indian Machiavelli'. Most political scientists still prefer the narrative that the pre-modern foundations of Political Realism are to be found exclusively in Europe with Thucydides, the ancient Greek Sophists, or the Roman historian Tacitus. Kautilya, Sun-Tzu of ancient China (*The Art of War*) or the medieval Persian political theorist Nizam ul-Mulk (*Siyasatnama* or *Book of Government*) seem to count for nothing (cf. Frankel 1996).

The denial of legitimate importance to Kautilya and the *Arthashastra* points towards the still prevailing Eurocentrism in Political Science and IR theory. But, strangely enough, Political Science and IR theory in India too have mostly disowned Kautilya. Almost a century ago, in 1919, Benoy Kumar Sarkar published his essay 'Hindu Theory of International Relations' in the *American Political Science Review* (cf. 1919). In this essay, Sarkar addresses, inter alia, Kautilya's foreign policy theorems and discusses their relevance for modern (Western) theorizing of inter-state relations. However, his early initiative regarding Kautilya's lasting relevance for IR theory was not taken up by Indian Political Science.[3]

That Western political scientists would have dismissed an essay on pre-modern Indian politico-strategic thought by an author from (then-colonial) India is hardly surprising. But equally ignored was Max Weber's engagement with Kautilya. He was the first Western social scientist to recognize the importance of Kautilya's *Arthashastra* in his *Politics as a Vocation*, and in his sociology of religion studies on Hinduism (cf. Weber 2008b; 2000). Weber's writings, in which he addresses Kautilya and the *Arthashastra*, were published between 1915 and 1919. During the subsequent decades of the twentieth century, Kautilya remained a distant and exotic figure for Western political scientists.[4] After the turn of the millennium, the American political scientist Roger Boesche published the book *The First Great Political Realist: Kautilya and His*

Arthashastra (2002a). During the following years, some Indian political scientists began to question 'the silence on Kautilya' in their discipline (cf. Behera 2007). In 2006, Rashed Uz Zaman had published the essay *Kautilya: The Indian Strategic Thinker and Indian Strategic Culture*, which was of special significance in that it addressed the contemporary relevance of Kautilya in a dedicated fashion.

In sum, Kautilyan ideas and concepts have remained practically untapped as a resource of Political Science. Equally so, the relevance of the *Arthashastra* for contemporary India's strategic culture, institutional evolution and its basic modalities of political thinking and behaviour have remained sadly under-theorized. Yet, during the second decade of the twenty-first century, there have been growing indications of an emergent interest in Kautilyan thought among political scientists in India and beyond.[5]

While Political Science and IR theory have mostly remained silent on Kautilya, Indologists and Sanskrit philologists have extensively engaged with the *Arthashastra*.[6] The Sanskrit philologist R. Shamashastry discovered the complete text of the *Arthashastra* (written in the seventeenth century on a bundle of palm leaves) in 1904 and published its first English translation in 1915. The Swiss-American Indologist Johann Jakob Meyer published the German translation (from the original Sanskrit) in 1926. Indologist R. P. Kangle has devoted his whole scholarly life to research on the *Arthashastra*—and his translation remains unsurpassed. Kangle thinks that the *Arthashastra* is characterized by such originality, conceptual coherence and methodological rigour that the assumption that it is a text compilation of various authors in different historical periods is not plausible.[7] While Indology has made the *Arthashastra* accessible for Political Science, the Indological perspective on the *Arthashastra* is one of philology and historiography. Indology's philological and historiographical research focus does clearly differ from the research approach of Political Science, which is interested in the political and strategic idea-contents of the *Arthashastra*. After all, Kautilya himself states in the very first paragraph of *Arthashastra* that his work is 'a treatise on the Science of Politics' (Kangle 2010a/1972, 15). Therefore, our approach aims at analysing and interpreting the

Arthashastra's core concepts in terms of political theory, comparative political theory, and IR theory. In this regard, the Political Science approach will apply the discipline's distinct methods, theories and vocabulary. The interpretive exposition of the *Arthashastra*'s political and strategic concepts necessarily involves the reconstruction of the text's latent idea-contents which are not specified as categories and thus cannot be adequately accessed via citations.

Besides the understanding and specification of the political and strategic concepts of the *Arthashastra*, Political Science is interested in the exploration of the influence of Kautilyan concepts upon patterns of thought and behaviour in the spheres of politics and strategy in historical and contemporary contexts. In that, the prime concern is the lasting legacy of Kautilyan thought in South Asian politics.

Thus, the research approaches of Indology and Political Science to Kautilya's *Arthashastra* are clearly distinct. As political scientists, we believe that an intellectual portrait of Kautilya's *Arthashastra* would fall short if it were limited to the exposition of the *Arthashastra*'s central concepts—although such undertaking is ambitious enough. An equally important objective of our research interest has been the significance of Kautilyan thought for everyday politics in contemporary India. That, we think, is *per se* an obvious research desideratum as well as the necessary completion of an intellectual portrait of Kautilya's *Arthashastra*. Thus, our study has two focal points:

1. The interpretive exposition of the core ideas and concepts of Kautilya's *Arthashastra* (section A)
2. The exploration of the relevance of Kautilyan thought for modern India (sections B and C)

Such dual focus is logically and empirically compelling since, without an adequate understanding of the political and strategic idea-contents of the *Arthashastra*, the exploration of the contemporary relevance of Kautilyan thought would be meaningless. Our portraiture of Kautilya's *Arthashastra* follows in tune with a sociology of knowledge: We go back to the text, to its interpreters and users—and thus we move from the more explicit to the surreptitiously implicit.

Scholarly literature addressing specifically the influence of Kautilyan thought in contemporary India is practically non-existent.[8] Therefore, we have chosen expert interviews in the Indian strategic community as the most promising avenue to collect data on the presence of Kautilyan thought in contemporary India.[9] For analysing and evaluating the data gained from the interviews, we have relied on the political sociology of Max Weber and Pierre Bourdieu as well as the concepts of 'hybridization' and 're-use of the past' (Mitra 2011a). Also, the concept of 'strategic culture' is an important tool for addressing the presence of Kautilyan thought in modern India.

However, exploring the empirical resonance of pre-modern politico-strategic thought for the structure and process of politics and modern political institutions of modern India necessitates addressing theoretically the question of an epoch-spanning 'idea-flow'. Fernand Braudel's concept of longue durée cultural continuity provides a conceptualization that allows for an adequate understanding of the oral and written transmission of Kautilyan thought up to the present. Without taking the singular staying-power and 'cohesive plurality' of Indian culture into account, within which the transmission of the *Arthashastra* thought has been embedded, the lasting presence of Kautilyan thought would remain incomprehensible. With the concepts 'hybridization' and 're-use of the past' we can understand why and how actors (re-)use Kautilyan thought to address contemporary political and strategic challenges. Bourdieu's concept of 'habitus' enables us to understand the (elusive) latent presence of Kautilyan thought, which implicitly influences the thinking and behaviour of Indian political actors in general and particularly so in the field of foreign and security policy. Kautilya—not Machiavelli or Hobbes—best represents the universe of the political man or woman in India, and the *Arthashastra* inspires the political analyst and institution designer much more than Western prototypes.

We argue that the roots of the discipline are to be found in pre-modern Asia and that many of its key ideas and concepts that appear to be of 'purely' European origin are in fact hybridizations of earlier Asian—notably South Asian—thinking. Sooner or later, Political Science and IR theory in the 'Global North' will realize that ignoring and marginalizing

Kautilya's *Arthashastra* comes down to an intellectual self-mutilation of the discipline. We believe that Political Science cannot afford not to use Kautilyan thought as an intellectual catalyst for theorizations addressing contemporary puzzles.

The book will proceed in three parts. The first part introduces the reader to some key theoretical and methodological concepts from Max Weber which are then juxtaposed to the key constituents of the Kautilyan state as delineated in the *Arthashastra*. The second part of the book dissects the Kautilyan components of modern India, using the concepts of 'longue durée' (Braudel) and 'habitus' (Bourdieu) as bridge principles that connect a classical thinker to the contemporary reality. This connectivity is then analysed in part three in terms of the ideas of Jawaharlal Nehru—for many, the founder of modern India—and through a systematic analysis of academic discourse on Kautilya in India. The analysis of discourse of the specialists of statecraft follows a maxim set by Milton Friedman. An expert billiard player, he has argued, does not know trigonometry. However, if one understands trigonometry, one can explain what makes him an expert! Thus, our elite respondents are not necessarily specialists of Kautilyan theory. However, if one is familiar with the teachings of Kautilya, one can understand the essence of their discourse. In other words, Kautilya's teachings on statecraft, the limits of authority and the social basis of legitimacy have become part of the deep knowledge of politics in Indic civilizations. The formal knowledge of Kautilya helps us understand the main lines of politics and strategic thinking that underpin the discourse of our conversations, which have been analysed in this section. Aside from the three major parts, the significance of Kautilya in the creation of the modern state and its resilience are analysed in the fourth part of the book. This text segment also prepares the ground for the discourse to move beyond Kautilya into global political theory in the fifth section which indicates, how, global political theory might restore the connectivity of the classical roots of major political systems of the world and the contemporary political processes, and the linkage of thinkers of the West with those from other parts of the world.

In putting Kautilya's contributions together with the emergent

Kautilya discourse in contemporary India and the re-use of Kautilya in the state structure, we hope that this study can be a contribution to a better understanding of the idea-contents of the *Arthashastra*, and to a yet-unwritten 'Genealogy of Global Political Thought'. In addition, it is our belief that without knowing Kautilyan thought, the analysis of India's political and strategic behaviour remains perfunctory. Our intention is to save the latter from losing out on the benefit of its significance.

SECTION A

An Interpretive Exposition of Kautilya's *Arthashastra*

1
THE WORK AND ITS AUTHOR

Kautilya's *Arthashastra* is one of the earliest examples of scholarly analysis of political and strategic affairs in the ancient world. It is an encyclopaedic work covering, inter alia, governance, public administration, economics, law, foreign policy and diplomacy, military affairs and intelligence. The text of the authoritative English translation extends over 511 pages.[1]

The Sanskrit word *arthashastra* has two components: *artha* and *shastra*. The original meaning of *artha* is 'thing' or 'object'. Its range of meanings includes: '1. the object of human pursuit, 2. the means of this pursuit, and 3. the needs and the desire suggesting this pursuit' (Zimmer 2011/1951, 36). *Artha* is translated as wealth, material benefits, power, politics or statecraft. The Sanskrit word *shastra* means 'authoritative textbook', 'manual' or 'compendium'. *Arthashastra* can be translated as 'textbook of politics' or 'compendium of statecraft' or 'manual of political economy', 'wherein are to be found all the timeless laws of politics, economy, diplomacy and war' (ibid.). The term *arthashastra* is the generic name for textbooks on politics, statecraft and economics. There are also *shastras* for other fields—for example *dharmashastras*, which treat religious-ethical and legal issues. Kautilya's *Arthashastra* is but one among a variety of political textbooks of ancient India, which, however, are all lost. Therefore, Kautilya's *Arthashastra* has become pars pro toto with respect to ancient Indian politico-strategic thought.

What do we know about the author of this *Arthashastra*? In the introductory chapter it says: *thus has this work on the science of politics been composed by Kautilya* (KA, I, 1, 19).[2] Whenever the author discusses the opinions of other authors on a subject matter and makes a judgement on them, there is the phrase: *So Kautilya [says]*. Thus, the author identifies himself in the text of the *Arthashastra*. On one occasion, however, in the final lines of the *Arthashastra*, the author does not call himself Kautilya but 'Vishnugupta'. This self-designation with two different names has led to some confusion. Moreover, in literary and *shastra* texts of the first millennium AD, Kautilya is often called 'Chanakya'. This naming is widespread if not dominant in India today. Kangle's explanation of the different names is: Kautilya is the family name, Chanakya the father's name and Vishnugupta the first name (cf. Kangle 2010b/1965, 112f). Finally, it should be noted that some scholars, for example Hartmut Scharfe or Charles Drekmeier, speak of 'Kautalya' instead of Kautilya.

In the Indological community, authorship and dating of the *Arthashastra* are intensely debated. Whenever Kautilya is mentioned among Indologists, there is a high probability that instantly a tense dispute would break out on the question of whether the *Arthashastra* is the work of the single author Kautilya or a text compilation of various (unknown) authors over an extended period of time. Most Indologists who have extensively researched the subject area are of the opinion that Kautilya is the sole author of the *Arthashastra*, who wrote the work at the turn of the fourth to the third century BC. But they do not exclude the possibility that, during the following centuries, smaller text passages were added to the original text—without, however, leading to substantive changes of the content and structure of the text. The Indologists who hold this position include R. Shamashastry, K. P. Jayaswal, R. P. Kangle, J. J. Meyer, H. Zimmer and L. N. Rangarajan. The Indological majority opinion is formulated by Heinrich Zimmer:

> The caustic and sententious style, literary facility, and intellectual genius displayed do high credit to the master of political devices who composed this amazing treatise. Much of the material was quarried from older sources, the work being founded on a rich tradition of earlier political teachings, which it superseded, but which is still reflected through its quotations and aphorisms, and yet the study as a whole conveys the impression of being the production of a single, greatly superior mind. (Zimmer 2011/1951, 93)

The opposing view suggests that the *Arthashastra* is a compilation of various texts which were written by various unknown authors between the fourth century BC and the second century AD. The text components were then compiled by unknown editors. Why such a collection of texts would have been attributed to a 'Kautilya' remains a mystery. The compilation thesis has been asserted, inter alia, by Indologists J. Jolly, M. Winternitz and A. B. Keith. T. R. Trautmann has tried to substantiate his claim that the *Arthashastra*'s multiple authors and text components stretch over a period of five centuries via a 'linguistic-statistical' computer analysis. Trautmann's conclusion is:

> Kautilya can not have been the author of the *Arthashastra* as a whole, but whether he wrote a part, and if so, which part, we can not decide without appeal to evidence outside the statistical study I have done. (Trautmann 1971, cit. in: Parmar, 11)

Patrick Olivelle also asserts forcefully that the *Arthashastra* has multiple authors and its composition stretched between the first century BC and the third century AD. Scharfe, whose detailed philological analysis of the *Arthashastra* is very helpful for the understanding of the work, compares Kautilya with Vyasa, the mythological figure who is credited with the authorship of the epic *Mahabharata* (cf. Scharfe 1968, 86).

The 'myopic-microscopic' debates (Meyer 1927, v) among Sanskrit philologists over the authorship and dating of the *Arthashastra* are fought out with philological weapons. Therefore, the layman in Sanskrit Studies who is intended to focus on the *Arthashastra*'s conceptual contents in a Political Science frame cannot but agree with Martin van Creveld who once wrote about such controversies:

> [I]t reminds one of the story of the philologist who, having spent twenty years in an effort to determine who composed the *Iliad* and the *Odyssey*, finally concluded that they had been written not by Homer but by another poet whose name was also Homer. (van Creveld 1999, 118)

The analysis undertaken in this book follows Kangle, Meyer and Zimmer and otherwise concentrates on Kautilya's ideas and concepts featured in the text, whose historical authenticity is not disputed by Indologists. The *Arthashastra* is characterized by such high degree of originality, conceptual coherence and methodological rigour that the assumption that it is a compilation with collective authorship does not seem plausible to us. We share Kangle's position who writes:

> We may, therefore, conclude that *there is no convincing reason why this work [Arthashastra] should not be regarded as the work of Kautilya*, who helped Chandragupta to come to power. (Kangle 2010b/1965, 106, emphasis added)

Kangle's finding gives an indication of the historical person Kautilya which is supported by Kautilya himself. In the closing lines of the *Arthashastra*, Kautilya writes that he—Vishnugupta, the author of this work—played a leading role in the overthrow of the Nanda dynasty. This is the only but crucially important hint by the author of the *Arthashastra* on his historical situatedness. The Nanda kingdom with its centre in Magadha (present-day Bihar) dominated north-eastern India during the fourth century BC. Historically certain are the overthrow of the Nanda dynasty and the establishment of the Maurya dynasty in its place 'around the year 320 BC' (cf. Kulke/Rothermund 1998, 80). The coup was led by Kautilya and Chandragupta who became the first ruler of the Maurya Empire. Under his grandson Ashoka, the Maurya Empire reached its greatest power and expanse, controlling the entire Indian subcontinent except the southern tip. Kautilya's statement in the *Arthashastra* that he played a leading role in the overthrow of the Nandas means that he was a near-contemporary of Alexander the Great, who died in 323 BC, and Aristotle, who died in 322 BC.

Except his own reference to the coup against the Nandas, we have no reliable biographical data on Kautilya. However, there are many legends about Kautilya's life: He was supposedly born and raised in South India. As a young man, he moved to Northern India to study at the University of Taxila (near modern Islamabad). After his studies, he took part in battles against the last remaining outposts of the Hellenic-Diadochi king Seleucus in the Indus area. Thereafter, he moved to Magadha and became a respected teacher in the capital Pataliputra. But then he was insulted by the Nanda king Dhana, and Kautilya swore revenge. To that end, he teamed up with Chandragupta—and their coup d'état ousted the Nandas (cf. Rangarajan 1992, 16f; Nehru 1962, 59f). For this legendary life story of Kautilya coming from literary and *shastra* texts of the first millennium AD, there exists no reliable historical evidence. But as Kangle emphasizes:

> [A]ll sources, Brahmanical, Buddhist and Jain, are, however, agreed on one point, that he [Kautilya] was responsible for the destruction of the Nanda rule in Magadha and the establishment of Chandragupta Maurya on that throne. (Kangle 2010b/1965, 108)

In the debate among Indologists over the historicity of Kautilya and the authorship of the *Arthashastra*, the Austrian-Czech Indologist Otto Stein takes a special position. He denies neither the authenticity of the *Arthashastra* and its author named Kautilya nor the historical existence of an ancient Indian statesman Kautilya aka Chanakya. But Stein claims that the statesman Kautilya and the author Kautilya are two different persons (cf. Stein 1921). He attempts to prove his thesis by comparing the *Arthashastra* with *Indica*—an ancient Greek account of India by the Hellenic diplomat and historian Megasthenes who was the ambassador of the Diadochi King Seleucus Nicator at the court of Chandragupta Maurya in Pataliputra.[3] Stein argues that the *Arthashastra* is not mentioned by Megasthenes in his *Indica*. Moreover, Megasthenes' descriptions of the administration, military, the economy and social life in the Maurya Empire differ substantially from what is written in the *Arthashastra*. From that, Stein concludes that the author of the *Arthashastra* could not possibly be identical with the political adviser of Chandragupta.

Stein's argument is not plausible for two reasons. First, of the complete text of the *Indica* only fragments have survived because they are cited in the works of later Roman historians. More importantly, Kautilya is not a historian, but a political theorist. The *Arthashastra* is not a historiographical work but a theoretical work on an ideal-type state and ideal-type statecraft. Thus, there is no need for Kautilya to provide a description of the Maurya Empire—it is not even mentioned in the *Arthashastra*. Thus, Charles Drekmeier notes: Kautilya '*never purports to give an account of a specific polity. It is a theoretical work*, and any attempt to deduce more than the broad outlines of the Mauryan administrative system from it must bear this in mind' (Drekmeier 1962, 167, emphasis added).

Nevertheless, the fragments of Megasthenes' *Indica* are quite helpful in giving us a time-congruent insight into the Maurya Empire and an understanding of the level of civilizational development in India during the fourth century BC. This is particularly true for his description of Pataliputra, the capital of the Maurya Empire, where Kautilya had lived and worked.

Given the lack of biographical data, Kautilya's historical location has to rely on the historically confirmed date of the political upheaval in the Nanda kingdom in 320 BC. About his activities in the subsequent period, we lack reliable information. We do not know, for example, how the relationship between Chandragupta and Kautilya turned out after their successful coup d'état. Did Kautilya become the 'chancellor' of the Maurya Empire, who guided the ruler almost like a student, as Nehru writes? (Nehru 1981, 123) If so, how long did he hold such a position as a kind of 'Richelieu', 'Mazarin' or 'Bismarck' of the Maurya Empire? Legend has it that Kautilya—after consolidating Chandragupta's rule—retired from active politics to devote himself entirely to his studies. Regarding the dating of the *Arthashastra*, we are thus left with the plausible assumption that the work was written after 320 BC, in the period of the turn of the fourth to third century BC.

2

THE *ARTHASHASTRA'S* ORAL AND WRITTEN TRANSMISSION

The question of the *Arthashastra*'s intellectual afterlife appears puzzling. The work was written at the turn of the fourth to the third century BC, but its 'rediscovery' occurred some 2300 years later by R. Shamashastry in 1904. Has the *Arthashastra* been 'lost' in the long interim period?

If the *Arthashastra* had been 'lost' or reduced to some legendary 'imagination' for more than two millennia, its 'rediscovery' in 1904 would constitute a quasi-archaeological discovery. In this case, the *Arthashastra* would be a kind of textual 'Troy' or 'Mycenae' and Shamashastry, an Indian Heinrich Schliemann. However, the facts contradict the assumption of such a quasi-archaeological rediscovery. Both in terms of logic and factuality, the 'rediscovery' of the *Arthashastra* in 1904 was only possible because of its continuous transmission over 2300 years through the inter-generational oral tradition of India. The two palm-leaf scripts with the complete text of the *Arthashastra*, which R. Shamashastry found in 1904 in Mysore, South India, were written down in the seventeenth and the early nineteenth century respectively. A text fragment of Kautilya's *Arthashastra* which was discovered in northern India dates from the twelfth century.[1] Alone on account of the perishability of palm leaves, the work had to be copied after a certain period of time (cf. Rangarajan 1992, 823). Thus, the 'rediscovered' manuscripts of the *Arthashastra* are not 2300 years old but were copied some four hundred to two hundred years ago. Therefore, the *Arthashastra* was not 'lost' at any time—not even in the era of Islamic rule from the thirteenth to the eighteenth century.

As significant as the textual transmission of the *Arthashastra* has been, much more important has been its oral transmission (parallel to the quantitatively very limited dissemination of the written text). Oral transmission means that the entire text is memorized and passed on in a continuous teacher-student cycle. Up to the late nineteenth century, oral transmission was the preferred mode of learning among Brahmin intellectuals. While it is impossible to estimate the number of persons who were familiar with the full text of the *Arthashastra* in the context of its oral and written transmission, the proposition remains valid that the key concepts of the *Arthashastra* were known to Indian intellectual elites ever since it was written twenty-three centuries ago.

However, for the academic discipline of Indology (dominated by European scholars), Shamashastry's discovery of the palm-leaf manuscripts of the *Arthashastra* in 1904 was indeed sensational news. In 1905, Shamashastry published an article about the *Arthashastra* in the British journal *Indian Antiquary* which contained lengthy excerpts from the original text. With that, Kautilya entered the discursive space of academic Indology. In 1909, Shamashastry published the full text, in the original Sanskrit, in book form, and six years later his English translation of the *Arthashastra* followed. Thus, for Indology, the intellectual afterlife of Kautilya's *Arthashastra* only began in 1905. From then on, the work and its author were systematically studied and analysed, and they became an important (and often controversial) subject of the Indological discourse.

However, there are indications of studies on Kautilya and the *Arthashastra* that were written well before Shamashastry's 1905 essay. It is still unclear whether the whole text or selected text passages of the *Arthashastra* were used as source material for these studies. The British Library in London lists the following books that need to be examined: N. Chiefale, *Kautilya*, Rome, 1825; E. Maneoseur, *Chanakya-Kautilya*, Paris, 1887; and Ramachandra Ghosh, *Morals of Chanakya*, Calcutta, 1891 (cf. Gupta 2015a; Gautam 2013a, 43). Another research lacuna concerns the written and oral transmission of *Chanakya niti*—collections of (putative) aphorisms and maxims by Kautilya. It needs to be explored to what extent the *Chanakya niti* were known beyond elite milieus in broader layers of the Indian population. Whatever future research on the history of the *Chanakya niti* may yield, it is a plausible proposition that 'imaginations' of the *Arthashastra*'s idea-contents and its author have been firmly established in broad layers of the Indian population for more than two thousand years.

The 'presence' of Kautilya's *Arthashastra* in the Indian cultural space over more than two millennia—as knowledge of the text or key concepts thereof—derives from the basic fact of its written and oral transmission. Such passing on of a classical asset constitutes one trait of politico-cultural continuity and is also a specific expression of the broader process of cultural continuity in India. The *Arthashastra*'s embeddedness in India's cultural continuity reveals itself not only through its oral and written transmission but equally so in the work's reception by outstanding figures of India's cultural sphere across the centuries. Particularly during the first millennium AD, the *Arthashastra* impinged profoundly on the works of outstanding Indian authors (cf. Kangle 2010b/1965, 60f, 279f; Scharfe 1968, 1ff). Brahmin, Buddhist and Jain authors quote from the work or comment on it. Classical poets and playwrights take recourse to Kautilya and the *Arthashastra*. Among them are:

- Asvaghosa (approx. 80–150 AD)
- Kalidasa (approx. turn of the fourth to the fifth century AD)
- Vishakhadatta (approx. fifth century AD)
- Dandin (approx. sixth century AD)
- Vatsyayana (approx. third century AD), author of the *Kamasutra*

India's second classical work of statecraft is *Nitisara*, probably written in the seventh or eighth century AD. Its author Kamandaka largely follows *Arthashastra* in form and content and calls Kautilya his guru. (cf. Upinder Singh 2010).

Of singular importance is the ever-popular classic play *Mudrarakshasa* by Vishakhadatta, in which Kautilya is the protagonist (cf. Fritze 1886). On this, historian Romila Thapar stated:

> Eight hundred years after Kautilya [...] Vishakhadatta refers to him also as Vishnugupta which was the name Kautilya had in the Gupta period. So it is almost as if it [*Arthashastra*] is a contemporary

text. Now that, I think, is an interesting comment on Kautilya by somebody who knows the text obviously very well, because the kinds of games that Kautilya plays in this drama are games that come straight out of the *Arthashastra* [...]. So, the *smriti* literature, the dharmashastra literature, the *Arthashastra* sort of literature that is written in the post-Gupta period and up to the early medieval period, they all list him, amongst the earlier writers. They list Kautilya. He did not vanish. Kautilya was known. (EI Thapar)[2]

The longue durée lore of Kautilya's *Arthashastra* is, of course, not a singular phenomenon in India. Other classical works such as the epics *Mahabharata* and *Ramayana*, the collection of animal fables *Panchatantra* or the *Manu-smriti*—the *dharmashastra* on social and ethical norms—have been handed down across time both orally and in writing. The elaborate and tedious passing on of these classical works over more than two millennia is an expression of the continuity of Indian culture despite great political upheavals.

3

A METHODOLOGICAL APPROACH TO KAUTILYA'S *ARTHASHASTRA*

Before we turn to the main ideas and concepts of Kautilya's *Arthashastra*, the methodological and theoretical orientation to their interpretive exposition need to be outlined. First, in our interpretive exposition we uphold the primacy of the text over the context of its origin. A classical text like the *Arthashastra* possesses autonomy, 'eigenvalue'—i.e., intrinsic worth—and timelessness. Contextuality—in biographical, social, cultural and historical terms—is only a subordinate aspect of the interpretation. Secondly, our interpretive exposition is situated in the framework of Political Science that includes the disciplinary subfields of Political Theory, Comparative Political Theory and International Relations theory. Thirdly, we draw on the vast research work on the *Arthashastra* done by Indologists to whom we owe the work's translation from Sanskrit into English (and German).[1] Yet, by its very nature, the Indological approach to Kautilya's *Arthashastra* is one of Sanskrit philology and historiography and thus tends to miss Kautilya's unique contributions to the evolution of political theory and statecraft. For us, as political scientists, Kautilya's *Arthashastra* is a foundational text of Political Science.

The main methodological guide to Kautilya's *Arthashastra* is provided by Max Weber. Social science is for Weber 'a science which aims at the interpretive *understanding* of social behavior in order to gain an explanation of its causes, its course and it effects' (Weber 1972, 29). Weber's sociological methodology of 'understanding' (*Verstehen*) and causal explanation of social reality aims at the reconstruction of the meaning (*Sinn* or *Sinngehalt*) of actions among human beings and/or objects generated by them—like texts, for example.

Because the meanings of social action and the objectifications it generates are mostly not obvious, these latent meanings need to be reconstructed through the social scientist's analytical research work. There is a significant conceptual overlap between Weber's notion of understanding and that of Hans-Georg Gadamer. Therefore, Gadamer's remarks on the interpretation of ancient, classical texts are quite relevant for the interpretation of Kautilya's *Arthashastra*. In *Truth and Method*, Gadamer writes:

> Not just occasionally, but always, the meaning of a text goes beyond its author. That is why understanding is not merely a reproductive but always a productive activity as well [...]. [Temporal distance] lets the true meaning of the object emerge fully. But the discovery of the true meaning of a text or a work of art is never finished. It is in fact an infinite process [...]. Interpretation here, then, does not [only] refer to the sense intended, but to the sense that is hidden and has to be disclosed. In this sense, every text not only presents an intelligible meaning but, in many respects, needs to be interpreted. (2013, 307, 309, 345)

As we will see in some detail later in this book, the intelligible meaning or the 'idea' of raison d'état is very much present in the *Arthashastra*, but Kautilya does not explicitly use that term. Thus, our interpretation often needs to 'transpose' latent meanings into concepts or categories. Moreover, we have to recognize that, in the first place, our very interpretation cannot proceed in the mode of 'pure' hermeneutics, that is, without any presuppositions. Since there is no 'direct' and 'immediate' cognitive access to the latent meanings of any text (and particularly not of ancient texts), interpretation is inevitably entangled with, if not dependent on prior-knowledge and preconceptions of the subject matters addressed in the text. Thus, when interpreting an ancient text like the *Arthashastra*, we inevitably have to draw on *post festum* concepts and categories that have been generated in the evolution of the social and political sciences centuries or even millennia after the *Arthashastra* was written. When we are 'applying' such post-Kautilyan categories in the interpretation, we must, however, not 'squeeze' the text's idea-contents into these categories. Instead of merely subsuming the *Arthashastra*'s pre-modern idea-contents under modern categories, we must seek their dialectical interface in order to generate concepts that are true to meaning, and have both explanatory power and theoretical value. That is what we mean by the methodological concept of 'transposition'.

That the interpretation of the *Arthashastra* along the methodological path of transposition based on the concept of structural homology is a valid proposition would be supported by Wilhelm Halbfass when he writes: 'The attempt to eliminate all Western constructs and preconceptions and to liberate the Indian tradition from all non-Indian categories of understanding would not only be impractical, but presumptuous in its own way' (1991, 12). Thus, the interpretive exposition of key ideas and concepts of Kautilya's *Arthashastra* must necessarily imply a comparative dimension.

In adopting this methodological approach, we orient ourselves on Max Weber's methodological core principle: 'the discursive character of our cognition'. That principle refers to 'the fact that we only grasp reality through a sequence of ideational changes' (2012, 127). At the core of Weber's research methodology, therefore, is 'a constant reshaping of those concepts by means of which we seek to grasp reality. The history of the sciences of social life therefore is, and remains, in constant flux between the attempt to order facts intellectually by means of concept formation; the breaking down—because of the broadening and displacement of the scientific horizon—of the mental images that have been arrived at in this fashion; and the new formation of concepts on this altered basis' (ibid., 134).

Weber's second methodological principle relevant for the Political Science-based interpretation of core ideas and concepts of Kautilya's *Arthashastra* is the 'ideal-type' concept, which is the logical conclusion of the just outlined process of understanding and explaining (latent) meanings of social action and objectifications thereof; in our case, a classical text on statecraft. The ideal type 'is obtained by means of a one-sided accentuation of one or a number of viewpoints and through the synthesis of a great many diffuse and discrete individual phenomena (more present in one place, fewer in another, and occasionally completely absent), which are in conformity with those one-sided, accentuated viewpoints, into an internally consistent mental image' (Weber 2012, 125). The ideal type is an intellectual construction of relations and coherence, which do not exist as such in the real world: 'In its conceptual purity, this mental image [ideal type] cannot be found empirically anywhere in reality' (Weber 2012, 125). However, the ideal type is a conceptual construction which allows heterogeneous 'empirical reality to be ordered intellectually in a valid manner' (Weber 2012, 137).[2]

The ideal type has a number of advantages compared to other methodological approaches: With the deductive or inductive nomological approach, the specific quality of the object of investigation is reduced to an attribute of some general rule or theory. The same applies to the classificatory approach that forms a generic category based on certain features which various social and/or cultural phenomena have in common. The descriptive approach excludes the possibility of theoretical generalization and also takes no account of latent meanings. The intuitive 'reliving' of or 'immersion' into social and/or cultural phenomena leads to results that are neither inter-subjectively verifiable nor generalizable. From these dilemmas, the concept of the ideal type provides a way out.

The rational-logical design process of the ideal type and its rational-logical internal structure are based on the—itself ideal-type—assumption of the tendency towards rationality in man: 'The rational construction of ideal types is therefore 'appropriate' because in the cultural reality of man, the tendency towards rationality is always present' (Henrich 1952, 100). However, the assumption of the disposition towards rationality does not imply that Weber would see rationality as the predominant feature of social action. Lastly, it needs to be emphasized that the ideal type is *not* a normative category that is articulating an 'ideal' of how social or cultural phenomena should be like: 'An "ideal type" in our sense of the term is totally indifferent to evaluative judgments; it has nothing to do with any other "perfection" than a purely logical one. *There are ideal types of brothels as well as of religions*' (Weber 2012, 130, emphasis added).

We feel, albeit indirectly, encouraged in adopting Weber's methodology for the interpretation of Kautilya's *Arthashastra* by the fact that Weber was the first western social scientist who recognized the significance of Kautilya. That is demonstrated by Weber's reference to Kautilya in his famous essay *Politics as a Vocation*, and this reference is probably the one and only occasion that Western social and political scientists might ever have encountered the words 'Kautilya' and '*Arthashastra*' (cf. Weber 2008a, 203; 1988b, 554f). Because of its significance for our methodological approach (and theoretical orientation as well), it needs to be emphasized that Max Weber did possess substantial knowledge of Kautilya and the *Arthashastra*. In his sociology of religion studies on Hinduism and Buddhism, he refers to the *Arthashastra* five times, including some paraphrasing of text passages. Weber's references are based on R. Shamashastry's article on Kautilya's *Arthashastra* in the journal *Indian Antiquary* (Vol. 34, 1905). This article contains a summary of *Arthashastra* and some text excerpts translated into English for the first time (Weber 2000, 349). Weber's exposition of Kautilya makes it very likely that he also read the essays of Hillebrandt and Jolly on Kautilya's *Arthashastra* which were published in 1907 and 1908 in the *Journal of the German Oriental Society* (cf. Garbe 1917, 1f).

In *Politics as a Vocation*, Weber rates Kautilya's *Arthashastra* as 'classic'. Indeed, in the history of political theory and theorized statecraft Kautilya has the rank of a classic (cf. Weber 2008a, 1988b; Hillebrandt 1923; Zimmer 1973; Kangle 2010b/1965; Sil 1989; Boesche 2002; Watson 1992). Classical texts are distinguished in that they remain significant beyond the historical context of their origin. Classics remain thought-provoking and provide intellectual inspiration across the ages.

However, Kautilya wrote his classic text on statecraft in Sanskrit—the language of the intellectuals of ancient India. Thus, our interpretive exposition has to rely on *Arthashastra*'s translations into English and German. In 1915, the first English translation of the full text of the *Arthashastra* was published by R. Shamashastry. In 1926, the German translation (from Sanskrit) of the Swiss-American Indologist Johann Jakob Meyer was published (re-printed in 1977). Between 1965 and 1972, R. P. Kangle's three-volume historical-critical edition of Kautilya's *Arthashastra* was published: Volume I, the original Sanskrit text; Volume II, the English translation (2010a/1972); and Volume III, a comprehensive commentary volume in English.

In the Penguin Classics series, a new English translation of the *Arthashastra* by L. N. Rangarajan was published in 1992. Most unfortunately, in this edition the original text structure is rearranged, supposedly to facilitate 'better intelligibility'.[3] This paperback edition has made the *Arthashastra* accessible to a wider reading public, but Kangle's translation remains the authoritative text version. In 2013, Patrick Olivelle, the Sri Lanka-born American Sanskrit philologist, published a new translation into English, titled *King, Governance and Law in Ancient India: Kautilya's Arthashastra*.

For our study, R. P. Kangle's English translation of Kautilya's *Arthashastra* is used as the prime source. In addition, we use J. J. Meyer's German translation which is meticulous in philological terms yet features a very vivid style of language—in contrast to Kangle's rather 'dry' style. For the Political Science-oriented interpretation of the *Arthashastra*, drawing on both is most helpful. Occasionally, Meyer's and Kangle's translations of text passages diverge both in style and semantic nuances. While Kangle's translation is the basis of our interpretive exposition of the *Arthashastra*, we do occasionally deviate from it and follow Meyer's translation of the text passage in question. When such a synoptic approach is taken with respect to Kangle's and Meyer's translations, we apply conceptual plausibility as benchmark.[4]

In spite of the advantage of being able to access the translations of both Kangle and Meyer, the fact remains that they both are Sanskrit philologists. Yet the *Arthashastra* is a foundational text of political theory and theorized statecraft. Most political scientists owe their access to Kautilyan thought to Sanskrit philologists like Kangle and Meyer. However, conversely, Kangle and Meyer lack the disciplinary background and vocabulary of Political Science when articulating Kautilya's ideas and concepts on the state and statecraft. Instead, they use an 'haute conversational language' in their translations. However, in order to adequately explain the central ideas and concepts of Kautilya's *Arthashastra*, the vocabulary of (modern) Political Science is indispensable.

Moreover, the problem here is not only one of philology and

linguistics. The issue of adequate vocabulary in terms of Political Science converges with the deeper methodological issue of how to explain latent ideas of the *Arthashastra*. In Meyer's and Kangle's translations, key categories such as 'state', 'security', 'interest', 'conflict of interest' or, as mentioned, 'raison d'état' are either completely absent or not consistently used. Yet the 'idea'—so to speak 'behind' these categories—is very much present in the *Arthashastra*, albeit often articulated by euphemisms and metaphors. Therefore, the interpretation of Kautilya's *Arthashastra* necessitates an adequate 'transposition' of these latent ideas into Political Science terminology. In other words: the mere citation of text passages of the *Arthashastra* will not (or not adequately) reveal the actual idea-content contained in them. However—and here lies the puzzle—such transposition must not compromise the intellectual originality and intrinsic worth of Kautilya's ideas. We feel encouraged in our approach by Charles Drekmeier who writes in his seminal work *Kingship and Community in Early India*:

> It is our responsibility to apply the refinements of methodology and the social sciences in *searching out the intended or latent sense of the ideas that confront us. The discovery of meanings that might otherwise remain hidden to us* is a nobler employment for our newer knowledge than its restriction to the essentially negative tasks of controverting and deriding. (Drekmeier 1962, 283, emphasis added)

The transposition concept in our study is derived from Helmuth Plessner's concept of 'covariance'. In his 1931 study *Macht und menschliche Natur* [Power and Human Nature],[5] Plessner speaks of 'covariant measurement systems' in 'the multiplicity of systems of meaning that have occurred in history.' His covariance approach is about the 'equal feasibility' of cultural and scientific achievements being generated in different historical periods and diverse cultures (cf. Plessner 2003, 217).[6] A similar approach is adopted by Eric Voegelin with his concept of 'equivalences of experience and symbolization in history' (cf. Voegelin 1990/1971) and by Adda B. Bozeman in her seminal work *Politics and Culture in International History* where she writes: 'certain other non-Western modes of comprehending the incidents of government seem, on examination, to refer to precisely, or nearly, the same values that Western nations are now trying to convey' (Bozeman 1960, 7).

In our study, covariance designates structural homology of ideas and concepts within a subject area that have been generated in historically and culturally distant contexts. In our case: pre-modern Indian ideas and concepts of statecraft are neither identical with nor qualitatively different from their modern Western homologues, but they are intrinsically related in the sense of a family resemblance. For clarification, let us take N.P. Sil's *Kautilya's Arthashastra: A Comparative Study* as an example. Sil compares Kautilya with Plato, Aristotle and Machiavelli. Kautilya, Plato and Aristotle lived in roughly the same historical epoch but in very different cultural contexts. In the case of Machiavelli, both the historical and cultural distance to Kautilya is very wide. Nevertheless, Sil concludes that the four thinkers 'appear to have derived their outlook on human society from a fundamentally similar ideological base. All of them have almost similar notions of human nature, the need for stability in the commonwealth, and the desirability of righteousness in collective political behavior' (Sil 1989, 9). Similarly, Max Weber has noted that Kautilya's understanding of statecraft is very similar to what we find in Machiavelli's political writings and that his understanding of the economy as the basis of state capacity conceptually corresponds to mercantilist and cameralist economic theory in Europe during the seventeenth and eighteenth century.

That the interpretation of the *Arthashastra* along a Weberian methodological path based on the concept of structural homology is supported by Halbfass, as cited above, stating that the attempt to purge the analysis of the Indian tradition from modern, non-Indian categories, 'would not only be impractical, but presumptuous in its own way' (Halbfass 1991, 12). Homologous thought-structures can be in different stages of their conceptual evolution. Therefore, the relation between an 'idea' and a 'category' can be understood in the sense of structural homology. Idea and category are intrinsically related thought-structures which have the same basic meaning but exhibit a different semantic morphology. Categories differ from ideas through a higher level of abstraction, precise definitional boundaries and the explication of the dimensions of meaning within these boundaries. One might say that the idea is the category 'in its youth'. And in their 'youth', one may add, thought-figures are intellectually most potent.

The transposition of Kautilyan ideas into (modern) categories of Political Science involves the risk that important nuances of Kautilyan thought could get lost because they may not have been addressed by modern Political Science. This is plausible, if we consider Helmuth Plessner's proposition that the development of humanities and social sciences is not a 'mono-linear' progression in which all pre-modern theoretical (and artistic) achievements have inevitably been absorbed and superseded by modern Western science (Plessner 2003, 149ff). Wilhelm Halbfass, too, repudiates the view 'that ancient and non-Western traditions are superseded by, (*aufgehoben*') in modern Western thought. They may, in fact, reach far beyond our current capacity of comprehension' (1991, 170). Thus, to restate the point made above, the intellectual eigenvalue of Kautilyan ideas and concepts must not be compromised. That means that the transposition of Kautilyan ideas must highlight the originality of Kautilya's intellectual achievements in the pre-modern evolution of Political Science. The second risk involved in the transposition of Kautilyan ideas is, as indicated above, drifting methodologically into a 'logic of subsuming': concepts and categories of modern Political Science are employed as classification categories under which Kautilyan ideas and concepts are subsumed in a manner that their originality and eigenvalue get lost.

We conclude by stating that the interpretation of Kautilya's *Arthashastra* by means of modern Political Science vocabulary involves necessarily comparative methodology that is valid as long as there is a heightened awareness of the '*cultural uncertainty relation*' that is inevitably associated with any comparative approach (Müller 2008, 105).

Our interpretive exposition of Kautilya's *Arthashastra* starts off with an outline of its basic conceptual features and characteristics, including Kautilya's epistemology and methodology. Next, the introductory part of the *Arthashastra*—'Book I'—is paraphrased rather extensively. This is done to provide insight into Kautilya's characteristic mode of argumentation and representation. In Book I, core ideas and concepts are introduced which feature in a more elaborate form in the subsequent parts of the work. Thus, the paraphrasing of Book I should help get a sense of the overall gestalt of the *Arthashastra*, as paraphrasing the entire volume is beyond the scope of our study. Next, the interpretation of Kautilya's *Arthashastra* proceeds with the analysis of three text-immanent concept clusters: 'the seven state factors' (*saptanga* theory), 'the six methods of foreign policy' (*shadgunya* theory), and 'the four basic principles of politics' (*upayas*).

4
KAUTILYA'S *ARTHASHASTRA* IN THE CONTEXT OF COMPARATIVE POLITICAL THEORY

Our interpretation of Kautilya's *Arthashastra* is guided by the methodological assumption that there are structural homologies between central ideas and concepts of this pre-modern treatise and key concepts and categories of Weberian social science and 'realist' thought in modern Political Science. Therefore, we need to explain the linkage of these modern concepts and categories to the classical ideas that underpin the *Arthashastra*. As with our methodological approach, much of the theoretical orientation for our interpretation derives from Max Weber, notably his categories of power, interest, conflict of interest and (patrimonial) state. In their core meaning, these categories are key components of the *Arthashastra*'s conceptual content. As we employ these modern categories for analysis and interpretation, these conceptual tools first need to be defined and explained in 'self-referential' terms.

In addition, we draw on Max Weber's sociology of religion studies on Hinduism and Buddhism, in which Kautilya's *Arthashastra* is repeatedly discussed, as a theoretical foil for the interpretation. In particular, we look at Weber's concept of the ancient Indian patrimonial state and its socio-religious foundations. Between April 1916 and May 1917, Weber published three sociological studies on Indian religiosity in the journal *Archiv für Sozialwissenschaft und Sozialpolitik*.[1] In 1921, a year after Weber's death, these essays were published as Volume II of the three-volume edition *Collected Essays on Sociology of Religion* (*Gesammelte Aufsätze zur Religionssoziologie*) (Weber 2008a).[2] Hereinafter, following the terminology chosen by Detlef Kantowsky, Weber's three essays are designated as 'Hinduism Study' (cf. Kantowsky 1986). The English-speaking reader depends on a highly problematic translation of Weber's three essays by Hans. H. Gerth and Don Martindale.³ This translation was published 1958 under the title *The Religion of India—The Sociology of Hinduism and Buddhism* (2000).

Can Max Weber's 'Hinduism Study'—a century after its publication—still provide a theoretical orientation for our study? We think it does. Weber's work is not outdated because it is neither a historiographical work nor an ethnographic and sociological analysis of colonial India in the early twentieth century. Rather it is a sociological analysis of the 'Hindu order of life' strictly following the ideal-type methodology. The 'data material' which Weber uses mostly are the formative, classical texts of ancient India as well as the research results of Indology in the early twentieth century, including those on Kautilya's *Arthashastra*. The Hindu order of life exhibits a unique structural continuity over more than twenty-five hundred years. The research path taken by Weber takes that into account by focusing—in the ideal-type mode—on the historical and ideational roots of this social order and its political framing at about the middle of the first millennium BC. Then, the ideational and social structures of this order were firmly established and the central 'value ideas' of the Indian *weltanschauung* and social practice have since remained largely intact, although political conditions have changed frequently and profoundly. That is also the position adopted both by the Indologist Michael Witzel and the political scientist Charles Drekmeier:

> It should be stressed that much, perhaps most of what is 'typical Indian', was formed already then [in ancient India]; though of course later on other traits (such as Islam, European influence) have been added. Therefore, much room is given [in Witzel's study] to the culture and the original ideas of the early Indians. During a prolonged stay in South Asia (in the case of the author's many years in the conservative Kathmandu Valley) one will realize that what had been documented in texts and pictures more than 2000 years ago, is indeed still alive in custom and imagination. (Witzel 2010, 7f)

The critical period of ancient Indian history was the age that spanned the Upanishads and the fullest development of Mauryan administration under Ashoka. In these formative years, roughly from the 7th to the middle of the 3rd century BC, the dimensions of Indian philosophical and social thought were established. All subsequent speculation was embellishment, the logical development of ideas, and the transformation of philosophy into ideology. (Drekmeier 1962, 282)

4.1 MAX WEBER'S POLITICAL SOCIOLOGY: KEY CATEGORIES

For Weber, 'struggle' (*Kampf*) designates a central social relationship in all communities (*Vergemeinschaftungen*)—ranging from clan to tribe to (patrimonial) states: 'A social relationship will be called struggle insofar as the behavior of one party is oriented purposefully towards making his own will prevail against resistance of other parties or another party' (Weber 1972, 85; 1956, 27). Struggle is the consequence of different and contrary interests of people within a community and between political communities. '*Interests (material and ideational), not: ideas, dominate directly the actions of men*' (Weber 2008a, 302, emphasis added).

When a struggle occurs with the intention that each of the opponents involved will enforce his respective will, 'power' decides the outcome of the struggle. Power decides who prevails and who must be subordinate: ' "Power" (*Macht*) is the probability that one actor within a social relationship will be in a position to carry out his own will despite resistance, regardless of the basis on which this probability rests' (Weber 1968, 53; 1956, 38). Thus, power is the actual capacity to enforce one's will. The instruments of power are highly varied, ranging from psychological and intellectual superiority to physical strength to material and financial wealth, and finally to the use of armed force. In principle, it does not matter whether the instruments of power are 'operationally' employed or the perception of their existence—'in being'—suffices to enforce one's will.

For Weber all 'politics' is based on the struggle for power: 'Anyone who engages in politics is seeking power [...] precisely because power is the inevitable means, and the striving for power is one of the driving forces, of all politics' (Weber 2008b, 156, 194; 1988b, 507, 547). Weber's definition of politics is: 'For us, therefore, "politics" means the attempt to gain a share of power or to influence the distribution of power, whether it be among states or groups of people living within a state' (Weber 2008b, 156; 1988b, 506).

In the evolution of social life, the starting point of politics is the creation of some sort of 'order' within communities which regulates the 'leadership' thereof. Once a community has organized leadership, it becomes a 'political association' (*politischer Verband*). For Weber, leadership is the central issue of all politics. The condition, the ultimate means, and the aim of political leadership, is power.

The exercise of leadership over a political association, Weber calls 'domination' (*Herrschaft*). Domination 'is the probability that a command with a given specific content will be obeyed by a given group of persons' (Weber 1968, 53; 1956, 38). Political domination in a given territorial area—i.e., obedience of the people to the political leader(s)— depends on the threat and/or application of physical force on the part of the political leadership. All communities encompassing a given territory and possessing a political order commonly follow that political leaders rule with the (ultimate) recourse to violence. This central feature is shared by tribal communities, patrimonial states and modern states. Weber defines the state as follows:

> [A] compulsory political organization with continuous operations (*politischer Anstaltsbetrieb*) will be called a 'state' insofar as its administrative staff successfully upholds the claim to the *monopoly of the legitimate use of physical force* in the enforcement of its orders [...]. Like the political associations that historically precede it, the state is a relationship of rule [domination] by people over people based on the means of legitimate force (i.e. force that is regarded as legitimate). In order for the state to prevail, the people ruled must therefore submit to the authority claimed by those ruling at the time. (Weber 1968, 54; 1956, 39; 2008b, 157; 1988b, 507, emphasis added).

For Weber, a state without the monopoly of the legitimate use of force ceases to be a state: 'If there existed social structures for which force as a means was unknown, then the concept of the "state" would have lapsed; then something that would be called 'anarchy', in this particular sense of the word, would have emerged' (Weber 2008b, 156; 1988b, 506). However, the actual use of force by the state to compel the obedience of the ruled is the exception. People are—most of the times—obedient to the state because they accept state power, based on the (monopolized) recourse to the use of force, as 'legitimate'. The legitimacy of the state leader(s) can be based on tradition and/or legality, the latter meaning submission under the law that is set and enforced by the state. Thus, the use of force is by no means the usual or only means of the state's exercise of power; but without it there is no state.

4.2 WEBER'S CONCEPT OF THE PATRIMONIAL STATE IN INDIA

Weber's 'Hinduism Study' presupposes his theory of patrimonial domination, which he, inter alia, sets forth in *Economy and Society* in the sections 'Traditional Authority' and 'Patriarchalism and Patrimonialism' (cf. Weber 1968, 226-40, 1006-68; 1956, 167-78, 703-832). The roots of patrimonial domination lie in the authority of the *pater familias* over his family and household. Patrimonial authority transforms patriarchal domination of one (extended) family into the rule over a 'political community' like a tribe from which a state-like entity can eventually evolve. Weber defines as the two basic elements of patrimonial domination: first, the *'power of tradition*, that is, the inviolability of what has always been (*des 'ewig Gestrigen'*)'; and second, *'loyalty and fidelity towards the person of the master'*—the ruler or king (Weber 1968, 1009; 1956, 741, emphasis added). 'Thus arose almost everywhere a legally unstable, but in fact very stable order which diminished the area of the master's discretion in favor of traditional prescriptions' (Weber 1968, 1012; 1956, 744). The patrimonial ruler needs to not be despotic because his subjects accept him, and the political order 'embodied' by him, as both traditional and legitimate: 'As a rule [...] the political patrimonial ruler is linked with the ruled through a consensual community which also exists apart from his independent military force which is rooted in the belief that the ruler's powers are legitimate in so far as they are traditional' (Weber 1968, 1020; 1956, 752).

The patrimonial state's organization and its functional organs are tied to the person of the ruler, who 'embodies' the state. That is, the state has not yet gained structural autonomy from the person of the ruler. From the 'household' or 'court' of the ruler arises the 'administration' of the state, which blends the (primary) personal allegiance to the ruler with the inherent logic and factual constraints of the administrative tasks. The senior servants of the ruler's household responsible for food procurement, the kitchen, the wine cellar, the household budget, horse stable etc., gradually turn into 'functionaries' of state administration—they become the patrimonial bureaucracy with functional or territorial administrative responsibilities. It is in the sphere of taxation where the trend towards rational bureaucratic administration first develops and then consolidates. Similarly, the ruler's body guard transforms into the (patrimonial) army and police force that, however, retain allegiance to the ruler personally. The patrimonial bureaucracy is therefore a hybrid of personal servitude and the execution of factual administrative or executive assignments. In the ancient Indian patrimonial state, the patrimonial bureaucracy came to full development:

> Kingly administration became patrimonial and bureaucratic. On the one hand, it developed a regulated hierarchical order of officials with local and functional competences and appeals, on the other hand, however, administrative and court offices were not kept separate […]. As shown by inscriptions, an elaborate filing system developed as early as the first dynasty of great kings (that of Maurya, 3rd and 4th centuries BC). As is well known from its innumerable edicts, in the administration of the great Buddhist king, Ashoka, an incredible love of writing developed. In a fashion characteristic of patrimonial bureaucracies, the regents of state territories were relatives [of the ruler]. (Weber 2000, 67f; 2008a, 620f)

With explicit reference to Kautilya's *Arthashastra*, Weber specifies the patrimonial bureaucracy of the ancient Indian state:

The *Arthasastra* ('political science') of Kautilya, edited by Chanakya, and ascribed to a minister of the great Maurya king, Chandragupta, supplements this picture. Comprehensive statistics were to form the basis of administrations. All inhabitants were to be registered by caste, sib, calling, possession, and income. The inhabitants were required to have passports and were to be controlled throughout their entire lives. For fiscal authorities the greatest danger to the state, next to subversion, was thought to be impairment of the 'will to work'; therefore, theatres and musical bands in the country[side], alcohol trade and inns everywhere were to be restricted. And the spies of the administration were to report upon the most intimate private life of the subjects. (Weber 2000, 68; 2008a, 621)

The economic system of the ancient Indian patrimonial state is characterized by Weber as both as 'mercantilist' and 'cameralist'.[4] Weber defined mercantilism as the state—mostly absolutist monarchies—adopting the 'acquisitive impulse' of private capitalist actors in the historical context of merchant and manufacture capitalism prior to the industrial revolution (cf. Weber 1956, 1040). Cameralism can be considered as a variant of mercantilism in the German territorial states of the seventeenth and eighteenth centuries, where the state systematically promoted economic development and controlled a significant part of the economy as the way to expand the state's power potential. To both, politico-economic formations applies:

> The purpose is to strengthen the power of the state leadership externally and internally. Thus, mercantilism means formation of the modern power state, directly by increasing state revenues, indirectly by increasing the population's capacity to pay taxes. (Weber 1956, 1040; transl. ML)

In contrast to mercantilism, which features a certain balance between the state and private economic actors, cameralism is characterized by the state or the state bureaucracy playing a dominating role with respect to private economic actors. In Weber's view, that corresponds to the conditions of the ancient Indian patrimonial state. Even in the ancient

Indian cities with their wealthy merchant-capitalist guilds and their highly productive and prosperous artisan guilds, 'the king and his staff have always remained dominant no matter what consideration they might have made in the single case to the power of the guilds' (Weber 2000, 90; 2008a, 640). In this sense, Weber uses the term 'cameralism' as the most appropriate characterization of the economic system of the ancient Indian patrimonial state:

> In India all science of social life remained in the form of a policing and cameralistic technology [*Kunstlehre*]. This can well compare with the contributions of our [European] 17th and early 18th century cameralism. (Weber 2000, 161; 2008a, 703)

4.3 SOCIO-RELIGIOUS FOUNDATIONS OF THE PATRIMONIAL STATE IN ANCIENT INDIA

The caste system (*varna*) was not only the social foundation of the ancient Indian patrimonial state—the state itself had a caste-structure.[5] Only one caste—the *kshatriya* caste—assumed political leadership in peace and war. The fact that the exercise of political power was reserved for the *kshatriya* caste is—as Weber emphasizes—based upon specific *dharma* of this caste: 'Classical sources ascribe to the Kshatriyas the function of "protecting" the population politically and militarily' (Weber 2000, 64; 2008a, 617).

The Brahmin caste provides the intellectual and ideological resources, notably including 'political advice', for the functioning of the state. The *vaishya* and the *shudra* castes ensure the material-economic base of the state. From the fact that the state itself had a caste structure follows that the maintenance of the order of castes was the central objective of the ancient Indian patrimonial state. Any threat to the *varna* order was a threat to the existence of the state. Weber's concept of the ancient Indian patrimonial state rejects the Orientalist and essentialist perceptions associated with the term 'oriental despotism' in the sense of an arbitrary and totalitarian tyranny. Even though the political power of the ruler of an ancient India state was in principle 'absolutist', there were firm limits to the king's actual exercise of power. His legitimacy depended on his adherence to the kingly *dharma* of safeguarding the security and welfare of his people. Another limitation of the patrimonial exercise of power resulted from the caste structure of the state, which prevented the combination of political and religious power in one person. A 'divine ruler' or a ruler heading a state religion was unimaginable in ancient India. In fact, there was no state religion.

Instead, Weber argues, there was a complex system of checks and balances via the *varna* order, notably between the (*kshatriya*) ruler and the Brahmins. The ruler's political actions had to be backed up by the religious-magical, and thus legitimizing, support of the Brahmins: '[A] king without a Brahman is simply said to be "without guidance"' (Weber 2000, 125; 2008a, 670). The Brahmins possessed not only knowledge of religious and magic but also politically relevant expert knowledge on which the ruler depended because outside of Brahmanism no independent sources of expert knowledge existed. The dependence of the *kshatriya* king on Brahmanism was not one-sided. Conversely, the Brahmins depended on the ruler providing protection and alimentation for them: '[R]eligious and secular power cooperated in the interest of the legitimate order' (Weber 2008a, 603; transl. ML).

In Weber's analysis, the connectivity between the caste system and Hindu religiosity is the key to the significance of both to the state structure.[6] Strict adherence to the respective caste duties (*dharma*) is the only possible 'way of salvation' (*moksha*) in Hinduism. For Weber—logically and historically—the Brahmins originated the caste system: By defining themselves as caste, the Brahmins produced also the caste system (where it is logically irrelevant whether there are one, two or three other castes). Brahmanism is a hereditary priestly profession, and the intellectual and ritual socialization, and professionalization of the Brahmins occur exclusively within the Brahmin family or by the Brahmin Guru. Becoming a Brahmin priest and/or intellectual is neither possible through 'following a vocation' nor by training in caste-independent religious-educational institutions.

Historically, Weber argues, Brahmanism intellectually designed the caste order. The background, but not the cause for designing and implementing the *varna* system, is the socio-economic transformation of nomadic Arya tribes into village communities of sedentary farmers (and mixing with the indigenous Dravidian population).[7] The Brahmin-designed caste system cemented via endogamy the status of the privileged groups of tribal society in the new socio-economic context. Tribal magician-priests composed the Brahmins, the tribe's political and military leaders became the *kshatriya*s, and wealthier tribesmen, *vaishya*s. The ideological resource and lever for the Brahmins' social engineering was their religious authority based on the monopoly of interpreting the *Vedas*. '[T]his well-integrated, unique social system could not have originated or at least could not have conquered and lasted without the pervasive and all-powerful influence of the Brahmans. It must have existed as a finished idea long before it conquered even the greater part of North India' (Weber 2000, 131; 2008a, 675).

In the new caste order, the 'common people', previously enjoying basic equality within the nomadic tribe, were 'transformed' into the negatively-privileged *shudra* caste—segregated from the three 'higher' castes by social and ritual barriers. Such social degradation of the majority of the population, argues Weber, could be enforced in two ways: either through the use of force and economic leverage, or by what he calls 'religious domestication' by the Brahmins. The latter attained the acceptance of the caste system by the negatively-privileged *shudra*s through the religious doctrines of *samsara* and *karman*. According to the *samsara* doctrine, human beings go through an eternal cycle of death and rebirth—'an eternally rolling "wheel"' of reincarnations (Weber 2000, 132; 2008a, 676). Despite its apparent strangeness from a European perspective, Weber reminds us that the idea of reincarnation existed also in ancient Greece—Plato and Pythagoras being examples. However, the *samsara* doctrine becomes truly consequential only in combination with the *karman* doctrine: 'All (ritual and ethical) merits and faults of the individual formed a sort of ledger of accounts; the balance irrefutably determined the fate of the soul at rebirth, and this in exact proportion to the surplus of one or the other side of the ledger' (Weber 2000, 119; 2008a, 665). However, the *karman* doctrine does not mean a universal principle of retribution but is intrinsically linked to a person's caste existence and identity. Punishment or reward ensue in regard to the caste status in the 'next life', i.e., penalty or gratification in reincarnation mean ascent or descent in the hierarchy of castes.

For Weber, the 'Karma doctrine transformed the world into a strictly rational, ethically-determined cosmos. It represents *the most consistent theodicy ever produced in history*' (Weber 2000, 121; 2008a, 667, emphasis added). The Brahmins' focus on the *samara* and *karman* doctrines resolves the problem of how the majority population would accept its social and ritual degradation as *shudra* caste. The individual born as *shudra* 'knows' the why that is so: bad conduct in terms of his or her (caste) *dharma* in the previous life. At the same time, the acceptance of the current caste status can be rationalized by the firm prospect of being reborn with an improved caste status. Thus, the *samara* and *karman* doctrines create the prospect of both social advancement and soteriological gratification. In summary, Weber writes:

> The combination of caste legitimacy with karma doctrine, thus with the specific Brahmanical theodicy—in its way a stroke of genius—plainly is the construction of rational ethical thought, and not the product of any economic 'conditions'. Only the wedding of this thought product with the empirical social order through the promise of rebirth gave this order the irresistible power over thought and hope of members and furnished the fixed scheme for religious and social integration. (Weber 2000, 131; 2008a, 675)

4.4 WEBER ON THE 'MACHIAVELLIANISM' OF THE PATRIMONIAL STATE IN ANCIENT INDIA

The obligation to safeguard the security and welfare of the people is one side of the *kshatriya-dharma*: 'That king is good whose subjects are prosperous and experience no famine' (Weber 2000, 64; 2008a, 617). The other side is the obligation to expand the power of the state, notably through the expansion of state territory: 'Conquest was, therefore, the *dharma* of the king' (Weber 2000, 54; 2008a, 608). Thus, it is not surprising that Max Weber writes: 'Machiavelli has predecessors in India' (Weber 2008a, 2). And in his *Politics as a Vocation*, he states:

> This ethical specialization enabled Indian ethics to achieve a continuous development of the royal art of politics, one that followed only the laws proper to politics and indeed enhanced them radically. *The classical example of a truly radical 'Machiavellianism', in the popular sense of the word, in Indian literature is found in Kautilya's Arthasastra*, which dates back to very early pre-Christian times, and is said to be from the time of 'Chandra Gupta'. *Compared to this, Machiavelli's 'Il Principe' is innocuous*. (Weber 2008b, 203; 1988b, 554f, emphasis added)

We have to keep in mind that Weber did not know the full text of the *Arthashastra* when he compared it with Machiavelli's *Prince*, but he had read the latter text well enough to differentiate between Machiavelli's core ideas and 'Machiavellism' as a popular metaphor for power politics without regard for ethics.[8] Weber also compares Kautilyan political thought with Thucydides' understanding of politics in *The Peloponnesian War*. Notably, Weber draws parallels between Kautilya's argumentation and that of the Athenians in the 'Melian Dialogue' who expound purposive political rationality in terms of power politics. For a ruler of an ancient Indian patrimonial state, the individual personality, the dynastic lineage or the recourse to 'divine authorization' were of secondary importance. What mattered were political leadership skills resulting in victorious wars and a population content in political and economic terms: 'Hence, success of the King was decisive' (Weber 2000, 145; 2008b, 686).

Weber was familiar with the 'warring states' period of ancient India. The two classical Indian epics *Mahabharata* and *Ramayana* bear witness to these neverending wars, in the course of which the number of (patrimonial) states steadily declined as the losing states were annexed or became vassals. Around the middle of the first millennium BC, there were sixteen territorial states in North India. Among them, Magadha, located in the eastern Ganga plains, emerged as the hegemonic power. Step by step, Magadha absorbed all competing states of northern India.

Towards the end of the fourth century BC, Chandragupta Maurya (ca. 360–300 BC) and his Brahmin chief adviser Kautilya established the Maurya Empire, which stretched from the Afghanistan to the Deccan Mountains and from the Arabian Sea to the Gulf of Bengal (cf. Kulke/Rothermund 1998). With this historical background, Weber writes:

> That a king should ever fail to consider the subjugation of his neighbors by force or fraud remained inconceivable to secular and religious Hindu literature [...]. The *dharma* of the prince was to conduct war for the sake of pure power per se. He had to destroy his neighbor by cunning and fraud and no matter what crafty, unknightly, and ruseful means, by surprise attack, when in distress, through instigation of conspiracies among his subjects, and by bribing his trusted friends. (Weber 2000, 64, 146; 2008a, 617, 687)

The ruler of the ancient Indian patrimonial state was not subject to any restrictions in his political actions, provided they served the purpose of maintaining and expanding the power of the state and did not infringe upon the welfare of the people. In terms of domestic policy, for the ruler that meant:

> He had to keep in check and tax his own subjects through spies, agent provocateurs, and a sophisticated [system of] cunning and suspicion. Here power politics (and to our mind quite unholy egotism of princes) were practiced for their own sake [and theoretically warranted]. All political theory was a completely amoral technology [theorized art] of how to get and hold power. It went far beyond what was familiar and average practice for the *signores* of the early Italian Renaissance in these respects and was devoid of any 'ideology' in our sense of the word. (Weber 2000, 146; 2008a, 687)

Max Weber's analysis of the politics in ancient India has the following features:

- The conduct of power politics—in inter-state relations and in domestic politics—was all-embracing and even more ruthless

than in Renaissance Italy (as typified by Cesare Borgia, for example).
- The practice of power politics was not negatively charged in ethical terms. Moreover, the advocacy of power politics was not camouflaged but explicitly, even offensively, postulated in ancient Indian political theory. 'And as in the Greek polis of classical times, so the princes in the epics of the Maurya epoch [*Mahabharata* and *Ramayana*] and more so in later times practiced as a matter of course the most naked "Machiavellianism" without objections on ethical grounds' (Weber 2000, 146; 2008a, 687).
- Power politics was perceived as an expression of political rationality and systematically theorized 'princely methods of warfare, politics, finance were rationalized, made subject to literary [exposition], and, in the case of politics, even quite Machiavellian theorizing' (Weber 2000, 3; 2008a, 567).

But why was there such systematic and profound theorizing of 'Machiavellian' power politics in ancient India?

Weber's analysis of the Indian patrimonial state sees its 'Machiavellian' power politics as a form of Brahmanical 'construction': 'The purely autonomous (Machiavellian) conceptions of the *dharma* of the princes resulted only partly from the political conditions [...] the other part came from consistent Brahmanical ratiocination' (Weber 2008a, 723, transl. ML). The characteristic of the Brahmanical rational thinking is 'to do justice, on their own terms, to the most varied spheres of life and knowledge, thus promoting the development of various scientific disciplines' (Weber 2008a, 687, transl. ML). Thus, Brahmanical thought is based on the recognition of ethical autonomy in accordance with the intrinsic worth of the different areas of life. From Brahmanism arises a political theory which ensures that 'the position of the prince and of politics generally is recognized with a peculiar, penetrating focus on the inherent dynamic and logic of politics' (Weber 2008a, 686, transl. ML).

In Max Weber's view, ancient Indian political theory is not the 'maid' of theology, nor does it submit to other metaphysical and ideological suppositions. Theorized statecraft is based on its inherent normative standards that are not compatible with the ethics of everyday life. Political theory is a scientific discipline which upholds the autonomy and the eigenvalue of politics. Kautilya's *Arthashastra* bears witness to that.

The analysis in the chapters that follow juxtaposes the conceptual ideal types of the Weberian patrimonial state with the structure of governance and institutions in Kautilya's *Arthashastra*. The first optimization of good life as laid down in the *dharmashastra* texts, and political order is the central organizing principle that interprets the minutiae of royal life, the complementarity of royal power and Brahmanic control, the judicious use of effective force, taxation, war, crime and just punishment.

5

THE KEY FEATURES OF KAUTILYA'S *ARTHASHASTRA*

In the *Arthashastra*, Kautilya treats political theory, governance, public administration, economics, law, foreign policy, intelligence and military affairs in 15 'Books' with a total of 150 chapters. The number of chapters per book varies greatly, ranging from only one chapter each in Books XI and XV up to 36 chapters in Book II. Roughly speaking, the first half of the *Arthashastra* (Book I-V) deals with domestic politics and the second part (Book VI-XIV) with foreign policy, diplomacy and warfare. The 15 'Books' can be summarized as follows:

Book I: The requirements to be met by the ruler and the human and institutional resources available to him in the exercise of power

Book II: The (patrimonial) state bureaucracy; the focus is on fiscal and economic policy

Book III: Legal system with emphasis on civil law

Book IV: Criminal law, including investigations and court proceedings

Book V: Monitoring and control of the state apparatus, using the intelligence service

Book VI: The 'seven state factors' (*saptanga* theory); the other focus is the constellation of states with their changing status as friend, enemy and neutral (*mandala* theory)

Book VII: The 'six methods of foreign policy' (*shadgunya* theory); the correlations of forces that determine the choice of one of the six methods

Book VIII: Causes for degradation of state factors (*prakriti*) and ways to counter that

Book IX: Planning foreign policy and/or military operations; the material and immaterial factors to be considered

Book X: The armed forces and its military branches; discussion of different forms of warfare and operational issues (mobilization, march, order of battle)

Book XI: Subversion and 'covert actions' against competing/hostile states; irregular warfare operations under pre-war and war conditions

Book XII: Use of diplomacy and intelligence operations by a weaker against a stronger state

Book XIII: Conquest of the enemy capital, its surrender should be achieved without storming it; mild and conciliatory treatment of the people of conquered territories

Book XIV: Means of deception and destabilization of the enemy: psychological warfare

Book XV: The methodological concepts underlying the work

Before we proceed to the substantive analysis of Kautilya's *Arthashastra* focusing on the three text-immanent concept cluster 'the seven state factors' (*saptanga*), 'the six methods of foreign policy' (*shadgunya*) and 'the four basic principles of politics' (*upayas*), we first list the basic characteristics of the work as a whole:

1. Kautilya's *Arthashastra* is a comprehensive, almost encyclopedic treatise of politics. It aims at systematically presenting and analysing all aspects of the state and statecraft.

2. The *Arthashastra* is a theoretical work on the state and statecraft, which builds on the earlier political theory of ancient India. The ruler, the state and statecraft, as designed by Kautilya, are ideal types.

3. The Kautilyan state is, on the one hand, an ideal-type conception and free of ideological suppositions, and on the other, a state model in a normative-instructional sense of how the state ought to be organized and operated.

4. Despite its references to state and society in classical India, the *Arthashastra* is not a descriptive and historical work. The Kautilyan state is not a portrayal of the Maurya Empire or of other historically antecedent or congruent states. There is no

historical role model for the Kautilyan ruler and his policies. Historical, mythological or empirical example cases are rarely used by Kautilya, and if so, only for illustrative purposes.

5. In the *Arthashastra*, Kautilya has not only intellectually digested earlier Indian political theory but draws heavily on his own experience in political practice. He himself states that the *Arthashastra* was written after *going through all the sciences in detail and observing the [political] practice* (KA, II, 10, 63).

6. Like all ideal-type concepts of political theory, the Kautilyan state has an historical context and an empirical foundation—i.e., it is not a utopian construction. The context dependency means that the Kautilyan state's institutional structure and modes of action are that of a patrimonial state.

7. For Kautilya, absolutist-monarchic rule is evidently the superior form of government. Thus, he does not engage in any comparative treatment of different forms of government, as Aristotle did. However, Kautilya at least mentions 'democratic'-oligarchical state structures (in ancient India).

8. Kautilya's theory of foreign policy is not structure-focused but adopts an actor-centred perspective: that of the *vijigishu*—the ruler, who, starting from his own state, pursues the strategic goal of politically uniting the Indian subcontinent.

9. The *Arthashastra* is a foundational text of Political Science in terms of units of analysis, ideas and concepts as well as methodology. Because of its comprehensive and theoretical character, the *Arthashastra* does not belong to the 'Mirrors for Princes' genre.[1]

Dietmar Rothermund describes Kautilya's *Arthashastra* as a 'political grammar of power accumulation, power distribution and power preservation' (EI Dietmar Rothermund).[2] This characterization should not be seen as a mere illustrative analogy. Grammar analyses the basic units of a language—word and sentence—and the structures that underlie and determine their moldings. Grammar is theoretical and analytical as well as normative because it upholds the general applicability of the (ideal-type) regularities theoretically extracted from the empirical language material. A grammar textbook serves not only the understanding of a language's inner structure as it is but as it ought to be. Relevant here is that grammar was 'invented' in India. Probably in the fifth century BC, Panini wrote the world's first grammar in which the basic linguistic terms such as root word, affix or syntax were developed and brought into systematic coherence. The methodology of Panini's Sanskrit grammar exerted profound influence on the entire ancient Indian *shastra* literature. Grammar 'has traditionally been considered as a fundamental and therefore most important science' in ancient India (Mylius 1983, 283). Thus, in Rothermund's view, 'Kautilya is congenial with the famous grammarian Panini, who is also amazingly modern' (El Rothermund).

With his 'grammatical' methodology, Kautilya extracts from heterogeneous political reality seven 'basic units'—*prakriti*—that are constitutive of the state: ruler, government, rural population, capital, treasury, armed forces and ally (foreign policy). The state can be theorized with this cluster of seven (ideal-type) concepts—*saptanga* theory. Kautilya analyses each of the seven elements of the state individually and in their interdependency. He shows in what manner they impact the state—positively or negatively—i.e., increase or degrade the power of the state, and the welfare of the people. Thus, the theoretical analysis gains also a normative dimension.

Next, Kautilya identifies the basic forms of political behaviour in general which aim at enforcing one's will against the resistance of others: the four *upayas*. The *upayas* are valid both for intra-state and for inter-state relations. Regarding inter-state relations, Kautilya derives from the *upayas* the concept cluster *shadgunya*, i.e., the 'six methods of foreign policy'. The *shadgunya* theory is logically and factually connected with the *saptanga* theory because the correlation of forces in terms of the *prakriti* determines which of the six foreign policy options is to be chosen. Again, each of these modes of foreign policy agency is analysed individually and in their interdependency. And that, too, is done in a normative framing: which of these foreign policy actions (or combination thereof) leads to the state gaining power or losing it, which, for Kautilya, also means an increase or decline in the welfare of the people.

The 'grammatical' methodology of Kautilya's *Arthashastra* demonstrates the theoretical and analytical nature of the work that transcends mere description and narration—and thus gives the normative dimension of the *Arthashastra* a firm conceptual grounding.

Kautilya not only asserts the systematic character of his work, but expounds explicitly and in detail the methodical tools that make it a scientific work. In Book XV of the *Arthashastra*, he presents a list of 32 categories of his scientific methodology by which he demonstrates the validity of the principle of sufficient reason and logical consistency in his work:[3]

1. 'object of investigation': The means to maintain and improve material existence, including maintenance and expansion of political power
2. 'individual treatment': The investigation of certain aspects of the object of investigation
3. 'practical application': The result of the investigation of a certain subject area which can be generalized
4. 'term': Definition of the meaning of a word
5. 'proof': Explanation of the cause of a thing
6. 'summary statement': Explanation of the interaction of different causes for a thing
7. 'interpretation': Exposition of different factors involved in a thing
8. 'maxim': Generally valid instruction
9. 'reference': Explaining a thing by referring to other authors' statements on it
10. 'back reference': Explaining a thing by something already elaborated
11. 'forward reference': Statement of a fact which is explained later
12. 'analogy': Explaining a (yet) opaque thing through a known empirical fact
13. 'consequence': A phenomenon necessarily resulting from the thing itself

14. 'point of doubt': Conflicting explanations for a thing cause
15. 'subsuming': A thing which is closely related to another subject that was previously treated
16. 'econtrario': Explanation of a thing by its opposite
17. 'supplement': A previous statement is enriched by additional information
18. 'acceptance': Relying on the statements of other authors
19. 'elaboration': Thorough explanation of a thing
20. 'etymology': Derivation of a term's meaning from the word or stem it is based upon
21. 'illustration': Explaining a thing by way of example
22. 'restriction': Reference to exceptions to a rule
23. 'innovative term': New term or new meaning of an existing term generated by the author
24. 'claim': Assertions by other authors about a thing
25. 'correction': Revising the views expressed by other (previous) authors and opinions about a thing
26. 'universal statement': A generally valid statement without exceptions
27. 'introduction': Presentation of a hitherto untreated thing without providing an instant explanation of it
28. 'background': Situating a thing in a context that has already been investigated
29. 'necessity': Logically and practically only possible conclusion
30. 'alternative': Mutually exclusive conclusions from a situation (either-or)
31. 'combination': Multiple, coexisting conclusions from a situation (as well as)
32. 'inference': Conclusion which is not completely based on empirical facts

Kautilya demands that a *shastra* text must have a clear and stringent conceptual structure—he speaks of the 'skeleton'—which then must be filled with factual content—'flesh and blood' as he puts it. This had to be done without repetitions, vagueness, digressions and grammatical errors (cf. KA, II, 10, 57–62)

For the general reader, these explanatory notes are of crucial significance because, at the first reading of the *Arthashastra*, Kautilya's logical stringency and sophisticated methodology will most likely not become evident. Among the author's idiosyncrasies complicating the understanding of the *Arthashastra* are: very extensive, detailed and complex listings and classifications of facts and procedures, as well as the extensive presentation of the spectrum of options for multiple boundary conditions of a situation. Often there are abrupt shifts from listing and analysing concrete facts to expounding abstract concepts and vice versa. Rather than enhancing comprehensiveness, repeated approaches to the same subject in different perspectives in successive segments of the text are straining for the reader. Therefore, the reader should keep in mind what Betty Heimann writes:

> Indian logic, therefore, searches for commonality rather than difference among the phenomena. Not delineating or defining, but problems of identity, equality and similarity, the concept of coherence, the concept of inter-penetration of phenomena (*vyapti*), these are the questions that Indian systematic logic deals with again and again. (1930, 208)

6

PARAPHRASE OF BOOK I OF THE *ARTHASHASTRA*
The Ideal Ruler

In the following segment of our study, Book I of the *Arthashastra* is paraphrased in a concise manner. In this way, a preliminary insight into Kautilya's characteristic reasoning and mode of argumentation can be gained. Moreover, in Book I some of Kautilya's core concepts are introduced which are treated in greater detail later on in the text. Thus, one can get a certain sense of the conceptual gestalt of the *Arthashastra* as a whole.

1. KAUTILYA'S INTRODUCTION TO HIS WORK

Kautilya dedicates his work to Shukra and Brihaspati who are the mythological creators of the science of statecraft. Moreover, in Indian mythology, Shukra is the teacher of the demons who do not have an entirely negative connotation. Brihaspati is the teacher of gods (cf. Meyer 1977, 1). The dedication is therefore not addressed to the demons or the gods as such but rather applies to their 'teachers'. The divine or demonic mode of existence does not *eo ipso* constitute the status and dignity of gods and demons—for that a certain competence has to be acquired which, in turn, requires education by teachers.

Next, Kautilya tells the reader that his compendium summarizes the key concepts of all antecedent *arthashastras*. That means that textbooks on politics existed well before Kautilya wrote his *Arthashastra* and were considered necessary for obtaining the necessary competence in statecraft. However, these early political textbooks were lost in the centuries after the *Arthashastra* had been written. From Kautilya's references to them we can deduce that they had a theoretical character and were not just mythological or historical narratives about past rulers, as to learn from their mistakes and achievements. Thus, the imitation of historical role models is not at the centre of educating the (future) ruler; the systematic and theoretical study of the principles and methods of the exercise of political power is.

Kautilya characterizes his own work in a very self-confident manner: The essentials of all political theories contained in antecedent *arthashastra*s are summarized by him; however, his *Arthashastra* is in form and content, better than the earlier works. His *Arthashastra*, he emphasizes, is coherent, precise and without repetitions and diffuseness. Kautilya sees his work as an innovative advancement of political theory and theorized statecraft. He sees himself as intellectually superior to the antecedent authors. Refrain-like he states in the *Arthashastra* that others have postulated this or that, but he—Kautilya—says it is that way and not otherwise, or should be that way and not otherwise. Kautilya agreeing with previous authors is rather the exception.

> *Easy to learn and understand, precise in doctrine, sense and word, free from prolixity of text, thus has this work on Political Science been composed by Kautilya.* (KA, I, 1, 19)

2. PHILOSOPHY IS THE BENCHMARK

In the course of his education, Kautilya states that the (future) ruler must master four sciences: philosophy, theology, economics and political science. He polemicizes against antecedent authors who did not acknowledge all four disciplines as science. Against them, Kautilya argues that only by means of all four sciences the realization of both *artha* (material gain) and *dharma* (moral good) is possible. That is the criterion for defining science and other disciplines beyond the four sciences as mere 'auxiliary sciences'.

However, among the four enumerated sciences (as well as other disciplines), philosophy takes the first rank. Philosophy stands above the other three sciences because it provides a frame and structure for them. Through philosophy, what is actually valuable in the theology of the *Vedas*, what is wealthcreating or loss-making in economics, and what meets the requirements of statecraft in Political Science, can be determined. For Kautilya 'the philosophy' consists of the teachings of *samkhya*, *yoga* and *lokayata*:

- *samkhya*: Founded by the legendary philosopher Kapila in the pre-Buddhist period, it is a dualistic ontology of spirit and matter in which life is the mixture of both. The soteriology of the atheistic Samkhya philosophy is the knowledge about the world through logical rational cognition (cf. Garbe 1917).
- *yoga*: Contemplative and psycho-physical techniques to catalyze the generation of logical-rational or spiritual-mystical knowledge; Kautilya is only interested in rational knowledge (cf. Glasenapp 1974).
- *lokayata*: Atheistic, materialistic philosophy which sees the mind as an attribute of matter. There are similarities between *lokayata* and the philosophical materialism of the pre-Socratics in ancient Greece (cf. Mehta 1992).

The main features of these three philosophical 'schools' are not elaborated in the *Arthashastra*. Kautilya apparently assumes that they are sufficiently known to his readers. He also does not explain why the other philosophical schools of ancient India remain unmentioned. Since Kautilya considers the combination of *samkhya*, *yoga* and *lokayata* as 'the philosophy', it is implied that he does not necessarily endorse all the propositions put forth by each of the three schools. Rather it seems that, in spite of their differences and even contradictions, the three schools complement each other and provide, in their entirety, the philosophical approach desired by Kautilya (cf. Glasenapp 1974, 58, 139).

Philosophy, as defined by Kautilya, is realistic, rationalistic and materialist and thus takes distance to metaphysical suppositions. Most remarkable is that theology is presented as 'science' and not as a religious belief system. And philosophy will tell what is valuable in the *Vedas* and other religious texts and what is not. Moreover, philosophy—not theology—provides clarity on the puzzles of life and generates the intellectual and practical skills for all life situations.

> *Philosophy is ever thought of as the lamp of all sciences, as the means of all actions and as the support of all laws and duties.* (KA, I, 2, 12)

3. THE CASTE ORDER: THE STATE'S SOCIAL FOUNDATION

Only after the treatment of philosophy does Kautilya address the *Vedas*— *Sama Veda, Rig Veda, Yajur Veda* plus *Atharvaveda* and *Itihasaveda*, the latter consisting of the ancient Indian epics *Mahabharata* and *Ramayana*. However, Kautilya does not address the religious contents of the *Vedas*. Instead, he is exclusively interested in the ethical and social norms derived from the *Vedas*. For Kautilya, the *Vedas* serve as the prime source and justification of the caste system (*varna*) which he sees as the unshakeable foundation of the social order. Among these norms he distinguishes caste-specific and general, caste-independent duties. About the latter he says:

> *Duties common to all are: abstaining from injury to living creatures, truthfulness, uprightness, freedom from malice, compassionateness and forbearance.* (KA, I, 3, 13)

Kautilya does not elaborate on these general ethical norms but pays great attention to the caste-specific norms. For each of the four castes— *brahmin, kshatriya, vaishya* and *shudra*—there is a set of specific ethical norms (caste *dharma*) which Kautilya describes in detail:

- *Brahmin dharma*: Studying, teaching, priestly ritual, which goes along the right to be alimented by the other castes.
- *Kshatriya dharma*: Military service and protection of the people, which includes political leadership and governance tasks; (self-)education and generosity.
- *Vaishya dharma*: Entrepreneurial activity in agriculture, trade and crafts, (self-)education and willingness to donate.
- *Shudra dharma*: Subordination to the three upper castes, and physical labour in agriculture, crafts, trade and services.

Only strict adherence to the respective set of caste-duties leads to individual salvation (*moksha*) in this world and in heaven. Speaking of salvation in heaven, Kautilya does not seem to match his statements on (atheistic- materialistic) philosophy in the previous chapter. One gets the impression that Kautilya's message is: everyone should be happy after his own fashion—provided there is strict adherence to the respective caste *dharma*. For Kautilya, the caste duties are primarily a political question because he sees in them being disregarded the cause of societal chaos and the consequent decline or even disintegration of the state. Firmly ensuring the inviolability of the caste order with its different *dharmas* is thus a central political task of the ruler.

In addition to the caste *dharma*, Kautilya demands strict adherence to a set of norms specific to each of 'the four stages of life' (*ashrama*). The four stages are: 1) the socialization and education phase up to adolescence; 2) the active phase of working life and raising a family; 3) the more contemplative phase after birth of the first grandson; and 4) the detachment from worldly matters in the final stage of life.

> *Therefore, the king should not allow the special duties of the different beings to be transgressed by them; for, ensuring adherence to each one's special duty, he finds joy after death as well as in this life. For, people, among whom the bounds of Aryan rule of life are fixed, among whom the varnas and the stages of life are securely established and who are guarded by the three Vedas, prosper and do not perish.*
> (KA, I, 3, 16–17)

4. THE RIGHT USE OF THE STATE'S COERCIVE POWER

First, Kautilya emphasizes the paramount importance of the economy. Agriculture and animal husbandry produce crops, livestock and raw materials, and trade in these goods generates pecuniary profits. The economy is the basis of the ruler's exercise of power both internally and externally. Through a prospering economy, the state coffers get filled and a strong army can be sustained.

The growth of the economy and thus the power of the state and the welfare of the people are secured by the 'rod' (sceptre) in the hands of the ruler. 'Rod' implies the penal power of the ruler or coercive state power. The right use of coercive state power is the central question of statecraft, which Kautilya defines as follows:

> [The rod's] right administration constitutes the science of politics, having for its purpose the acquisition of things not possessed, the preservation of things possessed, the augmentation of things preserved and the bestowal of things augmented on a worthy recipient. On it is dependent the orderly maintenance of worldly life. (KA, I, 4, 3-4)

Based on this axiomatic proposition, Kautilya puts forth the following maxim with respect to the way the ruler should use the rod:

> For, the king severe with the Rod, becomes a source of terror to his subjects, the king mild with the Rod, is despised. The king just with the Rod is honored. (KA, I, 4, 8-10)

The ruler who uses state power excessively and arbitrarily is hated by the people. If the ruler's use of the rod is driven by affect and irrationality, outrage and rebellion of the people—even family fathers and the elderly—will be the consequence. On the other side, the weak ruler who refrains from the proper use of coercive state power is not only despised by his people but will unleash anarchy: the 'law of the fishes' (*matsya-nyaya*)—the stronger devouring the weak—will come into force. However, the ruler who uses coercive state power wisely and in a measured manner is respected. The right use of the rod brings to the subjects virtue and material wealth and even sensual pleasures (*kama*). Thus, the life of the people will be peaceful and prosperous and the state will grow more powerful.

In the fourth chapter, Kautilya introduces four basic concepts:

- The economy is the basis of state capacity.
- The ruler's wise and prudent use of coercive state power is the precondition of the state's stability and prosperity.
- The irrational and arbitrary use of state power leads to rebellion of the people.
- A weak, passive state leads to social and political anarchy (*matsya-nyaya*).

5. THE SCIENTIFIC EDUCATION OF THE RULER

It is the scientific education of the ruler which determines whether he will exercise state power wisely or not. And that, in turn, decides whether he will bring security and prosperity to his people or anarchy. Education can only be acquired through hard work, but some talent and disposition are necessary. Scientific education presupposes that the student has thirst for knowledge and desire to learn and that he is open to logical thinking and criticism. But the decisive factor for educational success is to be seen in the teachers.

> *But training and discipline in the sciences are acquired by accepting the authoritativeness of the teachers in the respective sciences.*
> (KA, I, 5, 6)

Next, Kautilya presents the educational program of the ruler. From the age of three, he should learn to read and write as well as be tutored in arithmetic. Having mastered this, the young prince should start to study philosophy and the *Vedas* under the guidance of competent teachers. Next, he should be taught economics and the management of public administration by experienced officials as well as theoretically qualified teachers. Kautilya demands that education remains a life-long task for the ruler, which is why he needs to remain in constant association with men of science—i.e., learned Brahmins. In politics, practical experience is important, but it must always remain linked to science. A power instinct, as such, is not sufficient for governance.

After the longitudinal profile of the ruler's educational program, Kautilya presents the daily training schedule for the prince: In the morning, there should be military training in theoretical and practical terms. In the afternoon, the prince should listen to readings of the epics, philosophical writings, legal and political science texts, i.e., *dharmashastras* and *arthashastras*. Then, the prince should listen to his teachers' explications and comments of these texts.

> *During the remaining parts of the day and the night he should learn new things, familiarize himself with those already learned*

and listen repeatedly to things not learned. From continuous study ensues a trained intellect, from intellect comes practical application and from practical application results self-possession; such is the efficacy of sciences. For, the king, trained in the sciences, intent on the discipline of the subjects, enjoys the earth alone without sharing it with any other ruler, being devoted to the welfare of all beings. (KA, I, 5, 15–16)

6. POLITICAL ANTHROPOLOGY AND THE RULER'S CHARACTER FORMATION

There is a reciprocal relationship between the ruler's intellectual education and the process of self-disciplining of his character. Kautilya speaks of a *group of six of enemies* that the ruler needs to control within himself: *lust, anger, greed, pride, arrogance* and *foolhardiness* (KA, I, 6, 1).

Even the most powerful ruler will politically fail if he is unable to control his instincts and emotional impulses. As illustration, Kautilya refers to mythological rulers from the epic *Mahabharata* who lost their kingdoms because they failed to control the 'six enemies' inside themselves. Even submitting to one of them is enough to bring about disaster. As an example of a greed-driven ruler, he refers to excessive taxes being squeezed out of the people—leading to economic decline and political rebellion. The chapter ends with two examples of good rulers from the *Mahabharata* who successfully contained unbridled sensuality and irrational feeling states—and therefore ruled long and successfully.

Kautilya's thought figure of the 'six enemies' reveals his 'realist' political anthropology: That man's behaviour is driven by instincts and affects is a basic fact of life which needs to be acknowledged. However, based upon that recognition, instincts and affects can and must be controlled and sublimated. Man's anthropological condition of being driven by instincts and affects is also the cause of the 'law of the fishes', mentioned by Kautilya in the fourth chapter of the *Arthashastra*. Anarchy will rule if men are left to themselves and their affects. In society as a whole, the *six enemies* cannot be contained by relying on self-discipline; instead, coercive state power must enforce order and security and thus prevent *matsya-nyaya*.

Kautilya's maxim is: As with his intellectual education, the ruler's character formation through self-discipline is *conditio sine qua non* for successful governance.

7. MONARCHY IS NOT DESPOTISM: THE POLITICAL ANTHROPOLOGY OF POWER

In this chapter, first, additional character defects are addressed which obstruct the ruler's successful exercise of power. In the previous chapter the focus was on 'active' character defects; now Kautilya addresses 'passive' character defects: laziness, lack of motivation, vanity and wasting of time with useless persons, things and activities. Then follows a clarification regarding the ruler's sexuality: of course, he must not stay celibate, but he should act out his sexuality in ways as not to cause political problems. The proper balance needs to be found between action for material and political benefits (*artha*), norm conformity (*dharma*) and pleasure (*kama*).

However, right thereafter, Kautilya makes the categorical statement that in the triad of *dharma*, *artha* and *kama*, it is *artha* that has priority:

> Material well-being [*artha*] alone is supreme, says Kautilya. For spiritual good and sensual pleasures depend on material well-being (KA, I, 7, 6–7).

If the ruler fails to create conditions in which the material needs of his subjects are satisfied, he cannot expect the people to abide by the law, behave in accordance with morality and remain content with a quiet private life. Material misery provokes political discontent and rebellion. His affirmation of the priority of *artha* reveals yet another aspect of Kautilya's 'realist' political anthropology: Meeting the basic material needs of the people is the precondition of sustaining order in a polity.

Following that, a maxim comes which is quintessential for Kautilyan statecraft: The ruler cannot govern alone. The monarch depends on advisers and political-administrative officials—and he must heed their advice.

> Rulership can be successfully carried out only with the help of associates. One wheel alone does not turn. Therefore, he should appoint ministers and listen to their opinion. (KA, I, 7, 9)

In this chapter—as in the fourth chapter with respect to the wise and prudent use of coercive state power—Kautilya draws a dividing line to tyranny. The Kautilyan ruler is not an omnipotent autocrat and the Kautilyan state is not 'Asiatic despotism'. Instead, Kautilyan monarchy means a patrimonial state in which the ruler's decision-making is based on collective deliberation with his advisers and government officials. Kautilya's unequivocal message is: 'lonely decisions' are bad for the state and ruler himself.

8. SELECTING ADVISERS AND MINISTERS

First, Kautilya presents the opinions of seven antecedent authors about the criteria for selecting advisers and ministers. They recommend selecting friends from boyhood and youth, relatives, scholars or men experienced in practical politics. On top of this, prospective advisers and senior officials should have an affinity in character with the ruler, great strength of character, loyalty and also zealousness. Instead of rejecting the views of other authors, as he does most of the time, here Kautilya states they all were somewhat right.

However, for him, professional and executive competence matters most in the selection of senior officials. The way to evaluate such competence is to review the candidate's previous professional performance, which will also give insight into his character traits. Kautilya draws a distinction between those who function as ministers or senior officials with departmental responsibilities (*amatya*) and those with overall political responsibilities, notably the 'chancellor' (*mantrin*), belonging for this reason to the small circle of the ruler's personal advisers.

9. QUALIFICATION OF AND DELIBERATION WITH ADVISERS AND MINISTERS

Kautilya presents a 26-point requirement profile for advisers and ministers. In addition to the already mentioned character traits and attributes of professional competence, the requirements include: descending from a respectable family, good health, being strong-willed, personally modest, cooperative and diplomatic, and disposing of improvisation skills. Anyone who meets all 26 criteria is a perfect adviser or minister; he who meets 75 per cent is mediocre, and he who is below 50 per cent is barely acceptable as a senior official.

Clearly, Kautilya sets very high intellectual, character and professional standards for state officials. Even more significant is that Kautilya wants the selection of senior officials to be linked to rational and transparent criteria. He does not want to leave the selection of senior officials to the ruler's hunches and intuition. Moreover, Kautilya wants the personal background of prospective senior officials to be checked by interviewing acquaintances, teachers and colleagues of the candidates.

Next, Kautilya explains that governing the state means decision-making which depends on the availability of adequate information. He distinguishes three types of knowledge—raw and processed information—that provide the basis of decision-making at the top of the state:

- 'first-hand knowledge': information that is directly perceived by the ruler himself
- 'indirect knowledge': information supplied by others to the ruler
- 'inferences': conclusions derived from the two previous forms of knowledge, i.e., decision-making and policy-planning vectored into the future

In order to govern, the ruler is dependent on information, assessments and proposals for action by his advisers and other senior officials. The ruler alone cannot make adequate assessments of the situation nor sound policy decisions. Thus, governing is necessarily a collective and deliberative process, even though the ruler alone makes the final decision.

With respect to the implementation of the ruler's decisions, the ruler can only be at one location at a time, but his decisions are to be implemented as soon as possible throughout the state territory. Thus, the ruler depends on state officials located outside his residence to carry out his orders.

If the ruler has good advisers, deliberates with his senior officials and adheres to the principles of Political Science, state policy will be successful in meeting even the most difficult challenges.

10. VETTING ADVISERS AND MINISTERS

Kautilya demands that the ruler's closest advisers, ministers and other top officials be vetted not only before they are appointed but also after they have assumed their posts. In order to verify their loyalty and performance in office, merely collecting information about them is not enough. Kautilya recommends a method of investigation which Kangle translates as 'secret test' and Meyer as 'guileful probe'. In modern intelligence and police jargon, one would speak of 'sting operations': the target person is being probed by setting up a trap for him. Kautilya presents several examples of 'guileful probes' for senior state officials:

A senior official (who is 'on the inside') will be deprived of his office (a sham sacking, of course). The 'ousted' official feigns anger and vindictiveness and approaches the target person by asking him whether he was willing to participate in a conspiracy to overthrow the ruler.

A servant ('on the inside') of the ruler's harem tells the target person that the queen has fallen in love with him. Would he come to a secret rendezvous with the queen? We can assume that Kautilya's prime concern is not marital fidelity but the possibility of a political conspiracy arising from such an affair.

A senior official ('on the inside') invites his colleagues to a private dinner. In the middle of the dinner, the participants are arrested and charged with treason. In prison they are individually contacted by a 'fellow prisoner' who says that friends of his are preparing for the assassination of the ruler. His death would mean the release of all political prisoners. Would they welcome the plan to overthrow and kill the ruler?

Via guileful probes, argues Kautilya, it is not only that the loyalty of senior state officials can be determined. Their strengths and weaknesses in terms of professional performance can equally be identified. In particular, when there is suspicion of abuse of power or corruption, the method of guileful probes should be applied. However, Kautilya does not conceal that this method might create the opposite effect of what was intended: to spoil the unspoiled, i.e., officials who on their own would not have considered treason or other state crimes. While the ruler is the initiator of guileful probes and the recipient of their results, he personally should stay away from such sting operations. That, Kautilya strongly recommends, should be left to senior officers of the secret service.

11. THE SECRET SERVICE, PART I

For Kautilya, the 'secret service' or 'establishment of spies' takes a prominent role in the state structure. He is the first author, except China's Sun-Tzu (*The Art of War*), who treats intelligence not in the mode of episodic narratives but in a scholarly and comprehensive manner (cf. Liebig 2014c; Shoham/Liebig 2016). However, it must be remembered here that the Kautilyan state is a patrimonial state in which the state bureaucracy is still in its infancy. Consequently, the Kautilyan intelligence service must not be equated with the bureaucratic apparatus of twentieth-century intelligence services. Only the ruler and a small circle of his closest advisers are involved in the planning of intelligence operations and receiving the intelligence reports. Nevertheless, the Kautilyan secret service is an organizational entity, as we can see from an elaborate pay list of the state bureaucracy which also specifies what pay each category of secret agents should receive (cf. KA, V, 3). And, as described in the *Arthashastra*, the network of secret agents and informants is enormous and extends across the whole territory of the Kautilyan state.[1]

Kautilya emphasizes that the secret service is an imperative necessity for the state and its governance. Via the intelligence service, state goals can be realized that otherwise could not be achieved at all or only with great effort and cost as well as serious collateral damage. However, when it comes to how the Kautilyan intelligence service is organized and how it operates, much remains opaque and vague in the *Arthashastra*. Both Meyer and Kangle have obviously to contend with serious problems when translating text passages dealing with intelligence matters. With great philological meticulousness, Hartmut Scharfe has made an important contribution to a better understanding of the text passages on the secret service in the *Arthashastra* (Scharfe 1968, 233–76). While the account of intelligence matters in the *Arthashastra* is more thorough and extensive than that of any other author of antiquity, Kautilya, as an intelligence virtuoso, appears not to have been interested in revealing all he knew about the organization, methods and procedures of intelligence. Much about the inner modus operandi of the Kautilyan intelligence service remains unsaid or at least not explicitly said. Thus, Kautilya is no different from the leading intelligence actors at all times.

His treatment of the intelligence service begins with presenting the 'stationary secret agents'. The organizational and operational management of the stationary agents is the responsibility of the *mantrin*, the ruler's closest adviser and 'chancellor'. In the *Arthashastra*, four categories of stationary agents are listed:

1. The 'professional' secret agent (*kapatika*) carries out various intelligence assignments under changing covers: spying on certain individuals or groups; undercover investigation of suspicious occurrences; exploring the public mood or acting as agent provocateur. The *kapatika* is a salaried civil servant. From this category of secret agents, intelligence 'craftsmanship' would be expected, but no above-average skills in terms of intellect or character.

2. In contrast, the next category of secret agents—wandering ascetics—requires special intellectual and psychological skills. Whether such 'begging friars' are intelligence agents using a religious cover or genuine religious persons who (for unspecified reasons) also carry out intelligence work remains unexplained. But Kautilya tells us that the ascetics' religious and intellectual attraction is increased by material benefits they can offer their followers and students. The money is made available by the

state treasury so that secret agent and religious virtuoso can recruit a network of informants from among his followers.
3. Farmers, artisans and traders who have gotten themselves into business and financial troubles are recruited by the secret service as paid informants to report about acquaintances, neighbours, customers and business partners.
4. Another group of religious virtuoso—'holy men or women'—are recruited as paid intelligence informants because they offer religious-ritualistic, astrological or psycho-therapeutic services and thus have easy access to sensitive information of their clients. Kautilya notes that the standing and credibility of such ascetics/agents can be improved when the secret service arranges certain occurrences about which the ascetics had previously made 'prophecies'.

The most efficient and reliable among these secret agents are to be at least partially privy to the intentions of the government, so that they can carry out their intelligence tasks as purposefully and effectively as possible.

And if they do so, their pay should be generous. In case of justified complaints, the secret agents should receive material and psychological satisfaction. However, if secret agents disobey their instructions, deceive their superiors or provide false information over an extended period of time, they face 'silent punishment'—i.e., covert assassination, which is made to appear as a natural death, an accident or 'normal' crime.

12. THE SECRET SERVICE, PART II

The elite unit of the Kautilyan intelligence service consists of the 'mobile secret agents' (*sattrin*), who must meet high intellectual, character and psychological standards. *Sattrin* are directly attached to the ruler: they receive their orders only from him personally and, if possible, report back to him personally. If this is not possible, they send written, encrypted messages to him directly.

It needs to be underlined here that the *sattrin* constitute an intelligence unit which is sealed-off from the rest of the intelligence service, i.e., the stationary agents under the direction of the *mantrin*. Moreover, *sattrin* are authorized to spy on the *mantrin*. Thus, the Kautilyan secret service is divided in two separate departments; obviously, also with respect to intelligence, Kautilya adheres to the principle that control is better than trust.

A *sattrin* must come from a respected family because, inter alia, his missions include spying on the highest-ranking officials of the state. Among these target-persons are: the crown prince, the *mantrin*, the ruler's personal chaplain (*purohita*), the war minister, the commander-in-chief of the armed forces, the chief of the bodyguards, the chief of the harem guards, the head of court administration, the supreme tax collector, the minister of finance, the minister of justice, the chief of public administration, the head of the capital city's administration, the head of state-owned enterprises, the 'departmental coordinator', the police chief, the chief of the border guards and the chief of the forest areas (where the tribal people live). For monitoring these high dignitaries, the *sattrin* recruits informants among the servants of the officials or places agents under the cover of artists in their vicinity.

The second task of the *sattrin* is espionage and covert operations in foreign countries. There, they operate a network of local agents and informants. Espionage should not only be directed against enemy states but equally against allies, friendly states and neutrals. The main focus should be spying on the highest dignitaries of these foreign states. At the court of the respective state, secret informants (and also agents of influence) are to be recruited and/or secret agents are to be placed there. Also, traders and farmers should be recruited as informants on the general political and economic situation in the targeted state. (In the fourteenth and the sixteenth chapters, Kautilya will say more about espionage and covert operations in foreign countries.)

Sattrin are also responsible for counter-intelligence, i.e., the tracing and unmasking of enemy agents and/or turning them into double agents. Kautilya strongly endorses the use of double agents who can be exploited to one's own benefit because they can access information about the intentions of other states which are difficult to obtain otherwise.

Agents of one's own intelligence service should agree to recruitment if approached by a foreign secret service as to feed it disinformation.

On behalf of the ruler, *sattrin* are also authorized to carry out 'silent punishment'. For the covert assassinations of enemies of the state at home and in foreign countries, they employ specially trained killers, who in particular employ poisoning.

In this twelfth chapter, Kautilya tells us something about the transmission of secret reports of the stationary agents, who are located all over the country, to the king's residence. From the local 'stations', special messengers deliver encrypted reports to the *mantrin* in the capital. And we learn about the reliability of intelligence reports: Kautilya considers intelligence information reliable if and only if three spies deliver the same information independently. Lastly, it should be noted that Kautilya strongly supports the use of female agents—both for domestic and foreign intelligence operations.

13. INTERNAL SECURITY

The security of the state requires that not only the elites but also the people are to be monitored. The ruler needs to know what the mood among his people is. To explore popular opinion, Kautilya recommends that secret agents be placed at marketplaces or pilgrimage sites where they should start a political quarrel. One agent should sharply criticize the ruler, while the other praises him and his governance. The bystanders should be drawn into this staged political quarrel. From what people say, a sense of the popular mood can be gained. Moreover, if the 'positive' agents do their job well, popular opinion can be influenced to the advantage of the ruler.

If there is discontent among the people, the ruler must determine its causes and remedy legitimate grievances in order to appease the people. Kautilya tells the ruler to refrain from a knee-jerk reaction against the people finding fault with him. If individuals or groups protest against injustices, the ruler should listen to their complaints and treat them with kindness and generosity. If the ruler has remedied the grievances but the popular discontent does not diminish, the ruler must prevent disgruntled persons or groups from bonding. Instead, he must find ways, including the use of the secret service, to breed discord among them.

If figures of higher political and social status stick to their unruly attitude, they should be assigned to carry out functions that make them unpopular—for example, collecting taxes and fees. Alternatively, the ruler himself or the secret service can put pressure on their families and so force them into good behaviour. Kautilya's main concern is to prevent conspiracies and/or domestic opposition figures secretly linking up with foreign intelligence agents. If opposition leaders remain recalcitrant and an insurrection looms ahead, they must be quietly liquidated as internal enemies of the state.

Kautilya strongly recommends that in making policy decisions that might have repercussions on the internal security situation, the ruler must take a flexible attitude and not stick fixed patterns. In each concrete situation, the ruler must decide what the best way to deal with acute or potential opposition is. He offers four policy alternatives: accommodation, granting material benefits, dividing and isolating, or, lastly, use of force. This is a reference to the four basic forms of political action—the *upayas*.

With respect to domestic security, Kautilya demands that an 'early warning system' has to be in place. If potential or acute threats to domestic security are observed, he advocates that first a 'remedial approach' be adopted before a 'suppressive approach' is pursued.

> *The king should favor those who are content with wealth and honor. He should manage those who are discontent by means of conciliation, gifts, dissension or force. In this way, the wise king should guard against the secret instigations of enemies targeting those likely to be seduced and those unlikely to be seduced in his own territory, whether prominent persons or common people.* (KA, I, 13, 24–6)

14. SUBVERSION OF FOREIGN STATES

In this chapter, Kautilya deals with the topic of the previous chapter as it were a mirror image: not how to assure political stability and internal security but how to subvert and destabilize foreign states. The issue here is not so much about collecting information in a foreign country but using the intelligence service for the orchestration of factional strife within political elites and popular unrest—with the ultimate aim of overthrowing the foreign government.

Kautilya provides a list of sociological and psychological motives that can be exploited and corresponding incentives that can be offered for the recruitment of 'agents of influence'. Such secret collaborators should be persons in senior positions who are themselves willing or can be induced to commit high treason. Kautilya lists four groups of persons suitable for secret collaboration:

- Persons who have been treated badly and offended by the (adversary) ruler. Wounded honour and the resulting anger and resentment are a powerful motive for treason. This group offers excellent recruitment opportunities for the intelligence service.
- A second target group consists of persons living in fear. They might be politically prosecuted by the foreign ruler or some of his underlings, they might fear the detection of a misconduct or crime they had committed earlier or they might face financial difficulties and fear loss of their wealth. Kautilya says that fear and insecurity are most virulent among government officials of all ranks and within the extended royal family.
- The third target group includes persons driven by greed or affects. Particularly the addiction to money and sex offers great opportunities for the secret service to recruit agents of influence by providing them with what they desire so much.
- The fourth group of potential agents of influence is driven by unfulfilled ambition: persons who want to gain success, power and prestige by whatever means—and are thus ready to engage with a foreign intelligence service.

Next, Kautilya describes the methods of recruitment and particularly the argumentation to be used therein tailored to each of the four groups. Again, the four *upayas*—smooth words, gifts, sowing discord and (threat of) violence—are to be used to build a network of secret collaborators ready to subvert, weaken and overthrow the adversary government. As the enemy state been sufficiently undermined, its breakdown will not necessitate conducting war on a large scale.

> When they have agreed with the word 'So we shall do' and have become allied to him by the making of the terms, he should employ them according to their capacity in his own works, with spies to watch over them. And he should win over the seducible in the enemy's territories by means of conciliation and gifts and those not seducible by means of dissension and force, pointing out to them the defects of the enemy. (KA, I, 14, 11–12)

15. PLANNING AND CONDUCTING OPERATIONS AGAINST FOREIGN STATES

Strategic planning requires, first, that the ruler has firm control over the situation in his own country, secondly, that sufficient and good intelligence about the situation in the adversary state is available, and thirdly, that there is substantial deliberation of the ruler and his advisers on the situation and the policy decisions to be derived from it: *All [foreign policy] undertakings should be preceded by consultation* (KA, 1, 15, 2).

Planning meetings for foreign policy operations must be held in strict secrecy and the decisions taken must remain secret. Kautilya warns that through carelessness—while drinking alcohol or during sexual encounters—state secrets might be divulged. Even the body language of the ruler or his ministers might indicate secret intentions and plans. Compromising state secrets can be an existential threat to the state and must be prevented at all costs.

Next, Kautilya deals with the question of who should be involved in strategic planning. He refers to antecedent authors who recommend that 1) the ruler should decide alone; 2) because of the many imponderables, the ruler should deliberate with a large group; 3) the ruler should consult with several advisers without, however, disclosing his actual intentions; 4) the ruler should disclose his intentions and consult with those who possess the expertise needed for carrying out the planned operation.

Against these opinions, Kautilya asserts that strategic planning should involve not more than four advisers in order to assure secrecy. Consulting with only one or two advisers will lead to biased assessments and recommendations. Because of the uncertainty of all future-directed undertakings, the ruler's deliberation with three or four competent and experienced advisers will produce the best result. But, never content with fixed formulas, Kautilya adds: If the circumstances demand an instant decision, consulting with one or two advisers or the ruler deciding alone is better than delaying the decision.

Kautilya mentions five main points that need to be deliberated upon when planning foreign policy (or military) actions:

- the cause, trigger or pretext to start the operation;
- the quantity and quality of available human and material resources (one's own and the adversary's);
- the geographic and temporal scope of the operation;
- alternative options if things go wrong ('Plan B');
- the objectives for the successful completion of the operation

If these questions are answered satisfactorily, then the operation is to be launched without further delay. No time is to be wasted—neither through more internal deliberation nor negotiations with the adversary state. Instead, a 'steering committee' should be established for directing the operation. Various proposals of other authors on the numerical size of such a committee are rejected by Kautilya, who argues that the size of the staff depends solely on the tasks it has to fulfill:

- staying on top of things—one's own actions and those of the enemy;
- correcting omissions and mistakes in the conduct of the operation;
- improving the conduct of ongoing actions;
- determining whether the targeted objectives have been reached

The ruler should regularly consult with the steering committee on the progress of the operation. With those of its members deployed in the field, he should consult through written messages. Kautilya warns the ruler explicitly against 'lonely decisions'.

If we look at this and the preceding chapter, the foreign policy operations discussed here seem not to refer to a classical war. Rather it appears that Kautilya has a combination of diplomatic pressure, political subversion, covert operations and military threats in mind. Such an approach for achieving foreign policy objectives is clearly favoured by Kautilya. Key for the successful conduct of foreign policy are a) adequate intelligence on the adversary state, b) rapid information about the execution of one's own operations and c) collective deliberation and the ruler's decision-making based upon a) and b).

> *Indra has a council of ministers consisting of a thousand sages. He has that as his eye. Therefore, they call him the 'thousand-eye one', although he is only two-eyed.* (KA, I, 15, 55–7)

With characteristic self-confidence, Kautilya ends the chapter by saying that only the ruler who adopts the ideas contained in his *Arthashastra* is fit to be a good and successful ruler.

> *Just as a person not learned in the Veda does not deserve to eat the Shraddha meal of good persons, so a king who has not studied the Arthashastra and not learned the teachings of the science of politics is unfit to listen to counsel.* (KA, I, 15, 61)

16. DIPLOMACY

Corresponding to the three qualification levels of senior state officials as outlined in the ninth chapter, Kautilya submits three diplomatic ranks: plenipotentiary, envoy, and carrier of messages.

Before the diplomat embarks on his mission, he has to be prepared thoroughly. How should the ruler's message be delivered to the adversary king? How might the latter react to the message? And how should the ambassador react to the foreign king's reaction?

Already the diplomat's journey to the adversary's residence is to be used for intelligence collection: Are geographical and infrastructural conditions favourable for an invasion or do they favour the defense of the country? Are there recognizable war preparations in the adversary country? What on-site economic resources could be used in an invasion?

The diplomat should not limit himself to what he can see in the adversary country but should talk to people as to extract information from them.

When the diplomat submits his king's message, he must carefully study the reaction of the adversary ruler: what he says, how he says it, his body language and the protocol arrangements. From all of that, the trained diplomat can draw conclusions on the intentions of the other side.

Often the adversary king delays his response to the diplomat's message for a lengthy period of time. The diplomat must use the time spent at the residence for intelligence collection and subversion. He must ascertain political fractions, individuals or groups resenting the adversary king and other indications conducive to political subversion and high treason. In that, the diplomat must secretly cooperate with the *sattrin* intelligence officers operating in the adversary country. Of course, the diplomat must always be aware that he is under observation by the adversary secret service. Kautilya's message is clear: diplomacy and intelligence are two sides of the same coin.

> *Sending communications, guarding the terms of a treaty, upholding his king's majesty, acquisition of allies, instigation, dividing the enemy's friends, conveying agents and troops into the enemy's territory. Kidnapping the enemy's kinsmen and treasures, ascertainment of secret information, showing valour, helping in the escape of hostages, and resort secret practices—these are the functions of the envoy.*
> (KA, I, 16, 33-4)

17. THE PROBLEM OF ROYAL SUCCESSION, PART I

In this chapter the danger of conspiracies and treason within the royal family is discussed. Obviously, court intrigues—like conspiracies in general—are a very great concern of Kautilya. This danger is highly prevalent and harmful among the ruler's sons, wives and concubines, particularly so for the crown prince, the eldest son of the legitimate principal wife. The authors of antecedent *shastras* on statecraft had warned that the crown prince was the most serious threat to the rule of the king and suggested drastic counter-measures: keep the crown prince away from politics by having him indulge in sex, hunting and other amusements, remove him permanently from the royal residency or even kill him through silent liquidation.

These propositions are firmly rejected by Kautilya. Instead, the crown prince should be thoroughly educated and trained to qualify him for governance (as outlined in the fifth, sixth and seventh chapters). However, the crown prince should be monitored by the secret service, but, unlike with other senior state officials, the method of the 'guileful probe' must not be applied to him. Instead, intelligence officers (*sattrin*) should arrange 'pedagogic experiences' for the crown prince in which 'negative rewards' are attached to sexual adventures, excessive drinking, gambling or resentment against the father.

If such pedagogical measures do not produce the desired result, the king must place the crown prince under house arrest or send him off on journeys—under secret service supervision—in the hope that he will come to his senses. If that does not happen and the ruler concludes that the legitimate crown prince is unreasonable and unfit to be his successor, another son must be appointed crown prince. If there is no other son, the ruler should beget a son. Kautilya thinks of all eventualities: if the ruler is no longer capable of procreation, he should select a relative to have intercourse with the queen. Here, state interest takes precedence over the ruler's personal feelings because the prospect of the next ruler being unsound in character and intellect represents an existential threat to the state.

18. THE PROBLEM OF ROYAL SUCCESSION, PART II

Now Kautilya addresses the problem of succession as a mirror image of the preceding chapter. He adopts the perspective of a virtuous crown prince who is qualified for governance but rejected by the king. Here, the problem is not the son, but the father.

In this case, Kautilya recommends that the crown prince accepts the humiliation and goes to a wise *guru* to continue his education. Meanwhile, he should properly carry out all the duties assigned to him. The obligation of loyalty ends, however, when the crown prince has to fear for his life or, for Kautilya the weightier reason, the king's bad governance becomes a threat to the state. If the ruler's political misconduct threatens to provoke internal rebellion or foreign invasion, the crown prince has the right and duty to turn against his father, the king.

Kautilya develops a scenario of how the crown prince might re-assert his rightful place in the state. He ought to go into exile in a well-run state governed by a wise king. There, the crown prince should marry into a respectable, wealthy family. Next he should raise funds in order to recruit mercenaries. The exiled crown prince must be alert of his father's secret service tracing him in order to kidnap or kill him. Thus, the crown prince should take the initiative and secretly link up with the political enemies of his father back home. Endowed with funds and commanding a mercenary force, the crown prince should return to his home country and link up with the political enemies of his father in staging a coup d'état.

For Kautilya, overthrowing and even killing the king is legitimate under two conditions: first, if the king's political misconduct threatens to trigger internal rebellion or a foreign invasion; secondly, if the king intends to install a successor with inferior qualifications compared to the—repudiated—politically capable crown prince. In both cases, the king becomes a threat to the state and people and his removal serves the interest of the state and the people.

Obviously, Kautilya's sympathies lie with the virtuous and capable but repudiated crown prince. But as long as the ruler governs in a manner which does not endanger the state and selects a politically capable successor, his ethical misconduct against the first-born son is irrelevant. It is a personal tragedy, but not a matter of state.

19. THE RULER—THE FIRST SERVANT OF THE STATE AND THE PEOPLE

In Kautilya's view, energy and vigour distinguish the good ruler. The ruler's attitude shapes the attitude of the whole state-apparatus. His vigour will radiate to state officials of all ranks—and the state will thrive.

Conversely, the ruler's indolence will make his subordinates sluggish—and the state will go into decline.

Characteristic of Kautilya, the energy and vigour of the ruler are defined through a set of precise criteria: he must daily furnish the work of governance. In the work schedule submitted by Kautilya in the *Arthashastra*, daytime and night-time are divided into eight time intervals respectively. During daytime, the ruler has to do the following:

Interval 1: Receiving reports on the internal and external security of the state; reports on the status of public finances
Interval 2: Reviewing the situation of the population in rural and urban areas
Interval 3: Bathing and eating, reading and studying
Interval 4: Meeting officials on fiscal and administrative affairs
Interval 5: Consulting with ministers, correspondence with senior officials outside the capital; receiving secret (written) intelligence reports
Interval 6: Individual interviews, audience
Interval 7: Discussing military matters, troop inspection
Interval 8: Deliberating foreign policy and military strategic issues

Following sunset, the ruler has to attend to the following tasks:

Interval 1: Meeting with intelligence officers
Interval 2: Bathing, eating, studying
Interval 3–5: Sleeping
Interval 6: Wake up to music; thinking about tasks and the schedule for the day
Interval 7: Decisions on intelligence operations, assigning tasks to intelligence officers
Interval 8: Religious rituals with the *purohita*, consulting with personal physician, cook, etc.

Obviously, the rigid work schedule for the ruler is an 'ideal-type' scheme, yet it is Kautilya's way to 'operationalize' the ruler's 'energy' and 'vigour'.

> *Therefore, being ever active, the king should carry out the management of material well-being. The root of material well-being is activity, of*

> *material disaster its reverse. In the absence of activity, there is certain destruction of what is obtained, and of what is not yet received. By activity reward is obtained, and one also secures abundance of riches.* (KA, I, 19, 35–6)

Kautilya asserts that energetic governance is the ruler's true 'worship service' and 'sacred work'. J. J. Meyer opines that these formulations should not be seen as mere metaphors but reflect Kautilya's a-religious attitude: If good governance itself is 'sacred' and 'worship', the priestly performance of religious rituals loses its exclusivity. And, more importantly, the statesman no longer depends on the priests to provide religious legitimacy to his governance.

Most of the ruler's activities prescribed in the tight daily schedule occur *in camera*, but Kautilya demands that the ruler also allot sufficient time for audiences to which all subjects who wish to see him can put forth their concerns.

> *For a king difficult to access, is made to do the reverse of what ought to be done and what ought not to be done by those near him. In consequence, he may have to face insurrection of the subjects and subjugation by the enemy [...]. He should hear at once every urgent matter, and not put it off. An affair postponed becomes difficult to settle or even impossible to settle.* (KA, I, 19, 6–28 and 30)

The ruler himself must hear what the concerns and needs of the people are. An 'invisible' ruler is alienated from the people and this situation can be exploited by his internal and external enemies. Also, lacking direct contact with his people, the ruler can become hostage to the court and its intrigues.

Then, towards the end of this nineteenth chapter, comes a central maxim of the *Arthashastra*:

> *In the happiness of the subjects lies the happiness of the king and in what is beneficial to the subjects is his own benefit. What is dear to himself is not beneficial to the king, but what is dear to the subjects is beneficial to him.* (KA, I, 19, 34)

These two sentences contain the *Arthashastra*'s normative core message: The ruler is the first servant not only of the state but the people. It seems clear that Kautilya does not mean that in a declaratory sense.

20. THE PERSONAL SECURITY OF THE RULER, PART I

In this chapter, Kautilya writes extensively about the ruler's palace, but he does not deal with its architecture—neither in terms of aesthetics nor power symbolism. His sole concern is the ruler's personal safety. Therefore, secret doors and passages or underground escape routes in the royal palace are deemed mandatory and described in some detail. Arson, poisons or snakes are a serious danger to the life of the ruler. For the royal palace, Kautilya recommends the use of different plants and animals that react to toxins or kill snakes.

During his intimate encounters with women, the ruler's security is particularly endangered. Kautilya cites six mythological examples of kings getting murdered in the bed of their wives or concubines. Therefore, the ruler should receive women only in his own bedchamber and after they have been thoroughly checked. Personal relations of women—who work and/or live in the royal palace—with outsiders are seen as a security threat and should be prohibited.

21. THE PERSONAL SECURITY OF THE RULER, PART II

The ideal-type royal palace should have four security circuits—each separated by a wall. Each circuit is secured by a separate detachment of the royal bodyguards. In the fourth innermost palace sector, the ruler's personal residence and the harem are located. The ruler's bodyguards, protecting this most sensitive area, consist of a special female detachment, while the bodyguards responsible for the other three sectors are male.

For security reasons, the personal servants of the ruler should only come from families that have served the royal family for a long time. In regard to the safety of the ruler, the kitchen of the royal household is of particular importance: poisoned food is the preferred means of political murder. The royal chef is also the food taster; drinks and drinking water must also be tasted in advance. Once again, Kautilya lists various poisons and describes how they can be identified. Thus, at all times, the ruler has to be accompanied by poison experts and physicians. Whatever medication the personal physician intends to administer to the ruler, he first has to administer to himself. Also the clothes and cosmetics of the ruler have to be checked for poison. Artists performing in the royal palace as well as their instruments and equipment must be thoroughly searched for weapons and poison. The ruler must receive foreign ambassadors only in the presence of his bodyguards.

Outside the palace, the safety of the ruler is especially endangered when he is hunting. Therefore, Kautilya expounds preventive security measures in forests. In an urban context, the ruler should move only along wide roads—surrounded by his bodyguards, while additional guards are to be posted at the roadside. When the ruler participates in religious and popular festivities, security measures need to be further upgraded.

The *Arthashastra*'s two chapters on the ruler's personal security demonstrate the extraordinary significance that Kautilya accords to the issue of political assassinations and measures to foil them. The ruler's personal security is a matter of state—assassinating the ruler literally means the decapitation of the patrimonial state.

7

THE CONCEPT CLUSTER *SAPTANGA*
The Seven State Factors *(Prakriti)*

From the heterogeneity and complexity of political life, Kautilya conceptualizes as the key structural elements the seven *prakriti*—'the seven state factors' (Meyer's translation) or 'the seven constituent elements of the state' (Kangle's translation).

> *The king, the minister, the country, the fortified city, the treasury, the army and the ally are the seven constituent elements of the state.* (KA, VI, 1)

The *saptanga* cluster as such is presented right at the beginning of Book VI. Then the (ideal-type) qualities of the seven state factors are elaborated. In Book VIII, Kautilya investigates the consequences of the degradation of each of the *prakriti*. The *saptanga* theory is better understood if we list the *prakriti* as follows:

1. *swamin*: the ruler;
2. *amatya*: the minister (government/state bureaucracy);
3. *janapada*: the people (of the land);
4. *durga*: fortress (capital city);
5. *kosa*: state treasury;
6. *danda*: coercive power of the state (armed forces, secret service, police);
7. *mitra*: ally (in foreign policy).

Roughly speaking, the text structure of the *Arthashastra* as a whole follows the sequence of seven *prakriti*, starting with *swamin* in Book I. *Amatya, janapada, durga* and *kosa* are covered in Books II–V. *Danda* and *mitra* are treated in Books VI–XIV (cf. Hillebrandt 1923; Sharma

1968, 31–49). The first two state factors—ruler and 'government'—have primarily a cognitive, immaterial quality because they are concerned with policy-making and administration. The next four *prakriti* are material factors in demographic, economic- financial and military terms. The seventh state factor 'ally' takes a special position as it concerns relations to foreign states.

The ranking of the state factors indicates the importance and weight that Kautilya assigns them. He explains this weightage *e contrario* in Book VIII by showing the negative impact of a state factor's degeneration upon the next—and all successive ones:

> *Of calamities befalling the king, the minister, the country, the fort, treasury, the army and the ally, that of each earlier one is more serious. (KA, VII, 1, 5)*

The ranking of the *prakriti* is also an expression of a logical and substantive architecture according to their sequence of generation: The state factor *swamin* is the generative condition of the state factor *amatya*—without the ruler there are no advisers, ministers or bureaucracy. Ruler and 'government' establish the institutional framework of the territorial state within which its constitutive people lives (the vast majority thereof in the countryside)—i.e., *janapada*. The first three state factors combined are the prerequisites for the state factor *durga*—the fortified city or capital city of the state. There, in the capital, the ruler resides with his government that collects the tax revenues that are primarily extracted from the rural population. All that is the precondition of the accumulation of tax funds in the treasury (*kosa*). Without the treasury, the armed forces, police and the secret service—state factor *danda*—cannot be sustained. And lastly, the state factors 1 to 6 are preconditions for the state's foreign policy because depending on their status it can be decided whether an ally (*mitra*) is needed and, if so, how the ally is to be 'used'. Thus, we could speak of a logical 'verticality' of the seven state factors.

At the same time, the seven state factors are situated on a 'horizontal' plane—like balls on a pool table, so to speak. Instead of the hierarchical principle of the generative sequence, entanglements and intersections between various state factors come into play. The ruler cannot rule without the state bureaucracy and both cannot function without the rural population paying taxes which flow into the treasury. The fortified capital city is inconceivable without the treasury and armed forces.

This horizontal entanglement is reflected in the text structure of the *Arthashastra*: While each state factor is consecutively treated as the main subject of a text segment, there are also cross-references to other state factors. And frequently, aspects of these *prakriti* are discussed which, in their prior treatment, had not yet been addressed. Therefore, the full exposition of a state factor in the *Arthashastra* transcends the text passage in which it is the prime focus and is usually dispersed across the text as a whole. This mode of exposition seems to contradict Kautilya's otherwise systematic, stringent exposition. In fact, he seems to aim at explicating each state factor as exhaustively as possible by taking repeated approaches from different perspectives. And he does so at different places across the text, making it hard for the reader to follow. In that, the *Arthashastra* exhibits a characteristic feature of Indian thought and its exposition.

Thus, the reader of the *Arthashastra* needs to be conscious about the fact that Kautilya's key concepts—such as the *saptanga* cluster—are not explained in neat, self-contained thought-packages that can be intellectually 'consumed' like the subsequent courses of a grand menu. Kautilya does not spare the reader '*die Mühe des Begriffs*', as German academics would put it.[1]

7.1 STATE FACTOR SWAMIN: THE RULER

Book I of the *Arthashastra* reveals that the patrimonial state is framing Kautilya's political thought. Because the ruler (still) embodies the state, his competence in statecraft is decisive for the power of the state and the welfare of the people. Conversely one could say: 'the fish rots from the head'. The political incompetence of the ruler ruins the other six state factors—and thus the state and the people. For Kautilya, the ruler is the first and most important state factor because he is the 'independent variable', while the other six *prakriti* are dependent variables.

> It is the king alone who appoints the group of servants like the mantrin, the purohita and others, directs the activity of ministers and departmental heads, takes countermeasures against the calamities of the state factors, whether human or material, and secures their advancement. If the ministers are suffering from calamities, he appoints others who are not in calamities. He remains ever diligent in honoring those worthy of honor and suppressing the treasonable. And when the king is possessed of excellences, he makes the state factors perfect with their respective excellences. What character he has, that character the state factors come to have, being dependent on him in the matter of energetic activity and remissness. For, the king is in the place of their head. (KA, VIII, 1, 12–18)

The Kautilyan state is an 'absolutist' monarchy, but the monarch is not a despot who exercises unrestricted and arbitrary power. From Book I of the *Arthashastra* we already know the intellectual qualities and other characteristics which Kautilya requires of the ideal-type ruler. When treating the state factor *swamin*, Kautilya lists no less than sixty qualifications which a ruler must possess (cf. KA, VI, 1, 2–6). Among these, intellectual, if not scientific, prowess ranks high:

> Desire to learn, listening, learning, memory power, thorough understanding, reflecting, rejecting false views and intentness on truth—these are the qualities of intellect [the ruler must have]. (KA, VI, 1, 4)

Even if the ruler is full of energy and valour, he must be firmly grounded in the 'science of politics': *[The king] deviating from the science of politics, with his mind firmly fixed on what is contrary to science, ruins the kingdom and himself* (KA, VIII, 2, 12). But *the king with the eyes of intelligence and political science [...] can overcome even enemies who possess [great] energy and might* (KA, IX, 1, 15).

For Kautilya, advancing the state factors in quantitative and qualitative terms is the prime task of the ruler: *A king endowed with personal qualities endows with excellence the state factors not yet so endowed* (KA, VI, 1, 16). The starting point for realizing this task is not decisive: At first, a state may have only a small territory and population, moderate economic strength and a small-sized army. What matters is what the ruler's statesmanship makes out of such an initial situation. Through a policy of 'good governance', internal economic development, skillful diplomacy and/or the considered use of force, a small state can become a great and powerful state:

> A king possessing personal qualities, though ruling over a small territory, in combination with excellent state factors and adhering to the science of politics, does conquer the earth[2] and never loses. (KA, VI, 1, 18)

Kautilya sees the power of the state as fluid: *decline, stability and advancement* (KA, VI, 2, 4). States always go into a certain direction: they may drift towards weakness or march towards strength. States may stagnate for some time, but usually sooner than later their decline or rise becomes discernible. Such fluidity Kautilya does not present as the result of some 'cyclical regularity' in history. Whether states rise, stagnate or decline depends on the leadership quality of the ruler in facilitating the improvement of his state factors. Kautilya insists that the ruler must register the trend of the state factors early on and then must take appropriate measures to reverse the decline, advance from stagnation and consolidate the rise of state factors:

> He, who is well versed in the science of politics, should employ all the means with respect to advancement, decline and stable condition as well as weakening and extermination [of the enemy]. (KA, VII, 18, 43)

Kautilya's dynamic state conception is thus the opposite to the political inertia and ossification often associated with pre-modern Indian politics by Westerners. The same goes for the Western idea of the (supposed) backwardness and stagnation of the 'Asiatic mode of production'.

The energy and vigour which should characterize the ruler must not be misunderstood in the sense of arbitrariness in policy-making. The ruler is bound by the explicit normative commitment to the welfare of the people: *In the happiness of subjects lies the happiness of the king and in what is beneficial to the subjects is his own benefit* (KA, I, 19, 34). Kautilya's maxim is derived from the traditional coronation oath of ancient Indian rulers: 'Whatever good I have done, my heaven, my life, and my progeny may I be deprived of, if I oppress you [the people]' (Jayaswal 1943, 210). The ruler's commitment to the material welfare of the people and waiving its oppression should not be seen as declaratory. This obligation has an intrinsic normative value and is simultaneously an expression of political rationality. Satisfying the people's material needs and abstaining from bullying the subjects are a binding obligation of political ethics for the ruler, but it is at the same time an expression of purposive-rational political calculation: If materially satisfied and not oppressed, the people will be content with the ruler—thus political stability and state capacity are guaranteed. In contrast, the tyrannical and incompetent ruler who fails to expand and improve the state factors will not only undermine state power and capacity but also provoke anger and eventually rebellion among the impoverished and oppressed people.

In the *Arthashastra*, the concrete, vivid personality of the ruler retreats in the background. Instead, the ruler turns into an ideal-type 'abstraction'. There is not the slightest hint of adulation or flattery with respect to the ruler in the *Arthashastra*, which is so typical for the later 'Mirror of Kings' literature in both Asia and Europe. The ruler's personal privileges are not mentioned at all, but more so the qualifications he must possess and the tasks he must fulfill—laid down in a lengthy and detailed catalogue of requirements.

The 'abstract' state is not yet really detached from the (also increasingly 'abstract') person of the ruler. Yet the intrinsic value of the state does find expression in the objectives that Kautilya puts forth for the ruler: The state has to become larger and mightier as well as more capable and efficient. To achieve this goal, the economy must prosper and the people's welfare must increase, which are, in turn, the preconditions for fiscal strength and thus overall state capacity. These are objective necessities of state the ruler must comply with. If the ruler does not comply, he loses his legitimacy. Thus, the Kautilyan ruler is the very opposite of the Western stereotype of 'Oriental despotism'.

In Kautilya's *Arthashastra*, there is no ambiguity left that the ruler has effectively become 'the first servant of the state'—and the people. In Europe, it was not until 1756 when this idea was articulated by the Prussian King Frederick the Great (cf. van Creveld 1999, 137).

7.2 STATE FACTOR *AMATYA*: THE MINISTER (GOVERNMENT/STATE BUREAUCRACY)

The ruler alone cannot govern the state; he needs personal advisers, ministers, a state bureaucracy with several administrative levels and multiple administrative tasks as well as a functioning legal system and a law enforcement apparatus, including the secret service. The state apparatus, including the legal system, is described in great detail in Book II, III, IV and V of the *Arthashastra* which accounts for approximately half of the total text.

> *Rulership can be successfully carried out only with the help of associates. One wheel alone does not turn. Therefore, he should appoint ministers and listen to their opinion.* (KA, I, 7, 9)

The Kautilyan ruler 'embodies' the state, but with the state bureaucracy— already more than a mere extension of the royal household—the contours of the state as an abstract political institution becomes discernible. The Kautilyan state is a patrimonial state that is administered by a patrimonial state bureaucracy which is functionally differentiated and organized hierarchically: 'Function, merit, and initiative had actually long been components of the traditional justification of power [in ancient India]. They receive new emphasis in the Kautalyan model of the bureaucratic state and the theory of authority on which it was built' (Drekmeier 1962, 260).

In the twelfth chapter of Book I of the *Arthashastra*, the highest public offices have already been mentioned because they are to be monitored by the secret service in view of their importance for the ruler and the state: *mantrin*, *purohita*, crown prince, commander-in-chief of the armed forces and the key figures of the royal household. Then follows a long list of the most senior officials in the state administration who are responsible for fiscal and economic affairs, justice and law enforcement as well as the state bureaucracy as such. In Book V (3, 1–24), Kautilya presents a far more extensive listing of state officials including lower hierarchy levels and the corresponding salary brackets.

At the upper level of the Kautilyan state apparatus, three categories of politico-administrative offices can be distinguished:

1. The most senior and best-paid positions are those with overall executive responsibilities in the intersection of politics and administration:
    - The *mantrin*, the ruler's closest political adviser, is the 'chancellor' or 'prime minister' of the Kautilyan state. The *mantrin* also directs one section of the secret service.
    - The commander-in-chief of the armed forces seems to be involved not only in military planning but also in the conduct of foreign policy more generally. In case of war, the commander-in-chief—not the ruler himself—is leading the army in the field. Organizational and logistical matters of the armed forces are the responsibility of other senior state officials (like the 'chief of military logistics', 'chief of fortresses').
    - The crown prince with alternating political and military assignments. Together with the ruler, these three officials constitute the supreme body of political deliberation, policy planning and decision making of the Kautilyan state. These three most senior officials below the ruler have the largest authority but are also most exposed to the danger of falling out of favour with the ruler. As Kautilya stresses: *Self-protection must always be first secured by the wise adviser; for the conduct of those serving a king has been described as if staying in a fire* (KA, V, 4, 16).
2. In the next lower hierarchy level are the 'heads of departments' who need first of all professional competence for specific areas of responsibility. Among them, the supreme tax collector and the 'minister of finance' seem to be most influential. At this level we have also the chief justice, the head of public administration, the head of the capital city's administration, the head of state-owned

enterprises, the police chief, the chief of military logistics, chief of fortresses, etc.

3. In addition, and characteristic for the patrimonial state, there are the court offices: not only the *purohita*—the ruler's personal priest and confidant on personal and political questions—but also the chief of bodyguards, the chief of harem guards, or the heads of various other fields of duty at the royal household—food, drink, stables, entertainment, etc. Such court offices, which have historically been the origin of state administration, take a special position in the state apparatus: their administrative authority is limited to the court and court personnel, but the political influence which can be exerted through these offices can be great.

In the Kautilyan state apparatus, four functional priority tasks can be identified:

- taxes, finance and economics;
- legal system and law enforcement;
- external security: foreign and military affairs; and
- intelligence activities, both internal and external

Apart from the foreign policy field, each of these functional sectors of the Kautilyan state bureaucracy possesses a hierarchical administrative structure covering the whole country down to the proverbial 'last village'. An organizational chart of the administrative structure is missing in the *Arthashastra*, but there is a reference to 'administrative districts' of 800, 400 and 200 villages and the lowest administrative unit comprising 10 villages (cf. KA, II, 1, 4; Scharfe 1968, 178ff).

Obviously, tax collection plays a central role in the state bureaucracy's organizational structure. The principal task of that part of the state bureaucracy dealing with taxes and duties, fiscal administration and the state-run domains, manufactures, mines, forestry, etc., is to generate the highest possible surplus for the state treasure. Kautilya demands that the sum total of salaries of government employees must not exceed one-quarter of the state's tax revenue. The public servants down to the lower ranks must be able to read and write because their work results have to be documented in writing. This documentation will be reviewed by auditors. Inspectors also check the work of state officials of all ranks. Kautilya's paramount concern is corruption at all levels of the administrative apparatus. To combat corruption, alongside auditors and inspectors also the secret service is employed.

> *Just as it is not possible not to taste honey or poison once placed on the surface of the tongue, equally so it is not possible for someone dealing with the money of the king not to taste the money in however small quantity. Just as a fish moving inside the water cannot be know when drinking water, equally so officials carrying out works for the king cannot be known when appropriating money.* (KA, II, 9, 32–3)

Primarily in order to have a reliable basis for taxation, the Kautilyan state is endued with a comprehensive land registry and census system that collects data on demography, occupations, income and property. Another task of the Kautilyan state bureaucracy is the monitoring and enforcement of a comprehensive system of government regulations in the social-economic sphere, including consumer protection, trade control, labour inspection, weights and measures, animal protection and nature conservation. The state bureaucracy is also responsible for enforcing regulations relating to public health, the 'entertainment industry'—taverns and bordellos—or the transport infrastructure.

Kautilya covers the justice system and law enforcement in great detail in Books III and IV. We can only roughly summarize his very detailed elaborations on legal matters. The justice system is a core task of Kautilyan state and appears to be highly developed. There is a distinction between civil and criminal law. Cases of dispute in the sphere of civil law can be settled by village elders and by the leaders of professional guilds. Otherwise, the jurisdiction is the occupation of state-salaried judges. Court proceedings must be presided over by three judges. Kautilya specifies what is necessary for a fair trial: unbiased examination of both witnesses for the prosecution and defense witnesses, sworn statements, circumstantial evidence and/or well-founded evidence based on contradictory statements of the persons involved in the trial. Court rulings must be logically and substantially comprehensible. Judges who commit perversion of justice must be severely punished. In the initial investigation of a case, the suspect shall be subjected to interrogation, and incriminating as well as exculpatory evidence shall be collected and examined. In cases of serious crime, the defendant can be tortured under certain conditions.

The sentencing follows the principle of retaliation (*ex talionis*). Imprisonment is absent in the Kautilyan penal code—except pre-trial detention. The death penalty is limited to murder, aggravated robbery, arson causing death, rape (if the victim belongs to a higher caste) and state crimes (such as treason, counterfeiting or embezzlement of state property). Except for these serious crimes, corporal punishment—mostly mutilations—can be converted into monetary fines. Kautilya is strongly in favour of financial penalties, which accrue to the state treasury and thus finance the state-run justice system. This is yet another example of Kautilya's characteristic entanglement of normativity and political purposive rationality.

In summary it can be stated that the Kautilyan legal system, as part of the state apparatus, provides certainty of the law but no equality before the law. For the same offenses, different penalties are imposed depending on the caste status.

7.3 STATE FACTOR *JANAPADA*: THE PEOPLE OF THE LAND

K.P. Jayaswal is right when he writes that *janapada* 'really means the whole area of a kingdom minus the capital' (1943, 240). The demographic and economic base of the Kautilyan state is the rural population. The vast majority of the population lives in villages in the countryside engaged in agriculture and crafts. Agriculture ensures the material subsistence of the population and also generates a surplus product. One-sixth of agricultural produce is paid as tax to the state, making it the state's most important source of revenue.

> A populous country is better. For, a kingdom is that which has men. Without men, like a barren cow what could it yield? (KA, VII, 11, 23)

> *The countryside is the source of all undertakings, from it comes might.* (KA, VII, 14, 19)

> *The undertakings of the fort [capital city], the treasury, the army, water works and the occupations for livelihood have their source in the countryside. And bravery, firmness, cleverness, and large numbers of people are found in the countryside* (KA, VIII, 1, 29–30).

The agriculturists in the Kautilyan state are mainly small farmers of the *shudra* caste who own their own land and/or are tenants. Large landowners (mainly of the *vaishya* caste) employ landless farm workers or lease portions of their land to small farmers. Since the farmers produce the material foundation of the state, Kautilya is firmly opposed to any government harassment of peasants through excessive taxation, special levies or forced labour. In addition to the private land of *shudra* peasants and large landowners, there are state-run agricultural domains. The state employs (landless) farm workers in its domains and/or leases domain land to small farmers. In the Kautilyan state bureaucracy, there is a separate administrative unit responsible for the domains. The state owns all pasture lands and the forests as well as all bodies of waters. For the private use of these lands and waters, the state charges a rent. For the state-owned pasture lands, forests and waters, there are separate administrative units in the state bureaucracy (cf. Ritschl/Schetelich 1973).

In ancient India, vast territories were still unsettled. That should be kept in mind when looking at the first two chapters of Book II of the *Arthashastra* where Kautilya strongly advocates land reclamation as a means to increase economic output. His land reclamation policy has the following features: The state transfers unsettled land for cultivation to landless *shudra* peasants. The settlers become owners of the land, and during the start-up phase they are exempt from taxes and levies. Once the new villages have been built and the agronomy produces normal return, the *shudra* peasants have to pay regular taxes. Kautilya's land reclamation policy is exemplary for the optimization of the state factors: newly cultivated land means increased agricultural production, which leads to higher tax revenue enhancing state capacity.

In addition, the internal stability of the state is strengthened because landless *shudra* peasants become landowners—thus social tensions and potential political discontent are reduced. Moreover, the new settlements expand the effectively state-controlled territory by reducing the quasi-autonomous zones with tribal population.

> *The ruler should cause settlement of the country, which had been settled before or which had not been settled before by bringing people from foreign lands or by shifting the overflow of population from his country.* (KA, II, 1, 1)

In the countryside, large forests are located, which are of great economic (and military) importance. As the woodlands are state property, they are administered by a special unit in the Kautilyan state apparatus. Forests provide timber, the main building material of ancient India. Charcoal is used for production and processing of metal. Forests provide materials for wattle, textiles, medicines (and poisons), dyes and writing materials (ink and bamboo leaves). Above all, forests are the habitat of elephants. This habitat must be protected so that a sufficient number of elephants can be caught, which are then trained as working and war elephants. For Kautilya, the war elephant is a strategic weapon system; a state without a sufficient number of well-trained war elephants is risking its existence. The importance Kautilya attributes to elephants is evident from the fact that there is an administrative unit within the state apparatus that deals exclusively with elephants: securing the habitat, capturing, training, feeding, stables and veterinary care.

In the countryside, there are mines where iron ore, (surface) coal, gold, silver and other precious metals as well as gems are extracted. There are also the smelters in which the minerals are processed into semi-finished products. For the Kautilyan state, mines and smelting plants are of strategic importance—both in economic and military terms. Thus, they are invariably owned by the state and managed by a department of state bureaucracy which is headed by an 'Overseer of Mining and Metallurgy Works'.

Kautilya considers the rural population as having a stronger physical and mental constitution than the urban population. To keep it that way, he wants to ban urban-style entertainment—jugglers, prostitution, alcohol consumption, and gambling—in the countryside, in particular in newly cultivated areas.

7.4 STATE FACTOR *DURGA*: THE FORTRESS (CAPITAL CITY)

In the Kautilyan state, the vast majority of the population lives in villages where most of the economic output is generated. That is why Kautilya attaches to the countryside the quality of a 'state factor'. But there also many small and medium-sized towns as well as fortresses along the state borders. Of all urban constructs, Kautilya gives the attribute 'state factor' only to the fortified city in which the ruler resides. The capital city is the political-administrative and military centre of the state as well as the hub of trade and crafts. If the enemy captures the capital, the fate of the entire state is usually sealed.

> *Dependent on the fortified capital are the treasury, the army, silent war [intelligence operations], controlling one's own people, military operations and assistance from allies, repulsing enemy forces and forest tribes. And in the absence of a fortified capital city, the treasury will fall into the hands of enemies. For, it is evident that those with a fortified capital are not exterminated* (KA, VIII, 1, 37–40).

The beginning of Book II of the *Arthashastra* expounds how the ideal-type capital city should look like. The fortified capital should be located near the centre of the state territory and in the proximity of a river or another large body of water. Chapter 3 of Book II is devoted to a detailed description of the city's fortifications, and in the next chapter a detailed 'map' of the ideal-type capital city is presented: The city is divided into four districts—one for each caste. In the northern Brahmin quarters, the royal palace with its security facilities and annexes is located. The neighbouring *kshatriya* district encompasses the buildings of the state administration, courthouse, military barracks and depots, (state) elephant stables and storehouses. In the *vaishya* quarter, trading houses, retail shops, taverns, brothels and workshops of fine crafts are located. In the *shudra* district, there are the workshops of simple crafts.

The four districts are also the living quarters of the respective castes. En passant, Kautilya mentions temples of different deities, parks and artificial lakes in the capital city, but he does not elaborate on that. He pays no attention to the aesthetic dimension of urban architecture in the *Arthashastra*. Instead, Kautilya emphasizes that the capital city is an important fiscal resource: trade, crafts and 'entertainment industry' offer great opportunities for taxation and fees. Taverns, brothels and gambling halls are state-run and generate hefty profits for the treasury.

To get a more graphic sense of the state factor 'fortified capital city', it is helpful to take recourse to Megasthenes's description of Pataliputra. Earlier on, his account of the size and design of the capital of the Maurya Empire was regarded as exaggerated. But later archaeological and historical research has confirmed Megasthenes's report: Located at the confluence of the Ganga and its tributary Son, Pataliputra—with an outline like a parallelogram—covered an area of 25.5 square kilometres. The city was enclosed by a rampart extending over 33.8 kilometres. The fortification consisted of a moat and a 10-metre-high mound on which two rows of 4.5 metre high wooden palisades were placed. Along the fortification wall, there were 570 towers (at a distance of 53 metres) and 64 city gates. Pataliputra was the only big city in Indian antiquity which was fortified with wooden palisades; otherwise a brick wall capped the mound. In the city, the streets were parallel and crossed at right angles—a clear indicator of precise urban planning. The houses had two or three floors with a courtyard and were occupied by an extended family. Between the houses, there was a safe distance for fire prevention. However, there was neither a central fresh water supply system nor a sanitation system—as it had been the case in the cities of the earlier Harappa culture. Instead, each house had a well and a cesspit. Parks and man-made ponds complete the picture of ancient Pataliputra (cf. Schlinghoff 1969). The big cities of the European antiquity did not measure up to the capital of the Maurya Empire:

> Pataliputra leaves the cities of the ancient world far behind. Alexandria covered 1/3 of Pataliputra's expanse, and imperial Rome, within the 18.8 km long Aurelian Walls, covered an area

of 13.7 km² —that's little more than half of Pataliputra's area. Thus, *Pataliputra was the largest city of the whole ancient world.* (Schlinghoff 1969, 29, emphasis added)

7.5 STATE FACTOR *KOSA*: THE TREASURY

> *Acquired lawfully by his ancestors or the ruler himself, consisting mostly of gold and silver, containing various kinds of big jewels and cash, thus enabling [the ruler] to withstand a calamity even of long duration in which there is no income—these are the excellences of the treasury.* (KA, VI, 1, 10)

In the fortified capital city, the state treasury is located, on which the financing of the royal court, the state apparatus and the armed forces depends. Empty state coffers paralyse the ruler and the state as a whole. Kautilya stresses that a poor state of the armed forces can be improved rather quickly if sufficient financial resources are available, but even a powerful army is practically worthless without money.

> *All undertakings are dependent first on the treasury. Therefore, the ruler should look to the treasury first.* (KA, II, 8, 1)

> *Because it brings into being all objects, the calamity of the treasury is more serious.* (KA, VIII, 1, 52)

The guiding principle of the Kautilyan state's fiscal policy is that the maximum of tax revenue, special levies, customs duties and profits from state enterprises are accrued at the treasury. At the end of each fiscal year, state revenue must exceed government spending as to add the differential to the treasury's existing stock.

> *Thus the wise fiscal administrator should fix the revenue and show an increase in income and decrease in expenditure and should remedy the opposite of these.* (KA, II, 6, 28)

Like the secret service, the Kautilyan state's financial administration is split up into to two units: one responsible for the collection of taxes, another one managing the treasury. The two units are headed by the 'supreme tax collector' and the 'supreme treasure manager', who—after the *mantrin*/'chancellor', 'commander-in-chief' and crown prince—are the most important officials of the Kautilyan state.

As mentioned above, the main tax of the Kautilyan state (and of historical ancient India) is a tax in kind, 'the sixth': one-sixth of agricultural production output accrues to the state. What the state does not require for its current needs and stockpiling for emergencies is sold to wholesale merchants. In the Kautilyan state, there is a developed money economy with silver and copper coins. The coinage is made exclusively at state-run mints. The tax rate of 1/6 seems also to apply to the income from trade, crafts and various services, but as a money tax. Then there are the customs revenues from cross-border trade.

In addition to 'the sixth' standard tax, there are a variety of special levies. Over the entire text of the *Arthashastra*, Kautilya submits recommendations for special levies to be charged on alcohol consumption, gambling, commercial sexual services, and various other forms of entertainment, sales of jewelry, as well as road tolls, fees for using (state-owned) port facilities, ferries or irrigation facilities. In emergency situations such as natural disasters, epidemics, famines or wars, Kautilya advocates imposing special levies on the wealthy and even religious institutions. Resistance against such compulsory levies should be broken by using the secret service to exert pressure. As mentioned already, court-imposed financial penalties (substituting corporal punishment) are an important source of revenue for the state.

Regarding the 'entertainment industry', Kautilya takes a pragmatic stance: amusements of the people, as long as they don't get excessive, are necessary because they serve as relaxation from work and help making people 'depoliticized' and 'pacified'. However, the 'entertainment industry' is an important source of revenue for the state. That is particularly evident in the 'sex industry': houses of prostitution are not only licensed and supervised by the state but run by state via the department of the 'Superintendent of Courtesans'. Prostitutes are effectively state employees and their customers pay the state for their services.

Despite his systematic search for new sources of revenue for the state,

Kautilya has a clear understanding that excessive taxation is economically and politically counterproductive. Excessive taxation lowers economic output and pauperizes the people.

> *He [the ruler] should take from the kingdom fruits as they ripen, as from a garden; he should avoid unripe fruit that causes an uprising, for fear of his own destruction.* (KA, V, 2, 70)

> *Subjects, when impoverished, become greedy; when greedy they become disaffected, when disaffected they either go over to the enemy or themselves kill the ruler. Therefore, the king should not allow these causes of decline, greed and disaffection among his subjects to arise, or, if arisen, should immediately counteract them.* (KA, VII, 5, 27–8)

In this respect, Hillebrandt has pointed to the congruency between the *Arthashastra* and the epic *Mahabharata*: 'A reasonable king must milk his kingdom like a young cow. Well treated, it grows strong and can withstand difficulties. But too much milked, it won't work as it should. Equally so, an excessively milked kingdom does not do its work' (cit. in: Hillebrandt 1923, 132f).

An important means of keeping within limits the population's burden of taxes and duties are the state-run enterprises: domains, mines, smelting works and manufactures. In the state sector of the economy, profits can be generated that accrue directly to the treasury.

Once a year, the audit of state finances takes place, which is performed by a separate 'controlling' department in the state bureaucracy. This department is neither subordinated to the office of the supreme tax collector nor the administrator of the Treasury. Income, expenditure and cash balances of all state agencies are reviewed. If there are contradictory, incomplete or false accounts, the government officials involved—at whatever hierarchical level—face severe punishment. In case of faulty accounting, severe fines will be imposed. Corruption, embezzlement and misappropriation can carry the death penalty, in the case of senior officials' 'silent liquidation'. In addition to the 'controlling' department, the secret service is used against corruption and embezzlement in the state bureaucracy.

The 'Minister of Finance' is responsible for the safekeeping of the state treasure containing cash coins, precious metals and jewels. He also supervises the state depots where cereals and nonperishable food as well as 'strategic' goods and weapons are stored.

7.6 STATE FACTOR *DANDA*: COERCIVE POWER OF THE STATE (ARMED FORCES, SECRET SERVICE AND POLICE)

Only if the treasury is sufficiently endowed, the military can be sustained—besides police and secret service the most important organ of the state's coercive power. The military has to be properly armed, equipped, fed and trained. If these conditions are met, the state can defend itself against external enemies and/or pursue a policy of conquest. In the *Arthashastra*, the military as well as military strategy and tactics are treated in Books IX–XIII.

> *The army, indeed, is rooted in the treasury. In the absence of a treasury, the army goes over to the enemy or kills the king.*
> (KA, VIII, 1, 47–8)

The military of the Kautilyan state has also a dual structure: it consists of a command and an administrative organization. The command structure is led by the 'commander-in-chief of the armed forces' (*senapati*), who belongs to the innermost circle of the ruler. The *senapati* is responsible for military strategic planning and the conduct of military operations in the event of war. In combat in the field, he—not the ruler—commands the troops. The (separate) military administration is responsible for organizational, logistical and personnel issues. On top of the military administration are presumably the 'chief of military logistics' and the 'chief of fortresses'. In the *Arthashastra*, the importance of the logistic base of the armed forces is stressed. The Kautilyan state has a highly developed 'defense industry'. State-run manufacturers produce weapons, military equipment like chariots, siege engines, etc., as well as 'dual-use' equipment like tents, trolleys, etc. Besides military barracks, there are also stables for cavalry horses and war elephants.

Kautilya favours a standing army, because the mobilization of a militia army is too time-consuming. The officer corps is recruited from the *kshatriya* caste, i.e., (hereditary) professional warriors. The *kshatriya dharma* is roughly comparable to the ethos of European chivalry or the Japanese *shogun*. Kautilya has no high opinion of officers from the Brahmin and *vaishya* castes; in contrast, he appreciates the bravery and combat effectiveness of soldiers from the *shudra* caste.

Statements on the naval warfare are missing in the *Arthashastra*. The armed forces of the Kautilyan state do not include a sea-going navy. For Kautilya, maritime security threats seem not to exist nor does he ponder the use of a navy to conquer territories across the sea. As far as waterborne warfare is considered at all in the *Arthashastra*, it pertains to inland waters like rivers. This may be surprising, but it shows that Kautilya is only concerned with the political and military control of the Indian subcontinent. Beyond that, there is no inclination for military expansion.

In case of war, the standing army is supplemented by mercenary troops. These are trained military formations that are arrayed and commanded by local *kshatriya* leaders. Also tribesmen from the (autonomous) jungle areas are recruited, and they are mainly used as 'scouts' and for guerrilla-type operations. Kautilya is quite appreciative of the tribesmen's combat power. Under certain circumstances, the army is reinforced by contingents of allied countries and/or deserters from the enemy army. However, Kautilya expresses great skepticism about the loyalty and fighting power of allied troops and deserted units.

The Kautilyan army is divided into four services: infantry, cavalry, war elephants and chariots. For each service, there is a special department in the military administration; in addition, there is a department for combat engineering and the medical corps. The conduct of warfare follows the principle of 'combined arms': in battle, infantry, cavalry, elephants and chariots operate together in tactical formations— 'brigades' of about 4,000 men. The smallest tactical unit is a group of 10 infantrymen led by a 'sergeant' (cf. Schwalm 1986).

In the *Arthashastra*, Kautilya presents four basic orders of battle and multiple variations thereof. He also names the variables that must be considered when determining the concrete order of battle. Schwalm is right when he writes that Kautilya's theoretical treatment of military strategy proves thorough knowledge of warfare in ancient India, but it seems doubtful that this knowledge is based on personal combat experience (cf. Schwalm 1986, 226ff). When it comes to military strategy, Kautilya is no 'Indian Clausewitz'. While Clausewitz's *On War* is a dedicated work on military strategy that is based on intense combat experience in the Napoleonic Wars, Kautilya's genius is Grand Strategy which subsumes military strategy.

That said, of great conceptual importance for military strategy is Kautilya's differentiation of three basic forms of armed conflict in the sixth chapter of Book VII:

- *prakash-yuddha*: 'regular' war, i.e., opposing armies fighting according to 'chivalrous' rules
- *kuta-yuddha*: 'irregular warfare', i.e., ambushes and raids behind enemy lines
- *tusnim-yuddha*: 'covert operations', i.e., sabotage and targeted assassinations

War in the sense of 'classic' warfare—*prakash-yuddha* and *kuta-yuddha*—is ultima ratio in Kautilyan statecraft. Even a victorious war inevitably involves severe losses of personal and material not only for the losing but also for the winning party. In pursuing foreign policy aims, such losses should be avoided. As noted above, Kautilya knows no principal inhibitions to the use of force, but for both ethical and realpolitik reasons he firmly opposes unnecessary suffering and destruction. Consequently, the *Arthashastra* upholds rules of warfare which sharply differ from the brutalized conduct of war in European antiquity: it demands a quarter for the wounded fighters who surrender, no enslavement of prisoners of war, and protection of the civilian population. Abstaining from unnecessary violence and destruction is equally stipulated for the behaviour of the victor after the termination of hostilities: the population-at-large must be treated well, local customs and traditions must be respected and the economy must not be plundered or otherwise impaired.

If war has become inevitable, all efforts should be undertaken to avoid a protracted war. Offensive war is recommended by Kautilya only if there is overwhelming superiority over an already weakened opponent, i.e., victory must be highly probable, the duration of combat short and the losses minor. Unquestionably, Kautilya's preference is either 'diplomatic victory' or *tusnim-yudda*, i.e., victory through subversion and covert operations. In the 'silent war', what really matters are mental faculties: intelligence, foresight, psychological skills and ingenuity.

> An arrow, discharged by an archer, may kill one person or may not kill even one; but intellect operated by a wise man would kill even children in the womb. (KA, X, 6, 51)

In the *Arthashastra*, the armed forces take the penultimate place in the ranking of state factors. Military strength is one, but only one, prerequisite for the main strategic objective of the Kautilyan state: political control of the Indian subcontinent. The military is one tool, but not the only tool, to achieve this goal. Kautilyan statecraft does not favour a military strategy of 'blood and iron'.

7.7 STATE FACTOR *MITRA*: THE ALLY IN FOREIGN POLICY

In the ranking of state factors, *mitra* comes last. When it comes to allies and alliances, Kautilya's core recommendation to the ruler is:

> First he should care of his own affairs and put his own things on a firm ground, then he should get resolutely to grips with the affairs of the others. (KA, VII, 6, 12)

In the terminology of modern International Relations theory, one could say that Kautilya's priority is 'internal balancing'—developing the endogenous power resources by upgrading the six *prakriti*. The strengthening of one's own (relative) power position through engaging in alliances with other states—'external balancing'—is a secondary option for him.

In contrast to the six other *prakriti*, the state factor *mitra* is an 'external' factor that does not directly relate to the internal strength of the state. For Kautilya, this state factor is a temporary (or complementary) expedient in order to gain time for advancing the internal power resources. Therefore, the optimization of the state factor *mitra* differs from that of the other six 'internal' state factors. Here, optimization does not mean strengthening the state factors of an ally but, quite to the contrary, the maximum exploitation of the state factors of the ally to one's own advantage.

As long as a state's power resources are still underdeveloped relative to those of other states, Kautilya recommends entering into alliances because doing so can buy time for internal development. However, alliance-making involves inevitably dependency on the ally or allies and the reduction or even loss of the freedom of action in foreign policy. This can be temporarily accepted as the price to be paid for the unimpeded development of one's 'internal' state factors. However, the alliance should be terminated:

- if, on top of foreign policy restraints, the build-up of the 'internal' state factors gets impeded through the alliance;
- if, under the protective 'umbrella' of the alliance, the development of the 'internal' state factors has advanced to a degree that the position of weakness relative to other states no longer exists.

Under these conditions, the alliance and the allies have become an impediment for the state's power potential and a restriction of the freedom of action in foreign policy in terms of using this power potential. Ergo, the alliance must be terminated.

Alliances and allegiance among states have no normative eigenvalue for Kautilya. An alliance is exclusively the result of purposive-rational calculation with the aim to exploit the allies' resources to one's own political advantage. For Kautilya, alliance politics consists of four elements:

> *Of a treaty, there are (1) the desire to make a treaty not yet made, (2) clinging fast to a treaty made, (3) breaking a treaty, and (4) repair what is broken.* (KA, VII, 6, 16)

Thus, breach of treaty belongs intrinsically to Kautilya's understanding of alliances. The allies and 'friends' of today are the enemies of tomorrow—and vice versa. Just as there is no permanent allegiance, there is no friendship in inter-state relations. Kautilya's definition of a 'friend' in inter-state relations is clear enough:

> *Insofar and as long as one can derive benefits from a friend, insofar he is a friend; being of use for oneself, is the characteristic of being a friend.* (KA, VII, 9, 12)

For the Kautilyan state, there is only one way to gain the 'lasting friendship' of another state: not through the (temporary) exploitation of allied resources but through their permanent appropriation. The Kautilyan state's 'best friend' is a state giving up its sovereignty and becoming a vassal state. At this stage, the vassal's state factors are effectively 'incorporated' in the hegemonic state's aggregated power potential. Thus, the 'external' state factor *mitra* becomes de facto an 'internal' state factor.

8

THE SEVEN *PRAKRITI* CONSTITUTIVE OF STATE POWER

The *saptanga* theory—the concept cluster of the seven state factors—provides the key to Kautilya's understanding of 'state power'. First it should be noted that Kautilya—undoubtedly a theorist of power politics—refrains from any ideological or rhetorical overstatement of power. In the *Arthashastra*, no 'cult of power' is celebrated. Instead, power is the natural attribute of the ruler: the 'rod' with which he can, if necessary, strike at his subjects to make them comply with his will. Power is the ability of the ruler to use force—first personally, then by 'executive agencies' upon his command. The ruler's monopoly of the use of force enables him to maintain order in his kingdom and to prevent anarchy—*matsya-nyaya*. Power—the 'rod' or *danda*—is thus constitutive of the patrimonial state. A weak and powerless state will disintegrate internally or, more likely, be conquered by a more powerful state. But, equally so, the arbitrary and excessive use (or threat) of force—internally but also in external relations—is ruinous for the state because it will provoke resentment and rebellion among the subjects and hostile reactions of other states.

In addition to this basic understanding of political power, another critically important concept of power is introduced in the *Arthashastra*. Kautilya's idea of the state's power transcends its understanding in terms of means of violence at the disposal of the ruler. The (patrimonial) state's power is not limited to *danda*—there are six additional power factors. Thus, Kautilya states:

> *The king and his rule [state], this is the sum-total of the seven constituents of the state.* (KA, VIII, 2, 1)

Kautilya's conceptual breakthrough is the recognition that the 'sum-total' of the state factors constitutes the state's power. There are seven *prakriti*, of which only one—the sixth, *danda*—relates to means of violence. In addition to *danda*, the power of the state is based on six other state factors: ruler, government, people in the countryside, capital city, treasury and ('utilization' of) the ally. Thus, Kautilya transforms the conventional concept of state power, fixated on the means of violence, to one that is based on the status and development trend of all the seven *prakriti*. The aggregate of the seven state factors constitutes the power of the state.

Kautilya's innovative concept of state power not only transcends the understanding of power that remains fixated on military force; it is one that is both comprehensive and can be 'operationalized'. If the power of the state is the aggregate of seven state factors, then this aggregate power can also be de-aggregated into its seven components. Each of the *prakriti* can be analysed and evaluated in terms of its current status and estimated in terms of its development tendency. From that, to use a formulation by Marx, the conceptional 'return journey' of re-aggregating the now substantiated *prakriti* can be made. Thus, with the aggregate of the seven state factors, state power acquires its comprehensive and substantiated determination.

State power, as an aggregate of the seven state factors, can be quantified and thus measured in terms of human and material resources, for example, the number of tax-paying peasants or literate and trained administrative officials or the size of army personnel. Material resources that can be measured might be the volume of the grain harvest or the production output of iron or the weight of bullion in the treasury. However, also immaterial—intellectual and mental—resources are part of the aggregated state power, for example, the mastery of statecraft by the ruler or the administrative competence of the state bureaucracy or the skills and productivity of farmers and artisans. Thus, Kautilya's concept of (state) power has not only material substance but also intellectual and psychological dimensions. First there is the intellectual and deliberative quality of statecraft, followed by the economic and military resources of the state, before, lastly, leadership 'morale'—energy and valour—comes into play:

> *Power is the possession of strength [...]. Power is three-fold: the power of knowledge is the power of counsel, the power of the treasury and the army is the power of might, the power of valor is the power of energy.* (KA, VI, 2, 31 and 33)

> *The power of counsel is superior [...]. Thus the king, superior in each later one among the powers of energy, might and counsel, overreaches the enemy.* (KA, IX, 1, 14 and 16)

Kautilya offers a substantive concept of state power in the *Arthashastra*, which is equally comprehensive as it is differentiated in itself. This substantive concept of power provides the benchmark for state capacity. The seven state factors are the foundation of the Kautilyan state's capacity, and their status and development tendency determines the scope of the sovereign capacity to act—internally and externally. And this capacity to act, in turn, is the precondition to maintain and expand the power of the state—i.e., maintaining and upgrading the seven state factors.

In the *Arthashastra*, Kautilya develops a holistic-substantive idea of state power for which there is no precedent. The *saptanga* theory is one of Kautilya's truly outstanding theoretical achievements. The singular significance of the *saptanga* theory in the history of political ideas and for the evolution of Political Science becomes evident when we compare Kautilya's *Arthashastra* with the political writings of Niccolo Machiavelli. Neither in the *Prince* nor in the *Discorsi*, written some 1800 years after the *Arthashastra*, can one find a conceptualization of state power as systematic and comprehensive as Kautilya's *saptanga* theory. In the *Prince*, Machiavelli titles the tenth chapter 'How the strength of all states should be measured', where he writes:

> In examining the character of these principalities it is necessary to consider another point, namely, whether the prince has such a position as to be able in case of need to maintain himself alone, or whether he has always need of the protection of others [...]. I would say, that I consider those capable of maintaining themselves alone who can, through abundance of men or money, put together a sufficient army, and hold the field against anyone who assails them

[…]. [States unable to do this] are obliged to take refuge within their walls and stand on the defensive […]. A prince, therefore, who possesses a strong city and does not make himself hated [by the population], cannot be assaulted; and if he were to be so, the assailant would be obliged to retire shamefully. (*The Prince*, in Lerner 1950, 39, 40, emphasis added)

From this citation from the *Prince* we can derive that Machiavelli in explaining how the strength or power of a state should be measured is listing six equivalents of Kautilya's seven *prakriti*:

1. The ruler whose policies do not alienate his subjects would correspond to *swamin*.
2. A large population (who does not hate the ruler) would correspond to *janapada*.
3. A sumptuously filled state treasury would correspond to *kosa*.
4. A strong army would correspond to *danda*.
5. A well-fortified capital city would correspond to *durga*.
6. Allies, if one needs the protection of others, would correspond to *mitra*.

In other dispersed text passages of the *Prince* (and the *Discorsi*), Machiavelli elaborates on these six elements constituting the strength of a state. Government and administration—in Kautilyan terms, *amatya*—are not mentioned by Machiavelli as a component of the state's strength. However, in other text passages of the *Prince* and the *Discorsi*, Machiavelli has a lot to say about the ruler's advisers and senior state officials and much of it is conceptionally homologous with what Kautilya writes on the state factor *amatya*.

It is evident from the above that Machiavelli has a basic understanding of the elements that constitute state power and how to 'measure' it. But he does not form a systematic and coherent theory of state power which would parallel Kautilya's *saptanga* theory.

Even more impressive becomes Kautilya's *saptanga* theory when we relate it to Hans J. Morgenthau's theory of Political Realism in the mid-twentieth century. In his most famous book, *Politics among*

Nations, Morgenthau develops the concept of 'national power' which shows remarkable homologies with Kautilya's concept of state power (cf. Morgenthau 1951/1978, 105–70).

Morgenthau's concept of 'national power' includes the following components which are partly material and quantitatively measurable variables, and partly immaterial, intellectual-mental factors:

1. the geographical setting of a state (while sharply rejects the theory of geopolitics);
2. the availability of raw materials and agricultural products;
3. the industrial potential;
4. the population size;
5. the military potential of a state;
6. 'national character';
7. 'national morality'; and
8. the 'quality' of government and diplomacy

The very concept of 'national power' as put forth by Morgenthau points to a structural homology with Kautilya's *saptanga* theory. While Morgenthau's eight components of 'national power' do not exactly correspond to Kautilya's seven state factors, there is an evident 'family resemblance', to use an expression of Ludwig Wittgenstein, between the two concept clusters separated by more than two millennia. Morgenthau's categories 'population size' and 'availability of raw materials and agricultural products' would correspond to *janapada*; his category 'military potential of a state' to *danda*; his category 'industrial potential' to *durga* or *kosa* or both; his category of 'quality of government' to *swamin* or *amatya* or both; the category 'quality of diplomacy' to *mitra*.

Besides the similarities between Kautilya's concept of state power based upon the *saptanga* theory and Morgenthau's 'national power' concept, there are other thematic areas—notably political anthropology, as we shall see later in the text—where the pre-modern and the modern political theories seem to converge. As we said earlier, if there is structural homology between Kautilya's pre-modern ideas and concepts and modern theories of the state and statecraft, an independent but 'parallel' generation of thought-figures in different cultural and historical contexts is a plausible explanation. For this explanation, Helmuth Plessner's 'covariance' approach and Eric Voegelin's 'equivalences' approach would be relevant.

While we adopt the 'covariance' approach for this study, there is a second explanation for structural homology of pre-modern and modern thought-figures in theorizing statecraft. That second explanation might be described as 'idea-migration': in our case a 'westward' trans-temporal and trans-cultural 'flow' of Kautilyan thought or at least some of his thought-figures thereof. Naturally, in the course of such trans-cultural idea-migration, the original Kautilyan thought-figures undergo a process of 'hybridization' corresponding to the specific historical and cultural contexts in which they are absorbed and re-constituted (as hybrids) (cf. Mitra 2011a, 2012a; section C of our study).

When Kautilya and Morgenthau are concerned, the puzzle of 'idea-migration' comes down to the simple fact that Morgenthau knew of Kautilya.[1] Morgenthau had evidently studied the *Arthashastra* as indicated by four references to Kautilya in his book *Dilemmas of Politics* (Morgenthau 1958, 36, 48, 56, 67). With respect to the homology between Kautilya's concept of state power in terms of the *saptanga* theory and Morgenthau's concept of 'national power', the following quote from *Dilemmas of Politics* is relevant:

> Political science, like any other science, presupposes the existence and accessibility of objective, general truth. If nothing that is true regardless of time and place could be said about matters political, political science itself would be impossible. Yet the whole history of political thought is a living monument to that possibility. *The relevance for ourselves of insights which political scientists of the past, reflecting about matters political under the most diverse historic circumstances, considered to be true, points towards the existence of a store of objective, general truths which are accessible to us as they were to our predecessors.* If it were otherwise, how could we not only understand, but also appreciate, the political insights of a Jeremiah, a *Kautilya*, a Plato, a Bodin, or a Hobbes? (Morgenthau 1958, 36, emphasis added)

9

THE CONCEPT CLUSTER *SHADGUNYA*
The Six Methods of Foreign Policy

In Book VII of the *Arthashastra*, Kautilya sets forth that a state has six policy options for the conduct of its foreign policy—no more, no less: *These are really six measures, because of differences in the situations*, says Kautilya (KA, VII, 1, 5). The 'six methods of foreign policy' (*shadgunya* theory) are:

- peace (*sandhi*);
- war (*vigraha*);
- 'staying quiet', 'wait and see', neutrality (*asana*);
- 'marching', coercive diplomacy, mobilization for war (*yana*);
- 'seeking shelter', alliance building (*samshraya*); and
- 'dual policy', diplomatic duplicity (*dvaidhibhava*).

Unlike the cluster of the seven *prakriti*, there is no logical ordering among the six methods of foreign policy, nor does the *shadgunya* theory involve a normative ranking among the six options. The *shadgunya* cluster can be understood as a continuum of which peace and war are the poles, but neither peace nor war is normatively charged up by Kautilya. For him, peace and war can be equally useful instruments of a state's foreign policy, but for reasons of purposive political rationality, a policy of peace is preferred. That is so because war inevitably means the destruction of personal and material resources: one's own and the enemy's.

> *If there is equal benefit in peace and war, the ruler should resort to peace. For, in war there are losses, expenses, hindrances and absence from home [where in the meantime a coup might be staged].* (KA, VII, 2, 1)

If the enemy's state factors are destroyed, they cannot be seized and appropriated by the victorious power which, for Kautilya, is the true aim of fighting a war. That is why Kautilya speaks of 'injuring' and 'weakening', but not of destruction or annihilation of the enemy state. Beyond incapacitating the enemy state's fighting power, the destruction of his *prakriti* is counter-productive and actually harming the victor. For Kautilya, war is ultima ratio—not because of ethical considerations but a sober cost-benefit analysis with respect to one's own and the enemy's state factors. Often conditions exist where pursuing a 'pure peace policy' or fighting a war (in offensive or defensive terms) would be disadvantageous for the state. Therefore, Kautilya pays equal attention to the other four methods of foreign policy in between war and peace.

The selection of one of the six methods of foreign policy is not wholly dependent on situational factors, yet it follows an inherent logic. The guiding principle in determining which of the six foreign policy options is to be adopted derives from the intrinsic connectivity between the *shadgunya* and *saptanga* theories:

> *The circle of constituent elements [the seven prakriti] is the basis of the six measures of foreign policy [shadgunya].* (KA, VII, 1, 1)

> *The conqueror [vijigishu] should employ the six measures of policy with due regard for his power.* (KA, VII, 3, 1)

Particularly with respect to decision-making in foreign affairs, Kautilya distrusts a ruler's 'instincts' and 'intuitions'—and the consequent 'lonely decisions'. And even more so he rejects mixing political decision-making with magic, notably astrology. The eminent role played by magic in political and strategic affairs in antiquity (and beyond) can hardly be exaggerated. We may think of the role of the Oracle of Delphi in ancient Greece or Augury in ancient Rome. For Kautilya, magic must have no place in the conduct of state affairs[1]: *The object slips away from the foolish person, who continuously consults the stars* (KA, IX 4, 26).

9.1 THE CORRELATION OF FORCES

Instead, Kautilya wants an objective assessment of the situation. In inter-state relations, there are necessarily at least two independent actors involved. Therefore, in the foreign policy sphere it is not one's own state's power potential (*prakriti* aggregate) that is decisive but the ratio of the *prakriti* aggregates of two (or more) states. Before making decisions in foreign policy, the task of the ruler and his advisers is *ascertaining the relative strength or weakness of powers* (KA, IX, 1, 1). The ratio of *prakriti* aggregates or the correlation of forces is the key concept of the Kautilyan theory of inter-state relations. The seven parameters of the *saptanga* theory provide objective and substantive criteria for making a sound assessment of the correlation of forces between competing or adversary states and deciding on the course of action in foreign policy. The correlation of forces (in terms of *prakriti* aggregates) determines which of the six foreign policy methods has to be chosen.

As noted above, the correlation of forces does not only include material and quantitatively measurable state factors, which Kautilya calls economic-financial and military 'might'. The *prakriti* 'ruler' and 'government' have qualitative characteristics: the ruler's personal 'valour' or 'energy' and what Kautilya calls 'the power of counsel', which is the knowledge necessary for the conduct of foreign policy. We know from Book I of the *Arthashastra* that such knowledge consists of three components: 1) 'firsthand knowledge': information that is directly perceived by the ruler himself; 2) 'indirect knowledge': information supplied to the ruler by advisers, officials and intelligence officers and; 3) 'inferences': assessments and conclusions derived from the two previous forms of knowledge. Based on such information—aggregated and processed—the ruler and his advisers can make an assessment of the correlation of forces that is devoid of wishful thinking.

A sound assessment of the correlation of forces begins with one's own *prakriti*. As mentioned above, there is a comprehensive census system in the Kautilyan state. The state bureaucracy collects and documents the demographic, economic, fiscal and other data. Thus, one's own state factors *janapanda*, *durga*, *kosa* and *danda* can be estimated fairly accurately. For evaluating the performance of the government and state bureaucracy (*amatya*), however, Kautilya advises the ruler to (also) use the secret service. Additionally, Kautilyan statecraft requires that the ruler must judge his own performance soberly and self-critically. The comprehensive evaluation of the seven *prakriti* provides the assessment of one's own power potential.

Important is not only its current status but the development trend of one's power potential—rising, declining or stagnant. With a dedicated policy of 'internal balancing'—prioritizing the improvement of one's own *prakriti*—the ruler can best facilitate a favourable correlation of forces. That applies more if the opponent pursues policies that make his *prakriti* stagnate or decline. In addition, when assessing the correlation of forces non-anthropogenic, catastrophic events must be taken into account: drought, famine, floods or epidemics, which can afflict one or both conflict parties.

For knowing and assessing the capabilities and intentions of foreign states—competing or adversary—the Kautilyan secret service is indispensable. Most of the 'indirect knowledge' required in the conduct of foreign policy is 'intelligence' that only secret agents and diplomatic envoys can provide. They must collect the best possible information on the current status and trend of the *prakriti* of the foreign state(s). Much information about the political, economic and even military situation of a foreign country can be collected by diplomats and intelligence operatives keeping their eyes open and talking to both ordinary people and senior officials. However, collecting secret political and/or military information, particularly about the intentions of competitors or adversaries, necessitates the recruitment of local informants and agents of influence by one's own intelligence operatives. The incoming intelligence reports must be analysed and assessed via the parameters of the *saptanga* theory. Doing that allows a realistic assessment of the status and the development trend of the foreign state's *prakriti* as well as its aggregated power potential.

If all material and mental assets, trends and imponderables are included in the assessment of the situation, the result should be a reliable assessment of the correlation of forces, which, in turn, will determine which of the six foreign policy options is selected:

> *Situated within the circle of [the seven] constituent elements, he, the ruler, should, in this manner, with these six methods of foreign policy, seek to progress from decline to stable condition and from stable condition to advancement in his own undertakings.* (KA, VII, 1, 38)

Based on the objective assessment of the correlation of forces between one's own state and competing or adversary states, the right choice of one of the six methods of foreign policy can be made:

1. If the ruler's state is weaker than the enemy state(s): *sandhi*. The ruler should pursue a policy of peace and accommodation with superior adversaries. This is to buy time in order to develop one's own state factors as to get out of the position of inferiority. Once the weakness is overcome, new foreign policy options open up.

   > *When in decline as compared to the enemy, the ruler should make peace.* (KA, VII, 1, 13)

2. If the ruler is stronger than the enemy: *vigraha*. From a position of massive superiority, the war can be won within a short period of time and without incalculable risks, costs and casualties. Of the enemy state's *prakriti*, only the ruler and his army have to be crippled or destroyed, the remaining *prakriti* are appropriated by the victor.

   > *The ruler should go to war against the weaker state [...]. Being thus enriched with people, with counsel, with material resources and army, the ruler should march into the field and crush the enemies into the ground.* (KA, VII, 14, 29)

   However, once the enemy state is defeated and occupied, Kautilya's characteristic symbiosis of realpolitik and normativity comes into play: The winner must treat the vanquished with generosity and leniency because that is morally imperative as well as politically expedient.

   > *The ruler who were to kill or imprison those who have surrendered, and covet their land, property, sons or wives, he shall frighten the circle of kings and make them act in order to destroy him.* (KA, VII, 16, 30)

3. If the adversary or adversaries possess a power potential that is equal to the strength of the ruler: *asana*—waiting-in-neutrality. In the meantime, one's own *prakriti* must be upgraded. Once the correlation of forces shifts to one's advantage, waiting-in-neutrality must be replaced by an active (and offensive) foreign policy.

   When the ruler thinks, the enemy is not able to do harm to me, nor me to him, he should stay quiet. (KA, VII, 1, 15)

4. If one's own *prakriti* grow stronger, while the adversary's stagnate or decline: *yana*—coercive diplomacy and military mobilization. With the help of the secret service's covert subversion and destabilization operations, the adversary can be also pressured into making far-reaching concessions or even surrendering—without fighting a war.

   When possessed of a preponderance of excellent qualities, the ruler should mobilize. (KA, VII, 1, 16)

5. If there is no chance in the foreseeable future to surpass, by one's own efforts, the adversary's power potential: *samshrya*—alliance-building with other states. Such alliance may at first have a defensive character, but the ruler should work hard to give the alliance an offensive thrust against the main adversary.

   Submitting to another [state via an alliance treaty] is seeking shelter [...]. Depleted in power, the ruler should seek shelter. (KA, VII, 1, 10 and 17)

6. If the correlation of forces is very fluid: *dvaidhibhava*—diplomatic duplicity. For example: State X concludes a peace and friendship treaty with state Y while simultaneously entering with state Z into a secret pact targeting state Y. The actual intention of state X, however, is to attack state Z. Kautilya presents a variety of highly complex situations and configurations in inter-state relations, in which diplomatic double games are the appropriate foreign policy option.

> Resorting to peace with one state and war with another state is dual policy [...]. In an undertaking that can be achieved with the help of an ally, the ruler should resort to a dual policy. (KA, VII, 1, 11 and 18)

One can get the impression that the sixth foreign policy instrument *dvaidhibhava* is particularly congenial with the spirit of Kautilyan foreign policy. This policy is particularly demanding with respect to intelligence, assessment of the situation, foresight, deception and psychological insights. One feels reminded of the fact that the game of chess was invented in ancient India. As in this 'royal game', Kautilya aims at giving the ruler freedom of action as to change the status quo to his advantage. Thinking ahead by several moves, the opponent is to be driven into paralysis and surrender.

> The ruler who sees the six measures of foreign policy as being interdependent in this manner, plays, as he pleases, with kings he has tied by chains of his intellect. (KA VII 18, 43-4)

Kautilya's insistence that the conduct of foreign policy is restricted to a fixed array of policy options is shared by Hans J. Morgenthau:

> Governments might have been wise or unwise in their choice of policies, successful or unsuccessful in their execution; they could not have escaped the rational necessity of *selecting one of a limited number of avenues* through which to bring the power of their nation to bear upon the power of other nations on behalf of the national interest. (Morgenthau 1958, 66f, emphasis added)

9.2 THE STRATEGIC GOALS OF KAUTILYAN FOREIGN POLICY

Does the *shadgunya* cluster constitute a 'general theory' of International Relations or, at least, a key component thereof? In our view, the answer is in the affirmative. At minimum, the *shadgunya* cluster contains most valuable conceptual building blocks of a 'general theory' of inter-state relations. Adam Watson is right when he writes on Kautilya:

The Arthashastra deals with how to conquer and govern an Empire [...]. It has additional significance for us in that *it [Arthashastra] sets out a major theoretical analysis of international relations* as an integral part of the problems of statecraft [...]. But when we remember that the Greeks, who produced such outstanding analyses of the domestic government of a state, wrote nothing comparable about a state's foreign relations or about the workings of their international system, *we realize the importance of this pioneering Indian achievement.* (Watson 1992, 78f, emphasis added)

And Hans J. Morgenthau notes:

That men throughout the ages have thought little of a theory of international politics is borne out of fact that but rarely an explicit attempt to develop such a theory has been made; as rare instances of such attempts, *Kautilya* and Machiavelli come into mind. (Morgenthau 1958, 48, emphasis added)[2]

However, it must be kept in mind that Kautilya's *shadgunya* does not adopt an abstract, theoretical panorama view of inter-state relations. Instead, an actor-centric foreign policy perspective is adopted: that of the *vijigishu*—the ruler who seeks conquests.

The king endowed with personal excellences and those of his material state factors, the basis of good policy, is the would-be-conqueror (vijigishu). (KA, II, 2, 13)

Kautilya's foreign policy theory is not about preserving the status quo but its revision. However, 'conquest' does not mean imperialist aggrandizement as an end in itself. In the historical context of the *Arthashastra*'s origination, 'conquest' means the elimination of political fragmentation on the Indian subcontinent. 'Conquest' must serve the political unification of the Indian subcontinent in order to be legitimate. Kautilya sets such 'righteous conquest' against 'greedy' and 'demoniacal' conquest. The 'greedy' conqueror is exclusively interested in the spoils of war—*seizure of land and goods* (KA, XII, 1, 14). The 'demoniacal' conqueror's sole aim is pillage, enslavement and destruction.

> *There are three types of kings who attack: the righteous conqueror,*
> *the greedy conqueror and the demoniacal conqueror.* (KA, XII, 1, 10)

In the context of the *shadgunya* cluster, the term 'conquest' should not be misunderstood as (exclusively) 'military conquest'. In addition to war, there are five other methods to 'conquer' other states on the subcontinent, that is, deprive them of their sovereignty and appropriate their *prakriti*. The loss of sovereignty does not necessarily mean annexation but can also take the form of turning a state into a vassal of the *vijigishu*. Either way, what counts for Kautilya is the political unification of the Indian subcontinent. Once the *vijigishu* has completed the unification of the subcontinent, he becomes the *chakravartin*—the 'ruler of the earth'. But for Kautilya the 'earth' is the Indian subcontinent *between the Himalaya and the sea* (KA, IX, 1, 18).

Also, and this is a critically important point, the term 'conquest' in the *Arthashastra* should *not* be associated with 'imperialism' or 'expansionism' beyond the geo-cultural space of the Indian subcontinent. Once India is politically unified, Kautilyan foreign policy is essentially *saturiert*, to use here Bismarck's terminology. Beyond India's geo-cultural boundaries, the political status quo is not called into question. As noted above, in the *Arthashastra* there is not the slightest indication of intentions for military conquest of territories or states bordering the Indian subcontinent, nor is there any indication for maritime expansionism. Kautilya adopts a defensive stance of preserving the status quo vis-à-vis the Greco-Persian Diadochi states, China, the states in Central Asia and on the Indian Ocean rim.[3]

For Kautilya, the formation of a pan-Indian state structure has strategic, if not normative, weight. The political unification of the Indian subcontinent is Kautilya's conclusion from the strategic assessment of the political situation of his time. The necessity of establishing a pan-Indian state had been demonstrated by the Achaemenid-Persian occupation of north-western India since the middle of the sixth century BC and even more so by the attempted conquest of India-at-large by Alexander the Great in 326 BC. However, the impulse for politically uniting the subcontinent is much older. Drekmeier rightly notes that the 'concept of a state spanning the length and breadth of the subcontinent under the rule of a *chakravartin* goes back at least to the 10th century BC' (Drekmeier 1962, 203).

In Kautilya's strategic agenda of politically uniting the Indian subcontinent, we find a striking parallel with Machiavelli, whose political writings must be seen in the light of the strategic goal of Italy's political unification and liberation from foreign domination.[4] In Machiavelli's time, Italy was not only politically fragmented but suffered from serial foreign interferences and outright military invasions by the risings powers Spain and France and to a lesser extent the weakened German Empire. Drekmeier rightly notes: 'Kautilya was faced with the same need for political union in the face of disorder and external threat that confronted Machiavelli in northern Italy [...]. Northern India was comparable in this respect to the Italy of Machiavelli's time' (Drekmeier 1962, 206, 268). And Adam Watson writes:

> Just as Machiavelli wrote a treatise called *The Prince* as a guide to a man who might be able to conquer and unite Italy, so Kautilya wrote a manual called *Arthashastra* or Book of the State. In it he described in detail the nature of the Indian states system and the relations between one ruler and another, and explained how a prince, whom he called the conqueror, might exploit the pattern in order to bring all India into a Persian-type of Empire. Kautilya also found a man [Chandragupta Maurya] capable of doing this, which Machiavelli did not. (1992, 78)

9.3 THE *MANDALA* SCHEME AND SOME MISCONCEPTIONS THEREOF

In treating the Kautilyan theory of foreign policy, we must address also his *mandala* concept which is based on an ideal-type constellation of states. The *mandala* scheme can be sketched as follows: In the centre of concentric circles of states, the *vijigishu*'s state is located—like the hub of a wheel. Grouped around it, there are the immediate neighbour states, which are regarded as enemy states (*ari*). In the rear of the first circle of (enemy) states, there is a second circle of states. These indirect neighbours of the *vijigishu* are his friends (*mitra*) or potential allies because their relation to the first circle states—their direct neighbours—is hostile.

Beyond these two circles of states come two more. The ordering principle of the *mandala* scheme is: direct neighbour = enemy, indirect neighbour = friend. For the *vijigishu* state, the first and third circles tend to be hostile, while the second and the fourth circles are friendly. However, beyond friends and enemies there are neutral states (*madhyama*), bordering the *vijigishu* state and its allies as well as its enemies. And there are distant powerful states (*udasina*) which (at least temporarily) stay out of the conflicts in which the *vijigishu* state is involved.

The *mandala* concept is often described as the 'essence' of the Kautilyan theory of foreign policy. However, we think that this is a misconception. *Mandala* is more of a scheme designed to provide some basic foreign policy orientation for the *vijigishu* who is trying to form one dominant state out of a multitude of smaller states. We do not think that the *mandala* scheme defines a rigid friend-foe relation in the sense of a 'geometric' and /or 'geopolitical' determination. Kautilya's *mandala* scheme is certainly not some 'iron law' of inter-state relations that is universally valid. The central principle behind the relationship with neighbours is to minimize the use of overt force while keeping the entire system dynamic. One can see traces of the Kautilyan *mandala* theory in long years of balance of power in European politics, or, closer home, under long years of British colonial rule in India, in the complex policy of cooperation and intervention between central rule and the native Indian princes.

The *mandala* scheme is valuable insofar as it addresses the general problem of the common border between neighbouring states. The common border is constitutive for the territorial integrity of neighbouring states, but usually the borderline is not 'natural' as in the case of rivers, mountain ranges or the sea. And even if there is a 'natural' boundary, it is often not recognized as such by neighbouring states. Therefore, the common border is often a cause of conflict, and the probability of conflict is higher between direct neighbours than among indirect, geographically more distant neighbours. Hence, Kautilya's *mandala* concept points to an often observed phenomenon in inter-state relations, linked to the behavioural pattern of state actors for which we usually use the phrase 'the enemy of my enemy is my friend'.

However, the actual reason why the *vijigishu* state views its direct neighbours as enemies is the determination to conquer them and make them part of a pan-Indian state. Once these first-circle states have been conquered, the indirect neighbours and former friends of the second circle become the *vijigishu*'s enemies because they become the target of his policy of 'righteous conquest' in order to establish the pan-Indian state.

In fact, the Kautilyan theory of foreign policy is not at all schematic. Its basic assumption is the fluidity of inter-state relations. The status friend, foe, neutral or (dis-)interested third party changes all the time. For Kautilya, change is constant in foreign affairs. G. J. Roy is correct, when he notes: 'Thus, an element of dynamism characterizes the theory of mandala. This points to the ever-changing attitudes of states' (Roy 1981, 214).

Lastly we have to address the question of 'balance of power' in the Kautilyan theory of foreign policy. Hans J. Morgenthau argues that Kautilya is the first theoretician of the balance of power concept, even though the key political figures of antiquity were practitioners of that foreign policy principle (cf. Morgenthau 1958, 67). Authors who deny that, across the ages, balance of power has been a 'universal principle of politics, domestic and international,' Morgenthau says, are obviously ignorant of 'what Kautilya was writing about in the 4th century BC when he summarized the practical tradition of Indian statecraft in terms of the balance of power' (Morgenthau 1978, 64). The idea of balance of power is certainly present in the *Arthashastra*, even though the category is not explicitly introduced. The *shadgunya* cluster can be interpreted as an expression of the balance of power principle in foreign affairs since all six methods of foreign policy can be means of balance of power politics.

10

THE KAUTILYAN IDEA OF RAISON D'ÉTAT

To begin with a puzzling problem: In the *Arthashastra*, Kautilya's *idea* of raison d'état is omnipresent if it is defined as the 'unconditional imperative of the state's self-preservation' (Münkler 1987, 49). Yet the *category* 'raison d'état' is absent in the text.

Here, again, lies a fascinating commonality with Machiavelli. Both his *Prince* and *Discorsi* are so permeated by the idea of raison d'état that it is often believed that Machiavelli coined the term. However, the term 'raison d'état' (*ragion di stato*) is missing in his political writings. Instead, the idea of raison d'état is addressed, without further elaboration, as the ways and means 'to found a republic, maintain states, to govern a kingdom, organize an army, conduct a war, dispense justice, and extend Empires' (*Discorsi*, in Lerner 1950, 104).

If there are doubts about the formative presence of the idea of raison d'état in Kautilya's *Arthashastra*, the following citation from Friedrich Meinecke might help to dispense with them. What Meinecke writes about the absence of the category raison d'état in Machiavelli's political writings applies equally to Kautilya and the *Arthashastra*:

> We are concerned here with the thing itself, not with the name for it, which he [Machiavelli] still did not possess. Machiavelli had not yet compressed his thoughts on raison d'état into a single slogan. Fond as he was of forceful and meaningful catch-phrases (coining many himself), he did not always feel the need to express in words the supreme ideas which filled him; if, that is, the thing itself seemed to him self-evident, if it filled him completely [...]. [H]is whole political way of thought is nothing else but a continual process of thinking about raison d'état. (Meinecke 1962b, 29)

Roughly seven decades after Machiavelli's death, Giovanni Botero was the first to introduce the term 'raison d'état' in his book *Della Ragione di Stato*: He defines raison d'état as 'the knowledge of the means and measures that are necessary to establish, maintain and expand a state' (cit. in: Münkler 1987, 169). In essence, this definition corresponds to the central idea of the *Arthashastra*.

10.1 KAUTILYAN RAISON D'ÉTAT AS OPTIMIZATION OF THE STATE FACTORS

However, the Kautilyan idea of raison d'état transcends the abstract and indeterminate principle of the state's self-preservation and power-augmentation. Kautilya's *saptanga* theory allows for a substantive determination and explication of raison d'état. When Kautilya analyses each of the seven state factors, his interest is not limited to determining their current status (and the aggregate thereof defining state power at a given point of time). Instead, Kautilya wants to determine the development trend of the state factors—are they stagnant, rising or declining? The state factors are magnitudes of potentiality and dependent variables: they can change because they can be made to change. The ruler can change his ways of policy-making, he can change the government's mode of operation and he can change the policy contents which he and his advisers pursue. The ruler and his government, by adopting certain policy measures, can change the economic performance of the people in the countryside and urban centres. And that, in turn, can change tax revenue available for both internal development and foreign policy action.

> *And when the king is possessed of excellences, he makes the state factors perfect with their respective excellences.* (KA, VIII, 1, 16)

The directionality of change that Kautilya demands for the state factors is unambiguous: he wants the optimization of the state factors. The ruler should develop the best possible political leadership quality. The 'government' must advise the ruler to pursue the best possible policies, and the state bureaucracy must implement these policies in the best possible manner. The peasants in the countryside must increase agricultural output (notably by expanding the area under cultivation) and thus increase tax revenues. In the capital, the craftsmen should be as productive and the merchants as profitable as possible. The differential between government revenues and expenditures should be as large as possible, so that the state treasure can grow. The military should have the best fighting power and the intelligence service should be highly effective. Regarding the external state factor *mitra*, the allies' resources should be exploited to maximum extent to one's own advantage. In other words, using modern political science terminology, priority is to be given to 'internal balancing' via the strengthening and improvement of the seven state factors. The fundamental state interest and the supreme goal of Kautilyan statecraft is:

> *My state factors are full of energy, thriving and evenly developed, will carry out their works unhindered or will destroy the intents of the enemy.* (KA, VII, 4, 6)

In his seminal work *Die Idee der Staatsraison*,[1] Friedrich Meinecke writes: 'raison d'état is 'the State's first law of motion. It tells the statesman what he must do to preserve the health and strength of the State' (Meinecke 1962b, 1). And he adds an important supplementation: 'The State is an organic structure whose full power can only be maintained by allowing it in some way to continue growing; and raison d'état indicates both the path and the goal for such growth' (ibid.). Thus, raison d'état means that the preservation of the state's power necessitates its growth.

Meinecke's definition of raison d'état is accurate and at the same time applies for his supplementation—but both remain abstract maxims. What is missing is the 'operationalization' of raison d'état. What do 'health' and 'strength' of the state concretely mean? How shall we substantiate the ways and means to achieve the 'health' and 'strength' of the state?

Well, in the *Arthashastra*, Kautilya does explicitly tell the statesman what he must do to preserve and enhance the health and strength of the state: the state factors (*prakriti*) must be protected as well as quantitatively expanded and qualitatively improved. It is in the fundamental interest of the state that the seven state factors are being optimized—thus preserving and expanding the power of the state. Political action is in accordance with the imperative of raison d'état if and only if it leads to optimizing the state factors. Ergo, the optimization of the *prakriti* is raison d'état.

Thus, Kautilyan raison d'état loses the character of an abstract and indeterminate maxim. Instead, it acquires substantiality and can be operationalized. Whatever the situation might be, the statesman must pursue policies which optimize the *prakriti* quantitatively and qualitatively. The fundamental benchmark for all political action is the optimization of the state factors.

Like his *saptanga* theory and concept of state power as the aggregate of the seven state factors, Kautilya's idea of raison d'état represents a groundbreaking intellectual achievement in the history of political thought. Referring to ancient Indian political thought and particularly to Kautilya, Charles Drekmeier rightly notes: '*Thus does the problem of raison d'état develop [in ancient India]—before its appearance in the West*' (Drekmeier 1962, 203, emphasis added). While the category of raison d'état is an intellectual child of the modern period of European history, the idea of raison d'état was developed in ancient India—and Kautilya was the first to substantially theorize it.

Meinecke has undertaken an historical and intellectual genesis of the concept of raison d'état that begins with the early Renaissance in Europe, but he does not assert that the idea of raison d'état is exclusively anchored in the historical context of the European (early) modernity.[2] Instead, he states:

> An account of this process [the evolution of the idea of raison d'état] from the standpoint of universal history would have to embrace and compare all cultures; it would have to begin by examining the idea of raison d'état in the ancient world, and analysing its relationship with the spirit of that epoch. *For both the free city-states and the monarchies of antiquity are teeming with the problems of raison d'état and with attempts to formulate it.* (Meinecke 1962b, 25, emphasis added)

Regrettably, ancient India is beyond the scope of Meinecke's investigation of the evolution of raison d'état. If he had done so, he would have realized that Kautilya did intellectually advance a long way towards the (modern) category of raison d'état. Moreover, Kautilya substantiated raison d'état as the optimization of the seven state factors. Thus, we assert that Kautilya came off with an intellectual achievement in political thought that has not been matched for almost two millennia.

If raison d'état provides the 'strategic directionality' for statecraft, what about the concrete, 'tactical' policies that facilitate the advancement of the state factors?

Even if the statesman does know the strategic direction dictated by raison d'état, the exact pathway he chooses therein depends on situational factors and his political skills. In a given situation, the statesman might not be able to expand and improve all state factors at the same time and/or to the same extent. He will probably have to adopt policies that prioritize certain state factors for the time being. In the tactical sphere of political decision-making, a multitude of contingent factors and constraints come into play. Still, however multifarious those factors might be, Kautilya sees only a limited number of policy options when acting in accordance with raison d'état: the six methods of foreign policy (*shadgunya*) and the four basic methods of politics (*upayas*), which will be discussed below.

The Kautilyan idea of raison d'état is rooted in the *saptanga* theory. And, equally so, the *shadgunya* concept cluster is based on the *saptanga* theory because the choice of one of the six policy options depends on correlation of forces in terms of the state factors. Thus, we see a logical and substantive connectivity between the *saptanga* theory, the *shadgunya* concept cluster and Kautilyan raison d'état.

Hans J. Morgenthau rarely uses the term raison d'état and instead prefers the term 'national interest'. Also, Meinecke uses occasionally the term (fundamental) 'state interest' synonymously with raison d'état. We believe that Morgenthau's concept of (core) national interest is not only influenced by Meinecke's theory of raison d'état[3] but also by Kautilya's idea of raison d'état. That is plausible because of the homology between the Kautilya's *saptanga*-based concept of state power, which provides the basis for the Kautilyan idea of raison d'état, and Morgenthau's concept of 'national power', in which Morgenthau's concept of national interest is embedded. If we substitute the term 'raison d'état' with 'national interest', Morgenthau provides a good exposition of the operational transformation of raison d'état into political action, notably in the foreign policy sphere:

> The relative permanency of interest and threat is surpassed by the virtual immutability of the configurations through which *the reason of man transforms the abstract concept of national interest into foreign policy*. Faced with the necessity to protect the hard core of the national interest, that is, to preserve the identity of the nation, *all governments have resorted throughout history to certain basic policies, such as competitive armaments, the balance of power, alliances, and subversion, intended to make the abstract concept of national interest a viable political reality*. (Morgenthau 1958, 66, emphasis added)

10.2 KAUTILYAN RAISON D'ÉTAT: THE NORMATIVE DIMENSION

The 'operational transformation' of the concept of raison d'état inevitably raises normative questions. It has often been asserted that Kautilyan statecraft is 'pure' power politics bereft of any morality. We believe that this assertion is unsustainable. Kautilyan statecraft does have a normative framing—and his idea of raison d'état attests to this. Kautilya does not only analyse and synthesize his idea of raison d'état in terms of the *saptanga* and *shadgunya* theories but ascribes to it an intrinsic normative quality. When we examine the normative dimension of the Kautilyan raison d'état, we realize that it integrates two fundamental 'value ideas:'[4]

- maintaining and expanding the power of the state; and
- ensuring the welfare and security of the people.

The first value idea means political rationality that commits the ruler to the optimization of the seven state factors. The second value idea is the solemn commitment of the ruler to strive for the happiness of the people, as laid down in Book I of the *Arthashastra*: *In the happiness* of subjects lies the happiness of the king and in what is beneficial to the subjects is his own benefit (KA, I, 19, 34).

While the first value idea is evidently the intrinsic core feature of raison d'état, the second value idea might appear declaratory. Is the commitment to the welfare of the people merely an appealing 'ethical packaging' for raw power politics? We can safely assume that Kautilya's affirmation of the ruler's obligation to secure the welfare of the people is indeed genuine. On that, Charles Drekmeier remarks: 'By the 4th century BC there had been a notable increase in the welfare functions of the state in India. The king was obliged to promote education, religion, and the arts, charitable services, and agricultural and commercial development [...] this idea had the effect of making the king accountable for the general prosperity of the people' (Drekmeier 1962, 255).

For Kautilya, there is no dichotomy between enhancing the power of the state and enhancing the welfare of the people. He sees the ruler as the 'first servant of the state' and, equally so, as the 'first servant of people'. As Charles Drekmeier notes: '[F]or the author of the Arthashastra the welfare of the state meant ultimately the welfare of the people, and the well-being of his subjects must be rated higher than that of the king himself' (Drekmeier 1962, 203, emphasis added).

In the sphere of statecraft, Kautilya denies a fundamental contradiction between purposive political rationality—the state's inherent power logic or state interest—and political normativity in the sense of assuring the well-being of the people. On the entanglement of state interest and political normativity, Kautilya writes:

> For, by discarding the good and favoring the wicked and by causing unrighteous injuries [...] decline [of the state] as well as greed and disaffection are produced among the subjects. Subjects, when impoverished, become greedy; when greedy they become disaffected, when disaffected they either go over to the enemy or themselves kill the ruler. Therefore, the ruler should not allow these causes of decline [of the state] as well as greed and disaffection among the subjects to arise, or, if arisen, should immediately counteract them. (KA, VII, 5, 19-28)

> *If weak in power, the ruler should endeavor to secure the welfare of the people.* (KA, VII, 14, 18)

Moreover, in Kautilya's view, each of the two value ideas underpinning his idea of raison d'état—enhancing state power and the people's welfare—has a dimension of purposive political rationality and a dimension of political normativity:

On the one side, the optimization of the seven *prakriti* results from purposive political calculation: it is the way to maintain and expand state power. Yet the power of the state—manifested in the optimization of the *prakriti*—is the precondition for realizing the normative obligation to ensure the welfare of the people. The imperative of optimizing the state factors means to act according to political purposive rationality, but only by doing that can the normative imperative for the happiness of the people be realized. Without the optimization of the state factors, the people would get pauperized and succumb to *matsya-nyaya*—be that domestic anarchy or foreign aggression.

On the one side, the commitment of the ruler (the state) to strive for the happiness of the people and to prevent *matsya-nyaya* has an intrinsic normative value. Yet this ethical obligation is also an expression of political rationality: only if the people are materially saturated and not politically tormented and oppressed, will they remain content, accept the ruler as legitimate, and thus keep the state stable and strong—domestically, and in terms of its external security.

Purposive-rational political action to optimize the seven state factors constitutes Kautilyan raison d'état. The policy of optimizing the *prakriti*, dictated by raison d'état, also creates the sources of the welfare and happiness of the people—constituting the normative quality of raison d'état. The Kautilyan idea of raison d'état means the symbiotic entanglement of purposive political rationality—state interest—and political normativity.

Here we find a remarkable homology in the understanding of raison d'état between the pre-modern Indian political theorist Kautilya and the twentieth-century European theorist Friedrich Meinecke. For both, raison d'état has a double nature: 'The well-being of the State and of its population is held to be the ultimate value and goal [of raison d'état]; maintenance of power, extension of power, is the indispensable means [of raison d'état] which must—without any qualification—be procured' (Meinecke 1962b, 2f). The normative dimension concerns the 'well-being' of the state and people, while the dimension of political purposive rationality means political action to maintain and expand the state's power.

With respect to the duality of purposive political rationality and political normativity that are subsumed under the Kautilyan idea of raison d'état, we must distinguish 'political normativity' from 'general ethics'. For Kautilya, political normativity and general ethics are two different ethical spheres. In Book I of the *Arthashastra*, Kautilya has laid out the general ethical standards: *Duties common to all are: abstaining from injury to living creatures, truthfulness, uprightness, freedom from malice, compassionateness and forbearance* (KA, I, 3, 13). For Kautilya, 'private morality is valid only in the sphere of personal relations and not in politics' (Drekmeier 1962, 205). In the sphere of statecraft, other ethical standards are valid. All too often, the state commits lying, deception, betrayal, perversion of justice, breach of treaty, violent acts or even extra-judicial killings and ultimately war. Such acts of the state are damnable in terms of general ethics. For Kautilya, too, such acts are damnable if the state commits them for 'base motives'—i.e., motives that are unconnected with and contrary to preserving and enhancing the power of the state and welfare of the people. If, however, fundamental state interest is at stake, unethical state actions gain a different normative quality. If state actions violate general ethical standards but are congruent with raison d'état, they are legitimate for Kautilya. Charles Drekmeier notes on this problematic:

> There can never be a thoroughgoing divorce of politics and ethics for Kautalya; he never denies that the ultimate purpose of the state is a moral purpose, the maintenance of dharma [...]. [He] means that *moral principles must be subordinated to the interest of the state inasmuch as the moral order depends upon the continued existence of the state* [...]. The state was forced to take measures

that frequently ran counter to the accepted moral standards of the community. But Kautalya well knew that such policies were all that could save society from collapse. *He was led inevitably to a theory approximating the reason of state arguments of 16th century Europe.* But he thought to emphasize the fact that such actions were not irresponsible. Indeed, it is the duty of the ruler to his subjects that compels him to take drastic steps to ensure their welfare. Survival and progress are recognized as bestowing authority. (Drekmeier 1962, 201, 260, emphasis added)

Thus, Kautilyan raison d'état possesses a superior 'cardinality' in the hierarchy of ethical norms. We might speak of Kautilyan raison d'état as the 'supreme norm' for statecraft. As such, Kautilyan raison d'état stands above the generally accepted ethical norms. As long as the state acts according to raison d'état as the 'supreme norm', for Kautilya there is no fundamental ethical dilemma. As long as state action is guided by raison d'état, it is not immoral. What Meinecke writes applies to Kautilya as well:

> The ancient world was already familiar with these sins of raison d'etat, and did not omit to criticize them, *but without taking them very much to heart. The very secularity of human values in the ancient world made it possible to view raison d'état with a certain calmness* and to consider it the outcome of natural forces which were not to be subdued. (Meinecke 1962b, 29, emphasis added)

Kautilya's position that raison d'état stands above generally accepted ethical norms is echoed by Machiavelli. But in his case we can sense that he—unlike Kautilya—sees and feels the ethical dilemmas that are inevitably linked with political conduct dictated by raison d'état:

> *For where the very safety of the country depends upon the resolution to be taken, no consideration of justice or injustice, humanity or cruelty, nor of glory or of shame, should be allowed to prevail. What course will save the life and liberty of the country.* (*Discorsi*, in Lerner 1950, 528, emphasis added)

And Hans J. Morgenthau notes: 'We know that this is the way all nations are *when their interests are at stake—so cruel, so faithless, so cunning* (Morgenthau 1958, 64, emphasis added).

With respect to the accusation of promoting ethical nihilism in politics, leveled against ancient Indian political theory in general and Kautilya in particular, Alfred Hillebrandt has drawn attention to Plato's *Politea*—a foundational work of European political theory and political ethics:

> One may point to Plato, in whose 'The State' one will find the thought: If anyone, it is the rulers of a state who have the right to commit deceptions, that is lying, either because of the enemy or for the sake of the citizens, but surely for the benefit of the state. (Hillebrandt 1923, 36)

Plato, who theorizes the 'ideal state' in the *Politea*, acknowledges that specific and exceptional ethical standards apply in statecraft that, if applied in regular civil life, would be deemed damnable and punishable.

We come to the conclusion that Kautilya is the intellectual originator of the idea of raison d'état. He expounds the dual nature of raison d'état in terms of purposive political rationality as well as political normativity. Yet Kautilya's penetrating analysis also reveals, to use a formulation by Meinecke, that 'raison d'état demands [...] an ice-cold temperature' (Meinecke 1962b, 7). At the same time, the Kautilyan idea of raison d'état is an expression of what Max Weber calls the 'ethics of responsibility' in politics.

11

THE CONCEPT CLUSTER *UPAYAS*
The Four Basic Methods of Politics

The *upayas* are not an original Kautilyan concept but go back to the oldest sources of ancient Indian political literature (cf. Hillebrandt 1923, 150). In the *Arthashastra*, the *upayas* are explicitly introduced in the tenth chapter of Book II, but Kautilya comes back to them many times in course of the text.

> *The means [of politics] are conciliation (saman), gifts (dana), dissension (bheda) and use of force (danda).* (KA, II, 10, 47)

Following Max Weber, one may say that the *upayas* state how a political actor can enforce his will against resistance. While the four basic principles of political action apply to all fields of politics, the *shadgunya* cluster can be seen as a derivative of the *upayas* in the field of foreign policy. For Kautilya, there is a ranking among the *upayas*; its criterion being the amount of effort necessary to enforce one's will upon the other party.

> *This is the group of four means. In that, each preceding one in the enumeration is the easier and lighter one. Conciliation is simple. Gifts are twofold being preceded by conciliation. Dissension is three-fold, being preceded by conciliation and gifts. Use of force is four-fold, being preceded by conciliation, gifts and dissension.* (KA, IX, 6, 56–61)

With respect to conciliation (*saman*), Kautilya differentiates five dimensions of meaning (KA, II, 10, 47–56):

1. *Praising of merits*: The target person (or group) is praised for actual or fictitious qualities and accomplishments. The counterpart's concerns are treated with keen interest and

sympathy. Adulation softens up the counterpart with respect to one's own intentions upon him. If the desire for appreciation is satisfied, the motivation to resist one's will often erodes or even vanishes. Whether paying respect is sincere or feigned, is irrelevant for Kautilya. What matters is the outcome.
2. *Mention of relationship*: Cozy words appeal to the counter-party by pointing to (common) kinship, ethnicity or social status as well as commonalities of education, *weltanschauung* and taste. The purpose is to psychologically disarm the counterpart.
3. *Pointing to common benefits*: The counterpart is made to believe that by accepting one's own demands, the interests of both parties are equally served. Whether that is really so, is irrelevant.
4. *Showing benefits in the future*: The counterpart is made to believe that by accepting one's own demands, he will obtain material gains or other advantages in the future. Whether that will actually be so, is irrelevant.
5. *Placing oneself at the other's disposal*: With respect to claims of the counter-party, the prospect of concession and compromise is held out. Whether the concession and compromise offered will actually materialize, is another question.

Kautilya emphasizes that fancy words cost nothing, but they can psychologically disarm the counterpart. Of course, *saman* is a key feature of diplomacy.

If silken words are not enough to bring the counterpart to heel, then making gifts (*dana*) cannot be avoided. That may mean making cash payments, giving away valuables of any kind, making territorial concessions or handing over hostages. *Dana* means that a price has to be paid for the enforcement of one's own will. This price must be kept as low as possible, which is why *dana* is always to be combined with *saman*. *Dana* can also mean doing the counterpart a small favour through which the target person or group feels obliged to behave in a certain way.

Finally, *dana* also means bribery—in this case, by the state. Such bribery can be quite profitable for the state because short-term expenses can generate much bigger political and material gains in the future.

In the context of the Kautilyan state, bribing semi-autonomous clan leaders and tribal leaders in the backwoods is an effective policy instrument. With bribery, rebellions can be prevented, thus sparing the state costly actions to suppress them. However, the main field of bribery by the state lies in foreign relations. In foreign countries, the recipients are agents of influence and persons committing treason. Here, we see a fluid transition to the third *upaya*—sowing discord (*bheda*) in order to destabilize a foreign state. Otherwise, in foreign policy *dana* means to pay subsidies to allies. Or, with respect to stronger states which pose a security threat, it means to make cessions of land, and pay tribute in money or in kind. Regarding *dana* in foreign policy, Kautilya makes the following sophisticated differentiation, which comes down to the fact that out of five varieties of 'gifts' only one actually involves a net loss:

> Gift is five-fold: 1) relinquishing what is due [because of a predicament or contractually], 2) yielding to what the other has taken already [accepting a loss], 3) return back what one has previously appropriated, 4) bestowal of one's own possessions, 5) transfer to the ally of a share of the expected spoils of war. (KA, IX, 6, 24)

The third basic method of politics is *bheda*: sowing discord or *divide et impera*. Through selective preference or discrimination, actors are isolated from each other. Kautilya explains the use of *bheda* for different political situations: In case of a conspiracy among the domestic political elite, the ruler must separate the mere fellow travellers from the hard core perpetrators of high treason. The former must be won back for the ruler by *saman* and *dana*, but the hard core must be liquidated—preferably, in secrecy. In a popular uprising, a similar approach must be taken: the masses are to be separated from the ringleaders by *saman* and *dana*, while the latter must be killed.

> In the case of rebellion, the ruler should use against the citizens and the country people the three means [conciliation, gift and dissension], but not force. For, force cannot be used against a multitude of people. If used, not only will it not achieve its object, but it might lead to another disaster. But against the leaders of them, he should act as in 'the infliction of secret punishment'. (KA, IX, 6, 2–5)

The principle of competitive units is built into the structure of the Kautilyan state bureaucracy, that is, *bheda* is institutionalized: The royal bodyguards consist of different units, separated by gender, ethnicity, and area of responsibility in the palace. The financial administration is divided in the office of tax collection and the office of management of the treasury; in addition, there is a department for audit. In order to prevent military coups, the military has separate command and administrative structures. The secret service is divided into two sections, one of which is directed by the ruler himself, the other by the *mantrin* or 'chancellor'.

Finally, the *bheda* principle is underlying the very structure of ancient Indian society: the caste system. The people is divided into largely self-contained social groups: the four castes (varna)—and within each caste multiple sub-castes (*jati*), the outcasts (dalits), and the tribal groups (adivasis). This de-aggregation of society is a key factor for the exercise of power by the Kautilyan state. At the very beginning of the *Arthashastra*, Kautilya writes that the conservation of the caste order is a prime objective of the state.

> *The people, of the four varnas and in the four stages of life, protected by the ruler with the rod, and deeply attached to the occupations prescribed as their special [caste] duties, keep to their respective paths.* (KA, I, 4, 16)

Like *saman* and *dana*, *bheda* too is a characteristic feature of diplomacy. Alliances of states that threaten the security or the interests of one's own state must be broken up or, preferably, their formation must be prevented in the first place. Selective threats or benefactions are best suited not only to break up alliances but to isolate the state one is intent on harming. These three *upaya*s refrain from the use of force, albeit not the threat of force.

If *saman*, *dana* and *bheda* fail to enforce one's will against the resistance of others, then *danda*—use of force—has to be applied. This concerns first of all the execution of corporal punishment by the state agencies for law enforcement. In addition, there is the 'silent penal power': the covert killing of (usually high-ranking) enemies of the state on orders of the ruler in cases of treason, rebellion, corruption, and embezzlement of state property. The executions are carried out by the secret service and should carry the impression of natural death, accidents, family feuds, etc. The 'silent penal power' plays an essential role in the Kautilyan state's system of rule.

> The 'weeding of thorns' from the fortified city and the countryside has been explained [in terms of criminal justice]. We shall now explain that with respect to the 'thorns' of the ruler and the state. [...] He should apply 'silent punishment' towards his own subjects or the enemy without hesitation - for the benefit of the future and present. (KA, V, 1, 1 and 57)

In inter-state relations, the ultimate expression of *danda* is war. However, this form of *danda* is the most costly and also the riskiest. Therefore, in the sphere of foreign relations, Kautilya's preferred form of *danda* are covert actions—*tusnim-yuddha*. For Kautilya, sabotage and the assassination of leading figures of a targeted state are effective and legitimate means to enforce one's own state interests. Kautilya makes no difference whether foreign leaders harbour aggressive intentions or stand in the way of one's own policy of conquest. He appreciates the low cost of 'covert operations' relative to what can be gained from them. The covert killing of a foreign ruler determined to resist one's own expansionist intentions may mean that his state can be made into a vassal without the need of going to war. The covert liquidation of an adversary military commander can greatly reduce battle losses.[1]

We should keep in mind that, in the Kautilyan state, *danda,* including covert operations, is not without normative constraints. For wars of conquest or covert actions to be legitimate and 'righteous', they must serve the purpose of the political unification of the Indian subcontinent. If wars are mere means of plunder or indiscriminate destruction, they are morally reprehensible, if not 'demoniacal'.

Kautilya's directness in relation to the four main methods of politics will likely appear cynical, if not repulsive, to many modern readers of the *Arthashastra*. As Heinrich Zimmer noted: 'Most of the scholars could look with only pity and disgust on such documents as Kautilya's *Arthashastra*' (2011/1951, 139). We, however, agree with Alfred

Hillebrandt when he writes about Kautilya and other authors of the ancient Indian statecraft: 'They, like Machiavelli, *speak out openly and tell us of the things that happen in Europe too, but there they are hidden behind a veil of fine words*; the ancient Indians theorists differ from Western authors by much greater sincerity' (1923, 155, emphasis added).

Lastly, if there are similarities between Kautilya's concept of state power and his idea of raison d'état and Morgenthau's concepts of 'national power' and 'national interest', there are also 'echos' of the *upayas* in Morgenthau's writings. We speak of Kautilyan 'echos' because the *upayas* cluster would have undergone profound hybridization in its usage by Morgenthau. As P.K. Gautam points out, Morgenthau—in the section 'Different Methods of the Balance of Power' of his *Politics Among Nations*—seems to have been influenced by the *upayas* cluster in *Arthashastra* (cf. Morgenthau 1978, 185–8):

> Interestingly, without any reference to Kautilya, the pioneer of 20th century power politics theory, Hans J. Morgenthau, in the chapter of different methods of balance of power in his book *Politics Among Nations: The Struggle for Power and Peace* (1966) mentions that 'The balance of power can be carried on either by diminishing the weight of the heavier scale or by increasing the weight of the lighter one.' His chapter has sections on: 1) Divide and Rule; 2.) Compensation; 3.) Armaments; and 4.) Alliances. *The four sections are very close to the Kautilyan concepts of bheda (divide and rule), dana (compensation), danda (armaments) and sama (alliances).* (Gautam 2013e)

We believe Gautam's observation is correct and confirmed by Morgenthau's references to Kautilya in his *Dilemmas of Politics*.[2] In conclusion, we can certainly agree with G.J. Roy when he writes:

> The *chatur-upayas* and *sadgunyas* have not become anachronistic with the passage of time. Even today they have a considerable relevance in international politics. The modern states in some form or other adopt the strategies of *sama, dana, danda* and *bheda* and when their mutual relations drag them to the verge of war, they follow expedients similar to the *sadgunyas* in the context of modern circumstances. (1981, 216)

12

KAUTILYA'S POLITICAL ANTHROPOLOGY

The *upayas* concept cluster is based on certain assumptions about human nature and basic patterns of social behaviour. At the beginning of Book I of the *Arthashastra*, Kautilya tells us how he perceives man's basic anthropological dispositions like: instincts, affect-driven impulses, greed and striving for dominance: *lust, anger, greed, pride, arrogance and foolhardiness [...] the group of six enemies* (KA, I, 6, 1 and 11).[1] Kautilya demands that the ruler must control these basic anthropological dispositions in order to develop the character traits necessary for political leadership.

'Naturally', affect-driven impulses, greed and striving for dominance are basic anthropological dispositions of human beings in general, not just princes and kings. Kautilya's argumentation is dualistic: On the one hand, instincts and affects can and must be controlled and sublimated through personal self-discipline, education, ethics and law. But, on the other hand, these anthropological dispositions are an integral part of the *conditio humana* and thus cannot be erased from human existence. Politics, therefore, must not ignore or sideline this highly precarious anthropological duality. Shortly after affirming the necessity of reining in the 'six enemies', Kautilya writes:

> '*Material well-being [artha] alone is supreme*'... *For, spiritual good [dharma] and sensual pleasure [kama] depend on material well-being.* (KA, I, 7, 6–7)

While Kangle translates *artha* as 'material well-bring', Meyer's translation is 'worldly utility' [*irdisch Nützliches*]. The above sentence—in both translations of *artha*—demonstrates that Kautilya 'realistically' accepts the pursuit of material gain and power as 'facts of life'. These basic anthropological dispositions must be hedged, argues Kautilya, but they should not be denied and cannot be eradicated. Any attempt to the contrary would actually hurt the 'spiritual good'.[2]

Thus, Kautilya adopts a very 'realistic' position: Politics must soberly take the anthropological realities—man pursuing material gain and power—into account while avoiding their Sophist-style ideological adulation.[3] That is stressed by Kautilya repeatedly in the *Arthashastra*:

> *Since material wealth is the root of spiritual good and has pleasure for its fruit, the attainment of that utility means attainment of all gains.* (KA, IX, 7, 81)

> *Men without wealth do not attain their objects even with hundreds of efforts; objects are secured with objects, as elephants are caught through elephants set to catch them.* (KA, IX, 4, 27)

> *Material gain, spiritual good and pleasures: this is the triad of gain. Of that, it is better to attain each earlier one in preference to each later one.* (KA, IX, 7, 60–1)

Thus, Charles Drekmeier concludes that Kautilya 'assigns first importance to wealth and, anticipating the most outspoken of Western materialistic pronouncements, proclaims that the condition of righteousness is wealth' (1962, 194). Kautilya's pre-modern political anthropology is echoed some 1800 years later by Niccolo Machiavelli. N.P. Sil rightly notes that Kautilya and Machiavelli 'have almost similar notions of human nature' (1989, 9). In the *Prince* and the *Discorsi*, Machiavelli writes:

> *The desire to acquire possessions is a very natural and ordinary thing* [...]. *For it may be said of men in general that they are ungrateful, voluble, dissemblers, anxious to avoid danger, and covetous of gain* [...]. [L]*ove is held by a chain of obligation which, men being selfish, is broken whenever it serves their purpose; but fear is maintained by a dread of punishment which never fails.* (*The Prince*, in Lerner 1950, 13, 61, emphasis added)

> [W]*hoever desires to found a state and give it laws, must start with assuming that all men are bad and ever ready to display their vicious*

nature, whenever they may find occasion. If their *evil disposition* remains concealed for a time, it must be attributed to some [yet] unknown reason [...]. Men act right only upon compulsion [...]. The nature of men is ambitious as well as suspicious [...]. Whoever considers the past and the present will readily observe that all cities and all peoples are and ever have been animated by *the same desires and the same passions*. (*Discorsi*, in Lerner 1950, 117, 139, 189, 216, emphasis added).

Twenty-three hundred years after Kautilya and five hundred years after Machiavelli, Friedrich Meinecke writes:

The striving for power is an aboriginal human impulse, perhaps even an animal impulse, which blindly snatches at everything around until it comes up against some external barriers. And, in the case of men at least, the impulse is not restricted solely to what is directly necessary for life and health. *Man takes a wholehearted pleasure in power itself* and, through it, in himself and his heightened personality. *Next to hunger and love, pleonexia is the most powerful elemental and influential impulse in Man*. Moreover, it was this impulse which, going beyond the mere satisfaction of bare physical needs, awakened the human species to historical life. For without the crude grasping for power of the earlier despots and ruling castes, with all the attendant horror and frightfulness, the stage would never have been reached where States were founded and men were educated to the point of great tasks to be undertaken in common. (Meinecke 1962b, 4, emphasis added)

And, Hans J. Morgenthau states: 'Why is it that *all men lust for power; why is that even their noblest aspirations are tainted by that lust?*' (1958, 33, emphasis added)

Kautilya's political anthropology has a second basic feature: Because of their basic disposition of affect- driven impulses, greed and striving for dominance, human beings—individually and as a social group—pursue 'egoistic' or 'selfish' interests. As individuals, social groups or political entities pursue their own interests, conflicts of interest are inevitable and often lead to (violent) conflicts. For Kautilya, conflicts of interest are a self-evident fact of life and of all politics. Conflicts of interest and subsequent non-violent and violent struggles between individuals and social groups—family, clan, tribe or state—are an anthropological constant in human existence. For Kautilya, acknowledgement of this conflict-laden reality is a key premise of 'political science' and practical politics. Without reference to Kautilya, E.H. Carr, the twentieth-century British political realist, echoes the Kautilyan standpoint: 'The clash of interests is real and inevitable; and the whole nature of the problem is distorted by an attempt to disguise it' (1981, 60).

Usually, the resolution of conflicts of interest and struggles derived thereof means that the stronger party enforces its will upon the weaker party. This basic anthropological situation—*matsya-nyaya* or anarchy—is expounded by Kautilya already at the beginning of Book I of the *Arthashastra*: *[T]he law of the fishes (matsya-nyaya). For, the stronger swallows the weak in the absence of the wielder of the rod* (KA, I, 4, 13–14).

Charles Drekmeier sees the thought-figure *matsya-nyaya*—the fear of anarchy and the emphasis on the state's coercive power—as a general feature of ancient Indian political thought: 'The suspicion of human nature that dominates Hindu thought can be summed up in the words of Manu: a guiltless man is hard to find. A society without constraints is no society at all: men feed on one another as do the beasts of the jungle and the fish in the sea' (Drekmeier 1962, 249).

In Book I of the *Arthashastra*, Kautilya tells the story of two secret service agents who, in front of a crowd of people, stage a political debate. One agent exclaims that people ought to be grateful for being ruled by a king who collects taxes and enforces the law. Without the king wielding the rod, there would be *matsya-nyaya*: people would have to live in constant fear for life and property. The stronger ones would oppress, loot, enslave or even kill the weaker ones. The ancestors had suffered so badly through *matsya-nyaya* that they came to an agreement to select and install a ruler endowed with the instruments of power in order to end *matsya-nyaya*:

> People, overwhelmed by the law of the fishes, made Manu, the son of Vivasvat, their king. And they assigned one-sixth of the grains, one-tenth of the commodities and money as his share. Maintained by that, kings bring about the well-being and security of the subjects.
> (KA, I, 13, 5–7)

For Kautilya, *matsya-nyaya* is the anarchic 'state of nature' in social life. He anticipates what, some 1900 years later, Hobbes called the *bellum omnium contra omnes*. However, Kautilya expounds that *matsya-nyaya* can be contained and transformed to the benefit of society by making the ruler or the state strong and powerful enough as to terminate the violent resolution of conflicts within society. Again we find a Kautilyan concept that was taken up by Hobbes with his *Leviathan* theory: the people surrender to the ruler/state the use of force. Thus, the state 'domesticates' *matsya-nyaya* by monopolizing the use of force and thus denying it to its subjects. The state's superior power vis-à-vis its subjects establishes and enforces the law which means punishing those among its subjects who refuse to submit to the state's monopoly of violence by perpetrating murder, assault and robbery or similar violent crimes. It's the ruler and the state wielding the rod, that ends anarchy. If a weak state is incapable of exercising state power and thus fails to enforce the law (based upon the state's power) within its territory, *matsya-nyaya* would come back with a vengeance. Charles Drekmeier rightly notes that ancient Indian political theory as typified by the *Arthashastra* 'postulates a state of nature (*matsya-nyaya*) not essentially different from that of Hobbes and Spinoza, in which a strong authority is required to impose restraints on the natural appetites of the people. The state without sanctions is no state at all' (1962, 10).

In the above mentioned text passage of the *Arthashastra*, Kautilya presents a kind of 'contract theory' on the origins of the monarchical state. In this idealized construction, there is, first, a consensual agreement among the people to install a ruler endowed with instruments of power that are strong enough to 'domesticate' *matsya-nyaya* within the territory of the state. Secondly, there is a 'contract' between ruler and the people to the effect that the latter pay taxes to the king who, in return, provides internal and external security.

While *matsya-nyaya* can be 'domesticated' within the state, in inter-state relations 'the law of the fishes' reigns supreme. Kautilya does not even try to come up with some construction of a 'consensus' or 'contract' between rival states that might end the regime of anarchy in inter-state relations. In the *Arthashastra*'s historical context or origination, *matsya-nyaya* means that a multitude of rival states in the Indian subcontinent constantly fight each other by all means at their disposal. On that 'warring states' period of Indian history, Heinrich Zimmer writes:

> Ancient Indian affairs were pervaded by an atmosphere of danger, suspicion and threat. There was waged a kind of continuous white war of nerves [...]. Everyone feels always endangered. Every king—utterly vulnerable though armed to the teeth—is watching constantly to forestall surprise. No one is fully master of the situation for any length of time. Sudden changes bring death and disgrace. Intrigues and murder from within, intrigues and aggression from without, threats of surprise, upset the strong. Direct, crushing blows annihilate the weak. *Maya* [deception], fratricide, poison, and the dagger constitute the order of the day. (Zimmer 2011/1951, 111f)

Under such conditions of permanent warfare, the more powerful states force their will upon the weaker ones—effectively eliminating them as sovereign political entities. However, in Kautilya's view, inter-state *matsya-nyaya* should and could eventually be 'domesticated' in the Indian subcontinent, albeit not via consensus and contract. Instead, out of unending inter-state power struggles and wars, the *vijigishu* will eventually create a hegemonic state that will formally or factually incorporate all other rival states in the subcontinent. Thus, the *vijigishu* will become the *chakravartin*, the ruler of a politically unified Indian subcontinent on which *matsya-nyaya* would be eradicated.

To summarize: Kautilya's political anthropology rests on two basic assumptions:

- the preponderance of the pursuit of material gain and power; and

- the conflictual nature of social and inter-state relations.

These anthropological constants are neither philosophically elevated nor ethically abominated in the *Arthashastra*. As basic 'facts of life', these anthropological dispositions must be carefully considered in political theory as well as in practical statecraft—and that is what Kautilya does in the *Arthashastra*.

The (pre-modern) ideas of political anthropology expounded by Kautilya in the *Arthashastra* show a remarkable similarity with modern political anthropology, notably the theoretical approach of Helmuth Plessner.[4] As for all biological nature, self-preservation is constitutive for man. In this primal instinct, Plessner sees first of all man's self-protection in defending the integrity of his or her bodily 'boundaries' against the 'outside' and the 'other'. For man, protecting the boundaries of his or her body is a matter of survival. Even though humans are biologically created by the parents, socialized within the (extended) family and depend existentially on other human beings throughout their lives, each human being remains an individual within the boundaries of his or her body. Moreover, the body is forcing human beings to acquire material objects from the environment: food and protection (for the body) such as clothing and housing. In addition, human beings are forced to develop tools and weapons to ensure their food supply and protect themselves against predators and violent fellow-men. In view of these basic anthropological facts, Plessner considers the normatively charged terms 'egoism' or 'selfishness' as inappropriate. Moreover, the primacy of 'self-interest' in self-preservation does not mean that man is inherently anti-social since the basic nourishment and reproductive instincts push him or her into the community with other human beings—family and clan. However, due to the primacy of individual self-preservation, conflicts of interest do inevitably arise between human beings—especially when it comes to procuring indispensable but scarce goods.

The basic anthropological principle of bodily 'boundaries' among individuals is also efficacious with respect to 'social bodies' like family, clan, tribe or political communities such as the (patrimonial) state. All these 'social bodies' defend their 'boundaries' against intrusions from the 'outside' and by 'others'. Social groups—as do individuals—counterpose 'a familiar, native sphere to an unfamiliar, foreign sphere' (Plessner 2003, 231).[5] Due to the basic anthropological fact of 'boundaries' and self-interest, inevitably conflicts of interests arise among social groups (as among individuals), which can turn into a friend-foe relation: 'For man, the adversary is what is detrimental to his interests [...] [conflicts of interest] are the most natural and most familiar thing of the world [...] causing everyday quarrels and disputes about the smallest and biggest of things' (Plessner 2003, 194).

Like Max Weber, Plessner defines politics as the 'struggle for power in the interpersonal relationships of individuals, groups and organizations, peoples and states' (Plessner 2003, 139). He considers 'politics as the necessity, emanating from the basic human condition, to live in a situation of pros and cons and to safeguard, in the friend-foe relation, an intrinsic zone [*Eigenzone*] against an extrinsic zone [*Fremdzone*]' (Plessner 2003, 195). Thus, politics cannot escape anthropologically-grounded conflicts of interest and power struggles. But by acknowledging anthropological realities, '*politics can actually become the art of the possible—in the direction not of the maximum but the optimum for one's own situation*' (Plessner 2003, 232f, emphasis added).

The basic supposition of Plessner's political anthropology is: there cannot be a political community free of conflict and domination. In man's social existence, there is no power vacuum but power struggle. Whether as actor or recipient of politics, man is 'in politics', but it is also true that politics is 'in man'.

> Questions of power have always existed as long as people live together in a social order which means domination and subordination. Someone has to be on top—be it a tribal chieftain, a king or a tyrant, or as the result of an election, possibly a ruling body on behalf of the sovereign people. In all such cases, the dynamics of the power do not change. Somewhere, somehow decisions must be made. And who will decide? The one who has the power. (Plessner 2003, 261)

The sober and unbiased acknowledgement of the entanglement of human nature and politics does not inevitably lead to cynical power politics bereft of any ethics; rather, argues Plessner, it provides the '*anthropological foundations for statecraft* as a welcome help for the leader who has to stay sober and level-headed when deciding what is the right moment to engage in a fight or to quit it' (Plessner 2003, 145f, emphasis added).

Kautilya's understanding of political anthropology has found its intellectual continuation, albeit through hybridization, in early modernity by Niccolo Machiavelli. And conceptual homologies do also exist with respect to Kautilyan political anthropology and that of modern theorists such as Max Weber, Helmuth Plessner and Hans J. Morgenthau.[6]

13

KAUTILYA'S ASSUMPTION ABOUT POLITICS AND THE THEORY OF POLITICAL REALISM

Kautilya's anthropological assumptions with respect to politics can be correlated to the term 'Political Realism'. Roger Boesche writes that 'Kautilya was the first great, unrelenting political realist' (Boesche 2002, 1). This finding is correct, but there is the problem that the category 'Political Realism' does not show up in the *Arthashastra*. However, as in the case of Kautilya's idea of raison d'état, the idea cluster underlying the theory of Political Realism is very much present in the *Arthashastra*. 'Clearly, it was not described as 'realism' by Kautilya [...]. Yet it was more than evident in [...] [his] writings and actions,' notes W.P. Singh Sidhu (1996, 175, emphasis added).

Kautilya's realist attitude in analysing political phenomena is well captured by Max Weber in his *Politics as a Vocation*, speaking about '*the trained ability to gaze relentlessly on the realities of life, and the ability to bear them and have the inward strength to be equal with them*' (Weber 2008a, 204; 1988b, 558, emphasis added). Kautilya submits that his political theory is grounded in empirical analysis of political reality and is scientific in that his theory-building proceeds methodologically and according to the principles of causality and logical consistency. Based on these suppositions, his theorems are not derived from 'ideological' presuppositions—in religious, metaphysical, moralist or eschatological terms. As Max Weber notes, the *Arthashastra* is 'devoid of any "ideology" in our sense of the word' (Weber 2000, 146; 2008a, 687). Kautilya sees politics as an autonomous sphere with an inherent rationality in terms of theory and practice. Thus, we can already recognize here a central feature of the Kautilyan idea of Political Realism.

From the above explication of Kautilya's political anthropology in the *Arthashastra* we can identify the following thought-figures as constituting Kautilya's idea of Political Realism that encompasses the whole sphere of politics, not only the field on inter-state relations:

- the preponderance of the pursuit of material gain and power as anthropological constant;
- the preponderance of (self-)interest and consequent conflicts of interests as anthropological constant;
- the understanding of politics as struggle;
- the anarchic nature of inter-state relations;
- the centrality of power in politics; and
- politics as an autonomous sphere with inherent logic and inherent normativity.

Based upon this Kautilyan idea cluster, we argue that the *Arthashastra* is the foundational text of the theory of Political Realism, even though Sun-Tzu's antecedent *The Art of War* does already contain important realist thought-figures.

If there is a structural homology between central ideas of the *Arthashastra* and key categories of modern Political Realism, the logical conclusion is that the modern theory of Political Realism is built upon (premodern) Kautilyan thought. Our argumentation is backed by Hans J. Morgenthau who locates the conceptual starting point of his theory of Political Realism in ancient political philosophy—not only of Greece, as one would expect, but of China and India:

> Human nature, in which the laws of politics have their roots, has not changed since the classical philosophies of China, India, and Greece endeavored to discover them. Hence, novelty is not necessarily a virtue in political theory, nor is old age a defect [...]. [T]he fact that a theory of politics which developed hundreds or even thousands of years ago—as was the theory of the balance of power—does not create the presumption that it must be outmoded and obsolete [...]. To dismiss such a theory: because it had its flowering in centuries past, is to present not a rational argument but a modernistic prejudice

that takes for granted the superiority of the present over the past. (Morgenthau 1978, 4, emphasis added)

It is indeed most remarkable that Morgenthau traces his theory of Political Realism not only to the European tradition but to ancient political philosophy of Asia.[1] Morgenthau does not name any authors or works of ancient Chinese and Indian philosophy, but we know of his intellectual familiarity with Kautilya from his book *Dilemmas of Politics*.

In the first of his 'Six Principles of Political Realism', Morgenthau states that his theory articulates 'objective laws' that derive from 'forces inherent in human nature' and condition all forms of political interaction (Morgenthau 1978, 3f). Thus, Morgenthau anchors his theory in political anthropology.

Moreover, as we have seen, the core features of Morgenthau's political anthropology are broadly similar to Kautilya's theorems of the preponderance of the pursuit of material gain and power as well as the conflicting nature of social relations. But it is not only in the understanding of political anthropology that we find homologies between Kautilya and Morgenthau. We find them as well in the 'laws of politics' (rooted in human nature): the understanding of politics as struggle, the centrality of power in both domestic and inter-state politics and the anarchic nature of inter-state relations. In Morgenthau's theory of political realism, the terms 'power' and 'interest' take central positions. He defines power—in close analogy to Weber—as 'anything that establishes and maintains control of man over man' (Morgenthau 1978, 9). Again following Weber, Morgenthau defines 'politics', particularly 'international politics', as power struggle:

> *International politics, like all politics, is a struggle for power. Whatever the ultimate aims of international politics, power is always the immediate aim* […]. The aspiration for power being the distinguishing element of international politics, as for all politics, international politics is of necessity power politics. While this fact is generally recognized in the practice of international affairs, it is frequently denied in the pronouncements of scholars, publicists, and even statesmen. (Morgenthau 1978, 29, 35, emphasis added)

Also, Morgenthau's concept of 'interest' is oriented around Weber. In his *Politics Among Nations* he quotes the latter's dictum: *'Interests (material and ideal), not ideas, dominate directly the actions of men'* (Morgenthau 1978, 9; Weber 2008a, 302). Taking off from that, Morgenthau develops the core concept of his theory of political realism—'interest defined in terms of power':

> Realism assumes that its key concept of interest defined as power is an objective category that is universally valid, but it does not endow that concept with a meaning that is fixed once and for all. The idea of interest is indeed the essence of politics and is unaffected by the circumstances of time and place. (Morgenthau 1978, 8, emphasis added)

Morgenthau's conceptional orientation drawing on Max Weber is evident, but what matters for us here is the fact that both Weber and Morgenthau knew of Kautilya. And it was Kautilya who first developed a realist political theory that is based on political anthropology as well as the concepts of (state) power and state interest. The homologies between Kautilya's and Morgenthau's theories of Political Realism are evident in the following citation from *Dilemmas of Politics*:

> [The] denial of the existence and intelligibility of a truth about matters political that exist regardless of time and place implies a denial of the possibility of political theory both in its analytical and normative sense [...]. *[The theory of Political Realism] believes that the world, imperfect as it is from the rational point of view, is the result of forces inherent in human nature. To improve the world one must work with these forces, not against them. This being inherently a world of opposing interests and of conflict among them,* moral principles can never be fully realized, but at best be approximated through the ever temporary balancing of interests and the ever precarious settlement of conflicts. (Morgenthau 1958, 13, 54f, emphasis added)

In view of the evident conceptual homologies between Kautilya and Morgenthau, the established intellectual history of Political Realism is flawed and Eurocentric. In chronological terms, realist political theorizing begins with Sun-Tzu (ca. 544–496 BC) in ancient China, notwithstanding that the author of *The Art of War* focuses on the conduct of war rather than on politics and statecraft in general.[2] Yet most representations of the history of Political Realism omit Sun-Tzu and Kautilya. Instead, they start off with Greek antiquity. Usually Thucydides (ca. 454–396 BC) and his *The Peloponnesian War* are presented as the point of departure of Political Realism. Thucydides, however, is first of all a historian—not a political theorist. *The Peloponnesian War* does contain important realist thought-figures, notably his emphasis of interest and power as the driving forces of politics. Yet Thucydides's opus magnum is a historical narrative that includes realist theory by implication only.[3] Next, the ancient Greek Sophists are usually named in the intellectual history of Political Realism: Protagoras and Gorgias as well as Thrasymachus, Critias and Calicles who are featured in Plato's writings.[4] The Sophists are first of all rhetoricians who expound radical skepticism in epistemic and ethical terms: what appears as 'truth' is subjective and contingent, and 'right' is what best serves a given purpose. These thought-figures and the Greek Sophists' emphasis on 'might makes right' does not, however, constitute political theory or a theorization of statecraft.

With respect to political thought of European antiquity, the Roman historian Tacitus is often invoked as an early representative of Political Realism. To Tacitus applies what we noted above with respect to Thucydides: he is first of all a historian who also brings in some realist thought-figures. To summarize, none of the ancient European authors that are usually designated as constituting the lineage of Political Realism approximates the breadth and depth of Kautilya's theorization of Political Realism.[5]

Proceeding from antiquity to (early) modernity, Niccolo Machiavelli is unquestionably the central figure in the intellectual evolution of Political Realism.[6] E.H. Carr characterizes Machiavelli's core ideas as following:

> The three essential tenets implicit in Machiavelli's doctrine are the foundation-stones of the realist philosophy. In the first place,

history is a sequence of cause and effect, whose course can be analysed and understood by intellectual effort, not (as utopians believe) directed by 'imagination'. Secondly, theory does not (as utopians believe) create practice, but practice theory [...]. Thirdly, politics is not (as utopians pretend) a function of ethics, but ethics of politics. Men 'are kept honest by constraint'. Machiavelli recognized the importance of morality, but thought there could be no effective morality where there was no effective authority. Morality is the product of power. (Carr 1981, 63f)

Carr's assessment of Machiavelli is correct, except that he overlooks the fact that 'the foundation-stones of the realist philosophy' were laid long before Machiavelli by Kautilya. There are significant conceptual homologies among key concepts in the *Arthashastra* and Carr's *The Twenty-Years Crisis*. Yet in contrast to Morgenthau, there is no indication that Carr knew of Kautilya's *Arthashastra* (nor Sun-Tzu's *The Art of War*) since he writes:

> It was in the 5th and 4th century BC that the first serious recorded attempts were made to create a science of politics. These attempts were made independently in China and Greece. But neither Confucius nor Plato, though they were of course profoundly influenced by the political institutions under which they lived, really tried to analyse the nature of those institutions or to seek the underlying causes of the evils they deplored. (Carr 1981, 6)

The many comparisons between Kautilya and Machiavelli attest to the fact that many conceptional homologies exist between the two realist thinkers. Max Weber has already been mentioned as comparing Kautilya and Machiavelli, but the list of other scholars doing so is much longer (cf. Sarkar 1919; Hillebrandt 1923; Zimmer 1973/1945; Drekmeier 1962; Roy 1981; Sil 1987; Karnad 2002; Boesche 2002a, 2002b; Dixit 2003; Watson 1992; Gautam 2013c; Bajpai et al. 2014). A dedicated conceptual comparison between Kautilya's *Arthashastra* and Machiavelli's *Prince* and *Discorsi* is beyond the scope of our study. Thus, we limit ourselves to one basic homology that concerns the very methodological structure of

Kautilya's premodern treatise and Machiavelli's early modern political writings.

Kautilya states in the *Arthashastra* that his book was written 'after *going through all the sciences* in detail and *observing the [political] practice*' (KA, II, 10, 63, emphasis added). Machiavelli writes in the Introduction of the *Discorsi*: 'I have endeavored to embody in it [the *Discorsi*] all that *long experience* and *assiduous research* have taught me of the affairs of the world' (*Discorsi*, in Lerner 1950, 103, emphasis added). Kautilya's exposition of the state and statecraft is not meant to draw up 'visionary schemes of ideal communities' (Carr 1981, 7). The Kautilyan state and statecraft are no 'idealist' or utopian constructions, but rooted in the empirical analysis of political reality using ideal-type methodology. Machiavelli pursues a homologous approach. In the fifteenth chapter of the *Prince* he writes:

> But my intention being to write something of use to those who understand, it appears to me more proper *to go to the real truth of the matter than to its imagination; and many have imagined republics and principalities, which have never been seen or known to exist in reality*; for how we live is so far removed from how we ought to live, that he who abandons what is done for what ought to be done, will rather learn to bring about his own ruin than his preservation. (In Lerner 1950, 56, emphasis added)

If there is structural homology between key ideas and concepts of Kautilya and Machiavelli, two basic explanations seem plausible. First, there exists an independent and parallel generation of thought-figures in different cultural and historical contexts. The second explanation for such structural homology is that there has been a 'westward' trans-temporal and trans-cultural 'flow' or 'migration' of Kautilyan thought or at least of the thought-figures thereof. Charles Drekmeier has alluded to the possibility that Machiavelli might have been influenced by Kautilya (without, however, indicating how), writing: 'It has even been suggested that the Italian [Machiavelli] was inspired by the Arthashastra' (Drekmeier 1962, 204). And Bharat Karnad raises the question: 'Could it be, that the Arthashastra traveled to Europe, in the manner the so-called "Arabic" numerals, etc., originating in India had earlier done, and provided Machiavelli with the necessary inspiration?' (Karnad 2002, 11)

Investigating whether the evident homologies between Kautilya and Machiavelli are a case of 'covariance' or of 'idea migration' (or both) is beyond the scope of our study. But Karnad's question is indeed of great significance for future research. That the conditions have existed which would have made a transcultural 'flow' of Kautilyan thought across Eurasia possible seems a plausible proposition. Adda Bozeman (1960) has led the way in theoretical and methodological terms with her seminal work *Politics and Culture in International History*.[7]

Among serious scholars in academia and public life, Machiavelli's place in the lineage of the great thinkers of Political Realism is undisputed. Moreover, the intellectual connectivity between him and the well-known theoreticians of Political Realism in the twentieth century—E.H. Carr and Hans J. Morgenthau—is generally recognized. What is still sadly missing is the recognition that Machiavelli, Carr and Morgenthau are standing on the intellectual shoulders of Kautilya and his *Arthashastra*.

SECTION B

KAUTILYA AND MODERN INDIA
A Complex Resonance

1

KAUTILYA AND MODERN INDIA
Methodological and Theoretical Approaches

We have analysed the delineation of Kautilya's ideal-type state in the previous section. Now we turn to the exploration of the presence of Kautilya in the institutions and governance of the modern Indian state. The Constituent Assembly which framed India's constitution had no specific mandate to embed Kautilyan thought in the Constitution. Kautilya did, however, find his way into the structure of governance in postcolonial India. This chapter will attempt to discern Kautilya's implicit presence, beginning with an analysis of the writings of Nehru who, for many, is the founding father of the modern state in India. The more explicit method to detect the legacy of Kautilya is through in-depth conversations with scholars, political leaders and diplomats, who constitute a microcosm of the Indian elite.

With regard to the question of the contemporary relevance of the Kautilya's *Arthashastra*, the first problem to be addressed is the data to be used for the investigation. The search for scientific publications in which Kautilya's relevance for modern India is addressed in a dedicated fashion has yielded little of any substance.[1] If there is any resonance between Kautilya and modern India, it is neither simple nor direct. However, a review of literature provided some evidence that the research question has occasionally been touched upon, albeit only in passing, in some Indology, social science and historiography publications. In a few articles dealing with Indian strategic culture, Kautilya's influence has been thematized. In addition, there are some valuable journalistic articles that address Kautilya's contemporary relevance. Of special significance is Jawaharlal Nehru's *The Discovery of India*, in which, among other politico-cultural resources of India, Kautilya and the *Arthashastra* are treated in the political perspective of the Indian independence struggle.

Since the literature pertaining to Kautilya's contemporary relevance is sparse, conducting 'expert interviews' is the method of choice to generate additional data material. In journalism, an informant or a 'personal source' is questioned because the interviewer assumes that the interviewee possesses some 'special knowledge' beyond what is publicly available via 'open sources'. Expert interviews in the social sciences are, in principle, not different: it is about accessing expertise that is not available in the scientific literature and other open sources (cf. Girtler 2001; Wengraf 2001; Bogner et al. 2009; Behnke et al. 2010).

Thirty-four expert interviews were conducted and assessed during a three-month research stay in India in the Spring of 2012.[2] The interviewees came from the Indian strategic community and academia. What mattered in the interviews was not the interviewees' in-depth knowledge of Kautilya's *Arthashastra*, but the relevance of Kautilyan thought in modern India observed in what they had to share with us. In addition to the expert interviews, there were many informal discussions with Indian interlocutors on the research subject, notably in the context of seminars at the Institute of Defence Studies and Analyses (IDSA), the United Service Institution of India (USI), and the Vivekananda International Foundation (VIF).[3]

The expert interviews[4] were structured by the following set of questions. However, sooner than later, all interviews evolved into a narrative and discursive mode.

- What has been your personal 'encounter' with Kautilya's *Arthashastra* in primary socialization, education and professional life?
- Do you see Kautilya as an endogenous politico-cultural resource of India. What about other such resources?
- Do you see Kautilyan thought as having influence in contemporary India? If so, what are its manifestations? Do you also see a latent influence of Kautilyan thought-figures in Indian politics?
- How do you see the influence of Kautilyan thought specifically

in the Indian strategic community and in academia?
- What is your sense of Indian culture and cultural continuity, in which Kautilyan thought has been embedded?
- Is Indian politico-strategic culture shaped by 'realism' or 'idealism' or both?
- What do you make out of Nehru's treatment of Kautilya's *Arthashastra* in the *Discovery of India*?
- Considering India's status as a rising power in the multipolar world system, do you think the relevance of Kautilya will increase in the twenty-first century?

Our data analysis follows Weber's methodology of 'discursive cognition': the 'constant flux between the attempt to order facts intellectually by means of concept formation; the breaking down—because of the broadening and displacement of the scientific horizon—of the mental images that have been arrived at in this fashion; and the new formation of concepts on this altered basis' (Weber 2012, 134).

The aim of the evaluation of the expert interviews was to provide a theoretically structured and empirically saturated basis for answering the research question of Kautilya's relevance in modern India. Inevitably, the evaluation process faces a dilemma because it 'moves systematically between the Scylla of empirically illustrating a given theory and the Charybdis of meticulous, but non-theoretical description that pays for the wealth of information with the dispensation of explanation' (Allert 1998, 20). We believe that a certain degree of modesty regarding theoretical generalizations of analytical results is appropriate. In case of doubt, the evaluation of the expert interviews followed the dictum 'good description is better than bad explanation' (Behnke et al., 2010, 358).

Obviously, the interviewees' statements and assessments—even though they come from experts—can only be verified in terms of their plausibility—both during the interview and also in the subsequent analysis.[5] The interviewees provided not only factual information and assessments with respect to the research question as such, but they also contributed most valuable cultural and historical knowledge. Without the latter, the adequate understanding of the first would often have been difficult, if not impossible. Roland Girtler correctly emphasizes the necessity to complement data collection with in-depth analysis of the historical and cultural context. The researcher must interpret social phenomena 'both in their current situation and with respect to their historical background. That is what Weber or [Georg] Simmel did [...]. An effective social and cultural research thus requires both the study of the current level (planum) and the temporal depth (profile), right in the spirit of Max Weber' (Girtler 2001, 33). The validity of Girtler's statement is evident in the expert interviews. In discussing Kautilya's current relevance, the narration of most interviewees spontaneously drifted to questions of Indian culture and history. That follows from the inner logic of the research question which links pre-modern Kautilyan thought with modern India.

It is a specificity of our study that in the course of the three-year research process new possibilities to operationalize the research question emerged. Neither during the project design phase, nor during literature search and analysis, or during the interviewing process was it to be expected that, starting in 2012, a 'Kautilya discourse' would emerge in India—i.e., in parallel with the ongoing research work. This emergent 'Kautilya discourse' generated a wealth of new empirical material: articles, essays, speeches, video documents, press releases and even books. Thus, a third set of data became available—in addition to literature analysis and evaluating the expert interviews. Analysing the new data meant no additional methodological challenge. However, there was a sticky point: On the one hand, the rather dynamic 'Kautilya discourse' was a fortuitous development for our research project. On the other hand, greater temporal distance would have been preferable because it also usually means greater 'scientific distance' when analysing the object of investigation. However, this potential methodological problem must be balanced against the fact that the new arrivals of empirical data help decisively to come to valid findings on the question of Kautilya's contemporary relevance.

For the analysis of the data material on the contemporary relevance of Kautilya's *Arthashastra*, we credit the following theoretical concepts with particular exploratory power:

- The concept of longue durée history, developed by Fernand Braudel, is of paramount importance for the understanding of cultural continuity in India. Cultural continuity is the logical condition for the possibility of Kautilyan thought to have any influence in present-day India.
- The concept of 're-use of the past' (Mitra 2011a) refers to the 'reactivation' of pre-modern politico-cultural resources for dealing with contemporary politico-strategic challenges. Re-use—the strategic incorporation of the elements of the past to create a new, more robust and legitimate present—is the key for understanding the manifest presence of Kautilyan thought in contemporary India's political institutions and practices.
- The concept of strategic culture, notably in its conceptualization by Alastair Iain Johnston, who ascribes to the early strategic texts of a politico-cultural space a formative influence on the dispositions and preferences in foreign and security policy of the modern state evolved from it. For India, the *Arthashastra* is such a text, just as Sun-Tzu's *The Art of War*, is for China.
- The sociological concept of 'habitus', developed by Pierre Bourdieu, allows for an understanding of the latent presence of Kautilyan thought in modern India. Latent presence means that Kautilyan thought-figures are perceived and used as 'common sense', making their explicit attribution to Kautilya superfluous.

2

THE KAUTILYAN LEGACY EMBEDDED IN LONGUE DURÉE CULTURAL CONTINUITY

2.1 CULTURE AND LONGUE DURÉE HISTORY

Not only is cultural continuity the logical precondition of Kautilyan thought being efficacious in contemporary India, but the transmission of the *Arthashastra* over some 2300 years is itself an expression of cultural continuity. In our study, we don't delve into the cultural history of India but sketch an outline for a basic theoretical understanding of cultural continuity that draws primarily on Fernand Braudel's theory of history and the place on culture therein.[1] Next, we will turn specifically to Indian culture and cultural continuity in which the transmission of the *Arthashastra* has been embedded.

First, what is to be understood under the broad but evocative concept of 'culture'? As Braudel notes: 'Not even Arnold Toynbee seemed to have felt the need to give us a definition or an overview of what "culture" means to him. That goes without saying, isn't it' (Braudel 1992, 250). In actual fact, it is not at all self-evident what culture means. Braudel refers to the American anthropologists Kroeber and Klukhohn, who have come up with 163 different definitions of culture (ibid., 248). Among the multitude of meanings of culture, three aspects are essential for us:

- The anthropological dimension of culture: the unique human capacity to transform or 'cultivate' nature and, in doing so, generate material and immaterial artifacts that range from religion to technology. This creative human capacity of 'culture-making' is a political resource that—in principle—knows no limits (cf. Plessner 2003).

- The historical dimension of culture: the human transformation of nature occurs always in a social and intellectual context which has been formed by antecedent human beings, i.e., languages, socio-economic and political formations, customs and thought-traditions. Thus, past human existence—history—is inextricably linked with culture and 'culture-making'.[2]
- While we might speak of one 'civilization' (with universal features and standards), culture exists only in plurality. Cultures are distinguished by different languages, ecological contexts, collective experiences and traditions (cf. Todorov 2010). Thus, each culture constitutes a 'sphere of familiarity' for those who belong to it as opposed to other, 'unfamiliar' cultures.

The symbiosis of the anthropological and historical dimensions of culture provides a basis for the theoretical understanding of cultural continuity: The central characteristic of all cultures is continuity in historical change. At the same time, culture is an expression of the (in principle) unlimited creative potentiality of man—and thus the catalyst of historical change. We approach the examination of the interface of culture and history by turning to Braudel's theory of history. Braudel's distinguishes three '*temporalités*' or 'time structures':

- the time structure of current or contemporary 'events' that could also be called the 'journalistic time';
- the medium time structure of conjunctures, cycles or generations comprising decades;[3]
- the time structure of the longue durée which covers centuries or even millennia. Longue durée—the 'deep structure' of history—is the mode of existence of cultures.[4]

Each of these time structures has its own metric and rhythm. In 'journalistic time', a week may 'last long', while in the longue durée structure of cultures a century may be 'a short time'. For Braudel, history in its entirety or '*globalité*' can only be understood in the simultaneity and mutual overlay of 'event history', the 'history of conjunctures' and the longue durée history. In each moment of history, the three dimensions of history coexist and interact with each other (cf. Rojas 1999). And in this interaction, the respective 'pulse strength' can very much differ, which can manifest itself in 'stagnation' or in revolutionary ruptures in the course of history:

> Obviously, events and conjunctures do not represent the actual depth of the past and the present time. On the deepest level, we find a history almost at a standstill, passing by slowly, slowly, the longest of all the long histories; something like the secular trend, or rather the economists' multi-secular trend, which comprises many centuries. I speak of a deep, not a stationary history [...]. *In addition to the passing time, there is the time that persists, the deep past to which our lives are attached—mostly without us noticing it.* (Braudel 1993, 398, 401, emphasis added)

Comprehending longue durée history is obviously a lot more difficult than dealing with contemporary events. The study of the deep structures of history requires an almost impossible interdisciplinary approach[5] and, equally so, a precise understanding of the term 'structure'. Braudel designates structure as 'that part of history which can be singled out when applying the criteria of duration, repetition, and persistence,' i.e., what 'resists time in the major part of society, what persists, evades contingency and stands firm—tenaciously and successfully' (1993, 387f). Structure is 'not absolute immobility. It appears immovable only in relation to what is moving around it and develops more or less rapidly [...]. In short, the global history presents itself, if simplified to the utmost, in the perspective of a permanent dialectic between structure and non-structure, between continuity and change' (ibid.).

Braudel defines culture as a 'durable dynamic structure' congruent with longue durée history (1992, 255). He stresses that there are only cultures (in the plural) which are different because they have evolved under quite diverse environmental, linguistic and social conditions. For Braudel, each culture is characterized by 'coherence in space and length of time' (ibid., 273). Every culture has a material and a cognitive dimension. The material dimension has a geographical-ecological component and a social, economic and political component. Braudel argues that the geographical and the environmental conditions are essential for the singular inertia of culture. The cognitive dimension of culture consists of 'acquired reflexes and attitudes, fixed habits, ingrained tastes, which can only be explained by [the influence of] a slowly moving, barely conscious history that reaches way back'[6] (Braudel 1993, 384). What Braudel writes about inner characteristics of cultures in general, applies in a singular fashion to Indian culture:

> As realities of enormously long duration, cultures—with a virtually infinite adaptability to their fate—*exceed all other collective realities in longevity, they literally survive them all* [...]. In other words, cultures survive political, social, economic and even ideological upheavals—actually, at least in part, they covertly dominate them. (Braudel 1992, 283, emphasis added)

Braudel's concept of the longue durée history as a mode of existence of culture enables us to qualitatively deepen the understanding of cultural continuity: Cultures can have an immense staying power, and their time structure differs decisively from that of political history. Cultures are uniquely resilient and adaptive structures which can withstand socio-economic, political and ideological ruptures. Braudel tells us that cultural continuity is a reality—the efficacy of which is as profound as it appears opaque in conventional perspectives of social science.

2.2 CULTURAL CONTINUITY IN INDIA

Exploring the relevance of Kautilya's *Arthashastra* in contemporary India necessitates addressing the facticity of cultural continuity in India as a logical precondition. Problematizing cultural continuity in India may seem rather superfluous since Indian culture is evidently among the oldest cultures of the world. Yet, for our study dealing with the relevance of an ancient Indian text for modern India (in the framework of Political Science) we need to have a basic understanding of what culture and cultural continuity mean for India. Since historiography and Cultural Studies are not our fields of expertise, we draw primarily on statements on the subject of Indian culture and cultural continuity from the expert interviews. But first we take a look at Jawaharlal Nehru's *Discovery of India* that addresses the two concepts.[7] Nehru was, as he himself states explicitly, neither a historian nor a scholarly expert on the cultural history of India. Yet his broad historical and cultural knowledge and his penetrating intellect enabled him to provide a panoramic view of the key lines of development of India's history and culture. In *The Discovery of India*, Nehru states that his Western education had created a critical distance from Indian culture, but precisely it is that distance that enabled him to recognize its uniqueness.[8]

> I read her history and read also a part of her abundant ancient literature, and was powerfully impressed by the vigor of thought, the clarity of language, and the richness of mind that lay behind it [...]. *There seemed to me something unique about the continuity of cultural tradition through five thousand years of history*, of invasion and upheaval, a tradition which was widespread among the masses and powerfully influenced them. (Nehru 1981, 50, 52)

In contrast to the discontinuities of European cultures, in Indian culture

> there has *not* been such a break and *there is definite continuity* [...]. Like some ancient *palimpsest* on which layer upon layer of thought and reverie had been inscribed, and yet no succeeding layer had completely hidden or erased what had been written previously. All of these existed in our conscious and subconscious selves, though we may not have been aware of them. (Nehru 1981, 54, 59, emphasis added)

In the expert interviews, the *Arthashastra* was perceived as an integral part of Indian culture and its epoch-spanning transmission as embedded in the longue durée continuity of Indian culture. The interviewees used terms like 'flow', 'code', 'thread', 'trait' or 'legacy' in order to capture the phenomenon of cultural continuity in India. The variety of expressions indicates the paradoxical difficulty to conceptualize a cultural phenomenon that is perceived as 'natural' and 'self-evident'.

Since the Enlightenment, the mainstream Western understanding of history and culture has been focused on change and progress that leave the past behind. In Eurocentric historical thinking, cultural continuity appears rather as stagnation and 'lack of progress'. In contrast, the Indian tradition of thought is far more focused on continuity in the sense of a 'coexistence' of the past with the present. Old ideas and cultural assets do not lose their relevance for the present, even if they have survived only in the form of myths and legends. Paradigmatic ruptures or 'intellectual revolutions' are alien to Indian thought, favouring instead the synthesis of old and new ideas. The quasi-teleological notion of progress in the course of history is absent.

Betty Heimann has pointed out that the Indian tradition of thought prefers a 'non-temporal and horizontal' configuration of cultural achievements instead of their 'temporal and vertical' stratification as in the West. Past and present are rather positioned 'side by side' than as 'succession'. 'Thus one finds at all times and in all disciplines of Indian thought elements of primitive thought-figures interspersed within the most advanced cultural concepts' (Heimann 1930, 258). In view of the Indian tradition of synthesizing and time-transcending thinking, it is not surprising that there is no established tradition of (chronological) historiography in India, and no philosophy of history and culture that is anchored in the paradigm of progress.

In the context of our inquiry, we can state that cultural continuity is not only the logical precondition but the factual facilitator of the presence and efficacy of Kautilyan thought in today's India. Conversely, the transmission of Kautilya's *Arthashastra* across two millennia is one expression of the longue durée continuity of Indian culture.

An important factor impeding the understanding of cultural continuity in India is India's deep-rooted tradition of oral transmission of cultural assets. In European history, including the Jewish tradition, books and culture are inseparably tied together. Only what has been written down is regarded as truly valuable in terms of culture. The 'materialization' of idea-contents in books was seen as the precondition for their reliable transmission thus establishing cultural continuity. Yet while the written text has been the indispensable medium of cultural continuity in Europe, there has been no comparable hegemony of written texts in Indian culture. Even after the introduction of writing during the first half of the first millennium BC, the domination of oral transmission in India did not recede, and that remained so until the beginning of the twentieth century. Indian intellectuals continued to favour oral transmission even though they could perfectly well read and write:

> *There can be cultural continuity without books or written documents. From generation to generation, there has been oral transmission. It is a very strong element in Indian society throughout history.*
> (EI Rana Chhina,[9] emphasis added)

That anyone could learn by heart a vast tome such as Kautilya's *Arthashastra* is barely comprehensible in European cultural space—and that applies also to twenty-first century India. Nevertheless, until the late nineteenth century, many Indian intellectuals—Brahmin, Buddhist or Jain gurus—spent almost their entire life memorizing classical texts to pass them on orally to their students. The mental discipline and mnemonic virtuosity necessary for becoming a 'living book' exceed modern imagination.

The long-lasting dominance of oral transmission of cultural assets cannot be derived from the state of widespread illiteracy (even today) in India. Oral transmission has not been a symptom of 'cultural backwardness' but rather the result of a conscious preference of elites engaged with 'high culture'.[10] But mnemonic virtuosity is equally found among—often illiterate—'storytellers' who act in rural and urban contexts as 'living books'. Often they are able to retell, albeit in vernacular language, large sections of the monumental Sanskrit epics *Ramayana* and *Mahabharata* or the collection of fables *Panchatantra*. This is one reason why the classical texts of Indian culture have been disseminated among the uneducated masses and have been popular among common people across time.[11]

To summarize: up to the twentieth century, not only the central ideas and values of Indian culture but also its classical texts (mostly of great length), have mainly been transmitted by way of oral narrative, both among the intellectual elites as well as amid the (mainly illiterate) majority population. India is the case in point where cultural continuity over millennia can be based upon oral transmission, and does not depend on written texts.

2.3 DIVERSITY: THE BASIC PREMISE OF INDIAN CULTURE

If cultural continuity can be considered a fact since at least the middle of the first millennium BC, the question arises as to what are the structural features of Indian culture that bring forth its staying power over millennia and make it withstand most dramatic historical ruptures. Further, what role might the patrimonial state have played in sustaining the plural structure of this culture.

Most interviewees said that Indian culture is not only phenomenologically different from other major cultures but has other structural properties. In India, the very idea of culture is qualitatively different from that in Europe, the USA or China, they argued. Indian cultural space is characterized by ecological, ethnic, linguistic and religious diversity. In contrast, already the early stages of the formation of cultures in Europe or China were characterized by a relatively high degree of ethnic, linguistic and religious homogenization. Ancient Greece could serve as an 'ideal type' of cultural homogeneity: Here the Greeks, one ethnicity, language and religion, there the 'barbarians'. The inner dynamic of the cultures of Europe, the United States, China or Japan has been to steadily expand and deepen homogeneity—at least until the end of the twentieth century. It has not been so in India. Indian culture knows no homogenizing impulse. In the expert interviews, there was consensus that the issue of diversity vs. homogeneity offers a basic approach for conceptionalizing the structural difference between the Indian culture-type and other types of cultures.

The Indian subcontinent has always been inhabited by different ethnic groups: Indo-Aryans, Dravidians and a multitude of small ethnic groups. In India today, there are 22 constitutionally recognized languages belonging to four language families: Indo-European, Dravidian, Austro-Asiatic and Sino-Tibetan. In addition, there are at least 80 other local languages (cf. Rothermund 1995). However, India's intellectual and political elites of all ages have communicated via a *lingua franca*: Sanskrit,

Persian—parallel to Sanskrit—in the Islamic era, and then English in colonial and postcolonial times.[12] From a European perspective, it is rather puzzling that such linguistic diversity would not obstruct cultural (and political) cohesiveness. The interviewees thought otherwise and pointed to Pakistan where the suppression of linguistic diversity was an important factor for that state's break-up in 1971.[13]

Since ancient times, India has known no religious homogeneity. The Vedic-Brahmanical majority religion—today called Hinduism—is not a closed belief system and has never had the status of state religion. As early as the sixth century BC, the Vedic-Brahmanical religion was challenged by Buddhism and the Jain religion. Buddhism, originally more of an ethical stance without explicit reference to God than a religion, was until the end of the first millennium AD the second main religion of India next to Hinduism. The gradual disappearance of Buddhism in India was not the result of its suppression but occurred primarily through a metamorphosis of the Vedic-Brahmanical religion which significantly adapted to Buddhist teachings and religious practices. Although Buddhism has been marginalized since the end of the first millennium AD, it has probably been the most important 'cultural export' of India, from where it spread to Central Asia, China, Mongolia, Japan and Indochina.[14]

In order to accommodate the ethnic, linguistic and religious diversity on the subcontinent, Indian culture had to develop structural features that make it a unique culture type differing not only phenomenologically but structurally from other cultures.

2.4 THE PLURAL PARADIGM OF INDIAN CULTURE

In the expert interviews, it was argued that Indian culture was able to evolve and gain staying-power precisely because it has internalized diversity as its premise. The deliberate dispensation with the paradigm of homogeneity, the central feature of European and Chinese cultures, is the real strength of Indian culture, as the interviewees argued. Thus, the paradigm of plurality is constitutive of the Indian culture. The coexistence and inclusion of different 'sub-cultural' traits, based on the acceptance of ethnic, linguistic and religious diversity, have made it possible that 'the' Indian culture could evolve and persevere for three thousand years.

The Eurocentric point of view is confronted with the paradox that a 'structural deficit', namely the absence of homogeneity, should be the source of cohesiveness for the Indian culture. Can a—'one'—culture evolve out of structural pluralism? From an Indian perspective, it is the other way around: homogeneity is the 'structural deficit' standing in the way of cultural cohesiveness based on diversity. Max Weber wondered whether, in view of its enormous inner diversity of beliefs (and their toleration), the Hindu religion should be considered a—'one'—religion in the European sense. Analogous to that, Indian culture singularly features inclusive pluralism. Like the Hindu understanding of religion, the Indian concept of culture is structurally different from that of Europe and China. The structural contrast between the two great and ancient cultures of Asia—China and India—is particularly striking and was repeatedly highlighted in the interviews. The political unification of India and China respectively occurred at roughly the same time— between the end of the fourth and the end of the third century BC. But in that, two opposite cultural paradigms were politically consolidated: radical homogeneity—in terms of culture, language and organizational structures—in China under the Qin dynasty versus inclusive pluralism in India under the Mauryan emperor Ashoka (304–232 BC).

Ashoka not only 'tolerated' religious, linguistic and cultural diversity but made plurality the basic political norm of his state. After converting and becoming a fervent Buddhist, Ashoka did not raise Buddhism to the status of state religion nor did he discriminate against the Hindu majority. Ashoka communicated his political and ethical program via inscriptions on columns and rocks written in a variety of languages, including Greek and Aramaic. The locations of these inscriptions range from today's Afghanistan to South India. One such column (discovered in Afghanistan) has as inscription the '7th Edict' which not only decrees that all subjects may exercise their different religions freely but commits them to mutual tolerance and cooperation (Kulke 2005, 22f; Kulke/ Rothermund 1998, 83ff). The '7th Edict' codifies the paradigm of Indian culture: inclusive plurality based on the assumption that there is a 'higher plane of unity' within diversity.

> This goes back to Ashoka's 7th edict [...]. There Ashoka says that he, 'the Beloved of the Gods,' would wish that *all peoples and followers of different paths of religious belief live all together in his kingdom*. Although it is not explicitly stated, it is obvious that the contrast he had in mind were either people living in other states which were completely homogenized or living in the Maurya territory, but back to back rather than face to face [...]. *Ashoka's idea was that populations of different creed, language and ethnicity should always stay together. I think this Ashokan idea has continued throughout Indian history.* (EI Rajeev Bhargava,[15] emphasis added)

Thanks to its intrinsic pluralism, Indian culture gains a quality which could be described with the Hegelian term *Aufhebung* that integrates three dimensions of meaning: 1) undoing or overcoming, 2) preserving, and 3) raising to a higher level. In the expert interviews, it was pointed out that its inclusive pluralism gives Indian culture exceptional elasticity with respect to ethnic, linguistic and religious diversity. More generally, differences and contradictions tend to be accepted—'as-well-as' instead of 'either-or'—and eventually synthesized in some way instead of insisting on unilateral solutions.[16]

In the expert interviews, the political dimension of the cultural paradigm of inclusive pluralism was emphasized. Throughout Indian history, there have been different, if not opposing, theories of statecraft. Kautilya's *Arthashastra* may be the most influential politico-strategic tradition of India, but it never had the monopoly of political thought. The tradition of Kautilyan political realism has always coexisted and competed with idealist political thought, and out of that controversial interaction has emerged a synthesis of novel ideas. Not only in political theory but also in India's political practice it was argued that pluralism has been the predominant tradition because it is consonant with, and deeply rooted in, Indian culture.

In the development of the theory of state and political thought generally—at any point of time in India—there were always different, competing currents of thinking. There never was just one; even in Kautilya's time, there was not only one. *Now the Indian pluralistic system permitted that these multiple currents [of political thought] could flow together.* Thinkers did not agree, but they did not deny the right of having different views [...]. The basic undercurrent of the Indian political thinking has never taken a homogenous form. (EI Ajit Doval,[17] emphasis added)

2.5 COHESIVENESS WITHIN PLURALITY: THE 'VALUE IDEAS OF THE EPICS'

Even assuming the structural otherness of Indian culture, the question remains: What is it that constitutes cohesiveness within plurality? The answers in the expert interviews were puzzling. The main argument was that the historical continuity of inclusive pluralism in Indian culture is constitutive for 'the' Indian culture. In other words, 'the' (pluralist) Indian culture exists because there has always been cultural pluralism. This is obviously a circular argument in which the conclusion is already included in the supposition. A similar argument comes from V. R. Mehta:

> [O]n the whole, Indian society has up to the time of Gandhi worked and operated with the conviction of such a continuity. In other words, *we have always taken India to be a case of unity in diversity.* Throughout our history we have constantly referred to past writers, *habitually quoting or citing Manu, Valmiki or Vyasa,* as though these people shared the same idiom of thought. Even Abdul Fazal undertook the translation of the *Mahabharata,* the influence of earlier ideas is writ large in his writings. Similarly, writers like Aurobindo and Gandhi constantly referred to the past views; others like M. N. Roy refuted the dominant tradition but only to draw on the materialistic tradition in India. Mazumdar's and V. P. Varma's books have emphasized this historical continuity in the past or the present in which the older ideas are seen in

terms of timeless and permanent trends which still have some relevance. (Mehta 1992, 5f, emphasis added)

Mehta's view, which converges with most of the experts' opinions, comes down to the proposition that inclusive pluralism and cultural continuity are mutually constitutive. The durability of inclusive pluralism becomes the cause of the cohesiveness of Indian culture. Again, this is a circular argument which does not address the question of the ideational resources that generate and sustain the cohesive force of India's pluralist culture. However, Mehta does provide an important clue by mentioning the (*dharmashastra* text) *Manu-smriti* and the epics—Valmiki's *Ramayana* and Vyasa's *Mahabharata*.

The two epics, we believe, are of exceptional significance in the search for the ideational resources that constitute the cohesive force of Indian culture. We should remember that Kautilya writes, at the beginning of the *Arthashastra*, that the study of the epics *Ramayana* and *Mahabharata* has to have prominent place in the educational canon of the ruler (KA, I, 3, 1; I, 5, 12). The epics, particularly the *Mahabharata*, expound a complex array of paradigmatic ideas and norms. That the 'value ideas', to use Max Weber's term, contained in the *Mahabharata* do play a singular role in Indian culture is a reliable assumption which is supported not only by the expert interviews.

In his *Discovery of India*, Nehru raises the following question: '[S]urely India could not have been what she undoubtedly was, and could not have continued a cultured existence for thousands of years, if she had not possessed *something very vital and enduring, something that was worthwhile. What is this something?*' (Nehru 1981, 50, emphasis added) In the attempt to determine the 'something' which gives the Indian culture its unique structure and unbroken continuity, Nehru comes to the following conclusions:

- There has been a cluster of ideas that assure inner cohesion and continuity for Indian culture.
- The core gestalt of this idea cluster was generated already in the very early phase of India's cultural history.
- This idea cluster is not primarily religious and otherworldly

and certainly not world-denying.
- These ideas do not constitute a secret doctrine or esoteric knowledge.

In his attempt to grasp the ideational core of Indian culture, Nehru writes that engaging with members of the educated classes in India proved unsatisfactory. To his surprise—and Nehru came from a wealthy, well-educated and anglicized family—it was among ordinary people and illiterate peasants that he encountered the essence of Indian culture: the values and ideas of the epics *Ramayana* and *Mahabharata*:

> I found *a cultural background had exerted a powerful influence on their lives*. This background was a mixture of popular philosophy, tradition, history, myth, and legend; and it was not possible to draw a line between any of these. Even the entirely uneducated and illiterate shared this background. *The old epics of India, the Ramayana and the Mahabharata and other books, in popular translations and paraphrases, were widely known among the masses*, and every incident and story and moral in them was engraved on the popular mind and gave richness and content to it. Illiterate villagers would know of hundred verses by heart and their conversation would be full of references to them or to some story with a moral, enshrined in some old classic. (Nehru 1981, 67, emphasis added)

The apogee of the *Mahabharata* is the philosophical poem *Bhagavad Gita*, which Wilhelm von Humboldt characterizes as 'the most beautiful and perhaps the only true philosophical poem of all known literature' in the world (cit. in: Glasenapp 1955, 9). Also Max Weber emphasizes repeatedly the central importance of the epic *Mahabharata* and within it 'the very famous episode belonging to the repertoire of every story-teller and known by the name of Bhagavadgita' (Weber 2000, 182; 2008a, 723). Weber sees the *Bhagavad Gita* as the key text for the *weltanschauung* and basic ethical disposition of Indian intellectuals since ancient times. And he argues that, with a religious connotation, this also applies to the broader Indian population. Therefore, we summarize here Weber's interpretation of the *Bhagavad Gita* which, we believe, is particularly conducive for identifying its central value ideas.

The *Bhagavad Gita* features the discussion of the military commander Arjuna with the hybrid 'god-man' or *avatar* Krishna, who is a close companion in arms of Arjuna. The conversation takes place before the battle of Kurukshetra, in which the Arya tribes of the Pandavas and Kauravas stand against each other. Plagued by doubts, Arjuna hesitates to commence the battle since he will have to kill relatives and friends fighting among the Kauravas. Krishna tries to dispel Arjuna's self-doubts, and his philosophical and ethical arguments form the gist of the didactic poem. In the *Bhagavad Gita*, Weber sees three lines of argument by Krishna:

- The battle between the Pandavas and Kauravas is an inescapable fate—regardless of whether Arjuna would fight or not.
- His *kshatriya dharma* leaves Arjuna with no option but to fight. As a prince and military leader, not fighting would mean abandoning his people, and loss of honour.
- Ethically 'good' is energetic action in the world, while passivity and indecision are unethical. However, such action must abandon any fixation on reward.

The references to inescapable fate and the *kshatriya dharma* do not convince Arjuna. But Krishna's third argument does: *Do what is necessary in life, but do it with 'detachment' or 'inner distance'*. The basis for such action is the (philosophical) knowledge of the transience of worldly success. But shedding illusion does not lead to passivity in the affairs of world. Energetic and committed action in the world while dispensing with worldly gain and success is not only the supreme ethical obligation but the way of salvation in this world and the next world. Weber speaks of the 'soteriological aristocratism of knowledge. Only the men of knowledge possess the way of salvation' (Weber 2008a, 730).

2.6 INDIA AS 'GEO-CULTURAL SPACE'

However, besides the 'value ideas of the epics' there are other factors relevant for the cohesiveness and continuity of the Indian culture.

Among the factors mentioned in the expert interviews are: 'geo-cultural' community formation, the recourse to the political grandeur and cultural flowering of Indian antiquity, and Indian culture's singular mode of interaction with other cultures.

On the relation between geography and culture, Braudel writes: 'Of course the cultural sphere depends on geography, and far more so than anthropologists assume' (Braudel 1992, 273). On the one hand, geography has a significant impact on the boundaries and thus the spatial extension of a culture; on the other hand, geography influences both the character and the idea-contents of a culture. In the expert interviews, the dual significance of the geographical factor for Indian culture was emphasized. On the one hand, the fundamentality of geographical demarcation from other geo-cultural spaces—in the Northwest the desert and mountain ranges of Baluchistan and the Hindu Kush, in the Northeast the Himalayas, in the East, West and South the Indian Ocean—, on the other hand, the enclosure of subcontinental space by these geographic boundary conditions, makes it a distinct, and 'stand-alone', geo-cultural space.

Already at a very early stage, the interviewees argued, the inhabitants of the subcontinent developed a hazy imagination of a distinct geographical space in which people lived surrounded by high mountains and the sea. This geographical imagination did help transcend the enormous ecological diversity within the subcontinent. Although vaguely, the idea of a geographical space 'India' could emerge as well as that of some distinct commonality among the people living within this space—in spite of their differences in terms of ethnicity, language and customs. Thus, a first approximation of cultural cohesion could arise in the midst of diversity. From the idea of a distinct geographical space the idea of 'singular' geo-cultural space could arise.

> I think, *as a form of cultural landscape, the idea of something like India or bharatavarsha*, as it is usually called in the Sanskrit texts and other vernacular texts of the older times, *certainly seems to have been there*. People knew that this was a territory which was largely bounded by the Himalayas and stretching to the seas. And it was *a*

territory bounded by certain common cultural practices and certain kinds of commercial interactions [...]. I think there is something like a 'cultural territory' to which people could relate as to some broad reference point. (EI Srinath Raghavan,[18] emphasis added)

However, in order to develop the imagination of a 'geo-cultural community' within a vast subcontinent, 'inter-cultural' communication had to occur between geographically distant population groups, each having their local or regional customs, social practices and religious beliefs. In the Indian subcontinent, the process of acculturation began in the North—in the Indus and Ganges plains—during and after the immigration of the Arya tribes (ca. 1500–1000 BC). In this period, the mass of the previously nomadic population settled down in villages and became socially organized in the caste system. Despite the enormous expanse of northern India and its ethical, linguistic and religious diversity, this territory became largely consolidated as a distinct cultural space during the first half of the first millennium BC (cf. Kulke/Rothermund 1998; Weber 2008a). The catalysts of this process of acculturation in the Indus and Ganges plains were the Brahmin priest-intellectuals, as mentioned by Sircar and Raghavan in the interviews. The Brahmins were—besides the traders of the *vaishya* caste—the only mobile actors in ancient India, and they acted both as repositories and distributors of the cultural paradigm that is expressed in the 'value ideas of the epics'.

After the cultural consolidation in northern and eastern India, the Brahmins pursued cultural diffusion towards central and southern India. In a mostly peaceful manner, Brahmins facilitated the 'pan-Indian acculturation' and 'intra-Indian cultural integration' by making themselves indispensable as cultural, religious and political advisers to the (mostly Dravidian) territorial rulers of central and southern India (Kulke 1992, 34). The Brahmins supplied the southern rulers with an enhanced cultural status and normative legitimacy, enabling them to transform the previously existing social order into the caste system[19] (cf. Kulke/Rothermund 1998, 123f).

When summarizing the thematically relevant statements of the interviewees, we come to the plausible finding that already in early

Indian antiquity the elites' and people's imagination of the subcontinent as a distinct geographical space had become increasingly overlaid with a sense of cultural communality.

Friedrich Meinecke's concept of 'cultural nation' can be understood as a conceptual expression of cultural continuity (cf. Meinecke 1962a). The term 'cultural nation'—in contrast to 'nation-state'—can be applied if there exists among the inhabitants of a certain geographic area a historically evolved sense of 'togetherness' in terms of language, customs and ideational traditions. The cultural nation is based on 'some jointly experienced cultural heritage' (Meinecke 1962a, 3). The perceived cultural commonality might still be somewhat vague, but it must have preponderance over internal cultural deviations and include a sense of otherness with respect to 'outside' cultural spaces. The collective imagination of a 'cultural nation', however, lacks the political-institutional framing of a state—be that a pre-modern or a modern state. In Meinecke's view, the political will and the actual capability of state-building depend on the prior existence of the cultural nation. Thus, for Meinecke, the cultural nation is the logical and historical precursor of the nation-state. The cultural nation is superseded by the nation-state but still lives on within it, which means that the cultural nation persists as 'inner fabric' of the nation-state.

Obviously, Meinecke's concept of cultural nation is based on the European historical experience and thus the homogeneous European culture-type, which is structurally different from the pluralist Indian culture-type. Therefore, some interviewees hesitated to characterize India as a 'cultural nation'.[20] However, the actual issue is whether the concept of cultural nation is inseparably linked to the European homogeneity-centred culture. We believe it is not. In view of its explanatory power for cultural continuity, the reach of the concept of 'cultural nation' can and should be extended to the pluralist culture-type as well. In the case of Indian culture, the (self-)perception of cultural commonality does not depend on ethnic, linguistic, religious or ideological homogenization. So why not apply the concept of cultural nation to India? Provided that the pluralist structure of Indian culture is taken into account, several interviewees viewed the concept of cultural nation as an appropriate characterization of Indian reality from early antiquity up to the formation of the nation-state in 1947.[21]

Thus, also in the context of a pluralist culture-type, the collective self-perception of a cultural nation can emerge and sustain itself for very long periods of time—in the case of India, over more than three millennia. Moreover, such culture-vectored sense of community can be the catalyst for the political will to create a state structure. That was the case with the pre-modern, patrimonial state of the Mauryas and again with the modern Indian nation-state constituted in 1947. In the expert interviews it was repeatedly pointed out that Gandhi and Nehru, as leaders of the nationalist independence movement, did see India as a 'cultural nation', even if they did not use that term. They were determined to build the Indian nation-state upon the foundation of the Indian cultural nation going back to antiquity.

> India as a 'civilizational state' has existed since the *Mahabharata*. (EI Ajit Doval)[22]

Gandhi is the case in point. By addressing the 'cultural patriotism' of the Indian masses, Gandhi was able to transform the independence movement into a potent political force. Gandhi's understanding of the idea of cultural nation is clear enough:

> The English have taught us that we were not one nation before, and that it will require centuries before we will become one nation. This is without foundation. *We were one nation before they came to India [...]. I believe that the civilization India has evolved is not beaten anywhere in the world. Nothing can equal the seeds sown by our ancestors.* Rome went, Greece shared the same fate, the might of the Pharaohs was broken, Japan has become westernized, of China nothing can be said, *but India is still, somehow or other, sound at its foundations.* (Cit. in: Engelmeier 2009, 155, 213, emphasis added)

Indeed, it is hard to imagine that the Gandhi-led political movement would ever have developed its strength against the British if it had been based merely on the ideologies of nationalism and socialism imported from Europe. Instead, the leaders of the liberation movement were able to draw upon the paradigmatic value ideas and traditions that had been underpinning the Indian cultural nation for more than three thousand years. In Gandhi's case it is evident that the value ideas of the epics played a central role for his political 're-use' of India's cultural past since he wrote a study on the *Bhagavad Gita*. And the same is evident with Nehru's *Discovery of India*. In substance, albeit not in terminology, the concept of the Indian cultural nation is also expounded by leading authors of contemporary India. Jaswant Singh writes:

> Civilizationally, the Indian nation is a unity, a whole: diverse, multilingual, with numerous shades and varieties of faith and kaleidoscopic cultural distinctions, also varieties of belief, languages, dialects, dress, food—but always with indefinable, civilizational oneness: an Indianess. Thus, civilizationally there is but one India; politically, however, there has been greater diversity [...]. *Indian nationhood, being largely cultural and civilizational*, and Indians being supremely contended with what was theirs, feared no loss of it, for it—the civilizational—was as unconquerable as is the spirit. (1999, 10, 16, emphasis added)

And K. Subrahmanyam, one of the most prominent strategic thinkers of India, writes:

> *The concept of India as a civilization entity differentiated from the surrounding Sinic, Persian and South East Asian civilizations is, however, several millennia old.* While ancient civilizations—such as Egypt, Persia, Han China, Korea and Japan—can claim similar hoary civilizational traditions, India is the only instance where *multilingual, multi-ethnic and multi-religious populations share such a long continuity of common identity.* (Subrahmanyam/Malhotra 2005, 361, emphasis added)

The amazing staying power of the Indian cultural nation becomes evident when one considers the fact that it took more than three thousand years until the transition from the cultural nation to the modern nation-state was achieved. It is hard to imagine that the modern Indian nation-state could have been established and would have been able to preserve its political unity and territorial integrity thereafter if it were not rooted in the Indian cultural nation.

2.7 CULTURAL SPACE AND POLITICAL SPACE: THE MAURYA EMPIRE AS PRECEDENT

We have sketched the transition of a 'geographic imagination' of the Indian subcontinent to an internally acculturated geo-cultural space—the emergence of an Indian cultural nation. The logical consequence thereof would be the establishment of a political order encompassing this geo-cultural space and cultural nation. That did happen towards the end of the fourth century BC with the creation of the first pan-Indian state structure by Chandragupta Maurya and Kautilya. With the Maurya Empire the idea—one might also say, the ideal—of a politically united India had arrived in historical reality.

Under emperor Ashoka (304–232 BC), the Maurya Empire extended over the entire subcontinent with the exception of its southern tip. Ashoka's (patrimonial) state was, in regard to its territorial expanse, its political and administrative organization, and its economic strength and military power, the most important and powerful state structure in the subcontinent until the establishment of independent India in 1947. The Maurya Empire fused the inclusive-pluralist Indian culture with the idea of a pan-Indian state. Above, we have referred already to Ashoka's '7th Edict' which decrees that all his subjects may exercise their different religions and cultural habits freely, and commits them to mutual tolerance and cooperation.

With the Maurya Empire, a political precedent for the entire subsequent history of India was established. The majority of the interviewees thought that the Maurya Empire as historic role-model has been firmly engraved in the Indian collective memory throughout the past two millennia. Because political unity of the subcontinent had once been a real-life fact, the 'dream' of a pan-Indian state could be sustained even during the long periods of political fragmentation and foreign domination.

After the Maurya Empire had disintegrated in the second-century

BC, it remained the role-model for ever-new attempts of political unification: the Kushan Empire (ca. 30–250 AD), the Gupta Empire (ca. 320–550 AD) and the Mughal Empire (1526–1858). That also applies, paradoxically enough, to the British Raj, even though the British colonialists claimed that it was them who created for the first time a politically unified space in the Indian subcontinent. On that, K.M. Panikkar remarks:

> The age-old political tradition in India before independence was that of an administrating state. At all times, from the time of the Nandas in the 4th century BC, it was a vast bureaucracy that governed the country, collected its revenue, looked after the irrigation system and maintained law and order. *Basically the British system was not different from that of the Mauryas or the Moghuls.*
> (Panikkar 1963, 228, emphasis added)

As Lloyd and Susanne Hoeber Rudolph emphasize, Indians did not forget that they have had their own historical role-model of state-building:

> *The state in India was not a European import*, an ideological and institutional transplant from foreign climes rooted in India's exotic and alien soil [...]. The historical legacies of imperial states on the Indian subcontinent in the pre-Christian era established state conceptions and institutions that *provided models for the subcontinental multinational state of modern India [...]. [T]he subcontinental state conception was already realized in preclassical times, in the Mauryan Empire*, particularly under Ashoka (312–185 BC), and under the imperial rule of the Guptas (319–540 AD).
> (Rudolph/Rudolph 1987, 63f, emphasis added)

The interviewees alluded to the relation between political unity and cultural productivity in Indian history. During the Maurya Empire, and again during the Gupta Empire, India experienced a cultural 'golden age'. Between the fourth century BC and the sixth century AD, most of the classical texts were written or finally edited, which, in turn, decisively strengthened the cohesive force of Indian culture. For 2300 years, the cohesive force of Indian culture was not only backed up by the imagination of a singular geo-cultural space and by ideational resources like the paradigmatic value ideas of the epics, it was also backed up by the precedent(s) of a politically unified, pan-Indian state.

Lastly, the significance of the Mauryan precedent in India's collective memory is also linked to Kautilya. The popular perception of Kautilya in the life-world of today's India is not only that of the 'cunning and unflinching statesman, who gets things done whatever it takes'. In the popular perception, Kautilya is also the symbol and historical role-model of India's political unification. He is seen as the builder of the first all-Indian state in the subcontinent—the Maurya Empire.

2.8 EXTERNAL INFLUENCES ON INDIAN CULTURE

During the last two millennia, Indian culture was exposed to multiple and intense external influences which mostly came as a consequence of the serial foreign invasions of the subcontinent. On land, India was invaded by the Achaemenid Persians, the Greeks under Alexander the Great, the Greek-Persian Diadochi as well as a variety of belligerent nomadic tribes and patrimonial states from Central Asia, which had mostly adopted the Islamic religion and Persian culture. From the sea, India was invaded by the Portuguese, Dutch, French and British. All these invaders settled in India and exerted political domination during shorter or longer periods of time over more or less extensive territories. All of these invaders were 'outsiders' in ethnic, lingual and religious terms, who brought their respective cultures to India and backed up their cultural influence with hard politico-military power. However, until the consolidation of British rule in the nineteenth century, none of the many invaders was able control the entire subcontinent. The centre of impact of foreign cultural influence was northern and north-eastern India, where a large part of the population converted to Islam.[23]

In spite of all that, on the subcontinent as a whole, India's cultural continuity was not disrupted. Indian culture did successfully maintain its hegemonic status on the subcontinent. Where does India's *singular ability to absorb the culture of others and assimilate it without losing her own identity* come from? (Panikkar 1963, 16, emphasis added) In the expert interviews, two reasons for its cultural resistance and perseverance were mentioned: first, the elasticity and adaptability of Indian culture, and second, its unique capacity to absorb—i.e., effectively neutralize—foreign cultural influences.

The basic form of self-preservation of a culture is refusing to interact with a foreign culture. On such rejection, Braudel writes: 'Sometimes deliberately, from a clear-headed decision, sometimes blindly, as if a threshold or a latch prevents the passage [...]. Such rejection is of great significance (certainly the deliberate and consistent rejection even more so) because it is a decision by which a culture reaffirms itself' (Braudel 1992, 274f). The Indian attitude of cultural rejection is described by the Islamic polymath Albiruni (973–1048). His voluminous work *Tarikh Al-Hind* (History of India) is the first systematic and comprehensive description of Indian culture by a non-Indian. The work could even be considered as the starting point of Indology. Albiruni stayed for some time in India and translated philosophical and scientific Sanskrit texts into Arabic and Persian. In *Tarikh Al-Hind*, he complains that it is extremely difficult to get in touch with the 'arrogant' Indian Brahmins:

> [A]ll their fanaticism is directed against those who do not belong to them—against all foreigners. They call them mleccha, i.e. impure, and forbid having any connection with them [...]. The Hindus believe that there is no country like theirs, no nation like theirs, no kings like theirs, no science like theirs. They are haughty, foolishly vain, self-conceited and stolid. (Sachau 1992, 19, 22)

That there has been 'cultural refusal' was acknowledged in the expert interviews, but it was emphasized that it has not been the characteristic Indian way of dealing with foreign cultures. Far more than turning back to foreign cultures, Indian culture has taken an attitude of elastic adaptability: foreign cultural assets have selectively been integrated into Indian culture. As a result, Indian culture has gradually and slightly changed, but the adaptability does not apply to its ideational core substance. Most interviewees argued that foreign borrowings are limited to cultural attributes such as clothing, food habits, organizational matters, technical methods and procedures, and artistic styles, notably in architecture. Such foreign cultural imports were described as 'additives' or 'alloys' of Indian culture which have penetrated Indian culture, but in doing that, they themselves have changed and acquired a distinct Indian coloration. Western science and technology are the only major 'cultural imports' which have been adopted without modifications by Indian culture. In contrast, imports from Western humanities and social sciences would sooner or later acquire endogenous coloration and substantial modifications, the interviewees argued.

However, the main characteristic of Indian culture in relation to other cultures is its capacity to adapt to some attributes of non-Indian cultures while effectively neutralizing the rest. Most exogenous cultural influences literally vanish if exposed to Indian culture, the interviewees argued. After a certain period of time, foreign cultural influences evaporate in the proximity of Indian culture. In Indian history, the many foreign invaders—except the British—submitted to Indian culture, even if they continued to exert political domination. The foreign conquerors dropped their traditional ways of thinking and acting in favour of the culture of the conquered. In reference to Goethe's *Faust*, one might say that Indian culture has a 'big stomach' that easily 'digests' foreign cultural influences.

As an example of Indian culture's power of the assimilation, the Mughal Empire (1526–1858) was repeatedly mentioned in the interviews. The Mughal dynasty's Turko-Mongol origins lay in Central Asia; they adhered to the Muslim faith and were steeped in Persian culture. As rulers of (northern) India, the Mughal elite kept their Muslim faith and Persian as court language—but otherwise immersed fully into Indian culture. The prime example for such 'Indianization' is the most outstanding Mughal ruler, Akbar (1556–1605), whose secular and pluralistic understanding of culture and politics is in many ways similar to Ashoka's.

The major exception is the British colonialists. The British not only withstood the gravitational force of Indian culture but probably exerted a stronger and more durable influence upon Indian culture than any of their intrusive predecessors. However, the interviewees stressed that, during the nearly two hundred years of British rule, British culture was unable to undermine the ideational core of Indian culture. T. B. Macaulay's 1835 plan for a 'cultural revolution'—substituting Indian culture by a European-style culture—failed in colonial India.[24] The staying power of Indian culture proved superior. Only 89 years after the formal establishment of the British *Raj*, the British colonialists had to leave India.

> Indians do not think the way the British think. Yes, we might have taken their dresses—we are very fast in adapting. But we have not submitted to their way of thinking. Instead, we have integrated British thoughts into our culture, and in that sense the British have influenced our thinking. *British thought is an alloy of our culture, but has not substituted our culture.* It's difficult to judge the relative weight of this British alloy in our cultural mainstream, but it certainly has not had the quality to transform our culture. It's rather like a ferment. And there have been many such ferments in Indian culture and there will be more of them probably in the future. (EI Ajit Doval,[25] emphasis added)

In summary, one gets the impression that all forms of self-assertion of Indian culture—rejection, elastic adaptation as well as 'digestion' and neutralization of foreign cultural influences—derive from the Indians' deep-rooted sense of cultural superiority that goes back to early antiquity. What appears at first glance to be passive 'riding out' foreign cultural influences is rather an expression of cultural self-confidence which is guided by the conviction that foreigners, at least in the longer term, cannot escape being drawn towards, or even into, Indian culture. As Charles Drekmeier notes:

> Although India was unable to achieve a stable and enduring political unity, she constructed an effective and viable cultural unity and survived where vast empires, possessing political but no cultural cohesion, have disappeared. *This [cultural] strength enabled India to absorb foreign invasions and await the day the lessons of Kautalya could be relearned.* (1962, 271, emphasis added)

3

KAUTILYA'S *ARTHASHASTRA* AS AN ENDOGENOUS POLITICO-CULTURAL RESOURCE

3.1 THE TERM 'ENDOGENOUS POLITICO-CULTURAL RESOURCES'

The term 'endogenous politico-cultural resource(s)' is not (yet) established in the vocabulary of the social and political sciences. But more than half a century ago, Adda B. Bozeman did address the subject matter underlying this term. She criticized (Western) social sciences for the '*deliberate or involuntary devaluation of the native modes of thought and behavior*' in India and other countries outside Western cultural space (Bozeman 1960, 8). She pointed to the presence and efficacy of endogenous ideational resources that impact the political thinking and behaviour in what is now often called the 'Global South':

> Most of these indigenous patterns of life and thought became blurred during the centuries of European supremacy, when they were being integrated into the Occidental scheme of things [...]. However, when the non-Western peoples began to assume their places as modern political communities in the world so largely shaped by Western thought, it became increasingly apparent that *Western ideas were not the exclusive mainsprings of their political attitudes and actions.* Whether in India, Egypt, or Nigeria, men have been generally stimulated by the spread of literacy and the growth of nationalism to *probe their own pasts and to resurrect the realities and myths that antedated their knowledge and acceptance of the Western way.* (Bozeman 1960, 5, emphasis added)

In our study, the category 'endogenous politico-cultural resource' is understood in the following sense: Within each cultural space there are cultural assets that are perceived as having both timeless value and political significance. These are outstanding cultural artifacts, notably 'classic' texts that remain thought-provoking, inspire and/or provide aesthetic pleasure across time. Politically significant are cultural assets if they address issues of political life—within communities and between communities. Such issues of politics can be treated not only in scholarly works but also in literary or religious texts. In India, inter alia, the *Manu-smriti*, Kautilya's *Arthashastra* or Kamandaka's *Nitisara* have the status of endogenous politico-cultural resources, but equally so the epics *Mahabharata* and *Ramayana*, or the beast fables *Panchatantra*.

Endogenous cultural assets are the genuine product of a particular culture and/or articulate the peculiarity of a culture. That is, they are not obvious 'imports' from other cultural spaces. That said, there is, of course, the caveat that 'pure' endogenous cultural artifacts do not exist, as each endogenous artifact inevitably also contains elements of trans-cultural diffusion. To summarize: endogenous politico-cultural resources a) are part of the 'cultural capital' of a distinct space, b) are politically significant, and c) have epoch-spanning efficacy.

3.2 KAUTILYA IN THE SPECTRUM OF INDIA'S POLITICO-CULTURAL RESOURCES

Although not established in the social and political sciences, the term 'endogenous politico-cultural resource' was readily accepted without further questioning in all expert interviews. Kautilya's *Arthashastra* was consistently viewed as India's foremost classical text on politics and statecraft, and none of the interviewees questioned its characterization as an endogenous politico-cultural resource.

However, all interviewees emphasized that India has a broad spectrum of endogenous politico-cultural resources, among which Kautilya's *Arthashastra* is just one. They designated as endogenous politico-cultural resources classical texts like the epics *Mahabharata* and *Ramayana* or *Panchatantra*, but also 'politico-cultural' personalities like Buddha, emperor Ashoka of the Maurya empire, Mughal emperor

Akbar, the poet and philosopher Rabindranath Tagore, philosopher Sri Aurobindo, as well as Gandhi and Nehru. To all of them, principal equivalence was attributed in terms of their status as endogenous politico-cultural resources.

Naturally, the interviewees expressed subjective preferences. A minority favoured politico-cultural resources vectored to 'idealism'— Buddha, Ashoka, Gandhi or Tagore. The others preferred 'realist' politico-cultural resources, naming Kautilya, the *Mahabharata*, the *Panchatantra* or Nehru. The exceptional value of the *Arthashastra* was recognized across all expert interviews, but there were also some reservations that Kautilya should not get 'overrated'. As one interviewee put it, Kautilya should not be made the 'golden boy' of Indian politico-strategic thought. Conversely, several interviewees said that Kautilya does deserve an elevated position in the spectrum of politico-cultural resources and is of singular importance for contemporary India.

> So Kautilya stands apart, this is my opinion, and I feel that a lot of those who came after him, while their contribution is of course not insignificant, do not quite measure up to him. Some of them were great thinkers, scholars and doers in their own right, but they would rather have been influenced by Kautilya. So to that extent, I think Kautilyan philosophy, his thought, his concepts have a preeminence and a kind of a precedence which the others would lack. (EI Rana Chhina)[1]

3.3 WHY KAUTILYA'S *ARTHASHASTRA* IS VIEWED AS AN ENDOGENOUS POLITICO-CULTURAL RESOURCE

As there was consensus among the interviewees that Kautilya's *Arthashastra* is one of India's politico-cultural resources, the question arose as to why Kautilyan thought-figures would be particularly relevant for deserving this status. The multiple reasons given by the interviewees for designating Kautilya's *Arthashastra* as an endogenous politico-cultural resource can be arrayed as follows:

- Kautilya's holistic treatment of the state and statecraft;
- the normative dimension of the *Arthashastra*;
- Kautilya's secularism and his relativization of caste status;
- Kautilya's political economy;
- the *Arthashastra* in comparison with Western and Chinese political classics

3.3.1 Kautilya's holistic understanding of political theory and statecraft

Almost uniformly, the interviewees stated that the singularity of the *Arthashastra* consists of its 'comprehensiveness', because Kautilya examines all components of the state and their complex connectivity.[2] The synopsis of the arguments in the expert interviews includes the following elements: Kautilya expounds a theoretical analysis not only of the state but also statecraft. He submits a wide range of options for action in the various policy areas and for different constellations of domestic and foreign policy. He emphasizes the need for flexibility in state conduct and recognizes the interface of policies in different fields which must be taken into account when choosing a specific policy course.

Thus, Kautilya is the first theoretical proponent of 'grand strategy'. To that end, Kautilya critically processed the entire antecedent theoretical knowledge of statecraft, but he does not simply borrow traditional thought-figures and maxims. Instead, he scrutinizes antecedent ideas and then develops his own theoretical positions. Ergo, the combination of intellectual originality and his holistic approach make Kautilya a formidable politico-cultural resource.

However, one interviewee questioned Kautilya's originality and asserted that he merely 'distilled' relevant politico-strategic concepts from antecedent texts of ancient India such as the *Vedas*, the epics and the *puranas*.[3]

3.3.2 The normative dimension of Kautilya's Arthashastra

Maybe surprisingly, most interviewees firmly rejected the imputation that the *Arthashastra* is devoid of morality and Kautilya advocates 'naked power politics'. To the contrary, the interviewees argued, the *Arthashastra* does contain a normative-ethical dimension. Kautilyan statecraft is 'value-based' in that it combines 'hard realpolitik' with the promotion of the welfare of the people. While Kautilya undoubtedly advocates power politics vectored towards the maintenance and expansion of state power, such 'realpolitik' is embedded in political *dharma* which both hedges the ruler's exercise of power and bestows legitimacy upon him.[4]

Further, the interviewees argued that no despotism is touted in the *Arthashastra*. Instead, Kautilya demands that the political decisions of the ruler must be rational and have to be preceded by thorough deliberations with his political advisers. And, in the decision-making, normative considerations must be included. Several interviewees stressed that the Kautilyan conception of 'absolute monarchy' should not be confused with Karl Wittfogel's theory of 'Asiatic despotism'.[5] For the ruler, safeguarding the people's welfare is a binding obligation that is prominently and explicitly stated in the *Arthashastra*. The welfare of the people—not just in terms of material prosperity but also in security and the rule of law—is for Kautilya the cornerstone of the legitimacy of the ruler and the state.[6]

Some interviewees argued that the Kautilyan monarchy is based on a 'contract' between the ruler and the people: The ruler provides internal and external security, social stability (inviolability of the caste system), rule of law, private property and economic prosperity. In return, the people pledge allegiance and the payment of taxes. Thus, Kautilya turns the normative reciprocity in the relationship between ruler and people into a quite practical, almost business-like proposition: for the services rendered by him, the ruler can legitimately claim a 'compensation' in the form of taxes and duties. In that, Kautilya anticipated the theories of 'social contract' of early modernity in Europe.[7]

Several interviewees pointed to Kautilya's sharp and consistent condemnation of misconduct and corruption in the state bureaucracy as an important aspect of the *Arthashastra*'s normative dimension. For Kautilya, corruption represents per se the most serious ethical deviance, which, moreover, means materially and politically damaging the state. Kautilya does not confine himself to an abstract condemnation but puts forth a set of concrete measures to combat corruption—in terms of both administrative procedures and criminal justice.⁸

In domestic conflict situations—conspiracies, unrest and rebellions—Kautilya rejects the state's reflexive use of brute force, particularly collective punishment. Instead, he demands investigating and remedying the causes of popular discontent. Also the Kautilyan monarchy recognizes the need for a certain degree of local autonomy and subsidiarity.⁹ The interviewees argued that both Kautilya's normative and realpolitik-derived caveat with respect to (over-)centralization of the state, and his recognition of diversity and autonomy, are quite relevant for subsequent Indian history—in contexts from Ashoka to Akbar to the constitution of the Republic of India.¹⁰

Kautilyan foreign policy is usually considered to be devoid of any ethical considerations. However, in the expert interviews, it was stressed that normativity is very much present in those sections of the *Arthashastra* that are dealing with foreign affairs. Here, too, utilitarian political calculation connects with normative considerations. Interviewees noted Kautilya's great restraint with respect to going to war. For sure, Kautilya is no proponent of non-violence (*ahimsa*) in inter-state relations, but his foreign policy is the opposite of militarist adventurism. Several interviewees pointed to Kautilya's distinction between the 'righteous', the 'greedy' and the 'demoniacal' conqueror.

> So Kautilya very clearly told Chandragupta Maurya that whenever you [are] engaging with the adversary, it is so important to have a moral legitimacy, it is so important to have a framework where people perceive you as being just. It is not possible to win if you are seen as unjust. (EI Namrata Goswami)¹¹

However, if war has become inescapable, its conduct as well as post-war policies are subject to normative constrains. The interviewees noted that the *Arthashastra* contains principles of *jus in bello* that sharply differ from the brutal rules of warfare in Greek and Roman antiquity. Kautilya regards avoidable and unnecessary human suffering and material losses as ethically reprehensible. His emphasis on covert operations (subversion, sabotage, assassinations, etc.) should be seen as an 'ethical trade-off' since they can avert war with its inevitably vast human and material losses.[12]

The guiding principle of Kautilyan foreign policy is the political unification of the Indian subcontinent. Thus, Kautilya is not pursuing a foreign policy of 'aggrandizement' as an end in itself. Only what contributes to gaining political control of the whole Indian subcontinent is 'righteous' foreign policy.[13] The interviewees noted the complete absence of expansionist schemes beyond the subcontinent in the *Arthashastra*, which can be interpreted as equaling a normative barrier. All interviewees—including those with a critical attitude towards Kautilyan foreign policy—rejected the supposition that Kautilya is an early proponent of imperialism.

> Kautilya never says: let's invade Persia or China. We did not produce any Alexanders. Because the idea never occurred to anyone here.
> (EI Ajit Doval)[14]

Crucial for the legitimacy of a war of conquest is the behaviour of the victor after the termination of hostilities: the population-at-large must be treated well, local customs and traditions must be respected and the economy must not be plundered or otherwise impaired.[15]

In the expert interviews, multiple aspects of the normative dimension of Kautilyan statecraft were addressed which all add up support to the proposition that Kautilya's *Arthashastra* deserves the status of an endogenous politico-cultural resource.

3.3.3 Kautilya's secularism and his relativization of caste status

In the *Arthashastra*, a remarkable distance, if not indifference, to religious issues is exhibited. Or, to put it positively, Kautilya stands for the principle of religious and 'ideological' tolerance—and that well before Ashoka issued his edicts on plurality and tolerance.

While Kautilya's secularism should not be equated with the modern European secularism that gained traction with the Enlightenment, an emergent principle of separation of state and religion can be identified in the *Arthashastra*.[16] The Kautilyan ruler stays outside the religious sphere and does not draw his legitimacy from religious authorization. In the

Kautilyan state, there is no state religion. Even the interviewees with Muslim background, who took a rather critical attitude towards Kautilya, acknowledged his unbiased position towards religious minorities. As the interviewees noted, his indifference in religious matters is also the reason why Hindu fundamentalism in modern India has adopted a distant, if not disowning, attitude towards Kautilya.[17] Because Kautilya laid the foundation of the secular tradition of India's politics, he deserves, as most interviewees argued, the status of an endogenous politico-cultural resource.

Several interviewees pointed to Kautilya's reluctance to accept caste status as the prime criteria for judging a person's character qualities and professional qualifications. While Kautilya does not principally question the caste system, he refrains from claiming that caste status per se defines the value of a person or group. Thus, Kautilya at least relativizes caste status and gives increased weight to merit. That means caste status has to be earned through accomplishments. Merit and professional competence are not principally inferior to caste status.

Kautilya does not derive his superior intellectual prowess—to which he himself refers quite often and very self-confidently—from his being a Brahmin. Being born into the Brahmin caste does not suffice for intellectual and social distinction. Instead, Kautilya demands (self-)education, (self-)discipline and lifelong learning in order to justify the intellectual and social elite status of a Brahmin.

> The importance of Chanakya is not him being Brahmin but being an exceptional intellectual [...]. This should help us to adopt a dispassionate, realistic, non-politicized and a-religious view of Chanakya and the Arthashastra. If we take such a sober approach, we can forget about this utter misconception of Chanakya as some arrogant Brahmin [...]. So I am quite clear in my mind that Chanakya is not trying to sell his own Brahmanical caste—there is no need for him to do that. Because you had to be educated, trained, you had to prove your worth to be a Brahmin. What mattered was your intellectual caliber. (EI P. K. Gautam)[18]

None of the interviewees denied the social and economic discrimination of the *shudra* caste in Indian antiquity (and up to the present day). However, the social and legal status of *shudras* cannot be compared with that of the slaves in ancient Europe, they argued. European slavery meant the reification of human beings in legal terms, i.e., the slave was a 'thing' at the slave-owner's unrestricted disposal. In contrast, *shudras* have been an integral part of the social order and have not been without basic human rights. However, *shudras* have not only been negatively privileged in social and material terms but they have also been undermined legally. In the *Arthashastra*, the interviewees noted, the same crime committed by a *shudra* carried much harsher punishment when compared to a perpetrator from one of the three higher castes.

Kautilya does not put in question the negative privileging of the *shudra* caste, but he shows unusual appreciation for their skilled workmanship in agriculture and handicrafts. Kautilya puts forth a new, socio-economic understanding of the *shudras* as the actual producers of the material sustenance of society-at-large as well as providing the fiscal base of the state. In the *Arthashastra*, the emphasis is not on the *shudras*' ritual exclusion and socio-economic discrimination but on the recognition of their productive power in sustaining society and the state.[19]

Because Kautilya recognizes the productive power of the *shudras*, he is strongly propagating the development and melioration of new land by *shudra* peasants that is supported by the state through subsidies and tax benefits. Also Kautilya praises the combat skills of *shudra* soldiers. Similarly, he acknowledges the military qualities of the fighters from the tribal people in isolated jungle areas and calls for their recruitment in the armed forces. Kautilya's non-doctrinaire and pragmatic attitude towards *shudras* and outcasts was recognized and appreciated by leaders of the movement against caste discrimination in modern India. As an example, some interviewees referred to B. R. Ambedkar (1891–1956), who was the leader of the emancipation movement of the dalits.[20]

From the expert interviews, the conclusion can be drawn that Kautilya's distanced attitude to the self-postulated 'inherent qualities' of the higher castes and his sober and pragmatic attitude towards the lower castes have contributed to his recognition as a politico-cultural resource in contemporary India. This finding is also shared in the literature. N. Chakravarty writes:

> [O]ne cannot fail to note Kautilya's liberal and comparatively human attitude towards the Shudras [...]. Though Kautilya may not be called a social reformer as such, his ideas, particularly with reference to the Shudras, have considerable social significance. (Chakravarty 1992, 203)

And Charles Drekmeier states: 'The author of the Arthashastra emerges as something like the champion of the shudras, espousing their rights as free-born citizens' (1962, 198).

3.3.4 Kautilya's political economy

All interviewees considered Kautilya's treatment of the economy in the *Arthashastra* as groundbreaking. Nowhere in the ancient world has there been a comparable theoretical achievement with respect to the economy and its relationship to the state. His economic theory was listed as a key reason why Kautilya should be considered an endogenous politico-cultural resource.

> It is only in the Arthashastra that the question of statecraft is inseparably, inextricably interlinked with the question of economic matters and finance [...]. *About the centrality of economics in Kautilyan statecraft, there is absolutely no doubt. And the very idea is quite startling.* (EI Ranabir Chakravarti,[21] emphasis added)

Kautilya is the first theoretician to conceptualize the basic interrelationship between economic prosperity, higher tax revenues and increased state capacity—and vice versa. In addition, Kautilya promotes the concept that the state can and should facilitate economic development—primarily via the state-sponsored expansion of arable land and thus agricultural production.

> Kautilya tells us—which is quite mind-boggling—that the ruler should pursue a consistent policy of expansion of agriculture. That is always trying to create new villages, meaning sedentary

agricultural communities in areas which were previously not cultivated. (EI Ranabir Chakravarti)[22]

In the interviews, it was repeatedly stressed that Kautilya's economic theory and his economic policy recommendations have a discernible influence on modern India. The origins of the twentieth-century concept of the 'mixed economy' in India—the combination of the strong state sector with the private sector—can be ascribed to the *Arthashastra*.

Kautilya puts the state's economic strength on an equal footing with its military power. He recognizes that the state's economic power provides the indispensable basis for sustaining its military power. The interviewees pointed to Pakistan where the mismatch between strong military power and weak economic performance is particularly evident. In contrast, Indian governments have tried to balance military requirements and the build-up of economic strength. This strategic approach that can be traced back to Kautilya has remained a guiding principle of all Indian governments since 1947.

> Kautilya has embarked on a relationship between wealth and power. He believes both are very, very important. And that power, which means here a strong state and a strong military, is deeply dependent on a strong economy. You cannot have power or a strong state if it is not based on a wealthy state. So wealth and power go hand in hand, and the state therefore must be focused on doing both simultaneously. (EI Sujit Dutta)[23]

Kautilya also strongly advocates advancing economic development through the expansion of mining and iron works. The build-up of such ancient 'heavy industry' was the prerequisite for the productivity-enhancing use of iron and steel tools in agriculture and crafts—and, of course, weapons.

Kautilya's concept of the state as an economic actor is not merely concerned with satisfying the state's need of 'strategic goods', for example, weapons and other military equipment. On top of that, Kautilya demands that all state enterprises—manufacturing, agriculture, crafts and 'services'—operate profitably in order to obtain an additional source of income for the state on top of tax revenue.

In the expert interviews, the view was upheld that Kautilya's economic theory was not matched by European economics until the theory of mercantilism in the seventeenth century—some 1900 years after the *Arthashastra* had been written. For this reason alone, the Kautilya's *Arthashastra* should be considered an endogenous politico-cultural resource.

3.3.5 Kautilya and the political classics of other cultural spaces

Lastly, an important factor for attributing to Kautilya the status of an outstanding endogenous politico-cultural resource is his intellectual equality with the leading theorists of the state and statecraft in Europe and China—and not only those of antiquity.

Throughout the expert interviews, Kautilya's *Arthashastra* was perceived as a singular intellectual achievement in the field of political theory and statecraft. In contrast to the great thinkers of Eurasian antiquity who addressed political issues, Kautilya conceived of political science as an autonomous scholarly discipline. Thucydides was primarily a historian who also touched upon matters of statecraft in theoretical terms. Plato and Aristotle were primarily philosophers who were also dealing with questions of political theory, but they did not address statecraft in theoretical terms. Sun Tzu was first of all a theoretician of military strategy who also addressed issues of statecraft. It was Kautilya alone who theoretically addressed governance, statecraft, economics and military strategy and their interrelations within framework of political science. Thus, the interviewees argued that Kautilya's theorizing achieves a breadth and depth that is not matched by any thinker of the Euro-Asian antiquity.

It was not until the Early Modern Age that European thinkers began to address political theory and statecraft in a manner that is comparable with Kautilya's holistic approach of political science. In this context, the interviewees mentioned primarily Machiavelli, but there were also some references to Jean Bodin and Hobbes. However, it was noted, even these early modern thinkers rarely attain Kautilya's comprehensiveness and theoretical penetration of the state and statecraft.

Several references were made to Nehru who had written: 'Chanakya has been called the Indian Machiavelli, and to some extent this comparison is justified. But he was a much bigger person in every way, greater in intellect and action' (Nehru 1981, 123; cf. B 4.2). The interviewees mentioned also J. N. Dixit's statement that 'Chanakya's teachings in statecraft could have taught Machiavelli a lesson or two' (Dixit 2003, 24f; cf. section B 7.3). Therefore it is not only regrettable but absurd that Kautilya remains in the shadow of the European and Chinese classics of political theory.[24]

India's own intellectual engagement with Kautilya has been grossly deficient in recent decades; nevertheless, that there has been some political and scholarly interest is not altogether absent due to a certain pride with regard to the notion that India has produced a political thinker who can stand up to the classical political thinkers of Europe.

> Kautilya was definitely, to the extent that he was on par with great civilizational thinkers like Sun-tzu, Plato or Aristotle, to that extent there was something of pride about the depth of Indian civilization [...]. *The Arthashastra formed part of India's idea of what it was, and in a sense about its equivalence with the West* [...]. The depth of the *Arthashastra* is exceptional, even in the practical political aspects of it. It's a very much mundane, earthly, practical political philosophy as opposed to purely non-mundane philosophizing, which is what a lot of Indian philosophy could be dismissed as.
>
> *That probably contributed creating the Indian identity—in terms of providing the sense that we were not necessarily any worse, that we have things to be as proud of as others.* (EI Srinath Raghavan,[25] emphasis added)

Dietmar Rothermund's assessment of the significance of Kautilya's *Arthashastra* for pre-Independence Indian nationalism cogently explains why Kautilya's status as an endogenous politico-cultural resource is almost self-evident.[26]

4
NEHRU AND KAUTILYA

Nehru's fascination with Kautilya can be attributed to his deep sense of Indian history. Jawaharlal Nehru (1889–1964) was, next to Mahatma Gandhi and Sardar Patel, the key figure of the Indian Independence movement. As Prime Minister from 1947 to 1964, he was the dominant political figure of postcolonial India. If Nehru, whose formative influence on Indian politics still persists today, was engaged with Kautilyan thought, the proposition that Kautilya is relevant for modern India would be corroborated. And so it is.

Nehru has repeatedly referred to Kautilya, most extensively in his book *The Discovery of India*, which he wrote in 1944 while incarcerated in a British prison (cf. Nehru 1981, 122–7). Of course, Kautilya is not the only politico-cultural resource that Nehru treats in this book; he refers also to Buddha, Ashoka, Akbar, Tagore and many other political and intellectual figures. But the references to Kautilya are not made en passant, and Nehru does not confine himself to reviewing the historical figure Kautilya, but he deals with the theoretical and normative concepts of the *Arthashastra*.

Nehru's engagement with Kautilya has barely been addressed in the literature, and that includes biographical writings (cf. Tharoor 2006; Rothermund 2010). Once again, the expert interviews proved their worth by providing valuable insights into Nehru's perception of Kautilya and the influence of Kautilyan thought on his political stance.

4.1 NEHRU'S INTELLECTUAL ENGAGEMENT WITH KAUTILYA, 1930–44

Nehru was imprisoned nine times by the British colonial power. Between October 1930 and January 1931, he was incarcerated in the Naini Central

Prison near Allahabad. Shortly before his release on 26 January 1931, in his handwritten 'Jail Notes,' Nehru lists the books he had read during that prison term. Nehru's reading list includes Kautilya's *Arthashastra*. (cf. Nehru 1973, Vol. 4, 462) Besides the *Arthashastra*, the list includes inter alia works of Shakespeare, Trotsky, Radhakrishnan, Anatole France, Count Keyserling and the Persian poet Firdausi's *Shanameh*. While in prison, Nehru not only read literary, political and scientific works, but studied them thoroughly and made extensive notes: 'I had got into the habit of making in prison rather copious notes of the books I read [...]. I have thirty such notebooks to which I can refer and which help me in my subsequent writing' (Nehru 2003, Vol. 32, 575).

A first result of reading Kautilya's *Arthashastra* is found in a letter, dated 25 January 1931, to his daughter Indira, then thirteen years old. Each of the 194 letters which Nehru wrote to his daughter focuses, in a somewhat didactic fashion, on a historical or contemporary event or personality of Indian and world history. In 1934, the letters to Indira were published in book-form under the title *Glimpses of World History* (Nehru 1962). The theme of the eighteenth letter is 'Chandragupta Maurya and the *Arthashastra*' (Nehru 1962, 51-4). In that letter, Nehru writes:

> This is Kautilya's *Arthashastra*. Kautilya is none other than our old friend Chanakya or Vishnugupta, and *Arthashastra* means 'the science of wealth'. This book, the *Arthashastra*, deals with so many subjects and discusses such a variety of matters that it is not possible for me to tell you much about it. It deals with the duties of the king, of his ministers and counsellors, of council meetings, of departments of government, of trade and commerce, of government of towns and villages, of laws and law courts, of social customs, of the rights of women, of the maintenance of the old and helpless, of marriage and divorce, of taxation, of the army and navy, of war and peace, of diplomacy, of agriculture, of spinning and weaving, of artisans, of passports, and even of gaols. I could go on adding to this list, but I do not want to fill this letter with chapter-heads of Kautilya. (Nehru 1962, 52f)

Then Nehru emphasizes that Kautilya did not see the king as a despot;

instead, 'the idea of kingship in ancient India meant service to the people. There was no divine right of kings, no autocratic power. And if the king misbehaved, his people had the right to remove him and put another in his place. This was the idea and theory' (Nehru 1962, 53). It is remarkable that Nehru chose to tell his young daughter in some detail about the *Arthashastra*—after all, it is a complex theoretical work. It seems that Nehru wanted to make clear to Indira that ancient India had not only a highly developed culture but a political theory which assigns to the ruler the role of the first servant of the state. Nehru's acquainting his daughter with Kautilya and the *Arthashastra* has another significant implication in that it shows that the later Indian Prime Minister Indira Gandhi (1966-77 and 1980-84) was familiar with Kautilya and the *Arthashastra*.

In 1936, Nehru published the book *An Autobiography*, in which there is no reference to Kautilya. If Nehru does not mention Kautilya in his autobiography, one might conclude that Nehru's study of the *Arthashastra* was a marginal phenomenon which did not exert a lasting influence on him. But soon after the publication of his autobiography, we find Nehru's next documented reference to Kautilya. In November 1937, Nehru wrote an article entitled 'The Rashtrapati' which was published in the Indian journal *Modern Review* (Nehru 1976, Vol. 8, 520). For this article, Nehru chose the pen name 'Chanakya'.

In 1937, Nehru was the President of the Indian National Congress (INC) which was then torn apart by fierce infighting between 'moderates' and 'radicals'. The conflict pertained to the question of whether or not violence should be used in the struggle against British colonial oppression. The conflict also related to the question of whether the Congress should adopt a socialist or a national-liberal orientation. Given these bitter factional struggles, Nehru wanted to resign as INC President. In the 'Rashtrapati' article, he (self-)ironically presents an INC President who, if he remained in this post, could turn into a 'fascist leader'; therefore, this INC President had to be removed from office without delay. It is no far-fetched assumption that Nehru viewed his article about the need to oust a potential 'fascist' at the helm of the Congress as a 'Kautilyan ploy' in order to convey the message of his intended resignation. Equally so, Nehru's choice of the pseudonym 'Chanakya' can be interpreted in the sense of a realistic assessment of the situation: He saw himself as the wrong man, at the wrong place, at the wrong time. In any case, Nehru's choice of the pen name 'Chanakya' demonstrates that he considered Kautilya a significant political symbol. This view is shared by Andrew Kennedy, who writes: 'To be sure, Nehru appreciated the writings of Chanakya, the ancient Indian strategist, as suggested by the pseudonym he adopted in writing "The Rashtrapati"' (Kennedy 2012, 162).

In 1941, Nehru was imprisoned again. On 10 January 1941, he wrote a letter to the British historian Edward Thompson, a friend of his: 'Ranjit and I are here together at Dehra Dun Jail. Ranjit is busy translating an old Sanskrit play, the *Mudrarakshasa*, written about the 7th century during the Gupta period. *This is a political and historical play dealing with Chanakya and Chandragupta Maurya and is full of the wiles and stratagems of kings and their ministers. The world has not changed so much after all*' (Nehru 1972, Vol. 11, 528, emphasis added). In subsequent years, Nehru will repeatedly refer to the classic Sanskrit play *Mudrarakshasa* and the central role played by Kautilya in it.

4.2 KAUTILYA AND THE *ARTHASHASTRA* IN NEHRU'S DISCOVERY OF INDIA

For almost three years, from August 1942 to June 1945, Nehru was imprisoned in Fort Ahmednagar, some 120 km northeast of Pune. There he wrote *The Discovery of India* during the period April to September 1944. The book offers a panoramic view of India's political and cultural history, but it is not a work of academic historiography: 'I can not write academically of past events in the manner of a historian or scholar. I have not that knowledge or equipment or training; nor do I possess the mood for that kind of work' (Nehru 1981, 36). From his academic education in England, Nehru was a (natural) scientist and a lawyer. When writing the *Discovery of India*, he had already been in politics for almost three decades, therefore looking at Indian history and culture from the perspective of contemporary problems and challenges. Nehru writes that he does not intend to indulge in nostalgia and glorification of the past but has undertaken a kind of (macro-)'psychoanalysis' of the entanglements between India's past and present:

> The roots of that present lay in the past and so I made voyages of discovery into the past, ever seeking a clue, if any such existed, to the understanding of the present [...]. Past history merged into contemporary history [...]. It was this attempt to discover the past in its relation to the present that led me twelve years ago to write *Glimpses of World History* in the form of letters to my daughter. (Nehru 1981, 23)

Even though Nehru stresses that his approach to history and culture is not academic, namely, 'learning a mass of facts and dates and drawing conclusions and inferences from them' (ibid.), he was a man of vast reading who possessed broad and deep knowledge of Indian and world history. Nehru was thus in a position to grasp the crucial lines of development in Indian history and culture. Considering the fact that *The Discovery of India* was written in prison without sufficient access to literature, the work represents an extraordinary intellectual achievement which provides an excellent outline of India's history and its history of ideas. K.M. Panikkar is correct when he writes: 'So far the textbooks of Indian history read more like telephone directories, a vast jumble of names unrelated to each other, with emphasis on the period of British rule in India. *What gave to Indian history a perspective was Nehru's* Discovery of India—*a layman's attempt to understand the main currents of India's past*' (Panikkar 1963, 131, emphasis added). Panikkar's assessment of the *Discovery of India* was shared in most expert interviews.

Across six pages of book—in the sections 'Chandragupta and Chanakya: The Maurya Empire Established' and 'The Organization of the State'—Nehru covers Kautilya and the *Arthashastra* in a dedicated fashion. However, there are also references in other text passages:

- 'One book of inestimable value is Kautilya's *Arthashastra* of the 4th century B.C., which gives details of the political, social,

- economic, and military organization of the Maurya Empire' (Nehru 1981, 110).
- He writes of ancient Indian materialism (*lokayata*): '[I]n the famous Arthashastra, Kautilya's book on political and economic organization, written in the 4th century B.C., it [*lokayata*] is mentioned as one of the major philosophies of India' (Nehru 1981, 96).
- Nehru also refers to Kautilya in the context of ancient Indian drama *Mudrarakshasa*: '"The ignorant rely on Providence," says Chanakya contemptuously in the "Mudra-Rakshasa," they look to the stars for help instead of relying on themselves' (Nehru 1981, 163).[1]

At the beginning of the two sections that deal directly with Kautilya, Nehru sketches the historical development that 'amalgamate[d] the petty states and small kingdoms and republics; the old urge to build up a united centralized state had been working' (Nehru 1981, 122). Then, the failed invasion of India by Alexander the Great created the conditions for taking on the project of a pan-Indian state:

> Two remarkable men arose who could take advantage of the changed conditions and mould them according to their will. These men were Chandragupta Maurya and his friend and minister and counselor, the Brahmin Chanakya. This combination functioned well [...]. Chandragupta and Chanakya raised the old and ever-new cry of nationalism and roused the people against the foreign invader [...]. Within two years of Alexander's death [...] the Maurya Empire had been established [...]. For the first time in recorded history a vast centralized state had risen in India. (Nehru 1981, 122f)

Nehru introduces Kautilya first as a historical figure. The picture he draws of Kautilya is sober and positive, but certainly not idealizing. With reference to the classical drama *Mudrarakshasa*, he gives a cogent but by no means uncritical personal characterization of Kautilya:

> Bold and scheming, proud and revengeful, never forgetting a slight. Never forgetting his purpose, availing himself of every device to

delude and defeat the enemy, he sat with the reins of Empire in his hands and looked upon the emperor more as a loved pupil than as a master. Simple and austere in his life, uninterested in the pomp and pageantry of high position, when he had redeemed his pledge and accomplished his purpose, he wanted to retire, Brahmin-like, to a life of contemplation. There was hardly anything Chanakya would have refrained from doing to achieve his purpose; he was unscrupulous enough; yet was also wise enough to know that this very purpose might be defeated by means unsuited to the end. (Nehru 1981, 123)

This characterization is also revealing with respect to the importance Nehru attaches to Kautilya in terms of his own political stance and behaviour. It is not far-fetched when we assume that the intellectually and politically sophisticated Kautilya was a source of inspiration for Nehru.[2]

In the *Discovery of India*, Nehru considers Kautilya's *Arthashastra* as a historiographical account of the Maurya Empire, but at the same time he views it as a theoretical and normative work on the state and statecraft. Nehru conflates the historical and the theoretical reading of the *Arthashastra*, even though the first interpretation is hardly sustainable. Nehru calls Kautilya the 'great scholar' of the 'science of polity' who deals with almost all aspects of the theory and practice of the state (Nehru 1981, 123). He then refers to the widespread comparison between Kautilya and Machiavelli and comes to following verdict:

> Chanakya has been called the Indian Machiavelli, and to some extent this comparison is justified. But he was a much bigger person in every way, **greater in intellect and action**. (Nehru 1981, 123, emphasis added)

Nehru continues by stating that Kautilya anticipated the Clausewitzian dictum that the war is the continuation of politics by other means. Long before Clausewitz, Nehru writes, Kautilya postulated that war must not be an end in itself: '[T]he statesman's objective must always be the betterment of the state as a result of war, not the mere defeat and destruction of the enemy. If war involves both parties in common ruin that is the bankruptcy of statesmanship' (Nehru 1981, 123f). And then he adds that for Kautilya true statesmanship is not fixated on military strategy as such but pursues 'high strategy, which saps the enemy's morale and disrupts his forces and brings about his collapse, or takes him to the verge of collapse, before an armed attack. Unscrupulous and rigid as Chanakya was in the pursuit of his aim, he never forgot that it was better to win over an intelligent and high-minded enemy than to crush him' (Nehru 1981, 124).

In the next section, titled 'The Organization of the State', Nehru presents, on the one hand, the exposition of the state's organization and operations in the *Arthashastra* as a description of the historical state structure of the Maurya Empire, and on the other hand, he treats the Kautilyan state as a theoretical and normative conception. However, Nehru admits that there is an occasional incongruity of theoretical statements and historical reality. If we leave aside this complex conflation of the two categorical levels—Kautilya's ideal-type state and the historic state structures of the Maurya Empire—Nehru's representation of the Kautilyan state has the following focal points:

The centralized state serves the people: The Kautilyan state is autocratic, but not comparable to modern-age totalitarian dictatorships. Nehru emphasizes the obligations of the ruler to the people by quoting from the *Arthashastra*: 'In the happiness of the subjects lies his happiness, in their welfare, whatever pleases himself he shall consider as not good, but whatever pleases his subjects, he shall consider as good [...]. If a king is energetic, his subjects will be equally energetic.'[3] An incompetent or evil king forfeits his claim to rule—indeed he should be unseated.

The system of governance is centralized and operates through an extensive state bureaucracy, which regulates social life and the economy. At the same time there is a certain degree of local autonomy, both in the cities and in the country, which the ruler respects. The state must ensure external and internal security, for which sufficient tax revenues are necessary. Nehru mentions Kautilya's frequent references to the secret service, without, however, elaborating on that.

It is evident that Nehru has a rather positive attitude towards the emphasis on centralization in the Kautilyan state. It should be noted here that Nehru—in contrast to Gandhi—always favoured a strong and centralized executive, and a centralized state bureaucracy, and he followed that through in the design of the state structure of independent India.

The key role of the state in the economy: The second focus of Nehru's narrative on Kautilya is the economy and economic policy. He states that the *Arthashastra* deals with the full spectrum of the economy: agriculture, animal husbandry, horticulture, crafts, manufactures, trade, mining, fisheries, food processing, long-distance trade with China and western Asia, currency and financial matters. Striking is Nehru's emphasis on control and regulation of economic activities. He stresses that agriculture, crafts, trade, moneylending and services are supervised and regulated by the state in order to combat fraud, profiteering and corruption. The currency is a state monopoly, and weights and measures are standardized. The object of the government's economic policy is the maintenance and expansion of infrastructure, including roads, highways, waterways, ferries, bridges and irrigation systems.

Beyond the all-important link between the performance of the economy and the tax revenue as a fiscal basis of state capacity, Nehru is obviously impressed by the state's commanding role in the economy. The state itself is a major economic actor while adopting a 'dirigiste' policy stance towards the private sector. It is probably no far-fetched interpretation that Kautilyan economic policy, as set forth in the *Arthashastra*, comes rather close to Nehru's ideas of etatist dirigisme (with a strong socialist element added) and the actual economic policy during his tenure as Indian prime minister.

The state's welfare policies: Nehru describes how the Kautilyan state assumes social responsibility for the people. The state is running hospitals, enforces the observance of hygiene rules, and there is a kind of consumer protection by state. Widows and orphans receive government support. The government's stockpiling of food prevents famines in case of bad harvests. The state even looks after women's rights, including divorce and the remarriage of widows. Finally, civil protection measures in case of large fires, floods or other natural disasters are the state's responsibility. The paternalistic social policy, as put forth in the Kautilya's *Arthashastra*, comes close to Nehru's social policy aims which were strongly influenced by Fabian socialism.

Ancient India's international standing: Nehru points to the fact that the Maurya Empire, established by Kautilya and Chandragupta, maintained diplomatic relations with the Hellenistic kingdoms of the Diadochi in Eurasia and Egypt. He emphasizes the importance of long-distance trade between India and Central Asia, the Middle East, Greece, Egypt, China and Indochina. The level of civilization in the Maurya Empire, Nehru writes, was en par with that of the Hellenistic world. This applies to the standard of living, including luxury goods, as well as cultural activities such as literature, theatre, singing and dancing as well as more mundane forms of entertainment. Nehru puts special emphasis on the highly developed urban life in the Maurya Empire's capital Pataliputra. He notes that the predominantly wooden construction in the capital city was not a sign of civilizational backwardness but of far-sighted urban planning in view of the risk of earthquakes. In many respects, Indian science anticipated Europe's intellectual achievements by many centuries.

Nehru sees the Maurya Empire as a 'global player' of the ancient world. India was equal or superior to the other great empires of the ancient world—in terms of culture, science, military strength and economic performance. In addition, ancient India had produced with Kautilya a unique theorist of the state and statecraft, who, on top of this, was a key political actor in bringing about the political unification of the subcontinent.

From this historical perspective, it is not surprising what Nehru writes in a subsequent text passage of the *Discovery of India*—that is in 1944—about independent India's future role in world politics:

> *India, constituted as she is, can not play a secondary part in the world.* She will either count for a great deal or not count at all. No middle position attracted me. Nor did I think any intermediate position feasible. (Nehru 1981, 22, emphasis added)

Nehru's statements about Kautilya and the *Arthashastra* in the *Discovery of India* prove beyond doubt that he had thoroughly studied the *Arthashastra* and intellectually absorbed key concepts from it. Moreover, it is evident that Kautilya was a political and intellectual inspiration for Nehru.

4.3 KAUTILYA'S SIGNIFICANCE FOR NEHRU AS PRIME MINISTER

Next the question arises whether Kautilyan thought remained relevant for Nehru beyond the nationalist liberation struggle against British colonial rule. What can be said about Nehru's relation to Kautilyan thought after he had become the Prime Minister of independent India in 1947?

To our knowledge, a scientific monograph on Nehru's relation to Kautilya does not yet exist. Such a study would have to involve systematic research of the extensive stock of Nehru's writings during the post-1947 period. To our knowledge, much of this archive material is still classified and not accessible to research. A cursory review of Nehru's published texts shows that he did make references to Kautilya after 1947, albeit rarely (cf. Nehru 1972, 1993).

In a 1948 internal memorandum to the Indian Ministry of External Affairs regarding Indian policy towards Pakistan and Afghanistan, Nehru writes: 'According to both Machiavelli and Chanakya, India's interests would lie with countries on either side of neighbouring countries. That doctrine hardly applies in the modern world because of various developments, but there is something in it which can not be ignored' (Nehru 1993, Vol. II, 371). Here, Nehru evidently refers to Kautilya's *mandala* scheme whereby the immediate neighbours tend to be enemies, while the indirect neighbours—in the back of the immediate neighbours—can be regarded as friends. Nehru rightly notes that the *mandala* concept should not be misunderstood as a rigid geopolitical scheme of universal validity, but he acknowledges that it contains some elements of truth deserving attention. That the *mandala* scheme had some influence on Nehru's foreign policy approach is also the view of the Bangladeshi political scientist Rashed Uz Zaman, who writes:

'Nehru did develop a strategy similar to Kautilya's mandala or "circle of states" system. Given India's friendly relations with countries like Afghanistan, Vietnam and the Soviet Union, and its enmity with Pakistan and China, it seems that Nehru did understand the utility of Kautilyan ideas' (Zaman 2006, 241).

Another example of Nehru taking recourse to Kautilya is the speech 'Destiny of Asia' which he delivered at the conference of the Institute of Pacific Relations in Lucknow on 3 October 1950. In that speech, Nehru states:

> There is evil in the world, plenty of it, and that evil supports itself by armed strength. *We have to meet it with armed strength* […]. Now, unfortunately, when we enter the realm of warfare and the military mind, there is always that desire to go to the last limit, and in doing so, the objective for which the war is fought is itself often betrayed. If you have time or opportunity, I would advise you to read in your leisure moments an ancient Sanskrit play [*Mudrarakshasa*] written in the fifth century. It is a political play dealing with this particular problem of peace and war. *The great Indian [Kautilya], who was the hero of that play, was a master not only in statecraft but of war too. He waged war and established a powerful Empire.* He discusses it and says: It must always be remembered that war is fought to gain a certain objective. Victory is not the objective. War is fought to remove an obstruction, which comes in the way of your gaining an objective. If by victory you mean the removal of your obstruction, well and good. If victory itself becomes an objective, then you have forgotten your real objective. You have gone astray and therefore it is the end of it. You have gone off, the objective has gone somewhere else and new problems face you. *That is a very wise message indeed.* (Nehru 1993, Vol. 15/I, 502f, emphasis added)

Nehru's speech in 1950 connects with his repeated references to the play *Mudrarakshasa* and his remarks in the *Discovery of India* six years earlier, in which he points to Kautilya's anticipation of the Clausewitzian dictum that war is the continuation of politics by other means and not an end in itself. His characterization of Kautilya as 'the great Indian' and 'master of statecraft' indicates that nothing has changed in Nehru's appreciation of Kautilya. Also, close associates of Nehru testify that he did make references to Kautilya during his time as Prime Minister of India. B.N. Mullik, the long-time former director of India's Intelligence Bureau (IB), writes:

> The Prime Minister proceeded to stress how from the beginning of history everything depended ultimately on information and data [...]. [Nehru] referred to Chanakya's *Arthashastra* and said it was astonishing what a complicated system of intelligence Chanakya had built up. He said if intelligence was so important 2000 years ago, it has assumed much greater importance in the present age of swift communication and transportation. (Mullik 1971, 70)

The quote from Mullik's book confirms what is evident from Nehru's own statements: He was not only intellectually familiar with Kautilyan thought but used it in his political work as prime minister.

However, at least with respect to his foreign policy approach, there might be doubts about the influence of Kautilyan thought on Nehru. In the final part of the *Discovery of India*, Nehru sharply condemns the theory of geopolitics referring to its British originator Halford Mackinder, the German Karl Haushofer and the American N.J. Spykman. Nehru denounces foreign policy stances that are based on 'geopolitics', 'imperial expansion', 'spheres of influence', 'encirclement' or 'balance of power' as 'supremely foolish' (Nehru 1981, 540). Doesn't this harsh verdict apply to Kautilya's realist foreign policy doctrine as well? We don't think so. Geopolitical and imperialist power politics as postulated by Mackinder, Haushofer or Spykman cannot be equated with Kautilya's realism in foreign policy. Kautilya's strategic and normative aim was the political unification of the Indian subcontinent. Thus his foreign policy revisionism was restricted to the subcontinent (as a distinct cultural space) and not based on imperial expansion or geopolitics. Moreover, Nehru's own statements on Kautilya and his realist foreign policy concepts exclude any conflation with modern imperialist power politics of the geopolitical or ideological variety.

Nehru's understanding of foreign policy realism is unconventional, but it is not incongruent with Kautilyan realism. In the *Discovery of India*, Nehru writes: '*Realism, of course there must be*, for no nation can base its domestic or foreign policy on mere good-will and flight of imagination' (Nehru 1981, 539). But such realism is quite different from the 'realism' that is based on imperialist, geopolitical power politics, as the latter 'is more imaginative [imaginary] and divorced from today's and tomorrow's problems than much of the so-called idealism of many people' (ibid., emphasis added).

Nehru has also quite an unconventional understanding of 'idealism' in foreign policy, which he explained in a speech before the Indian Parliament on 7 December 1950: '*Idealism alone will not do*. What exactly is idealism? Surely it not something so insubstantial as to elude one's grasp. *Idealism is the realism of tomorrow*. It is the capacity to know what is good for the day after tomorrow or for the next year and to fashion yourself accordingly' (cit. in: Michael 2008, 98, emphasis added). Thus defined, Nehru's understanding of idealism in foreign policy does—quite in line with Kautilyan realism—not exclude use of military force. Right after becoming Prime Minister in 1947, Nehru ordered the deployment of the Indian army in Kashmir. And in 1961, he ordered the Indian army to seize the Portuguese colony of Goa. There is no doubt that Nehru saw the use of military force as ultima ratio. However, when vital national interests were at stake, he did not hesitate to resort to military force. And herein Nehru stands in the realist Kautilyan tradition. In a speech to the Indian Parliament on 15 February 1956, Nehru said: 'I am not aware of our government having ever said that they have adopted the doctrine of ahimsa to our activities. They may respect it, they may honor the doctrine, *but as a government it is patent that we do not consider ourselves capable of adopting the doctrine of ahimsa*' (cit. in: Michael 2008, 311, emphasis added).

A fascinating insight into Nehru's foreign policy realism is provided by his assessment of the global-strategic situation in the late summer of 1944. In the *Discovery of India*, he writes that the United States and the Soviet Union will be the only true victors of World War II. But, as both powers are set for imperial expansion, they are moving towards bipolar rivalry and confrontation. While Britain is clinging to the status of a colonial and imperial world power, that effort is doomed. Even at the apparent British triumph of 1918, the decline of the British Empire had already set in—and will further accelerate after the end of World War II. The same fate awaits Europe's other colonial powers: France, Spain, Portugal and the Netherlands. As European colonialism is coming to an end, a federation of nation states might be established in Europe. Nehru concludes his 1944 assessment of the global-strategic situation, stating:

> *The Pacific is likely to take the place of the Atlantic in the future as the nerve center of the world.* Though not directly a Pacific state, India will inevitably exercise important influence there. India will also develop as a centre of economic and political activity in the Indian Ocean area, in South-East Asia and right to the Middle East. *Her [India's] position gives her an economic and strategic importance in a part of the world which is going to develop rapidly in the future.*
> (Nehru 1981, 536, emphasis added)

His own statements in the *Discovery of India* and elsewhere confirm beyond reasonable doubt that Nehru was influenced by Kautilyan thought. For Nehru as one of the leaders of the independence movement against British colonialism, Kautilya was important because he gave Indians political self-confidence and the certainty of standing in a grand tradition of endogenous politico-strategic thought. Nehru had thoroughly studied the *Arthashastra* and knew the *saptanga* theory and the concept clusters *upaya*s and *shadgunya*. Thus, Kautilya offered to Nehru a broad range of foreign policy options. And within this spectrum, both the realistic and the 'idealistic' aspects of Nehru's foreign policy approach could be accommodated. It is not difficult to identify the 'Kautilyan spirit' in an internal government memorandum that Nehru wrote in 1947:

> *Whatever the present position of India might be, she is potentially a Great Power.* Undoubtedly, in future she will have to play a very great part in security problems of Asia and the Indian Ocean, more especially of the Middle East and South-East Asia. Indeed, India is

the pivot around which these problems will have to be considered. I need not go further into this matter as the importance of India to any scheme of Asian security is vital. *It is absurd for India to be treated like any small power* in this connection. (cit. in: Michael 2008, 149, emphasis added)

4.4 NEHRU'S RELATION TO KAUTILYAN THOUGHT IN THE PERSPECTIVE OF THE EXPERT INTERVIEWS

4.4.1 How profound was Nehru's study of Kautilya's Arthashastra?

All interviewees had read Nehru's *Discovery of India* and some of them remembered vividly the text passages on Kautilya and the *Arthashastra*. Regarding the question of Nehru's relation to Kautilyan thought, two thematic issues dominated the expert interviews. First, how profound was Nehru's intellectual and political engagement with Kautilya's *Arthashastra*; secondly, if Nehru's overall policy stance—and his foreign policy in particular—stood in the tradition of Kautilyan political realism or if it was predominantly shaped by the 'idealistic' traditions of Indian political thought.

There was a consensus among the interviewees that Nehru was the dominant political figure in independent India until his death in 1964. There was also a consensus that Nehru has continued to exert formative influence on Indian politics—in the domestic and the foreign policy sphere—since after his death up till the 146 present. But in the perception and appraisal of Nehru's foreign policy, the interviewee took remarkably controversial positions. Here, three positions can be distinguished:

- Nehru was a political realist and markedly influenced by Kautilya. What appears 'idealistic' in his foreign policy is actually derived from realistic assessments of the situation.
- Nehru's foreign policy was shaped by idealistic goals and policies in the tradition of Ashoka and Gandhi—i.e., Nehru is not at all or only marginally influenced by Kautilyan thought.
- Nehru's policy stance was a singular synthesis of political

realism and idealism. He combined the Kautilyan and Ashokan traditions and also absorbed Western political theories.

A large majority of the interviewees adopted the first and third positions, while a minority labeled Nehru a political 'idealist'—and that too, with surprising vehemence.

Most interviewees had not known that Nehru had actually studied the *Arthashastra*, assuming that his knowledge of Kautilya had come from secondary sources. However, two interviewees who had done scholarly studies on Nehru noted that a copy of Kautilya's *Arthashastra* can be found in the library at Anand Bhavan, the home of the Nehru family in Allahabad. General agreement existed among the interviewees that the rationalist and secular Kautilya had great intellectual appeal to Nehru. One might even speak of a mental affinity towards Kautilya in the sense of intellectual brilliance coupled with political sophistication. However, as the interviewees noted, Nehru kept his distance as his critical mind would not allow a quasi-ideological identification with any political and/or intellectual role-model.[4]

Although most interviewees held the view that Nehru had a lasting and profound intellectual and political interest in Kautilya, some asked why, precisely in the year 1944, did Nehru focus so much on Kautilya's *Arthashastra*. Two contradictory explanations were offered:

The first explanation refers to the deep crisis of the Indian independence movement during the years 1942 to 1945. Negotiations over India's future between the Congress leadership and the British Special Envoy Sir Stafford Cripps had failed in 1942. The negotiations had vectored towards a compromise: India should get autonomous status under British suzerainty, but all policy areas vital for the war effort would remain under British control. However, such compromise could be understood as an intermediate step towards full independence after the war. That was probably the reason why British Prime Minister Winston Churchill rejected the compromise plan. After the negotiations with Cripps had broken down, Gandhi launched the 'Quit India' campaign against the British which led to violent unrest in large parts of India during the summer of 1942. The British authorities responded with the arrest of the entire Congress leadership, including Gandhi and Nehru. Gandhi was imprisoned from August 1942 to May 1944 and Nehru was detained until June 1945 (cf. Rothermund 2010, 140–61).

Under these most adverse conditions, *The Discovery of India* was written. In doing that, the interviewees argued, Nehru was intent to instill self-confidence into the battered Independence movement (including himself). To that end, he expounded the great political achievements in the ancient history of India and the stamina of Indian culture. And that is why Nehru highlighted Kautilya as the co-creator of the first pan-Indian state, the Maurya Empire, and the political theorist on par with Western political thinkers.[5]

> *The Discovery of India* is written at a time when the present looked very gloomy. So there is an attempt by Nehru to turn to India's past and say, this is a country which has been through all of this horrific stuff but still retained that central element of vitality [...]. I think *the book is a product of its moment* which may not necessarily capture everything of what we know about Nehru. Having said that, *the sections on Kautilya's Arthashastra, however, are very interesting because Nehru was very engaged with the text.*
> (EI Srinath Raghavan,[6] emphasis added)

At the same time, Nehru wanted to correct intellectual and political deficits of the Independence movement via his book *The Discovery of India*. In spite of the fact that Kautilya and the *Arthashastra* had gained significant political weight for the Independence movement, the interviewees opined that most Congress leaders and nationalist intellectuals lacked deeper knowledge of Kautilyan thought and used it primarily for political rhetoric. In contrast, Nehru had thoroughly studied the *Arthashastra*, and his aim was to use Kautilyan politico-strategic thought as an intellectual catalyst for giving the Independence movement a sharper political edge against the British under particularly adverse circumstances.

The second line of argumentation in the interviews did not focus on the gloomy context in which the *Discovery of India* was written—it was quite the opposite. Some interviewees argued that, in 1944, Nehru saw light at the end of the tunnel. In his book, Nehru writes that Britain will emerge from World War II in a decisively weakened condition—in spite of belonging to a group of victorious powers. Thus, Britain would not be able to deny India its Independence much longer. With Independence approaching fast, Nehru knew that he was the likely candidate for prime minister of sovereign India as he was second only to Gandhi in the Congress leadership. Therefore, the argument went, Nehru sought inspiration and conceptual input from Kautilya preparing him for his impending role as the chief of state of Independent India—that is why Nehru turned his attention to Kautilyan statecraft in 1944.

> My reading is that [in 1944] Nehru thought he is going to be the Prime Minister of India, and he thought that he could learn something from the *Arthashastra* in preparing him for this position, especially with respect to administrative matters. So I think he did engage in Kautilya to train himself. Though he is not following Kautilya outright, he found many things there to be implemented in practical governance [...]. That's why he was so interested in Chanakya—his statecraft, administrative skills and his method of analyzing the situation. (EI P. Chandramohan)[7]

4.4.2 Nehru: A political realist in the Kautilyan tradition

Three years after writing the *Discovery of India*, Nehru had indeed become the first Prime Minister of Independent India. He held this office from Independence Day—15 August 1947—until his death on 17 May 1964. During this period, Nehru was in personal union also foreign minister. In the following segment, we report on the views of those interviewees who considered Nehru a political realist in the Kautilyan tradition.

As Prime Minister, Nehru followed the Kautilyan role-model of the highly educated and disciplined statesman. Fully conscious of his political charisma, Nehru never abused his power as prime minister towards establishing an authoritarian regime (as in neighbouring states). Ever thoughtful of legitimacy, Nehru did not take any personal advantage of his office, and his self-conception was that of the first servant of the people. He developed a policy approach for gradually overcoming the economic, scientific-technological, social and educational backwardness of India. Given the conditions of postcolonial poverty and underdevelopment, Nehru used his power and charisma to maintain the stability and internal cohesion of the new Indian state. His personal prestige was also a key factor for the high reputation that India enjoyed on the global political stage—in spite of its lack of hard power resources. All that, the first group of interviewees argued, adds up to a stance of political realism in the Kautilyan tradition.

> If you look at Kautilya in a more subtle framework, then I think there is a case to be made that *Nehru could be seen as someone who falls within that Kautilyan tradition* [...]. I would say that it is the more so because of Nehru's own engagement with the text, even though, of course, it is not the only thing he read and liked. But the *Arthashastra* was an influence on him. (EI Srinath Raghavan,[8] emphasis added)

Nehru adopted for India the Western model of parliamentary democracy, but he insisted on a strong, centralized state as enshrined in the Constitution of India.[9] The Kautilyan tradition is also evident in the centralized state bureaucracy, to which Nehru attached extraordinary importance. He decided to take over the entire Indian staff of the colonial Indian Civil Service so that, right from the beginning, Independent India had a centralized state bureaucracy—the Indian Administrative Service (IAS). Also the colonial police forces, intelligence agencies and armed forces were taken over from the British without any political purges as to avoid a power vacuum. Nehru's decision to make the Ashokan 'Lion Capital' and the 'Ashoka Chakra'[10] the state emblems of Independent India can be seen as a conscious re-connection with the tradition of the centralized state in India—starting with the Maurya Empire. In that, Nehru prevailed against Gandhi, who wished a replication of a spinning wheel as India's state emblem.

> I'm not sure if even Pandit Nehru was not influenced by the theory of centralization featured in Kautilya's *Arthashastra* when he became India's Prime Minister. *Under Nehru there is a tendency towards centralization,*

because it was seen as a way of promoting the common good for the people of India: political centralization, the role of the state in controlling economic activity and in building up basic infrastructure. (EI Ranabir Chakravarti,[11] emphasis added).

However, several interviewees critiqued that Nehru did not opt for an American-style presidential democracy, which would have been closer to the monarchical Kautilyan tradition and better suited for underdeveloped India than British-style parliamentary democracy. As long as Nehru himself was on top of the affairs of state, India was practically a presidential democracy, but thereafter the weaknesses of parliamentarianism became evident. Also criticism was directed against Nehru's inclination to give too much weight to a select group of advisers and to delay urgent decision-making by protracted deliberations. This criticism was voiced by the interviewees who otherwise saw Nehru's overall policy stance as being in the tradition of Kautilyan realism.

All interviewees, including those who attributed political idealism to him, agreed that Nehru's economic policy followed the Kautilyan principle that the economy is the foundation of state capacity. Nehru's economic policy, which gave the state a leading role in the economy, stood in the Kautilyan tradition of etatist dirigisme. The widespread emphasis on the influence of the Soviet-planned economy model and the British war-economy system has tended to blur the Kautilyan background of Nehru's economic policies. Via the state's promotion of scientific and technological research as well as scientific-technical educational institutions, Nehru laid the foundation for India's industrial development.

> *I think Nehru was more Kautilyan*, because he took the industrial growth model. He rejected Gandhi's 'small is beautiful' policy based on villages. He pushed ahead science and technology, he set up the National Defence Academy, he got the Indian Institutes of Technology, he got the nuclear plan going, he brought nuclear energy to India with policies spelled out by Homi Bhabha, the nuclear physicist. (EI Namrata Goswami,[12] emphasis added)

In keeping with Kautilyan thought, Nehru emphasized the connection between economic development and military power. He knew that building up India's defense capabilities depended on indigenous industrial development and overall economic growth generating sufficient tax revenue. Therefore, Nehru prevented a unilateral military build-up at the expense of overall economic development—the opposite of what was done in neighbouring Pakistan.

> So if you look at Nehru's pronouncements, both in terms of speeches and letters, it is quite clear that he is saying from the very beginning that getting an industrial, technological base in the economy is the prerequisite for building up defense capabilities in India. (EI Srinath Raghavan)[13]

Most interviewees denied that Nehru had neglected the Indian military. In spite of being a 'civilian' through and through, Nehru recognized the importance of the armed forces for national security. In spite of the scarcity of economic, fiscal and technological resources, the Indian armed forces were expanded and upgraded during Nehru's tenure. Nehru recognized the importance of technologically advanced weapon systems for the Indian armed forces, notably the air force. And he also acknowledged that India had to be capable of endogenously developing and producing state-of-the-art weapon systems—to not to have to depend on the goodwill of foreign states. For example, in 1956, the Indian government contracted the German aircraft designer Kurt Tank who developed the first operational jet fighter to be endogenously produced in a developing country.[14]

> Many people falsely accused Nehru of having ignored India's defense. The Indian army, the army India received at the time of Independence, was 240,000 strong. By the time of the 1962 war, its manpower had nearly doubled. The number of air force squadrons went up from some 8.5 to 30 or something. Naval expenditure rose four times. And Nehru laid the ground work for nuclear program [...]. So *Nehru did develop India's military and technological capabilities. And of course, he understood that*

> *economics is the foundation for all this.* (EI S. Kalyanaraman,[15] emphasis added)

Nehru did not hesitate to deploy the Indian armed forces when he saw vital national interests threatened: in 1947-49, in Jammu-Kashmir against Pakistan; in 1948, for the military occupation of the 'State of Hyderabad' in south-central India, which had been formally independent during the colonial era and refused to accede to the Indian Union; and, in 1961, for the military annexation of the Portuguese colony Goa. Under Nehru, India was also involved in 'covert warfare'—Kautilya's *tusnim-yuddha*. After the Sino-Indian war in 1962, the Indian army and intelligence services supplied and trained—in cooperation with the CIA—Tibetan fighters who waged a guerrilla war against the Chinese government. However, during Nehru's seventeen-year term as prime minister, military force was rarely used altogether. His reluctance to use force is in line with Kautilyan realism treating war as ultima ratio. Kautilya as well as Nehru gave preference to the five methods of foreign policy other than war.

> In some ways you could argue that Nehru falls into that [Kautilyan] tradition about the role of force: The role of force is more to persuade someone to change the way he is behaving towards to you, rather than to put him in a spot and say this is what I want you to do, so do it. *In that persuasive rather than operational fashion, Nehru usually thought of the role of force.* (EI Srinath Raghavan,[16] emphasis added)

Of particular technological, economic and military-strategic importance was the Indian nuclear program, which was decidedly expedited by Nehru. He worked very closely with Homi Bhabha, the outstanding physicist and visionary head of India's nuclear program. Nehru was first and foremost interested in the peaceful uses of nuclear energy, but he had always been conscious of the military potential of India's atomic research program. Nehru wanted no nuclear weapons for India, but equally so he did not want to renounce the option of being able to develop them. He campaigned vigorously for global nuclear disarmament but insisted that India could only forgo something that it actually possessed. Therefore,

Nehru gave his personal friend Homi Bhabha free rein for the nuclear research program and did not insist on blocking avenues of research that opened up the possibility of future military use.

> To the extent you are talking about development of capabilities which could at some future point result in the acquisition of nuclear weapons capabilities, I think both Nehru and Homi Bhabha knew very well which direction they were going. They were not children. Bhabha knew exactly what the civilian nuclear program would be and what its potential strategic military implications could be. If you pushed it in certain directions—you could take it all. So I think they got into that very much with their eyes open. (EI Srinath Raghavan)[17]

This assessment of Nehru's nuclear policy stance is also supported in the literature. C. Raja Mohan writes: 'Nehru and Bhabha were clear in their minds that India should not give up the option to make nuclear weapons in the future' (2003, 9). And Marcus Kim writes: 'Although Nehru, the first Indian prime minister, largely took an anti-nuclear stance, he never dismissed the possibility of nuclear deterrence, particularly in the form best known as "non-weaponized deterrence"' (2004, 85).

The political scientist Bharat Karnad was the sole interviewee who thought that there was a tacit agreement between Nehru and Homi Bhabha to actually develop nuclear weapons. Karnad bases his assessment on his own participant observation: His father had worked in a leading position in the Indian nuclear program and Bhabha had been a frequent guest in his parents' home, where young Karnad could often listen to their conversations. Karnad also took a singular position among the interviewees, in that he believes that those aspects of Nehru's policy stance which appear to be 'idealistic' were in reality deliberate camouflage of his realpolitik in the Kautilyan tradition. In the interview, Karnad reiterated what he had written in his book *Nuclear Weapons and Indian Security*, published in 2002:

> *Nehru, for his part, was an old-fashioned realpolitik-minded statesman,* who was alive to the imperatives of national security

and wise to the uses of military power of the state [...]. Nehru's moralpolitik was, therefore, a diplomatic toll to enlarge India's political maneuvering room (Karnad 2002, xxii, xxxi, emphasis added).

Not only Karnad but most interviewees expressed the view that the essence of Nehru's foreign policy—non-alignment—was based on Kautilyan realism. What benefit would India have achieved if it had joined one of the two ideological and military blocs and submitted to one of the two superpowers? Pakistan had gone this way, and that choice has not paid off in the long run—neither in terms of its internal development nor in terms of its foreign policy status. Instead, Pakistan's involvement in the shifting strategic interests of the United States has contributed to bringing the country to the brink of political and economic ruin. India, in contrast, greatly benefited from keeping a distance from the Cold War superpowers and 'playing them off against each other'. In the 1950s and 1960s, India obtained urgently-needed grain shipments from the USA, weapons from the United Kingdom, engineering goods and expertise from Western Europe, and industrial plants and weapons from the Soviet Union. Thus, Nehru's non-alignment policy can be characterized as soberly calculating realpolitik which allowed for economic development and preserved India's freedom of action in international affairs. What else is foreign policy in the Kautilyan tradition of political realism?[18]

Notably the American government deeply resented Nehru's refusal to join the US-led Western block which meant that relations between Washington and Delhi remained precarious throughout his tenure. Among the American political elites, Nehru was sometimes treated as a 'crypto-communist'—in spite of his tough stance against the Indian communists or his refusal to diplomatically recognize communist East Germany. Conversely, Stalin viewed Nehru as a sophisticated tool of British imperialism, and the Indian communists acted accordingly. Moscow's attitude towards India became more friendly after Khrushchev took over, and Soviet-Chinese relations began to deteriorate. Nehru has often been lambasted for his alleged condoning of the Soviet Union's brutal suppression of the Hungarian uprising in in 1956. That was, as several interviewees noted, not an expression of genuine pro-Soviet sympathies but realist foreign policy—after all, the USA and NATO did not actively intervene in favour of the Hungarian insurgents and thus accepted the Cold War status quo in Europe. An equally realist foreign policy, they opined, was Nehru's high-profile diplomatic stance against the Anglo-French-Israeli attack on Egypt in the same year 1956. Nehru denounced the 'Suez crisis' as an act of neo-colonialism and neo-imperialism threatening world peace. Ultimately, even American President Eisenhower came to a somewhat similar conclusion and forced Britain, France and Israel to terminate their military operations against Egypt.

Nehru saw his non-alignment policy also as a way to ease tensions between the two power blocks and mediate in conflict situations. Reducing East-West confrontation and the risk of war carried normative eigenvalue for Nehru, but at the same time it was a matter of India's self-interest: Nehru considered a more peaceful and stable world as favouring India's internal development. In his efforts to reduce tensions between the US- and Soviet-led power blocs, Nehru gave much weight to the United Nations, although India was denied a permanent seat at the UN Security Council. His attitude towards the UNO, the interviewees argued, should been seen as an expression of foreign policy realism: The UNO and its sub-agencies were the only institutional format of international politics in which non-aligned states like India could a) articulate their interests at least in terms of public diplomacy and b) at least formally interact at the same level as the established powers. Nehru's efforts to reduce international tensions and confrontation—in the framework of the UNO and beyond—have yielded little immediate results, but that does not mean they were useless.

Kautilyan realism demands that every available opportunity in foreign policy is used to promote state interests even if—as with chess—tangible results can be expected only in the longer run.

> Nehru often suggested, especially on things like disarmament, that India, because it was not part of this alliance system, could find ways to reduce the differences between the two blocs, as an honest

broker, in a creative kind of space. So I think non-alignment was a bit richer than simply manipulating the super powers to get the best out of them and stay out of their clutches. That too is part of non-alignment. *And, you could say it is also a Kautilyan element in Nehru's foreign policy stance.* (EI Kanti Bajpai,[19] emphasis added)

In the South Asian region, Nehru's foreign policy realism was particularly evident, the interviewees argued. Here, Nehru employed robust diplomatic pressure tactics—*yana*, the fourth method of foreign policy in Kautilya's *shadgunya* cluster. As a consequence, the small Himalayan states Bhutan and Nepal became effectively Indian client states and Sikkim was eventually incorporated in the Indian Union. Nehru's policy vectored towards the formation of an Indian-controlled buffer zone with respect to China (cf. Singh 2005).

Perhaps surprisingly, most interviewees opined that, prior to 1962, Nehru's policy with respect to the disputed border with China in the Himalayas had been quite assertive. India repeatedly declined Chinese offers to engage in diplomatic negotiations on the border demarcation. However, what might appear as robust realism was actually a fateful policy mistake based on an utterly wrong assessment of Chinese capabilities and intentions. The Chinese leadership waited patiently until the Soviet Union and the United States were completely absorbed by the Cuban Missile Crisis of October 1962. Right then, China launched a surprise attack against India and occupied large chunks of disputed territory in the Himalayas. Moreover, Nehru failed to order the deployment of the superior Indian Air Force to cut off the Chinese supply lines over the Himalayan passes. That sealed the humiliating defeat of the Indian army. All interviewees agreed that the 1962 Sino-Indian border war was the nadir of Nehru's foreign policy. At this point, he had lost connection with Kautilyan thought and political conduct.

Three interviewees with intelligence background unanimously stressed that the Indian intelligence agencies had provided sufficient information on the Chinese preparations for the attack in the Himalaya. But Nehru and his close advisers ignored or misjudged the intelligence reports. However, the interviewees argued, this gross misjudgment was singular, albeit with traumatic consequences for India and Nehru personally.[20] One should not conclude from his failure in 1962 that Nehru would have been disinterested or even aversive to intelligence matters. He knew of the value of intelligence—a key factor of Kautilyan policy-making.

> Nehru did not want publicity about India's external intelligence capability, but *do not underestimate what has happened with respect to intelligence during the Nehru period*. (EI Srinath Raghavan,[21] emphasis added)

Nehru's commitment to *Panchsheel*—'The Five Principles of Peaceful Coexistence' in inter-state relations, which formed the ideological basis of the NonAligned Movement—should not be misunderstood as 'pure idealism' in foreign policy. Several interviewees argued that *Panchsheel* as a leitmotif of the anti-colonial struggle for emancipation of the Third World was based on a realistic assessment of the global realities in the 1950s and 1960s. *Panchsheel* upgraded India's prestige and status in world affairs—and thus substantially increased its agency.

> *This assumption that Nehru was entirely idealistic does not really hold up in light of Nehru's actual conduct of foreign policy. He was definitely a lot more pragmatic, more realist. Nehru was not looking at the acquisition of power as to end in itself, but he really understood the role of power in international politics.* He can not be accused of not knowing what power means, which is what a lot of people do. The trouble is that they do not know their Nehru. (EI Srinath Raghavan,[22] emphasis added)

The above listed assessments of the interviewees are supported by the literature. C. Raja Mohan, for example, writes: 'India's first Prime Minister and Foreign Minister, *Jawaharlal Nehru, was quite a realist in his thinking about foreign policy* and the importance of protecting national interest, while the public articulation of India's foreign policy had the mark of idealism [...]. *Nehru was by no stretch an idealist or moralist in his thinking about foreign relations*' (Mohan 2003, xxi, 38, emphasis added).

Among the interviewees, only two experts had a Muslim background. These interviews were conducted at the University of Kashmir in Srinagar. On the question whether Nehru was influenced by Kautilyan thought, the answers were emphatically in the affirmative. The interviewees argued that Nehru was a ruthless and cynical master of power politics while outwardly preaching political morality. The purely declaratory nature of his 'idealistic' political pronouncements would be evident in his policy stance towards the Kashmir issue. Nehru's Kashmir policy was described as a breach of promises and agreements combined with outright repression. These views of Nehru obviously reflect the specific, conflict-laden conditions in Kashmir since 1947. In support of this assessment of Nehru, the case of Kashmir leader, Sheikh Abdullah Muhammud, was brought up in the interviews. Sheikh Abdullah, who was known as the 'Lion of Kashmir', was initially a political ally of Nehru. However, in 1953 he was arrested and charged with conspiracy to foment separatism. He spent eleven years in Indian jails until he was rehabilitated in 1972. Thereafter, until his death in 1982, Sheikh Abdullah was Chief Minister of Kashmir.[23]

Both interviewees from Kashmir emphasized that they would not want to mix up their view of Nehru's relation to Kautilya with the evaluation of Kautilya and the *Arthashastra* in terms of Political Science. While most Muslims in the Indian subcontinent have little interest in or appreciation of Kautilya, they said, the significance of Kautilya's *Arthashastra* for the history of political thought is indisputable.

4.4.3 Nehru as 'political idealist'

The many statements in the interviews that Nehru's political thinking and actions were shaped by political realism in the Kautilyan tradition are now contrasted with the opposite opinion. In the expert interviews, no precise definition of the term 'political idealism' was offered. Instead the term was used pragmatically in the sense of *argumentum contrario*: political idealism is what deviates from political realism in the Kautiylan tradition or explicitly contradicts it. However, it must be noted here that the interviewees who thought Nehru was a 'political idealist' (mis-) understood Kautilyan realism as 'pure' power politics devoid of any normative objectives. Moreover, they judged Nehru's understanding of idealism as 'realism of tomorrow' as mere quibbling.

Considering Nehru's deviation from Kautilyan realism as going so far that they characterized him as a 'political idealist', some interviewees denied that Nehru had some knowledge about Kautilya and the *Arthashastra*. However, they asserted that whatever Nehru had said affirmatively of Kautilya in the *Discovery of India* was not derived from an actual grasp of Kautilyan thought and therefore was inconsequential. From the (supposed) contradiction of his praising Kautilya while denouncing Western power politics and geopolitics, the conclusion was derived that Nehru did not understand the *Arthashastra* at all—or, at best, only superficially so.[24]

These interviewees opined that Nehru's intellectual and political stance was irreversibly shaped by his long stay in England. Through his close ideological ties to British Fabianism, Nehru adopted socialism and the idea of equality and friendship between nations as his principal political values, which he put above state interests and raison d'état. Despite his undeniable pragmatism and very sobering political experiences, Nehru kept faith in political idealism of Fabian provenance. In addition to the British Fabianism, Nehru's political idealism was also fed by the Indian tradition of 'peace-loving' politics going back to Buddha and Ashoka. Therefore, what Nehru writes on Buddha and Ashoka in the *Discovery of India* is far more important for his political thought and action than what he states on Kautilya.[25]

All interviewees who labeled Nehru a 'political idealist' acknowledged, however, that Nehru had followed Kautilya in that he saw economic power as the basis of state capacity and thus energetically promoted economic development. However, while for Kautilya the transformation of economic strength into military power was paramount, Nehru neglected the strengthening of the armed forces. Nehru did not recognize the central importance of military power for the state's agency in external affairs; moreover, he harboured an aversion against the military which was nourished by his ideological beliefs and intellectual arrogance. As Prime Minister, Nehru abolished the General Staff and made the Service Chiefs subordinate to the Minister of Defence, which in practical terms meant the senior civilian bureaucrats of the Ministry of Defence. Nehru and his closest advisers rarely consulted the military leadership and excluded them from the government's decision-making on issues of national security. Instead, Nehru almost exclusively relied on his (civilian) defense minister, Krishna Menon.

The assumption that the 1961 military occupation of the Portuguese colony Goa had been a manifestation of realist power politics is not valid, the second group of interviewees argued: With respect to Goa, Portuguese dictator Salazar had been completely isolated on the international stage. Even the American government pressured him to give up Goa. Salazar would have backed down within a short period of time and Goa would have been peacefully returned to India just as it had happened with the French colonial enclaves on India's eastern coast a few years earlier. In spite of this, Nehru ordered the military invasion Goa. The quick defeat of the hopelessly inferior Portuguese forces did not demonstrate India's strength but exposed India's 'peaceloving' postulates as duplicitous and thus damaged its international standing.

Nehru was unwilling to accept that only 'the sum of hard power'— strong state plus strong economy plus strong armed forces—will assure agency in foreign affairs. This attitude of denial proves that political realism in the Kautilyan tradition remained alien to him, the interviewees argued. Therefore, Nehru was also blind to the 'hard' power politics of the Chinese leadership that, after militarily annexing Tibet in 1954, was determined to force through a geo-strategic realignment of the Himalayan boundaries. While China—with this objective—was preparing a military attack on India, Nehru put faith in China's ideological and diplomatic declarations and relied on his own diplomatic finesse. Some interviewees felt that Nehru might simply have got it wrong. 'Nehru felt that the Chinese assault was a betrayal of whatever was agreed with Beijing [...]. *He never expected the Chinese to play to that extent realpolitik that they actually did. Nehru was, I would think, too much influenced by moral values and idealism*' (EI Rana Banerji,[26] emphasis added).

Nehru never recovered from the humiliation at the hands of the Chinese leadership in 1962. Yet even though the foundations of his foreign policy stance had been shattered, he did not break with his 'idealism', some interviewees argued. Already at the end of the 1950s, Nehru had received sufficient intelligence that China was working hard building nuclear weapons, but he refused to draw the necessary lessons from that intelligence information. Even after the humiliating defeat of 1962, Nehru refused to redirect the Indian nuclear program towards a nuclear weapons capability. In October 1964—five months after Nehru's death—China conducted its first nuclear weapons test. Only thereafter, under Nehru's successor Lal Bahadur Shastri and then his daughter Indira Gandhi, a correction of the previous 'idealist' foreign policy began.

From the perspective of the second—minority—group of the interviewees, the assumption that Nehru had a special relation to Kautilya in intellectual and political terms is based on a 'misunderstanding': His statements on Kautilya in the *Discovery of India* are just 'declaratory' and had no impact on his actual policy-making. Instead, Nehru pursued 'idealist' policies to the detriment of India's national interests. This view is shared by Jaswant Singh, former Foreign and Defence Minister, who speaks of '*Nehru's idealistic romanticism*' (1999, 34, emphasis added).

4.4.4 'Nehruvianism' as synthesis of realism and idealism

The third group of interviewees thought that Nehru's policies cannot be adequately conceived via the dichotomy of political realism in the tradition of Kautilya or political idealism in the tradition of Ashoka. Instead, Nehru's policy stance contains both realist and 'idealist' features—and both derive from Western sources as well as Indian traditions. The relative weight of the multiple ideational elements within Nehru's overall political stance is a matter of argument, but ultimately this argument is not expedient because it misses the peculiarity of his political personality.

The third group of interviewees emphasized the influence of Western ideas—including both liberalism and socialism—on Nehru's understanding of politics. Nehru was not only a well acquainted with the Western political and cultural discourse but a well-travelled man. In the course of his many, often long-lasting trips to Europe, the United States and Asian countries, Nehru developed a large network of friends and acquaintances who mostly occupied very senior positions in the political and intellectual spheres. From these mostly left-liberal and 'progressive' sources, he adopted ideas and concepts and moulded them into his very own political weltanschauung.

> In my book, *War and Peace in Modern India*, I say that Nehru is a mixture of the liberal tradition and the realist tradition in international relations. (EI Srinath Raghavan)[27]

> Nehru is the inheritor of the tradition which is both looking at the realities of the world and keeping idealism in the forefront. (EI Krishnappa Venkatshamy)[28]

In the expert interviews, it was argued that Nehru was equally open-minded and adaptive to Western political ideas as well as to the dual—realist and idealist—traditions of Indian political thought. His political thinking and behaviour was described as a singular synthesis of realist and idealist elements taken from both Western and Indian traditions. Nehru's 'integrative' political thinking, these interviewees argued, plainly corresponds to the pluralist and inclusive structure of Indian culture.

> Nehru was not a thinker in polarities. Nehru was an integrative thinker [...]. Of course, Nehru himself does not explain his own way of strategizing. I think it was very clever on his part to be inclusive in terms of historical resources he draws upon [...]. *Nehru was a synthesizer and an integrative mind; he did not fixate on polarities and conflicts*. He always saw some other point of view which needs to be reconciled. (EI Krishnappa Venkatshamy,[29] emphasis added)

In the expert interviews, Nehru's singular style of political thought and action was termed 'Nehruvianism'.[30] Asked how to best define 'Nehruvianism', some interviewees referred to the above-quoted dictum of Nehru that 'today's idealism is tomorrow's realism'. This sentence would express the dialectical relationship between political realism in the Kautilyan tradition and political 'idealism' in the tradition of Ashoka—along with Western ideational influences. Others pointed to J.N. Dixit who had written: 'Over the years, since independence (in August 1947),

India's foreign policy had moved from its idealistic and romantic phase to more realistic moorings and Panditji [Nehru] progressively adjusted to the political realities *and emerging trends in world politics as well as to the surrounding pressures born out of these trends on India'* (Dixit 2003, 75, emphasis added).

Even though the influence of Kautilyan realism is evident, Nehru perceived Kautilya in his own way, some interviewees said. His interpretation of Kautilyan realism draws a distinction to the Western understanding of 'pure' power politics which Nehru explicitly rejected for its normative emptiness. Nehru's subtle understanding of power and force was, as noted above, more indirect and persuasive than direct and operational.

> *Nehru gives Kautilya a certain interpretation which is* not quite a realist interpretation. *He does not consider him as an arch realist. He appropriates him to his own political visions, in support of his own visions of a pragmatic, realistic statecraft, but driven by idealism of sorts,* anchored in idealism. (EI Krishnappa Venkatshamy,[31] emphasis added)

Already the textual composition of the *Discovery of India* shows that Nehru had wanted to connect his treatment of Kautilyan realism with that of Buddha's and Ashoka's idealism. Nehru was fascinated by the Buddhist Ashoka because Ashoka was both an ethically 'good' ruler whom the people held in veneration as well as a politically 'successful' ruler who led the Maurya Empire to unprecedented levels of power, wealth, culture and international reputation. Even though, with respect to the sphere of politics, Buddhist ethics might appear not only as hyper-idealistic but world-negating, Ashoka had proven that Buddhist ethics and realist statecraft can go hand in hand. Several interviews who had done scholarly studies on Nehru reported that of all religious beliefs, the agnostic Nehru felt most strongly attracted to Buddhism.

> Here is a truly great Indian thinker—Kautilya, along with Chandragupta Maurya's grandson Ashoka—a Buddhist [...]. Nehru tackled both Kautilya and Ashoka in one stroke. (EI P.K. Gautam)[32]

We can conclude that Kautilyan thought was an integral part of Nehru's political thinking and conduct. That said, the question of the relative weight of Kautilyan realism within the ideational composite of 'Nehruvianism' is really secondary.

Our finding that Nehru did substantially relate to Kautilya derives from Nehru's own written and spoken accounts; it is supported by the majority of the interviewed experts, and also backed by scholars and political insiders. The influence of Kautilyan thought on Nehru—intellectually and in terms of political practice—is a key indicator of Kautilya's ideational presence in modern India.

4.4.5 The Kautilyan triumvirate of modern India: Gandhi, Nehru and Sardar Patel

Between the end of World War I and India's Independence in 1947, the Indian Independence movement was led by a 'triumvirate': Gandhi, Nehru and Sardar Vallabhbhai Patel.[33] Several interviewees objected to the widespread opposition of Nehru, the 'political realist' in the Kautilyan tradition, versus Gandhi, the 'political idealist' in the tradition of Buddha and Ashoka. With distinct emphasis they denied that Gandhi was a 'pure' idealist.[34]

Unquestionably, Gandhi put forth genuinely idealistic positions: He rejected the modern nation-state with its bureaucratic apparatus. He idealized the village community of farmers and craftsmen. He rejected modern industry and scientific-technical progress as well as capitalist profit-making. But Gandhi was not an unworldly, contemplative philosopher but a political activist determined to force the British colonial power out of India. This political objective to which Gandhi devoted his life sprung not only from spiritual and ethical ideals but also from the experience of being rejected by the 'British system' in a humiliating fashion. During his Law studies in England, Gandhi was quite fond of the British upper class lifestyle. But when he tried to establish himself as a socially accepted barrister in South Africa, his aspirations were rudely shattered. Disillusioned, he became an activist against racial discrimination of South Asians in South Africa and, upon his return to India, a passionate Indian nationalist and freedom fighter.

Several interviewees noted that, according to legend, Kautilya had a similar humiliating experience at the hands of Dhana Nanda, the ruler of Magadha. Revenge for that humiliation, they said, became a key motive of Kautilya for overthrowing the Nanda ruler.

Gandhi's strategy of non-violent resistance is not only an outgrowth of ethical idealism, some of the interviewees argued. His renunciation of violence as a means of gaining India's independence can also be seen as an expression of Kautilyan realism. Gandhi's strategy was based on the sober realpolitik calculation that, under conditions of British military superiority, armed liberation struggle would be hopeless, while non-violent resistance of the Indian people would psychologically wear down the British resolve to hold on to India. Mass-scale civil disobedience and non-cooperation were also forms of power politics, the interviewees argued. The great *satyagraha*s of the 1920s and early 1930s that were led by Gandhi were no spontaneous protests but meticulously planned and organized in an almost general staff-like manner—mainly under the direction of Sardar Patel. Gandhi and Patel took the calculated risk that *satyagrahi*s would not only be beaten up and wounded but might get killed by the colonial authorities. Even Gandhi's repeated hunger strikes and his threat of fastening to death could be seen as a 'negative' variation of power politics: Gandhi knew that the British were aware that his death would not only make him a martyr for the Indian masses but would ruin both the legitimacy and the morale of the British colonial power. Moreover, his death would likely trigger a violent mass insurrection.

Gandhi, as the interviewees noted, was not a man for whom democratic rules were inviolable and who always sought consensual decisions. Already in his Sabarmati Ashram, Gandhi's regime was rather authoritarian. And one gets a sense of Gandhi's actual political leadership-style when he proclaims: '[T]he Congress must be in the nature of an army [...] the Congress, conceived as a fighting machine, has to centralize control and guide every department and every Congressman, however highly placed, and expected unquestioned obedience. The fight cannot be fought on any other terms' (cit. in: Balraj 2013, 185). Subhas Chandra Bose, the Congress president in 1938 and 1939, was determined that India should stay out of any future war that Britain might get involved in. He demanded mass resistance if the British government would again draw India into a World War as they had done in 1914. Gandhi strongly opposed Bose's position and tried to prevent his reelection as Congress president for 1939. When he failed in that, Gandhi broke away from Bose and engaged in intra-party obstructionism that forced Bose to resign as Congress president.

In the interviews, it was repeatedly stressed that Gandhi did not consider his *ahimsa* principle as a dogma. Not only did he justify the use of force in personal self-defense situations, he also granted the Indian state the right of military self-defense. One interviewee referred to Gandhi's book *The Gita and Satyagraha*, where he writes:

> *I do believe when there is only a choice between cowardice and violence, I would advise violence.* Thus, when my eldest son asked what he should have done, had he been present when I was almost fatally assaulted in 1908, whether he should have run away and seen me killed or whether he should have used his physical force which he could have wanted to use, and defend me, I told him that it was his duty to defend me even by using violence [...]. *I would rather have India resort to arms in order to defend her honor than that she should, in a cowardly manner, become or remain a helpless witness to her dishonor.* (cit. in Menon 2012, 5, emphasis added)

In 1914, Gandhi had strongly endorsed India's involvement in World War I. He put ethical and ideological consideration aside because he calculated that Indian support for the British war effort would, in return, lead to British concessions on the path to independence. That turned out to be a political miscalculation. In 1939, Gandhi did not firmly resist India's involvement in World War II as a major military and logistical resource of Britain.[35] And, as one interviewee noted, Gandhi remained silent for almost a year on America's nuclear bombing of Hiroshima and Nagasaki. He kept quiet because he did not want to alienate the American government from the cause of Indian Independence through the moral condemnation of their actions against Japanese civilians. Lastly, in 1947, Gandhi consented to the deployment of the Indian army in Kashmir.

In his published writings, Gandhi refers to Kautilya and the *Arthashastra* only three times.[36] Gandhi, was therefore, not unfamiliar with Kautilyan thought. We can safely assume that Gandhi not only knew the four *upayas*, for his political conduct reveals that he applied the first three *upayas*—*saman, dana* and *bheda*—and was not dogmatic with respect to *danda*.

> Gandhi—like Kautilya—was a person who was having the pulse of politics; he carefully calculated the correlation of forces. He searched for the politically weak flanks of the adversary. And Kautilya suggested ways to achieve political goals without going to war [...]. I say: On Mahatma you can agree or disagree, but *Gandhi was certainly a realpolitik man*. And in pursuing his realpolitik, Gandhi was willing to sacrifice—even his being a sage wearing Indian dress. (EI Partha Ghosh,[37] emphasis added)

Gandhi's political realism comes also to the fore by his choice of Nehru as his deputy and successor. Gandhi made this choice in spite of the considerable political and ideological differences between him and Nehru. He knew that Nehru was determined to build up a centralized and industrialized Indian state that would contradict his own ideals in many respects. But Gandhi was political realist enough to know that an 'idealist' alternative to Nehru would not have been in India's interest.

Lastly, a note on Sardar Vallabhbhai Patel, Gandhi's 'chief of staff' in the 1920s and 1930s. After India's Independence, Patel, who was Deputy Prime Minister, became known as 'India's Iron Man' who created the unified Indian state by integrating the 550 nominally independent princely states into the Indian Union. The way Patel acted politically before and after independence has led his biographer Krishna Balraj to the conclusion that Patel possessed '*the political acumen of a Chanakya*'. Sardar Patel '*followed Chanakya's four-fold policy* of persuasion (*sama*), money (*daam*), punishment (*dand*) and division (*bhed*)' (Balraj 2013, 366, 420, emphasis added). V.V. Giri, India's President from 1969 to 1974, remarked that Patel possessed '*the astute statesmanship of Chanakya*' (cit. in: Balraj 2013, 417, emphasis added). And Prime Minister Narendra Modi compared Patel with Kautilya, saying, 'The country can never forget Sardar Patel. Centuries ago, Chanakya conducted a successful experiment of establishing a strong state set up by uniting small princely states [...]. Post Independence, the same great work was done by the man whose birth anniversary we are celebrating today, Sardar Vallabhbhai Patel' (*Times of India*, 31 October 2014).

5

THE MANIFEST PRESENCE OF KAUTILYAN THOUGHT IN MODERN INDIA

Nehru's multiple references to Kautilya and the *Arthashastra* are 'materially recorded' in the *Discovery of India* and other texts. He refers to Kautilya explicitly, engages intellectually with thought-figures of the *Arthashastra* and often relates them to contemporary political contexts. Thus, we can ascertain an empirical expression of Kautilyan thought in modern India. Such manifest presence of Kautilyan thought needs to be distinguished from its latent and subconscious influence, which we will explore later.

The manifest presence of Kautilyan thought necessarily involves explicit referencing to Kautilya and/or the *Arthashastra*. Such explicit references can occur in two ways: as discursive recourse, as in the case of Nehru, or as non-discursive recourse. In contrast to an intellectual, argumentative engagement with Kautilya in mostly 'elite' contexts, the non-discursive recourse, mostly occurs in a 'life-world' framing.

In this section, we examine first the non-discursive dimension of the manifest presence of Kautilyan thought. The obvious choice for approaching the non-discursive recourse is a phenomenological perspective. After examining the symbolic and media objectifications of Kautilya in the Indian life-world, we turn to the discursive recourse to Kautilyan thought in the political sphere, where Kautilyan thought-figures are likely to be 'used' in some way for tackling contemporary political issues. Such 'active' presence in the political realm, as typified by Nehru, is best captured by the concept of 're-use of the past' (Mitra 2011a).

5.1 KAUTILYA'S NON-DISCURSIVE PRESENCE IN THE CONTEMPORARY INDIAN LIFE-WORLD

5.1.1 A survey in a phenomenological perspective

When one travels through India, one will sooner or later encounter Kautilya in a perfectly normal daily life context: on the street, in some print media, on television or on (Indian) websites. Someone who is interested in Kautilya and the current relevance of his ideas will probably consciously look for 'manifestations' of his presence in the Indian life-world. The 'normal' Indian, however, will quite unintentionally 'run into' Kautilya, for example, when he or she searches for some popular novel and finds it behind a stack of 'Chanakya guide booklets'.

A sociological analysis of Kautilya's phenomenological presence in the Indian life-world would certainly be in itself a fruitful field of research. However, in this study our aim is merely to show that there is indeed a phenomenological presence of Kautilya in the life-world in today's India. That will be illustrated by the following examples, which have merely the character of anecdotal evidence:

- The extensive embassy district in New Delhi is named Chanakyapuri and within it there is a street named Kautilya Marg. The assumption is plausible that in other Indian towns and cities also, streets, squares and parks are named after Kautilya and Chanakya respectively.
- In the entrance hall of the Political Science department of Jamia Millia University in Delhi, one of the leading Indian universities, hangs a portrait of Kautilya—next to pictures of Western political theorists. Whether Kautilya is a subject of research and teaching at the faculty is not our concern here. What is important for us is merely the fact that a portrait of Kautilya has been placed on the wall of a university building and each day students and teachers walk past that portrait.
- Many public and private educational institutions in India contain Kautilya/Chankakya as part of their names: in Mumbai, there

is a 'Chanakya Institute of Public Leadership' and a 'Chanakya Institute of Management Studies and Research', in Patna (Bihar), the 'Chanakya National Law University' is located, and in Jaipur (Rajasthan) we have the 'Kautilya Institute of Technology & Engineering'. The listing of Indian universities, academies and institutes named after Kautilya could be continued. What role, if any, Kautilya plays in the curricula of these educational institutions is not relevant here. What matters for us is that anyone who has anything to do with these institutions will inevitably encounter Kautilya—simply by walking through the entrance gate and seeing the name of the educational institution or reading a newspaper article about the graduation celebration at an educational institution named after Kautilya.

- A multitude of Indian commercial enterprises have made Kautilya/Chanakya a part of their names, including hotels, consulting firms, real estate companies, firms offering financial services or businesses in the IT sector. They are called, for example, 'Kautilya Management Consultants', 'Kautilya Technical Services Ltd.', 'Kautilya Media Networks' or 'Club Kautilya'.[1] It is remarkable that private businesses would want to adopt Kautilya's name or claim his ideas (whatever their [mis-]interpretation might be). The firms' business activities seem not to matter in their naming. A substantial connection between Kautilyan ideas and hotels, engineering firms or IT companies is difficult to construct. In any case, the firms' owners or managers seem to be convinced that 'Kautilya' in the company name is conducive to their business. But again, what really matters for us here is the fact that Indian consumers and businessmen will likely encounter companies which carry the word 'Kautilya' in their names.

- In a major newspaper *The Times of India*, S.D. Pradhan, a former Deputy National Security Adviser, titles his columns with 'Chanakya Code'. Earlier, Jairam Ramesh, who served as minister in the central government and was a leading figure of the Congress, signed his comments in the Indian weekly *India Today* with 'Kautilya'. Both columnists are not concerned with a substantive treatment of Kautilyan ideas but deal with issues of day-to-day politics. Relevant for us here is that the columnists must have viewed the choice of the pen name 'Kautilya' as expedient and many Indians have encountered the pen name 'Kautilya' or 'Chanakya' when reading newspapers and magazines.

- In every well-assorted Indian bookstore, the *Penguin Classics* paperback edition of Kautilya's *Arthashastra* (in English) is offered. The purchase and especially the reading of this book, however, is probably a marginal phenomenon of the Indian life-world (and belongs rather to the Indian discursive sphere). Certainly no marginal phenomenon of the Indian life-world are the countless books and pamphlets containing a collection of Kautilyan aphorisms and maxims (in vernacular languages). There are multiple versions of such *Chanakya niti*. Most interviewees thought that the selection criteria of the *Chanakya niti* are arbitrary and, still worse, the authenticity of many aphorisms cannot be corroborated in the text of the *Arthashastra*. Nevertheless, *Chanakya niti* is quite popular. In addition to the *Chanakya niti*, there are books and pamphlets addressing issues and problems of everyday life while claiming to be based on 'Kautilyan wisdom'. Such guide books and booklets, mostly written in regional languages, will tell the reader how to run a profitable business and/or making a successful professional career by offering some aphorism and maxims ascribed to Kautilya plus 'practical interpretations' thereof. One relatively recent example is R. Pillai's bestseller *The Corporate Chanakya: Successful Management the Chanakya Way*. There have been several editions of this book 2010 and it is also available in Hindi, Marathi, Bengali, Gujarati and Tamil.

Chanakya niti and the 'Kautilya guide books' are sold primarily through the myriad of book kiosks and stalls on the street. While strolling along a busy Indian street, it is almost inevitable to run into (fictional) Kautilya portraits on the cover of various books or pamphlets. Finally, there are the popular 'Chanakya' comics by Amar Chitra of which also smartphone apps exist. Thus, there is a manifest presence of Kautilya on the streets and in the railway stations and airports of modern India. Passersby and travellers do encounter Kautilya on book covers. Whether the many books by and (much more so) about Kautilya are not only bought but also read, and what conclusions the readers draw from them, is not our concern here. What is important is that a wide range of print media by and about Kautilya is part of the Indian life-world.

- The 47-part Indian television series *Chanakya*—a historical drama about Kautilya's life from childhood to the establishment of the Maurya Empire—was a 'blockbuster' when aired in 1991–92. Since, there have been several reruns of the series, and it is still a commercial success being sold in DVDs. Similarly successful was the TV series *Chandragupta Maurya*—Kautilya being the second lead character—with 105 episodes in the years 2011–12. Both series were broadcast in Hindi or dubbed in other regional languages. Several interviewees pointed to the outstanding popularity of these TV series in all walks of life and age groups.[2]

- When entering the search term 'Kautilya' in *Google*, the number of entries cross fourteen lakhs and they are mostly from India. When entering the more popular name 'Chanakya', the number crosses twenty lakhs. These impressive figures of web entries are a key indicator of Kautilya's cyber presence in the Indian life-world.

5.1.2 Kautilya's presence in symbolic and media objectifications

The anecdotal evidence listed above shows that Kautilya's phenomenological presence in today's India manifests itself in the form of symbolic and media objectifications. Symbols are perceptible objects (in the widest sense) that represent something else that is not directly perceptible.[3] In our study, we speak of symbolic objectification when the 'sign' (name) 'Kautilya' or 'Chanakya' is attached to certain 'things' of the Indian life-world like streets, universities or businesses. In the context of our study, media objectifications mean references to Kautilya outside the 'discursive spheres' of politics and academia, i.e., texts, films, comics or websites dealing with Kautilya that aim at 'information' and 'advice' (both in the widest sense) as well as entertainment.

For our study, it is of particular importance that these symbolic objectifications depend on the precondition that the 'recipients' of the perceptible symbol do have some prior understanding of the non-perceptible message 'behind' the symbol. If streets, universities or companies are named after Kautilya, the name-givers send out a 'message' which they believe will somehow be understood because its recipients have at least some vague idea of 'Kautilya'. In India, Kautilya is of symbolic significance because many, if not most, people are able to associate, albeit hazily, certain attitudes, principles and thought-figures with him.

Among Kautilya's media objectifications, the above-mentioned collections of (putative) aphorisms—*Chanakya niti*—and the 'Kautilya guide books' don't aim at theoretical discourse but have the purpose of utilizing (putative) ideas of Kautilya for better organizing daily life, notably career promotion and business success. Such books and booklets are on display at railway kiosks and stalls on the street because the booksellers assume that many travellers and passersby have some vague idea of Kautilya as well as some interest in him. As with the symbolic objectification, Kautilya's media objectifications necessitate an antecedent receptivity in the general public. TV series featuring Kautilya would not have been produced if the producers had not been confident that, in the public, there is some interest in Kautilya and people want to learn more about him, albeit in terms of entertainment. The concomitant tendency in these TV series to trivialize Kautilya and his thought is not relevant here. What matters are the existence of a certain 'foreknowledge' and an attitude of interest towards Kautilya in the Indian society.

Even though our evidence is only anecdotal, it suffices to prove that symbolic and media objectifications of Kautilya are part of the Indian life-world. Moreover, from such phenomenological presence of Kautilya we can deduce that a widespread receptivity and resonance potential for Kautilyan thought does exist in contemporary India.

5.1.3 The 'Kautilya metaphor'

The simplest form of an explicit but non-discursive reference is the mere mentioning of the name 'Kautilya'. If one is interested in more than measuring the statistical frequency of the use of the word 'Kautilya' in certain contexts, the question of the 'semantic content' of this word comes up. In semiotic terms, it's not the 'signifier' but the 'significatum' that we are concerned with. What does it mean when Kautilya's name is frequently pronounced without any deeper reflection (and without further explication)?[4]

The Kautilya metaphor can be understood as a set of selective attributions of meaning derived from an 'imagination' of Kautilya as a historical figure and/or from a superficial and fragmentary knowledge of Kautilyan thought. As P.B. Mehta notes: 'Like all the iconic texts, the *Arthashastra* was fated to be known more than read' (Mehta 2009). Thus, the Kautilya metaphor is based on certain hazy ideas about Kautilya that are partly accurate, partly imputations. Without exception, the interviewees confirmed Rothermund's observation of the Kautilya metaphor and considered it the most common articulation of taking explicit recourse to Kautilya in modern India.

However, the Kautilya metaphor should not only be seen as a trivialization of Kautilya, as the interviewees argued. In spite of representing a selective and reductionist perception of Kautilyan thought, the Kautilya metaphor symbolizes 'best practice' in governance and statecraft. That symbol is being 'understood' in the breadth of Indian society and is therefore suitable for ubiquitous use irrespective of social and/or educational status. Because of the Kautilya metaphor's reduction of complexity, Kautilyan thought has seeped in day-to-day politics and popular politicking. As a political symbol, the Kautilya metaphor is an integral part of India's 'popular' political narrative. The interviewees argued that, thanks to the Kautilya metaphor, Kautilya is not an esoteric or elitist phenomenon in contemporary India. However, the Kautilya metaphor is also widely used in Indian intellectual milieus. Among

Indian intellectuals, the reflexive and explicative recourse to Kautilya is the exception rather than the rule—just as in the rest of the population.

The Kautilya metaphor can also be conceptualized in the context of Pierre Bourdieu's theory of the 'logic of practice,' which is 'based on the principle of the economy of logic' and 'a sacrifice of rigour for the sake of simplicity and generality.' Within the logic of practice, 'symbolic systems owe their practical coherence,' on the one hand, to 'their unity and their regularities, and on the other, their 'fuzziness', and their irregularities and even incoherencies, which are both equally necessary' (Bourdieu 1990, 86). The selectivity and the inconsistencies of the Kautilya metaphor are offset by its intellectual economizing and situational usefulness.

With respect to the prime meaning of the metaphor—Kautilya as the symbol of cunning and unflinching statecraft—the interviewees noted positive and negative connotations in normative terms. On the one hand, Kautilya is a role-model for tackling big and important (political) projects in a resolute manner. He symbolizes the political 'doer' who fully commits himself to a cause and pushes it through against all odds. Kautilya is perceived as an antipode of the failures of India's political class—gridlock, procrastination and corruption. He is neither fickle nor opportunistic. Morally questionable means are applied only for the sake of the matter—not for personal gain. Kautilya is associated with a simple, even ascetic lifestyle in high office which contrasts not only to that of the political class but more generally the 'consumerist' attitude gripping particularly the Indian middle class. Lastly, in the Kautilya metaphor, there is also the meaning of the integral teacher from whom one can learn 'how the world really works.'[5]

On the other hand, the Kautilya metaphor means 'Kautilya the Crooked' who stands for ruthlessness and amorality in politics. In that, a purely linguistic association may play a role because the Sanskrit word 'kutila' can be translated as 'crooked' or 'devious' (cf. Kangle 2010a/1965, 112). Thus, the Kautilya metaphor stands for political action, which subordinates morality to the realization of political goals. Duplicity, lies, breach of promise or other immoral actions are deemed justified in political conduct and in affairs of the state.

> Kautilya is a metaphor and the connotation is the stereotypical image of the cunning and crooked Brahmin (EI P.K. Gautam)[6]

In this second meaning, the Kautilya metaphor is similar to the term 'Machiavellianism' which essentially means that, irrespective of ethical considerations, political ends justify any means. Of course, 'Machiavellianism' too is a metaphor and one that grossly misrepresents Machiavelli's actual body of thought. But 'Machiavellism' is a catchy and practical construct to express the complexity and the dilemmas of political action. In the milieu of Indian intellectuals, the equalization of the Kautilya metaphor with 'Machiavellianism' has led to the habit of using Machiavelli as code for Kautilya. The ironical consequence is that the 'Machiavellianism' metaphor is employed to 'explain' the Kautilya metaphor.

> Kautilya is the ruthless, cunning politician—the same metaphor like Machiavelli. It may be an injustice to their actual thoughts, but it is the reality. (EI Noor Achmad Baba)[7]

> The simplistic picture is: Kautilya is identified along with Machiavelli or Sun Tzu. The complexity of Kautilya is blanked out. (EI Rajesh Rajagopalan)[8]

However, beyond symbolizing cunning, unflinching statecraft and its dual normative connotations, the Kautilya metaphor has still another dimension of meaning: Kautilya as the symbol and historical role-model of India's political unification. In this second meaning, Kautilya is seen as the builder of the first all-Indian state on the subcontinent—the Maurya Empire. Kautilya symbolizes 'the old and ever-new cry of [Indian] nationalism' (Nehru 1981, 122f). This dimension of the Kautilya metaphor is an integral part of the 'national narrative' of India.

In a newspaper commentary on the hundredth anniversary of R. Shamashastry's first print publication of Kautilya's *Arthashastra*, P.B. Mehta described how Kautilya is perceived in contemporary India. All the elements of his perception mentioned by him have found their way into Kautilya metaphor:

Like all iconic texts *Arthashastra*, or more accurately its putative author Kautilya, had a long mythology woven around him, particularly in literary productions. At one level he became the personification of the etymology of his name: *kutila*. But he also became a kind of Great Legislator, the savior of India from internal dissension and external attack. While his teaching came to signify ruthlessness in a political cause, the opposite cautionary message could also be drawn. If politics requires you to be ruthless you better be sure that it is for the welfare of the subjects, and it is done with supreme detachment from personal ambition. (Mehta 2009)

Even more than Kautilya's symbolic and media objectifications, the ubiquitous Kautilya metaphor is evidence that Kautilya's manifest presence in modern India is not limited to the sphere of political and academic discourse—it's a life-world reality.

5.2 KAUTILYA'S DISCURSIVE PRESENCE IN CONTEMPORARY INDIA: 'RE-USE OF THE PAST'

Recourse to Kautilya is discursive if it involves a content-related and argumentative engagement with the *Arthashastra* and its author. In that, Kautilya is either treated as an 'intellectual gestalt' or selective ideas and thought-figures from the *Arthashastra* are addressed. The depth of the intellectual engagement with the text and author is of secondary importance. It may range from a thorough study of the *Arthashastra* to the mere reading of the text or parts thereof, to reading more or less valuable secondary literature about Kautilya.

The obvious places of discursive reference to Kautilyan thought are educational and academic milieus—primarily those concerned with Sanskrit philology, historiography, philosophy and, one would think, the social and political sciences. However, for the moment, Kautilya's manifest presence in academic contexts is not our focus.[9]

Instead, we will concentrate on the discursive recourse to Kautilyan thought in the political sphere. Since politics and statecraft are the subject of the *Arthashastra*, the political sphere is the natural place for discursive reference to Kautilyan thought. Moreover, in this context, discursive recourse to Kautilyan thought will likely mean that it is deemed valuable enough to be 'used' for tackling current political issues.[10] Thus, our investigative interest is the 'active' presence of Kautilyan thought in Indian politics. We want to explore the tangible influence of Kautilyan thought on the political (and strategic) thinking and behaviour in contemporary India. Such 'active' presence is best captured by the concept of 're-use of the past' (Mitra 2011a, 2012a). Nehru's explicit and discursive recourse to Kautilya is a case in point of 'the strategy and vision of modern political actors of re-using the past' (Mitra 2012b, 107). In the *Discovery of India*, Nehru writes:

> [T]he past is ever with us, and all that we are and that we have, comes from the past. We are its products and are immersed in it. Not to understand it [the past] and feel it as something living within us, is not to understand the present [...]. If I felt occasionally that I belonged to the past, I felt that the whole of the past belonged to me in the present. (1981, 21, 23)

Mitra characterizes the modern Indian state and the Indian political system as a singular hybrid of elements of the modern Western liberal-democratic state (mostly of British provenience) with elements of the endogenous state tradition that goes back to Indian antiquity.

> Those unfamiliar with India would be amazed to see *how far and how much India's pasts live on in the midst of modern institutions and practices*, not necessarily as exotic rituals but as competing partners. (Mitra 2011a, 215, emphasis added)

Because of its amalgamation of pre-modern and modern institutional structures, thinking patterns and modes of behaviour, Mitra views the Indian political system as eluding the established classification categories of Political Science, notably its sub-discipline Comparative Politics. Indian polity, argues Mitra, is a political system sui generis that cannot be mechanically equated with its Western counterparts.

> [T]he state of India resembles a manifold—an embodiment of the 'avatars of Vishnu' (Rudolph and Rudolph 1987). *The state of India is a hybrid*—one which diverges from the Western state 'in the importance it accords to "pre-modern" political forms [...] because they express different cultural values and traditions that form part of the cultural heritage.' (Mitra 1990b, 6; Mitra 2012a, 107, emphasis added)

However, the political recourse to tradition features not only in modern India. Since the primordial beginnings of political formations on the subcontinent (embedded in the continuity of Indian culture) has there been recourse to tradition as the primary means for addressing the political problems of the day. Across millennia, argues Mitra, whenever Indian political formations were faced with aberrations and/or new challenges, they adapted with recourse to the tradition. The first reference point has always been Bharat—the mythological, primordial Indian kingdom. With respect to the recourse to tradition as key corrective in politics, Mitra points to the *Bhagavad Gita*:

> This spirit of renewal, essential to the *conservative dynamism of pre-modern India*, is summed up in an oft-repeated sloka from the Gita: Whenever, scion Bharatas! Righteousness declines and unrighteousness prevails, I manifest myself. (Mitra 2012a, 113, emphasis added)

Since the dawn of (patrimonial) state formation in India, during the first millennium BC, Mitra sees a complex and dynamic symbiosis of politico-cultural tradition and political change. This modus of using tradition as the catalyst for political change, Mitra argues, has prevailed during the entire pre-modern history of India—including the centuries of Islamic rule. Until the onset of British colonial rule, the political and cultural past has always been an integral and 'active' part of the 'conservative reformism' of Indian politics.

The political elites of modern India use endogenous political and cultural resources generated in the course of India's long history to address current political problems and develop solutions for them. The reason for the political effectiveness of the 're-use of the past'—not the least its provision of political legitimacy—is that the recourse to tradition is itself a tradition. Thus, the reactivation of political and cultural resources is far more than just an opportunist, tactical 'political technique' by the elites. The 're-use' of the past is politically effective and at the same time confers legitimacy because tradition is so deeply rooted in the Indian population at large. In that, Mitra points to the enormous popularity of the TV adaptations of the ancient Indian epics *Ramayana* and *Mahabharata*.

For Mitra, the strategic 're-use' of politico-cultural traditions is perhaps the most decisive factor for the stability and resilience of India's political system. The 're-use' of tradition reduces social tensions and makes it easier to find solutions to political conflicts by situating current socio-political contradictions in a wider historical and cultural context. By adopting such a longue durée perspective, 're-use' can facilitate a 'supra- political identity' (Mitra 2011a, 227), which means that the acute political situation is not the exclusive framework for finding solutions for conflicts of interest. Instead, the political 'here and now' gets transcended (and put into perspective) through the authority of politico-cultural tradition.

> The *continuity of the past in the midst of the change* is yet another element that is distinctive to India compared to China or Western democracies [...]. India's incremental change has entailed frequent re-use of the past, which has become a general practice, and as such, is not confined to ambitious politicians drawing on the legacy of illustrious predecessors, or on Indian tradition in general [...]. *The past in the country is present, not just as exotic relics of distant memory but instead, as a contender, jostling for space, attention and power within the modern structure and public sphere.* (Mitra 2011a, 216, emphasis added)

Mitra's concept of the political 're-use' of endogenous politico-cultural resources is not only a crucially important theoretical contribution to understand the manifest presence of Kautilyan thought in modern India. The deep-rooted latent presence of endogenous politico-cultural resources, like Kautilya's *Arthashastra*, is the precondition of the possibility of accessing and actively 're-using' them in the context of modern Indian politics. This will be dealt with in greater detail in Section C (Kautilya redux) of this book.

5.3 THE 'RE-USE' OF KAUTILYAN THOUGHT IN POLITICAL DISCOURSE

In this segment, we shall show that Nehru's discursive recourse to Kautilya—i.e., his 're-use of the past'—is no isolated case. We will provide some select examples of the discursive 're-use' of Kautilyan thought in India's political sphere and in the Indian strategic community. Later, in the sections addressing India's strategic culture and the emergent 'Kautilya discourse' in the past few years, we shall examine additional examples of explicit and discursive recourse to Kautilya and the *Arthashastra*, and we will examine the explicit and discursive recourse to Kautilyan thought in the section dealing with Kautilya's role in Indian educational institutions and academia. While in these sections of our study, we will focus on the content of these discursive references, here, we intend to verify if there is a manifest presence of Kautilya in contemporary India in terms of the discursive 're-use' of Kautilyan thought in the political realm.

K.M. Panikkar (1895–1963) was an Indian historian, journalist and diplomat. He was Indian ambassador to Beijing, Cairo and Paris. In 1956, he published *The Principles and Practice of Diplomacy*—a book based on lectures to Indian diplomats. In it, Panikkar prominently addresses Kautilya and the *Arthashastra*. He refers to Kautilya as the founder of the theory of diplomacy, whose concepts have remained significant up to the present:

> Kautalya in his *Arthashastra* gives the most elaborate rules for the conduct of diplomatic relations, and the doctrine of sama-dana-bheda-danda—conciliation, concession, rupture and force—*still remains the basis of all diplomacy*. (Panikkar 1956, 3f, emphasis added)

Panikkar extracts two principles from Kautilya's *Arthashastra* which, in his opinion, have remained valid across time:

[1] What produces unfavorable results is bad policy; that is, a policy is to be judged by the results it produces. *Diplomacy is not concerned with ideals but with achieving practical results for the state.* Kautalya defines the six-fold policy of a state as peace, war, observance of neutrality, war- preparedness, alliance and separating of enemies. In the case of a militarily weak country, he advises a policy of peace and development and non-involvement in quarrels and alliance with stronger states [...]. [2.] No king shall keep to that form of policy which causes him loss of benefit from his own action but which entails no loss for the enemy [...]. *These instructions [of Kautilya] are as valid today as they were when written in the fourth century BC.* (Panikkar 1956, 5, emphasis added)

Panikkar does not use the term 'political realism' with respect to Kautilya, but his statement that idealism is misplaced in diplomacy and the following sentences leave no doubt that he considers Kautilya as a representative of the 'realist' approach to international relations:

The primary object of all diplomatic relations is the *safeguarding of the interests of one's own country.* The basic interest that every state has is, of course, its own security [...]. Diplomacy, used in relation to international politics, is *the art of forwarding one's interest in relation to other countries.* (Panikkar 1956, 21, 71, emphasis added)

Further on in his book, Panikkar analyses Kautilya's four *upayas* and explains their meaning under the conditions of the twentieth century. For example, *bheda*—applying pressure—would mean downgrading or severance of diplomatic relations, economic sanctions, boycotts, blockades or actions of political propaganda to discredit and isolate other states.

What is important to note in Panikkar's remarks is his discursive engagement with Kautilya from which he concludes that Kautilyan theorems on foreign policy are as valid now as they were at the time they were written in Indian antiquity—and that they ought to be 're-used' for the current conduct of diplomacy.

Next we turn to the former President of India, Pranab Mukherjee (whose term began in July 2012) and who was previously also Foreign, Defense and Finance Minister in the central government.[11] The Indian media described Mukherjee as follows:

> He is five feet one inch tall. He looks up to the portrait of Kautilya on his wall ... He is a voracious reader, and reads three books simultaneously, but 'Arthashastra' by Kautilya, the ancient Indian treatise on statecraft, economic policy and military strategy is his favorite book which he often quotes during his budget speeches. (Bragta 2012)

When key figures of Indian politics repeatedly make explicit and discursive recourse to Kautilya and the *Arthashastra*, we can state in the affirmative that Nehru was not a lone exception.

6

THE LATENT PRESENCE OF KAUTILYAN THOUGHT IN MODERN INDIA

6.1 THE PUZZLE OF KAUTILYA'S LATENT IDEATIONAL PRESENCE

A latent (ideational) presence of Kautilya in modern India could be assumed if Kautilyan ideas and concepts are used without naming their author. The reason for the absence of explicit reference could be that Kautilyan thought-figures are 'taken for granted' or perceived as 'common sense'. For that, there are two explanations: First, there is some knowledge of the originator of these ideas, but explicit mentioning of Kautilya is deemed unnecessary: 'it goes without saying.' Secondly, Kautilyan thought-figures may be used, but those using them are not aware of the fact that Kautilya is their originator. None of the interviewees denied these variants of Kautilya's latent ideational presence in modern India.

> All I can say is that Kautilyan wisdom, Kautilyan doctrines have been practised, are practised without acknowledgement. You must remember that many a practice here is not footnoted. In India, authorship is the least important. (EI Jawhar Sircar)[1]
>
> In a sense, what Kautilya has said is common sense. He wrote it, and then his thought has permeated politics throughout [...]. You can call it collective wisdom, or you can call it the teachings of Kautilya. (EI Vinod Anand)[2]

Some interviewees considered that Kautilya's latent ideational presence as an actuality can be intuitively perceived. What P. K. Gautam writes in his study *One Hundred Years of Kautilya's Arthashastra*, he also expresses in the interview: 'It is clear intuitively that Kautilya is relevant even today' (Gautam 2013c, 14). However, it is exceptionally difficult to satisfactorily identify and verify such intuitively perceived latent presence of Kautilyan thought-figures. Thus, addressing Kautilya's latent ideational presence means facing a conceptual puzzle.

> Kautilya is never absent in Indian politics, even though we cannot precisely tell how he is present. And we know that he's not the single factor of influence. (EI Ajit Doval)[3]

The expert interviews disclosed strenuous intellectual efforts for the adequate understanding of Kautilya's latent ideational presence. Some interviewees referred to Nehru's metaphor of 'palimpsest': Kautilyan ideas are 'inscribed' and remain efficacious in the collective memory, and have become part of the collective subconscious; they are as such, no longer empirically evident.[4]

P.K. Gautam confirms the subconscious presence of Kautilyan thought-figures when he writes: 'This subconscious part [of Kautilya's presence] is thus borne out with my personal observations in attending various seminars in India and most of them at the IDSA [Institute for Defence Studies and Analyses]' (Gautam 2013c, 67). Other interviewees pointed to J.N. Dixit, who writes in his book, *Makers of India's Foreign Policy*:

> Two contradictory trends have impacted on the wellsprings of India's foreign policy *at the subconscious level*. One trend is rooted in the school of thought led by Chanakya, the great chief minister and advisor to Emperor Chandragupta Maurya [...]. The second trend *influencing the collective subconscious* also ironically originated in the thought processes and political impulses generated by another Mauryan emperor, Ashoka the Great, who was influenced by the teachings of Lord Buddha. (Dixit 2004, 39, emphasis added)

Noteworthy is how Shivshankar Menon (India's National Security Adviser, 2010–14) addresses the latent presence of Kautilyan thought in contemporary India—both in the strategic community as well as among the Indian people in general. In his speech at the Institute for Defence

Studies and Analyses (IDSA) on 8 October 2013, Menon said: '[T]here is no gainsaying the fundamental importance of the *Arthashastra* in our thinking [...]. *Much of this is unselfconscious and instinctive today*' (Menon 2015b, xviii, emphasis added).

Finally, some interviewees used the metaphor 'DNA' to describe the latent ideational presence of Kautilya and other endogenous politico-cultural resources in contemporary India. The metaphor of the biochemical repository of genetic information is quite helpful because DNA is a structure that does exist but can only be identified with the tools of science. DNA may be described as a structure that a) has been structured by the past, b) structures the present and c) pre-structures the future.

Because the latent presence of Kautilyan thought-figures is not an empirically evident phenomenon, it must (and can) be deduced from empirically manifest indicators like symbolic and media objectifications that necessitate a prior 'foreknowledge' and 'receptivity' with respect to Kautilya. However, in order to do that, we require a theoretical concept that allows for adequately capturing the—diffusive and elusive—latent presence of Kautilyan thought in modern India.

6.2 PIERRE BOURDIEU'S SOCIOLOGICAL CONCEPT OF HABITUS

Bourdieu's concept of 'habitus' is a rather difficult concept. That is inevitably so because it is designed to intellectually capture phenomena of social life that are real but as such not empirically evident. That, however, is precisely the reason why the concept of habitus meets the requirements for conceptualizing the latent presence of Kautilyan thought in modern India.

Bourdieu's intellectual development began with philosophy before he turned to social science—first, ethnology during four years of field research in Algeria and then, back in France, sociology. In his encounter with a non-European culture and its intellectual processing, there is a parallel between Bourdieu and Fernand Braudel, who also spent several years in Algeria. The special profile of Bourdieu's sociology lies in the symbiosis of a philosophically grounded theoretization, alongside ethnological and sociological field work. Bourdieu himself has repeatedly stated that his sociological theory owes much to Max Weber, who writes:

> For the most part, *real behavior proceeds at the subconscious or inarticulate conscious level* of the subjective meaning. *The person behaving in a certain way 'feels' this vaguely*, rather than being explicitly aware of the source of this behavior. *Mostly his behavior is governed by habit or instinct* [...]. Really effective, that is, truly conscious and clearly meaningful behavior, is in reality always a marginal case. Every historical and sociological investigation engaged in the analysis of empirical facts, has to take this into consideration. (Weber 1972, 54f, emphasis added)

Bourdieu's concept of habitus is strongly oriented towards the physical: 'The relation to the body is a fundamental dimension of the habitus' (Bourdieu 1990, 72). A primary articulation of the habitus is 'body language' as well as the 'habits' of eating and dressing or hair-styles. At the same time the habitus has a cognitive-psychic dimension— affective dispositions as well as patterns of perception and thought. In a first approximation, one can define Bourdieu's habitus as the characteristic ensemble of values, thought patterns and behavioural dispositions of an individual (or a group). The habitus is not innate but acquired—particularly in primary socialization. The acquisition of habitus is not a conscious and intentional learning process but takes place—much like 'learning' the mother tongue—in the way of cognitive internalization of 'role-models'. Behavioural dispositions and value ideas of the family (and its social environment) are 'naturally' accepted and internalized—they 'become part of our flesh and blood', so to speak. 'The habitus is spontaneity without consciousness or will' (Bourdieu 1990, 56). Thus, a human being cannot deliberately choose his or her habitus.

Bourdieu insists that the habitus is an objective structure that shapes or at least influences basic dispositions of thought and behaviour— independently of willful intentions. He does not view structure as an a-historical *a priori* but as constituted by its historical and social genesis: the habitus is a structure that is produced by history and that structures the thoughts and behaviour of people, thus pre-structuring the future course of history.

> The habitus, a product of history, produces individual and collective practices—more history—in accordance with the schemes generated by history. It ensures the *active presence of past experiences*, which, deposited in each organism in the form of schemes of perception, thought and action, tend to guarantee the 'correctness' of practices and their constancy over time more reliably than all formal rules and explicit norms. This system of dispositions [is] a present past that tends to perpetuate itself into the future. (Bourdieu 1990, 54, emphasis added)

So the habitus connects the past with the present—and the future. The past makes the habitus into what it is. That, however, is not to be misunderstood as quasi-mechanical determinism. Bourdieu has firmly rejected all suppositions that the habitus means an inescapable fate. Instead, the habitus is the modality of (subconscious) 'pre-selection' from a wide range of possible thoughts, attitudes and actions. Yet, the habitus of individuals or groups is also responsive and adaptive to changing circumstances and new experiences. Thus, it produces dispositions which have high inertia but are not rigid and unchangeable. The habitus constitutes a robust yet 'elastic' framing for thinking, attitudes and behaviour.

> As an acquired system of generative schemes, the habitus makes possible the free production of all the thoughts, perceptions and actions inherent in the particular conditions of its production—and only those. Through the habitus, the structure of which it is the product governs practice, not along the paths of a mechanical determinism, but within the constraints and limits initially set on its inventions. This infinite, yet strictly limited generative capacity is difficult to understand only so long one remains locked in the usual antinomies—which the concept of the habitus aims to transcend—of determinism and freedom, conditioning and creativity, consciousness and the unconscious, or the individual and society. (Bourdieu 1990, 55)

Man can only have one habitus—not two or three. Since the habitus has a certain elasticity, it can be modified but neither be taken off nor put on like a piece of clothing. Attempts to consciously adopt another habitus usually end up in the loss of personal authenticity as in the case of the petty-bourgeois who wants to be a 'real' bourgeois or the *nouveau riche* who purchases an academic degree or a title of nobility in order to appear as a man of esprit, taste and distinction.

So far, the habitus was considered as structure. And as such, the habitus is, of course, no empirically identifiable phenomenon but needs to be addressed through its concrete emanations: a specific body language, specific patterns of perception, a specific style of thinking, specific values and the specific mode of behaviour of a person or group. The ensemble of these (specific) elements constitutes the real-life habitus which can be observed and described. In his comprehensive sociological field survey *La Distinction*, Bourdieu examined the empirical manifestations of the habitus in various social classes and cultural 'fields' in the French society of the 1970s (cf. Bourdieu 1982).

The paradoxical presence of past experiences and ideas in the habitus is tackled by Bourdieu also in a different perspective. So far, the habitus was considered primarily at the individual level. The habitus is indeed acquired individually, but it is also a collective formatting of thought and behaviour patterns in different social groups or 'fields' of society. It combines individuality with collectivity. The habitus of a specific social group or a particular 'field' in society is the 'subjective, but non-individual system of internalized structures, common schemes of perception, conception and action' (Bourdieu 1990, 60). Field and habitus belong together because in real life there is no 'habitus-in-general'. The habitus is inevitably tied to specific fields of society—in socio-economic, institutional or cultural terms.

Bourdieu's concept of 'field' is far less developed than that of the habitus, and it is far more difficult to understand. 'It [the field] is among the more problematic of Bourdieu's theoretical constructs: because there is a lack of clarity in nearly all of his many explanations of the concept. Matters are further complicated by the fact that Bourdieu rarely ever explains the field in exactly the same way twice' (Jackson 2008, 166). In

Le sens pratique, Bourdieu speaks of 'the almost miraculous encounter between the habitus and a field, between incorporated history and objectified history' (Bourdieu 1990, 66).

One may understand Bourdieu's field as a 'social space' in terms of political, socio-economic, functional, institutional or cultural frameworks. Each of these fields has its (historically evolved) specific character and inner logic. And each field generates 'its' corresponding habitus, which in turn reproduces 'its' field. Eva Barlösius sees Bourdieu's concept of field closely related to Max Weber's concepts of 'sphere of life' and 'value sphere' (Barlösius 2011, 95). In this dualistic perspective, the field would be both an objectification in the sense of an institution or institutional practices and an 'ideational space' with a characteristic set of ideas and values. This ideational dimension of the field includes specific ideas, thought patterns and values that arise from the intrinsic logic of the field and are adapted to it. The field-specific ideas are absorbed into the field-specific habitus and remain 'stored' therein.

6.3 THE HABITUS AS REPOSITORY OF LATENT IDEA-CONTENTS

Bourdieu's concept of habitus relates not only to 'incorporated' history but also to 'incorporated' history of ideas. If the habitus 'contains' past ideas and 'value ideas', how do such ideas underpin the habitus of a person or a social group? Bourdieu argues with the paradox that the habitus 'carries along' past ideas or values by blocking them out from consciousness—they are 'forgotten': 'The habitus—embodied history, *internalized as a second nature and so forgotten as history*—is the active presence of the whole past of which it is the product' (Bourdieu 1990, 56, emphasis added). In the habitus, past ideas and values are forgotten without being actually forgotten, because they remain unconsciously present and active.[5] In the habitus, tradition is silent,' but it remains efficacious in the present (Bourdieu 1979, 330). Bourdieu explains the paradox of the 'unforgettable forgotten' with a quote from Emile Durkheim:

> In each of us, in differing degrees, is contained the person we were yesterday, and indeed, in the nature of things it is even true

that our past personae predominate in us, since the present is necessarily insignificant when compared with the long period of our past because of which we have emerged in the form we have today. *It is just that we don't directly feel the influence of these past selves precisely because they are so deeply rooted within us. They constitute the unconscious part of ourselves.* Consequently, *we have a strong tendency not to recognize their existence* and to ignore their legitimate demands. By contrast, with the most recent acquisitions of civilization we are vividly aware of them just because they are recent and consequently have not had the time to be assimilated into our collective unconscious. (cit. in: Bourdieu 1990, 56, emphasis added)

When past experiences and ideas of a collective are 'unforgettably forgotten', they will be 'taken for granted'. The subconscious patterns of perception, ideas and values which got absorbed into the collective habitus become 'common sense'. What is 'self-evident' need not be explained.

Bourdieu refers to the epistemic realm of common sense as 'doxa'. The modus operandi of doxa is the 'logic of practice'. The non-reflexive and practical logic of everyday life (of a social group or in a 'field') follows 'an implicit and practical principle of pertinence' (Bourdieu 1990, 90). The logic of practice is precisely no scientific logic which is 'a mode of thought that works by making explicit the work of thought' and thus makes the results of the thought process logically verifiable (Bourdieu 1990, 91). The logic of practice is under time pressure and must economize on the intellectual effort; thus, it does not know the 'luxury' of scientific synopsis that 'owes its scientific efficacy precisely to the synchronizing effect it produces (after much labor and time) by giving an instantaneous view of facts which only exist in succession and so bringing to light relationships (including contradictions) that would go otherwise unnoticed' (Bourdieu 1990, 82). The practical logic 'presupposes a sacrifice of rigour for the sake of simplicity and generality.' In the habitus operates an 'approximate, "fuzzy" logic' because in the mode of doxa logically stringent, causal explanations are superfluous

(Bourdieu 1990, 86). The habitus makes the explication of the ideas and values underpinning it unnecessary: What is taken for granted 'you can safely forget about'.

The significance of Bourdieu's concepts of habitus and the field for our study is that they can give 'conceptual materiality' to the latent presence of ideas and values within a given field. Bourdieu speaks of the 'materialization of collective memory' (Bourdieu 1990, 54). The (field-specific) habitus is thus the 'repository' or the 'carrier' of (field-specific) ideas, thought patterns and values which thus 'keep them in activity, continuously pulling them from the state of dead letters, reviving the sense deposited in them, but at the same time imposing the revisions and transformations that reactivation entails' (Bourdieu 1990, 57). The concept of habitus enables us to address the subconscious and 'forgotten' idea-contents of a certain field, for example, that of the Indian strategic community.

Since the individual and collective habitus is always inextricably tied to a specific field, it is logical that with an undifferentiated expansion of the field the contours of the habitus would become ever more diffuse. A concept 'habitus of mankind' would have little meaningfulness and even less explanatory power. The more delineated the field, the more meaningful will be its habitus for the researcher.

The question as to whether there is—beyond the manifest presence—also a latent presence of Kautilyan thought in modern India is central for our study. With respect to this central question, the theoretical application of Bourdieu's twin concept of habitus and field means that the habitus of only one field is relevant for us: 'the field of Indian politics'. However, the proposition of the 'habitus of the field of Indian politics' would appear rather stretched as both field and the habitus would be too undifferentiated. Consequently, an attempt to identify Kautilyan thought-figures as one of the ideational ingredients of such equally fuzzy field and habitus would be problematic. Therefore, in the course of our exposition, 'the field of Indian politics' will be deaggregated to more compact fields—like the Indian strategic community—and correspondingly to a habitus with sufficient density and contour.

But before we do that, we keep the overstretched proposition—'habitus in the field of Indian politics'—as heuristics. Abstracting from empirical analysis, we ask whether Kautilyan ideas can be identified in the 'value sphere' or 'ideational dimension' in 'the field of Indian politics'. And staying within the heuristic approach, we ask if Kautilyan thought is an ideational ingredient of the habitus of that field.

Obviously, Kautilyan thought-figures do 'match' the field of (Indian) politics. Kautilya has generated classical concepts of politics which express the inner logic of this field. If we perceive 'the field of Indian politics' as a structure that is structured by the past and that structures the present, Kautilyan thought is necessarily an essential element of the ideational genesis of that field. Consequently, Kautilyan ideas are efficacious in the 'value sphere' of the field of Indian politics. Since field and habitus are mutually constitutive (and reproductive), each field has 'its' corresponding habitus (and vice versa). Such dialectics equally apply to ideational dimension or value sphere of both field and habitus. Therefore we can conclude that Kautilyan thought-figures and patterns are not only an essential element of the ideational genesis of 'the field of Indian politics' but must also be part of the habitus in that field. Or, to be more precise, Kautilyan thought must be an essential ingredient of the ideational dimension of the habitus in 'the field of Indian politics'.

This heuristics-grounded derivation using Bourdieu's habitus/field theory establishes that—logically—there should be a latent presence of Kautilyan thought in modern India. With this theoretical derivation as background, it needs to be stressed that most interviewees considered latent presence of Kautilyan thought in Indian politics as a natural, intuitively noticeable fact. The naturalness of its idea-contents is an essential characteristic of the habitus. The idea-contents of the habitus figure are 'common sense' in the respective field. Because it is based on ideas that need no further explanation, the habitus is ubiquitous and resilient in its respective field.

The habitus is the repository of latent idea-contents that cannot be adequately apprehended otherwise. The latency of its idea-contents—precisely because they are perceived as common sense—is a central feature of the habitus. Without the latency of its idea-contents, the habitus would be no habitus but intentional, consciously calculating thinking and behaviour.

The absorption of idea-contents into the habitus occurs in a mainly subconscious mode. Their influence on a person's (or group's) thinking and behaviour remains also predominantly subconscious. But via the habitus we can conceptually access subconscious ideas and values that influence or unconsciously steer thinking and behaviour. Within the conceptual framework of the habitus, the latency of its idea-contents gains 'materiality'. The 'substantive latency' of the idea-contents of the habitus is not an oxymoron because the habitus 'forgets' as well as 'preserves' its idea-contents—*Aufhebung* in Hegelian terms. In simpler words, in the habitus, forgotten ideas and values are not really forgotten.

In the indicated heuristic frame, we can conclude through theoretical derivation that Kautilyan thought is part of the habitus in 'the field of Indian politics'. We can logically conclude that the habitus of 'the field of Indian politics' is necessarily the repository of Kautilyan thought-figures. In this theoretical perspective, the 'sedimentation' of Kautilyan ideas in the habitus in 'the field of Indian politics' becomes plausible. With that, we exit the heuristic framework and turn to the question of how that might occur empirically.

6.4 THE LATENT PRE-UNDERSTANDING OF KAUTILYAN THOUGHT VIA THE INDIAN LITERARY CLASSICS

How do Kautilyan ideas, thought-patterns and values 'enter' the habitus in the field of Indian politics? The assumption of Kautilya's latent ideational presence is plausible if it can be derived from expressions of his manifest presence. Therefore, we take as starting point for the exploration of his latent ideational presence the expressions of Kautilya's manifest presence, specifically his non-discursive presence with the Kautilya metaphor and his symbolic and media objectifications in the Indian life-world. As noted above, all these non-discursive expressions of manifest presence are subject to the condition that some prior, semi-conscious perception of Kautilya already exists. A resonance of disposition towards Kautilya is the condition of the possibility to communicate in a meaningful manner with respect to Kautilya. The Kautilya metaphor necessitates some pre-understanding of Kautilya. Kautilya's symbolic and media objectifications can only be understood if there had been some prior imaginations and associations about him. But what are the sources that feed the semi-conscious, latent pre-understanding of Kautilya?

The habitus is primarily formed in the course of primary socialization. Therefore, Kautilyan ideas, thought-patterns and values must have been internalized and 'incorporated' into the ideational dimension of the habitus during primary socialization. The expert interviews provided important leads with regard to how that occurs. The interviewees emphasized that, regardless of the singular originality of Kautilya's *Arthashastra*, this work has to be situated in the context of classical literary texts of ancient India. Among these, the classic epics—*Ramayana* and *Mahabharata*—play the most prominent role. As noted above, Nehru points in the *Discovery of India* to the unbroken and profound significance of the two epics among the Indian people and particularly among the mostly illiterate peasants and artisans:

> The old epics of India, the *Ramayana* and the *Mahabharata* and other books, in popular translations and paraphrases, *were widely known among the masses*, and every incident and story and moral in them *was engraved in the popular mind* and gave richness and content to it. Illiterate villagers would know hundreds of verses by heart and their conversations would be full of references to them or some story with a moral, enshrined in some old classic.
> (Nehru 1981 67, emphasis added)

Some 70 years after this statement by Nehru, the interviewees agreed on the continued popularity of the ancient epics. Irrespective of recipients' social and educational status, *Ramayana* and *Mahabharata* have remained popular because of their oral transmission primarily within the context of family. In addition, the epics are spread by wandering storytellers or street theatres as well as via children's books and, lately, films, television series and the Internet.

Part of the *Mahabharata* is the *Bhaghavad Gita*, to which we have referred to earlier on (cf. B 2.6). It is widely regarded as the culmination of ancient Indian classical literature. On one hand, the epics are literary texts saturated with dramatic action. There are heroes, heroines, anti-heroes and anti-heroines; there are human beings, gods, avatars and demons. They all are involved in bloody wars and mean intrigues; they have deep friendships and passionate love affairs. But the drama in the epics is not an end in itself. The literary form provides the framework to raise profound ethical and philosophical questions. Ethics and philosophy are not mere accessories of the literary narrative but are explicitly—often in an almost scholarly fashion—discussed. Max Weber writes: 'The *Mahabharata* is in form and content a manual of ethics in terms of examples—no longer a poem' (Weber 2000, 160; 2008a, 703). And in his history of Indian literature, Indologist Helmuth von Glasenapp writes about the epics: 'Above all, the level of ethical considerations and the depth of philosophical knowledge, which—in the midst of the bizarre and platitudes—are expressed in the epics, are never even approximated by Homer's works' (Glasenapp 1929, 81).

Not only are ethical and philosophical questions explicitly addressed in the epics, but also fundamental issues of politics and statecraft. And here we find the link to Kautilya's *Arthashastra*. Indologist Alfred Hillebrandt writes in his book *Altindische Politik* (Ancient Indian Politics) that the *Mahabharata* has to be seen as a key text of ancient Indian statecraft which stands in conceptual coherence with Kautilya's *Arthashastra*. In particular, Hillebrandt refers here to the lectures of Bhishma, who as political leader and the Kauravas' military commander is one of the main characters of the *Mahabharata*:

> In particular, it is said Book 12 [of the *Mahabharata*] which provides an *outline of the main features of ancient Indian political wisdom*. It does so vividly, appearing psychologically truthful and without undue detail—and *in substantial congruence with Kautilya* [...]. To the exiled king Yudhisthira, Bhishma gives a series of lectures about the nature of politics and the role of the king which cover all areas of statesmanlike thought and action. Yudhisthira asks, Bhishma answers, and the latter does so in such an elaborated

manner that one could speak of lessons that are saturated with experience and a profound understanding of politics; *it is a kind of political propaedeutics*. (Hillebrandt 1923, 7, emphasis added)

Hillebrandt judges similarly the treatment of statecraft in the epic *Ramayana*: 'Not only with respect to its technical, but also substantial features, the author of the *Ramayana* exhibits *complete familiarity with the nature of politics*. His political psychology that is featured especially in the 6th book, is *no less valuable than that of Bhishma's lectures*. (ibid., 11f, emphasis added)

Hillebrandt's view of the conceptual coherence between the epics and Kautilya's *Arthashastra* on the topic of statecraft is widely shared in the Indological literature—and that view was also shared in most expert interviews:

> If you look at the epics, at *Mahabharata* and *Ramayana*, at the Puranic stories, *just about everything that is there is also in the Arthashastra*. (EI Bharat Karnad,[6] emphasis added)

The conceptual connectivity between the epics *Mahabharata* and *Ramayana* and Kautilya's *Arthashastra* on matters of statecraft, which rather often amounts to identical positions, is of critical importance for exploring the question of Kautilya's latent ideational presence in India today. The analysis of relevant Indologist literature and the expert interviews leads to the conclusion that the epics a) serve as an 'access route' to Kautilyan ideas, b) establish a pre-understanding of Kautilya and c) contribute indirectly to the diffusion of Kautilyan thought.

Several interviewees pointed to *Panchatantra* as another source of the pre-understanding of Kautilyan ideas. The *Panchatantra* is an ancient Indian collection of animal fables which is probably older than Kautilya's *Arthashastra*. Via Persian and Arabic translations, the *Panchatantra* came to Europe in the fifteenth century, where some parts of it were included in Jean de la Fontaine's collection of animal fables. In spite of its literary format, the *Panchatantra* 'is seen and used as a *full-fledged scientific textbook of statecraft*' (Heimann 1930, 196, emphasis added). And Hillebrandt writes:

> The samples of political wisdom, which can be found in the *Panchatantra*, a book of fables designed *for the instruction of princes*, unfortunately failed to attract attention for Indian statecraft [in Europe]. The main reason for that is its garment in the garb of the fable which made it appear more as a book of entertainment rather than for instruction. The European eye, which is accustomed to stricter forms of treatment of such issues [of politics], lacks familiarity with the graceful art to teach insights into human affairs via the fable. (1923, 2f, emphasis added)

In India, the *Panchatantra* still enjoys popularity and is understood as a work dealing with the basic issues of politics and statecraft. Thus, much like the epics, it provides a means to understand Kautilyan ideas. For the purpose of illustration, we briefly summarize here the story of the 'clever mouse Palita', in which issues of statecraft like interest, conflicts of interest, alliances, and the impact of changing circumstances on interests and alliances are treated in literary form:

In front of Palita's mouse hole, a cat is caught in the net of a trapper. The cat begs the mouse to gnaw away the net and offers eternal friendship in return. But Palita knows what to expect from the cat after her being freed from the trap. While relishing the fatal situation of her mortal enemy, the mouse Palita realizes that an owl is about to dash down on her and also a mongoose is sitting in front of her mouse hole. Now, cat and mouse—generally foes—are both facing mortal danger by third parties: trapper, owl and mongoose. A new situation and a new constellation of interests have arisen.

Thus, Palita slips into the net and hides under the cat who thus grants her friendly protection. After the owl and mongoose have left in frustration, the cat says: 'Palita, I have saved your life and we have become best friends. Therefore, I ask you to gnaw away the net without further delay.' However, the clever mouse responds by saying: 'Let us stay together here in close friendship'—and enjoys her situation until finally the trapper approaches. Only then does Palita bite through the net and quickly slips into her mouse hole, while also the cat escapes to safety.

After the disappointed trapper has left, the cat comes back to the mouse hole: 'Palita, why don't you come out? Haven't we become best friends?' Palita, however, remains in her mouse hole and states: 'When we were both mortally threatened by others, it was right to become friends, even though we were previously mortal enemies. Whether enemies become friends or friends turn into enemies is not a matter of feelings but of interest and utility in a given situation. Because the danger posed by third parties against both of us has passed, it is in your interest again that I serve thee as food. Therefore, I will not be swayed by your utterings of friendship and rather stay in my mouse hole' (cf. Hillebrandt 1923, 41ff).

The conceptual proximity of the *Panchatantra* fables to Kautilya's political realism is obvious. Adda Bozeman remarks: '*It [Kautilya's Arthashastra] restates in the language of a systematic political philosophy the cold wisdom that India has traditionally rendered in its celebrated beast fables*' (Bozeman 1960, 129, emphasis added). Bozeman's view was confirmed throughout the expert interviews. The strength of the mental imprint by the literary classics of ancient India was demonstrated by an interviewee who spontaneously referred to a *Panchatantra* fable as to illustrate Nehru's policy of non-alignment with respect to the American and Soviet power blocs:

> So how can I make use of the fact that these two warring blocs of nations are there for me to exploit? Very simple. There is a tale from Panchatantra [...]. The tale of the monkey and the two cats who have a pack of butter. Each cat wants the larger size of the pack of butter. So the monkey says, ok, I'll balance it for you, I'll give both of you an equal amount, so he keeps tipping the balance—and keeps eating the excess. The monkey says, do not worry, I am balancing it. This is the Panchatantra tale. I did not put it in my book, but the point is, that is what Nehru was doing. (EI Bharat Karnad)[7]

In the expert interviews, multiple references were made to the classic play *Mudrarakshasa* by Vishakhadatta, in which Kautilya is the central figure. The play was most likely written in the fifth century AD and has been very popular across time, as Nehru's above mentioned references show. The play describes how Kautilya operates in consolidating the newly established Maurya Empire and how he foils the attempts of the ousted Nanda dynasty to recover their power.

The plot of the play can be roughly sketched as follows: Kautilya's former allies in the overthrow of the Nandas have since become allies of the defeated Nanda because Kautilya had refused to cede some territory to them. The coalition of the Nandas and Kautilya's former allies tries to reconquer Magadha and overthrow Chandragupta and Kautilya. As is to be expected, Kautilya not only has an excellent intelligence picture about their intentions and capabilities but a sophisticated plan to sow discord in the enemy coalition. To that end, all means of diplomacy and intelligence are employed: disinformation, duplicity, intrigue, spies, double agents and covert assassinations. As on a chessboard, Kautilya 'plays' friends and foes alike. But in all of that, Kautilya pursues a higher aim: he wants to win over the highly respected Rakshasa, chancellor of the ousted Nanda ruler and his main adversary. Moreover, Kautilya wants to make Rakshasa the chancellor of the Maurya Empire and thus his own successor. And in the end he succeeds (cf. Fritze 1886). Vishakhadatta's message in the play is that Kautilya is not driven by lust for power but wants India's political unification through the Maurya Empire and the best-qualified statesman to lead it. Thus, the classic play *Mudrarakshasa* also provides a pre-understanding of Kautilyan thought-figures and contributes to the diffusion of Kautilyan ideas.

The four literary classics of ancient India—*Mahabharata, Ramayana, Panchatantra* and *Mudrarakshasa*—form a central part of Indian culture and have remained most popular in all walks of life up to the present. The norms and values, patterns of thought and politico-strategic concepts contained in these classical works are closely related to core concepts of Kautilya's *Arthashastra*. Thus, these literary works make a significant contribution to a prior understanding of Kautilyan thought in contemporary India. That is the main reason why there are, in India, hardly anyone who is 'clueless' with respect to Kautilyan thought.

The expert interviews showed how the foil of the ancient Indian classics—impregnated by Kautilyan thought—comes about in the course of family socialization. In their childhood, most interviewees were strongly influenced by the literary classics—in particular, the epics *Mahabharata* and *Ramayana*. As quoted above, formulations were used like having 'grown up with the epics' or having internalized them 'like mother's milk'. Since early childhood, they had listened to their parents and grandparents telling them tales from the epics—and thus they absorbed (quasi-)Kautilyan thought-figures and thought-patterns. All that occurred not in a purposeful and formal atmosphere but in a playful manner. The interviewees were of the opinion that their personal experiences can be generalized. Thus, in the kindergarten age, Indian children from all layers of life are introduced into a world of thought that has close affinity to the idea-contents of the *Arthashastra*.

> Take our epics. *As little children we were brought up on the Ramayana, Mahabharata and all that.* We assimilated all the positive values that exist together with the negative; there were also negative aspects to it. One was brought up in that. (EI Satish Nambiar,[8] emphasis added)

The interviewees reported about discussions within the family circle—mostly involving three generations—on the ethical and political-strategic issues raised in the epics. As with the exciting stories from the epics, the children had also closely followed these discussions which often extended to other classical authors and works of ancient India—including Kautilya and the *Arthashastra*.[9]

The intensity of the encounter with Kautilyan ideas within family socialization differs sharply from that within educational socialization. All interviewees said that their acquaintance with Kautilya during school education was casual and superficial. Kautilya was treated almost exclusively in history lessons, and the history textbooks presented him as the chancellor and key adviser of Chandragupta Maurya. In this context, the *Arthashastra* was mentioned, but without consideration for its contents. That and far more than that, as most interviewees noted, they had already known from their parents and other members or friends of the family. Only one interviewee reported that he had read some excerpts from Kautilya's *Arthashastra* at school, but that was so because he had Sanskrit as optional subject. Even during college and university, most interviewees had heard little of Kautilya. That includes interviewees from 'elite' universities like Jawaharlal Nehru University (JNU) and University of Delhi (DU), where most of them had studied.

As is evident from the above contrast in how Kautilya is disseminated, the formation of the habitus, including its ideational dimension, occurs within family socialization. One way or the other, the playful and semiconscious encounters with Kautilyan thought 'sink in' the minds of Indian children—and remain efficacious throughout their later lives.

An interesting example of the encounter with Kautilyan thought in childhood is Rabindranath Tagore (1861–1941), the Nobel Prize-winning Indian writer and poet. In his memoirs, Tagore writes: '[M]y introduction to literature began, by way of the books which were popular in the realm of the servants [at his family home]. *The most important ones were a Bengalese translation of Chanakya's aphorisms and the [epic] Ramayana*' (Tagore 2004/1917, 9, emphasis added).

6.5 KAUTILYAN THOUGHT AS LATENT IDEATIONAL INGREDIENT OF THE HABITUS OF THE INDIAN STRATEGIC COMMUNITY

The expert interviews offered the possibility of de-aggregating the rather amorphous 'field of Indian politics' by focusing on the Indian strategic community. The latter is concerned with the assessment of the situation in terms of capabilities and intentions of both the state and other (competing and hostile) state actors, the definition of state interests and goals, as well as generating policy options to enforce these interests and realize these goals (cf. Liddell Hart 1967; Kovac/Marcek 2013). The strategic community includes, on the one hand, persons with operational, political responsibilities within government, notably the intelligence services and the armed forces. On the other hand, there are persons outside government who—mostly in the context of universities and think tanks—address issues of 'grand strategy' analytically and conceptually. This latter group includes social and political scientists, economists, former government officials, retired military officers, and specialized journalists. The expert interviews were conducted only with representatives of this second group in the strategic community.

So as to avoid misunderstandings, we do not intend to produce a comprehensive sociological profile of the Indian strategic community. Nor do we intend to present an in-depth analysis and thorough description of the habitus of the Indian strategic community. Rather we examine the significance of Kautilyan thought for the habitus of the Indian strategic community. What is the (relative) weight of Kautilyan thought in the ideational dimension of the habitus of Indian strategic community? What is the semiconscious influence exerted by Kautilyan thought on the perceptions, attitudes, preferences and thought-patterns of the Indian strategic community? Whether, or to what extent representatives of the Indian strategic community do explicitly and discursively refer to Kautilya and Kautilyan thought is not the issue here. Our investigation is exclusively centred on the latent presence of Kautilyan thought in the field of the Indian strategic community.

Some hints of Kautilya's latent ideational presence in the Indian strategic community can be found in the political science literature. Kanti Bajpai seems to refer to such latent influence when he speaks of '*Kautilyan echoes*' in the Indian strategic discourse (Bajpai/Mallavarapu 2005, 27). Arndt Michael, who has examined Kautilya's impact on India's foreign policy stance towards the South Asia region, cites a senior Indian strategic expert, saying: '*Kautilya is the DNA of India's foreign policy*' (2008, 99, emphasis added). Here the same metaphor 'DNA' is used, which we encountered in the expert interviews to describe Kautilya's latent ideational presence—though not specifically related to the Indian strategic community.

In the interviews, there was a confusing ambiguity in the responses to the question of latent influence of Kautilyan thought in the Indian strategic community. On the one hand, such latent presence was emphatically affirmed. Kautilyan influence could be 'felt' in the attitudes and preferences of the strategic community and was also clearly detectable by scholarly analysis of politico-strategic documents. On the other hand, great skepticism was expressed that there was any latent presence of Kautilyan thought in the case of the Indian strategic community—although, in principle, a latent presence of Kautilyan thought in contemporary India was not disputed. The skeptics asserted that, since the explicit and discursive recourse to Kautilya in the Indian strategic community was rare, the latent presence of Kautilyan thought must be equally negligible.

Paradoxically enough, an important reason for the puzzling divergence of perceptions is likely due to the fact that the question of Kautilya's latent ideational presence in the Indian strategic community was directed to persons belonging to this community. The skepticism was mostly based on the argument that persons with professional qualification in strategic affairs who do not explicitly and discursively refer to Kautilya, either know nothing about him or do not want to know anything about him. If Kautilya is absent in the conscious cognition and discursive articulation of members of the strategic community, a latent presence of Kautilyan thought must be discounted. For professionals in the field of strategic affairs, it seems to be particularly difficult to recognize that 'latent knowledge' can exist, i.e., a knowledge which is not the result of a conscious intellectual effort. They cannot imagine that subconsciously assimilated ideas can influence perceptions, attitudes and preferences. This 'incomprehension' is apparently the stronger the more immediately one's own (intellectual) field of work is concerned. The strong skepticism with respect to Kautilya's latent influence in the strategic community comes down to a seemingly clear-cut position: You know your Kautilya or you don't—*tertium non datur*. That position shows why Kautilya's latent ideational presence and influence is so difficult to comprehend without drawing on Bourdieu's concept of habitus, which resolves the apparent paradox that ideas and values whose semiconscious acquisition has been 'forgotten' do nevertheless remain efficacious in thinking and behaviour.

The other group of interviewees viewed the latent presence of Kautilyan thought in the Indian strategic community as a verifiable fact—without however resorting to Bourdieu's concept of habitus. Several interviewees referred to J.N. Dixit—a leading representative of the Indian strategic community—who states that Kautilyan thought is one of the main subconscious influences shaping India's foreign and security policy (cf. section B 6.2). In India, they said, one could not get past Kautilya in the field of politics and strategy because he had laid down the conceptual foundations of that field. Therefore, these interviewees argued, it does not really matter whether strategic experts explicitly and discursively refer to Kautilya or treat his ideas as 'common sense'; in the politico-strategic field, that needs no further explication.

In the perspective of Bourdieu's approach, what had earlier been said on Kautilya's latent influence in 'the field of Indian politics' equally applies to the field of the Indian strategic community: Kautilya belongs intrinsically to the 'ideational sphere' of the field of statecraft because he was the first thinker to theorize statecraft and grand strategy in a systematic and scholarly fashion. Consequently, Kautilyan ideas are an integral part of the habitus of the Indian strategic community. Thus, the habitus of the Indian strategic community is the repository of latent Kautilyan idea-contents, even if strategic experts—'on top of it'—do discursively refer to Kautilya.

The interviewees who affirmed the latent influence of Kautilyan thought in the Indian strategic community stated that such latent presence can be reliably substantiated by examining the intellectual products of that community: documents, books, articles or lectures. Regrettably, they said, in most of these texts explicit references to Kautilya are rare or missing altogether, but scholarly content analysis of strategic texts proves beyond reasonable doubt the latent presence of Kautilyan thought.

> I could give you a lot of documents relating to India's internal and external policy where *the Kautilyan tradition is clearly recognizable*. It may not be obvious and explicitly stated, but as a political science researcher you can draw this conclusion without going into unsound speculation. (EI Namrata Goswami,[10] emphasis added)

It was with a reference to the United States that Goswami elaborated her view that the underlying but not explicitly stated ideational sources of contemporary strategic texts could be identified. If in India, Kautilya is the key source of strategic thinking; in the USA, Clausewitz and Alfred Thayer Mahan play a comparable role.[11] The comparison is also fitting because only few Indian strategic experts have actually studied Kautilya's *Arthashastra* in a systematic fashion, and the same is true for their American counterparts with respect to Clausewitz's *On War* and Mahan's *The Influence of Sea Power Upon History*. Nevertheless, thought-figures of both Mahan and Clausewitz are very much present in the American strategic community, and their latent influence is clearly detectable in contemporary American texts on foreign and security policy. Using content analysis, Goswami argued, the 'hidden' sources of and influences on current strategic texts can be laid open—without resorting to intuition or guesswork.

> Let me put this way: Take any strategic policy documents of any other country. For instance, if you look at the influence of say Mahan or Clausewitz. I do not think any US national strategy document states explicitly that it is conceptionally based on Mahan or Clausewitz. But as a political science researcher you can analyze the document and make comparisons—and you will recognize, yes, it does contain Clausewitzian or Mahan concepts. I do not think George Bush or any other American president has ever said: I am following Morgenthau's political realism. But he will say that use of force remains an indispensable option for America, the ability to develop technology is crucial for America's position in the world. And as a researcher, I can identify him as being a realist, following the Morgenthau or Kenneth Waltz tradition. (EI Namrata Goswami)[12]

The following example, which was not brought up in the interviews, illustrates the latent influence of Kautilyan thought in the Indian strategic community. On 11 September 2010, Jayant Prasad, then Special Secretary in the Indian Ministry of External Affairs, gave a lecture on India's security policy at a conference of the International Institute for Strategic Studies (IISS) in Geneva.[13] In his paper, Prasad did not mention Kautilya by name but used an important thought-figure of Kautilya: the *mandala* scheme—the concentric constellation of states grouped around the state in the hub.

> *India's interaction with the world begins in concentric circles around India*, beginning with the countries of South Asia Association

for Regional Cooperation (SAARC), including Afghanistan, and China. *The next circle* extends to much of the Indian Ocean Littoral: from the West to East, it stretches from Aden to Singapore; from Iran, the Central Asian Republics and the Gulf countries to the countries of ASEAN. It stretches, in the North, from Russia, as a Eurasian power, to Seychelles, Mauritius and Indonesia in the South. *The next circle* encompasses Turkey, the countries of the East African seaboard, stretching from the Horn of Africa to South Africa, the Koreas, Japan and Australia. The United States is a significant, de facto, Asian player present in our neighbourhood. Finally, together with other major Asian countries, India has maintained its traditional traction with Europe and a growing one with Africa and Latin America. (Jayant Prasad at IISS, Geneva, 2010, emphasis added)

Neither Kautilya nor his *mandala* concept is referenced in Prasad's speech. However, anyone familiar with Kautilya's *Arthashastra* will instantly recognize that Prasad uses a Kautilyan thought-figure to depict India's current foreign policy situation. He describes India's strategic environment in the form of three concentric circles of states. In addition, outside of the three circles of states, but very much involved in their affairs, are the powerful United States—*udasina* in Kautilyan terms. In addition, there are three other 'outside' power centres of lesser weight: Europe, Africa and Latin America. With respect to a senior Indian foreign policy official like Prasad, the most plausible assumption is that using Kautilya's *mandala* scheme is something so 'natural' that it requires no further explanation or reference. Prasad's IISS lecture is a case in point that the proposition of the latent presence of Kautilyan thought-figures in contemporary India's basic foreign policy posture can be verified.

The interviewees made some recommendations with regard to texts that from the Indian strategic community should be selected and analysed in order to prove the latent presence of Kautilyan thought-figures. The selection criteria were a) the document has a certain level of representativeness for the strategic community and, b) does not contain any explicit recourse to Kautilya or Kautilyan thought-figures. Such a text's content should then be analysed as to whether latent Kautilyan thought-figures or thought-patterns are recognizable.

6.6 THE LATENT PRESENCE OF KAUTILYAN THOUGHT-FIGURES IN THE STRATEGIC DOCUMENT *NONALIGNMENT 2.0*

The criteria set above apply to a document which deals with the strategic directionality of India in the twenty-first century. The document, published in 2012, is titled: *NonAlignment 2.0—A Foreign and Strategic Policy for India in the Twenty First Century* (Centre for Policy Research 2012).[14] At the discussion forums from which the document emanated, also had the then-National Security Adviser Shivshankar Menon and his two deputies as participants. Thus, the text can be considered as being representative of the thinking in the Indian strategic community. In fact, Rajesh Rajagopalan has criticized the document as 'establishmentarian' (Rajagopalan 2012).

In the sixty-four-page document on India's strategic orientation, Kautilya is not mentioned. Machiavelli, Gandhi, Tagore, Nehru and Ambedkar are mentioned, but just *en passant*. If Kautilyan ideas are latently present in the habitus of the Indian strategic community, one should be able to identify them in the *NonAlignment 2.0* document. If Kautilyan thought really belongs to the 'DNA' of India's foreign and security policy, at least 'echoes' of his thought would have to be detectable in this text.

6.6.1 Grand strategy and 'hard' realism

The document covers not only foreign and security policy in a narrow sense but is actually about grand strategy. In addition to foreign policy and military-strategic issues, internal security, the state, governance, social issues, science, technology and education are discussed in some detail. The authors use the term 'Grand Strategy' which ought to be designed like a 'chess grandmaster's game' where 'each move will have to be mindful of several other pieces on the board and the game is played as part of a long strategic interaction' (91).[15]

Rather obviously, the authors' comprehensive understanding of strategy stands in the Kautilyan tradition. Of course, the international strategic discourse has shifted in recent decades towards an extended concept of security, and that has certainly influenced the document. But that does not alter its mooring in India's Kautilyan tradition, which is characterized by a holistic understanding of strategy—exactly, grand strategy.

That the *NonAlignment 2.0* document covers extensively foreign policy issues and military strategy is *per se* not remarkable, but it is indeed striking how that is done. Already after reading the first pages, it is clear that the document is characterized by sober, hard and blunt realism in the assessment of the situation. Semantic camouflage of strategic objectives and abstract indeterminacy of policy options are absent. Not only the conceptual content of key statements but its blunt style is reminiscent of Kautilya's *Arthashastra*. Instead of phrases like 'if deterrence fails' or 'state of defense', which are typical for comparable Western documents, we read here: 'Due to unresolved boundary disputes and other potential political issues *there is also threat of war that demands military preparations*' (38, emphasis added).

With respect to world politics, 'great power competition of a classical kind' is diagnosed (10). And with respect to Asia, there are 'strategic rivalries' (12). For India, great power status is claimed, so it 'can assume its rightful place in the world' (69). If India uses its resources properly, 'there are few limits to India's global role and influence' (7). On India's geo-strategic sphere of influence, the document states: '*We should be in a position to dominate the Indian Ocean region*' (41). Essential for India's great power status is the possession of nuclear weapons:

> *The pursuit and maintenance of nuclear capability has been integral to India's quest for strategic autonomy since Independence.* There has been a consensus amongst successive governments on this issue— even in the face of immense international pressure and sanctions. In the absence of a credible nuclear deterrent, India would have few options when confronted with adversaries possessing nuclear weapons. (54, emphasis added)

India's nuclear forces must be upgraded in order to ensure the survivability of the nuclear arsenal in case of a first-strike nuclear attack. Moreover, India must gain an assured second-strike capability through sea-based nuclear systems, that is, first of all, nuclear-powered and nuclear missile-armed submarines. In addition, India must have operational missile defense and space-based systems for reconnaissance and communication. If other powers try to put pressure on India by claiming its nuclear build-up would lead to a nuclear arms race in Asia, they confuse cause and effect: India acquired nuclear weapons decades after the other nuclear weapon powers had done so, and its nuclear strategy is based on the principle of 'credible minimum deterrent' and 'no first use' (54).

There is little prospect of normalization of relations with Pakistan, states the document. India must be prepared for more irregular warfare and terrorist attacks that are covertly steered by Pakistan. In the foreseeable future, there is also little prospect of a diplomatic solution with respect to the disputed border demarcation with China in the Himalayas. Therefore, India has to be prepared for military conflicts along the border with China. With most unusual openness, the document discusses India's military options in case of military conflicts with Pakistan or China. If attacked, India must offensively retaliate. The key military-strategic lever against both Pakistan and China must be India's ability to control the Indian Ocean and thus block the sea routes to the Middle East and the Atlantic:

> 'In practice, the only direction in which India has greater freedom of projection is towards the Indian Ocean. Therefore the fundamental design that must underpin the shaping of India's military power should be the leveraging of potential opportunities that flow from peninsular India's location in the Indian Ocean, while concomitantly defending its country borders against Pakistan and China. The development of military power must therefore attain a significant maritime orientation. Presently, Indian military power has a continental orientation. *To emerge as a maritime power should, therefore, be India's strategic objective.* (38, emphasis added)

In case of limited military conflicts with Pakistan or China, the Indian air force, in particular, has to launch counter-strikes. Also cyberwar capabilities are getting increasingly important for asymmetric retaliation. In addition, if attacked by China, India should have the option to organize and logistically support insurgencies in Tibet. The same retaliation option should be available with respect to Pakistan—for example, in the Balochistan province. The document also does not refrain from stating that—below the threshold of state collapse—Pakistan's internal instability can be in the interest of India.

Such blunt statements in a strategic document that is available to the public do indicate 'Kautilyan echoes', even though the maritime dimension is absent in Kautilya's understanding of military strategy. Another indicator of the Kautilyan tradition of realism is the *si vis pacem, para bellum* principle which permeates the document. War is ultima ratio, but a range of military options in case of aggression is laid open: regular war, irregular (guerrilla) war and also covert operations, albeit without using that term. We can recognize the Kautilyan triad of military strategy.

The *NonAlignment 2.0* document repeatedly emphasizes that the assessments of the situation and policy recommendations expressed therein do not represent the policy of the Indian government. Whether this is indeed the case remains to be seen. For the purposes of our study, the essential observation is that the security policies put forth in the document are consistent with Kautilyan realism. The following sentence cannot be understood otherwise: '*The role of hard power as an instrument of state is to remain ready to be applied externally or internally in pursuit of political objectives*' (38, emphasis added).

6.6.2 Strategic autonomy

The state's sovereign freedom of action is of paramount importance for Kautilya as it is the prerequisite for the effective enforcement of state interests and goals in foreign and security policy. Dependency on other powers through alliances should be avoided except when the state is under threat by a superior adversary. The *NonAlignment 2.0* document draws on this Kautilyan foreign policy principle with its central concept of 'strategic autonomy'. However, no reference is made to Kautilya. Instead, 'strategic autonomy' is situated in the context of Nehru's non-alignment strategy (as if that had come from nowhere).

> *Strategic autonomy has been the defining value and continuous goal of India's international policy ever since the inception of the Republic [...]. The challenge is to renovate that value and goal for the twenty-first century—thereby enabling the continuous and cumulative pursuit of India's interests in a world at once full of uncertainty and of great opportunity.* (iv, emphasis added)

The severe conflicts of interest, if not strategic rivalry between India and China—mutual territorial claims to the Himalayan border and China's refusal to accept India on a level playing field—contrast with much lower-level conflicts of interest with respect to the United States. Should India therefore commit itself to alliance with the United States and thus increase its strategic leverage against China? Although India could benefit from an alliance with the United States in various fields, it would lose its strategic freedom of action and risk dependency on American foreign and security policy. Therefore, an alliance with the USA is not endorsed in the *NonAlignment 2.0* document.

> Given that India has more interests in 'direct' competition with China, and less with the US, it may be tempting to conclude that the U.S. is a likely alliance partner. But this conclusion would be premature. While there may appear to be attractions for India to exploit its derivative value, the risk is that its relations with the U.S. could become a casualty of any tactical upswing in Sino-American ties. Nor is it entirely clear how the U.S. might actually respond if China posed a threat to India's interests. The other potential downside is that India could prematurely antagonize China [...]. The U.S. can be too demanding in its friendship and resentful of other attachments India might pursue. *The historical record of the United States bears out that powers that form formal alliances with it have tended to see an erosion of their strategic autonomy. Both India and the U.S. may be better served by being friends rather than allies.* (32, emphasis added)

The singular value of strategic autonomy also implies that India should take a sober, differentiated and critical position towards ideologically charged values and norms for which universal validity is claimed. If such normative standards are internationally established, they should not be rejected, but adhering to them applies the condition that they are not contrary to essential national interests:

> Norms in the international system often mask the exercise of raw power. They are also hostage to the fact that enforcement of these norms is selective. It is often a pretext for the application of power. (36, emphasis added)

The discourse reflected an attitude of skepticism towards international institutions such as the United Nations, the IMF, World Bank, etc.—at least in their current structure which discriminates against India:

> They [international institutions] are *the creatures of an era still dominated by the West*, and quite inappropriate for a world that has seen the end of the European Empires and the rise of Asia's economic dynamism. *These institutions require fundamental reform to reflect the new distribution of power in the world.* India must actively pursue a more influential role in these institutions—a position not just *commensurate with its growing power but also with its expanding range of global interests.* (33, emphasis added)

With respect to the fact that India is constructively participating in the international institutions—in spite of the present condition of inequality—one must always bear in mind that these institutions still are 'a medium of projecting national power' (34).

The Kautilyan principle of the state's sovereign freedom of action in its foreign relations clearly permeates the *NonAlignment 2.0* document. The respect for international standards is made conditional on their compatibility with basic national interest. India's strategic stance must never be made hostage to ideological positions—home-made or exogenous. Here, we can observe political realism in the Kautilyan tradition, of which Max Weber says that it is 'devoid of any "ideology"' (Weber 2000, 146; 2008b, 687).

6.6.3 The state and state capacity

In the *NonAlignment 2.0* document, the state has an intrinsic normative value. The state is not only the institutional frame but also the purpose of national security. For sure, the state is also seen in functional terms providing public goods and services, yet it is a lot more than that. The system of parliamentary democracy is considered as constitutive of the Indian state, but the pride on the stability of Indian democracy seems not to translate into a normative prevalence of democracy relative to state capacity:

> In terms of constitutional vision, India is the most 'Western' and liberal among the non-Western powers. But *we are rooted in Asia* [...] [and] *we do not 'promote' democracy or see it as in ideological concept.* (31, emphasis added)

One could understand the last sentence as follows: In Asia—including in India—we should have democracy, but the state we must have. Its democratic system yields for India enhanced legitimacy—internally and externally—as well as domestic political stability. So far so good. But it seems that the authors of the *NonAlignment 2.0* document are not particularly eager for 'more democracy' in India. In any case, calls for further democratization of state structures are missing, and the following remarks convey rather the opposite impression: '[W]e need a strategic culture and public discourse that is willing to keep its eye on the long term and not get distracted by the "noise" generated by our democracies' (16). Moreover, 'the state seems to be riddled with all kinds of perverse incentives that hinder internal decision making' (65). Greatest importance is assigned to the decision-making power of the executive branch, in particular 'the Prime Minister's Office, Planning Commission and National Security Council' as to assure agency (66). The authors seem quite concerned that cumbersome decision-making processes in democracies compromise state capacity:

> Democracies elect leaders, and ultimately there can be no getting away from the fact that the political leadership has to take responsibility [...]. No amount of structural reform of the state,

or continuous economic growth, will yield the necessary dividends *if political leadership is indecisive, irresponsible or indifferent*. (68, emphasis added)

As a leitmotif, the demand for expansion, for strengthening and improving state capacity runs through the *NonAlignment 2.0* document: '*Enhancing state capacity in all respects* must therefore be recognized as a basic element of India's strategic conception' (11, emphasis added). It is stressed that 'the accomplishment of India's strategic goals is bound up with the capacities of our state. We must ensure that these strategic goals do not founder because of any weakening of these capacities [...]. In fact we need to strengthen dramatically these capacities' (66).

One needs no in-depth analysis to recognize that the paramount role and normative eigenvalue assigned to the state in the *NonAlignment 2.0* document are Kautilyan thought-figures.

6.6.4 Economic development and national security

Another leading theme of the *NonAlignment 2.0* document is the importance of the economy for state capacity—and thus national security. For the most part, the economy is seen as an autonomous sphere of private actors and the post-1991 economic reforms are endorsed. However, the economy is not considered a self-referential system of private economic actors, for which the state merely provides the political-institutional and legal framework. Instead, the private business community has the task and obligation to promote economic development—that is, to contribute '*to build national power*' (8, emphasis added). That the state itself remains an economic actor in 'strategic' sectors, and the necessity of the 'Planning Commission' for economic development, are not called into question.

Such economic policy perspective is certainly no 'liberalist' conception of the relationship between the private sector and the state. Rather it is an 'etatist' conception of economics in the Kautilyan tradition that views the strengthening of the economy as a means to strengthen the capacity and power of the state. It is certainly not the Anglo-Saxon model of liberal capitalism that is advocated here; rather it is an 'etatist-dirigiste' model of economic development whose origins we know from the *Arthashastra* and one that was taken up again by Nehru.

The *NonAlignment 2.0* document welcomes the Indian economy's dispensation from the quasi-socialist system of the 'Licence Raj' with its excessive regulations. But, in principle, the 'mixed economy' development model should remain valid. 'While much of the attention of economic reform focused on getting the state out of certain areas, there was much less attention to *areas where the state needed to get in - to expand its presence*' (65, emphasis added). The (mainly private) economy has to generate the tax revenue that strengthens and expands state capacity in terms of social security, education, science, technology, infrastructure and defense. As in a circle, a thriving economy advances state power and the welfare of the people, which, in turn, advance economic development:

> The crossroads in terms of state capacity is this. If India grows at 8–9% a year on average for the next decade, it will lead to unprecedented *expansion of resources available to both the state and society at large*. India has, by comparative standards, a relatively low tax to GDP ratio. This will rise with growth […]. There must be a consensus on augmenting India's resource base. But resources are not likely to be as binding a constraint for the Indian state as they once were. (64, emphasis added)

As economic and technological achievements in the private sector are seen as contributions to the advancement of 'national power', the development of India's economy should focus on its domestic market of 1.2 billion people. While the Indian economy should be open to the world economy and integrate into it, a 'globalist', export-oriented economic strategy of producing mainly for the world market is not advocated. The priority of internal economic development also includes the endogenous development of the Indian defense sector, which, in this case, means reducing the import dependency with respect to defense-related goods:

> The main challenge is to leverage India's burgeoning defense market to ensure progress towards greater *defense industrial self-reliance.*

The choice we face is between techno-nationalism and techno-globalism. We need to move from techno-imitation to techno-innovation by unleashing the power of the private industry and energizing *state-owned defense industry institutions*. (62, emphasis added)

The *NonAlignment 2.0* document promotes a 'mixed economy' model of economic development which tries to balance private sector dynamism and 'etatist-dirigiste' policies. That is clearly an 'echo' of economic principles put forth in the *Arthashastra*, although the recourse is not to Kautilya but to Nehru's economic development model.

6.6.5 The importance of internal security

Eight pages of the *NonAlignment 2.0* document are devoted to internal security issues—that is the most extensive section of the text.[16] The greatest threat to internal security is the weakness of the state in certain regions—'*state abdication*' (44). The absence or compromising of administrative structures, police, judiciary and educational institutions creates a vacuum that is penetrated by insurgents building up counter-structures to control the local population: 'So much of our discourse of the state has been about taking the state out of particular domains. *We have neglected to ask where we need to bring the state back in*' (44, emphasis added).

The second threat to internal security arises if the state is perceived as oppressor by certain population groups—like ethnic and religious minorities or social groups suffering from economic deprivation and marginalization. The sense of oppression and the consequent readiness to support insurgent groups is triggered by arbitrariness, discrimination, corruption and excessive use of force of state organs. The document points out that the national paramilitary security forces of India (excluding those of the federal states and the regular police) have a manning level of two million (almost twice as large as the Indian armed forces). Nevertheless, the security situation in several regions of India is precarious up to conditions of armed insurgency: 'Indeed, these regions have been subject to very ambivalent treatment by the Indian state, which has been simultaneously very accommodating and repressive, producing what might, in Machiavelli's words, be called a state that is neither feared nor loved' (46).

This diagnosis appears correct and corresponds with estimates in the expert interviews. It is puzzling, however, that Machiavelli, not Kautilya, is referenced. Already in the first pages of the *Arthashastra*, Kautilya writes that excessive use of the state's coercive power leads to resentment, unrest and rebellion among the people, while the impotent state leads to anarchy. For Kautilya, a central task of the intelligence service is to identify grievances of the people and their causes, preferably before resentment among the people turns into unrest or outright rebellion. Without delay, the ruler must remedy the causes of such grievances in order to calm down the people. But if, in spite of remedial action, a rebellion breaks out, the people should not be punished collectively. Instead, they should be treated leniently and thus be separated from their leaders. If they later refuse compromise or submission, they should be crushed by force. The conclusions on internal security in the *NonAlignment 2.0* document are essentially congruent to Kautilya's, even though there is no reference to him:

> In some respects, it will be the failure of the state, if it needs to resort to hard power for domestic security. The Emphasis should be on *preventive measures and political solutions*, including, eventually negotiations and peace talks. But in the eventuality that hard power has to be used domestically, it needs some restructuring [...]. First, we need to build a credible state that makes citizens feel secure. Second, we need to further develop models of inclusive governance that can address the sense of disempowerment in certain sections of the population. Third, *we need a political culture that is attuned to defusing conflict rather than exacerbating it.* (50, emphasis added)

Rather surprisingly, India's Intelligence Bureau (IB) and the foreign intelligence service Research & Analysis Wing (R & AW) are mentioned only en passant in the document. That is really puzzling in view of the fact that intelligence services are of paramount importance for both internal and external security—today, as in Kautilya's times. Why the intelligence services are not addressed in the *NonAlignment 2.0* document is an issue about which one can only speculate. Perhaps it is due to an excessive 'culture of secrecy' in today's India. In contrast, Kautilya was rather outspoken with respect to intelligence matters. In any case, the assumption seems not far-fetched that the actual role of intelligence agencies in today's India is not that much different from what is written in Kautilya's *Arthashastra* on that subject.

Kautilya considers internal security an issue of paramount importance—and that also applies to the *NonAlignment 2.0* document. Internal security is at risk if the state is either weak or oppressive. Internal Security is ensured if the state is strong and at the same time recognizes its own failures—and remedies them. These Kautilyan principles resonate throughout the document. Although only Machiavelli is referenced and the role of intelligence services is blanked out, the document's section on internal security does contain latent Kautilyan thought-figures.

6.6.6 Contemporary Kautilyan echoes: Epiphenomenon sans conceptual depth?

In the *NonAlignment 2.0* document, Kautilyan thought-figures can be identified in terms of grand strategy, foreign policy, military strategy, the character of the state, the relation of economics to 'national power' as well as internal security. But in spite of its latent interspersion with Kautilyan thought-figures, the *NonAlignment 2.0* document is not a 'Kautilyan text'. In the document, other ideational factors of influence are recognizable—factors which are derived from 'idealist' politico-cultural traditions. Such non-Kautilyan thought-figures in the text are mostly latent, but, in some cases, they are explicitly introduced. The programmatic title of the document—*NonAlignment 2.0*—demonstrates that its authors intend to build on Nehru's strategic paradigm. Thus, the conceptual basis of the document can be characterized as 'Nehruvianism' which conflates both the Kautilyan realist tradition as well as the idealist political tradition going back to Buddha and Ashoka:

> All of India's great leaders—Gandhi, Tagore, Nehru, Ambedkar—had one aspiration: that India should be a site for an alternative

universality [...]. These values gave India enormous moral and ideological capital [...]. India must remain true to its aspiration of creating a new and alternative universality [...]. *In international relations, idealism not backed by power can be self-defeating. But equally, power not backed by the power of ideas can be blind* [...]. *India should aim not just at being powerful: it should set new standards for what the powerful must do.* (69f, emphasis added)

While idealist positions with respect to politico-strategic affairs are doubtless present in the *NonAlignment 2.0* document, they do not define its main orientation. When the document is viewed as a whole, in our judgement, the realist positions in the Kautilyan tradition are predominant. For the purposes of our study, however, the determination of the relative weight of Kautilyan realism and the idealist positions in the text is not required. What matters is the finding that the presence of latent Kautilyan ideas and concepts in the *NonAlignment 2.0* document can be validated. The latent presence of Kautilyan thought-figures in the Indian strategic community can thus be considered verified by this document being representative for the community's mainstream views, even though the text is devoid of any explicit reference to Kautilya.

6.7 LATENT KAUTILYAN THOUGHT-FIGURES IN THE FIELD OF 'POPULAR POLITICIZING'

In the final segment of this section, we address the question of the latent presence of Kautilyan ideas in the field of 'popular politicizing' in India. Obviously, this vast and amorphous field is very different from that of the Indian strategic community which is compact and structurally almost uniform. In spite of this problematique, we take up the exploration of the latent presence of Kautilyan ideas in the field of popular politicizing because several interviewees strongly recommended it as a way to gain additional insights in the latent presence of Kautilyan thought in contemporary India.

The field of popular politicizing does not involve the Indian 'political class' which professionally engages in politics. Instead, popular politicizing involves political 'laymen' who talk and debate about politics in everyday situations. However, even by 'commenting' on politics, these political laymen do necessarily participate in the sphere of ideas and values in the field of Indian politics.

The concept of everyday politicizing may at first glance have a somewhat pejorative connotation, but such perception is inappropriate since popular politicizing is a widespread social practice that is not less 'valuable' than the elitist political discourse. In this sense, Bourdieu has not shied away from the term 'people' and the analysis of their 'logic of practice'. Because 'talking politics' is an important component of the communicative practice of 'common people' in India (as elsewhere), it is appropriate to search for central ideas and thought-patterns therein.

In the expert interviews, it was stressed that politicizing among the Indian people is a deep habit. Although there is no European-style tradition of bar-room politics, politicizing within the (extended) family or circle of friends, during the bus and train ride or during breaks at work is habitual in India. According to some interviewees, the politicizing in the countryside is at least as prevalent as in urban environments. In most Indian villages, there is a square at which usually a tea house is located where the (male) villagers meet daily to discuss local politics as well as 'high politics'. Such talking politics is mostly not about political ideologies or party programs; rather it is made up of sober and realistic assessments of the political situation—domestically and beyond—based on experience and tradition.

Inevitably, the question arises whether the habitual politicizing of the Indian people—after all, some 1.2 billion people—can be adequately captured with Bourdieu's concepts of field and habitus as to identify the political idea-contents carried by them. The term 'mentality', as expounded by Theodor Geiger, might appear to be more suitable for such a large population. Geiger defined mentality as the 'man's immediate mental imprinting through his social life-world and the experiences made therein' (Geiger 1932, 77). Geiger's concept of mentality, which he distinguishes from ideology, has some similarity with Bourdieu's concept of habitus in that he describes mentality as 'skin' which thus cannot be taken off or put on like cloth. However, because Geiger's concept of mentality is tightly linked to socio-economic classes or strata, it does not provide increased exploratory power relative to Bourdieu's concepts of field and habitus which can be applied to fields that are not (only) defined in socio-economic terms. Moreover, Bourdieu's concept of field and habitus allows accessing the latent idea-contents 'contained' therein. And that really matters when searching for latent Kautilyan ideas in the field of popular politicizing in India.

The finding that the Indian people not only like to politicize but do so 'habitually' might at first appear rather banal. Not trivial is the question of the semiconscious, 'natural' perceptions, thought patterns, ideas and values that permeate popular politicizing. The assumption seems plausible that popular politicizing is done in the doxa mode, which Bourdieu defines as the 'logic of practice' in everyday life. When politicizing in the doxa mode, people inevitably draw on the ideas and values of the political field which are expressions of its internal logic and its ideational genesis. But the people don't do so discursively, i.e., they don't reflect upon these political ideas and values or their origins. Instead, they access these political ideas and values via metaphors, puns and thought-figures that cut through logically separate category levels. Politicizing in the doxa mode means economizing the intellectual effort: Political ideas and values are perceived as a matter of course and are not further problematized because they have been 'incorporated' in the habitus of the field of popular politicizing. This phenomenon is cogently described by Nehru in the *Discovery of India*. He reports about his political campaigning across rural India. In his speeches, Nehru addressed not only the oppressive social and economic conditions of the peasants but also 'high politics'—politics of the day as well as world political issues. He was surprised by the profound political understanding which he found among the rural masses. Nehru writes:

> Sometimes, as I reached a gathering, a great roar of welcome would greet me: Bharat Mata ki Jai - 'Victory to Mother India'. I would ask them unexpectedly what they meant by that cry, who was this Bharat Mata, Mother India, whose victory they wanted? *My*

> question would amuse them and surprise them. (Nehru 1981, 60, emphasis added)

For the Indian peasants, fighting and winning the national liberation struggle against British colonialism was a matter of course that needed no further explanation or justification. Now it was Nehru's turn to be surprised. In trying to understand what he had experienced, he points to the impressive 'background' of politico-cultural common sense among India's rural masses:

> [A] mixture of popular philosophy, tradition, history, myth, and legend, and it was not possible to draw a line between any of these. Even the entirely uneducated and illiterate shared this background [...]. Often I was surprised by some such *literary turn given by a group of villagers to a simple talk about present-day affairs*. (Ibid., 1981, 67, emphasis added)

Nehru contrasts his own discursive thinking with Indian peasants' political common sense that draws on a broad array of profound ideas but does not require discursive effort. Next, the question arises whether popular politicizing drawing on the melange of literary narrations, philosophy, traditions and myths, as described by Nehru, would also include Kautilyan ideas. Does the habitus of popular politicizing 'carry along' Kautilyan thought-figures? Several interviewees responded in the affirmative:

> You will go to some village, and you do not have to wait for long, *you will see the shadow of ancient Indian thinking in the villagers' behaviour*. Just wait another moment: *practices, rituals, reaction patterns. You cannot but recognize it: Oh, there is a Chanakyan strain in that* [...]. The pure expression of the tradition of any particular thinker or a school of thought is not discernible in the composite modern thinking of India. *But if there is one person whose continuous influence is the highest, it is Kautilya. Whether consciously or unconsciously, people are following his way of thinking—even if they are not aware of Kautilya's name.* (EI Ajit Doval,[17] emphasis added)

Bajpai has used the expression 'Kautilyan echoes', albeit with respect to the discourse in the Indian strategic community. Other interviewees, like the just cited Ajit Doval, do recognize 'Kautilyan echoes' in the everyday situation of popular politicizing. This is also the view of Shivshankar Menon who observes among *'common Indians'* a *'formative influence'* of Kautilyan thought, which however is mainly *'unconscious'* and *'instinctive'*: *'Kautilyan ideas [...] are part of the popular vocabulary and thinking on politics'* (Menon 2015b, xvii-xxix, emphasis added).

In line with Doval's and Menon's views, several interviewees stated that this political realism in the Kautilyan tradition features prominently in popular politicizing. Among the Indian population, a remarkable homogeneity of basic positions regarding key issues of 'high politics' can be observed—with respect to both domestic and foreign policy. Of course, political realism is not understood as a theoretical concept, nor does it imply explicit reference to Kautilya as its originator. Rather, political realism is the 'natural' attitude in the perception and assessment of political events. The focus on sober, pragmatic and 'hard' realpolitik, the interviewees argued, is the main feature of the political thought patterns among most Indian. The realist stance is largely independent of the political affiliations as well as socio-economic and educative status. The realist pattern is also not dependent on shifting political conjunctures but remarkably constant. Deviant attitudes among political-ideological or religious minority milieus do not tangibly impact the realist mainstream orientation.

Concerning the role of Indian media, which unquestionably do influence popular politicizing, the interviewees argued that they too are enfolded in the predominant realist pattern of perception and thought. Thus, the Indian media mainly 'ride out' the established trend rather than re-shaping the basic political dispositions of their recipients. That, of course, does not exclude occasional media hypes, notably pushing ultra-nationalism. Since the media mainly follow the firmly rooted core positions of popular politicizing, Indian 'public opinion' exhibits a high degree of consistency, if not inertia. Among the Indian people, the broad consensus on political realism in the Kautilyan tradition comprises the following core positions: the central role of the state, inviolability of sovereignty, raison d'état, enforcing state interests, power politics in the sense of highlighting 'hard' power, and also the acceptance of war as ultima ratio.

Kautilyan realism, the interviewees argued, is also a factor of influence in public opinion when it comes to negotiations and peaceful conflict resolution in domestic or foreign policy crises. In matters relating to the national interest, compromises would only be sought after one's own weakness had been overcome. Once a position of strength had been regained, compromise can be struck. As an example, the Kargil conflict in early summer 1999 was mentioned: Only after the infiltrated Pakistani troops had been militarily repulsed—without, however, going for a military counter-escalation—India did engage in political negotiations with Pakistan. This firm but balanced attitude of the Indian government had the full backing of the Indian population. The realist reaction pattern of the Indian population also applies to the field of internal security. In cases of separatist or other insurgencies, a tough response is demanded before turning to a negotiated solution—and Indian governments usually behave accordingly:

> I have been following these counterinsurgency operations for quite some time. Typically, at first the Indian state was brutal in terms of use of force when there was internal dissent; in the beginning, using massive force and zero tolerance. But when the realization dawned that these insurgents had a kind of moral legitimacy, which is why there was popular support for these movements, then the state shifted to the classic Kautilyan advice: you need to have negotiation. (EI Namrata Goswami)[18]

Among most Indians, it is not the power of the state that is feared but its weakness—internally and externally. Harsh criticism of the inefficiency and arbitrariness of state organs and political corruption is not directed against the state as institution. Strengthening of the power of the state is generally considered positive and desirable. Here, too, the people's understanding of the state is embedded in a realist tradition that goes back to the Kautilyan state conception.

Finally, the interviewees pointed to the broad appreciation of military power in India, even though, due to the *ahimsa* tradition, the Indian people have no militaristic proclivities. Yet Indians do have a realist view of the need for military power—primarily as deterrence, but also accepting war as last resort. Independent India has been involved in several wars: four wars against Pakistan in 1947–48, 1965, 1971 and 1999, the 1962 war with China and a number of smaller military conflicts like Goa 1961 or the Indian military intervention in Sri Lanka in the late 1980s. It should be noted that, except the Goa conflict, all wars were not started by India. Therefore all these military conflicts were seen as legitimate and firmly backed by the Indian population.

Despite India's enormous internal problems—notably poverty and lack of education—there is a broad consensus in supporting the armed forces. That backing also includes India's nuclear weapons arsenal. Ever since the early 1960s, a wide majority of Indians has endorsed the acquisition of nuclear weapons—as demonstrated by the great popular support for the nuclear weapon tests in 1998. Most Indians are proud that India has become a nuclear weapon state. In April 2012, the authors of this study witnessed the proud reaction of Indian students to the successful testing of 'Agni V'—India's first nuclear-capable intercontinental ballistic missile.[19] The Indian people's appreciation of military strength—without militarization of society, state and foreign policy—reflects a political paradigm that is grounded in the Kautilyan tradition of realism.

It might be argued that this basic pattern of political realism that permeates popular politicizing in India is not due to the endogenous Kautilyan tradition but simply an expression of postcolonial nationalism. Some authors, notably Elie Kedourie, have argued that Indian nationalism—as that of other 'young' nation states with colonial past—is merely a transplant from Europe: European nationalism was 'exported' to India and assimilated not only by the political elites but the population at large. In this perspective, Indians have succumbed to European-style nationalism, albeit spiced up with some endogenous traditions (cf. Kedourie 1970; Engelmeier 2009).

Surely, India's nationalist independence movement was also influenced by European nationalism. But Indian nationalism has always been a phenomenon sui generis. Indian nationalism is no ideological import from Europe peppered with Indian idiosyncrasies. Indian nationalism can be grasped with Lloyd and Susanne Hoeber Rudolph's concept of 'modernity of tradition' (1967, 3). The Indian struggle for independence started in 1857 with a popular armed uprising—what the British called the 'Indian Mutiny'. The actors of this insurgency were not inspired by European nationalism, which at that point of time wasn't yet an exportable commodity. The uprising was driven by ideas, values and symbols of the Indian tradition going back some three millennia. In the first half of twentieth century, the nationalist independence movement transformed into a politically potent mass movement precisely when Mahatma Gandhi re-connected it to the ideas, values and symbols of (ancient) Indian tradition. In that, Gandhi, Patel and Nehru fused the tradition of nonviolence going back to Buddha and Ashoka with the equally deep-rooted Kautilyan tradition of realist quest for power.

In summary, it can be stated: The basic pattern of political realism in everyday politicizing among the Indian people is significantly influenced, if not shaped, by Kautilyan thought. Political realism in the Kautilyan tradition is the key ideational ingredient in the habitus of politicizing Indians. Although Kautilya is mostly not mentioned at all, and if mentioned, that is mostly as metaphor, the latent presence of Kautilyan thought can be diagnosed in the popular politicizing of modern India.

7
KAUTILYA AND THE STRATEGIC CULTURE OF INDIA

7.1 THE CONCEPT OF STRATEGIC CULTURE

The concept of 'strategic culture' was developed in the late twentieth century when the bipolar world order began to be transcended by multipolarity in world politics.[1] The roots of this concept can be traced to the term 'political culture', which in turn is derived from the term 'civic culture' that was developed in the United States by Gabriel Almond and Sidney Verba in the early 1960s. In the late 1960s, Lucian Pye provided a still valid definition for the concept of political culture:

> Political Culture is the set of attitudes, beliefs, and sentiments which give order and meaning to a political process and which provide the underlying assumptions and rules that govern behavior in the political system. It encompasses both the political ideals and the operating norms of a polity. Political culture is thus the manifestation in aggregate form of the psychological and subjective dimensions of politics. A political culture is the product of both the collective history of a political system and the life histories of the members of that system, and thus it is rooted equally in public events and private experiences. (Pye 1968, in Sills 1968)

The concept of political culture is grounded in the basic, perhaps banal assumption that nation states—in addition to different ecological conditions and varying sociological characteristics—have also different historical experiences and thus different collective memories. Like culture as such, political culture exists only in the plural—as a diverse manifold of political cultures. The analytical usefulness of the concept of political culture is recognized in the Political Science literature. Harald Müller speaks of the 'political importance of the cultural factor' and the 'cultural shaping of state policy' (Müller 2008, 96f). Jepperson, Wendt and Katzenstein argue: 'Cultural environments affect, not only the incentives for different kinds of state behavior but thus the basic character of states—what we call state "identity"' (Jepperson et al. 1996, 33). Morgenthau's terms 'national character' and 'national morality' have significant affinity with the concept of political culture. Dirk Berg-Schlosser is right when he writes: 'In spite of many criticisms and varying emphasis, the concept of political culture is here to stay' (Berg-Schlosser 2010, 48).

Strategic culture can be understood as a subset of political culture—vectored on the field of security policy. As for culture as such and political culture, the principle of plurality applies equally to strategic culture—there are multiple and diverse strategic cultures. If one accepts the relationship of strategic culture to political culture, both of which are grounded in (a specific) culture, then, in turn, the above mentioned problematique of defining what 'culture' is comes into play. Therefore, in a study on Kautilya and Indian strategic culture, Rashed Uz Zaman warns that '[f]or any student of strategic studies, *the concept of strategic culture is as dangerous as an unmarked minefield on a dark night*' (Zaman 2009, 69, emphasis added). If we understand culture as the anthropological potential whose realization is bound by the given historical setting (cf. section B 2.1) and if we understand political culture in the sense of Lucian Pye, then, the term strategic culture refers to historically evolved perceptions, ideas and behaviour with respect to the internal and external security of a (particular) state.

For each state, its security has a 'strategic' quality because it relates to the threat of use of force or the actual use of force, thus bearing upon the most fundamental state interest—that of self-preservation. As stated by Weber, the capacity to employ physical violence constitutes the essence of the state. In other words: without the ability to use force, there is no sovereign state. When it comes to threats to the internal and external security of the state or, equally important, perceptions thereof, we enter the field where the actual use of force is most likely and, in fact, does occur most often. If the state's security has a strategic quality because it pertains to the use of force and thus (in certain circumstances) to the very existence of the state, Stuart Poore is right when he writes that the concept of strategic culture is 'considering the relevance of the "cultural context" in influencing strategic preferences' of a state (2003, 45). Thus, the concept of strategic culture assumes that the strategic policy thrust of different states is neither uniform nor the contingent result of ad hoc decisions.

Beyond the fundamental state interest of self-preservation, security is no objectively definable category because it is determined by the 'subjective' perception of actors. For one state, security may mean defensive preservation of the status quo, while another state may see its security only guaranteed by aggressive revisionism of the status quo. The respective 'subjective' perceptions of the state's security and the threats to it are shaped by attitudes and ideas which, in turn, have significantly been influenced, if not conditioned, by the culture and history of that state.

However, it is precisely this assumption that cultural and historical factors do significantly affect the security policy of a state that has been vigorously disputed in the Political Science sub-disciplines of International Relations (IR) and Security Studies. Culture and history are often considered to be negligible factors of influence in inter-state relations. Instead, it is claimed that all actors in the field of foreign and security policy follow the same, universal logic. A closer look, however, would rather diagnose that this assumption is based on 'ethnocentric universalism', which projects the patterns of perception, thought and behaviour in security policy prevailing in the hegemonic state (or political space) onto actors in the security field of other states with very different cultural backgrounds and historical experiences.

Starting in the late 1970s, some scholars in IR and Security Studies began to express doubts whether there really was a symmetry of perception, thought and action in military strategy between the United States and the Soviet Union. In view of the enormous differences in historical experience and culture between the two superpowers, the Soviet leadership might have other threat perceptions and reaction patterns than their American counterparts. Such questions gained particular (and existential) significance with respect to the nuclear-strategic postures of the two superpowers. Similar questions had already earlier come up with respect to the Vietnam War, where the asymmetry in military strategic thinking and behaviour between the Americans and Vietnamese had been evident.

With the end of the Cold War, the main theatres of military conflict shifted to the 'Global South', that is primarily Asia and Africa. The ideological premises of the East-West conflict—liberalism and capitalism versus communism—had both been an offspring of the Occidental cultural space. After the end of the Cold War, the template of the 'clash of civilizations' became fashionable. Irrespective of the shallowness of Samuel Huntington's construct, historical and cultural factors impacting security postures have gained much greater attention in the IR and Security Studies discourse since the 1990s. However, while the concept of strategic culture has gained increasing acceptance, the disciplinary debate over its definition and explanatory power has continued unabated.

The largely conformable definitions of strategic culture of Alastair Iain Johnston (1998), Alan Macmillan, Ben Booth and Russell Trood (1999), and Darryl Howlett (2006) can claim a certain representativeness within the discipline of Security Studies, and are conducive for examining the role of Kautilyan thought in Indian strategic culture:

> Strategic Culture is an integrated system of symbols (i.e. argumentation structures, languages, analogies, metaphors, etc.) that acts to establish pervasive and long-lasting grand strategic preferences by formulating concepts of the role and efficacy of military force in inter-state political affairs, and by clothing these conceptions with such an aura of factuality that the strategic preferences seem uniquely realistic and efficacious [...]. A strategic culture exists and persists if preference rankings are consistent across objects of analysis from deeply historical, formative periods up to the period of examination. (Johnston 1998, 36, 38)

> Strategic Culture is a distinctive and lasting set of beliefs, values and habits regarding the threat and use of force, which have their

roots in such fundamental influences as geopolitical setting, history and political culture. These beliefs, values and habits constitute a strategic culture which persists over time, and exerts some influence on the formation and execution of strategy. (Booth/Trood 1999, 8)

Strategic culture is an ensemble of shared beliefs, assumptions, and modes of behavior, derived from common experiences and accepted narratives (both oral and written), that shape collective identity and relationships to other groups, and which determine appropriate ends and means for achieving security objectives. (Howlett 2006, 3)

In these largely consonant definitions of strategic culture, there are two aspects of particular importance for our study: First, strategic culture is characterized by durability and inertia—a consequence of the longue durée-structure of culture. Secondly, strategic culture does not mean that cultural and historical factors determine the patterns of perception, thought and action with respect to the internal and external security of a state. Rather, strategic culture refers to specific dispositions and preferences in a state's security policy. Thus, it is a specific set of dispositions and a specific ranking of preferences that characterize the strategic culture of a state. In the strategic culture of state X, the disposition for risk avoidance may be predominant, while in the strategic culture of state Y the readiness to take risks in conflict situations may prevail. There may be a disposition for threatening military action early on or, conversely, for diplomatic conflict resolution. The preference may be using the intelligence service for covert operations or for relying on economic sanctions in exerting pressure on other states. The concept of strategic culture presupposes that such dispositions and preferences are not merely the product of situational 'pragmatism' but are conditioned by the respective state's culture and history.

When undertaking the empirical analysis of a state's strategic culture, the difficulty of operationalizing the concept of strategic culture becomes apparent. So it is not surprising that a large proportion of the literature on strategic culture is self-referential, that is, it mainly consists of intra-disciplinary disputes over theoretical and methodological issues.

A.I. Johnston has blisteringly criticized his academic colleagues for their supposed lack of methodological rigour with respect to strategic culture. However, in spite of his acrimony, he has developed a methodological approach for identifying a state's strategic culture that is very valuable. First, he asks the right questions:

> To what sources does one look as repositories or representations of strategic culture? From which time periods should these sources be taken? Why are certain historical periods considered formative sources of strategic culture and others not? How is strategic culture transmitted through time? (Johnston 1995, 39)

Johnston's answer to these questions is: Search the history of the respective state for early, formative texts dealing with strategic issues. These texts are then examined for patterns of strategic dispositions and preferences:

> It is important, therefore, that the analysis of strategic-cultural objects begins at the earliest accessible point in history, where strategic-cultural preference rankings may reasonably be expected to have emerged [...]. From this point one moves systematically forward. (Ibid., 50)

The key features extracted from politico-strategic texts of early periods of history are then compared with those of such texts of later historical periods—down to the present day. If a substantive congruence of strategic dispositions and preferences across time can be ascertained, a continuity of strategic thinking and thus the existence of a strategic culture can be assumed:

> [A] strategic culture can be said to exist and to persist if one finds consistency in preference rankings across objects of analysis from formative historical periods up to the period under examination [...]. The longer the period across which this congruence stretches, the more powerful and persistent the strategic culture. (Ibid., 48f)

In his book *Cultural Realism—Strategic Culture and Grand Strategy in Chinese History* (1998), Johnston goes back to the oldest available source material on strategic issues in China: *The Seven Military Classics*. From this starting point, he shows the continuity in strategic thinking and action during the subsequent periods of Chinese history. *The Seven Military Classics* are a collection of strategic writings from the second half of the first millennium BC, which includes *The Art of War* by Sun-Tzu. *The Seven Military Classics* are not exclusively confined to military strategy but also address some broader questions of statecraft. The compendium was canonized in the eleventh century AD by Emperor Shenzong and has since been mandatory reading for the Chinese state bureaucracy.

Using content analysis methodology, Johnston derives from *The Seven Military Classics* a clear preference for 'hard realpolitik' and a 'parabellum strategic culture' (Johnston 1998, 220). He then examines the role of this strategic paradigm in the diplomatic and military policies of the Ming Dynasty (1368–1644). He concludes that during the Ming period, roughly a millennium after the *The Seven Military Classics* had been written, the strategic culture of China was still characterized by 'hard realism'. In his essay *Cultural Realism and Strategy in Maoist China*, Johnston analyses several texts on strategic issues by Mao Tse-tung. Again he comes to the conclusion that even under Mao's communist regime, the strategy paradigm of *The Seven Military Classics* has remained efficacious in Chinese foreign and security policy:

> *Maoist strategic culture does indeed represent continuity with the past* [...]. The evidence suggests as well that China's conflict management behavior after 1949 has been generally consistent with hard realpolitik strategic axioms. The fact that these axioms have persisted into the 1980s and 1990s [...] suggests that China's realpolitik behavior *is rooted ideationally*. (Johnston 1996, 221, emphasis added)

In summary, it should be emphasized that Johnston's approach to identify the strategic culture of a country via endogenous, historically early and formative texts dealing with politico-strategic affairs is a very fruitful research avenue. It seems natural that this approach should apply also to the strategic culture of India—and that means taking Kautilya's

Arthashastra as the starting point for ascertaining its basic features. This view is also shared by Darryl Howlett:

> Many analysts regard key texts as important in informing actors of appropriate strategic thought and action. Traditional analyses of peace and conflict have long pointed to the influence of such texts throughout history and in different cultural settings. This may follow a historical trajectory from Sun Tzu, who was considered to have written the Art of War during the time of the warring states in ancient China, through *the writings of Kautilya in ancient India*, and into western understanding as a result of Thucydides' commentary on the Peloponnesian Wars and Clausewitz's writings on the nature of war as a result of observations of the Napoleonic period. (2005, emphasis added)

If a state's strategic culture is a culturally and historically conditioned framework of dispositions and preferences with respect to its security, it would be natural to apply Bourdieu's concepts of habitus and field to the concept of strategic culture. Bourdieu's description of habitus as the 'system of dispositions—a present past that tends to perpetuate itself into the future by reactivation in similarly structured practices' (1990, 54f) does apply to strategic culture. Interestingly enough, Johnston speaks of strategic cultures as 'states' body language' (1995, 40). Unfortunately, relating Bourdieu's habitus theory to the concept of strategic culture with its 'habitual' patterns of thought and behaviour in the context of a state's security policy is an intellectual enterprise yet to be undertaken.[2] That is the more regrettable as Bourdieu's habitus approach could help to identify the 'subtle distinctions' between states' strategic cultures.

To summarize, oriented on Bourdieu's concept of habitus, we define strategic culture as an ideational framework of (conscious and subconscious) dispositions and preferences in perception, thinking and behaviour with respect to the internal and external security of a state that has been structured by the culture and history of the respective state.

7.2 INDIAN STRATEGIC CULTURE

Before we turn to India's strategic culture and Kautilya's place therein, we have to address a somewhat odd question: Does India actually have a strategic culture? Not long ago there were renowned personalities in academia and even in the Indian strategic community who denied the existence of an Indian strategic culture (while accepting that other states do have one). And even at present there are scholars who acknowledge Indian strategic culture but firmly deny that early and formative politico-strategic texts emanating from India—like Kautilya's *Arthashastra*—have any influence on Indian strategic culture.

We begin with an eerie debate in the early 1990s. It centred on the controversy whether or not India ever had a tradition of strategic thought and thus a strategic culture. The debate was triggered in 1992, when George Tanham's study *Indian Strategic Thought: An Interpretive Essay* was published (Tanham 1992). The 92-page study was written on behalf of the U.S. Department of Defense and published by the American think tank RAND Corporation. The core thesis underlying Tanham's study is the supposed '*absence of strategic thinking*' in India—past and present (Tanham 1992, 50, emphasis added). In Tanham's view, India 'has produced little formal strategic thinking [...]. The lacunae in strategy and planning derive largely from India's historical and cultural development' (ibid.). Tanham offers three reasons for the alleged absence of strategic thinking:

- Throughout its history, India has lacked the experience of a pan-Indian state formation. Until the British Raj, the subcontinent was politically fragmented.
- Hindu culture lacks the concepts of time and history.
- The Hindu understanding of human life is marked by mysticism, spirituality and traditionalism.

Obviously, Tanham's characterization of Indian history and culture is essentialist and superficial, which is admitted even by those who accept his thesis of the 'absence' of strategic thinking (cf. Bajpai/Mattoo 1996). His stereotype imagination of Indian history and culture is for Tanham not only the reason for the lack of strategic tradition but also the cause of continuous military weakness and the inability to militarily resist foreign invaders. Having been serially defeated and conquered became an additional factor preventing Indian from strategic thinking and thus the formation of strategic traditions. So much for Tanham's thesis. But what about Kautilya?

Tanham mentions Kautilya a few times in footnotes referring to the *mandala* concept: 'Kautilya, a Brahmin adviser to the Mauryans, used the mandala concept in describing his work on the art of government' (Tanham 1992, 23). Tanham's superficial understanding of the *mandala* scheme as well as his incorrect or missing references would indicate that he probably never studied or even read the *Arthashastra*. Tanham's understanding seems to remain at the level of the Kautilya metaphor. Yet it's a mystery how the 'absence' of an Indian tradition of strategic thinking can be proclaimed without seriously studying Kautilya's *Arthashastra*. For Tanham, strategic thought started in India with the British Raj; therefore, pre-colonial strategic thought is irrelevant and can be ignored. With one notable exception, the interviewees firmly rejected Tanham's assertions on Indian strategic thought:

> Some of these American scholars have made the point that India lacks a strategic culture. I think that is not correct. Look at Kautilya some two thousand years ago. So I think Indian strategic culture was very much there. (El Satish Nambiar)[3]

In his essay *Of Oral Traditions and Ethnocentric Judgements*, W.P. Singh Sidhu has critically examined Tanham's study. He notes that the *Arthashastra* and other texts of formative influence on Indian strategic culture were primarily transmitted orally over more than two millennia. That great literary and scientific works should not have been transmitted in writing is obviously beyond the comprehension of Tanham (and most Westerners): 'And when there does not appear to be any document or physical evidence, the inclination is to assume that history was not "discovered" or *that strategy or doctrine "does not exist"*' (Sidhu 1996, 174, emphasis added).

Sidhu identifies two basic trends of strategic thought in India, both of which originate in antiquity: the idealist tradition, which goes back to Ashoka and leads to Gandhi, on the one hand, and the realist tradition that dates back to Kautilya, on the other hand. Sidhu criticizes Tanham's superficial treatment of Kautilya as typified by his reductionist understanding of *mandala*, and he wonders why Tanham ignores the timeless significance of the *shadgunya* approach for realist foreign policy.

> *Another obvious strand of Indian strategic thought, which has remained constant since the time of Chandragupta Maurya*, through even Gandhi's non-violence era and right till the present day (but has been mentioned only in passing in the [Tanham's] essay under review), *is the concept of realism. Clearly, it was not described as 'realism' by Kautilya, the official strategist for the Mauryan Empire, as for that matter by Gandhi or Nehru. Yet it is something more than evident in their writings and in their actions* [...]. The mistake most analysts make in interpreting the relevance of the *Arthashastra* is to study modern Indian policy in the specific context of the mandala concept [...]. This however, does not conform to the modern reality of India and its neighbors and shows the dangers of interpreting the *Arthashastra* narrowly [...]. The relevance of the *Arthashastra* is to be found in its broader and strategic philosophy. (Sidhu 1996, 175f, emphasis added)

In February 1994, a seminar on Tanham's thesis of the 'absence' of strategic thought in India was held in Delhi at the Institute for Defence Studies and Analyses (IDSA), at which Tanham was personally present. In 2005, K. Subrahmanyam, a leading Indian strategic expert and longtime head of IDSA, wrote the following about that seminar:

> Of the large number of retired defense and civilian officials and academics [at the seminar], *the majority contested his [Tanham's] thesis. Did not India have Chanakya as a strategic thinker? They asked. True indeed, but Chanakya lived some 23 centuries ago. What of the centuries since?* (Subrahmanyam/Malhotra 2005, 7, emphasis added)

Subrahmanyam admits that, with Kautilya, India did have an outstanding strategic thinker in ancient times, but he denies that Kautilya has exerted any tangible influence on Indian strategic thought. Thus, Subrahmanyam effectively endorsed Tanham's thesis that there is no tradition of strategic thought in India.

Eighteen years after this memorable seminar, when the expert interviews were conducted in the spring of 2012, Tanham's thesis and Subrahmanyam's tacit endorsement of it were past history. While Tanham has been dismissed altogether, some interviewees argued that Subrahmanyam had later mitigated his judgement on Kautilya's alleged irrelevance for India's strategic culture. In the same 2005 book in which he wrote about the 1994 'Tanham seminar', Subrahmanyam remarks: 'The tenets of our ancient wisdom [...] prescribe that in dealing with adversaries and friends a ruler should use all four aspects of strategy— sama, dhana, bheda, danda (engagement, buying off, dividing the enemies and force as the last resort)' (Subrahmanyam/Malhotra 2005, 25). The four *upaya*s to which Subrahmanyam refers here without, however, mentioning Kautilya are one of the key concept clusters of the *Arthashastra*. From the 1960s to about the turn of the century, Subrahmanyam was probably India's most influential strategic thinker. His dismissal of Kautilya's relevance for Indian strategic culture is indeed puzzling, and the expert interviews offered no satisfactory explanation of his attitude.

In 2006, fourteen years after Tanham's study, the U.S. Department of Defense commissioned another study on the same subject. Titled *India's Strategic Culture*, the study's author, Rodney W. Jones, comes to conclusions that are diametrically opposed to Tanham's. For Jones, India does have a distinct strategic culture and Kautilya is one of the essential components thereof:

> India's strategic culture is not monolithic, rather is mosaic-like, but as a composite is more distinct and coherent than that of most contemporary nation-states. This is due to its substantial continuity with the symbolism of pre-modern Indian state systems and threads of Hindu or Vedic civilization dating back several millennia [...]. It [Indian strategic culture] therefore draws on Chanakya's (Kautilya's)

> secular treatise, the *Arthashastra*, which closely parallels Niccolo Machiavelli's *The Prince*, as an exposition of monarchical statecraft, realpolitik in inter-state balances of power, and the practices of war and peace. (Jones 2006, 3, 8, emphasis added)

In 2012, the supposition that India does not possess an endogenous strategic tradition had evaporated in the strategic community. What most interviewees thought about Indian strategic culture is cogently summarized in a 2013 newspaper comment by Namrata Goswami:

> [S]trategic culture is an ideational milieu by which the members of the national strategic community form their strategic preferences with regard to the use and efficacy of military power in response to the threat environment. Each country has its own way to interpret, analyze and react to external opportunities and threats. *As a member of the Indian strategic community, let me assure you that we do have a strategic culture* where we closely assess the external environment and debate on the efficacy of the use of military power in addressing external threats. That India tends to give priority to dialogue over the use of military power in foreign policy does not mean it did not have a strategic culture; it just means that the strategic preferences are different from the normal understanding of how Great Powers behave. (Goswami 2013, emphasis added)

7.3 THE ROLE OF KAUTILYA IN THE ACADEMIC DISCOURSE ON INDIAN STRATEGIC CULTURE

Our investigation of Kautilya's role in Indian strategic culture draws primarily on the literature which contains a fair amount of research-relevant material. Statements on Kautilya and Indian strategic culture from the expert interviews are referenced only en passant because they essentially match the argumentation in the literature. The relatively extensive and detailed treatment of Kautilya's significance for Indian strategic culture in the Political Science literature and in other forms of scholarly discourse is per se remarkable and also further evidence for the explicit and discursive reference to Kautilya in India today. Thus, we gain additional empirical corroboration of the manifest presence of Kautilyan thought in modern India.

The Political Science discourse about Indian strategic culture has evolved since the turn of the millennium. In most of the studies on the subject, Kautilya is considered a key factor of influence in Indian strategic culture, although the relative weight given to Kautilyan thought vis-à-vis other ideational factors differs among authors. In the 2004 edited volume *Neorealism versus Strategic Culture* (Glenn et al. 2004), Marcus Kim submits an analysis of Indian strategic culture. He argues that the Indian understanding of strategic affairs is primarily based on endogenous politico-cultural resources:

> *The roots of India's strategic thought lie in its ancient history.* It is with the formation of Chandragupta's Maurya [Empire] that the collective 'Indian' identity started to emerge. Alongside this development, the ideational origins of India's strategic thought were further advanced through the Vedic literature and especially through the *Mahabharata*. (Kim 2004, 99, emphasis added)

Kim does not see modern Indian nationalism as an ideological import from the West but as robustly anchored in India's intellectual history. Since more than two thousand years, India has a geo-cultural identity strong enough to withstand all foreign invasions and occupations. The Maurya Empire, with its central figures Chandragupta Maurya, Ashoka and Kautilya, remains an essential reference for Indian strategic thinking. Also, the strategic practices of the Mughal Empire were absorbed into Indian strategic culture, and the Mughal rulers assimilated the antecedent politico-cultural traditions of India. Such 're-use' of endogenous resources was interrupted by the British colonial power which transformed India considerably in political and institutional terms. But, emphasizes Kim, 'the ideology that dominated [Indian politics] from the time of independence had its origins in India's ancient culture and history' (2004, 86).

According to Kim, Indian strategic culture rests on two ideational pillars: on the one hand, Kautilya's *Arthashastra*, and on the other hand, the ideas of Gandhi which, in turn, have been influenced by the philosophical and religious thought of the Vedas, Buddhism and Jainism. While Kautilya's political thought is primarily rational, pragmatic and strategic, there is also a normative dimension, *rajadharma*: the duty of the king to secure the welfare of the people. In contrast, the nature of Gandhi's ideas is spiritualistic and ethical—*ahimsa* occupying the central place. Gandhi does not see the state as a political institution exercising power internally and externally but as a self-governing community (*swaraj*) of truth-seeking (*satya*) and *dharma*-aspiring people. However, Gandhi did not exclude the use of force under certain condition like to defending the dignity and honour of a person or a community.

> If Kautilya contributed the bases of political rationalism to the dynamics of modern Indian politics, Gandhi reinforced the moral logic that has existed for centuries [...]. *The Kautilyan and Gandhian ideas are 'strategic' in the sense that they have existed and influenced, through oral tradition and texts, Indian politics for almost three millennia. In this respect, these ideas have become integral part of the cultural context of Indian political and strategic thinking* [...] [T]he Kautilyan sense of power and interest for both the glory and well-being of the nation has also been reflected in the policies adopted. Indian strategic culture thus entails a degree of flexibility in the sense that by nature and over time it is adaptable to new ideas and circumstances [...]. This conflict of ideas still exists between the Gandhian and Kautilyan traditions. (Kim 2004, 93, 97, emphasis added)

Because Indian strategic culture can draw on endogenous ideational resources of which Kautilyan and Gandhian thought are by far the most important, Kim thinks that Indian strategic thinking does not depend on the import of Western ideas—although there are such influences, too. Indian strategic culture has shown a great adaptability with respect to political, economic and technological change—without, however, losing its inner characteristics. That, argues Kim, is evident in relation to the nuclear armament of India: 'In India's nuclear development, a culture of self-reliance is in evidence [...]. *With reference to the role of its nuclear weapons*, there exist *Kautilya's political rationalism* and the striving for a sense of "greatness"' (Kim 2004, 97, emphasis added). In sum, Kim argues convincingly that Indian strategic culture is the outgrowth of two traditions: Kautilyan-realist and Gandhian-idealist. Kim assigns to Kautilya's *Arthashastra* a key role in shaping the strategic culture of India which follows from the fact 'that *India had a strategic conception that predated much of Western thinking in that area*' (ibid., 99, emphasis added).

Teaching at the University of Dhaka (Bangladesh), Rashed uz Zaman has examined Kautilya's significance for the strategic culture of India in his essay *Kautilya: The Indian Strategic Thinker and Indian Strategic Culture* (Zaman 2006). Like Kim, Zaman sees a variety of ideational factors influencing Indian strategic culture; however, he attaches greater weight to Kautilya than Kim does.

> Indian strategic culture has manifold influences and one such is the thinker Kautilya [...]. [H]is ideas are important for the understanding of Indian strategic culture [...]. *We propose that, amongst other influencing factors, Indian strategic culture is influenced by the ideas of Kautilya codified in his book The Arthashastra*. (Zaman 2006, 231f, emphasis added)

A large part of Zaman's essay is taken up by a rather detailed exposition of the foreign policy theorems in Kautilya's *Arthashastra*: the concepts of *vijigishu/chakravartin*, *matsya-nyaya*, *mandala*, *shadgunya* and *upayas*. Zaman rejects the claim that India has traditionally been committed to non-violence and peaceful conflict resolution. He takes on Ashoka to prove his point. Ashoka led a particularly cruel war of aggression against the state of Kalinga (today's Orissa) to enlarge the Maurya Empire. After winning this war, Ashoka converted to Buddhism and proclaimed *ahimsa* as the guiding principle of his politics. However, Ashoka never thought of returning to the status quo ante or dissolving the armed forces of the Maurya Empire. 'Ashoka by no means gave up his imperial ambitions'; '*the teachings of Kautilya were never far from the mind of the emperor*' (Zaman 2006, 239, emphasis added).

The fixation on the (supposed) idealism of Buddha and Ashoka concealed the political and strategic Sanskrit literature which, according to Zaman, 'bear[s] testimony to the incorrigible militarism of the Hindus and reminds us that few communities have been more warlike and fond of bloodshed' (Zaman 2006, 240). Such stereotypical attributions are not rare to find among Muslim authors from Pakistan and Bangladesh (cf. Kiessling 2011; Hali 1999; Niaz 2008, 2013). For Zaman, Kautilyan thought was efficacious in India ever since the *Arthashastra* was written, but it is in modern, independent India that Kautilyan influence is stronger than ever.

> Thus, ideas espoused by Kautilya, especially the concept of realism, not only were relevant for Chandragupta Maurya but also for people such as Mahatma Gandhi or Jawaharlal Nehru [...] [which does] strengthen the conviction that *Kautilya's ideas indeed are relevant in today's India* [...] [W]hile medieval India certainly was influenced by Kautilyan ideas, *it is really in independent India that we see the implementation of Kautilyan policies*. (Zaman 2006, 240f, emphasis added)

Although explicit references to Kautilya have been rare in post-Independence Indian politics, as Zaman writes, Nehru's foreign policy shows that the Kautilyan *mandala* concept had been adopted: conflictual relations with the direct neighbours Pakistan and China but friendly relations with indirect neighbours such as the Soviet Union, Afghanistan or Vietnam. Zaman quotes independent India's first Foreign Secretary, K.P.S. Menon, saying: '[The] realism of Kautilya is a useful corrective to our idealism in international politics' (ibid.).[4] On the diplomatic stage, Nehru presented himself as a proponent of peaceful conflict resolution, but he did not hesitate to use military force, Zaman argues. Admittedly, Nehru subordinated military spending to economic development; nevertheless, in 1962 India had the largest navy and air force of all countries bordering the Indian Ocean and one of the largest land armies of the world. Thereafter, the Indian arms build-up accelerated further. Zaman does not see Nehru's non-alignment policy as a manifestation of an idealist foreign policy but, quite the contrary, as Kautilyan realism:

> It [Nehruvian nonalignment] was a strategy to use diplomatic or, when the situation permitted, military means to gain influence despite material weakness. Simply put, nonalignment was a low risk strategy to gain influence on the cheap [...]. *The Kautilyan brand of realism seems to pervade the Indian policy of nonalignment*, which has been a cornerstone of Indian foreign and security policy since India's independence. (Zaman 2006, 242, emphasis added)

Finally, Zaman affirms his view that, after the heyday of non-alignment during the Cold War, Indian foreign and security policy has firmly remained under the influence of Kautilyan realism. He sums up his findings on Kautilya's importance for India's strategic culture as follows:

> Under such changed [post-Cold War] circumstances, does it make sense to explore the *Arthashastra* for understanding of Indian culture strategic? For the reasons described herein, this article argues it does [...]. *The Arthashastra is important to understanding Indian strategic culture*. It is not the sole work shaping India's strategic behavior, but is an important one and, accordingly, should be studied [...]. Thus, *a thorough understanding of Kautilya's ideas is useful in deciphering Indian strategic culture*. (Zaman 2006, 244, emphasis added)

Zaman is a political scientist from Bangladesh—a country with an ambivalent attitude towards India. Bangladesh owes its existence as a state to India's military intervention in East Pakistan in 1971. Since then, however, relations between the two neighbours have been rather precarious. Correspondingly, Zaman's critical and distanced attitude towards India is evident in his essay. However, despite or maybe because of that, the essay is characterized by convincing argumentation as far as Kautilya's significance for Indian strategic culture is concerned.

Both Kim and Zaman come to the same findings: first, Indian strategic culture is an undeniable fact, and, secondly, Kautilyan thought is an essential source and component of Indian strategic culture. In contrast to Kim, Zaman rates Kautilyan realism as the dominant factor in Indian strategic culture. While the arguments and conclusions of both authors are mostly sound and coherent, they both back them up by drawing on relatively few explicit references to Kautilya (and other politico-strategic resources) by political, strategic and academic actors in India. Regrettably, the latent influence of Kautilyan thought on Indian strategic culture remains completely factored out.

In his essay *Indian Strategic Culture*, Kanti Bajpai distinguishes two dimensions of strategic culture: on the one hand, central, paradigmatic assumptions about national security, on the other hand, grand strategy, i.e., operational concepts and strategies that are derived from these paradigmatic assumptions (cf. Bajpai 2003). Because there is a characteristic ensemble of basic assumptions and dispositions in the Indian strategic community, Bajpai argues, Indian strategic culture is a fact. Referencing A. I. Johnston, he states that the safest way to identify the basic patterns of thought and behaviour that make up a strategic culture is the analysis of politico-strategic texts. However, Bajpai makes a sharp deviation from Johnston—both in conceptual and methodological terms—in that he is exclusively concerned with contemporary authors, actors and texts related to foreign and security policy. He asserts that only in the contemporary context it is possible to analyse and understand Indian strategic culture. Bajpai justifies his approach by claiming that India does not have a canon of ancient and classical strategic texts comparable to the Chinese *Seven Military Classics*, writing: 'Indians have not recorded their strategic thinking in written texts, the only exception being the ancient classic, Arthasastra [...]. *[In India] there are no established canonical texts except for the Arthasastra*' (Bajpai 2003, 246f, emphasis added).

Bajpai's argumentation is puzzling, to say the least. If Kautilya were India's one and only outstanding strategic thinker and the *Arthashastra* its one and only classical strategic text, why should Kautilya's *Arthashastra* be neglected as source and factor of influence of Indian strategic culture? Yet, strangely enough, that is exactly what Bajpai does.

Bajpai argues against overemphasizing the role of military power in the context of strategic culture and grand strategy and urges the inclusion of internal security as well as economic, cultural and other non-military factors. In view of the fact that the *Arthashastra* does feature a grand strategy approach, one would think that Bajpai might revise his exclusion of Kautilya as a factor of the ideational genesis of India's strategic culture. But when it comes to Kautilya, Bajpai is obstinate. He twists his previous line of argumentation by claiming that outstanding military-strategic texts are the precondition for Johnston's historical-genetic approach to strategic culture. And because there are no classical Indian texts on military strategy, except the *Arthashastra*, Johnston's approach is not valid for Indian strategic culture: 'There are no ancient "military" classics [in India] as far as we know apart from Kautilya's *Arthasastra*. *As for the Arthasastra, it does not have the status of the Western or Chinese military classics. It would be hard to show, for instance, that its tenets were widely known historically*' (Bajpai 2003, 250, emphasis added).

Again, Bajpai's argumentation is really perplexing. Since he cannot deny that military-strategic issues are extensively treated in the *Arthashastra* which thus can be characterized as an 'ancient military classic', Bajpai claims that the *Arthashastra* has inferior status relative to European and Asian military-strategic classics. True or not, such status would be irrelevant for Kautilya's influence on Indian strategic culture. Lastly, Bajpai claims—as Subrahmanyam had done in 1994—that knowledge about the tenets of the *Arthashastra* has vanished in the course of history. Since Kautilya had allegedly been forgotten, he would disqualify it as a source and factor of influence of Indian strategic culture.

Thus Bajpai turns away from the past and Kautilya's *Arthashastra* and focuses on the present to where he thinks the true sources and expressions of India's strategic culture are to be found. His central thesis is that Indian strategic culture is shaped by three contemporary strategic schools of thought: 'Nehruvianism', 'neoliberalism' and 'hyperrealism': 'I argue that Indian strategic culture can be understood in terms of an identifiable set of basic assumptions about the nature of international relations, some are shared between the three schools and some are not' (Bajpai 2003, 246). The intersection of the basic positions of the three schools forms the foundation of Indian strategic culture; its actual shape depends on a fluid mix of the three schools' non-convergent positions which, in turn, depend on the relative weight of the three schools at the given point of time. The ideational genesis of these three schools of thought seems not to interest Bajpai.

What really matters for our study is the role played by Kautilyan thought in Indian strategic culture. With respect to Bajpai's analysis of Indian strategic culture, our finding is that he does refer to Kautilya but, at the same time, tries hard to demonstrate his supposed irrelevance for Indian strategic culture. In the preface to a new edition of his essay *Indian Strategic Culture*, Bajpai reiterates his twisted arguments as to why Kautilya's *Arthashastra* must not be considered a component of India's strategic culture (cf. Bajpai/Pant 2013).

> Where might strategic ideas and strategic culture come from? In the case of India, we could begin with antiquity or some classical period. Is there a clearly identifiable canonical text that has had lasting influence? Some would argue that the Hindu epics—the *Ramayana*, *Mahabharata* and *Bhagavad Gita*—constitute the canonical texts of antiquity. In addition, there are the Vedas, Upanishads, Puranas, the Laws of Manu, the Sutras, Vedanta, and Dharma Shastras, amongst others. Perhaps the most often cited as relevant to discussions of strategic thought is Kautilya's *Arthashastra*. *The problem here is that it is almost impossible to show that these various texts have any valence amongst those who think about national strategy.* Although the epics are transmitted orally amongst Hindus and therefore have the quality of influential, 'living' texts, it is hard to claim this for any of the others. *Very few Indians of any social, religious, or caste background are familiar with these other texts: such as the Arthashastra. It is doubtful that elite Indians also know much about them.* (Bajpai/Pant 2013, 4, emphasis added)

This quote corresponds essentially to what Bajpai said in the expert interview about Kautilya's relevance in modern India: Because there is no knowledge of the *Arthashastra* in the strategic community of today's India, Kautilya is no factor of influence for Indian political discourse.

Lastly, Bajpai's complex relation to Kautilya is not likely to end soon: He comes back to him again and again—only to turn away from him and disparage the *Arthashastra* by proclaiming that Kautilya is no match for Machiavelli. The following quote of Bajpai's introduction of the edited volume *India's Grand Strategy - History, Theory, Cases*, written in 2014, illustrates the point:

> Before we get to the essays in this section, *it is worth saying a word on some obvious omissions in the volume. A fairly glaring one is Kautilya and his Arthashastra, the great Indian book on statecraft. Kautilya's work is often cited as a key instance of Indian strategic thinking that ranks with Machiavelli's The Prince. Whether it has that status is an open question. Our sense is that it does not do so.* While there are certainly some maxims from it that have almost canonical status, it is a text that has largely been caricatured. Understanding of the text is not deep in India. It is most likely taught in the military academies of India, but there is little Indian reflection on it, and the text does not seem to have been deeply internalized by Indian leaders, officials and military officers. (Bajpai et al. 2014, 10, emphasis added)

Bharat Karnad has not written a monograph on Indian strategic culture, but in his book *Nuclear Weapons and Indian Security: The Realist Foundations of Strategy* he spells out his understanding of India's strategic culture (Karnad 2002). Like Kim, Karnad sees Indian strategic culture as a configuration of opposing strategic traditions: on the one hand, 'machtpolitik' or power politics and political realism and, on the other hand, 'moralpolitik' or pacifist idealism. For Karnad, India's original strategic tradition is power politics which goes back to the Vedic period and permeates the classical Sanskrit texts. The opposing tendency of 'moral politics' set in with the rise of Buddhism and Jainism and later post-classical Hinduism adapted to their pacifist and idealist ideas.

Karnad draws on Nehru's metaphor of 'palimpsest' to describe Indian strategic culture: In the course of Indian history, the tradition of power politics was frequently 'overwritten' by 'moralpolitik', but the original tradition never lost traction and reasserted itself time and again: 'Machtpolitik in the Indian mind has perpetuated at the grassroots level using the classical methods of transmission in an oral culture' (Karnad

2002, 27). For him, it is the realist tradition of power politics that has shaped Indian strategic culture the most:

> [A]ncient Indian politico-military thought [...] had a policy slant, as if first passed through a fine sieve of pragmatic realism. There is nothing elsewhere [in the world] of comparable vintage, certainly nothing with this vision, complexity and practical value [...]. These politico-military ideas have evolved over time, reforming gradually. But the change in emphasis in this or that aspect of policy and of instrument of state *did not disrupt the basic framework and contours of the policy prescriptions which paid premium on armed might and its considered use.* (Karnad 2002, 3, 6, emphasis added)

Realistic politico-strategic thought originating in ancient India is of undiminished importance for the strategic culture of contemporary India. Therefore, the supposition of Tanham and others that India lacks an efficacious tradition of strategic thought and behaviour is utterly untenable:

> [T]he rich Indian strategic literature of yore and its current relevance: it helps us leap several Ages by hinting at the resonance between the ancient Indian system of war [...] and the modern international reality [...]. *At the very least, the ancient Hindu texts on strategy and statecraft provide the context in which to relate to the present day development of the Indian nuclear weapons, longrange military capabilities and related policies. And, in a major way, they undermine the notion popularized in the 1990s, which has since become a cliché, that India's strategic culture and thought are distinguished by their absence.* (Karnad 2002, 26, emphasis added)

From Karnad's point of view, Kautilya is of paramount importance for the realist tradition and strategic culture in India: the *Arthashastra* is '*the single most comprehensive tome on statecraft*' (Karnad 2002, 4), and Kautilya '*refined the traditional thinking to produce his classic text on realpolitik*' (Karnad 2002, 10, emphasis added). Karnad comes to this assessment even though he is of the opinion that Kautilya draws mostly on antecedent politico-strategic thought in ancient India.

The Kautilyan approach to foreign policy is dynamic, Karnad argues, because it is the duty of the ruler to set his sights high. He must set new objectives for the state and forcefully implement them, instead of being satisfied with the status quo. However, Kautilya did not advocate political and/or military adventurism. Instead, he considered use of force only as last resort. His insistence on the primacy of political over military objectives and the careful assessment of the situation anticipates Clausewitzian thinking. In Karnad's view, the continuing impact of Kautilyan realism finds its clearest expression in Nehru's grand strategy. The careful analysis of Nehru's actual policies provides an unique insight into the realist foundations of Indian strategic culture:

> The essentially *ultra-realist Nehru* has been lost in the mist of his own writings and speeches, which feature grand and evocative language about India's 'tradition of non-violence', its human mission in the world, of 'Gandhian' values the countryside represents, etc. It is another matter that such rhetoric shielded *the more down-to-earth policy he actually practised*. (Karnad 2002, 167, emphasis added)

Nehru's policy of non-alignment was the application of the ancient Indian strategic principle of *asana*: neutrality vis-à-vis two similarly strong powers. *Asana* is the third method of foreign policy in Kautilya's *shadgunya* cluster. *Asana* is not an end in itself but a well thought-out policy that takes one's own relative weakness into account and provides the latitude for building up one's own strength. In the expert interview, Karnad had illustrated the realist gist of Nehru's non-alignment strategy with a narrative from the *Panchatantra* (cf. B 6.4). Anchored in the Kautilyan tradition of realism, Nehru created the economic and technological basis that would make India a great power in world politics. In that, the decisive factor was the build-up of India's nuclear capabilities which Nehru drove forth in close collaboration with Homi Bhabha. Although Nehru did not directly aim at nuclear armament, he made India a 'virtual nuclear power' (cf. B 4.4.2).

For Karnad, another central piece of evidence for the continuing impact of the realist tradition, are the nuclear weapon tests in the year

1998 through which India made itself a nuclear weapon state. The nuclear tests and the subsequent build up of nuclear forces on land, sea and air make abundantly clear that the realist dimension of Indian strategic culture is ultimately decisive.

Some of Karnad's positions have been criticized by other members of the strategic community. Nevertheless, Karnad's main line of argument is conclusive: There is a deep-rooted tradition of politico-strategic realism in India that goes back to the Vedic period. In a systematic and scholarly fashion, Kautilya has codified the idea-contents of this realist tradition in the *Arthashastra*. And, this politico-strategic realism is the dominant feature of Indian strategic culture.

We turn now turn to authors who investigate the characteristic patterns of thought and behaviour of Indian foreign and security policy, but do not use the term strategic culture. Instead, they more generally speak of 'traditions' or specific constellations of 'values and norms' that underlie Indian foreign and security policy. And, occasionally, the term 'foreign policy culture' of India is used. However, the meaning of such terminology is roughly comparable to that of strategic culture because the characteristic dispositions and preferences of Indian foreign and security policy are traced to the classical sources of strategic thought in ancient India—including, notably, to Kautilya.

J. N. Dixit was an Indian diplomat and Foreign Secretary; from 2004 until his death in 2005, he was National Security Adviser. In 2003, Dixit published his book *India's Foreign Policy 1947–2003*, which is considered the standard work on the foreign policy of Independent India. Dixit writes that independent India could draw on a consolidated identity as a 'collective self'—i.e., its national identity did not have to be created anew with state formation in 1947. A major source of Indian identity is the collective pride in the civilizational status and the political, economic and military might of the Indian empires of pre-modern times. The great cultural figures and achievements of Indian antiquity have always been present among the people and elites, Dixit argues. And the same applies to the politico-strategic thinkers and their classical works, notably the *Arthashastra*. Several interviewees pointed to the following text passage in Dixit's book on the history of India's foreign policy:

While assessing the twin dimensions of self-confidence on the one hand and imperfect comprehension of realpolitik characterizing India's foreign policy in the initial stages after independence on the other, it would be relevant to speculate on the deeper philosophical underpinnings of such policy in terms of civilizational history. *India's foreign policy was governed perhaps by two schools of thought down the centuries going back almost to the 4th century BC.*

One school of thought (or orientation) was articulated in legendary terms by Shakuni (a character in the epic *Mahabharata* known for his expertise with dice) and in terms of recorded history by Chanakya, the great political mentor of, and minister during the reign of Emperor Chandragupta Maurya. Using power as an instrumentality to further one's objectives and to resort to stratagems and conspiratorial measures to further one's political interests was considered a necessity by these historical figures [...]. Our militant and aggressive nationalism of the late 19th and early 20th centuries *descended from the Chanakyan school of thought*, whereas the moderate, rational and non-violent orientation of Indian nationalism and the Indian freedom struggle originated in the teachings of Buddha and his successors—like Emperor Ashoka.

It is very important to note however *the moderate and rational approach to politics and inter-state relations* in each stage of the evolution of Indian history as an independent political entity followed a process of political consolidation which *required the application of concepts and prescriptions of Chanakya who pre-dated Machiavelli nearly 2000 years. (Chanakya's teachings in statecraft could have taught Machiavelli a lesson or two.* (Dixit 2003, 24f, emphasis added)

Like most other authors addressing the basic features of Indian foreign and security policy, Dixit too propounds a genetically-evolved twin constellation of the realist tradition coming from Kautilya and the idealist tradition that dates back to the Buddha and Ashoka. In addition, two aspects in this quote by Dixit are remarkable. First, he refers to Kautilyan thought as one of the 'philosophical underpinnings' of independent

India's foreign policy stance. Secondly, he presents Kautilya as an extraordinary strategic thinker, who not only preceded Machiavelli by many centuries but is intellectually superior to him. It is also noteworthy that Dixit locates the Kautilyan realist and the idealist traditions in the *'collective subconscious'* of Indians (Dixit 2004, 39, emphasis added; cf. B 6.1). Although Dixit does not elaborate on this thought-figure, it can be understood as an indication of the latent presence of Kautilyan thought in the strategic culture of India.

In the expert interviews, it was stressed that Dixit not only possessed a deep theoretical understanding of Kautilya's *Arthashastra* but had operationally implemented Kautilyan concepts in India's foreign and security policy. Thus, Dixit 'personifies' the presence of Kautilyan thought in India's strategic culture as well as operational foreign policy:

> J. N. Dixit was one of the most influential Foreign Secretaries India ever had. *And he was the man who did follow the dictions of Kautilya [...].* Dixit is clearly veering towards the Kautilyan tradition. Look at his lectures, his articles—he has written a lot more than that book on the history of Indian foreign policy. I had the fortune to listen to him when he gave courses at JNU. *Dixit surely veers toward the Kautilyan tradition.* His argument is that India needs to have the economic hard power in very material terms to be able to sustain its military capability—*which is what Kautilya said.* India must have very strong and capable intelligence agencies. India needs to be very good in terms of technology, advanced technology. *All in the Kautilyan tradition.* (EI Namrata Goswami,[5] emphasis added)

Political scientist (and formerly Reader at Delhi University) V.N. Khanna, mostly shares Dixit's conclusions with respect to the basic underpinnings of Indian foreign policy. In his book, *Foreign Policy of India*, Khanna writes:

> India has the heritage of an ancient civilization and culture. The foreign policy that India formulated after independence reflected our culture and political tradition. *Our foreign policy makers had*

before them the teachings of Kautilya, the realist, who had recognized war as an important instrument of power and foreign policy. They were also impressed by the Buddhist traditions of Ashoka the Great, who advocated peace, freedom and equality. (1997, 13, emphasis added)

The dual nature of the foundations of India's foreign policy is also diagnosed by Arndt Michael, who investigates Indian foreign policy with regard to regional multilateralism in South Asia (2008). He uses the term 'foreign policy culture' that is grounded in endogenous ideas, values and traditions: '*India follows a unique foreign policy*. In her foreign policy conduct, India possesses certain idiosyncrasies, what in short can be called the "Indian way", *with her own distinct traditions and objectives*' (Michael 2008, 112, emphasis added). The central feature of Indian foreign policy culture is the focus on cultural and historical continuity, Michael argues. Within this tradition-oriented self-conception of India's foreign policy, there are two conflicting currents that are always matched anew— Kautilyan realism and idealism going back to Buddha and Ashoka:

> The traditional values of India's foreign policy can be traced back to ancient scriptures like the Vedas, the *Arthashastra*, the *Manu-smriti* or the *Mahabharata*. India possesses the heritage of an ancient civilization and culture, yet this culture is full of inner contradictions and opposing ideas which necessitated that conflicting strands of normative standards, ideals and ethics had to be reconciled, with one or the other prevailing at times. On the one hand, there were *the teachings of Kautilya (3rd century BC), the 'first political realist,'* recognizing war and practically every means available as an important instrument of power and foreign policy. On the other hand, the politicians who formulated the foreign policy were guided by the Buddhist emperor Ashoka, who advocated peace, freedom and equality, and of course by the teachings of Mahatma Gandhi. (Michael 2008 79f, emphasis added)

Michael examines in detail the central thought-figures of both dimensions of India's foreign policy. With respect to the idealist dimension, they are: tolerance, the equal valuation of means and ends and the *ahimsa* principle; in the dimension of Kautilyan realism: the concepts of the seven *prakriti, matsya-nyaya, mandala, shadgunya* and the four *upaya*s. He also addresses Nehru's treatment of Kautilya in the *Discovery of India*. Michael's conclusions regarding Kautilya's significance in Indian foreign policy are clear enough:

> Kautilya and the Arthashastra are inextricably linked with India's foreign policy culture. The *Arthashastra* has served as a manual of statecraft which influenced generations of Indian thinkers and politicians […]. The ancient 'Kautilyan realism' forms an important pillar of India's foreign policy culture. (Michael 2008, 90, 99, emphasis added)

7.4 KAUTILYA AND INDIAN STRATEGIC CULTURE IN THE POLITICAL DISCOURSE

In the last segment of this section dealing with Kautilya's role in Indian strategic culture, we report on two figures of the Indian strategic community who held very senior positions in government: Jaswant Singh and Shivshankar Menon. Both have written and lectured about India's strategic culture and Kautilya's place therein. However, they expressed their views on Indian strategic culture in contexts that are rather political than strictly academic.

From 1998 to 2002, Jaswant Singh was India's Foreign Minister in the government of A.B. Vajpayee and, during 2000–1, also Defense Minister. During 2004–9, he was the leader of the opposition Bharatiya Janata Party (BJP) in the Indian Parliament (Lok Sabha). Prior to his political career, Singh was an officer in the Indian Army.

In 1999, Singh published his book *Defending India*, which is generally seen as a reverse image of 'Nehruvianism' in the realms of Indian foreign and security policy—and probably was meant exactly to be that way. The first chapter deals with the question of India's strategic culture. J. Singh presents several definitions of strategic culture, including that of A. I. Johnston. His own conception of strategic culture is focused on the term 'state power' which subsumes military power, diplomacy, economics, the power of ideas and the power of example. Then he writes: 'In our search for its strategic culture, the origins of the cultural impulses of India are the first building block [...]. Indian culture and Indian society are at the core of the Indian nation. *Thus Hinduism*' (J. Singh 1999, 4, emphasis added).

The equation of the structurally pluralist Indian culture with 'Hinduism' is puzzling, to say the least. Thus, Singh's concept of strategic culture acquires an essentialist connotation. While he admits that Indian strategic culture has been decisively influenced by Kautilya, it seems that he feels not at ease with him—maybe the cause of this distance is Kautilya's secularism. In any case, while he states that Indian strategic culture has absorbed Kautilyan thought, he sees this influence as problematic, if not outright negative.

Singh associates Kautilyan thought with a fixation on internal security and an overemphasis of the secret service. Moreover, historically, Kautilyan thought has concentrated India's strategic outlook on conflicts within the subcontinent—instead of addressing competing and hostile powers beyond its borders. Therefore the repulsion of foreign invaders had failed so often in India's history. In effect, J. Singh blames Kautilyan thought for these political and strategic failures—without, however, explicitly saying so. The clearest sign for his inner distance to Kautilya is the fact that, except internal security, Singh does not mention any of the *Arthashastra*'s key concept clusters—notably the *saptanga* or *shadgunya* theories which would be most relevant for India's strategic culture and foreign policy.

Singh's book creates the impression that the concepts he views as best suited to serve India's strategic interests were generated during the British colonial period. Consequently, British strategic thinking has deservedly become a major influence on Indian strategic culture. Regarding the weight that Singh attributes to British strategic thought, the following observation by C. Raja Mohan might be relevant:

> For sections of the Indian foreign policy elite who have long dreamed of a powerful role for India in its surrounding regions,

Curzon[6] *remains a source of strategic inspiration* [...]. *Jaswant Singh, India's external affairs minister from 1998 to 2002, belongs to the Curzonian school* in defining India's role in its neighborhood. He is sharply critical of the failure of Jawaharlal Nehru in creating a strategic culture suited to its geographic requirements. (Mohan 2003, 204, 205, emphasis added)

Following his discussion of the negatively connoted Kautilyan factor of influence and the positively connoted British factor of influence in Indian strategic culture, Singh turns to the Indian traditions of pacifism and what he calls 'ersatz pacifism'—Buddhism, Jaina and (Hindu) Bhakti religiosity. These religious movements, he argues, have produced an idealist disposition in Indian politics, notably in foreign affairs. Consequently, the realist dimension of Indian strategic culture got undermined and weakened. For Singh, Nehru was the embodiment of political idealism in modern India: 'His [Nehru's] economic policy, his foreign policy and consequently his defense policy [...] *was based less on a cool, calm assessment of facts giving due weight to human greed and human deceit than on idealism*' (1999, 24). According to him, '*Nehru's idealistic romanticism*' (ibid., 34, emphasis added) left a negative imprint on Indian strategic culture and became a heavy burden for India's foreign and security policy. His verdict could hardly be harsher:

> Nehru's legacy, whether still relevant or not, remains dominant, in the process providing a kind of continuity to independent India's strategic culture, even if that continuity be of negative attributes like veneration of the received wisdom; an absence of iconoclastic questioning, a still continuing lack of institutional framework for policy formulation; lack of sense of history and geography, an absence of sufficient commitment to territorial impregnability; and a tendency to remain static in yesterday's doctrines, even form.
> (J. Singh 1999, 58)

From the perspective of J. Singh, there is a historically evolved strategic culture of India, which, however, became increasingly detached from its

'Hindu' roots of political realism. In that process, (secular) Kautilyan thought has played an ambiguous, if not negative, role. With Nehru, the softening up of India's strategic culture through political idealism reached its apex. Consequently, J. Singh calls for resolutely reversing that negative trend in Indian strategic culture by turning back to 'Hindu realism' in foreign and security policy.

In the expert interviews, Singh's view of Kautilya and his place in Indian strategic culture were not shared. However, one interviewee, while disagreeing with Singh's view of Kautilya, agreed with his view of Indian strategic culture and the role played by Nehru therein.

> The dominant strategic culture has been the Nehruvian strategic culture post-independence. This strategic culture does not believe in the Kautilyan way of analyzing the world or achieving goals that the country has set for itself [...]. If there is realism, it is reactive, it is adaptive, it is a response, it is not a coherent realism [...]. Element of realism have come in, but the paradigm is still not a Kautilyan paradigm, the paradigm remains basically an adapted form of the Nehruvian paradigm. (EI Sujit Dutta)[7]

Shivshankar Menon has dealt extensively with the issue of India's strategic culture. He did so, inter alia, in a lecture entitled *K. Subrahmanyam and India's Strategic Culture*, which was published in *Air Power Journal* (Menon 2012). He begins his lecture with a reference to George Tanham's claim that India lacks a strategic culture: '*Frankly speaking, for a civilization and state like India not to have a strategic culture is impossible [...]. [O]f course, we in India have a strategic culture. It is an indigenous construct over millennia*, modified considerably by our experience in the last two centuries' (Menon 2012, 2f, emphasis added).

Menon then refers to Kanti Bajpai's proposition that 'Nehruvianism', 'hyperrealism' and 'neoliberalism' underpin Indian strategic culture. What the three schools have in common forms the substance of the strategic culture of India. But, right after that, Menon adds that the essence of Indian strategic culture is derived from the classic politico-strategic texts of ancient India, notably Kautilya's *Arthashastra*, the Bhishma dialogues in the *Mahabharata* and Ashoka's edicts. Those who criticize, for example, India's military intervention in East Pakistan which led to the establishment of the state of Bangladesh have not understood the ideational sources of Indian strategic culture, states Menon. Such critics should have read the epics *Mahabharata* and *Ramayana*. And if they had done so, they would have understood that the use of military force is both necessary and justified under certain circumstances—like those existing in 1971. Menon quotes a passage from Gandhi's book *The Gita and Satyagraha*, in which Gandhi justifies the use of force against unprovoked aggression, and adds: 'In saying so, *Gandhiji was expressing ideas and a political rationalism whose roots one can trace back to India's ancient history, to Kautilya or Ashoka, whichever you prefer*' (Menon 2012, 5, emphasis added).

Nehru had seized upon the classical heritage of Indian strategic culture and applied it to the foreign policy of Independent India. Despite the dramatic changes of Indian politics—internally and externally—since the early 1990s, the core positions of India's foreign and security policy, as articulated by Nehru, remain essentially valid, states Menon. India must preserve and extend its strategic autonomy. Non-alignment must not be seen in ideological terms but as a realist strategy. Indian realism, however, should not be confused with the Western realism because it combines the pursuit of national interests with the basic values of Indian polity—secularism, democracy and pluralism. Here, Menon speaks of 'realism-plus', which means that India is following its own tradition of political realism that does not exclude normative considerations in foreign and security policy.

The challenge facing India today is designing a 'Grand Strategy for the first half of the 21st century' that is based on '*our own culture and tradition of strategic thought*.' To that end, there is a need to '*develop our own strategic culture, vocabulary and doctrine* [...]. So, if anything, the need for, and the rewards of [,] studying our strategic culture will grow with time.' Today's complex and uncertain world situation is one 'with which the Indian state system was familiar for most of our pre-modern history. *A world where Krishna and Bhishma and Kautilya would all feel equally at home*' (Menon 2012, 10f, emphasis added).

According the Menon, also K. Subrahmanyam, who was instrumental in developing the Indian nuclear doctrine, was firmly rooted in the ancient strategic traditions forming the basis of Indian strategic culture and applied creatively this politico-strategic heritage to the conditions of the late twentieth and early twenty-first century. However, Menon does not mention Subrahmanyam's defense of Tanham nor his denial of continuing influence of Kautilyan thought.

In the expert interviews, Menon—like Dixit—was described as a person who possesses a profound theoretical understanding of Kautilya's *Arthashastra* and is also committed to the operational implementation of Kautilyan concepts in Indian foreign and security policy.

> Now when you talk to people who are actually involved in that process of security policy, for instance, if you talk to Shivshankar Menon, who is the National Security Advisor. *Well, he does take his clues from Kautilya because he has read it [Arthashastra]. So you see, there are senior government people who have actually read the Arthashastra.* (EI Namrata Goswami,[8] emphasis added)

In conclusion, it can be stated that both the academic and political discourse on Indian strategic culture broadly converge in the position that Kautilyan thought is an essential ideational component of India's strategic culture. Most authors see a duality of realistic and idealistic tendencies but assign to the realism of the Kautilyan tradition the predominant role in Indian strategic culture. As mentioned above, most of the opinions expressed in the expert interviews with respect to Indian strategic culture concur with what is stated on this subject in the academic political science or political discourse. What Raghavan said in this regard reflects the basic trend of most expert interviews:

> [M]odern Indian figures did have some intellectual engagement with this ancient political-strategic tradition, and that engagement has laid the basis for strategic culture as it operates today, or ideas of strategic culture that you find in India today […]. This means not to say: from Kautilya there and then straight ahead to Manmohan Singh here and today. Instead, it means that in the interim there was intellectual engagement with Kautilya which resulted in certain

categories, concepts, frameworks. Nehru's *Discovery of India* being a prime example of that process. (EI Srinath Raghavan)[9]

Our finding is: Kautilya's *Arthashastra* is the central ideational source of Indian strategic culture, but there are idealist factors of influence too. Kautilyan thought is influencing the dispositions and preferences in perception, thinking and behaviour of actors in the field of Indian foreign and security policy.

8

A DISTANT RELATIONSHIP
Kautilya and the Social and Political Sciences in India

In this section, we investigate the question why, until very recently, Kautilya has been marginalized in the Indian academia. First, we outline, mainly on the basis of expert interviews, the conspicuous absence of Kautilyan thought in the curricula of Indian universities and other institutions of higher education—with a focus on the historical and structural factors relating to this. Subsequently, we examine the peculiar constellation of social and political science 'schools', whose theoretical and methodological characteristics have contributed to the disturbing fact that Kautilya's *Arthashastra* has barely been used as an intellectual resource of the social and political sciences. Research and teaching on Kautilya in the context of Sanskrit Studies, Indology, philosophy and historiography can only be touched upon.

8.1 KAUTILYA'S ABSENCE IN INDIAN ACADEMIA

The status of Kautilya in research and teaching at Indian universities can be summed up with the following observation by P.K. Gautam: 'There is a near-total absence of knowledge and understanding of Kautilya in any structured curriculum of the Indian education system and in the resources available for strategic policymaking, academia and think tanks of the country' (2013c, 14).

This sobering assessment corresponds to the findings from the expert interviews that were conducted during Spring 2012. At that point of time, Kautilya was not included in the social and political science curricula of Jawaharlal Nehru University (JNU) in Delhi with its renowned School of International Studies (SIS). In 2012, this was also true for the University of Delhi (DU), where, however, in the meantime, changes have occurred that are discussed in the subsequent section B 9. Also, at Jamia Millia University in Delhi, Kautilya was barely noticeable in research and teaching. These three universities in Delhi belong to the 41 universities that are maintained by the Indian central government and have 'elite' status. The social science faculties of JNU and DU are role-models for the respective faculties of the more than four hundred other universities in India. That applies in particular for Political Science and its sub-discipline International Relations (IR), where the points of contact with Kautilyan thought are multiple. In the expert interviews, it was consistently reported that, at the three universities in Delhi, research and teaching on Kautilya depended exclusively on the personal initiative of teachers. Occasionally, some professors do substantially address Kautilya in their research and teaching, but, mostly, students have to be content with sporadic and superficial impartation of Kautilyan theorems—usually as a byproduct of the thorough treatment of Western political theory.

Equally so, at the institutions of higher education of the Indian military—National Defence College, Defence Services Staff College and the Indian Military Academy—Kautilya has mostly been absent in the curricula and in research. And the same applies to the educational institutions of the Ministry of Foreign Affairs (MEA) and the Indian Administrative Service (IAS).[1]

Of course, there are some exceptions. Some valuable academic works on Kautilya's *Arthashastra* have emerged from the social sciences departments of Indian universities in recent decades. One such example is Aradhana Parmar's *Techniques of Statecraft: A Study of Kautilya's Arthashastra* (Parmar 1987). Although there are indications that the marginalization of Kautilyan thought in Indian social and political sciences is gradually ending, the assessment of the diplomat Krishnan S. Rana still holds true. He writes in his book *Inside Diplomacy*:

> The statecraft genius Chanakya [...] left behind the epic work *Arthashastra*. It may astonish an outside observer *that neither this nor any other of the old texts relevant to the diplomatic profession*

figure in the Indian curriculum, which seems as curious omission [...]. The main reason is that the Indian education system is West-oriented, with a strong Anglo-American influence. (Rana 2000, 41f, emphasis added)

8.2 THE ANGLO-AMERICAN INFLUENCE IN INDIAN UNIVERSITIES

In the expert interviews, several explanations for Kautilya's marginalization in the academic field were brought up. One causation repeatedly mentioned was the 'power-knowledge matrix'. Long before Michel Foucault, Karl Mannheim (1965) theorized that the production of knowledge is not (only) a 'self-referential' cognitive activity but is significantly influenced by social contexts and the political and socio-economic power relations therein. Power relations do not only exist within a given social context but also between different (political) contexts. Thus, knowledge productions in a political entity with inferior power potential will be significantly influenced by the knowledge production in entities of superior political and economic power. Such opaque but efficacious influence of political power can be observed with respect to the structures as well as the teaching and research contents of formally autonomous academic institutions. This is succinctly formulated by Kanti Bajpai: '*[P]ower in the academic system lies with the Anglo-Americans*' (Bajpai/Mallavarapu 2005a, 8, emphasis added). The tenor of the expert interviews was in line with this observation:

> Nobody says Machiavelli is the 'Italian Kautilya'. Here, I would say, it is power in international politics—and its reflection in academia. Had India been the imperial power for the last 400 years, things would have been very different. British, American, German, French curricula would have included Kautilya. Here comes the question of power and influence. European thinkers became so important because that is the way of power. (EI Partha Ghosh)[2]

Until 1947, political power in India was exercised by Britain. Towards the end of the nineteenth century, the colonial power began to establish universities in India whose organization as well as teaching and research contents carbon-copied the British model of academia. These British-style institutions of higher education were intended to marginalize existing endogenous educational institutions, whose teaching was in Sanskrit, Persian and regional languages. The strategic thrust of the colonial education system was formulated by the British historian and politician Thomas Babington Macaulay (1800–59). In 1835, he wrote in his *Minute on Indian Education*:

> I am quite ready to take the oriental learning at the valuation of the orientalists themselves. I have never found one among them *who could deny that a single shelf of a good European library was worth the whole native literature of India and Arabia. The intrinsic superiority of the Western literature* is indeed fully admitted by those members of the committee who support the oriental plan of education [...]. We must at present do our best to form a class [of Indians] who may be interpreters between us and the millions whom we govern—*a class of persons Indian in blood and color, but English in tastes, in opinions, in morals and in intellect.* (Macaulay 1835, emphasis added; cf. Rothermund 1998, 313)

The colonial 'program of education', so blatantly articulated by Macaulay, remained valid until 1947, the interviewees said. But even after Independence, the habitual preference for the curricula, research topics, theories and methods at British universities persisted in the Indian academia. However, rather rapidly American academia positioned itself as the second point of reference for Indian social scientists. Most of them aspired to find recognition within this externally defined discursive space. In the early 1990s, V. R. Mehta came to the following findings:

> What is, however, unfortunate is the little attention being paid in university courses to the development of social and political thought in India. *Our students know more about Rome and England than about their own country with the result that they remain largely ignorant about their own traditions of thought.* (Mehta 1992, 2, emphasis added)

These assessments of Mehta in 1992 and of Rana in 2000 were confirmed in the 2012 expert interviews.

> For most of us—now I am talking of the somewhat educated elite—our thoughts are more Anglo-Saxon than going back to our real roots, to the culture in the sense of the Arthashastra. (EI Satish Nambiar)[3]

Paradoxically, the Anglo-American discourse dominance in Indian social science was exacerbated by the rapid build-up of the Indian university system. During the first decades after Independence, the interviewees noted, the social and political sciences—as well as the humanities—played only a secondary role in the overall system of higher education. Natural sciences, engineering and economics were prioritized, because first and foremost qualified cadres for the economic and technological development of the country were needed. Given India's strained financial resources and the need to overcome the underdevelopment, this priority is quite understandable. However, it meant poor infrastructure, inadequate staffing and low academic career opportunities for the social sciences and humanities. As a result, an exodus of Indian students and graduates of these disciplines set in. They went mainly to American and British universities where they could hope for scholarships and fellowships and subsequent academic careers. The scholarly output of Indian social scientists in the USA or the UK featured almost exclusively 'Western' theories and research topics which, in turn, radiated back on Indian academia. Thus, not surprisingly, there was no impetus from the academic diaspora in the United States and England to take up Indian traditions of political thought. Also, the thematic foci of the internationally established social and political science journals—most of them Anglo-American—practically excluded the intellectual traditions of India to the extent that, if 'Indian topics' were addressed at all, that was done strictly within the theoretical framework of Western schools of social science.

During the past three decades, along with the expansion of the Indian university system, the relative weight of Indian social sciences—quantitatively and qualitatively—has increased significantly. However, the Anglo-American influence on research and teaching has remained dominant:

> Most of the books used in India for teaching political science and international relations, including strategic studies, are American. (Subrahmanyam/Malhotra 2005, 12)

> IR has in the past and continues to be very much the discipline of the hegemon [...]. It is not misplaced to characterize the discipline [IR] as an 'American social science' both in terms of its reigning paradigms and content of investigation. (Bajpai/Mallavarapu 2005b, 3)

> Indian IR scholars, like many others outside the Anglo-American academy, have fairly rationally concluded that there is a division of labor internationally, within which they must work. In that division of labor, it is theirs to use theory (at best); it is not theirs to make theory. (Bajpai/Mallavarapu 2005a, 8)

In the expert interviews, another reason for the 'Gramscian hegemonic status' of Anglo-American theories over endogenous intellectual resources was brought up (Acharya/Buzan 2007, 294). The proclivity for Western theories was traced to the 'unresolved problem' why India had not been capable of repulsing Western colonialism. Among many Indian intellectuals it was argued that there is a deep sense of disappointment and frustration that Indian culture had generated neither the scientific and technological achievements nor the political-strategic thinking necessary to resist British colonialism. Out of this state of mind in the intellectual milieu, distrust and even resentment against culture and scholarship in pre-colonial India evolved. Because endogenous thought supposedly failed the 'test of history' when confronted with colonialism, the value of India's intellectual traditions for the present was contested.

> I think there was a sense that Indian thought could be troublesome [...]. There was some embarrassment. The elephant in the room was, if there was all this grand thought and culture back then, how come we screwed it all up in India? How did we fall under

the sway of the Europeans? There is a sense of, well, maybe Indian thought is not all that great actually, otherwise it should have helped us resist the conquest, and it did not. So let's not bother with that stuff, it actually got us into trouble. It was a dead end, and it was not a strong enough body of thought to produce a progressive modern India that found its own way to modernity and power. (EI Kanti Bajpai)[4]

The latent sense of 'failure' with respect to endogenous intellectual traditions tends to discourage the scholarly engagement with India's pre-modern politico-cultural resources. This bias is not openly expressed through outright rejection; it rather takes the form of defensiveness, which is tantamount to simply refraining from dealing with endogenous politico-cultural resources. Also, some interviewees argued, Indian social scientists are reluctant to focus on the endogenous political and cultural resources because they harbour an exaggerated fear of supposed 'nativism' in the Indian social or political sciences.

The danger of this [research] agenda is, as noted earlier, it will fall prey to nativism […] the view that pristine, indigenous thought and practice which is superior to alien counterparts and which more or less transparently contain answers to contemporary problems. (Bajpai/Mallavarapu 2005b, 32)

However, the majority of the interviewees did not share such fear of intellectual 'nativism'. Although understanding was shown for insisting on a critical and methodological approach towards endogenous politico-cultural resources, first of all one had to get on with the work instead of discouraging it in the first place.

8.3 SANSKRIT: ATROPHY OF LANGUAGE SKILLS

As a further explanation for the marginalization of Kautilya and other classical politico-cultural resources, interviewees referred to the fact that ever fewer Indian intellectuals master Sanskrit (cf. Pollock 2011). The mastery of Sanskrit would be important for social and political scientists because it can foster the analysis and interpretation of classical texts in the sense of adequately expressing their actual idea-contents and, simultaneously, stimulate fresh conceptual approaches in the current social and political science discourse.

Currently, academic Sanskrit Studies in India are predominantly philological and focus on literary, religious and philosophical texts, the interviewees opined. Sanskrit Studies contribute very little to render the classics accessible for the social and political sciences. Instead of linking philological and hermeneutic text analysis with social and political science perspectives, there is a 'firewall' between Sanskrit Studies and Political Science. Interviewees noted that Sanskrit philologists tend to view the *Arthashastra* as their 'intellectual property' and resent the idea that the *Arthashastra*'s interpretation can transcend the philological-hermeneutic domain—which is theirs—as to include the explication of its political and strategic idea-contents in terms of Political Science. In simple words, Sanskrit philologists tend to miss the fact that the *Arthashastra* is a foundational text of Political Science and International Relations theory. Thus, interdisciplinary cooperation between Sanskrit Studies and Political Science is mostly absent—in India and internationally.[5]

In the expert interviews, it was also noted that Sanskrit Studies are increasingly conducted at religiously oriented institutions of education. That means for many secular Indian intellectuals entering a gray area towards Hindu religious fundamentalism and Hindutva ideology. The actual or imputed proximity of Sanskrit Studies to the Hindutva ideology has a fatal consequence: Sanskrit Studies or even mere learning Sanskrit becomes suspect for many secular intellectuals. On the left of the political spectrum, almost aggressive opposition against 'Sanskritism' is widespread. Even many left-liberal and centrist intellectuals take a distance to Sanskrit because of diffuse fears that there might be some connection between Sanskrit and the Hindutva ideology. Thus, many intellectuals simply stay away from learning Sanskrit or even studying texts that were (originally) written in Sanskrit.

The non-reflective association of Sanskrit with Hindutva ideology in the intellectual milieu tends to get projected on the classical works of

Sanskrit literature, the interviewees noted. Thus, the epics *Mahabharata* and *Ramayana* or even Kautilya's *Arthashastra* are treated with suspicion. Such perceptions are neither logical nor factual, but nonetheless they are virulent in the Indian academic milieu. Since such preconceived opinions are often resistant against rational arguments, pointing to the fact that Kautilya represents secular and even materialist positions is usually to no avail. This applies also to pointing out that Hindu-nationalist organizations and their ideologues have shown no interest in politically appropriating Kautilya. In the works of the leading Hindutva ideologues, V.D. Savarkar (1883–1966) and M.S. Gowalkar (1906–73), there is no reference to Kautilya, the interviewees said. In the political programs and in the daily politics of Hindu nationalist organizations, Kautilya is absent.

The sad consequence of the aversion to 'Sanskritism' in the academic milieu is a kind of discourse-denial: Kautilya will not be criticized but simply ignored. Since the *Arthashastra* is studied only in rare cases, stereotypes of Kautilya and his thought are virulent even among social scientists. In addition, the widespread but wholly fictional 'portraits' of Kautilya keep intellectuals at distance because they relay the stereotype of the arrogant, caste-fixated Brahmin.[6]

8.4 SOCIAL SCIENCE 'SCHOOLS' AND THE MARGINALIZATION OF KAUTILYAN THOUGHT

This segment deals with methodological and theoretical 'schools' in the social and political sciences which have subtly contributed to the marginalization of Kautilyan thought in Indian academia. The schools and doctrines treated here are examined only in one respect: what theoretical and methodological characteristics tend to blank out Kautilya's *Arthashastra* in the academic discourse. By no means is an overall assessment or even valuation of these schools intended. The sole selection criterion for the schools and doctrines treated below are references to them in the expert interviews when the question of Kautilya's marginalization in Indian academia was discussed.

8.4.1 The positivist approach

As mentioned above, during the early stages of Independent India, the social sciences played a secondary role in the university system. Therefore, the interviewees noted, social scientists had first to secure a recognized place in Indian academia. In order to gain such recognition, they mainly followed the established path of Anglo-Saxon social science which borrows heavily from 'positivist' methods of natural sciences. Thus, turning to research of endogenous classics like Kautilya's *Arthashastra* seemed ludicrous for social scientists in a nascent discipline still yearning for recognition. Moreover, the positivist approach is neither suitable for researching the history of ideas nor for interpreting classical texts nor for the theoretical analysis of classical works in view of current research issues.

> We really have all become empirical positivists. And so something as theoretical as Kautilya tends to get sort of skepticized. (EI Romila Thapar)[7]

Positivist social scientists, 'interested in observable, quantifiable data, understandably tend to find culture a frustrating and unattractive ingredient of theory' (Engelmeier 2009, 70). Such suspicion equally applies to politico-strategic traditions going way back into Indian antiquity. And, of course, such skepticism is particularly virulent when the research subject is the nexus of an ancient Indian text like Kautilya's *Arthashastra* with the realities of contemporary India. In fact, the theoretical and methodological tools of the positivist approach are not applicable for the search of verifiable connections between an ancient work of statecraft and the politico-strategic thinking and practice in today's India—at least when it is not just about measuring statistical frequencies of the explicit mentioning of Kautilya in contemporary contexts. Therefore it is not surprising at all that positivist-oriented social scientists are utterly disinterested in engaging with Kautilya's *Arthashastra*.

8.4.2 Marxism and Indian social sciences

Parallel to (Anglo-American) positivism, Marxism has been a considerable factor of influence in Indian social and political sciences, particularly during the first decades after independence. In the interview, Dietmar Rothermund said that Karl Marx was highly esteemed by many Indian intellectuals because he appeared to them as a European version of the typical Brahmin scholar and *Das Kapital* seemed structurally akin to classical *shastras*. Consequently, whatever Marx had written about India possessed the highest intellectual authority for Indian social scientists with Marxist orientation. Therefore, we need to look a bit more closely at Marx's own writings on India in order to assess the attitude of Indian Marxists towards Kautilya.

During the 1850s, Marx wrote several articles on India for the *New York Herald Tribune*. On one hand, Marx showed great sympathy for the misery of the people of India under British colonial rule and also a certain, albeit rather superficial, understanding of Indian culture. On the other hand, he looked at Indian society as an expression of structural backwardness characterizing the 'Asiatic mode of production' and 'Oriental despotism'. In his article *The British Rule in India*, Marx writes:

> Now, sickening as it must be to human feeling to witness those myriads of industrious patriarchal and inoffensive social organizations disorganized and dissolved into their units, thrown into a sea of woes, and their individual members losing at the same time their ancient form of civilization, and their hereditary means of subsistence, *we must not forget that these idyllic village-communities, inoffensive though they may appear, had always been the solid foundation of Oriental despotism, that they restrained the human mind within the smallest possible compass*, making it the unresisting tool of superstition, enslaving it beneath traditional rules, *depriving it of all grandeur and historical energies*. We must not forget the barbarian egotism which, concentrating on some miserable patch of land, had quietly witnessed the ruin of Empires, the perpetration of unspeakable cruelties, the massacre of the population of large towns, with no other consideration bestowed upon them than on natural events, itself the helpless prey of any aggressor who deigned to notice it at all. We must not forget that

> *this undignified, stagnatory, and vegetative life,* that this passive sort of existence evoked on the other part, in contradistinction, wild, aimless, unbounded forces of destruction and rendered murder itself a religious rite in Hindostan. We must not forget that these little communities were contaminated by distinctions of caste and by slavery, that they subjugated man to external circumstances instead of elevating man the sovereign of circumstances, that they transformed a self- developing social state into never changing natural destiny, and thus brought about a brutalizing worship of nature, exhibiting its degradation in the fact that man, the sovereign of nature, fell down on his knees in adoration of Hanuman, the monkey, and Sabbala, the cow. (Marx 1853a, emphasis added; German version: Marx 1960a, 132f)

And in his article *The Future Results of the British Rule in India*, Marx postulated:

> India, then, could not escape the fate of being conquered, and the whole of her past history, if it be anything, is the history of the successive conquests she has undergone. *Indian society has no history at all,* at least no known history. What we call its history, is but the history of the successive intruders who founded their Empires on the passive basis of that unresisting and unchanging society. The question, therefore, is not whether the English had a right to conquer India, but whether we are to prefer India conquered by the Turk, by the Persian, by the Russian, to India conquered by the Briton. *England has to fulfill a double mission in India: one destructive, the other regenerating the annihilation of old Asiatic society, and laying the material foundations of Western society in Asia.* (Marx 1853b, emphasis added; German version: Marx 1960b, 220f)

For Marx, the combination of colonialism and capitalism thus fulfilled a historic mission of social and technological progress. It's through colonialism that India advances to Western modernity. Only on the basis of European civilization and the capitalist system can India proceed on the path of political and social self-liberation. The assumption that India might extract the intellectual and political resources for self-liberation from its own history and culture is unsustainable for Marx, for he shares 'not the opinion of those who believe in a golden age of Hindostan' (Marx 1853). Not through recourse to its classical traditions but through effective Westernization can India overcome colonialism and socio-economic backwardness.

But Marx has some idea of Indian culture when he describes India as a country 'whose gentle natives are, to use the expression of Prince Soltykov, even in the most inferior classes, *plus fins et plus adroits que les Italiens*' [more subtle and adroit than the Italians], a people whose submission even is counterbalanced by a certain calm nobility, who, notwithstanding their natural langor, have astonished the British officers by their bravery, whose country has been the source of our languages, our religions, and who represent the type of the ancient German in the Jat, and the type of the ancient Greek in the Brahmin' (Marx 1853).

Despite such empathy, Marx lacks a deeper understanding of Indian culture and history. The ancient Indian classics and the works of the leading Indologists of his time were outside the scope of his knowledge and interest.[8] In the expert interviews, Marx was consistently perceived as a leading representative of Eurocentric modernity who wanted India to be westernized via British colonialism and capitalism:

> Marx is promoting a modernist regime. Marx has a kind of static, unchanging concept of India in terms of this Asiatic mode of production. But what is it that Marx—and also Weber—are really interested in, what is that one thing? Is it not Western modernity that they are really interested in? [...] People here are critical of Marx for promoting high Orientalism in social theory, for constructing a social theory of modernity which is coloured by Orientalism. (EI Mohinder Singh)[9]

Marx's view of India as having no endogenous historical and cultural resources to draw upon for the struggle against British colonialism (after the latter had fulfilled its historical mission of socio-economic Westernization) provides little or no motivation for Marxist social scientists to engage in ancient Indian political theory and statecraft. One might think that Marxists would be quite interested in Kautilya's political economy. However, the interviewees opined that Marxist-oriented social scientists see Kautilya's expositions on political economy in the *Arthashastra* primarily as ideological articulations of 'early feudalism'. On the implications of this label, P.B. Mehta writes: 'The minute you pronounced a text feudal or bourgeois no longer had you to read it, in any serious sense of the term reading' (Mehta 2009).

As always, exceptions confirm the rule. The interviewees pointed to the Marxist historian (and polymath) D.D. Kosambi (1907–66). In his *An Introduction to the Study of Indian History*, Kosambi devotes a whole chapter to Kautilya's *Arthashastra* (cf. Kosambi 1975). What Kosambi writes about Kautilya is superb scholarship and very insightful. Overall, however, the study of the *Arthashastra* and its use as a resource for the social and political sciences has not been a desideratum for Marxist-oriented social and political scientists in India.

8.4.3 Kautilya and International Relations (IR) theory in India

In 1919, Benoy Kumar Sarkar published in the *American Political Science Review* his essay *Hindu Theory of International Relations* (cf. Sarkar 1919). In this, Sarkar addresses the foreign policy theorems in Kautilya's *Arthashastra* and discusses their relevance to Western theorizing of inter-state relations. He sees Kautilya as one of the originators of the concepts of 'power politics' and 'balance of power' in IR theory. However, Sarkar's early initiative regarding Kautilya's lasting relevance for IR theory was *not* taken up by Indian Political Science.

The tenor of the expert interviews was that, up to the present day, most Indian political scientists do not connect the term 'Political Realism' with Kautilya but with Hans J. Morgenthau and his work *Politics Among Nations*: 'Every generation of Indian [political science] students can be relied upon to have read or be conversant with Hans Morgenthau's famous text and his formulation' (Bajpai/Mallavarapu 2005b, 28). At the same time, Indian Political Science has completely missed out on the conceptional homologies between Kautilyan thought and Morgenthau's theory (cf. Section A, 8–12). If there has been interest in the intellectual sources of Morgenthau's Political Realism, the focus has been European intellectual history: Thucydides, Machiavelli and Hobbes. Morgenthau's own hint in *Politics Among Nations* that the political philosophy of ancient India is a key source of his theory of Political Realism and his explicit references to Kautilya in his *Dilemmas of Politics* have been ignored by Indian Political Science.

From the 1980s onwards, Kenneth Waltz's 'neorealism', as expounded in his *Theory of International Politics*, has become the second dominant track of IR theory in India—in competition with Morgenthau's theory. The dominating presence of Morgenthau and Waltz in Indian Political Science is to a significant degree due to American scholarship programs, the interviewees said. A high percentage of Indian political scientists working on IR theory have passed through these programs. In this regard, interviewees mentioned the Fulbright Program of the U.S. Department of State, the Ford Foundation and the Carnegie Endowment. Thus, Morgenthau's realism and Waltz's neorealism gained the status of 'orthodoxy' in Indian IR theory.

Morgenthau's theory of Political Realism is comprehensive. Its focus is international relations, but it is not limited to them. Anthropological, historical and cultural factors are not excluded. Moreover, Morgenthau's approach is agency-centred. In contrast, Waltz's neorealism sees international relations as a structure whose systemic logic is similar to that of capitalist 'free market'. That logic forces actors to continuously produce 'added value' in economic terms respectively in terms of security in order to successfully persist in economic respectively inter-state competition. Within the logic of the system, security is achieved by balancing power differentials between states. That can be achieved by the build-up of internal power resources ('internal balancing') and/or through alliance-building with other states ('external balancing'). The balancing of power differentials by increasing the respective power potential, however, does not lead to a sustained balance of power constellation (and thus stable security). The gain in power (and thus security) of one state means relative loss of power and security of another state. Therefore the other state must in turn—driven by the system's logic—compensate the relative loss of power and security through further strengthening of its power potential. Thus, the next round of power build-up is triggered.

In Waltz's theory of neorealism, states are the units of the system in which they (via rational calculation) do what the system's logic dictates them to do. The peculiarity of states consists alone in the quantitatively measurable differences of their military and economic power potentials. Here, one might think, Waltz's theory offers some conceptual points of contact with Kautilya's *saptanga* and *shadgunya* theories. But neorealism is based on ahistorical and acultural axioms; thus, this theory itself knows no ideational genesis. Moreover, endogenous characteristics of states, in terms of their political leadership, institutional evolution and strategic traditions, are of no interest. Ideational factors influencing the behaviour of states in their foreign relations do not figure in neorealist theory (cf. Glenn et al. 2004, 20–44; Schörnig 2006, 65–92).

Consequently, in the context of neorealism, there is no room for Kautilyan thought. The question whether or to what extent ideational factors like Kautilyan thought might influence India's strategic culture and operational foreign policy is meaningless in the context of neorealism. While, initially, Kautilya's premodern realism was literally 'buried' under Morgenthau's modern realism in Indian IR theorizing, for the disciples of neorealism Kautilya is simply irrelevant.

But there are some Indian political scientists who have both diagnosed and critiqued the exclusion of Kautilya from IR theory. Navnita Chadha Behera deplores '*the intellectual dependency of Indian IRT, which does not acknowledge India's own history and philosophical traditions (e.g. Kautilya) as a source of IRT*' (Behera 2007, 341, emphasis added). She then turns explicitly to Kautilya's marginalization in Indian IR theory:

> The impoverishment of traditional IR's political thought becomes further evident on its chosen ground—political realism—that *does not recognize our own Indian political philosopher, Kautilya, as 'the father of realpolitik'*. Kautilya is not taught in any 'principal IR theory courses' and though *Arthashastra* has much to offer for theorizing IR, the universal applicability of his ideas is not

acknowledged—almost universally [...]. The disciplinary subject matter of *traditional IR only offers silence on Kautilya*. (Behera 2007, 352f, emphasis added)

Behera regrets, a) that Kautilyan concepts are not recognized as a key historical and theoretical foundation of IR theory, and b) that the *Arthashastra*'s conceptual potential is not being used for innovative theoretizations in IR. Although Kautilya had stringently developed the core concepts of Political Realism long before Machiavelli or Morgenthau, his theoretical achievements are denigrated by locating them in a context of Oriental intellectual immaturity or even obscurantism. Therefore, Kautilya gets either completely ignored or turned into an inchoate 'approximation' of much later Western political theory.

> [T]he 'pre-modern' world of Kautilya is *disowned or excluded by traditional IR's modern worldview* [...]. So, Kautilya is reduced to becoming an 'Indian Machiavelli' and his ideas hold value, because they approximate those presented in Hobbes's Leviathan or Machiavelli's Prince and not vice-versa. (Behera 2007, 353, emphasis added)

Besides Behera, Amitav Acharya has criticized that Indian IR theory has ignored its endogenous intellectual sources and thus misses the opportunity to use them for theory building with respect to current issues. For Western realism it is a matter of course to position itself in the European intellectual tradition of Thucydides, Thomas Aquinas, Machiavelli and Hobbes—and claim universal validity for its propositions. In contrast, Indian Political Science neglects its endogenous intellectual resources: '[S]tuck as we are with the idea of Kautilya being an Indian Machiavelli, rather than Machiavelli being a Euro-Mediterranean Kautilya' (Acharya 2011, 628).

8.4.4 Social constructivism

Even though social constructivism is theoretically and methodologically a very heterogeneous approach, one might describe it as follows: The 'subjective' and 'situational' dimension of knowledge and social action is highlighted against the 'objective' existence of social phenomena: 'As we come to recognise the conventional and artifactual status of our forms of knowing, we realise that it is ourselves and not reality that is responsible for what we know' (Schapin/Schaffer cit. in: Shahi 2015, 63). Social reality is (mentally) 'constructed' by human beings within their contingent social contexts. Such 'construction' does not occur in the sense of arbitrary subjectivity but by means of 'collective identities' that are constituted by a fluid mix of formal and informal rules within a given social context. Thus, out of contingent social contexts, 'identities', 'worldviews', 'imaginations' and 'practices' are 'constructed' (cf. Kubálková 2001, 56–76; Ulbert 2006, 409–40). In some ways, (post-)modern social constructivism is reminiscent of the epistemic theorizing of ancient Greek Sophists like Protagoras and Gorgias.

One might think that history and culture would gain outstanding theoretical significance within social constructivism—as opposed to 'structuralist', ahistorical and acultural approaches in social science. After all, history and culture do impact perceptions, thinking and behaviour of human beings. However, history and culture are anathema for social constructivism. In the edited volume with the programmatic title *The Social Construction of the Past: Representation as Power*, its editors state categorically that social constructionists '*do not assume histories and cultures to be concrete realities*' (Bond/Gilliam 1994, 2, emphasis added).

Continuity and structure are intrinsic features of both history and culture, but social constructivism cannot accept the 'objective existence' of structures and continuity in social reality. While the structures underlying history and culture do have a social and historical genesis—and thus are neither a-priori nor immutable—history and culture do have an objective, substantive existence and efficacy (cf. Bourdieu, 1992, 135ff). In particular longue durée continuity—in historical and cultural terms—is anathema for constructivism. Consequently, constructivists prefer to substitute pluralistic 'pasts' or 'historical narratives' for history and a plurality of 'cultural practices' for culture. Consequently, the social constructivist approach boils down to the 'deconstruction' (in the literal sense) of history and culture. That, in turn, has most unfortunate consequences for the way how cultural assets of past times are viewed:

Their factual idea-contents get squeezed out by the contingent contexts of their reception. The dedicated intellectual engagement with cultural assets as such is sidelined by the focus on their contexts—not of their origination but their reception under contingent circumstances at various points of time. We will elaborate on this problematique by examining two relatively recent texts that deal in a constructivist perspective with the political history and strategic culture of India, including Kautilya's role therein.

Pursuing the social constructivist approach, Tobias Engelmeier (2009) has analysed the 'project' of Indian 'identity construction' in the context of post-Independence 'nation-building'. He discusses the impact of such 'identity construction' upon the strategic culture and the foreign policy of India. In examining his study, we try to determine whether the social constructivist approach—unintentionally or not—contributes to the neglect of endogenous politico-cultural resources such as Kautilya's *Arthashastra*.

Engelmeier concedes that 'it would be foolish to argue that contemporary India is not related to the Indias of the past and that "Indian culture" is nonexistent' (2009, 55). Noteworthy is that he uses the formulation 'the Indias of the past' (instead of 'India's past') and puts the term 'Indian culture' in ironic quotation marks. These formulations express Engelmeier's basic assumption that there has been neither historical nor cultural continuity in India. Consequently, he sees no quasi-genetic Indian identity that has accrued from that historical and cultural continuity. Instead, he argues, India's *identity is a unique construct* [...]. The past is but a resource in this endeavor, important as stabilizer, as a ready identity-glue to be used by leaders' (Engelmeier 2009, 133, 163, emphasis added). This 'identity construction' was undertaken in the first half of the twentieth century by India's nationalist elites in a top-down mode: 'Agents (especially Gandhi, Nehru) created a specific Indian political identity [...] [and] craft[ed] an abstract pan-Indian national identity' (ibid., 24, 27). Gandhi and Nehru 'claimed that the country which they seek to represent has an ancient lineage, a primordial "national" identity"' (ibid., 151). To support their pretension that there is a historically evolved 'Indianess', Gandhi and Nehru would have drawn on the reservoir of ancient Indian myths and narratives, 'mak[ing] skillful use of the available identity raw materials' (ibid., 111).

Thus, Indian history and culture are 'deconstructed' into a melange of myths, legends and other narratives that serve as 'raw materials' and 'glue' for Gandhi's and Nehru's 'project' to 'construct' an Indian identity. Indian nationalists 'use the primordial raw materials at hand in such a way as to serve their particular purpose—taking some, leaving others, combining them, and possibly importing further materials' (ibid., 152). Moreover, with respect to the nationalist 'construction' of an Indian identity by drawing on 'raw materials' from 'the Indias of the past', Engelmeier raises the question: 'What relationship is there between the material and the construction? It could be possible that the material itself already is the construction' (ibid.). Does not Engelmeier insinuate here that not more than a few 'fabrications' or forgeries underpin the nationalist 'constructions'? Whatever, we are presented with a multi-layered construction: 1) the nationalist 'construction' of Indian history and culture, based upon 2) historical and cultural 'raw materials' which are likely 'constructions' too, and 3) these dual 'constructions' are then used for 'constructing' an 'abstract pan-Indian national identity'.

Because in the first half of the twentieth century no Indian identity existed, claims Engelmeier, Gandhi and Nehru had no choice but to construct a synthetic 'national identity'. Their project of constructing an Indian identity ultimately served its purpose because the construction '*somehow resonates with something already there*' (ibid., 112, emphasis added). Although the objective existence of Indian history, culture and an identity accrued from both are denied, at least it is admitted that 'something' in terms of history and culture was 'already there' that 'resonates' with the nationalist 'identity construction'.

Part of the Indian 'identity construction' and nation-building was the 'construction' of a strategic culture for Independent India. Again, writes Engelmeier, nationalist elites drew upon the reservoir of ancient politico-strategic 'raw materials' like the realism of Kautilya's *Arthashastra* or the idealism of Ashoka's edicts. Such materials 'can be used almost at will by elites to incite the masses both to non-violence as well as communal rioting, to justify Panchsheel as much as realpolitik' (ibid., 56). From this perspective, India's strategic culture has not accrued from its history and its traditions of strategic thought. Instead, strategic culture is a 'construction' of nationalist elites who selectively use some politico-strategic 'building blocks' from putative traditions that are probably 'constructed', too.

> *That is not to say, however, that there is no Indian strategic culture. There is one—but it is not defined by ancient tradition.* It is defined, rather by the modern imagining of the Indian nation, by what nationalists have interpreted and institutionalized as Indian political culture. From a diverse cultural legacy, a certain view of Indian culture was constructed by way of emphasis, selection, and interpretation. *Strategic culture is the product of the dynamics created by nationalism.* Nationalism in turn references aspects of traditional culture. (Ibid., 57)

Consequently, Engelmeier is firmly opposed to the view *'that contemporary Indian strategic thought and practice is influenced by (or at least, stands in the tradition of) certain texts, some of which date back thousands of years* [...]. To argue that the Indian government today makes a decision because of anything *Ashoka or Kautilya or Akbar* did centuries ago or because of holy texts written even longer ago, would be misleading' (ibid., 46, 56, emphasis added).

Apart from the 'constructivist' representation of the concept of strategic culture as such, what attracts attention is Engelmeier's radical assertion that its ancient texts and traditions do not exert any influence on the politico-strategic thinking and practice in contemporary India. The contestation that realist Kautilyan thought as well as idealist thought in the tradition of Ashoka are of any relevance for Indian strategic culture is the result of constructivist axioms: Pre-modern politico-strategic ideas are no 'concrete realities' and thus have no history of intellectual efficacy. Instead, such pre-modern ideas are mere 'raw materials' for actors' contingent projections into the past. While some of these projections 'somehow resonate with something already there', others might be outright fabrications serving political expediency. The essential point here is that pre-modern politico-strategic thought as such is of no interest for constructivists.

The case study has shown why the inner logic of the social constructivist approach contributes to the marginalization of classic texts like Kautilya's *Arthashastra*. While the text itself and its idea-contents are pushed into the background, the (contingent) context of the text's reception becomes all important. Not what Kautilya actually states in the *Arthashastra* is of prime interest but its perception and utilization by Indian nationalists and other political actors. Kautilya's *Arthashastra* shrinks to a mere ideological accessory of Indian nationalism or other political interests. So, why bother to study the *Arthashastra*?

In the expert interviews, the social constructivist approach to Indian culture, history and strategic culture caused mostly skeptical smiles. For the Indian interviewees, the 'power of ideas'—particularly endogenous classical ideas, radiating efficaciously across time—was common sense.

> Cultural currents coming from the distant past may have been stronger or weaker. But they did not get cut off, there was no total break. *The idea that India's cultural identity is the exclusive creation by the early 20th century nationalists or by proto-nationalists of the late 19th century is not sustainable. Obviously, there is something terribly wrong with this thesis.* (EI Rajeev Bhargava,[10] emphasis added)

The study *Interrogating International Relations* by Jayashree Vivekanandan (2011) professes to shed light on the conceptual deficits in Indian IR theory—from a social constructivist (and postcolonial) perspective. She sharply criticizes Morgenthau's anthropological realism and Waltz's neo-realism, accusing them of being ahistorical and acultural. At first, it seems Vivekanandan wants to stress the importance of history and culture for IR theory, but then comes an eerie twist—the inclusion of history and culture in Indian IR theory is sharply critiqued: '[T]he cultural and historical turn in IR has not always presented a welcome shift. Studies that frame culture in self-referential terms run the risk of essentialism' (Vivekanandan 2011, 4). The assumption that there could be a 'self-referential'—objectively existing—cultural continuity that has not been 'constructed' retroactively is untenable for Vivekanandan:

> Katzenstein rightly observed that *culture must not be viewed as 'a child of deep continuities in history',* but the focus should be on the political processes by which *norms in different time frames are contested and contingent, politically made and unmade in history.* (Ibid., 193, emphasis added)

Nehru's *Discovery of India* is chosen as object of Vivekanandan's critique because this work is a typical example of the 'search for timeless essence and continuing traditions' (ibid., 93). Inconceivable for Vivekanandan is the assumption that politico-strategic ideas and traditions going back to Indian antiquity might radiate efficaciously into the present and influence the thinking and practice in the field of political and strategic affairs: '[T]he *exercise of extending ancient and medieval strategic traditions to the contemporary would be unviable*' (ibid., 7, emphasis added). We know such argumentation from Engelmeier: Not the past and the ideas and traditions generated therein impact the present, but present actors 'construct' the past and make up the traditions that fit their current interests and political needs:

> The compulsions behind constructing a grand tradition are rooted in contemporary concerns. In *'writing history backwards'*, proponents of lineages are more interested in substantiating their own theoretical claims by pointing out its historical antecedents. (Ibid., 42, emphasis added)

Faithful to the constructivist cause, Vivekanandan tells us that modern India's 'grand traditions' are really a case 'writing history backwards'—i.e., retroactive projections from the present into the past. But already on the next page of her book, she writes with explicit recourse to Kautilya:

> Theorising inter-state relations has had a long history in India. *Indigenous writings on statecraft and diplomacy date back to ancient India when strategists such as Kautilya theorised* […]. It is ironical that despite *this long and sustained history of strategic thought,* it was the European theorisations that went on to dominate subsequent

studies on India. (Ibid., 43, emphasis added)

Now, we are told, there is indeed a long and sustained history of strategic thought in India. And one wonders whether Vivekanandan would include social constructivism among the 'European theorisations' she critiques for sidelining endogenous traditions.

Vivekanandan also dislikes the concept of strategic culture which is why she mostly speaks of 'strategic practices'. She criticizes strategic culture as a 'self-referential' and 'essentialist' concept, just as she had done earlier with respect to cultural continuity and politico-strategic traditions.

> The basic tenets of strategic culture studies agree with the essentialist version of the [Morgenthau's] anthropological approach. Its assertion that communities as repositories of culture are clearly defined constancies sits well with the anthropological approach [...]. The tendency to mine history for substantiations of our contemporary concerns therefore stems from seeking contrived linkages with the past. *This is particularly true in the case of Indian strategic culture, an area that has thrown up a clutch of colonial caricatures invoking India's pristine antiquity.* (Ibid., 17f, 211, emphasis added)

Nevertheless, Vivekanandan reaffirms in unambiguous terms that India does possess an old and sustained tradition of strategic thought, in which Kautilya figures prominently:

> However, this is *not to discount the importance of theorisations that existed in ancient India* [...]. Although many of the ideas prevalent then may be lost in contemporary times, *they would serve as a useful beginning towards theorising about strategic practice in India.* This may necessarily involve referring to ancient Sanskrit texts that are popularly known as Hindu scriptures, and the genre is often termed the Hindu tradition of warfare. (Ibid., 85, emphasis added)

Such obvious contradictions are bound to occur since Vivekanandan tries to address India's politico-cultural and strategic traditions within the framework of social constructivism which aims at 'deconstructing' history, culture and politico-strategic traditions. However, at one point of her study, Vivekanandan breaks free of the constructivist corset: her substantive analysis of strategic thinking and practice during Mughal era in the sixteenth and seveneteenth centuries. She affirms that Mughal strategic thought is a continuation of—or at least significantly influenced by—strategic thought of Indian antiquity as expressed in the epic *Ramayana*, Kautilya's *Arthashastra* or Kamandaki's *Nitisara*:

> The central argument here is that *while Akbar innovated with his policies, to a great extent he drew from existing ancient and medieval traditions of kingship* [...]. Akbar consciously fashioned his image on the line of the traditional Hindu king [...] whose vital function entailed protecting the realm of norms and beliefs. (Ibid., 100, 193, emphasis added)

Vivekanandan also points out that the strategic thinking of the Mughal era is an important ideational component of India's strategic culture. And, as Mughal strategic thought and practice were significantly influenced by the epics, Kautilya and Kamandaki, she acknowledges, at least indirectly, that Indian strategic culture is indeed the outgrowth of a long and sustained tradition of endogenous politico-strategic thought.

Vivekanandan refers repeatedly to Kautilya and takes note of his theoretical achievements in the *Arthashastra*. Similarly, she is appreciative of Kamandaki's *Nitisara*, a political and strategic work that builds on the *Arthashastra* but was written centuries later—and thus proves the continuity of Kautilyan thought. Evidently, there is an inner contradiction in Vivekanandan's study: on the one hand, allegiance to the social constructivist approach of 'deconstructing' cultural continuity and, along with it, politico-cultural traditions and strategic culture; on the other hand, acknowledgement of the significance and continuing influence of India's ancient strategic traditions as typified by Kautilya.

The good intention to remedy conceptual deficits of Indian IR by turning the attention to endogenous politico-strategic resources is visible in Vivekanandan's study. But choosing the social constructivist approach to that end means straining an intellectual trip wire. The result is conceptual contradictions and inadequate attention to the idea-contents of classical source texts like Kautilya's *Arthashastra* that are feeding and shaping India's strategic culture.

8.4.5 Postcolonial theory

An unprejudiced observer might think that Kautilya's *Arthashastra* is 'in good hands' at postcolonial theory since this work is an endogenous politico-cultural resource of a formerly colonized country. Moreover, one might expect that the postcolonial school would engage in the intellectual rehabilitation of Kautilya countering his marginalization by Eurocentric theorizing. In addition, many leading figures of the postcolonial school come from India, and one would thus expect some extra intellectual openness towards Kautilya. However, all these assumptions prove to be incorrect. Postcolonial theory has cold-shouldered Kautilya.[11] As to why that is so, the following factors need to be considered:

Postcolonial theory is a very amorphous theory. Its founding document, so to speak, is Edward Said's 1978 book *Orientalism*. Said describes 'Orientalism' as an intellectual formation of the colonial and postcolonial West 'for dominating, restructuring, and having authority over the Orient' (Said 1979, 3). Parallel to Said, who deals with Orientalist representations of India only in passing, the 'Subaltern Studies' school, originating in India, forms a second source of postcolonial theory. Subaltern Studies, inspired by Antonio Gramsci's 'history from below', has aimed at reconstructing the ignored and repressed history of the Indian 'subalterns'—i.e., the peasant majority as well as other marginalized social groups. The subalterns are seen as the repository of an 'authentic' people's culture that stands opposed to Brahmin 'high culture' (cf. Prakash 1994; Nanda 2003). About this 'authentic' Indian culture, Gyan Prakash, a leading Indian representative of the postcolonial school, writes: 'These [Subaltern Studies] scholars have sought to uncover *the subaltern's myths, cults, ideologies, and revolts* that colonial and nationalist elites sought to appropriate and that conventional historiography has laid waste' (Prakash 1994, 1479, emphasis added).

In addition to Said and the Subaltern Studies theorists, Gayatri Spivak and Homi K. Bhabha are regarded as the leading figures of postcolonial theory.[12] The two Indian-born literary scholars, living in the USA and the UK, shifted postcolonial theory towards cultural studies at a highly abstract discourse level. The focus moved away from subaltern issues in colonial and postcolonial contexts towards postmodern discourses of subalternity and hegemony in general. The postcolonial discourse became a 'catachrestic combination of Marxism, poststructuralism, Gramsci and Foucault, the modern West and India, archival research and textual criticism' (Prakash 1994, 1490). This shift of discourse probably explains why postcolonial theory got rapidly established at British and American universities. Firmly anchored in Western academia, postcolonial theory radiated back into Indian social and political sciences (cf. Castro Varela/Dhavan 2005; Loomba 1998).

As postcolonial theory was getting established in Western academia, the deconstruction of Orientalist representations of the 'Global South' mutated into the radical 'deconstruction' of the principles of reason and scientific-technological progress—the Enlightenment paradigm. In the Indian context, Meera Nanda has critically examined postcolonial theory and social constructivism (cf. Nanda 2003). Responding to the critics of her critique, she writes:

> [P]ostcolonial theory is, above all, an epistemological critique of the very possibility of knowledge that can capture some aspect of reality truthfully, regardless of the context of its production. Postcolonial theorists, to the last man and woman, decry this 'empirical-realist' epistemology (Roland Inden's term) as Eurocentrism masquerading as universal reason [...] [O]nly those who excel at rubbishing the Enlightenment can speak for India these days. (Nanda 2005, 178)

For the postcolonial school, colonialism is wedded to the Enlightenment paradigm because the colonial peoples were subjugated in the name of European-style civilizational progress. Also the nation-state and nationalism are inextricably linked to the paradigm of Enlightenment. Therefore, the Enlightenment paradigm, nationalism and the nation-state are the ideological enemy images for postcolonial theory.

In the postcolonial perspective, the indigenous elites of colonial space take a hybrid position: on one hand, they are the (privileged) subalterns in conflict with the colonial power, on the other hand, they have a position of dominance over the 'real' subalterns—the negatively-privileged masses in the colonies. In their political resistance to the colonial power, the indigenous elites have submitted to the colonialists' epistemic regime. By adopting for themselves the ideas of Enlightenment, nationalism and the nation-state, the anticolonial elites have committed their most momentous crime—at least from the postcolonial point of view. Partha Chatterjee, a leading proponent of Subaltern Studies, writes about the political thinking of the Indian nationalists: '[I]t is born out of the encounter of a patriotic consciousness with the framework of knowledge imposed upon it by colonialism' (Chatterjee 1986, 79).

Postcolonial theory cannot deny that Indian nationalism was primarily formed through referencing the (pluralist) traditions of Indian culture. Indian nationalism began as 'cultural patriotism' and was thus not an ideological carbon-copy of nationalism in Europe. However, for the postcolonial school, indigenous cultural patriotism was as bad as the imported ideology of European-style nationalism as such because it supposedly meant pushing 'Sanskrit high culture' at the expense of the 'authentic' subaltern culture of the Indian masses.

Chatterjee sees Gandhi as an exception because he supposedly rejected basic ideas of European Enlightenment like the nation-state or industrial development. Instead, he reached out to the subaltern culture of India, which, according to Chatterjee, is demonstrated by Gandhi's supposed anti-utilitarianism, utopianism and spiritualism.[13] Nevertheless, Chatterjee laments, the Mahatma got himself inseparably tied up with Indian nationalism: 'And so we get, in the historical effectivity of Gandhism as a whole, the conception of a national framework of politics in which the peasants are mobilized but do not participate, of a nation of which they are part, but a national state from which they are forever distanced' (Chatterjee 1986, 125).

While the postcolonial critique of Gandhi is somewhat ambiguous,

Nehru is seen as the true incarnation of Indian nationalism. Nehru's *Discovery of India* is seen as the key programmatic document of Indian nationalism and the blueprint for building a European-style nation-state in India. Thus, claims Chatterjee, Nehru was intent to politically disempower the subaltern masses and strangle the 'authentic' (subaltern) culture of India. Gyan Prakash sums up his arguments:

> Chatterjee's work contains an extended analysis of Jawaharlal Nehru's *Discovery of India*, a foundational nationalist text, showing the use of History, Reason, and Progress in the normalization of peasant 'irrationality'. The inescapable conclusion from such analyses is that 'history', authorized by European imperialism and the Indian nation-state, functions as a discipline, empowering certain forms of knowledge while disempowering others. (Prakash 1994, 1485)

As already indicated, in addition to nationalism and the nation-state, 'Sanskrit high culture' is the ideological enemy image of the postcolonial school. The thrust of the criticism is threefold:

- Via the hegemony of Sanskrit high culture, the 'authentic' subaltern culture of India is to be suppressed, if not eradicated.
- Sanskrit high culture is the linchpin of Indian nationalism 'that upheld the ancient Hindu civilization as the bearer of the original Indian identity' (Vivekanandan 2011, 71).
- Sanskrit high culture is inseparably connected with European Orientalism: 'Indology and its attendant variants were intrinsically linked to the colonial project' (ibid., 37).

The postcolonial school's bitter opposition not only to Sanskrit high culture but to Indology as well deserves to be looked at more closely for herein may lie an important cause for the marginalization of Kautilya and other endogenous politico-cultural resources. How does the summary condemnation of Indology as an accomplice of colonialism come about? Meera Nanda describes the 'logic' behind apodictic postulates of the kind we have seen from Vivekanandan:

> The following syllogism is at work here; a. There is a. no representation free of power, b. The West exerted power over India, its most prized colony; c. Therefore, all colonial representations of Indian society—its sciences, culture, and religion—were meant to serve the Western interests in controlling India [...] [resulting in a] sweeping condemnation of all Western representations of India-regardless of whether they are factually valid or not—*as a colonial mutilation of India's original cultural gestalt*. (Nanda 2005, 179, emphasis added)

Undoubtedly, it was the Europeans who established (modern) Indology. The first (amateur) Indologists were members of the British colonial administration who collected Sanskrit texts and conducted archaeological field work. They were followed by academic Indologists—mainly philologists engaging in the Sanskrit Studies in Britain, Germany, France, Russia and other European countries—who translated the classical works of ancient India into European languages and thus made them accessible to the world. By the second half of the nineteenth century, Indology had matured into an established academic discipline with professorial chairs at many European universities.

In an insightful essay, Peter Hees has dealt with the postcolonial school's essentializing of European Indology as an auxiliary force of colonialism (Hees 2003). He comes to the conclusion that there were indeed condescending and patronizing as well as romanticizing attitudes among European Indologists of the colonial era. However, in most cases such problematic tendencies did not compromise the scientific integrity of their Indological research. Hees also deals with the beginnings of Indology in India itself, in particular Aurobindo Ghose's Indological studies. While Aurobindo strongly resented the often condescending attitude of European Indologists, he did not question their scientific quality of their works. Aurobindo wanted to establish Indology back home in India, but he did not seek ideological confrontation with European Indology. Thus, the summary accusation of Indology aiding and abetting colonialism is hardly sustainable—certainly not for non-British Indologists who had no political interest in the continuation of

British rule over India. The German Indologist Max Müller, who moved to England and spent most of his academic life at Oxford University, is a special case. But to him as well as most other British Indologists applies what Meera Nanda writes: 'I worry not about the political motivations of the Orientalist knowledge, but about the objective validity of their claims. I hold on to the idea that even those motivated by power can still sometimes find out some facts about another culture which are objectively true' (Nanda 2005, 179f).

In the view of the postcolonial school, European Indology has not only been complicit with European colonialism but also with the Brahmin caste representing Sanskrit high culture. In line with their *divide et impera* or *bheda* policies, the British privileged the Brahmins at the expense of India's other castes, religions and ethnic groups. Supposedly, European Indology and the Brahmins shared the common goal of consolidating the hegemony of Sanskrit high culture at the expense of Muslim or Buddhist culture and in particular 'subaltern culture' (cf. Chatterjee 1986; Rösel 1982).

The wholesale dismissal of the European Indology as Orientalist has fatal consequences for its research topics—notably classical Sanskrit texts. Because they have been researched and interpreted by (allegedly) Orientalist Indologists from Europe, the classical texts themselves appear as 'epistemically stained'. Thus, classical Sanskrit texts appear as tools of an epistemic exercise of power against the subalterns and their 'authentic' culture at the hands of colonialism, Indology and indigenous nationalist elites. Against this background, it is not surprising that Kautilya and the *Arthashastra* are met with deep suspicion by the postcolonial school. Such suspicious, if not aversive, attitude would be fueled by the following factors:

- Kautilya was a Sanskrit writing Brahmin, a prominent representative of (ancient Indian) rationalism and secularism, and the builder of the first pan-Indian state.
- The *Arthashastra* is an essential part of Sanskrit high culture, and European Indology has figured prominently in the work's scholarly investigation.

- Kautilya has gained great importance for Indian nationalism and modern Indian politics.

For the postcolonial school, these factors add up to 'guilt by association'. Its 'punishment' for Kautilya's *Arthashastra* is to give it the silent treatment. Not only, but especially the postmodern schools of social constructivism and postcolonial theory have subtly contributed to marginalizing Kautilya's *Arthashastra* in the Indian social and political sciences. But there is an important addendum to this finding: its expiration date is already foreseeable.

9

TREND REVERSAL
A 'Comeback' of Kautilya?

In the preceding section, we have investigated factors that have contributed to Kautilya's marginalization in the Indian social and political sciences. Now we turn towards the opposite trend. Since the turn of the millennium, there have been some indications for renewed interest in endogenous politico-cultural resources in Indian social and political sciences (and the Indian strategic community). This cautious process of re-orientation refers not only to Kautilya's *Arthashastra* and other classical texts of Indian antiquity. To some extent, politico-cultural sources of the Mughal period and politically relevant contributions of authors of Indian modernity like Tilak, Aurobindo or Tagore have been taken up in the social and political science discourse. During the first decade of the twenty-first century, the opening towards endogenous politico-cultural resources was still rather viscous, but it has gained momentum since. This pertains in particular to Kautilya's *Arthashastra* as we will show with two examples: the thematizing of Kautilya and the *Arthashastra* at the Faculty of Social Sciences, University of Delhi (DU), and at the Institute for Defence Studies and Analyses (IDSA) in New Delhi. First, however, the contradictory and fragile opening process in the first decade of the twenty-first century will be outlined.

9.1 A 'PROGRAM OF RECOVERY' FOR ENDOGENOUS POLITICO-CULTURAL RESOURCES

Particularly in the Political Science sub-discipline International Relations (IR), the fixation on theories originating from Europe and North

America gave rise to growing criticism among Indian IR scholars. In that, neither the paradigm of modern science has been questioned, nor has there been a call for an 'Indian IR theory'. The issue has not been the substitution of Western theories of Political Science but rather supplementing them by endogenous politico-strategic resources and theoretical concepts derived from them. This opening process was shaped by two opposing tendencies which have already been discussed in the previous section B 8: on the one hand, a great intellectual discomfort with the dominance of Western theories and the consequent 'division of labour' reducing Indian political scientists to licensees of Western theories; on the other hand, a deep-seated fear that theory-building drawn upon endogenous sources might turn into intellectual 'nativism'. Nevertheless, some proposals have been made as to what Indian political thinkers should be addressed as potential resources for theory-building in Political Science and particularly, IR theory.

A first initiative for revisiting endogenous politico-strategic resources came from Kanti Bajpai whose ambiguous relation to Kautilya we have already noted. In 2005, Bajpai (with Siddharth Mallavarapu) published the edited volume *International Relations in India—Bringing Theory Back Home*. The volume contains an essay by Bajpai with the same—programmatic—title (Bajpai/Mallavarapu 2005b, 17–38). In this essay, Bajpai submits a 'program of recovery' with the aim of tapping endogenous politico-cultural sources for Political Science and IR theory. He proposes that V.R. Mehta's work *Foundations of Indian Political Thought* be used for orientation (cf. Mehta 1992). Therein, Mehta lists eighteen—partly mythological—thinkers and writers who have had formative influence on political thought in India:

- Valmiki: author of the epic *Ramayana*
- Vyasa: the legendary author of the epic *Mahabharata*
- Surya: a mythological sage and teacher in the Vedas
- Brihaspati: the mythological author of a lost work on statecraft
- Kautilya
- Mahavira: the founder of the Jain religion, who probably lived in the sixth century BC

- Manu: the legendary sage and putative author of the *Manusmriti* ('The Laws of Manu'); this *dharmashastra* contains a canon of religious, ethical and legal norms
- Buddha: the philosopher turned into the founder of the Buddhist religion who most probably lived in the sixth century BC
- Somadeva: author of the work *Nectar of the Science of Polity* (tenth century AD)
- Barni (Barani): Islamic historian and political theorist (early fourteenth century AD)
- Abu al Fazl: vizier and biographer of the Mughal ruler Akbar (late sixteenth century AD)
- Aurobindo Ghose: political activist and philosopher (1872–1950)
- Balbhadra Sahu: author of philosophical and political work *Desik Shastra* (1921)
- Mahatma Gandhi
- N.M. Roy: political activist and philosopher (1887–1954)
- Jawaharlal Nehru
- R. M. Lohia: political activist (1910–67)
- Rabindranath Tagore: Indian poet, writer and philosopher (1861–1941)

Oriented on Mehta's list, Bajpai proposes to put together a comparable list of endogenous politico-strategic resources that should be investigated from the point of view of their relevance for IR theory. The research objective should be to tap the idea-contents of such thinkers in a critical and methodologically controlled manner for theory-building:

> A program of recovery will be crucial to the development of a self-conscious, critical, and confident International Studies [IS]. Braced by seeking a program the Indian field will be given a chance to go beyond the plaint that theory is something Westerners do. The process of recovery will energize IS in India in two ways. First, it will provide a series of 'exemplars'—role-models to put it crudely. This will invigorate the view that *Indians have a history of thought which contemporary students can critically draw on, and*

> that theory is a vital—i.e. living—component of their intellectual and political tradition. Second, *a recovery of a 'tradition' will help to construct a research program* in which Indians should have a comparative advantage. Indian scholars will have physical, linguistic, and philosophical access, particularly to older materials which outsiders, in general, will find hard to match. (Bajpai/Mallavarapu 2005b, 31, emphasis added)

Bajpai is proposing here a comprehensive research program on India's politico-strategic resources from antiquity up to the twentieth century. He insists that 'uncritical nativism' and an 'essentialist "Indian" vision' must be avoided: 'The danger of this agenda is, as noted earlier, that it will fall prey to nativism [...] the view that it is pristine, indigenous thought and practice which is superior to alien counterparts and which more or less transparently contains answers to contemporary problems' (Bajpai/Mallavarapu 2005b, 32). However, the real danger for the proposed research program on India's politico-strategic resources was different: disinterest and silence among Bajpai's Indian colleagues. For the rest of the first decade of the twenty-first century, no positive response to the proposed research agenda materialized—at least not in the sense of 240 tangible research results. Neither Kautilya nor the other endogenous sources listed by Mehta were studied or researched in a Political Science context as Bajpai had proposed.

However, in 2007, political scientist Navnita Behera published an essay which has a thrust similar to Bajpai's 'program of recovery'. Her essay, entitled *Re-Imagining IR in India*, has been mentioned already (see section B 8.4.3). Her critique is directed against the lack of intellectual autonomy of Indian IR theory which tends to take after fashionable Western theories. Indian IR theory 'does not acknowledge India's own history and philosophical traditions (e.g. Kautilya)' (Behera 2007, 341). But Behera does not stop at mere criticism; instead, she proposes a research agenda that is similar to Bajpai's:

> The second line of inquiry calls for IR scholars to undertake a thorough re-reading of the Indian history and *analysis of the political thought of various Indian philosophers and political thinkers*

> *including Manu, Valmiki, Buddha, Iqbal, Sri Aurobindo, Dadabhai Naroji, Tagore and political leaders: such as Gandhi, Nehru, Sardar Patel, Maulana Azad among others. In view of our analysis of Kautilya's Arthashastra, the issue of 'how to' read history is of critical importance.* (Behera 2007, 360f, emphasis added)

Behera sharply criticizes the marginalization of Kautilya and demands that special attention be given to the *Arthashastra* in terms of scholarly analysis and conceptual utilization for theory-building. While in Bajpai's case some self-doubts were detectable about whether his 'program of recovery' would actually be taken up by his colleagues in IR theory, Behera got personally involved in the implementation of such a research agenda. In that, her role in the transformation of Political Science curricula at the University of Delhi is of particular significance (see below B 9.2.2 and B 9.2.3).

Besides Behera, there were some other encouraging signs with respect to the 'recovery' of classical politico-strategic resources—at least in the sense of keeping the issue alive. Also in 2007, Amitav Acharya and Barry Buzan published an essay titled "Why is There No Non-Western International Relations Theory." Therein, they called for tapping not only pre-modern Indian but other Asian politico-cultural sources as well:

> [I]n parallel with Western international theory's focus on key figures such as Thucydides, Hobbes, Machiavelli, Kant, etc., there are Asian classical traditions and the thinking of classical religious, political, and military figures, e.g. *Sun Tzu, Confucius, and Kautilya*, on all of which some secondary 'political theory' type literature exists [...]. Attempts to derive causal theories out of these do exist, but have been rare. (Acharya/Buzan 2007, 302, emphasis added)

Acharya and Buzan criticize the marginalization of Kautilya, but they do not elaborate on the *Arthashastra* and its idea-contents. Instead, they propose to investigate the relevance of Gandhi and Nehru for IR theorizing and do the same for other nationalist leaders of Asia, including Mao Tse-tung, Aung San of Burma, Jose Rizal of the Philippines, and Sukarno of Indonesia:

> [E]xamine the historical, political and philosophical resources of the [Asian] country/area concerned (e.g. key historical experiences, key political leaders, key ideological traditions, key philosophical thinkers), with an evaluation of how these do or do not play into the debates about IRT, and assess how they might form the basis of an indigenous, non-Western IRT. (Acharya/Buzan 2007, 309)

In his 2011 essay, titled "In Search of International Relation Theories Beyond the West," Acharya raises once more the issue of scholarly utilization of endogenous politico-cultural resources for Political Science and IR theory. He mentions Kautilya's *Arthashastra*, but unfortunately, again, without further elaboration of its idea-contents. Noteworthy is his proposal to analyse the epic *Mahabharata* as a resource of IR theory:

> The Hindu epic *Mahabharata*, which describes a fratricidal conflict between the Kauravas and Pandavas, should be a rewarding source of concepts and theories of IRT, it is after all a metanarrative of just and unjust wars, alliances and betrayals, self-interest and morality, and good and bad governance. (Acharya 2011, 634)

Since then, Amrita Narlikar and Aruna Narlikar (2014) have published the study *Bargaining with Rising India—Lessons from the Mahabharata*, in which they examine negotiating strategies in the epic *Mahabharata* and correlate them with those of post-1947 India. In the study, they address the question: 'to what extent does India's bargaining behaviour, as a rising power, reflect cultural continuities' (Narlikar/Narlikar 2014, 2). They write:

> A study that brings together scholarship on modern-day negotiation behavior and classical readings may appear to be unusual at first glance. In fact, the engagement between classical theories and current problems is well rooted in an established repertoire of writings, such as the works that apply to the tenets of Clausewitz, Machiavelli, and Sun Tzu to understanding concerns of modern statehood, statecraft, war, and bargaining. *What is surprising, though, is that Indian classical theories have been put to only limited use with reference to today's problem; bar a few stray*

applications of Kautilya's Arthashastra with regard to understanding or recommending foreign policy strategies, the rich classical Indian scholarship that refers directly or indirectly to bargaining remains sparingly utilized. We aim to address this gap. (Narlikar/Narlikar 2014, 2, emphasis added)

In the first decade of the twenty-first century, the postulation for tapping endogenous politico-cultural resources was articulated, and in that, Indian IR theorists took the lead. But some years had to pass until practical consequences from this postulation became visible. In the meantime, the inclusion of Kautilyan thought and that of other endogenous politico-strategic thinkers in Political Science curricula and/or research projects was left to the personal initiative of a few teachers and scholars. However, since the beginning of the second decade of the twenty-first century, evidence is accumulating that research roughly along the agenda proposed by Bajpai, Behera and Acharya begins indeed to materialize.

In the expert interviews, it was pointed out that the sparse offerings in terms of teaching and research on Kautilya and other politico-strategic resources at Indian universities stand in marked contrast to the interest of students in that subject area. It seems that the intellectual impetus coming from a small group of social scientists has found significant intellectual resonance among students and younger faculty members. And this resonance is not limited to the field of International Relations theory. At a seminar of the (private) think tank *Vivekananda International Foundation*, a lecturer at University of Mumbai reported that a 'Kautilya study group' had been constituted at his faculty which enjoyed great interest among students and teachers (Conversation with R.C. Pillai, 29 March 2012).

P.K. Gautam of the IDSA project *Indigenous Historical Knowledge* has been trying to get an overview of Kautilya's presence in teaching and research at Indian universities. His general conclusion, as stated above, is very sobering: Only in a fraction of the more than four hundred Indian universities Kautilya is addressed in Political Science teaching and research. Gautam lists University of Mumbai, University of Delhi, South

Asia University in Delhi, Banarass Hindu University in Varanasi (Uttar Pradesh), Gorakhpur University (Uttar Pradesh), Jadavpur University in Kolkata and University of Rajasthan (EI P.K. Gautam, 25 April 2012).

9.2 KAUTILYA AT THE UNIVERSITY OF DELHI

9.2.1 *Kautilya's Arthashastra finds its way into the Political Science curricula*

The University of Delhi—usually called 'Delhi University' or 'DU'—with about 130,000 students, is among the Indian elite universities.[1] In 2012, changes were also made in the mandatory course 'Political Theory' to include Kautilya and other endogenous political thinkers, as Dr Mohinder Singh, Assistant Professor in the Department of Political Science (at the time of the interview), reported in the expert interview. The interview gives an insight into the process of change in the Political Science syllabus at DU—and the place of Kautilya's *Arthashastra* therein. At first, M. Singh described his personal intellectual interest in the field of political theory:

> It's only now that I am planning to read the Arthashastra systematically [...]. I have worked on German thinkers of the 20th century: Hannah Arendt and Walter Benjamin. *Now my interest is shifting to Indian political thought.* But I am familiar with the arguments of the Arthashastra from reading secondary works and commentaries, etc. I think *Kautilya's Arthashastra is a text that has intrinsic value. My sense is it's a classic.* And therefore, one needs to think of it in terms of reviving the intellectual histories or systems of political thought—political thought from India's ancient and medieval periods that have been subjugated by colonialism. (EI, Mohinder Singh,[2] emphasis added)

However, the shift of his personal research interests does converge with a broader trend, Mohinder Singh said. Indian political scientists no longer accept that Kautilya is referred to as the 'Indian Machiavelli'. The *Arthashastra* has a theoretical eigenvalue which makes its intellectual access via Machiavelli not only superfluous but counterproductive. Instead, a comparative approach should be chosen in which Machiavelli and Kautilya stand on an equal footing. From his own experience during the recent years, the question has become increasingly urgent why scholarly engagement with European political theories is valued highly than that with Indian political thought. In that, the word 'value' had to be taken quite literally: So far, in the Political Science curricula a thesis dealing with European theories could yield double the number of credit points relative to one on Indian political theory—such as Kautilya, for example. In 2012, Mohinder Singh said that the distortions of curricular contents and grading criteria were in the process of getting remedied. He noted a growing openness of left-oriented social scientists with respect to endogenous traditions of political theory. Such open-mindedness, as evidenced by the reorganization of the curricula, was still absent till only a few years earlier, he stressed.

While DU has adopted a leading role in the inclusion of Kautilya and other endogenous politico-strategic resources in teaching and research, other universities have been hesitant. Yet an opening process seems to be taking place at at the School of International Studies (SIS) at Jawaharlal Nehru University (JNU) as well as the South Asia University in Delhi.[3] In the expert interview, Dr Siddharth Mallavarapu, (then) a Political Science lecturer at the JNU, said:

> This text, the Arthashastra, is a really important text. *There is now a recognition that we need to more systematically approach Indian strategic thought. In that context, Kautilya is particularly interesting [...]. But I do not want to suggest that Kautilya is our 'golden boy.'* I am interested in Kautilya: because I want to know if it is worth. I want to look at what he had to say, what the extent of sophistication in his thinking is. I think it is fair to ask: Are there certain generic principles of statecraft which have a resonance of life in the world we are living? (EI Siddhart Mallavarapu,[4] emphasis added)

Revisiting the Indian tradition of political theory is not limited to Kautilya. As Mohinder Singh explained, at DU's Political Science department also a module on the *Manu-smriti* is being introduced.

He acknowledged that mastery of Sanskrit is a rare exception among Indian social scientists, but good English and Hindi translations of most source texts make that problem manageable. He emphasized the need to move beyond classical Hindu texts and tapping Buddhist, Jain and Muslim traditions of political thought for Political Science. Moreover, correcting the fixation on European and North American political theory should not be limited to the study of Indian sources. Instead, other Asian traditions of political thought—in particular those from China and Japan—should be tapped as well and become part of the Political Science discourse in India. On that basis, one could demand from political scientists in Europe, the USA and in other parts of the world that they, reciprocally, pay attention to the Indian traditions of political thought, notably Kautilya's *Arthashastra*.

Noteworthy was Mohinder Singh's focus on the idea-contents of the *Arthashastra* and other politico-cultural texts. He said that, in Political Science, the previously dominant focus on the reception contexts and political instrumentalization of Kautilya seems to be receding:

> Now there are different ways of reading *Kautilya—for the sake of understanding Kautilya rather than treating him as a figure who is important for asserting Indian nationalism.* That is much more interesting. That opens up Kautilya for the eigenvalue approach. The same goes for *Manu-smriti* actually [...]. Things are changing.
> (EI Mohinder Singh,[5] emphasis added)

Further indication of the Kautilya revival in the Indian academia can be seen in terms of the submission of doctoral theses[6] and the commitment of younger faculty members at DU's Political Science department to teaching of Kautilya.[7]

9.2.2 'Postmodernism meets Kautilya'

An assistant professor of political science at the University of Delhi, Dr Deepshikha Shahi (lecturer at the time of the presentation) presented a paper entitled "Arthashastra Beyond Realpolitik: The 'Eclectic' Face of Kautilya" (Shahi 2015) on 9 April 2013, at the 'IDSA Workshop on Kautilya: Creating Strategic Vocabulary'. We briefly examine this paper because it gives an insight into the perception of Kautilya among the younger generation of Indian political scientists, whose intellectual socialization has been significantly influenced by postmodern theories—social constructivism, post-structuralism, postcolonial theory and gender studies. Shahi exemplifies a new trend in Indian Political Science: The affinity to postmodern theories does no longer block the engagement with the idea-contents of endogenous politico-cultural resources like Kautilya's *Arthashastra*. Of course, when intellectual interest in the text as such goes along with the application of postmodern theories and methodologies, conceptual contradictions are inevitable. There are some similarities between Vivekanandan and Shahi, but the latter is clearly focused on the idea-contents of Kautilya's *Arthashastra*. Thus, at the beginning of her essay, Shahi states unequivocally:

> *Kautilya's Arthashastra has increasingly become a source of intellectual inspiration* for the scholars who are particularly interested in exploring the possibilities of theorization in Indian International Relations (IR). Their objective is not to institutionalize an Indian School of IR, but to acknowledge and appreciate the 'thinking capabilities' of the Asian world. (Shahi 2015, 63, emphasis added)

Shahi criticizes that Political Science has positioned Kautilya almost exclusively as an 'amoral political realist'—as typified by Roger Boesche's book on Kautilya. Therefore, the *Arthashastra* has to be 'liberated' from the 'prison' of naked power politics. She rightly emphasizes that a fresh approach to the *Arthashastra* is often frustrated by the fact that even political scientists with intellectual interest in Kautilya have not studied the text and, instead, rely on secondary literature. Shahi also correctly notes that such superficiality is also the reason why the *Arthashastra*'s profound theorems of political economy have largely been ignored by Political Science.

In view of this state of affairs, Shahi submits her own theoretical and methodological approach to Kautilya's *Arthashastra*: Multiple theoretical and methodological positions should be fused into an innovative 'eclectic' approach, within which, however, social constructivism is of particular significance. Such an approach would be conducive, she asserts, since the *Arthashastra* itself is an 'eclectic' work. Next, Shahi turns to Michel Foucault and his proposition of the intrinsic connection between power and knowledge. Since India has become an 'emerging power' in economic and military terms, its rise cannot remain without consequences for its knowledge production. But, so far, India's upgraded 'hard' power status has not yet arrived at the field of theory-building of Indian Political Science and IR theory. Shahi deplores that Indian IR theory continues to limit itself to 'sub-systemic' topics—i.e., those below the level of world politics. Therefore, it is urgent that Indian political scientists on their own volition develop the vocabulary and theoretical concepts that not only reflect India's growing power status but help to advance it further. That is indeed a puzzling position since Shahi's reference to the 'Foucauldian knowledge-power paradigm' does not serve as means to critique or 'deconstruct' India's growing power status, as one would expect, but aims at the exact opposite. In order to overcome the mismatch of hard and intellectual power, Shahi argues, Indian Political Science must turn to Kautilya. With him, India possesses a classical thinker of statecraft who can provide concepts for the autonomous development of 'systemic' IR theory. To meet this challenge, Kautilya is, as Shahi expressly states, more suitable than Gandhi, Nehru, Tagore, Ambedkar or Aurobindo. If Kautilyan concepts of statecraft were applied to the present world situation, Indian Political Science would advance its ability for theory building that would not lag behind that of Western academia.

While Shahi denounces the categorization of Kautilya as an 'amoral political realist', not much later she admits that the *Arthashastra* does indeed contain a lot of political realism. In order to avoid a one-sided fixation on Kautilyan realism, she argues, the *Arthashastra* should be approached via Alexander Wendt's social constructivist IR theory. For Wendt, anarchy in inter-state relation is not an objective fact that is either anthropologically determined or enforced through the international system's inherent logic. Instead, anarchy is 'made' (or 'constructed')— by the states' choice of attitude to each other. Shahi applies Wendt's proposition of 'three cultures of anarchy' to Kautilya's *mandala* concept of friends, foes and neutrals in inter-state relations: 'Kant culture' = friendly cooperation, 'Hobbes culture' = enmity, and 'Locke culture'

= peaceful rivalry. Which of the three options is adopted depends on the 'construction' of the respective (national) identity and the identity ascribed to other states. In the 'construction' of one's own identity and that of others, ethical considerations play an important role. That, according to Shahi, applies to Kautilya too, who rejects aggression against prosperous and well-governed states as violation of political ethics. Next, Shahi tries to prove the applicability of her constructivist thesis to Kautilya's *shadgunya* theory: identity 'construction' and identity attribution to other states determine which of the six methods of foreign policy is to be adopted.

> A careful reading of the Arthashastra reveals a striking resemblance with Wendt's Social *Constructivism* [...]. Kautilya's rational preoccupation with the notion of 'justice' discloses the 'eclecticism' in *Arthashastra* that includes both a realist concern for safeguarding selfish interests, and a constructivist awareness of designing foreign policy on the basis of the perceived identities of foreign states that are subject to change with the continuous interactions between the states. (Shahi 2015, 72, 74f, emphasis added)

Her 'reinventing the *Arthashastra*' via her 'eclectic' approach is conducive, Shahi argues, because Kautilya's work itself is 'eclectic' in that it propounds ethically refined realism as well as a social constructivist stance on foreign policy (Shahi 2015, 65). On that basis, and with its economic dimension added, the *Arthashastra* can become a key catalyst for autonomous theory-building in Indian Political Science.

Here is not the place for a conclusive assessment of Shahi's 'eclectic' interpretation of Kautilya's *Arthashastra*. What matters for our study is the finding that Shahi's paper demonstrates a substantive intellectual engagement with the idea-contents of the *Arthashastra* and an attempt to use Kautilyan thought-figures for theory-building regarding current issues of Political Science:

> Arthashastra, as developed in the 4th century BCE, is an ancient Indian script and *demonstrating its contemporary relevance* can serve the purpose of asserting the original thinking of the Asian epistemic communities. (Shahi 2015, 63, emphasis added)

As an indicator of a certain trend, Shahi's paper shows that the fixation on the reception contexts and the political instrumentalization of classical endogenous politico-strategic texts is giving way to an intellectual curiosity regarding their idea-contents. In this new approach, younger social scientists continue to carry their packet of postmodern theory, but that no longer prevents the substantive engagement with the ideas and concepts of Kautilya's *Arthashastra*.

9.3 THE KAUTILYA DISCOURSE AT THE INSTITUTE FOR DEFENCE STUDIES AND ANALYSES (IDSA)

In this segment, we reconstruct how, beginning in 2012, a 'Kautilya discourse' has come into being at the leading Indian strategic think tank, the Institute for Defence Studies and Analyses (IDSA) in New Delhi. For a rough orientation, one can compare IDSA with think tanks such as the Royal Institute of International Affairs (RIIA or 'Chatham House') in Britain or the German Institute for International and Security Affairs (SWP) in Berlin. IDSA is funded by the Indian Ministry of Defence and advises the Government of India. Research Fellows at IDSA come mainly from academia, the military and the Ministry of External Affairs. IDSA describes itself as

> a non-partisan, autonomous body dedicated to objective research and policy relevant studies on all aspects of defence and security. Its mission is to promote national and international security through the generation and dissemination of knowledge on defence and security-related issues [...]. Over the last fifty-plus years, IDSA has played a crucial role in shaping India's foreign and security policies. (http://www.idsa.in/aboutidsa)

IDSA's concept of security is very broad and includes military strategy, foreign policy and IR theory, area studies, economics and environmental issues. In addition, IDSA has thematized, albeit rarely before to 2012, endogenous traditions of politico-strategic thought that are relevant for India's strategic culture. On the topics listed, IDSA has been organizing conferences, notably the annual Asian Security Conference, Fellows'

Seminars and guest lectures. It also publishes several periodicals as well as research reports and studies in book form and/or as ebooks.

IDSA was founded in 1965. During the subsequent decades, the think tank paid no attention to Kautilyan thought. From 1968–75 and again 1980–87, K. Subrahmanyam headed IDSA. At a 1994 IDSA seminar on Indian strategic culture, Subrahmanyam had said that Kautilya was indeed a great strategic thinker, but that had been 2300 years ago—in other words, his relevance has evaporated since (cf. section B 7.2). Many Fellows at IDSA did not share Subrahmanyam's opinion of Kautilya, but that remained without consequences during the subsequent years. Then, in 1999, IDSA published a compilation of essays, titled *Sun Zi and China's Strategic Culture*. The edited volume contains K.N. Ramachandran's essay *Sun Zi and Kautilya—Towards a Comparative Analysis*. The author contradicts Subrahmanyam's statement that Kautilya has become irrelevant, writing:

> [T]here are striking similarities between Sun Zi and Kautilya in delineating strategic and tactical issues relating to war and peace [...] *[T]he wisdom of the two strategists on the basic issue of how to approach war and peace and on issues of intelligence and foreign policy is as fresh today as it was in their epochs.* (Ramachandran 1999, 76, emphasis added)

However, also during the first decade of the twenty-first century, Kautilya remained a non-issue at IDSA. It was only at the beginning of the second decade that things began to change with respect to Kautilya and the *Arthashastra*—not only at IDSA but more generally in the Indian strategic community. As P.K. Gautam notes:

> It is my observation that in the second decade of the 21st century the Indian strategic thinkers often quote the *Arthasastra*. For them Indian strategic thinking is highly informed by the *Arthasastra* and *Panchatantra*. *This trend is a sharp contrast to the strategic thinking of the last decade [...]. The trend now has reversed.* Often, more of Chanakya is being alluded to by top security and policymakers and journalists. (Gautam 2013c, 67, 78, emphasis added)

9.3.1 The IDSA Kautilya discourse in 2012

A key person for thematizing Kautilya and the *Arthashastra* at IDSA has been Col. (ret.) P.K. Gautam. After a distinguished career in the Indian Army (1970–2000), Gautam joined IDSA in 2005 as Research Fellow. His initial research foci were non-traditional security, notably environmental security, and area studies on Tibet. Later, Gautam's research focus shifted to the history of Indian strategic thought, in particular Kautilya's *Arthashastra*. That interest had been sparked by Tanham's 1992 paper on the 'absence' of strategic thought in India and Subrahmanyam's dismissive remarks on Kautilya in 1994. In 2012, Dr Arvind Gupta took over as IDSA Director General,[8] and it seems that he opened the way for dedicated research on Kautilya's *Arthashastra* within IDSA's overall research agenda—and Gautam was ready to get on with it.[9]

Towards the end of 2011, Gautam began to contact academics—Sanskrit philologists, historians and political scientists—who had done research work on Kautilya. He visited several Indian universities and research institutions where he had meetings and gave lectures on Kautilya. In the Spring of 2012, it was on Gautam's initiative that an initially informal working group of half a dozen IDSA Fellows was formed doing research on Kautilya's *Arthashastra* and its relevance for current Indian security policy. That was the starting point of the 'Kautilya discourse' at IDSA. On 19 April 2012, a Fellows Seminar was held at IDSA, at which M. Liebig, co-author of this study, gave a talk on 'Endogenous Politico-Cultural Resources: Kautilya's *Arthashastra* and India's Strategic Culture'.[10] In the Summer of 2012, the 'Kautilya working group' was transformed into a formal IDSA research project, named *Indigenous Historical Knowledge*.[11] In the context of this project, an IDSA seminar, titled *One Hundred Years of Kautilya's Arthasastra*, was held in September 2012. Among the panelists were IDSA researchers, the former senior diplomat K.P. Fabian, and political scientist Navnita Behera of the Delhi University. The report on the seminar on the IDSA website quotes from Gautam's seminar paper:

> Kautilya, the ancient strategic thinker of India, has been neglected and not been given his due in the Indian strategic thinking. It

> [the IDSA project *Indigenous Historical Knowledge*] seeks to revive the study of Kautilya's Arthasastra and establish it in the contemporary security studies [...] [T]he Kautilya moment has now arrived [...]. There is a need for state patronage, sponsorship and financial backing for the study of *Arthasastra*. Research and training for this purpose must be undertaken and encouraged at all the levels. (http://www.idsa.in/event/OneHundredYearsof%20 KautilyasArthasastra, emphasis added)

The IDSA has been a pioneer in spearheading the Kautilya revival as a part of its academic research. The Institute has sponsored several high profile conferences and has embarked upon an ambitious program of publication. A first major conference on Kautilya's *Arthashastra* and its relevance for contemporary India was held on 18 October 2012 at IDSA. In his welcome remarks, IDSA then-Director General Dr Arvind Gupta set forth the following as objectives of the conference (cf. Gupta 2015a):

- Bring together Indian security experts and academics in an interdisciplinary approach of engaging in-depth and systematically with Kautilya and the *Arthashastra*.
- Demonstrate the untenability of the claim that India lacks traditions of strategic thought and show that Kautilya's *Arthashastra* is a key factor for Indian strategic culture.
- The yield from the cooperative scholarly effort should help getting Kautilya his rightful place in the international strategic discourse, alongside Sun-Tzu and Machiavelli.
- The study of Kautilya's *Arthashastra* must be linked to the intellectual engagement with other classical politico-strategic texts of the Indian subcontinent, like the *Mahabharata*, *Panchatantra* or the South Indian Tamil Sangam literature.

The most prominent speaker at the October 2012 conference was the then-National Security Adviser Shivshankar Menon. He began by stating that he had studied the *Arthashastra* more than once and thus has gained, time and again, fresh insights that have helped him in his politico-strategic assessments and decision-making. The *Arthashastra* is a manual of statecraft, which contains both theoretical insights and offers conceptual assistance for politico-strategic practice. The work provides a realistic sense of what it means to lead a state. India's alleged lack of traditions of strategic thought is a 'colonial construct' because in all periods of Indian history—before and after the *Arthashastra*—there has been a rich tradition of strategic thought and practice. However, tapping these strategic traditions for theoretizations has so far been regrettably inadequate, yet he was confident, Menon said, that this task will now be embraced by younger Indian political scientists.

Menon spoke of the 'contemporary resonance' of many Kautilyan concepts like the 'polycentric state system' with asymmetric distribution of power or 'diplomacy of tous azimuth'. Such Kautilyan concepts are congruent with the multipolar world political situation and therefore of great value for IR theory. The strategic cultures of most other countries—Menon mentioned China here—lack the affinity to the concept of multipolarity in inter-state relations which has been characteristic of Indian strategic thought going back to antiquity. Thus, the study of strategic traditions can help to better understand the 'non-uniform' behaviour of states in the foreign policy sphere.

Menon regretted that strategic thinking in India is still dominated by 'derivative' concepts, doctrines and vocabulary that have been imported from other cultural spaces. Such derivative concepts do not meet India's requirements for designing its foreign and security policy. Nehru had laid the foundations for the modern strategic thinking in India, but that needs to be developed further. To that end, the reservoir of ancient Indian strategic thought, which includes, but is not confined to, Kautilya's *Arthashastra*, needs to be tapped.

> [R]eading Kautilya helps us by broadening our vision on issues of strategy. It will, naturally, take time and practice for us *to develop our own strategic vocabulary and doctrines*. This will require patience, but must be done if India is to truly seek the broadest possible degree of strategic autonomy. After all autonomy begins in the mind. As I said earlier, fortunately the younger generation of Indian

scholars shows signs of doing the necessary work and are thinking for themselves. (Menon 2015a, xvi–vii, emphasis added)

Menon ended his speech by expressing the expectation that in the context of the IDSA project *Indigenous Historical Knowledge* more such conferences will be held on Kautilya as well as other strategic thinkers of pre-modern India.

A good insight into the motivations and aims of the IDSA project *Historical Indigenous Knowledge*—the mainspring of the Kautilya discourse at IDSA—is provided by the conference speech of Dr. S. Kalyanaraman, titled *Arthashastra, Diplomatic History and the Study of International Relations in India*:

> There are three main reasons [why] Kautilya's *Arthashastra* must be studied. First, it is the earliest treatise on statecraft written anywhere in the world and being Indian in origin there is a need to celebrate this heritage by providing it a prominent place in the Indian discourse on International Relations. Second, *the Arthashastra continues to be relevant because of the key insights it provides about the enduring nature of the state and of the inter-state system* as well as because of the framework of thought and action it prescribes for states to navigate through this system [...]. *The third and even more important reason for studying the Arthashastra is to provide a boost for the discipline of International Relations in India*, a discipline that is widely acknowledged as continuing to wallow on the margins of the global discourse in this field [...]. It is within this broader focus upon the diplomatic history of pre-1947 India that the study of ancient Indian treatises such as the Arthashastra as well as many other classical texts needs to be located. Studying this history will enrich the Indian discourse in International Relations including by providing a laboratory to test and enrich the concepts and theories postulated both by contemporary scholars as well as by classical Indian thinkers like Kautilya. (Kalyanaraman 2015, 1f, 3, emphasis added)

With the October 2012 conference, the Kautilya discourse at IDSA had advanced qualitatively. The conference had an 'institutional' character: Besides the then-NSA Menon, senior representatives of government agencies, the military, the strategic community and academia participated.[12] The conference demonstrated that Kautilya was no longer a niche topic of a few academics and security experts. Moreover, one should keep in mind that IDSA has 'a certain attachment to the levers of power' in India (EI Kanti Bajpai, Frankfurt am Main, 25 September 2012).

9.3.2 The IDSA Kautilya discourse in 2013

In January 2013, an article by Gautam appeared in the peer-reviewed journal *Strategic Analysis*, which was published by Routledge in cooperation with IDSA. The article contains conceptual leitmotifs that since have continued to come up in the Kautilya discourse. Gautam's essay starts off with a programmatic statement: 'The community of scholars needs to study Kautilya's *Arthasastra* and apply his concepts to political theory and other fields of inquiry, such as intelligence, internal security, war, foreign policy, sociology, political psychology, law, accounting and management' (Gautam 2013a, 21). In this article, as well as in three more during 2012–13 (cf. Gautam 2013b, 2013d, 2013e), Gautam polemicizes against the habit of 'studying' Kautilya via secondary literature; reading *Chanakya niti* or commentary texts on the *Arthashastra* must not be substituted for the study of the text itself. If the text cannot be read in the original Sanskrit, Kangle's authoritative English translation of the *Arthashastra* is the only acceptable alternative. Because of the length and complexity of the text as well as the *Arthashastra's* diversity of topics, Gautam suggests a 'pedagogical' approach in order to capture the core concepts of the *Arthashastra* which he designates 'UPSRVY 4-7-6-12-3-3'. This 'mnemonic acronym' at first appears rather strange, but it is conducive to identifying and memorizing the key Kautilyan concept clusters by combining their initial letters and numbers: four *upayas*- seven *prakriti*-six *shadgunya*-twelve *rajamandalas* (constellations of inter-state relations)-three *vijay* (normative types of conquest)-three *yuddhas* (basic forms of warfare).

Gautam's article in *Strategic Analysis* shows that the IDSA Project

Indigenous Historical Knowledge had begun to pass beyond programmatic declarations, turning to methodological and didactic questions of addressing Kautilya's *Arthashastra*. That was also demonstrated by the lectures on Kautilya that Gautam delivered at universities and research institutions outside Delhi. The IDSA website reports about such lectures at University of Mumbai, University of Kolkata, Maulana Abdul Kalam Azad Institute of Asian Studies (Kolkata) and Upadhyay Gorakhpur University, Uttar Pradesh.

In April 2013, the IDSA research group *Indigenous Historical Knowledge* held a smaller-sized seminar, titled *IDSA Workshop on Kautilya: Creating Strategic Vocabulary*. Among the speakers were Dr Deepshikha Shahi of Delhi University, two doctoral students from the Nelson Mandela Centre for Peace and Conflict Resolution at Jamia Millia University, Delhi, and Jean Langlois-Berthelot from the École des Hautes Études en Sciences Sociales (EHESS) in Paris. This Kautilya seminar shows an effort to involve in the Kautilya discourse younger political scientists (with postmodern affinities) and, for the second time after April 2012, a non-Indian researcher. In the course of 2013, two more seminars of that format took place at IDSA: one on comparing Kautilya with Sun Tzu and another on Kautilya's relevance for IR theory.

In July 2013, the 149-page book *One Hundred Years of Kautilya's Arthasastra* by P.K. Gautam was published in the IDSA Monograph Series. The study has three thematic features:

- giving an overview of the current status of Kautilya's *Arthashastra* in academia and in the strategic community;
- summarizing the work done by the IDSA Project *Indigenous Historical Knowledge* during its first year of existence; and
- setting out goals for further advancing and broadening the Kautilya discourse.

With respect to the presence of Kautilyan thought in India's academia and in the strategic community, Gautam's findings remain sobering:

> As a political scientist and strategist, Kautilya's work is still enduring and relevant. However, his ideas have not been employed

> confidently by Indian scholars on security studies [...]. The absence of the study of the text (leaving aside Sanskritists) by political scientists and security experts is one main reason for the work still lying mostly unknown and understudied in the academic and policy world at both national and international level. (Gautam 2013c, 12, 59)

Gautam's list of causes that have led to Kautilya's marginalization is largely congruent with the findings of our study. But naming the causes why Kautilya has been sidelined is not Gautam's main concern; his aim is to point out ways to overcome it.

> *Kautilya or Chanakya must re-emerge and take his rightful place in the social science discourse of international studies.* [...] If early 20th century witnessed the discovery of Chanakya's manuscripts and commentaries during the freedom struggle, 21st century may be regarded as the second freedom struggle to rediscover him and cleanse him of all the loose and unjust interpretations of his work in comparative analysis with other great minds [...]. *Scholarship on the work [Arthashastra] must now come to the second stage of re-discovery. The need is to introduce the study of Kautilya for policy related work as it pertains to foreign policy, intelligence, war, internal security and administration.* (Gautam 2013c, 16, 21f, emphasis added)

In the 'second rediscovery' of Kautilya's *Arthashastra*, Gautam argues, IDSA's *Indigenous Historical Knowledge* project has taken a catalyst role. The IDSA Kautilya conference on 18 October 2012 should be seen as the starting point for the 'migration' of the Kautilya discourse to the social science departments of Indian universities and beyond. To that end, Gautam presents a kind of 'outreach program', in which he makes the following proposals:

- The *Arthashastra*—in Kangle's edition—should be made widely available via India's 'National Book Trust'.[13] Also, this edition of the *Arthashastra* should be translated into the major regional languages of India.

- In the curricula of the disciplines Political Science, History, Philosophy and Public Administration, the teaching and study of Kautilya's *Arthashastra* must be given adequate room. The textbooks in these disciplines must devote sufficient space to Kautilya, including citations of text passages from the *Arthashastra*.
- A scholarship program should be set up for faculty members and post-graduate students who want to do research on Kautilya and related subjects.
- Scientific projects should be funded that relate Kautilyan thought to current politico-strategic issues, notably in the disciplines International Relations, Security Studies and Intelligence Studies.
- Introducing teaching and research on Kautilya must apply not only to universities but also to the higher educational institutions of the Indian armed forces, the Ministry of External Affairs and the Indian Administrative Service (IAS).
- All of the above must be undertaken with the perspective of introducing Kautilyan thought in the international Political Science discourse.

For the implementation of the proposed outreach, Gautam calls for 'state patronage, sponsorship and finance' (Gautam 2013c, 118). However, such (hoped for) state support must be kept free of political interference. Any political, religious or ideological influence would compromise the Kautilya research program. The stringent necessity to exclude political and/or ideological interference in the teaching and research on Kautilya has been stressed by Gautam time and again. He sums up his outreach program, stating:

> There is a need for value-addition (in business language) by identifying the opportunities and gaps in knowledge which now require a new multidisciplinary impetus of research. Kautilya's contribution to political thought and theory needs to be placed at a high pedestal using his work which encompasses disciplines of linguistics, political science and theory, military science,

international relations, philosophy and history. All nations and countries of the [Indian] subcontinent need to claim him. However, Kautilya is not the end, but the means to improving and understanding political theory. (Gautam 2013c, 115)

Almost exactly one year after the first conference, on 8 October 2013, the second IDSA conference on Kautilya was held under the title *Developing Indigenous Concepts and Vocabulary: Kautilya's Arthashastra*. What is noteworthy is that IDSA's second Kautilya conference was co-funded by the Indian Council of Social Science Research (ICSSR), the premier funding council of the Indian state for social science research. The conference attracted an impressive array of diplomats, strategists, defence personal, and scholars.

IDSA's then-Director General Dr Gupta started his welcoming speech with a review of the Indian Kautilya discourse since the first conference in October 2012: The work of tapping the *Arthashastra* for concepts relevant for IR theory and Security Studies had made any significant progress. A still small but growing number of social scientists and experts have begun to situate Kautilyan concepts in the context of the contemporary politico-strategic issues and relate them to modern political science theory. These scientists do not want to juxtapose Kautilyan thought and Western IR theory in opposition or even substitute an 'Indian IR theory' for established Western IR theory. Instead, Kautilyan thought should be used productively for enhancing the political science discourse: 'The *Arthasastra* should be reclaimed as a global and not merely a nationalistic text. It should find its place alongside Sun Tzu, Clausewitz and others. This can happen only if Indian scholars study the text seriously and dispassionately' (Gupta 2015b, xv).

Gupta noted that the IDSA project *Indigenous Historical Knowledge* was engaged in building up cooperation with academic researchers working on Kautilya's *Arthashastra* in Europe and the United States. As a result, an active 'network' of Kautilya researchers had formed whose participants came not only from India but from Bangladesh, the USA, France and Germany. Therefore, Gupta said, IDSA was planning for 2014 a conference on Kautilya's *Arthashastra* with international participation.

As in the previous year, then-National Security Adviser Shivshankar Menon gave the 'Keynote Address' at the 2013 Kautilya conference too. He acknowledged the progress made in tapping key concepts of the *Arthashastra* over the past twelve months: 'We have come a long way in the year since your first seminar. My congratulations to Arvind Gupta and all those who have contributed to this exercise' (Menon 2015b, xvii). He noted that the research work done by IDSA and its external collaborators has been productive and valuable because 'mechanical' and 'schematic' applications of Kautilyan thought-figures on contemporary issues have been avoided. Menon stated that the study of the *Arthashastra* is necessary because many of its thought-figures and the Kautilyan thought-style remain valid in contemporary contexts. First, there are structural parallels in the international system then and now:

> *The world which we face today* (of multiple states, of several major powers, of an uneven but lumpy distribution of power among those major states even while the system has one predominant military power), *is similar to the world that Kautilya operated in when he built the Mauryan Empire* to greatness. (Menon 2015b, xvii, emphasis added)

Secondly, there are constancies in political behaviour—within states and between states—that were identified and theorized by Kautilya:

> While our technologies and experiences may be very different from those Kautilya knew, human nature, *politics and state behaviour do not appear to have changed quite as much or so drastically as to be unrecognizable*. In other words, since Kautilya's time theories have multiplied and changed drastically, politics has not. (Ibid., emphasis added)

Menon emphasized the exceptional importance of the *Arthashastra* for Indian strategic culture—both as a conscious reference and as a subconscious factor of influence:

> *But there is no gainsaying the fundamental importance of the Arthashastra in our thinking [...]. Much of this is unselfconscious and*

instinctive today. Your work here is therefore important in bringing us to the next stage of self-aware thinking on these issues. (Ibid., xviii, emphasis added)

Generating strategic concepts that fit Indian conditions and needs, stressed Menon, 'cannot result from the wholesale borrowing of concepts and ways of thinking from abroad, but has to draw on the indigenous strategic traditions as well'—notably the Kautilyan tradition of strategic thought.

No doubt, IDSA's manifold activities with respect to Kautilya's *Arthashastra* and its contemporary relevance since the beginning of 2012 have been the key for catalyzing the evolution of the Kautilya discourse in India. In early 2012, IDSA was the initiator and sole repository of this discourse, but already the Kautilya conference of October 2012 showed that the discourse was beginning to radiate into the strategic community and some Indian universities. By the time of the second Kautilya conference in October 2013, that process had consolidated, even though IDSA continued to be the main driving force behind the Kautilya discourse.

During 2013, there were also some developments outside the context of IDSA that are relevant for the Kautilya discourse. In January 2013, Patrick Olivelle published a new English translation of the *Arthashastra* titled *King, Governance and Law in Ancient India: Kautilya's Arthashastra*. The Sri Lanka-born Sanskrit philologist teaches at the University of Texas. It remains to be seen whether Olivelle's new translation actually provides added value or may even replace Kangle's as the authoritative translation. The apodictic fervour with which Olivelle asserts that the *Arthashastra* has multiple authors and was compiled over several centuries signifies yet another episode in the 'Hundred Years' War' among Sanskrit philologists and is vexing for readers who are primarily interested in gaining the best possible access to the ideas and concepts of Kautilya's *Arthashastra*.

In May 2013, the *Indian Journal of Diplomacy* published an article by Pravin Chandrasekaran entitled *Kautilya: Politics, Ethics and Statecraft* (2013). The article has a somewhat subjectivist slant and does not dig deep into the idea-content of the *Arthashastra*. That said, the author does present the *mandala* and *shadgunya* concepts and states that Kautilya can stand up to Plato, Aristotle or Machiavelli. These Western theoreticians too promoted absolute monarchy and wanted no changes in the social structure—for which Kautilya is often criticized. Chandrasekaran argues that Kautilya's understanding of diplomacy remains valid across time. Astonishing enough, Chandrasekaran's essay was originally written at Harvard University in 2006, but its publication in a specialized journal occurred in 2013. The assumption seems plausible that the editors of the *Indian Journal of Diplomacy* responded to the emergent Kautilya discourse in the Indian strategic community and academia.

In June 2013, the leading Indian journal of international affairs, *India Quarterly*, published the article *Kautilya's Relevance for India Today* (Liebig 2013). The article contains a summary outline of key findings of our study and has since attracted significant interest as indicated by the ranking in the journal's 'most-read-articles'.

9.3.3 The IDSA Kautilya discourse in 2014

On 9 April 2014, IDSA held its third conference on Kautilya. The conference was distinguished by its international character—researchers from the United States, Germany and Bangladesh participated. As in 2013, the IDSA event in 2014 was co-funded by the Indian Council of Social Science Research (ICSSR). The conference was not only international but trans-disciplinary in that political scientists, Sanskrit philologists, philosophers and economists addressed multiple aspects of the *Arthashastra* and the contemporary relevance of Kautilyan thought-figures.[14] Again, it was the then-NSA Shivshankar Menon who gave the 'Keynote Address' to this third IDSA Kautilya conference. He began his remarks by stating that IDSA's Kautilya initiative had really gained strength over the previous three years:

> You have prompted scholars in India to undertake fresh and valuable research on Kautilya and the *Arthashastra*, and have also put us in touch with scholars on these subjects from across the world. What you have achieved through these seminars and

conferences on Kautilya is important and relevant to a practitioner like me.[15]

Kautilya's theory of inter-state relations, said Menon, differs from the Westphalian system in that it is not 'based on an idealised and immaculate sovereignty' but includes various forms of dominion or suzerainty. Kautilya's pre-modern state conception has many affinities to the state in the twenty-first-century world where absolute sovereignty has been made porous by non-state actors and technological advances. Since the Kautilyan state is situated in a multipolar setting, it needs to be investigated how Kautilya's principle of maximizing state power can be realized within a multipolar context—then and now. Next, Menon turned to the normative dimension of the Kautilyan state, which aims at consolidating and expanding state power but is grounded in the *dharma* of the King who must benefit his subjects and the state and not himself:

> And the choice of policy instruments [*upayas*], whether *sama, dana, bheda or bhava* [*danda*], depends on what serves that higher purpose and not on the individual preference or whim of the King. This is not a text on the divine right of Kings or Mandate of Heaven. Instead it is a text on how to achieve noble goals in an ignoble world, to achieve political and social progress in an unstable and unpredictable environment. *Here again Kautilya is remarkably modern in his ideas and has considerable contemporary resonance.* (That Kautilya managed to establish the Mauryan Empire shows the efficacy of what he prescribes). (Emphasis added)

Menon argues that both the pre-modern Kautilyan state and the modern twenty-first-century state face a similar problem: 'a binary opposition between *dharma* and *artha*, between norm and purpose, or between aspiration and instrumentality.' In conclusion, Menon states:

> Thanks to your efforts and those of several scholars around the world *we may be at another 'Kautilyan moment'*. The last was when the national movement drew reassurance of Indian statecraft from the *Arthashastra* in the early twentieth century, seeking to establish an independent and realist tradition of our own in the

collision between Indian nationalism and Imperial historiography. The *Arthashastra* itself emerged from the collision of India's 6th century BC Enlightenment (Upanishads, Buddhism, reason) and the power politics of the Magadhan and North Indian state system in subsequent centuries. Both were worlds in rapid change. We seem to be at an analogous historical moment again.

At the event in April 2014, IDSA announced that selected papers submitted at the three Kautilya conferences will be published in three edited volumes.[16]

Just a few days after the third IDSA conference on Kautilya, India's nationwide public TV station *Doordarshan* aired the political talk show program *Wide Angle*. The subject of the talk show on 14 April 2014, was 'Kautilya and his relevance'. The host, well-known journalist and strategic analyst C. Raja Mohan had a discussion with Dr S. Kalyanaraman (IDSA), Dr Medha Bisht (South Asian University) and Ambassador H.H.S. Visvanathan (Observer Research Foundation). Two years earlier, talk show host C. Raja Mohan had caused a bit of a stir in the Indian strategic community when he wrote: 'Internal balancing, alliances, asymmetric approaches are as old as statecraft. They are not inventions of the modern strategic thought from Europe, but date back to the era of Kautilya's *Arthashastra* and Vishnu Sharma's *Panchatantra*. Unless Delhi is willing to grapple with the basics of statecraft and *reconnect with its own traditions of strategy*, India will find it increasingly hard to deal with the unprecedented challenges arising from the rise of China' (Mohan 2012, 29). The April 2014 talk show can be seen as yet another indication that the process of 'reconnection' with the endogenous traditions of strategic thought is underway in the Indian strategic community. Indeed, Kautilya's *Arthashastra* is no longer a niche topic of some isolated academics and security experts.

In 2002, the American political scientist Roger Boesche published his book *The First Great Political Realist: Kautilya and His Arthashastra*. Boesche's book leaves much to be desired in methodological and theoretical terms, but it has made an important contribution to arouse some interest in Kautilya and the *Arthashastra* in academic milieus outside South Asia. And Boesche will be proven right making the following prognosis:

> Soon professors who teach political thought will have to know—because of pressures from students, other professors and foundations—the traditions of political thought in China, India, Africa, and the Islamic world from Morocco to India. (Boesche 2002a, XI)

With that in mind, we conclude this section of our study by pointing to the 'Fourth Global International Studies Conference', which was held at Goethe University, Frankfurt, Germany in August 2014. The conference was organized by the World International Studies Committee (WISC), a leading international network of IR scholars. The theme of one of the panels of the Frankfurt WISC conference was '*Kautilya's Arthaṣhastra & Discourse on International Relations Theory and Practice*'. Panelists were: Professor Navnita Behera, Professor Subrata K. Mitra, P.K. Gautam, Dr Deepshikha Shahi and Dr Michael Liebig. The well-attended Kautilya panel at the WISC conference was remarkable in that, for the first time, Kautilya and the *Arthashastra* were addressed in a dedicated fashion at a major international event of Political Science and IR theory.

SECTION C

KAUTILYA REDUX?
Re-use of the Past and the Making of the Modern Politics of India

Kautilya's *Arthashastra*—a magnum opus on state theory and statecraft—was written over two millennia ago. Does this ancient text still have any significance in contemporary India? What role do the lessons of this classical text have in the making of the 'modern' state and in politics in contemporary India? (cf. Rudolph/Rudolph 1967; Mitra 2009a) Those unfamiliar with India's classical heritage might see this question as romantic nostalgia for a Hindu 'golden age' or, even worse, as a patriotic urge to revive a past that has no resonance with the present.[1] We have contested such views in this book through a detailed presentation of the basic text, and through an analysis of the resonance of this classical text in the discourse of a section of India's opinion-leaders. We argue here that the post-Independent state of India and the strategic thinking of India's political leaders draw on the intellectual bequest of the *Arthashastra* and the political culture of ancient India of which this text is an integral part. We argue, further, that the resilience of the Indian state—whose durability is an exception in the ephemeral world of postcolonial states—arises from the ability of the designers of modern Indian institutions to tap into the endogenous reservoir of stateness.

Our main argument is that the state and politics in India today are the results of a seamless evolution from the pre-modern past.[2] Modern India's institutions are the result of strategic adaption of some imported institutions in order to make them compatible with its deep-rooted traditions in the political sphere. Such hybridization of exogenous institutions and practices with their endogenous homologues is the consequence of two complementary processes: first, the conscious strategies of political actors to 're-use the past' (cf. Mitra 2011a, 2012a; B 5.2 and B 5.3) in addressing contemporary problems; secondly, the semi-conscious attitudes and thought-patterns that can be described as the 'habitus' in the field of Indian politics. Based on Pierre Bourdieu's sociological concept, 'habitus' is understood here as the repository of past ideas, patterns of thought and practices that subconsciously influence present thinking and acting in the political field. Thus, the habitus enables the 'flow' of ideas and attitudes across time—independent of their conscious transmission in discursive contexts (cf. Bourdieu 1990, 52–97; Liebig 2014b, 90–6, 276–312; B 6.2 and B 6.3).

The exegesis of the re-use of the Kautilyan state conception in the institutions of modern India is the main goal of this section. Its second goal goes beyond the specific case of India and aims at a generalization of state-formation in transitional societies. We argue that the designing of the modern state in India through the politics of re-use, hybridization and innovation by Gandhi, Patel, Nehru and their lesser-known acolytes is not an idiosyncratic feature of Indian history and culture. Instead, we assert that this narrative is a variation on the general theme of state-formation in transitional societies. To that end, we set forth a brief introduction into the key concepts of hybridity, re-use and resilience, and a brief perusal of institutional arrangements of the state in India in terms of these categories.

1

HYBRIDITY AND THE POSTCOLONIAL STATE

India, though in most senses a modern state with an emerging economy, still retains some features of a 'third world' country. Modern politicians in ethnic garb, mass poverty, urban squalor, traditional rituals in the public sphere and subsistence agriculture coexisting next to state-of-the-art technology mark the landscape of the vast country. With her continental dimensions, ancient traditions, living religions, huge ethnic and linguistic diversity, expanding market, steady economic growth and an effective but noisy democracy, modern India is a bundle of contradictions. Even for visitors who come equipped with prior knowledge of the country, surprises abound. The whole idea of the 'modernity' of India's politics can therefore lead to a sense of uncertainty among Western students of Indian politics for whom such politics is exotic and confusing.

There are contradictions at every corner. A country that still cherishes the non-violent legacies of Gautama Buddha and Mahatma Gandhi, India is nonetheless a proud possessor of the atom bomb. The bickering within India's political establishment over nuclear policy and ambiguity of the nuclear doctrine leads to confusion about the real objectives of India's nuclear strategy. India's general elections, the largest in the world in scale, are mostly free and fair, but armed troops need to be deployed for the safe conduct of the polls. Power changes hands peacefully through democratic elections, but an alarming number of legislators at local and regional levels carry criminal records. Beyond politics, one comes across the same welter of images that are at once baffling and contradictory. Internet cafes, slums and beggars jostle for space in crowded cities; vicious inter-community riots and terrorist attacks come and go, and yet life continues at an even pace, apparently undisturbed. The modern state, secular by law and in spirit, still appears to equivocate about the role of religion in politics.

India, the 'bomb and Bangalore' notwithstanding, is a transitional society and an emerging economy where the symbols of radical change in the short span of one generation are clearly visible. The significant point here is the deeper cultural unity and political consensus that underpin the strife at the surface of the political landscape. The combination of diversity and inequality, the bane of many developing societies, does not appear to disturb the stability of India's political system. The distinctive style of Indian politics is the result of hybridization of the pre-colonial past and the modern European politics that colonial rule introduced into the vast Indian Empire. The rulers of post-Independence India to whom the British transferred power have chosen to re-use this legacy in their design of the modern institutions of India. India, we learn from Rudolph and Rudolph, Nandy and Bozeman,[1] is not alone in the strategic incorporation of the past into the present in order to generate a modernity that is both legitimate and appropriate for the context.

To explain the hybrid Indian system as coherent to skeptical Western students of Indian politics is a challenging task for which the contribution of Bozeman is a significant landmark. To quote:

> Most of the indigenous patterns of life and thought became blurred during the centuries of *European supremacy*, when they were being integrated into the Occidental scheme of things. Many were officially discarded because they seemed to impede the attainment of the political and social goals associated with the cause of progress, as suggested by voluntary or involuntary contacts with the West. Others simply withered away with the social structures to which they had given support. However, when the non-Western peoples began to assume their places as modern political communities in the world so largely shaped by Western thought, it became increasingly apparent *that the Western ideas were not the exclusive mainsprings of their political attitudes and actions.* Whether in India, Egypt, or Nigeria, men have been generally

> stimulated by the spread of literacy and the growth of nationalism *to probe their own pasts and to resurrect the realities and myths that antedated their knowledge and acceptance of Western ways.*
> (Bozeman 1960, 5, emphasis added)

Why have Bozeman's prescient comments on the nature and course of political change in ancient civilizations facing the challenge of modernization, voiced five decades back, not been taken up more widely? This general incomprehension of 'the modernity of tradition', or more particularly in the case of India, the democratic achievements of the country based on a political system that some specialists of democratic theory dismiss as 'merely hybrid' (e.g., Wolfgang Merkel; cf. Croissant/ Merkel 2004) results from a deeply held belief in the superiority of the 'pure' as against the 'impure'. Hybrid species—cross-breeds, half-castes, amalgams and bastards—do not have an easy time in most societies. High cultures, high society, high art and the high church dictate purity as the norm. Hybridity—a generic expression for its opposite—is seen as the aberration that one has to put up with for practical and pragmatic considerations.[2] Beyond the pale of everyday life, purity is also the norm of modern science. Clear concepts, precise measurements and causal models constitute the essential tool kit of the modern scientist. Purity is essential to order, and the modern state is the ultimate upholder of purity and order. In the iconography of ideological purity, Danton, Robespierre and the unfailing guillotine, meting out revolutionary terror to the 'un-citizen' and the impure, remain the quintessential symbols of the Jacobin state, being the defenders of its single minded quest for virtue and perfect citizenship.[3]

The normative asymmetry of the pure and the hybrid, where the former is automatically endowed with superiority, has marked the comparative politics of transitional societies. Just as apprentice physicists must learn to define and measure atoms and even smaller particles; chemists, the periodic table; biologists, genes and chromosomes—so must the beginners in comparative politics learn to distinguish between democracy and dictatorship, the modern and the traditional, the developed and the developing as 'pure' categories, and to measure the hiatus between the ideal and the actual with quantitative, qualitative or discursive tools.[4] However, the world, seen through the lens of comparative politics based on 'pure categories', can produce unsatisfactory results. The catch—landed by the net of comparative analysis—is often difficult to classify, while some big fish escape the net of measurement altogether (cf. Diamond 2002). The interstices of 'pure' categories like democracy and dictatorship are full of substances that are real but not measurable in terms of the pure categories that define the polar opposites of the scale—that, too, only in terms of the ideal types that define them normatively.

In the era of globalization and trans-cultural, border-crossing citizenship, the political landscape of postcolonial societies and vast pockets of the Western world bear witness to the existence of hybrid structures—of institutions, practices and artistic design—that are fence-sitters, straddling different worlds and difficult to classify in terms of the canon on comparative politics. 'Caste associations', 'fixers (culture brokers)', 'mixed economies', *satyagraha* (the concept of mass civil disobedience coined by Gandhi in South Africa and subsequently introduced to India) and *gram panchayat*s (modern, elected village councils that are based on a classical concept of village self-governance; cf. Fürstenberg 2015)—each carrying a tenuous link to their original (root) concepts, to which new impulses and experiences have been strategically added—are part and parcel of the vigorous political life in these countries.

We question the normative asymmetry of purity and hybridity in the light of the Indian experience and seen through the prism of Kautilya. In that, we address the following questions whose empirical domain extends beyond the case of India:

- What are the salient hybrid features of the state in India, what led to their incorporation into the modern state that the constitution aimed at, and how do they connect to the pre-modern Kautilyan state conception?
- Is hybridization of the state—resulting from the strategy and vision of modern political actors in re-using the past—the

essential factor behind the resilience of the Indian political system? Finally, in everyday life, is hybridity the essential reality behind the chimera of a universal modernity, not bound by time and space?

2

CORE FEATURES OF THE KAUTILYAN STATE

In order to understand the hybrid nature of the contemporary Indian state, which is drawing on pre-modern endogenous and modern exogenous elements, we first have to outline the basic features of the Kautilyan state. We treat as the primary conceptualization of the pre-modern state in India what is stated in the *Arthashastra* about the state and its conduct.

2.1 THE QUINTESSENCE OF THE MODERN STATE AND THE KAUTILYAN IDEA OF RAISON D'ÉTAT

The state, as expounded in Kautilya's *Arthashastra*, is an ideal-type and not an exact description of the historical state structure of the Maurya Empire (or another polity in ancient India). That does not mean, however, that Kautilyan state is a utopian imagination. First, and most important, the ideal-type Kautilyan state in the *Arthashastra* is a theoretical derivation from the historical reality of the state in ancient India and based upon the ancient traditions of state conduct—thus the Kautilyan state conception is empirically saturated (cf. A 6, 7, 8 and 10). Secondly, Kautilya draws on the state conceptions of earlier political theory in ancient India, most of which got lost (cf. Kangle 2010a/1965).

To be precise, the Kautilyan state, as we have argued earlier in this book, is a 'patrimonial state', in Max Weber's terminology. That means that the ruler and the state still form a conflation, however one that begins to drift apart. The ruler still 'embodies' the state, but the state has already gained significant eigenvalue which manifests in an institutionalized 'state bureaucracy' that performs 'objective' functions dictated by the inherent logic of the state. Moreover, the intrinsic worth of the Kautilyan state transforms the nominally absolutist ruler into the 'supreme functionary' or 'first servant' of the state—the very opposite of 'Asiatic despotism'.

If the state bureaucracy is the institutional expression of the state's eigenvalue, the inherent logic of the state's conduct is expressed in Kautilya's idea of raison d'état: preserving and expanding the power of the state. The 'power' of the state is neither limited to its ability to use force (*danda*) nor is it an abstract principle. Instead, Kautilya puts forth a substantive definition of the state's power via the seven 'state factors' (*prakriti*): the ruler, the minister or government, the people in the countryside, the fortress or capital city, the state treasury, the armed forces (plus police and the secret service) and the ally or foreign policy. The aggregate of the seven *prakriti* constitutes the power of the state. If Kautilyan raison d'état means preserving and expanding the power of the state, the 'operationalization' of raison d'état means preserving and expanding each of seven *prakriti* and thus their aggregation. The optimization of the seven *prakriti*—and thus the qualitative and quantitative expansion of state power—is Kautilyan raison d'état.

However, Kautilyan raison d'état is not only the expression of the intrinsic logic of the state's existence but equally so the 'basic norm' guiding the state's actions. Raison d'état is the ruler's *dharma*. With respect to its foreign policy conduct, the Kautilyan state appears to be committed to 'pure' power politics. However, Kautilyan foreign policy has a directionality which is both 'strategic' and normative: the political unification of the Indian subcontinent. With this aim, neighbouring states can and should be 'conquered'—preferably by non-military means. Such 'conquest' for unifying the subcontinent is legitimate. Kautilya's apparent expansionism and revisionism does not see the territorial 'aggrandizement' of the state as an end in itself. For him, overcoming the political fragmentation of the subcontinent can only be realized if there is one state with the will and power to 'incorporate' the anarchic multitude of states on the subcontinent into one pan-Indian state. In ancient India, this state was Magadha which was transformed into the Maurya Empire by Kautilya and Chandragupta.

Beyond the geo-cultural space of the Indian subcontinent, Kautilyan foreign policy knows neither revisionism nor imperial expansionism. With respect to China, the Greco-Persian states or the states of the Indian Ocean rim, Kautilyan foreign policy is vectored on a non-revisionist 'balance of power' realpolitik.

2.2 THE KAUTILYAN STATE AND THE PEOPLE

As indicated above, the Kautilyan idea of raison d'état is not reducible to 'pure' power politics but has a normative dimension as well. The ruler's *dharma* is not only to strengthen state power but to assure the security and the material well-being of his subjects: 'In the happiness of the subjects lies the happiness of the king and in what is beneficial to the subjects is his own benefit [...]. Therefore, being ever active, the king should carry out the management of material well-being' (KA, I, 19, 34–5; Kangle 2010a/1972, 53).

Contrary to the despotic figure that the King is made out to be in Orientalist imagination of Eastern authority, the Kautilyan prince is the quintessential regulator, entitled to his first share—*bhaga*—of the produce. 'Manu says that if the king does not afford protection (yet) takes his share as King, his taxes, tolls and duties, daily presents and fines, he will soon sink into hell (Trautmann 2012, 169). Might one then talk in terms of a rudimentary form of social contract in Kautilya or even an early form of rule of law and a sense of collective law making in India? Trautmann (2012, 154) hints at the existence of such tradition of '*shanghas*' and '*ganas*' in ancient India. As proof, he refers to the official title of the Indian government, 'Bharat Ganarajya'.

The state's obligation of improving the welfare of the people constitutes a normative commitment, but it is one that Kautilya sees fully integrated in the basic norm of raison d'état: only the optimization of the seven *prakriti* will secure the welfare of the people, and only under conditions where the people's lives are secure and prosperous can the state build up its power in terms of the seven *prakriti*. The strong state will provide internal security and the rule of law as well as external security against foreign aggression. If the people feel secure and are prosperous, will they be politically content, and the state, stable.

Finding the balance among contradictory forces is the ultimate challenge of Kautilya. This could not have been easy then, as it is not now. Trautmann comments:

> There is no magic formula by which the King can ensure his success and avoid catastrophe. Everything depends upon his finding a proper balance among overlapping and sometime, competing ends: a full treasury, a strong army, a prosperous people and effective means of resolving disputes to maintain the peace of the kingdom. The *Arthashastra* cannot guarantee success but it shows Kings and their ministers the way to a rational approach in making choices. (2012, 143)

Kautilya sees the relationship between the ruler—the patrimonial state—and the people in almost contractual terms: the ruler delivers vital services—security and a political framework conducive to economic prosperity—and, in return, he can demand the payment of (non-excessive) taxes and duties.

2.3 THE POLITICAL ECONOMY OF THE KAUTILYAN STATE

For Kautilya, the economy is the material foundation of state capacity. The state has the obligation to promote economic development and growth because increased economic output translates into increased tax revenue (without unduly burdening the people). Tax revenue fuels state capacity: government and administration, the armed forces, the legal system and infrastructure. In accordance with Kautilyan raison d'état, the state promotes economic development, notably through the expansion of arable land and 'strategic industries' as well as infrastructure-building.

The Kautilyan political economy is a 'mixed economy'. Most of agriculture, crafts and trade are private, but the state is an economic actor on its own right who controls and runs the 'strategic sectors' of the economy: mining and metallurgy, manufactures for military goods, precious metals and infrastructure. What is notable is that the state also runs the 'entertainment industry'—taverns, brothels and gambling. Kautilya demands that all state enterprises must be profitable and thus provide a second source of state income on top of taxes and duties.

To a large degree, the Kautilyan economy is a money economy with a state monopoly of coinage. The Kautilyan state is conducting comprehensive supervision and regulation of the private sector, including consumer protection, trade control, labour inspection, weights and measures, animal protection and nature conservation. Thus, the economic policy of the Kautilyan state is etatist and dirigiste and exhibits remarkable similarities with mercantilism in Europe between the sixteenth and eighteenth century (cf. Weber 2000, 161).

2.4 THE KAUTILYAN STATE: CENTRALIZATION AND AUTONOMOUS SPACES

The Kautilyan state aims at centralization, but it does not strive for maximum centralization. The state accepts diversity and plurality in terms of ethnicity, language and religion—the central characteristics of Indian cultural space. The state pursues no homogenization drive: no 'state language' is enforced, nor is there a 'state religion'. In short, the Kautilyan state is a secular state. As Max Weber rightly observed, Kautilya exhibits an extraordinary degree of indifference towards religions and 'ideologies' of any kind (2000, 161).

The Kautilyan state respects a certain degree of autonomy of village communities in the rural areas and professional 'guilds' in urban contexts. Kautilya strongly advocates a policy of respecting local customs and habits in areas that have been conquered and annexed. That applies even more so for states that have been made vassals by diplomatic or other means.

However, on a deeper level, since society is segregated into castes, the Kautilyan state too is 'de-centralized'. First, the state's foundation is the caste system (*varna*), and its preservation is explicitly proclaimed a state goal by Kautilya. The senior positions in government and administration are reserved for the *kshatriya* and Brahmin castes, but between the two castes there is a barrier which prevents that political and religious-cultural power conflates into one 'ruling class'. Moreover, economic and financial power lies mainly with the *vaishya* caste which in turn is separated from the *kshatriya* and Brahmin castes. Thus, there is a singular distribution of power and corresponding 'checks and balances' within the state structure. Consequently, the ruler of the Kautilyan state is neither an 'Asiatic despot' nor a Roman Empire-style 'pontifex maximus' who unites worldly and religious-ritual power.

While strongly affirming the *varna* order as the social foundation of the state, Kautilya expounds some pragmatic relativization with respect to an a-priori valuation of caste status. For him, caste status has to be earned. In the balance of meritocratic and caste considerations, Kautilya tends to favour professional competence. His merit-based attitude to caste is visible with respect to the *shudras* whom he sees as the actual producers of national wealth and the bravest of soldiers in combat.

2.5 THE KAUTILYAN STATE AND ITS LEGAL SYSTEM

The Kautilyan state has an expansive and elaborated legal system. Three chapters ('Books') of the *Arthashastra* are devoted to legal matters: one for civil law, one for criminal law, and one for extra-judicial prosecution of 'enemies of the state'.

The justice system is a core task of Kautilyan state, and jurisdiction is the occupation of state-salaried judges. Kautilya specifies the requirements for fair trial and the prevention of perversion of justice. Sentencing follows the principle of retribution (talion), but, except high crime, corporal punishment—mostly mutilations—can be converted into money fines which are cashed in by the state. State crimes, such as treason, counterfeiting, corruption or embezzlement of state property, are punished extra-judicially by decision of the ruler and his closest advisers. 'Enemies of the state' are killed by special operatives of the secret service, and their death is made to appear as natural death or accident.

In summary, it can be stated that the Kautilyan legal system, as part of the state apparatus, provides certainty of the law but no equality before the law. For the same offenses, different penalties are imposed, depending on the caste status. However, the punishment of 'state crimes' lies outside the regular legal system.

2.6 SOCIAL HIERARCHY AND RATIONAL BUREAUCRACY

As mentioned above, the society on which the Kautilyan state rests is de-aggregated via the caste order. While the upper hierarchy of governance and administration is the prerogative of the *kshatriya* and Brahmin castes, 'the people' is segregated into *vaishya*s and *shudra*s (and dalits and adivasis) in social, ritual, economic and legal terms—each caste having its own, specific *dharma*.

The de-aggregated society is encapsulated by the multi-layered state bureaucracy whose functions include inter alia: tax collection, law enforcement and supervision and regulation of economic activities. The Kautilyan state bureaucracy is subject to the principles of rationality and efficiency. Its members need to have professional expertise in their area of functional responsibility, which means that most of them have to be literate.

The state bureaucracy is organized in 'competing units'. For example, the finance administration is divided in a department for tax collection, a department of the treasury and an audit department that controls the two other departments. That is to increase efficiency and combat corruption and embezzlement—both of paramount concern for Kautilya. Moreover, all elements of governance and administration, irrespective of their hierarchical status, are monitored by the secret service. Interestingly enough, the secret service itself is compartmentalized in two units—one attached to the ruler, the other to the 'chancellor' (*mantrin*) (cf. Scharfe 1968, 233-76).

Science, philosophy and other 'higher knowledge' is reserved for the Brahmins, but literacy is not the privilege of the upper casts. Practical knowledge is deemed necessary for all people.

2.7 THE KAUTILYAN CAPITAL CITY

The *Arthashastra* contains a rather detailed description of the Kautilyan state's ideal-type capital city (*durga*). Remarkable in this city design is Kautilya's exclusive focus on considerations of security and functionality. The fortification of the city is described at length and in detail. And, equally so, the design of the royal palace is primarily following security concerns, i.e., concentric security zones, secret escape routes, etc. Otherwise, the ideal-type design of the capital is guided by strictly functional considerations: fresh water supply, waste management, hygiene, fire protection, rectangular streets and housing blocs, etc. The one 'ideological' factor in Kautilya's city design is its division into four districts, one for each of the castes. Aesthetic considerations are completely missing in Kautilya's design: neither with respect to the royal palace nor other public or sacred buildings.

Kautilya exhibits a keen interest in science and, to a somewhat lesser extent, technology, but the arts are a non-issue in the *Arthashastra*. Political authority and legitimacy derives from the austere leader's competence in statecraft backed by a well-functioning state bureaucracy. Political aesthetics like monumental architecture and other forms of politically charged symbolism seem irrelevant for Kautilya. Is that so because Kautilya is genuinely disinterested in (political) aesthetics, or is it something so obvious for him that it is not worth writing about it?

3

KAUTILYAN THOUGHT, 'RE-USE OF THE PAST' AND 'POLITICAL HABITUS'

Kautilya's *Arthashastra* is a blueprint and manual on the structure, organization and functioning of the (patrimonial) state. Many Kautilyan principles of the state and statecraft have been adopted in the state structures of the Maurya, Gupta and Mughal empires—and even, paradoxically enough, in the British Raj (cf. Panikkar 1963, 228). Rudolph and Rudolph state:

> The historical legacies of imperial states on the Indian subcontinent in the pre-Christian era established state conceptions and institutions that provided models for the subcontinental multinational state of modern India. (1987, 63)

Even a cursory review of the political patterns of thinking and behaviour as well as the institutional make-up of contemporary India reveals manifold 'traces' and 'echoes' of the Kautilyan state. What is the 'connection' between such an ancient text and political reality in contemporary India? How does hybridity of pre-modern political thought and modern political practice come about?

Bozeman uses the concept of 'syncretism' in order to express the result of a dialectical interaction of the traditional and the modern in order to generate an authentic, context-relevant 'modernity'. To quote:

> Each nation, each culture, each region is [...] today a separate stage upon which local, communist, and Western European systems of reference and belief interact; and, barring the contingency of an ultimate obliteration of one or the other by conquest, *each is likely to evolve its own syncretic system for the ordering of life within its contours and the projection of its interests abroad*. In other words,

> the realities of world affairs today are not adequately rendered when conveyed in the simple myth of a bipolar world; *for between the poles of the contemporary cultural and political map of the world there are numerous well-defined civilizations as well as many others that are just beginning to define themselves.* (Bozeman 1960, 5–6, emphasis added)

Conventional theoretical approaches of Political Science tend to offer skeptical silence on the evident hybridity of pre-modern and modern political thought and practices. We adopt here a rather 'unconventional' theoretical approach by turning to Pierre Bourdieu's concept of 'habitus'. One can define habitus as the efficacious presence of past patterns of thought and behavioural attitudes in the present. That includes the 'active presence' of past ideas that have been 'forgotten' because they have become 'natural' or 'common sense'. The habitus is the repository of past ideas, in which these ideas are silent and 'forgotten' yet remain intact and efficacious (cf. Bourdieu 1990, 52–97).

Our assumption is that Kautilyan thought has 'lived on', albeit mostly latently, in the 'collective memory' of not only Indian elites but the population at large (cf. Dixit 2004; Menon 2015b, xviii). As Maurice Halbwachs, who developed the concept, stresses, collective memory involves a 'conscious' as well as a 'subconscious' or 'semiconscious' dimension (cf. Halbwachs 1991). Nehru cogently described India's collective memory as a 'mixture of popular philosophy, tradition, history, myth, and legend,' and with respect to the active presence of the past ideas in the present he uses the term 'palimpsest' (Nehru 1981, 59, 67).

We argue that Kautilyan ideas are indeed influencing the basic patterns of thought in the field of Indian politics and strategic affairs. Kautilyan thought-figures are an ideational ingredient of the habitus of those involved in Indian politics and strategic affairs. In other words, Kautilyan thought is a key component of India's politico-strategic culture (cf. Zaman 2006).

However, besides or 'on top of' the latent presence of Kautilyan thought, there has been its manifest presence—phenomenologically and discursively. The text of the *Arthashastra* has been continuously transmitted over the past 2300 years—orally, and in writing. Throughout this timespan, there have been Indian cognoscenti who studied, learned by heart or copied the *Arthashastra*. Moreover, Kautilyan thought has been addressed and absorbed in a multitude of scholarly writings, literary works, playwrights and popular narratives across the centuries. In 1904, the *Arthashastra* was 're-discovered' for Indology and for political actors of the Indian independence movement, but it had never been 'lost' in the preceding centuries.

Because the Kautilyan thought has 'nested' in India's collective memory—both its unconscious and conscious sphere—it can be efficiently 're-used' in addressing the political challenges of the time. Thus, our proposition is that Kautilyan thought has been re-used throughout India's political history—in the Maurya Empire, the Gupta Empire, the Mughal Empire and in post-1947 India. In other words, re-using (politico-strategic) traditions is a deep-rooted Indian tradition.

The relevance and efficacy of the Kautilyan thought for contemporary Indian politics derives from a singular constellation: Those political actors who have consciously and intentionally taken recourse to Kautilya's ideas and concepts in order to use them for resolving the strategic (and even tactical) problems of the day can build upon on their latent presence in the 'political habitus' among the elites as well as the people of India. The case in point is Jawaharlal Nehru who studied the *Arthashastra* and presented his findings in the *Discovery of India*. In whatever Nehru learned from studying the *Arthashastra* and then applied to building the modern Indian state, he could count on a ready receptivity towards Kautilyan thought in the Indian elites as well as the broader population.

Because of the dialectical entanglement between 'political habitus' (including its latent pre-modern idea-contents) and the deliberate 'political re-use' of such pre-modern ideas in India, the practical political outcomes of the re-use show such high degree of viability and resilience—in terms of hybrid institutions and institutional practices, notably the strategic directionality of foreign and security policy.

4

THE POSTCOLONIAL CONDITION
The Hybridity of the 'Modern' State in Transitional Societies

There are four parameters that underpin the state and modern politics in India, each with a bearing on the Kautilyan heritage. They are: 1) a bureaucratic state machinery that combines policy responsiveness and law and order management; 2) contribution to agenda setting by local protest movements; 3) political elites using two-track strategies that combine both institutional and non-institutional modes of action; and 4) constitutional change as a political resource (cf. Mitra 1999b; Mitra and Singh 2009).

The most important aspect of the modern state in India is that it draws on the Kautilyan heritage of the King as a provider of order, a party to an implicit social contract and a guarantor that disorder and civil war—*matsya-nyaya*, a condition of incessant conflict where big fish eat small fish—do not break out. This is the legacy on which Indian democracy and the political culture of election draw on—which makes it possible for India to develop an endogenous democratic culture. The important contribution of Bozeman (1960) helps appreciate the links between India's pre-modern political culture and context, and their re-use in the modern Indian state.

The state in pre-modern India made a distinction (not a dichotomy, however) between righteousness (*dharma*) and material power (*artha*).[1] The priestly group of the Brahmins and the rulers (*raja*) were responsible, respectively, to strike the balance between the two. Royal power, thus, rather than being identified with the divine mandate of the King—like the Pharaoh of Egypt or the Son of Heaven in China—was the outcome of a social contract. 'Anointed by the Brahmin high priest, the king was an executive, but in himself, he was nothing' (Bozeman 1960, 121).

Kings who exceeded their authority were subject to multiple censure. This pre-modern idea of countervailing forces has been re-used in the modern constitution where the Supreme Court of India has emerged as the ultimate arbiter of right and wrong and the referee in the incessant competition for power between individuals, groups, regions as well as the whole process of representation and election.

The application of these core ideas has led to a hybrid political system that is both modern and deeply traditional. The norms generated through this strategic and critical re-use of India's politico-cultural heritage has created a modern Indian nation that can aspire to membership of the global society and yet remain ensconced in its own tradition. These norms which are constantly evolving have helped the Indian state and society to 'lock-in' and generate democratic governance.[2]

The process of state formation in India distinguishes itself from the trajectory suggested by modernization theory and the structural-functional approach. The former tracks the process of transformation to the penetration of traditional societies by exogenous impulses, mostly of war, innovation and colonization, but also of trade and the global diffusion of norms. The structural-functional variant of modernization theory explains the growth of new structures in response to the functional needs of a traditional society undergoing rapid transformation.[3] There is no clear sense of endogenous agency in these approaches as the political momentum is generated by exogenous actors and processes. In India there is, as we notice in leaders like Jawaharlal Nehru, a clear sense of strategy and vision. His 'methodological individualism'—the tactical moves to build coalitions with like-minded endogenous and exogenous allies, his successful incorporation of rules as an endogenous variable and the specification of cultural and historical contexts as exogenous constraints—accounts for the spectacular success in creating modern institutions that found solid anchors in Indian society.[4]

Why was the Nehruvian approach more successful than the equivalent leadership in Pakistan? In the Indian model, the new social elites were themselves the outcome of a process of fair and efficient political recruitment through democratic elections, who drew on endogenous cultural and political resources that successfully connected their modern visions with India's classical heritage. Such was not the case in Pakistan. The Indian leader—at the levels of the nation, region and locality—could play a two-track strategy that could conflate the imported with the endogenous, creating in the process an endogenous modernity with a Kautilyan flavour. The Indian method of state-formation thus entailed the processes of law and order management, social and economic reform as well as the accommodation of identity as an operationally testable model—all of which is reminiscent of the Kautilyan heritage. The key function of this model is to focus attention on the policy process by identifying the key role played by the decision-making elite[5] (see Figure 1 below).

The Indian achievement of democratic governance is by no means trivial and deserves a brief explanation of how the conditions that led to them were institutionalized. Much further research is necessary to understand how and for which strategic reason the founding fathers of modern Indian politics such as Gandhi, Nehru and Patel adapted the pre-modern past to the challenges thrown up by colonial rule and Indian resistance to it and how the resultant institutional insights found their way into the Indian constitution. While the three leaders often diverged in their responses to specific issues, what held them together was their understanding of the need to re-use the past to produce an authentic Indian modernity. That made them more receptive to the whole notion of hybridity—an idea that was not so popular either for the leaders of revolutionary anti-colonial movements nor for those whose sole objective was to gain power through the mechanical imitation of the norms and institutions of colonial rulers. Since the notion of hybridity is relatively unknown in comparative politics, we make a brief mention of this concept in other disciplines.

In terms of its origin in biological sciences, hybridity is an attempt to overcome binary opposites through the creation of a third species that combines some characteristics of the two. Critical theorists find a positive appreciation of syncretism in this phenomenon (Fludernik 1998, 10). Hybridization is a motivating factor—an attempt to devise a 'third space' (e.g., between colonizer and the colonized or between dominance of race and nationalism) which combines elements of the original duality but folds them together in a functional, coherent way. Bhabha, to whom we owe this seminal concept, transforms hybridity by adding the concept of the imaginary from Fanon, Lacan and Bakhtin.[6] Fludernik comments: 'The term hybridity, from its moorings in sexual cross-fertilization, racial intermixture and intermarriage, has now drifted free to connote (rather than denote) a variety of interstitial and antagonistic set-ups which are clearly linked to a "subaltern" perspective and a positive re-evaluation of hybridity' (Fludernik 1998, 21f).

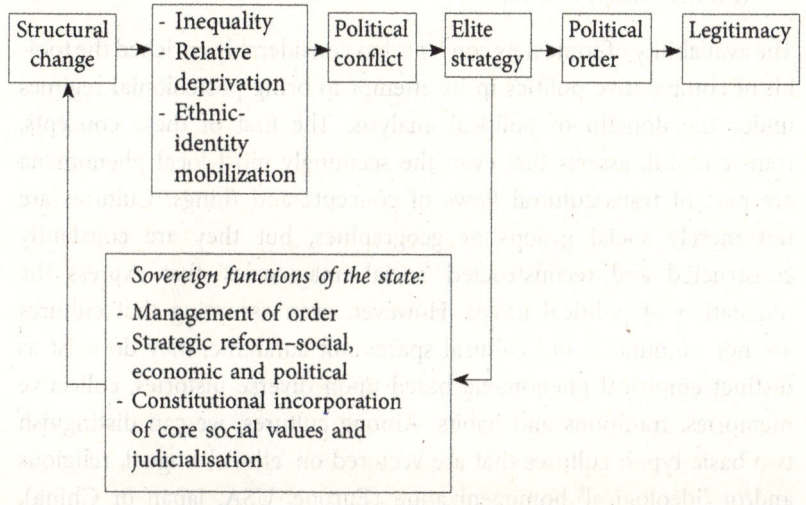

Figure 1: A dynamic neo-institutional model of innovative governance
Source: Adapted from Mitra (2005)

The research on hybridity runs parallel to the concept of re-use, emanating from art history, which has gradually found its way into the larger field of social and political investigation (cf. Hegewald/Mitra 2012). Referring to the presence of the past in the interstices of the present, Morris-Jones, a leading early chronicler of politics in India, writes:

> The political systems of modern states are usually developments from earlier, sometimes much earlier, times. The systems undergo change in response to changes in other aspects of human behaviour and thought; they also have the capacity to exert independent

influence on these other aspects. If, in haste, we speak of a political system 'reflecting' social conditions, we would recognize that the process of reflection is one which changes both the instrument and the subject [...]. India's political leaders inherited under this heading of government still more than the accumulated sum of psychological capital; they received the more tangible equipment and machinery of government. These may be considered first as organization, structure and procedures, and, secondly, as personnel. (Morris-Jones 1964, 13, 17)

The availability of some new concepts has considerably enriched the toolkit of comparative politics in its attempt to bring postcolonial regimes under the domain of political analysis. The first of these concepts, trans-cultural, asserts that even the seemingly most local phenomena are part of trans-cultural flows of concepts and things. Cultures are not merely social groups or geographies, but they are constantly constructed and reconstructed 'social imaginaries' that express the fluctuation of political forces. However, even assuming that cultures are not immutable and cultural spaces not autarchic, they do exist as distinct empirical phenomena based upon diverse histories, collective memories, traditions and habits. Among cultures, we can distinguish two basic types: cultures that are vectored on 'ethnic', lingual, religious and/or 'ideological' homogenization (Europe, USA, Japan or China), and cultures that are characterized by inclusive plurality in terms of ethnicity, language, religion and ideology—Indian culture being the case in point of the pluralist culture-type.

The hybrid institutions and practices are empirical evidence of what Bhabha calls the 'third space'. Hybrid institutions are necessarily a part of a larger political project, one where elites and counter-elites seek to amend the rules to produce new designs and imbue them with a new spirit, geared to a political goal. The flow diagram in Figure 1 (above) depicts how elites might seek to do this in the context of a changing or challenged society through the combination of three tactics, namely, the political management of identity, strategic reform of laws and the constitutional incorporation of core social values.

In their solicitude to gain legitimacy and enhance governance, elites look broadly across the social spectrum, and deeply into local, regional and national history, to identify useful resources for governance and legitimacy and bring them into the mainstream. Not bound by doctrine or ideology, India's colonial rulers, the nationalist leaders and subsequently the leaders of the postcolonial state could afford to be 'trans-lingual, trans-cultural and trans-disciplinary' in the sense that there was no political or scientific taboo against the search for things that would 'work'.[7] These huge experiments in colonial dominance, anti-colonial resistance, nation-building, democratic transition, economic growth and justice, governance and legitimacy produced a whole new range of hybrid political institutions and practices.

The empirical analysis below will focus on colonial forms of hybridization that retained the façade of tradition while changing its underlying power dimension as an act of imperial domination of the Indian population; Gandhian counter-hybridization as an act of resistance; and postcolonial hybridization as a project of nation-building and legitimacy in the context of a deeply divided and diverse society that takes democracy seriously. Postcolonial hybridization drew on Kautilyan thought by bringing tradition back in again into the fold of an endogenous modernity.[8]

5

HYBRIDIZATION AS A POLITICAL STRATEGY OF DOMINANCE AND RESISTANCE

The British, masters at indirect rule, innovated a number of hybrid institutions to rule India in an orderly manner. This sustained the Raj over two centuries—never in history have so few ruled so many with such little use of overt force. But this came at the cost of arrested growth and the severing of India's colonial present from the pre-modern past. We learn from scholarly accounts of everyday life in classical India that the society, polity and the economy evolved in continuous symbiosis in the course of the millennia of its early, settled existence (cf. Auboyer 1965; Edwardes 1965). While self-contained, India was not insulated from external inspiration because there were various forms of conceptual flow that continuously enriched Indian life. There were pilgrims and visitors from abroad, some international trade and military invasions. However, society had mastered the art of accommodation of difference and the art of re-use of the past to construct new, hybrid structures that could cope with changing times. This spirit of renewal, essential to the conservative dynamism of pre-modern India, is summed up in an often-repeated *sloka* from the *Bhagavad Gita*: 'Whenever, scion of Bharatas, righteousness declines and unrighteousness prevails, I manifest Myself.'

With the loss of political autonomy and destruction of the knowledge-generating universities and scholarly communities around temples through Islamic invasions that began in the eighth century, India started losing this capacity for endogenous self-renewal. There were local instances of fusion and innovation in art and architecture between Islam and Hinduism, Jainism and Buddhism, a process which reached a national scale under the rule of the Great Mughals.[1] But society as a whole had lost the vibrant capacity for efficient, endogenous evolution via politico-cultural re-use of the past. The coup de grace to this moribund structure was dealt by the colonial intrusion from Europe, starting in the eighteenth century. By 1858, with the defeat of the 'Sepoy Mutiny', the victorious British proclaimed the ultimate intellectual, moral and political subjugation of the Indians at the Delhi Durbar.

While India has been no stranger to invasions through the Northwest passes in the high Himalayas, British rule was special in terms of its representation of the Indian past. Up to the arrival of the British, in India, the past and the present had lived in a complex and dynamic symbiosis. But, under the British, the past really became the past. The point is made by Metcalf in his seminal *The Ideologies of the Raj* where he analyses aesthetics and power under colonial rule.[2]

While the British continued the tradition of 'appropriating the politically charged forms of their predecessors as a way of legitimising their own regime' (Metcalf 1998, 14), their method of depicting the past differed radically from their predecessors. Previous rulers of India had added their visions and symbols to existing designs so that the past and present could appear as part of a continuous flow. However, in British public buildings and political institutions, the past was depicted definitely as the 'past' whose only function was to serve as a foil, on which the British present could shine brighter while staying aloof and distant. In a memorable passage Metcalf recounts how the British *durbar* was traditional in form but thoroughly modern in content. In his 1903 *durbar*, Curzon sought to utilize the 'familiar' and even sacred form of 'the East'. As he proudly proclaimed, the entire arena was 'built and decorated exclusively in the Mughal or Indo-Saracenic style'. Yet Curzon refused to sanction an exchange of presents, or *nazr*s, which had formed the central binding element of pre-colonial *durbar*s. Instead, he had each prince in their turn mount the *dais* and offer a message of congratulation to the King-Emperor. Curzon then simply shook hands with the chief as he passed by. Incorporation and inclusion, so powerfully symbolized by *khillat* and *nazr*, had given way, despite the Mughal scenery and pretense, to a wholly colonial ritual.[3]

In aesthetics as in politics, the colonial strategy consisted in the incorporation of the past—Indian tradition in this case—within the present in a subsidiary capacity. Nandy adds in the same vein: 'Modern colonialism won its great victories not so much through its military and technological prowess as through its ability to create secular hierarchies incompatible with the traditional order' (1983, ix). The British told Indians that their past was truly a past: the way forward consisted in learning new, modern ways from European science, technology, institutions and morals. The hybridization of the Mughal *durbar* in this case was part of the colonial strategy to seal off the vital links of the colonial present with the pre-colonial past. A cluster of European publicists combined forces to teach the 'childlike' Indians new, better, modern ways and to punish them when they were 'childish', refusing to learn.

The hybridization of the Mughal *durbar* was part of the successful strategy of ruling the Empire through native intermediaries with very little use of overt force. The successful experiment spawned its variations in many other areas of administration, architectural design and city planning as well as in public life. The examples of re-use of colonial institutions in post-Independence politics are plentiful. Though not always so clearly visible to those who are unfamiliar with India's colonial interlude, specialists recognize the British derivation of the rules, procedures and rituals of the Indian Parliament.[4] The *Devaswam* Boards in South India and their equivalents in other parts of the vast country—departments of religious property, also set up during the British rule—are in charge of administration of old temples as of the new. Government ministers of democratic India hold court—much like their colonial and pre-colonial predecessors held *durbar*—and transact state business with a motley crowd of visitors, with the same display of power, privilege and pomp. Independent India has clearly moved on and shown, once again, the country's capacity to achieve change without revolution.

6

SATYAGRAHA

The Gandhian Conflation of Modernity and Tradition

This trend of uninterrupted and unhindered conceptual flow from Europe to India was challenged once Gandhi got to the centrestage of India's politics, fresh from the successful application of *satyagraha* as a novel, hybrid form of peaceful political resistance. Under his moral and political leadership, Indian freedom fighters learned to gain new insights on their home ground, which found singular expression in Nehru's *Discovery of India*, including his treatment of Kautilya and the *Arthashastra* therein. The process of introspection and selective re-use intervened during the process of the writing of the Indian constitution. The defining moment came with the celebrated Nehru speech 'Freedom at Midnight' in which he announced to a skeptical world the birth of the Indian nation-state when he said, 'the soul of a nation, long suppressed, finds utterance'. Today, the Indian state—cutting edge of the process of self-assertion of Indian society—is both structure and agency of the indigenous evolution and resilience of the political and social systems.

The Congress party, at the height of colonial rule, had become the vehicle of the synthesis of the two main strands of Indian nationalism—the liberal constitutionalists like the 'moderate' Gopal Krishna Gokhale and the radical 'extremists' led by Bal Gangadhar Tilak. Following its foundation in 1885 by a retired British civil servant—Sir Alan Octavian Hume—the Indian National Congress gradually acquired a complex, hybrid character—of collaborator and competitor, movement and party, purveyor of modern rules, committee meetings, minute taking and sporting the *khadi*, *charkha* and *satyagraha* as its main political instruments—combining participation and protest action as a two-track strategy of power (cf. Rudolph 1987; Parekh 1999). After Independence, when its rival, the Muslim League, left India for Pakistan, the Congress, complete with its party organization, Nehru as Prime-Minister-in-waiting, its core ideas about planning, foreign policy and state-building already shaped, was more than ready for succession to power.

Mahatma Gandhi, the most outstanding leader of India's struggle for Independence and a continued source of moral inspiration, was trained as a barrister in England. He developed the method of *satyagraha*—a quintessentially hybrid concept that re-used a Jaina ritual, turning it into a tool of nonviolent resistance—while he was in South Africa working for an Indian law firm. The South African experience also taught Gandhi the importance of cross-community coalitions, a theme that he subsequently transformed into 'Hindu-Muslim unity'. This became a salient feature of Gandhi's politics upon his return to India in 1915 and a hallmark of the politics of the Congress party, which found it useful as a political instrument to fend off its challengers—the Hindu Right, the Muslim League and their British patrons. Under his leadership, the Indian National Congress became increasingly sensitive to the gap between the predominantly urban middle-class Congress-party and the Indian masses, thus shifting its attention to the Indian peasantry. Under Gandhi's leadership, the Indian National Congress steadily broadened its reach both in terms of social class and geography. To mobilize mass support, Gandhi introduced a number of indigenous political practices like fasting and general strikes or *hartal* (a form of boycott accompanied by a work stoppage). He combined the techniques of political negotiation with more coercive direct action (such as *hartal, satyagraha,* etc.)— one wonders whether his staging of mass civil disobedience is not a variation of 'power politics'. Gandhi derived both the political resources and the methods from within Indian culture and history, and he knew the potency and stamina that these endogenous resources had among the Indian masses.

The distinct character of Indian politics derives in no small measure from the trickling down of the norms of British constitutionalism and hybrid colonial institutions, and the 'trickling up' of Indian tradition and custom, and hybrid forms of cooperation and contest. The most important of the legacies consists of the modern political institutions, the process of parties and interest groups, and the quintessential Indian political strategy that combines institutional participation and political protest. The main legacy of pre-Independence politics to post-Independence practice is the effort on all sides to bring political competition into the ambit of the rule of law, moderate politics and political institutions. When rules appear too restrictive or not sufficiently legitimate and the game threatens to get out of hand, the state intervenes with its own mixed strategy of suppression and accommodation in a manner that is both akin to that of its British predecessor and Kautilyan statecraft. With some exceptions such as the continuing conflict in Kashmir and the North East, this strategy has worked out successfully, adding layers of new elites and political arenas into the political system. The modest origin of decentralization has matured into a full-fledged federal system, comparable to the now defunct Soviet federal system in its institutional complexity but endowed with far more vitality, as one can see from its resilience. And in this federal system, we can clearly identify 'Kautilyan sediments'.

7

THE HYBRID POSTCOLONIAL STATE AS BOTH STRUCTURE AND AGENCY

With the coming of Independence, the state emerged both as the structure within which nation-building and development were to take place and the main agency for these projects. Just like their British predecessors, the leaders of Independent India put the institutions of the state to task to achieve these political objectives. But democracy made the difference; the national agenda got taken over by the subaltern social groups who increasingly moved on to the offices of power and prestige. However, the game continued to be played on the rules laid down by the Independence generation.

India's new social elites—people with ambition and skills, emerging from lower social orders—became the vital link between the modern and the traditional India, and as a hinge group in Indian society, charged with the task of acting as culture-brokers, they innovated new political practices, implemented through hybrid institutions. This section illustrates the core argument by drawing some examples from the structure of the modern state in India and the process of its interaction with traditional society and the traditions of political practice (and thought) going back to Indian antiquity. The section below discusses why and how the postcolonial state has come to play a catalytic role in reviving the interrupted links of the present to the past, thus restoring the vital process of self-reflexive and authentic evolution through its hybridization.

7.1 ONTOLOGY OF THE STATE: INDIVIDUALIST AND COMMUNITARIAN

Though the Constitution of India was greatly influenced by its British origin (two-thirds of the written constitution came from the Government of India Act, 1935, passed by the British Parliament), it nevertheless established the departure from colonial practice—by conflating the individual and the community, modernity and tradition, the exogenous cultural flow and the indigenous tradition, in a novel manner. Article 1 of the Constitution announced: India, that is *Bharat*, shall be a Union of States, thus affirming the dual origin of the Indian political system from the cultural flow from Europe through the conduit of colonial rule, and the resurrection of the ruptured links with *Bharat*—the mythical kingdom of pre-modern India. Similarly, the choice of the Ashokan 'Lion Capital' and the 'Ashoka Chakra' as the state emblems of independent India highlights the reference to the past. The hybrid constitution, part liberal, part communitarian, provides a third space between the rational, utility maximizing individual and the collectivity, keen on solidarity and policing the common bonds.

The Indian state moved beyond the canon of its liberal name-sake and ascribed to itself a variable space between the ideals of the neutral enforcer of norms—the essential feature of both Weberian bureaucratic modernity and the pre-modern Kautilyan bureaucracy—and the partisan defender of the traditional, the patrimonial and also the marginal.

> Like Hindu conceptions of the divine, the state in India is polymorphous, a creature of manifold forms and orientations. One is the third actor whose scale and power contribute to the marginality of class politics. Another is a liberal or citizens' state, a juridical body whose legislative reach is limited by a written constitution, judicial review, and fundamental rights. Still another is a capitalist state that guards the boundaries of the mixed economy by protecting the rights and promoting the interests of property in agriculture, commerce, and industry. Finally, a socialist state is concerned to use public power to eradicate poverty and privilege and tame private power. Which combination prevails in a particular historical setting is a matter of inquiry. (Rudolph/Rudolph 1967, 400f)

Rudolph and Rudolph also note that 'state in India was not a European import'; instead, the 'historical legacies of imperial states on the Indian subcontinent in the pre-Christian era established state conceptions and institutions that provided models for the subcontinental multinational state of modern India' (1967, 63f). Needless to say, the Kautilyan conception of the state is an important factor of influence on the design of modern Indian state—not only in terms of 'state philosophy' but basic institutional structures and procedures.

7.2 THE CONGRESS 'SYSTEM': BRIDGING COLONIAL RULE AND COMPETITIVE POLITICS

The transition from colonial rule to competitive party politics within a democratic framework was facilitated by a conglomerate of interests, personalities and beliefs that drew as much on the indigenous idiom as on liberal democratic politics. With Jawaharlal Nehru at the helm of affairs, the Indian National Congress, located at the fulcrum of national politics, constituted the core of a one-dominant-party system. For about two decades, the INC ruled from Delhi and practically in all the Indian federal States. Elections were free and held regularly, but the Congress, which never won a majority of votes, regularly won a majority of seats thanks to the first-past-the-post voting system and came to be known as the party of governance. The opposition parties, scattered around it, practically never held office but exercised power and influence in implicit coalition with factions within the Congress party. This made it possible for India to reinforce a political culture of bargaining, reform and orderly social change without party alternation. This unique constellation of forces came to be known as the Congress System, which, in retrospect, was the vital link between autocratic and democratic rule.

In the diagrammatic representation of the Congress System (Figure 2), the axes represent major issues facing the country, at the centre of which stood the Congress party. On each issue, left and right wing opinions were arrayed on either side of the Congress represented by the dark inner circle. The next circle stands for the opposition parties. The Congress System held the Indian National Congress in legislative power, but that was a power which could not swing the country in a clear political direction.

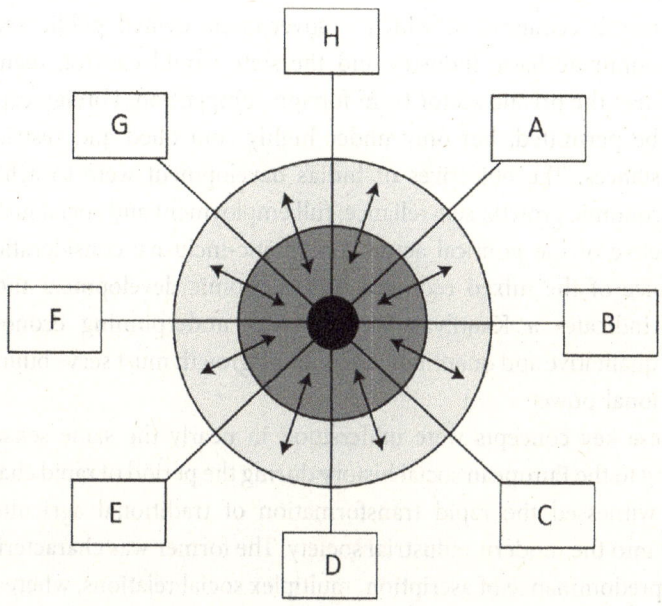

Figure 2: The Congress system of India
Source: Adapted from Morris-Jones (1966, 419)

7.3 THE ECONOMY—MODERN, TRADITIONAL, LIBERAL, SOCIALIST AND GANDHIAN, ALL AT THE SAME TIME

The 'mixed' economy, combining features of Soviet style planning and the free market with rather articulate 'echoes' of Kautilyan political economy, became the mainframe of India's economic life. The 'Indian' model of democratic development emerged from a series of strategic choices made during the early years after Independence. These choices, in turn, were based on a set of compromises that attempted to blend the experience of wartime planning and controls, domestic pressures for a policy of economic nationalism and the liberal, Gandhian and socialist ideological crosscurrents that existed within the nationalist movement. The model that grew out of these strategic choices evolved incrementally into a set of policies that became the basis of India's development consensus. It called for a system of centralized planning and a mixed economy in which a government-owned public sector would dominate basic industry and the state would control, regulate and protect the private sector from foreign competition. Foreign capital would be permitted, but only under highly controlled and restricted circumstances. The objectives of India's development were to achieve rapid economic growth, self-reliance, full employment and social justice. Irrespective of the political actors' pragmatic-inclusive considerations, the choice of the mixed economy and economic development model clearly indicates a Kautilyan directionality underpinning economic policy: qualitative and quantitative economic growth must serve building up 'national power'.

These key concepts were understood in nearly the same sense as referring to the European social history during the period of rapid change which witnessed the rapid transformation of traditional agricultural society into the modern industrial society. The former was characterized by the predominance of ascription, multiplex social relations, where one individual would play a variety of roles, and a deferential stratification system, ensconced within primordial kin networks. A modern society, on the other hand, was seen as one based on the predominance of universalistic, specific and achievement norms, high degree of social mobility, specialization and occupational differentiation, an egalitarian class system based on generalized patterns of occupational achievement and the prevalence of association of specific groups not based on ascription.

The mixed economy gave an institutional shape to the liberal, socialist and communitarian values that constituted the three main strands of the Freedom Movement and dominated the proceedings of the Constituent Assembly. The liberal values were given a clear and incontrovertible shape in the fundamental right to the freedom of trade, occupation and ownership, Article 19 of the Constitution. The socialist values were less explicit but nevertheless clearly discernible. One can argue that socialist values have subtly been arched over by the Kautilyan etatist and dirigiste tradition of political economy.

Instead of the concept of due process—open to judicial

interpretation—the Constitution settled for the concept of 'procedure established by law' which made 'national' interest more compelling than the interest of the individual, a doctrine that paved the way for land reforms and laws aimed at curbing the full play of capitalist enterprise. Articles 39, 41, 43, 46 of the Directive Principles of state policy recommended that the state pursues policies that aimed at bringing about right to an adequate means of livelihood, the distribution of the ownership and control of material resources of the community in a manner that best serves the common good, avoiding the concentration of wealth, a living wage, decent standards of living and full enjoyment of leisure, and social and cultural opportunities for the entire population. Finally, even though there was no staunch 'Gandhian lobby' in the Constituent Assembly, communitarian values such as welfare of *harijans*, backward classes, women and children, village and cottage industries, educational and economic interests of weaker sections, cattle welfare and banning slaughter of milch cattle found their way into the body of this elaborate text.

7.4 SELF-RULE AND SHARED RULE: COMBINING CULTURAL DIVERSITY AND THE FEDERAL STRUCTURE

Apart from academic disputation about the nature and even the 'authenticity' of India's federal system as defined in the constitution lies the reality of an enormous country whose cultural heterogeneity is expressed in the federal organization of power (cf. Mitra 2000). Since state reorganization in 1953 and 1956, state boundaries have roughly coincided with historically rooted linguistic and cultural regions. The differences reinforce the effects of size and continue in the federal system the tensions between regional kingdoms and subcontinental Empire that have characterized the history of the state in India since antiquity. The debate about federalization—the subject of numerous studies, conferences and commissions, beginning in the early 1970s with the Rajamannar Committee in Tamil Nadu (cf. Government of Tamil Nadu 1971) and continuing till today—reflects the crucial role it plays in national politics. The fact of the matter is that Indian federalism is very much a hybrid endogenous creation, combining imported concepts of power-sharing with indigenous methods of consensus and accommodation. During the dominance of the Congress party, the 'Union' government (a sign of hybridity—for the constitution recognized the federal government simply as the Union) and most state governments were ruled by the same party; thus, conflict resolution could take place informally within party channels, causing some authors to question the Indian brand as authentically federal. However, Indian-style federalism has gained endurance and legitimacy, and it found a new lease of life by developing an intricate set of informal channels and formal mechanisms to continue effective conflict resolution. The territorial state has seen many changes, particularly at the level of the regions. New regions have been created to give more salience to regional identity, language and economic needs. But unlike in neighbouring Pakistan which, mainly as a result of regional imbalance, split into two in 1971, the territorial integrity of India continues to be stable.

7.5 INDIAN PERSONAL LAW: CONFLATING THE SECULAR STATE AND SACRED BELIEFS

India's Personal Law, governing family, marriage, divorce, adoption and succession, is a unique blend of the double commitment of the state to the rights of the individual and to group identities (cf. Mitra/Fischer 2002; Ghosh 2007). Ironically, the collective rights and group identities were rooted in the history of representation under British rule. The British, who at home conceived of the political community in terms of equal citizens, in India saw it in terms of distinctive groups, which was taken to be a unique feature of Indian society. The same held also for the leaders of India's freedom movement who sought to realize a political community composed of equal citizens but early on realized that they could not build a nationalist movement without recognizing cultural and territorial communities. Political safeguards to minorities were a key element of British efforts to represent groups in Indian society. They were first elaborated in the Morley-Minto constitutional reforms of 1906, then in the Montagu-Chelmsford scheme of 1919 and finally in the constitutional framework that received the royal assent in 1935.[1]

The constitutional design and the structure of institutions that were intended to give concrete shape to the idealistic goals of the Republic, as enshrined in the preamble, adopted methodological individualism as the cutting edge of social change. However, such principles as individual rights and representation based not on group identities but individual interests and structured along the lines of political majorities, seen in the context of a society based on hierarchy and tightly-knit social groups, could only lead to conflicts based on values and interests of everyday politics. Free and fair elections, universal adult franchise and extension of the electoral principle into all realms of social power were intended to articulate, aggregate and eventually incorporate endogenous political norms and alien political institutions within the structure of the political system of the postcolonial state.

The fuzzy, hybrid practice of combining individual rights and group identity came to a sore test in the Shah Bano case where the Supreme Court upheld the appeal of a divorced Muslim woman for her individual right to alimony against the practice prevailing in the Muslim community of India of leaving such matters to the community. However, in the face of strong opposition to the extension of a 'pure' construction of individual rights to the Muslim community, Prime Minister Rajiv Gandhi introduced the (Muslim women) Protection of Rights on Divorce bill in 1986 and restored the hybrid solution to the complicated relationship of Islam and the secular state.

7.6 THE MODERN STATE AND CULTURAL DIVERSITY: THE THREE-LANGUAGE FORMULA

Many postcolonial states, following Independence, set up a single national identity—one state, one legal system, one national language and one state religion—as the basis of their statehood. Pakistan—the 'land of the pure'—became an advocate of this form of purity, whereas India stood for a more inclusive identity. In its solicitude to distinguish itself from secular and diverse India, Pakistan opted for Urdu as the national language, refusing to dilute this unity through official recognition to other major languages like Bengali. India, on the other hand, after a brief spell of disorder on the issue of national language, devised a formula in course of the States' Reorganisation Commission to encourage large sections of the people to learn a language other than one's mother tongue. Once again, the idea of hybridity has found a hospitable corner.

7.7 SOCIAL HIERARCHY AND RATIONAL BUREAUCRACY

The modern men and women to whom the British transferred power in 1947 had their task cut out for them. Echoing the spirit of the times, India's first Prime Minister Jawaharlal Nehru outlined his vision of the future of Indian state, society and economy in a famous oration that has since become a landmark on modern India. Nehru, a quintessential renaissance man, had presented this modernist agenda on the background of the carnage that followed the Partition of British India into Pakistan, carved out as a homeland for India's Muslims, and the Indian republic that chose to remain a secular state. As India's first Prime Minister, Nehru, who was a social democrat by temperament and intensely aware of the urgency of a concerted effort to remove mass poverty and ignorance, sought legitimacy through the promotion of general welfare. Democracy, a sense of community and modernization were values that were to lead the way into the promised future. At that moment of euphoria, the fact that such principles were of alien provenance did not matter.

Therefore, the modern message of Nehru and his generation of leaders was carefully wrapped in traditional, Indian symbols and conveyed through the hybrid institutions that formed part and parcel of the Indian political system. Nehru's generation of leaders who took over the mantle of hybrid modernity from their predecessors has been able to institutionalize the genre of the *neta*—typically Indian leaders. At the crucial nodes of this complex system, one increasingly found the Indian *neta*—Hindi for leader—who became a two-way culture broker, constantly conflating the modern and traditional idioms of Indian politics. In their attitude and rhetoric as in their person, these hybrid *neta*s represented a quintessential Indian genre—much like Mahatma Gandhi before Independence. A picture of charismatic Laloo Prasad Yadav shows how these political entrepreneurs combine traditional symbols and modern institutions and technology to produce a superb conduit for the flow of power, communication and legitimacy.

A key feature of the modern Indian state is its centralized bureaucracy. Both Nehru and Sardar Patel recognized the indispensability of a centralized state bureaucracy. They made sure that the Indian Civil Service of colonial times was wholesale taken over by the new state—just like the armed forces, the police and the intelligence service. However, centralized state bureaucracy in India was not invented by the British. India has an endogenous tradition of state bureaucracy that goes back to the Maurya Empire—and its conceptual design is laid down in Kautilya's *Arthashastra*. As Panikkar notes:

> The age-old political tradition in India before independence was that of an administrating state. At all times, from the time of the Nandas in the 4th century BC, it was a vast bureaucracy that governed the country, collected its revenue, looked after the irrigation system, and maintained law and order. Basically the British system was not different from that of Mauryas or the Moghuls. (Panikkar 1962, 228)

7.8 PUBLIC BUILDINGS AND IMAGES OF THE HYBRID STATE

The architecture of public buildings of India and the city planning provide the final evidence of hybrid modernity. The British colonial rulers laid down the plans of capital buildings with broad avenues (optimal for military marches as much as for showcasing the street plans of modernity) but nevertheless adorned with the architectural symbols of traditional India—the Mughal water garden, the Buddhist *stupa*, the Islamic minarets and the Hindu *chhatri*s that would make the native feel comfortable in the modern set up (cf. Hegewald 2012). The 'traditional' designs and architectural forms that the British drew on were themselves hybrid in nature, based on a re-use of local and regional forms as well as on a conceptual and cultural flow from outside the country.[2]

The British strategy of domination, which took into account the enormous gain in legitimacy through the reuse of the institutions and sacred symbols of those defeated by it, consisted of selected incorporation of some elements of the Indian past and conspicuous rejection of the rest. Imperial design and utilitarian ideology converged in the Anglo-Indian style—in architectural as much as institutional—design. The sole opportunity for colonized Indians to advance, as they saw it, consisted in the acceptance of modern (i.e., European) science, technology and values. The coming of Gandhi and, subsequently, India's Independence challenged that, opening up, in the process, the flood-gates into India's pre-modern politico-cultural past for those fighting for freedom from colonial rule.

Colonial aesthetic and colonial politics were of one piece. The architecture of colonial rule worked to one common purpose—the selective incorporation of traditional elites, de-linking them from their ancestral moorings and justifying their power in terms of the common purpose of progress, of which colonial rule was proclaimed the indispensable instrument. The Archaeological Survey of India preserved India's monuments—both sacred and administrative—in a state of 'arrested decay' (Metcalf 1998, 18). Thus, they were to be kept isolated and distanced from the community of which they used to be an integral part. So did the new British-established political and administrative institutions which presented the Indian past as inferior to the British present and, by the same analogy, the modernity symbolized by colonial rule as the superior future.

The 'Transfer of Power' to the successor regime of Nehru passed on this hybrid structure. The new stakeholders—many from lower social orders who quickly adapted themselves to their new social and political circumstances—found a useful tool of order and legitimacy in these new, modern institutions and re-used them by incorporating minimal but necessary changes in the inner architecture of space.

8

A DIALECTIC OF THE 'PURE' AND THE 'HYBRID'
Implications of the Indian Case for a General Theory of State Formation in Transitional Societies

In its search for pure categories in terms of which to compare the diversity of states, comparative politics has left behind the pragmatic empiricism of Aristotle which saw experience (and as such, actors' preferences) rather than superior knowledge as the basis of legitimacy.[1] Instead, the inspiration of Plato's 'ideal' state construction has dominated the field.

Examples of the ever present search for pure categories, and the failure to fit the world into them, are plentiful. A seminal attempt to classify contemporary political regimes (192 of them, to be precise) into democracy and authoritarian categories found 38 per cent belonging to the pure class of liberal democracy. The rest were distributed over 'electoral democracy' (16 per cent), ambiguous regimes (8.9 per cent), competitive authoritarian (10.9 per cent), hegemonic electoral authoritarian (13 per cent) and politically closed authoritarian (13 per cent) (Diamond 2002, 26). A subsequent attempt at a similar classification came up with a deeply pessimistic conclusion with regard to the tendency of transitional regimes to move firmly away from the lure of authoritarianism, smuggled into the structure of pure democratic institutions by the way of hybridization.[2] These unfruitful attempts to bring errant hybrid regimes into the net of neat classification hold out the portents of hope for trans-disciplinary analysis and a wider model encompassing insights gained from the new research on cultural flow that can take in 'pure' as well as hybrid cases.[3]

The status of the state in India as a modern, consolidated, electoral democracy is well established.[4] But, while the country responds positively to most items on formal check lists of stateness and democracy, doubts persist about its authenticity as a democracy because of its anomalous character. The authoritarian 'emergency' provisions built into India's constitution, the practice of relinquishing state power to the military under the Armed Forces Act, hybrid legislation that combine features of modern and religious laws, capitulation to social actors and ethnic groups in communal riots and, most importantly, glaring failures to protect secularism and individual rights—the ultimate symbols of high modernity—are pilloried as 'functional' lapses by the defenders of modernity. India's political system, which combines liberal democratic institutions and elements of her pre-modern past—notably Kautilya's state conception—continues to puzzle (cf. Lijphart 2009).

In their prescient study on the 'modernity of tradition' which analysed how 'modernity and tradition' do 'infiltrate and transform each other', Lloyd and Susanne Rudolph had laid down the ground work for issues raised by us here (Rudolph/Rudolph 1967, 3). India, thanks to the mismatch between pre-conceived categories and her empirical complexity, occupies an ambiguous position in global ranking of democracies (cf. Mitra 1999b). The empirical analysis of the features of the Indian state show, however, that rather than being merely a diminished sub-type of liberal democracy, the state in India is a modern state in its own right, but one which diverges from the Western state 'in the importance it accords to "pre-modern" political forms [...] because they express different cultural values and traditions that form part of the cultural heritage' (Mitra 1990, 6). It is the quintessential unity in diversity, for the state is the fulcrum around which diverse ideologies, cultures, beliefs and economic regimes revolve. In the words of Lloyd and Susanne Rudolph (1987), the state in India is a 'manifold'—an embodiment of the 'avatars of Vishnu'.

The hybrid elements in the modern state of India are the outcome of the historical genealogy of the state tradition, notably the Kautilyan state conception, and its discontinuities, the cultural and geographic diversity, and the deep class conflict that underpins Indian society. Besides analysing the conditions that have affected the emergence of the state, we need to consider the theoretical bridge that connects the process of state formation to its ultimate product, namely the institutional structure of the state.

The anomalous character of India in terms of the comparative politics of democracy helps link a debate specific to comparative politics with the larger issue of hybridity that has dominated critical theory and postcolonial literature. A brief foray into the larger theoretical landscape can help to establish a course for empirical analysis of the Indian case and provide the basis of an analytical tool box that extends the conventional rational choice neo-institutional model of the state by drawing on trans-lingual, trans-cultural and trans-disciplinary aspects of state formation. On the basis of this heuristic model, we can analyse the underlying process that has made the state in India what it is, thus explaining why the state has become a key element in the resilience of India's political system.

In our concluding remarks, we return to the issue of the relationship of the pure and the hybrid in Political Science and open it up for a general, cross-disciplinary debate. The focus on hybrid structures generates the space for the understanding of phenomena of cultural and conceptual flow and the emergence of hybrid institutions as a consequence of the conflation of the endogenous and the alien categories and institutions. We have outlined the theoretical puzzles associated with the 'modernity of tradition' of the post-1947 state in India. And we have specifically sketched the contours of the intellectual and tangible influence of the Kautilyan state conception upon modern Indian politics. Our examination has led us to the finding that there is a latent influence of Kautilyan thought upon political actors as well as the active re-use of Kautilyan thought by modern political actors. That duality of latent resonance and active re-use is the key for understanding the hybrid nature of the institutions and practices of India's political system.

We have argued that hybridization is part and parcel of Indian politics as actors, in their search for autonomy, coherence, resilience and development, transform rules and designs as they see fit. A solution where the bulk of stake-holders simultaneously reach or expect to reach their best outcomes, once achieved, yields a 'lock-in' from which they would find it difficult to exit. Each hybrid institution carries a 'lock-in' at its core. Drawing on Douglass North, we have asked, 'Why do institutions work in South Asia, sometimes?' (North 1990, 94; Mitra 1999a, 422) Not all innovations or amendments work, of course, but when they do, or, as North puts it, when a cluster of actors 'lock-in' around a particular design or set of rules, the result—a new hybrid institution—can become enduring.

Left to their own devices, people connected to these hybrid institutions do not necessarily see them as aberrations or diminished forms of the real thing. Despite their stretched, mixed or altered forms, or precisely because of them, hybrid political structures have a real life, full of vitality, social significance and the capacity for self-regeneration. Rather than being merely transient, many flourish over long stretches of time and space.

Not all hybrid structures are treated kindly by different scientific disciplines; their academic standing varies from one discipline to another. The intellectual indulgence that critical theory, postcolonial literature, cultural anthropology and social history have shown to hybrid structures, concepts and institutions contrasts sharply with comparative politics. In its Jacobin mode, comparative politics usually approaches the political process of postcolonial states with 'pure' categories of European provenance, thus running the risk of parts of the empirical world escaping the classificatory project altogether, or worse, the analyst, having failed to classify or explain, turning into a moralist out of sheer desperation! (cf. Mitra 1999b, 39–86) Little does one realize, however, that concepts—when they travel beyond their place of origin—still carry their birth marks of cultural and contextual assumptions built into them. The mechanical application of 'pure' concepts of European origin to alien soil can lead to 'conceptual stretching'[5] or violent retribution by the way of radical rejection of all that go under the banner of such concepts, leading to a post-revolutionary frenzy.[6] Inducting hybridity and cultural flow in to the pure categories of comparative politics might contribute to firmer measurements—and a more benign world.

Looking back at the Indian past through hybrid eyes yields surprises. One comes to realize that modern institutions of India, nationalist sentiments notwithstanding, are a true British legacy. In the second place, a critical analysis of British rule and Indian resistance to it helps explain why democratic institutions have worked more effectively in India as compared to her neighbours.[7] That the synthesis of British constitutional norms and political forms with India's indigenous political tradition as typified by the Kautilyan state conception led to a different outcome than the other successor states ensues from India's tradition of re-use, where the past continues within the present as a fundamental politico-cultural reality that is being drawn upon by deliberate political design. And such conscious re-use has been possible because tradition is so firmly rooted in the collective subconscious. The British pursued their own colonialist variation of re-use with respect to Indian tradition, but that eventually collided with the Indian nationalists' strategy of re-use.

Avid re-users, post-independent India's leaders have not only re-used their endogenous politico-cultural resources but also appropriated many of the symbols and institutions of their colonial predecessors and cloaked them in Indian garb. This blending of indigenous tradition and imported institutions explains both the ability of the British to rule for so long with little recourse to overt force and the smooth transition from colonial rule to multi-party democracy.

Effective accommodation of the past within the structure of the present is not necessarily a problem of mechanical accumulation. It also entails the need for leaders to strategically pick and choose; the process is marked by violence and leaves behind a trail of bitterness and anxiety. This helps explain the juxtaposition of successful state formation and persistence of inter-community conflict and regional secession movements in India.[8]

Seen in this light, the claim of high modernity in its Orientalist avatar to the 'pure' and to use the resultant power to authenticate its claim to the high moral ground, fending off any claims to familiarity by the subaltern (in the sense of the hybridity, pollution *métissage*, solecism, mimicry...), comes across as theory playing the hand maiden to politics.[9] The research on hybridity questions the dominance of one society over another in the name of modernity. Whereas 'the West had strung the tape at the finish line for others to break, for us it has become apparent that there are multiple races and many finish lines, and the tapes are manufactured also in Tokyo and Beijing' (S. H. Rudolph 1987, 732). The symbolic presence of the past constitutes a link of modernity with collective memory. Susanne Rudolph generalizes from these observations to the need to look at the universal claims of a particular variant of modernity afresh.[10]

Where, then, does comparative politics (and comparative political theory) go from here?

A number of theoretical developments in the social sciences and humanities since the halcyon days of structural functionalism—conceptual stretching, bounded rationality, two level games, entangled history, habitus, re-use of the past and cultural flow—point in the direction of new pastures that one can visit in order to enrich the basis of comparison that is relevant to our times.[11] The biggest challenge is to bring the two worlds—of comparative politics and conceptual flow—together and make it methodologically possible for them to draw strength from one another. Even as we celebrate the value added character of hybridity for conventional research on the state and modernity, one should nevertheless be weary of too hasty a rejection of the rigour of logical positivism at the core of comparative politics. Hybridity research stands to gain enormously from retaining the epistemological links with historical development of comparative politics as a distinctive field. Re-use rather than replacement is the best scientific way forward because, important as the heuristic value of hybridity is, progress in the field of research on modernity and the state is contingent on rigorous fieldwork that is the most valuable legacy of structural-functionalism. To measure the length, breadth, depth and stability of hybrid substances, we still need categories and tools that are themselves not hybrid. The alternative is to bring in a form of radical relativism that denies any possibility of inter-personal communication or replication.

The crucial issue is not to lose sight of the fact that political concepts and institutions—pure as well as hybrid—are political constructions that are, as such, contingent on a cluster of interests, stakeholders and their contextual setting. As long as the values, beliefs and interests of the stakeholders are served well and the world at large leaves it alone, an institution and its underlying concept can remain stable over long periods of time. However, today, in the age of trans-national citizenship and global communication, they are as much subject to the inward flow of concepts as to the outward. Most of all, thanks to the new research on hybridity, the ontological status of the 'pure' has become contested. Hybrids do not necessarily think of themselves as impure, and it is quite conceivable that the so-called 'pure' is actually a special case of the hybrid. As one notices the helpless search for a way to accommodate Islam on European soil, with the Jacobin state and global Islam locked into a stalemated conflict, one looks wistfully at the success of the hybrid Indian Personal Law and the hybrid modern state with its pre-modern Kautilyan roots that has kept the divisive issues of the sacred and the secular within the bounds of the rule of law.

SECTION D

KAUTILYA, INDIA AND GLOBAL POLITICAL THEORY
Democratic Aspirations and Institutional Evolution in the Non-Western World

India's counterfactual democracy continues to be a puzzle for students of democratic theory. How did India, at Independence in 1947, a postcolonial, poor society, steeped in social hierarchy and deep ethnic cleavages, make a successful transition to multi-party democracy? The case-specific question leads to a more general query. Is democracy a quintessentially 'Western' idea, exclusively applicable to Western society and culture, or do all societies carry the potential to achieve the democratic form of government, without necessarily having to imbibe Western culture and ethical values? With major contributions on political systems and cultures in Africa and the Greater Middle East, states of South, South-east and East Asia, and with a cogent summation of the lessons of the case studies in the 'general rules and regional specifics' of democracy transition and consolidation, Kautilya's contribution to the origin and evolution of democracy in India helps us join the debate about this most controversial question of our times. Its massive scope provides a foil on which the main arguments of the global democracy project can be analysed by pitching them against aspirations and institutional evolution in the non-Western world. In the vast range of political spaces from the non-Western world, one can ask as to whether there is only one democratic form which fits all societies or can be made to fit all societies by molding their cultures into the western model, or whether it is the democratic prerogative of all societies to develop their own models to their unique design.

The battle for democracy defines the high points of Western history. Transition to democracy and its consolidation are the connecting threads that join the critical junctures of Western history. This connects 'the glory of Athenian direct democracy to the formalization of Roman law, the proclamation of the dignity of man, the institutionalization of universal franchise and, finally, the democratic citizenship based on universal human rights' (Mitra 2017a, 673). Making the world safe for democracy was the justification of the World Wars on fascist regimes and, in more recent times, of the war in Vietnam against Marxist challengers. The fall of Soviet Communism was the final, defining moment of the victory of democracy over authoritarian rule and the forces of darkness

One tends to speak of Western civilization and liberal democracy almost interchangeably. Three problems arise out of this putative homology. First, liberal democracy as a value and a form of rule are seen as quintessential to Western civilization. The victory of Democracy over its rivals is often attributed to its innate strength, not to the local opportunity structure, contingent on global political conditions. Democratization thus becomes the equivalent of Aristotelian teleology, with the potential to spread globally. The success of democracy over its rivals is seen as *ideological* and not *political*, leading to a firm belief in the inevitability of its global spread. Finally, democracy gives the license to Western states to engage in violent regime change in non-Western societies in the name of making the world safe for democracy.

In asking 'Is non-Western democracy possible?' we draw on Kautilya's contribution to our understanding of orderly rule and the role of consent in India and the feasibility of democracy in a comparative context. The question helps bring comparative politics back in again to the field of comparative analysis of non-Western democracy which has sadly lapsed into polemics. With contemporary India as the case in point, these general questions have great comparative relevance. In decreasing order of 'purity' the key questions are as follows: Is there a standard democratic form that fits states of all kinds? Is there a generic form of which operational democracies are variants? Do the hybridized forms, and the democratic variants—Christian Democracy, Guided Democracy, People's Democracy and others of this genre—share a 'family resemblance'[1], or are they different from one another that one should cease to describe them as democracies altogether and simply settle down for a world where each state develops a form of rule appropriate to its unique situation?

A second set of questions emerge from the political momentum that underpins the drive for democratization. Is the democratic impulse essentially endogenous, or is the yearning of democracy a minority movement to begin with, which is subsequently quickened by its entanglement with external power, force of ideas or material incentives? Or is democracy transition necessarily a case of conceptual flow from exogenous quarters, transported by trade, aid, force or occupation? The third question relates to convergence. It is true that all societies evolve over time. But must the evolutionary paths lead towards the democratic form, i.e., rule based on popular consent, expressed through universal adult franchise? The fourth and final question refers to the main driver of the democratic impulse: Is democratization the result of democratic culture,[2] modernization of the economic structure or 'political capital', a variable which is described below at some length because of its relative novelty? The question has deep significance for India—the 'largest' democratic system in the world and for others merely a flawed, political democracy which lacks the essence of a liberal political culture.

1

CULTURE, STRUCTURE OR POLITICAL CAPITAL?
Some General Lessons of India's Counterfactual Democracy

Lipset's *Some Social Requisites of Democracy* (1959) which occupies a canonical status in the academic literature on democratization had made a pessimistic prognosis of the chances of democracy in the non-Western world which, as he saw it, lacked the essential drivers for the transition to democratic rule. The four key variables mentioned by him are: 'wealth, industrialization, urbanization and education' (Lipset 1959, 75).

> Given the existence of poverty-stricken masses, low levels of education, an elongated pyramid class structure, and the 'premature' triumph of the democratic left, the prognosis for the perpetuation of political democracy in Asia and Africa is bleak. The nations which have the best prospects, Israel, Japan, Lebanon, the Philippines and Turkey, tend to resemble Europe in one or more major factors, high educational level (all except Turkey), substantial and growing middle class and the retention of political legitimacy by non-leftist groups [...]. Given the pressure for rapid industrialization and for the immediate solution of chronic problems of poverty and famine through political agencies, it is unlikely that many of the new governments of Asia and Africa will be characterized by an open party system representing basically different class positions and values' (Lipset 1959, 101–2)

To the negative assertion of the feasibility of democracy in non-Western societies that lack Christian values and the four drivers of economic growth, India can be cited as a counter-factual (cf. Mitra 2014). Seen in the regularity and fairness of India's general elections that lead to smooth transition of parties in power and empowerment of social groups that have languished at the bottom of the social pyramid for centuries thanks to the relentless operation of the institutional machinery of democracy, one can argue that India's democracy is neither sham nor idiosyncratic. Colonial India's transition to democracy and its subsequent consolidation are not based on the democratic essence of Indian culture. Instead, they are the outcomes of general variables such as path dependency, adroit institutional arrangements, strategic policy reform and political capital (defined below). As such, India's democracy is a special case of a general model. The resultant hybrid political systems that conflate Western liberal democratic forms and non-Western cultures can pave the way for democracy in its most universal meaning, namely, enfranchisement, entitlement and empowerment of the citizens, and the creation of a sense of efficacy, social justice, legitimacy and trust among them.

India at Independence in 1947, emerging out of British colonial rule, was a poor, socially and spatially fragmented country with low literacy, still recovering from memories of vicious Hindu-Muslim riots that marked Partition and the formation of the new Republic. An overwhelmingly large percentage of its population—illiterate, poor and steeped in subsistence agriculture—was suddenly catapulted to the world of modern competitive politics. Still, the country made a successful transition to democracy and went on to consolidate it, despite the absence of the requisite social and economic conditions at the outset.[1] This makes India stand out as an exception to the rule. A second aspect of India's transition to democracy also deserves careful consideration. In South Asian comparison, India's democracy appears even more puzzling. Within South Asia, though all the states emerged from the same form of colonial rule, the common origin has nevertheless led to dissimilar outcomes, for democracy has not fared well among India's neighbours. In consequence, often and quite unwittingly, one starts thinking about *Indian* democracy rather than 'democracy in India' as if there was something essential and mystical about the connection between Indian culture and democracy.

The empirical evidence of the functioning of Indian democracy helps us understand the deeper and more general dimensions of democracy in the light of India's 'counter-factual'[2] democracy in order to explore a theoretical answer to democracy transition and consolidation in non-Western societies.

2

THE IMPACT OF PATH DEPENDENCE ON TRANSITION TO DEMOCRACY AND ITS CONSOLIDATION

The largely peaceful Transfer of Power by British colonial rulers to the leaders of the Congress party at Independence ensured the continuity of British institutions and practices in post-Independence India. These expanded enormously in order to take in the norms and values of Indian society and culture in the 1950s, once universal adult franchise and competitive elections ushered millions of local elites into the political arena. The incorporation of organic, collective identities within the structure of institutions based on methodological individualism was facilitated by the interaction of the caste system with large, general constituencies and by simple majority electoral rules. All this happened under the watchful eye of the independent Election Commission and the Supreme Court of India. This helped adapt European institutions to the reality of India's regions and localities.[1] A 'lock-in'[2] between elite interests, mass aspirations and the process of democratization took place. In consequence, India's democratic institutions survived the assault on their autonomy and integrity during the Emergency of 1975-77. The legacy of resistance to authoritarian rule lived on in the form of India's civil rights movements and activists who went on to play an important, moderating role. They contained the excesses of the bureaucratic authority of the state in places like Kashmir or the North East and curbed the excesses of ideology in the wake of the rise of Hindu nationalism in the 1980s.

A brief comparison with India's South Asian neighbours will help showcase the role of path dependence in securing democracy transition and consolidation. The Indian story starts with the incremental devolution of power and the exercise of ministerial responsibility by leaders of the Freedom Movement. This has had a long history that predates India's Independence in 1947. In retrospect, the 'one-dominant-party system' (1947–67) with the Indian National Congress (INC) at its core and opposition parties at the periphery, exercising power indirectly through coalitions with the factions within the Congress party, appears to have been a training ground for office-holding and power-sharing for India's regional and local leaders. Even when the Congress party lost its hegemonic position following its loss of power in several Indian states and the reduction of its absolute majority in the Parliament to a simple majority in 1967, the system of democratic rule survived pretty much intact through the turbulent years of unstable coalitions that followed. The 'lock-in' of political actors at federal and regional levels, parties, interest groups, civil servants and army, paramilitary and police forces that is crucial to the Indian political system was already created in the 1950s. It has held fast through the trying years of the Indian Emergency (1975–77) and, beyond it, during the ascendency of Hindu nationalism and the retreat of the state, following the liberalization of the economy in the early 1990s.

The form of elite mediation between the modern state and traditional society incorporated into the model of transition was the main plank of the social vision of the Indian National Congress and its policy of consensus and accommodation during the long years of the Freedom Movement. Following Independence, democratic *economic change* was accepted as the normative objective of the modern state, and parliamentary democracy was based on methodological individualism as its preferred method of achieving it. The juxtaposition of the modern state and traditional society, and the evolution of India's hybrid modernity have been at the basis of democratic transition and consolidation. The consequence has been the generation of a high stock of 'political capital'—an effective combination of structure and agency variables such as law and order management, strategic reform and constitutional incorporation of core social values on the one hand and efficacy, legitimacy and trust on the other—which has helped sustain the lock-in of the modern state and the traditional society.

3

MAKING DEMOCRACY WORK
India's Political Capital

We learn from Robert Putnam's social capital theory (Putnam 1993) that the necessary ingredients for liberal democracy are social attributes such as high interpersonal trust, voluntary social networks and norms that are shared across social group. India's caste-bound, hierarchy-ridden traditional society hardly meets these requirements (Mitra 1999). India's anomalous democratic transition can be explained by the country's *political* capital more than social capital. India's political system and process rather than its social structure have become the main agents of change. This concept subsumes a number of factors such as elections, modern political institutions and their interaction with traditional society, which create level playing fields, strategic social and economic reform, accountability and India's multi-layered citizenship. These democratic capital-generating institutions and processes are briefly described in the arguments that follow.

3.1 ELECTORAL MOBILIZATION AND APPROPRIATE PUBLIC POLICY

Regular and effective elections, based on universal adult franchise, to all important offices and institutions at the central, regional and local levels of the political system are one of the most significant factors to explain the success of India's democracy. An independent Election Commission oversees elections in India. It is ably supported by an independent judicial system pro-active in the defense of human rights and marginal social groups. Elections have helped induct new social elites in positions of power and replace hereditary social notables. The electoral process from its early beginnings about six decades *before* independence has grown enormously, involving a massive electorate of about six hundred million men and women, of whom roughly sixty per cent take part in the polls. The fact that in spite of terrorist attacks and insurgency an election could be held in Kashmir in 2008 speaks to the strength of India's democratic electoral processes.

While the constitutional structure of India's elections has remained more or less constant over the past six decades, the electoral process—evidence of the dynamism of social empowerment—has undergone significant changes. The general elections of the 1950s were dominated by traditional leaders of high castes. However, as the logic of competitive elections sunk in, cross-caste coalitions replaced 'vote banks' that were based on vertical mobilization, where dominant castes dictated lower social groups. 'Differential' mobilization of voters, which refers to the coming together of people from different status groups, and 'horizontal' mobilization, where people of the same status group coalesce around a collective political objective, have knocked vertical social linkages out of the electoral arena. Today, sophisticated electoral choices based on calculations that yield the best results for individuals and groups are the rule. Electoral empowerment has brought tribes and religions in all social strata into the electoral fray. The political coalition put together by Mayawati, who leads the Bahujan Samaj Party, has skillfully drawn support from dalits (former 'untouchables'), the upper Hindu castes and Muslims.

Differential and horizontal electoral mobilization of socially marginal groups has resulted in policy changes that further demonstrate the deepening of democracy in India. Successive governments have introduced laws to promote social integration, welfare, agrarian relations and social empowerment. Over the past two decades, broad-based political coalitions have forced more extreme ideological movements such as the champions of Hindu, Sikh and Muslim or, for that matter, linguistic and regional interests to moderate their stance. The percentage of people under the 'poverty line' has decreased from nearly half of the population in the 1960s to a little over a quarter during the past decade. Though the rapid growth India achieved in the decades following the liberalization of the economy in the 1990s has decelerated and high inflation and dwindling Indian rupee have taken the edge off India's success story, the gains have not been entirely lost and India still remains poised to be a major economic force in the international arena. In domestic politics, coalitional politics at the centre has stabilized India's major policies. The government has managed to maintain the pace of the liberalization of the economy, globalization, dialogue with Pakistan and nuclearization.

3.2 INSTITUTIONAL ARRANGEMENT AND COUNTERVAILING FORCES

India's record at successful state formation and, more recently, the progressive retreat of the state from controlling the economy, but without the ensuing chaos seen in many transitional societies caught in similar situations, speak positively of the effectiveness of her institutional arrangement and political processes. These institutional mechanisms are based on constitutional rules that allow for elections at all possible levels and areas of governance and therefore promote, articulate and aggregate individual choice within India's federal political system. Since the major amendment of the constitution in 1993 that created an intricate quota system, India's six hundred thousand villages have become the lowest tier of the federal system, bringing direct democracy to the door-step of ordinary villagers and guaranteeing the representation of women, dalits (former 'untouchables') and forest dwelling tribals.

The juxtaposition of the division and separation of powers, the fiercely independent media and alert civil rights groups, and a pro-active judiciary has produced a level playing field to facilitate democratic politics. Many of these are colonial transplants that have been adapted by repeated use and re-use to local custom and need. It is significant to note that India's main political parties do not question the legitimacy of India's modern institutions. Although they differ radically in their ideological viewpoints, parties such as the Communist Party or Hindu-nationalist parties like the Shiv Sena or the Bharatiya Janata Party all share the norms of democracy in contrast to the rest of South Asia where even the governing parties want to change institutions and constitution. Not even parties that draw their strength from mobilizing religious cleavages or class conflict object to the right to democratic participation.

3.3 ASYMMETRIC BUT COOPERATIVE FEDERALISM: BALANCING 'UNITY AND DIVERSITY'

India's federation has simultaneously succeeded in differentiating the political and administrative landscape of India whilst holding on tightly to the unity and integrity of the state as a whole. The boundaries of the federal states have been re-drawn on the lines of mother tongue, making regions coherent cultural and political units. Within this reorganization, a 'three-language-formula' has emerged, under which the bulk of regional governance is done in the local language but Hindi and English are retained as link languages. This helps to generate support for the national principle of 'unity in diversity'. The fears of 'balkanization' that marked the rise of language movements in the 1950s have not borne out. Meanwhile, the economy and the development of political coalitions that strive to accommodate small political groups have helped to promote national unity. The liberalization of the economy in 1991 and the gradual opening of the Indian market to international investors have given the states the incentive to emerge as promoters of regional interests.

Simultaneously, regions have also emerged as sites of governance in their own right by the transformation of regional movements into parties of power. Coalitions have transformed rebels into stakeholders. The Indian state has devised an ingenious system of enhancing the stability of the political system through an indigenous scheme of federalization. By creating new regional and sub-regional governments, federal units can be rearranged. Short-term, constitutionally permitted central or even army rule can substitute representative government when the regional political system is unable to sustain orderly rule. Such emergency rule at the regional level is usually withdrawn when the need for the suspension of the normal functioning of parliamentary politics is no longer tenable. The legal responsibility for law and order rests primarily with the regional government, but it is under the watchful eye of the centre. While the state governments control the regional police, the Constitution of India provides for their superseding by direct rule from Delhi when they fail to maintain lawful governance. In reality, however, the maintenance of law and order has become more of a joint venture of Delhi and the federal states. After the end of the 'one dominant party system' (1947–67), the Indian National Congress ruled both at the centre and in the states. However, since the 1960s, the federal states have increasingly acquired autonomy and an authentic political voice in conjunction with Delhi. Successive elections have consolidated India's transition to a multi-party democracy, national unity and political stability.

Within the framework of a national constitution, the Indian political system has managed to safeguard regional identity. The process of regional differentiation is, however, far from over. In view of the difference in time period and in context of their formation, regions experience the problem of governance in different ways. For example, caste and class conflict, feeding into violent groups like the Naxalites, challenge orderly rule in Bihar and Jharkhand. Similarly, the decision to grant statehood to the Telengana movement has intensified similar movements in India's North East. However, India has evolved a process of centre-state cooperation to resolve such conflicts. Many of these regional specificities and vulnerabilities are protected by the constitution of India. Tribal land, for example, cannot easily be transferred to people of non-tribal origin. Special representation is provided to tribal populations and former 'untouchables'. Backward regions are allocated extra recourses by the national Finance Commission for their economic advancement. National planning and the deployment of regular and paramilitary troops help local and regional governments to maintain orderly rule and the respect for due process. The induction of local elites into the structure of governance through elections and cooption has strengthened the linkage of India's traditional society with modern institutions.

In brief, the successful transformation of a colonized population into citizens of a secular, democratic republic has contributed to the sustainability of democracy. The main strategy has consisted in the encouraging of rebels, the alienated and the indifferent to become national stakeholders. The strategy's components are: (a) India's institutional arrangement (the Constitution), (b) laws meant to implement the egalitarian social visions underlying the constitution, (c) the double role of the state as a neutral enforcer and as a partisan supporting vulnerable social groups in producing a level playing field, (d) the empowerment of minorities through law and political practice, including India's Personal Law which guarantees freedom to religious minorities to follow their own laws in the areas of marriage, divorce, adoption and succession, and, finally, (e) judicialization which safeguards individual and group rights.

4

DEMOCRACY IN GENERAL AND IN THE NON-WESTERN CONTEXT

From the point of view of comparative theories of democratic transition and consolidation, the relevance of Kautilya's *Arthashastra* for the contemporary world where the battle-lines are drawn between 'the West and the Rest' can hardly be overstated. The contributions to comparative analysis of democratization in Africa and Asia brought together by Alexei Voskressenski help relativize the negative expectation of the feasibility of non-Western democracy by concepts like 'Oriental despotism',[1] deeply embedded in Western imagination of Asia and Africa. It is important to note that the general tone of the entire volume is analytical and empirical—aimed at an incremental expansion of the models of democratization rather than a blanket rejection of 'Western' models.[2]

Just as the concept of the 'Western' model tends to gloss over the radical differences in the context of the countries lumped together under the 'Western' label, so does the concept of the non-West tend to ignore important contextual differences. As such, we must also take into account the radical variation in the potential for transition to democracy and its consolidation in the vast spaces of Asia and Africa opened up for new political experimentation and innovation, following the end of colonial rule and the onset of modernization. Even in South Asia where democracy has had a better prospect, the picture is mixed. The success of India's democracy, in sharp contrast to its arrested development or outright failure in the neighbouring countries, bears significant implications for the comparative analysis of transition to democracy and its consolidation in the non-Western world. India's secular, democratic, federal path leaves Pakistan, Sri Lanka and Bhutan, which attach a different salience to the relationship of religion and politics and to the indivisibility of unitary power of the nation, with an invidious choice between their national identity as written into their constitutions and a radical change in their institutional arrangement in order to achieve Indian-style liberal democracy. We have attempted to overcome this India 'bias' by developing a more general model of democratization that would pay adequate attention to the specific contexts of the countries concerned. Rather than suggesting tolerant Indian culture and secularism as indispensable to the success of democracy, the approach taken here develops a general variable called 'political capital' which constitutes an efficient path for the transition from authoritarian rule to popular democracy. Beyond this general stance, the decision-making elites in each country have to find their specific way to democracy, making appropriate choices among alternatives offered by their local context.

India's success with democracy has been brought about through a power-sharing political process ensconced in a hybrid political culture that dovetails modernity and tradition. The success of India's democracy, properly understood, has important significance for democracy in South Asia as well as for broader democracy theory. It shows that strategic reform, accountability and social policies that balance efficiency with justice can sustain the progress of democracy and development in a postcolonial context. India's successful conflict-resolution, compared to other new democracies, has been immensely helped by the fact that India's social cleavages are cross-cutting rather than cumulative, and that key intermediaries for conflict-resolution such as the judicial system and party politics have been available for a considerable length of time prior to independence. India's national, regional and local elites, leaders of ethnic groups and social activists have mastered the art of political manipulation and power-sharing. Through a deft combination of protest and participation, they have formulated political strategies that combine cultural, symbolic and religious values with material interests.

In a comparative perspective, one must still ask if there are institutional arrangements other than that of India, particularly with regard to secularism and federalism as practised in India, to facilitate transition to democracy in South Asia. More particularly, is the institutional arrangement consisting of secularism, federalism, a multi-party system and civilian control over the military merely an Indian specificity, a path-dependent outcome reacting to the critical junctures of Indian history, or are democratic political systems conceivable where the majority ethnic identity becomes the basic foundation stones of democratic institutions? These questions require empirical research to be directed at identifying the basis for institutional arrangements that are appropriate to the culture and context of non-Western countries, arrangements which can build on the democratic longing of the people and combine cultural authenticity with a firm link to the general parameters of democracy.

The hybrid models of democracy as in India, but also those that Voskressenski offers based on a 'synthesis of Western and Eastern worldviews,' conflating 'moral laws and precepts' (2017, 568) and modern, plural political institutions, and the concluding statement of Voskressenski, deserve serious attention of the scholars of comparative democratization.[3] There is an important lesson here for students of non-Western democracy: In a world where the future of non-Western democracy is being written in the killing fields of the Middle East, in the cities and citadels of Europe where home-grown suicide terrorists are trading their arguments against lives, their own and that of their hapless victims, India's democratic resilience remains a sterling reminder of the feasibility of non-Western democracy. We have argued in this book that societies which have the comparative advantage of a classical tradition and the resources to build their modern institutions on the classical heritage might have a firm basis for rule by the consent of the governed. This heuristic insight into the requisite foundation of modern institutions is the ultimate lesson that the designers of institutions in transitional societies can draw from a close reading of Kautilya's *Arthashastra* and its valuable legacy for modern India.[4]

SECTION E

THE 'KAUTILYAN MOMENT', THE POWER-KNOWLEDGE MATRIX AND THE GENEALOGY OF GLOBAL POLITICAL THEORY

CONCLUSION
The Emergent 'Kautilyan Discourse' in India

In the middle of the second decade of the twenty-first century, there are clear signs of an emergent Kautilya discourse in India. Explicit and discursive recourse to Kautilya can be observed in the strategic community and academia, in political and media contexts. Such manifest presence comes along with the predominantly latent presence of Kautilyan thought—transmitted not only by the 'political habitus' of India's elites but through its politicizing of the people as well. Although the Kautilya discourse is still nascent and involves relatively few actors, it marks a significant change compared to the past decades. What might account for the Kautilya revival?

In the expert interviews, it was said that Indian foreign and security policy has undergone a 'learning curve' over the past decades. Since independence, realist Kautilyan thought has been an integral part of politico-strategic thinking and practice in India. However, it was argued that during the first decades of Independent India the Kautilyan impulse remained largely subcutaneous. Nehru spoke of India's potential power that had to be transformed into real power, but his message was garbed by *Panchsheel* declarations. In a learning process of negative experiences (along with some positive ones), the interviewees argued, Indian foreign and security policy has gradually metamorphosed towards an explicitly realist stance. Among the negative experiences in independent India's foreign relations, interviewees listed the following events and developments:

- The British colonial power's policy of 'divide and quit', which linked the end of colonialism on the subcontinent with its political fragmentation.
- The alliance of the United States with Pakistan since the latter's

accession to the Southeast Asia Treaty Organization (SEATO) in 1954; thus, the USA rejected democratic India's striving for a partnership that would respect its strategic autonomy.
- China's war of aggression in the Himalayas during October–November 1962, which was consistently characterized in the interviews as a traumatic experience.
- The threat of force by the U.S. government against India during the Indo-Pakistani War of 1971; then President Nixon and his chief adviser Henry Kissinger deployed the nuclear-armed aircraft carrier *USS Enterprise* in the Bay of Bengal to intimidate India.
- The continuing terrorist attacks on India, which are considered as steered by Pakistan, which in turn is allied with the United States and China.
- China's refusal to treat India as an equal partner, support her claim for a seat in the UN Security Council, and resolve the border dispute in the Himalayas.

These negative experiences have taught India, as the interviewees said, that any attempt to defend diplomatically national interests is bound to fail if diplomacy is not adequately backed by economic and military power. Through these experiences India learned that ideological and/or normative positions merely camouflage the power politics of other states.[1]

India's positive experiences in foreign affairs, the interviewees argued, were the result of its own strenuous efforts to build up its political, economic and military power base. Only to the extent that India gained in power and correspondingly pursued its interests did other states adopt a more friendly and cooperative attitude.[2] In this regard, interviewees brought up the following events as positive experiences for India:

- The build-up of India's scientific-technological and industrial foundations as well as a high level of agricultural self-sufficiency in the first three decades after independence;
- The enhancement and build-up of the Indian armed forces,

- including the nuclear weapons option, following the military and foreign policy humiliation in the 1962 war;
- The diplomatic firmness and military clout during the Indo-Pakistani War of 1971, which led to the establishment of the state of Bangladesh;
- The upswing in the Indian economy since the reforms of the 'license raj' in the early 1990s;
- The nuclear tests in 1998, in spite of massive international pressure, and the recognition of India as a nuclear weapons state by the United States in 2008.

In summary, it can be said that Indian foreign and security policy has undergone a process of transformation over the past seven decades. In spite of his idealist rhetoric, Nehru pursued a predominately realist foreign policy. But under his successors, during the remainder of the twentieth century, the Kautilyan realist impulse in Indian foreign and security policy grew stronger and became more articulate. This trend was particularly accentuated during the terms of the Prime Ministers L. B. Shastri (1964–6), Indira Gandhi (1966–77 and 1980–84), Rajiv Gandhi (1984–89), Atal Bihari Vajpayee (1998–2004) and, since 2014, Narendra Modi.

It is a truism in social sciences that processes of gradual change in social reality are intellectually captured only after they have advanced to a certain stage. Since the beginning of the second decade of the twenty-first century, it seems that the Indian strategic community is increasingly becoming self-conscious of the underlying realist transformation of India's foreign and security policy. While the realist impulse in the Kautilyan tradition has been there all along, its maturation—finding its expression in the gradual accumulation of India's political, economic and military power base—took a considerable length of time. In other words, since Independence, India has been striving for a great power status—fueled by an inner impulse of Kautilyan realism. Since the turn of the millennium, India has begun to reap the fruits of this striving for power. Now India has become one of the great powers in a multipolar world. Thus, the development process and its underlying impulses have reached the threshold of perceptibility. Therefore, it is not really surprising that the Kautilya discourse has emerged just at that point of time. In the words of an interviewee:

> I think the point to make is that Indian policy and the establishment are getting more grounded in the real world, which makes Kautilya and that kind of traditional statecraft more credible. It does not mean, however, that the Indian leaders have suddenly discovered Kautilya and his precepts, or that they are now really familiar with them. That is not the case, as I told you. They are still too detached from those roots as to say Kautilya is the answer, or the Arthashastra has the answers. No. *But you may say as a scholar looking at these things that India is finally rediscovering its Kautilyan past in terms of exercising realpolitik* rather than being mesmerized and fixated on rhetoric and moralpolitik, as I have called it. We are now beginning to exercise real power; we are beginning to appreciate the real power factors of the country. Material factors tend to matter more than the spiritual domain. Well, in that sense *you may say we are moving towards Kautilya.* (EI Bharat Karnad,[3] emphasis added)

What Bharat Karnad says about India's present power base is evident: Despite persistent severe internal problems—poverty, lack of education for the poor, infrastructure deficits—today's India is the tenth largest economy in the world if the GDP-OER standard is used. If the GDP-PPP standard is applied, India is the fourth largest economy in the world (cf. CIA World Factbook). The Indian economy will continue to grow—probably somewhat slowly but steadily. Already today, the well-educated Indian middle class is larger than the total population of the United States. The Indian armed forces are among the largest in the world and include land-, air- and sea-based nuclear weapon systems. India's political weight in the international arena is steadily increasing. What Karnad says about the connection between the advance of India's power and the new discourse priorities in the Indian strategic community was also addressed by Kanti Bajpai:

> If you are a future great power, a rising power, you have to start thinking more strategically, so it is obvious then that you are going to start mining your own tradition, in part at least. I expect that is actually going to be the case. So in that sense, Chanakya's theory provides some fresh input. (EI Kanti Bajpai)[4]

Now that the foundations of India's political, economic and military power do exist, the conditions are in place to address in a dedicated fashion the ideational resources which have been the latent driving forces of this power build-up. Among these ideational resources, Kautilyan thought takes the central position, but it is not the only ideational factor influencing Indian foreign and security policy. In the expert interviews, it was repeatedly stated that it is only now that India disposes of sufficient 'free energy' in terms of manpower, expertise and financial resources to systematically address Kautilyan thought and other politico-cultural resources as well as their impact on contemporary thinking and behaviour.

> India is emerging from its colonial shadow and becoming a major actor on the world scene. Nehru was right, in the immediate aftermath of independence, to forge a strictly independent approach to foreign policy. Since, the world order has been evolving, and India is one of the players who will matter, if it does not already […]. I would say that India needs Kautilya today more than ever before. (EI Rana Chhina)[5]

The timing of the emergent Kautilya discourse in India can also be seen in a broader historical perspective. At the 2013 'Munich Security Conference', then-National Security Adviser Shivshankar Menon, a man with profound knowledge of Kautilya's *Arthashastra*, insisted that India is not an 'emerging power' but a 're-emerging power'.

> In a speech at the Munich Security Conference in the first week of February 2013, India's National Security Adviser Shivshankar Menon argued indeed contrary to the Western discourse calling ancient civilizations as emerging powers as incorrect. Reemerging is a proper term as countries: such as India and other civilizations

are in process of *restoring the historical norm in the international hierarchy and distribution of power*. (Dikshit 2013, emphasis added)

Menon sees India's political identity anchored in its cultural and civilizational continuity which dates back millennia. For him, the congruence between the cultural and civilizational status of a nation and its political, economic and military power status is 'historical normality'. In the case of India, British colonial rule had interrupted this 'normality' for about two centuries, during which the nation was dramatically weakened in political, economic and military terms. Yet, the stamina of Indian culture remained not only unbroken but proved to be the catalyst for India's political and material regeneration—and thus, 'historical normality' was eventually restored.

Menon's argumentation can also be seen as an illustration of Subrata Mitra's concept of the 're-use of the past'—the traditional mode of action of Indian politics going back to the Indian antiquity. The challenges of historical change are not dealt with by breaking with tradition but by actively 're-using' tradition. If changed circumstances require new thinking and practices, that is done through recourse to traditional ideas and practices. In the politico-strategic sphere, such recourse or 're-use' inevitably (also) involves Kautilyan thought. Such 're-use' is based on the assumption that there is no ontological divide between past and present. Instead, there is an indissoluble interface since the historically distant objects of 're-use' are semiconsciously present in the present. Or, to put it in Bourdieu's terminology, since past ideas and practices are incorporated in the habitus, they can be reactivated.[6]

Through Mitra's concept of the 're-use of the past' one can better understand why just now—in the second decade of the twenty-first century—a discourse is emerging with reference to a political and strategic thinker of Indian antiquity. Since Independence, realism in the Kautilyan tradition has subtly guided India's build-up of power. Once India had (re-)gained great power status, it was confronted with new internal and external challenges. Is it not natural that, in addressing these challenges, Indian political and strategic actors would take discursive recourse to Kautilyan thought?

The Kautilya discourse in India is still nascent, but remarkable, since therein lies the role of younger political scientists (and postgraduate students). They have an unbiased attitude towards Kautilya and other endogenous politico-cultural resources—unburdened by the epistemic legacy of colonialism. And they think that India's intellectual resources should be used for innovative knowledge production—not substituting, but complementing the knowledge structures of the 'Global North'. Their healthy intellectual self-confidence and curiosity no longer accepts that India's wide range of endogenous political and cultural resources, including Kautilyan thought, should remain sidelined and undertheorized.

> The point is, till very recently and even today, these cultural treasures of India are largely still buried, they are not out in the open. Imagine we continue to be more or less in the same state as Europe was before the great Greek treasures became accessible to the people in Europe and to the world at large. (EI Rajeev Bhargava)[7]

For the younger generation of Indian intellectuals it is a self-evident reality that India is a great power—its enormous existing internal problems notwithstanding—and they resent the discrepancy between India's growing political and material power and its meagre knowledge production in Political Science and IR theory. They do not accept any longer the 'division of labour' between the theory-suppliers of the 'Global North' and the theory-licensees of 'Global South' that Kanti Bajpai had analysed already in 2005.

What we see here is a reflection of the 'power-knowledge matrix'. The knowledge production in postcolonial India with its still weak-power potential was significantly shaped by the knowledge regimes of the United States, Britain and continental Europe with their vastly superior power potentials. Such epistemic influence (riding on 'hard power') applies particularly to academic institutions—their research topics, theories, methods, vocabularies and publications. Within academia, Political Science and IR theory are most affected by hegemonic power-knowledge regimes. However, since the turn of the millennium, the growth of India's political, economic and military power has become part of the global power shifts towards Asia. In congruence with the power-knowledge matrix, the relative decline of hard power in Euro-Atlantic space inevitably affects knowledge production of the 'Global South'. As the hegemony of Western thought systems in Political Science and IR theory begins to erode, the inclination to address long-neglected endogenous intellectual resources tends to grow. China is tapping its Confucian and 'Legalist' legacies and has already established Sun-Tzu's *The Art of War* in the canon of strategic classics. However, in India too, the global power shifts inevitably impact the academia, notably in Political Science and IR theory. Therefore, it is not really surprising that younger Indian intellectuals turn increasingly to the large and diverse but mostly untapped reservoir of endogenous politico-cultural resources. With respect to Political Science and IR theory, Kautilya's *Arthashastra* is of singular importance among these endogenous resources. Consequently, the times when Kautilya was wholly ignored or treated as the 'Indian Machiavelli' in Indian Political Science and the strategic community, are surely coming to a close.

The growing power-potential of India and the power shifts of the multipolar world also bring up the question of India's soft-power positioning—and the role of endogenous politico-cultural resources therein. India's self-representation in terms of soft-power is essentially confined to expounding its democracy and freedom of expression. That surely distinguishes India from China. However, the self-portrayal as 'the world's largest democracy' has lost attractiveness since most emerging countries in the 'Global South' have also become functioning democracies. The 'spirit of Gandhi'—in the sense of strict nonviolence and ethical rigour—has also lost much of its earlier appeal, notably so in Asia. In the expert interviews it was strongly contested that Bollywood movies, folklore and exotic tourist destinations would jazz up India's soft power appeal. Instead, the interviewees argued that India's soft-power standing must be derived from its high culture, whose greatest achievements are not as spiritualistic, otherworldly and a-political as the familiar stereotype would suggest. They pointed to the epics *Mahabharata* and *Ramayana*, the *Panchatantra* and Kautilya's *Arthashastra* as well as

Ashoka, Akbar, Tagore or Sri Aurobindo. However, before becoming the cornerstones of India's soft-power portfolio, these diverse politico-cultural resources need to be 'unlocked' through scholarly research which, however, must strictly refrain from nativist narrow-mindedness and ideological enmeshment. Only if a stringent scholarly yet liberal approach is taken, will the presentation of India's cultural treasures to the world become a meaningful and conducive exercise. Interviewees argued that there is, around the world, great interest and receptivity for India's politico-cultural resources, which will likely grow in the future. The political scientist Rajeev Bhargava situated India's soft-power portfolio—thus defined—in the broader perspective of a 'global deficit of unspent ideas'.[8]

Bhargava's observation is surely true for Political Science and IR theory, where the search for fresh theoretical approaches is evident. Such theoretical innovations, however, will not come *ex nihilo*. Innovative ideas are the product of a critical intellectual engagement with past ideas, notably those that have been 'overlooked' because they seemed not to fit the established academic paradigm. When Machiavelli opened up the modern paradigm of Political Science, he first turned to political thought and practice of ancient Rome, Greece, Achaemenid Persia and, we believe, hybridizations of ancient Indian political thought. What he learned from the past he related productively to the problems and challenges of his age. Thus he was able to break free of the habits and mental constraints that surrounded him and develop concepts of lasting theoretical significance.

Machiavelli's intellectual encounter with the great political thinkers and actors of European and Asian antiquity provides a helpful lead to what needs to be done in the present. New conceptualization in Political Science and IR theory will have to draw on those past thought-structures which so far have been ignored and marginalized. For Political Science, the largest reservoir of untapped intellectual resources is waiting in the 'Global South'—and particularly so in India, which, along with China, possesses the oldest continual culture on the planet. Just as Machiavelli five hundred years ago, political scientists need to engage in a 'virtual dialogue' with Kautilya and correlate his political thought with the problems and challenges of the twenty-first century multipolar world. If that is done, we are sure that productive and innovative theory will be generated that can contribute to advancing Political Science and IR theory.

Kautilya's *Arthashastra* and its living memory teach us that India's pre-modern political thought is not a matter of 'dead letters' buried in archives. Pre-modern political thought is 'alive' in India in the sense of the 'modernity of tradition' and 're-use of the past'. Kautilyan thought is implicitly present in the strategic thinking and behaviour patterns of the Indian elites. The core concepts of Kautilya are a part of the strategic culture of India. Kautilyan ideas are a latent factor, ingrained in the basic political thought patterns of the Indian people. Furthermore, over the last few years, there is an emergent Kautilya discourse in the Indian academia and the strategic community. This trend, keeping in pace with a re-emerging India, might pave the way for a global political theory that can constitute an epistemological bridge among the divided political communities of our globalized world.

ENDNOTES

INTRODUCTION

1. That said, while references to Kautilyan thought are infrequent, they are not altogether absent. Many among modern India's political and strategic elites have engaged with Kautilyan thought. Among them are not only India's first Prime Minister Jawaharlal Nehru (in *The Discovery of India*, cf. Nehru 1981, 122–7) and the former President of India Pranab Mukherjee, but we know of at least three Indian National Security Advisers who have been cognoscenti of Kautilya and the *Arthashastra*: J. N. Dixit (2004–5), Shivshankar Menon (2010–14) as well as the current NSA Ajit Doval and the Deputy NSA Arvind Gupta. Sardar Patel, co-founder of the modern Indian state along with Nehru, has not left an oeuvre like Nehru, but he can be seen as the archetypical Kautilyan political actor in the modern context. Former Indian President V. V. Giri stated that Patel possessed 'the astute statesmanship of Chanakya' (Balraj 2013, 417).
2. 'Recipe knowledge', cf. Berger and Luckmann (1966).
3. There were exceptions: cf. Jayaswal (1943), Sharma (1968), Roy (1981), Parmar (1987), Mehta (1992), Zaman (2006), Behera (2007), Parekh (2010) and Shah (2010). In the second decade of the twenty-first century, the attitude of Indian Political Science towards Kautilya begins to change.
4. Again, there were some exceptions: Morgenthau (1958), Bozeman (1960), Drekmeier (1962), Modelski (1964) and Watson (1992). The German political scientist Harald Müller wrote in 2006 about 'the great ancient thinker Kautilya, who is, together with Sun Tzu in China and Thucydides in Greece, the most important and profound analyst of strategic affairs ante dominum' (Müller 2006, 233).
5. A good but not complete overview of the post-2011 literature on Kautilya is given on the website 'Indigenous Historical Knowledge' of the Institute for Defence Studies and Analyses (IDSA): http://www.idsa.in/history/publications.html.
6. Of the Indological literature on Kautilya's *Arthashastra* we have drawn on Hillebrandt (1923), Meyer (1927), Zimmer (2011/1951), Kangle (2010b/1965), Scharfe (1968), Ritschl/Schetelich (1973), Rangarajan (1992) and Olivelle (2013).

7. Whenever Kautilya is mentioned among Indologists, the likelihood is high that instantly a tense dispute would break out on the question of whether the *Arthashastra* is the work of the single author Kautilya or a compilation of various text segments of various (unknown) authors over an extended period of time (cf. Meyer 1977/1926; Kangle 2010b/1965; Zimmer 2011/1951; Trautmann 1971; Olivelle 2013). We accept Kangle's view of a single authorship (some later interpolations notwithstanding).
8. Except for the literature on Indian strategic culture, which, however, often suffers from an inadequate understanding of the *Arthashastra*'s core concepts and mostly neglects the latent influence of Kautilyan thought.
9. Thirty-four expert interviews were conducted with members of the Indian strategic community and academia in Spring of 2012. Field research in India was financially supported by the Fritz Thyssen Foundation, Cologne, Germany.

SECTION A
AN INTERPRETIVE EXPOSITION OF KAUTILYA'S *ARTHASHASTRA*

Chapter 1
1. R. P. Kangle (2010a/ 1972). The value added of Patrick Olivelle's (2013) translation of the *Arthashastra* in relation to Kangle's is yet to be seen.
2. KA stands for Kautilya's *Arthashastra*, the Latin number designates the 'Book' (15 altogether), the first Arabic number indicates the chapter within the respective 'Book', and the second Arabic number the paragraph—mostly only one (often long) sentence (*sutra*) in the chapter.
3. The kingdom of Seleucus Nicator, stretching from present-day Turkey to Afghanistan, bordered on the Maurya Empire in Northwest Pakistan.

Chapter 2
1. Charles Drekmeier notes: 'Since the ruling groups had an interest in limiting the circulation and preventing popularization of the *Arthashastra* treatises, it is not surprising that few of these works have survived' (Drekmeier 1962, 190f).
2. 'EI' stands for expert interview, and henceforth this abbreviation will be used across the text. EI Romila Thapar, historian, New Delhi, 27 March 2012.

Chapter 3

1. Kangle (2010a/1972) and Meyer (1977/1926); in the 1950s a Russian and in 2011 an Italian translation from the Sanskrit original text was published.
2. It should be noted here that Kautilya too adopts an ideal-type approach to his analysis and exposition of the state and statecraft in the *Arthashastra*, as we shall elaborate further on in this text.
3. Yet Rangarajan is right when he notes: 'All translations into English or other foreign languages have been made by Indologists and Sanskrit scholars who were concerned with preserving literary exactness, with the result that comprehensibility has been sacrificed for fidelity to the [Sanskrit] text' (1992, 38).
4. Because our quotes from the Arthashastra are mostly but not always identical with Kangle's translation text, we are omitting quotation marks and page numbers. Instead, the citations are in italics and referenced via the *Arthashastra*'s 'Books', chapters and sutras which conform in Kangle's and Meyer's translations.
5. Unfortunately, Plessner's *Macht und menschliche Natur* (2003/1931) has not yet been translated into English.
6. Plessner's covariance concept is not promoting 'post-modern' cultural relativism. The achievements of European culture and science are not put in question. Rather, foregoing Eurocentrism and 'European exceptionalism' open up new perspectives and intellectual opportunities: 'Relinquishing the supremacy of the European system of values and categories, the European spirit will gain the horizon of the original manifoldness of historically developed cultures and their world views' (Plessner 2003, 164).

Chapter 4

1. The three essays are titled: *The Hindu Social System, Orthodox and Heterodox Holy Teachings of the Indian Intellectuals* and *The Asiatic Sects and Redemption Religions*.
2. Weber's sociology of religion studies on India was not well received. Indologists have simply ignored it. Social scientists, if they have not done likewise, have been extremely critical of the work—some of them nonchalantly accusing Weber of methodological and theoretical incompetence (cf. Schluchter 1984; Kantowsky 1986). However, when looking more closely at these critics, the idea suggests itself that they might not have studied Weber's text all too closely. Such an attitude applies also to most Indian scholars. Kantowsky diagnosed a 'rather scanty and more or less negative reaction in the [South Asia] region to Weber's study

on Hinduism and Buddhism' (Kantowsky 1986, 9). A major reason for this he sees in 'the distorted image of Weber as an agent of capitalist progress and development' who allegedly attributes to Hindu culture passivity and world-negation (ibid., 28). Therefore, writes Kantowsky, the task is 'to put Weber back on his German feet in order to show that he was in fact the very opposite of what he is represented as in India, namely a development theorist, determined to obtain global acceptance for the occidental interpretation and rationalization of the world' (ibid., 210). It is often being asserted that Weber's interest in India was to prove *e contrario* the central thesis of rationality and economic dynamism as distinct features of the West in his *The Protestant Ethic and the Spirit of Capitalism*. In this vein, Weber has been criticized by Indian historian Romila Thapar for 'setting up a model of Indian society in order to prove a series of theses regarding modern European society. The non-European tradition was essential to his analysis not only as a contrasting study but more specifically in order to explain the absence of the emergence of capitalism in areas other than Western Europe' (Thapar 2000, 26). No doubt, the comparative question is present in Weber's 'Hinduism Study', but it is by no means the only or even dominant aspect of Weber's analysis. His research interest is understanding the nature and the intrinsic value of the Hindu order of life. That is admitted by Chaturvedi Badrinath, who otherwise ascribes to Weber an utterly wrong understanding of Indian culture. The initial question whether Hinduism might explain the lack of capitalist development in India is quickly pushed into the background, he acknowledges, because Weber 'seemed to have been bewitchedly drawn deeper and deeper into what he called the magical garden of Indian religion' (Badrinath 1986, 46). It should be noted that the term 'magical garden' resp. 'enchanted garden', which Weber uses in *Economy and Society* (Weber 1968, 630; 1956, 485), does not refer to Hinduism and is never used in his sociological studies on India.
3. Unfortunately, we too have to use Gerth's and Martindale's translation. When we quote from the 'Hinduism Study', we indicate both the page number of Gerth's and Martindale's translation and the original German text (Weber 2008a). However, when translation errors are too severe, we translate ourselves from Weber's original German text (transl. ML). 'Unbelievable', writes Hermann Kulke, is the 'extent of translation errors distorting the meaning [by Gerth and Martindale]' (Schluchter 1984, 297).
4. Weber's view is shared by Charles Drekmeier, who writes that 'a number of similarities exist between arthashastra and nitishastra thought and the

cameralist system that developed in Germany at the beginning of the modern era' (1962, 256).
5. Weber emphasizes that the established categories of Western social analysis are not suitable for the Hindu caste order. Instead, the *varna* order is a social system sui generis. Therefore, the caste system cannot be defined as: a) an order of socio-economic classes and strata; b) a feudal order of mutual rights and obligations; c) a professional order of guilds or similar professional associations; d) a social order based on ethnic or racial criteria. Each of the four castes—as well as the dalits and adivasis—has some features that correspond to these categories. However, each of these categories as well as their aggregation miss the appropriate characterization of the caste system.
6. While using the terms 'Hinduism' or 'Hindu religion', Weber questions the applicability of the 'Western' understanding of religion to Hinduism with its amorphous and non-dogmatic belief structure. 'Broader religious tolerance than this in a single religion is hardly conceivable. In truth, it may well be concluded that Hinduism is simply not a 'religion' in our sense of the word' (Weber 2000, 23; 2008a, 583). The main tenet of Hinduism is the fundamental recognition that the Vedas are uncreated-eternal sacred scriptures: 'One of the few essentially binding duties of Hindu "faith" is not—at least not directly—to dispute their authority' (Weber 2000, 26; 2008b, 586).
7. A nomadic tribe was a 'survival community' in which, while individuals must completely submit to the collective on the one hand, on the other hand, enjoy a certain degree of equality. These conditions changed radically when nomadic tribesmen turned into sedentary farmers and villagers.
8. Cf. Knoll (2015), who mentions in his essay Weber's comparison with Kautilya.

Chapter 5

1. 'Mirrors for Princes' are didactical and instructional texts for (future) rulers. Such texts originated in ancient India, from where they spread to medieval Persia and Europe. A late example of a 'Mirror for Princes' text is Erasmus of Rotterdam's *Education of a Christian Prince*, written for Emperor Charles V in the early sixteenth century.
2. EI Dietmar Rothermund, historian, Heidelberg, 9 January 2012.
3. Here, we follow Meyer's translation, since, for this segment, we find it to be more appropriate and coherent than Kangle's version.

Chapter 6
1. Literature on Intelligence in ancient India: cf. Roy (1981), Trivedi (1984), Chakraborty (1990), Rohatgi (2007) and Wilhelm (2009).

Chapter 7
1. Can be roughly translated as 'one's own intellectual labour of conceptualization'.
2. For Kautilya, 'the earth' means the Indian subcontinent, not the whole globe (see KA, IX, 1, 17-20).

Chapter 8
1. Besides Morgenthau's immediate knowledge of Kautilya, as indicated by his direct references to him, there is also an indirect intellectual connection via Max Weber. In several public and private statements, Morgenthau expressed his intellectual attachment to Weber. Morgenthau had thoroughly studied the writings of Weber in which the latter refers to Kautilya: See *Politics as Vocation* and his *Sociology of Religion Studies on Hinduism and Buddhism*. From the latter work he inserted a citation in *Politics among Nation* (Morgenthau 1978, 4; cf. Frei 1994).

Chapter 9
1. We have noted earlier that the secular-minded Kautilya has an instrumental understanding of religion—and the same applies to magic. While rejecting magic in political and strategic decision-making, Kautilya has no objections to the political exploitation of magic beliefs of other actors. Such use of magic for political purposes comes down to 'psychological warfare'—in war and also in peace. In that sense Book XIV of the Arthashastra, in which multiple magic practices are described, should be understood.
2. Indeed, it is remarkable that Aristotle in his *Politics* would not address foreign policy.
3. Such defensive stance is confirmed by the war that Chandragupta Maurya and Kautilya fought against the Diadochi ruler Seleucus I Nicator. This war aimed at re-taking the territories in today's Pakistan and Afghanistan that Achaemenid Persia had conquered in the sixth century BC and which remained Greek-occupied after Alexander the Great had aborted his invasion attempt of India. After expelling Seleucus I Nicator from these northern territories, the Maurya Empire refrained from any further offensive military action and made peace with the Seleucid Empire. For

the duration of the Maurya Empire, its relations with the Seleucid Empire remained peaceful.
4. Cf. Machiavelli's *Prince*. Its final chapter is an 'exhortation' to end Italy's political fragmentation and domination by foreign powers.

Chapter 10
1. English translation, cf. Meinecke 1962b.
2. The assertion that raison d'état is the unique intellectual product of early modernity in Europe, is, for example, made by Herfried Münkler (1987).
3. Hans J. Morgenthau notes that with respect to 'the debate on the reason of state (raison d'état), Friedrich Meinecke has given the definite account' (Morgenthau 1958, 55). Morgenthau explicitly acknowledged Meinecke's influence on his own thinking; in August 1929, he wrote in his diary: 'Have abandoned the plan [to write a book on] "Machiavelli", because Meinecke's "Raison d' E'tat" already contains very much of it [Morgenthau's own thoughts]' (cit. in: Frei 1994, 129). And, on 11 March 1969, he wrote in a letter to T. W. Robinson: 'You are entirely correct in assuming that I have been very much influenced by Weber and [Karl] Mannheim. I would add ... Meinecke' (cit. in: Frei 1994, 233).
4. The term 'value idea' (*Wertidee*) was coined by Max Weber and designates 'fundamental' ideas shaping social action in general and specifically political behaviour like 'rationality', 'ethics', 'power', 'religion' or 'secularism'.

Chapter 11
1. It should be noted here that up to the present, covert operations of intelligence services, including the assassination of foreign leaders, have been a standard instrument of foreign policy. That applies not only to totalitarian states but also to democratic states like the United States or Britain (cf. von Bülow 1998, 424ff). The main difference between then and now is that Kautilya wrote openly and without semantic euphemism about covert operations and assassinations, while modern states, in most cases, would not admit the 'wet work' of their intelligence services. And, usually, political scientists stay away from this 'dark side' of foreign policy and leave it to investigative journalists or NGOs.
2. It is often alleged that Morgenthau promotes a fatalistic understanding of foreign policy and politics in general, which is based on pessimistic anthropological assumptions. However, *Politics Among Nations* contains a sharp critique of nationalism, racism and militarism. And it is often overlooked that Morgenthau was one of the sharpest critics of American

government's policy during the Vietnam War (cf. Reichwein 2010).

Chapter 12

1. The latter two dispositions might be subsumed under the term 'hubris'.
2. Here one may think of the many 'ethical dictatorships' throughout history that have tried to create a political order based on the utopia of a 'new man' exorcised of his 'selfish' anthropological dispositions. The inevitable consequences have been bloody oppression, civil wars and wars.
3. Cf. The 'might is right' argumentation of the Sophists Calicles and Thrasymachos in Plato's *Politea*.
4. Helmuth Plessner (1892–1985) was a German-Jewish philosopher and sociologist with intellectual ties to Wilhelm Windelband, Edmund Husserl, Max Weber, Max Scheler, Nicolai Hartmann and Theodor W. Adorno. Before turning to philosophy and sociology, Plessner, son of a physician, had studied biology. In 1933, Plessner emigrated to Holland, where he taught at Groningen University. After World War II, he returned to Germany, where he headed the Institute of Sociology at Göttingen University.
5. Plessner's 1931 study *Macht und menschliche Natur* (Power and Human Nature), to which we refer here, has not been translated into English. All citations from Plessner refer to the original German text and are translated by Michael Liebig.
6. Morgenthau mentions Plessner's *Macht und menschliche Natur* in his 1933 study *The Concept of the Political* (2012, 106). Further insight into his reception of Plessner could come from his unpublished essay *Über die Herkunft des Politischen aus der Natur des Menschen* (The Origins of the Political from the Nature of Man), which still awaits scholarly analysis (cf. Morgenthau 2012, 49). On the conceptual similarities between Plessner and Morgenthau, William Scheuerman notes: 'Reminiscent of the conservative German theorist Helmuth Plessner, author of an influential book on politics and human nature, Morgenthau argued that an antagonistic model of politics required a deeper grounding in psychology and philosophical anthropology. Not only did a realistic or sociological approach demand recourse to the laws of politics, but basic political laws derived from fundamental features of human nature' (Scheuerman 2009, 37).

Chapter 13

1. Is it not puzzling that, for the past sixty years, no political scientist has followed up on Morgenthau's own statements about the intellectual roots of his theory of Political Realism in ancient India or his direct references

to Kautilya? What is even more puzzling is that Indian political scientists have not addressed these issues.
2. The edited volume *Roots of Realism* (Frankel 1996) does not even mention Sun-Tzu.
3. Cf. Laurie M. Johnson Bagby: *Thuycidian Realism—Between Athens and Melos*, in Frankel (1996, 169–93).
4. Cf. Thomas J. Johnson: *The Idea of Power Politics—The Sophistic Foundations of Realism*, in Frankel (1996, 194–247).
5. The history of Political Realism must include Nizam ul-Mulk (1018–1092 AD), vizier of the Persian-Seljuk Empire and author of the *Siyasat-nameh* (Book of Government) (cf. Schabinger 1987). This work of theorized statecraft is the most outstanding Persian example of the medieval 'Mirrors for Princes' genre—manuals of political instruction for prospective rulers—and features key thought-figures of Political Realism. Moreover, many such thought-figures in the *Siyasat-nameh* exhibit astonishing homologies with ideas and concepts in Kautilya's *Arthashastra*. However, Nizam ul-Mulk has been ignored in the Eurocentric perspective on the history of theorized statecraft and Political Realism.
6. Hobbes too is one of the key figures in the evolution of Political Realism in early modernity.
7. Regrettably, Bozeman's pioneering work was not followed up by political scientists in the subsequent decades.

SECTION B
KAUTILYA AND MODERN INDIA

Chapter 1
1. The literature search was mostly conducted at the Jawaharlal Nehru Memorial Library in Delhi, and the library of the South Asia Institute, Heidelberg University.
2. In addition, seven expert interviews were conducted in Germany.
3. Does a small sample of expert interviews provide an adequate knowledge base for generating reliable research results? Moreover, 32 interviews were conducted in Delhi and only two outside the capital—at the University of Kashmir in Srinagar. We think, the 34 expert interviews do constitute a sufficient database and provide enough information for valid conclusions. As Tobias Engelmeier notes: 'Today, the, narrowly defined, strategic community consists of at least a couple of hundred individuals based predominantly (but

not exclusively) in New Delhi. Compared to the size of India, geographically and demographically, this is still a relatively small group, of which a representative sample can be taken' (2009, 83).
4. The expert interviews were digitally recorded and processed. The interview texts were analysed and evaluated using qualitative methodology and drawing on *MAXQDA* software. *MAXQDA* is based on Anselm Strauss' and Barney Glaser's 'Grounded Theory' approach using theoretical and/or text-extracted categories (codes) for analysis (cf. Kuckartz 2009). Non-transcribed interviews were 'conventionally' analysed using notes and memos. Both *MAXQDA* and 'Grounded Theory' are compatible with Max Weber's methodology, which meant for the evaluation of the expert interviews 'to stick methodologically to the subject matter, and not to execute a pre-imposed methodical program' (Allert 1998, 23).
5. As Tom Wengraf notes: 'Interviewing someone can only tell you what that person thinks or feels or values about what they think is real. It can never tell you what is actually real now or was actually real in the past' (2001, 57). However, the interview statements are per se, and irrespective of their factual correctness, valuable for the social scientist. That said, all statements in our study that are directly derived from the expert interviews should neither be seen as conclusively verified facts nor theoretical findings.

Chapter 2

1. Braudel has addressed the relationship of history and culture in two truly remarkable essays: *Cultural History: The Past Explains the Present* (Braudel 1992) and a series of ten articles published in 1982–83 in the Italian newspaper *Corrriere della Sera* (Braudel 1993). The following citations of Braudel have been translated by us from the German edition of these essays.
2. One can think here of the famous phrase of Karl Marx in his *The 18th Brumaire of Louis Bonaparte*: 'Men make their own history, but they do not make it as they please; they do not make it under self-selected circumstances but under circumstances existing already, given and transmitted from the past' (Marx, 1969, MEW, Vol. 8, 115).
3. An example would be the 'Kondratiev waves' which refer to cycles of basic technological innovations and paradigm shifts, occurring roughly every fifty years since the end of eighteenth century (cf. Schumpeter 2008).
4. Longue durée can also be the mode of existence of social or economic formations like, for example, slavery, the cast order, feudalism or capitalism.
5. For Braudel, the adequate understanding of longue durée history necessitates

a comprehensive approach that includes 'geography, demography, economics, political science, anthropology, cultural history, sociology and history of events' (Braudel 1993, 388).
6. Braudel explains the powerful impact of culture on human life by referring to his own person: 'Take my whole way of life and thinking: It has been developed centuries ago. And, if I am ever so desperately trying to free myself from that way of thinking, fact is: I do not succeed. I'm stuck with the Christian heritage that still surrounds me, outwits me, accompanies me, but also helps me' (1993, 387).
7. Nehru's treatment of Kautilya and the *Arthashastra* in his *The Discovery of India* will be examined in later chapters in our study (cf. section B, chapter 4).
8. The only culture that is comparable to Indian culture in terms of staying power is the Chinese culture, argues Nehru.
9. EI Rana Chhina, military historian, New Delhi, 26 April 2012.
10. Widespread illiteracy made the development of outstanding mnemonic capabilities a practical necessity for the common man in India. The interviewees remembered illiterate traders and craftsmen who take large and complicated orders, memorize them, and then carry them out precisely.
11. Another aspect of oral transmission in India relates to 'historiography' in terms of family histories and biographical knowledge. In the interviews, reference was made to the importance of genealogy up to the present day. While genealogy in Europe is predominantly a reserve of the nobility, it has been very popular in India—across all social strata. The knowledge about the family history is orally passed on from one generation to the next. Thus, there is an enormous reservoir of latent historical knowledge in India that is, however, not perceived as such: 'I know that there is a common belief that people are not very historical minded in this country, but that is not really true. For instance, I know my village, I know that we, our family, have settled there for ten generations. I can name you my forbears over ten generations ... Yes, there is a deep sense of continuity' (EI Rana Chhina, New Delhi, 26 April 2012).
12. 'If you take up an Indian currency note, you will find English and Hindi about the denomination of the currency note in perhaps bolder and larger letters, but you will find 14 other languages printed there in 14 different scripts. All these 14 languages are considered as national languages—and all of them on one Indian currency note. I consider this the cultural strength of India which I would like to cherish' (EI Ranabir Chakravarti, historian, New Delhi, 23 April 2012).

13. The original state of Pakistan founded in 1947 consisted of West Pakistan—on the territory of today's Pakistan—and East Pakistan—which is Bangladesh today. This state-structure collapsed in 1971 when the Pakistani central government refused to accept the regional language Bengali as the second official language next to the Urdu. Thus, the attempt to consolidate Pakistan by linguistic homogenization led to its break-up. And one may add, the religious homogeneity of today's Pakistan has hardly contributed to its political cohesiveness and stability.
14. 'In India there are such a large number of religious beliefs and practices. And we do not even know many of the religious practices and beliefs of the many tribal groups in India. The term Hindu is a misnomer in imposing this religious-cultural matrix onto the Indian scenario of pre-modern times. You have the Vedic religion, from which the Puranic religion differs a lot. They may refer to the Vedas, but what the Puranas are preaching or are upholding is quite different from the Vedic religion. And in the Puranas you have many sects of Brahmanical divinities like Vishnu or Shiva or Goddess cults. You have a completely different position of the Buddhists, the Jains, and, of course, what is called the materialist schools of thought going back to antiquity. How much of it is philosophy, how much of it is what is considered religious in terms of Western theology is difficult to determine' (EI Ranabir Chakravarti, New Delhi, 23 April 2012).
15. EI Rajeev Bhargava, social scientist, New Delhi, 9 May 2012.
16. 'Do you know what is the real mantra of India? I can give it to you in two words: "Kindly adjust." Indians will come and sit on your lap in the bus and say "kindly adjust." They will stamp on your feet and say "kindly adjust" [...]. *This "kindly adjust" is the elasticity that holds things together.* It is elasticity. Anybody who has tried to make things rigid in India has failed—politically, religiously, and culturally. Nobody going that way has ever succeeded here, because if you try to make things rigid, they crack up, and you crack up' (EI Jawhar Sircar, former CEO of Prasar Bharati, New Delhi, 18 May 2012, emphasis added).
17. EI Ajit Doval, former Director of India's domestic intelligence service, Intelligence Bureau (IB), and since May 2014 National Security Adviser of the Narendra Modi government, New Delhi, 2 May 2012.
18. EI Srinath Raghavan, historian and strategic analyst, New Delhi, 15 May 2012.
19. The assumption seems plausible that the extension of the caste system across the entire subcontinent reinforced the imagination of a distinct 'geo-cultural' space.

20. These interviewees also feared that the term 'cultural nation' could be instrumentalized by Hindu-nationalist, anti-pluralist and anti-secular political forces. Hindutva ideology aims at constructing a 'pure Hindu' cultural tradition while marginalizing the Buddhist, Islamic and secular traits of Indian culture. Although the Hindutva ideology strongly critiques Western culture influences, it covertly sympathizes with the European homogeneity paradigm, the interviewees argued.
21. In the interviews, the terms 'culture' and 'civilization' were used synonymously—as it is common in the English language area.
22. EI Ajit Doval, New Delhi, 2 May 2012.
23. However, conversion to Islam in the north and east of the sub-continent, even on a mass-scale, cannot be equated with undoing Indian culture.
24. Cf. section B, 8.2.
25. EI Ajit Doval, New Delhi, 2 May 2012.

Chapter 3

1. EI Rana Chhina, New Delhi, 26 April 2012.
2. 'Kautilya understood the national security paradigm in a holistic manner. That has immense relevance, and it is becoming increasingly clear so that many aspects of it are still extremely relevant today' (EI Sujit Dutta, political scientist, New Delhi, 11 April 2012).
3. *Arthashastra* is a codification, it is not really original. Nevertheless, the reason Kautilya felt the need to codify it, in the year 322 BC, is important. He felt the Vedic concepts were being lost. The audio culture was being lost. He felt he had to preserve the record so that the king and the people hereafter know. That is important' (EI Bharat Karnad, political scientist, New Delhi, 20 April 2012). But even in this line of reasoning, the *Arthashastra* was considered an outstanding endogenous politico-cultural resource because Kautilya preserved the most valuable political and strategic concepts of Indian antiquity for posterity.
4. 'I think the major chunk of Kautilya's thinking was very much based on a value-oriented structure, and I do not think he separated values from interest. Kautilya saw values as a subset of interest. So having values is also a very important interest in terms of statecraft, which is very fascinating to me' (EI Namrata Goswami, political scientist, New Delhi, 26 April 2012).
5. On Kautilya's *Arthashastra* in the context of Wittfogel's theory of Asiatic despotism cf. Witzens (2002, 82–102). Several interviewees viewed the term 'Asiatic despotism' as an ideological construct that lacked historical foundation.

6. 'I would say that Kautilya definitely places before the ruler certain very lofty ideals of governance. A ruler's arbitrary actions would not bear him any fruit. The ruler must not indulge into what makes him happy. Try to put the happiness of the subjects before your own happiness. In other words, Kautilya is saying that if and when subjects are happy, the King's happiness will emanate from subjects' happiness. This is something unusual for a very staunch royalist school of thought. At the same time, Kautilya considers how you make the people happy. For him, the two foremost duties of the ruler, sacred duties, are protection and maintenance' (EI Ranabir Chakravarti, New Delhi, 23 April 2012).

7. 'Kautilya says: the ruler performs or has to perform these two very sacred duties of protection and maintenance that make him entitled to demand taxes. And the people in general have to yield taxes to the ruler because they receive protection from him [...]. So I am not saying that there is a typical European social contract theory, but at least there are two parties, the ruler and the ruled. Both sides have been given at least theoretically their own sets of ideal norms and what is their entitlement. If the ruler protects, the ruler gets taxes, because he has rendered some duty. In that sense, the taxes demanded by the ruler are almost like his wage or salary' (EI Ranabir Chakravarti, New Delhi, 23 April 2012).

8. 'Amazingly, Kautilya did address corruption! And I was so impressed that even in ancient India thinking this concept is taken up, which is so popular now—everybody talks about corruption [...]. Here was a man, who would grapple with this situation that the king's ministers, actually anybody handling public funds, are prone to be corrupt. Therefore, the king should be on guard. I was amazed' (EI Partha Ghosh, political scientist, New Delhi, 15 May 2012).

9. 'If Kautilya is on the one hand speaking of the encroachment and expansion of royal power, he is also sensitive that sometimes there are autonomous spaces. And you better refrain from interfering in these autonomous spaces [...]. This element of multiplicity, of plurality, of hybridity, it is also present in Kautilya's *Arthashastra*. He recognizes the importance of locality, of local aspirations. If there is a very powerful monarchical state, there is also the question of autonomous space' (EI Ranabir Chakravarti, New Delhi, 23 April 2012).

10. 'Kautilya himself says that this text is a manual for an intelligent aspirant political leader. If we compare the recommendations of the Arthashastra with statements in Ashoka's inscriptions, Ashoka the great Mauryan ruler, there is convergence' (EI Ranabir Chakravarti). 'There is a legacy which

lives on that practically every ruler in India has had to adopt something like Ashokan ways of statecraft in order to rule [...]. You will be astonished to see how many of the things that Akbar says are similar in some respects to what Ashoka says' (EI Rajeev Bhargava, New Delhi, 9 May 2012).

11. EI Namrata Goswami, New Delhi, 26 April 2012.
12. 'Subversion yes, but do not get into a straightforward war. Because in war, Kautilya says, there will be inevitable loss of life, property and resources. Why should the king take this burden if there are other means available? Kautilya's idea is: never stick to a static sort of politics. His idea is expansive politics, but with the least amount of confrontation and destruction. That is something very significant! For a theoretician who always considers the ruler's interest to be foremost and for whom the ideal ruler should aspire for a paramount position all over the sub-continental space, for him to suggest that the ruler should aspire to become that without necessarily taking recourse to mobilization of the army and war-fighting, that is something very significant' (EI Ranabir Chakravarti, New Delhi, 23 April 2012).
13. 'Kautilya's ideal is that one power will ultimately become paramount on the subcontinent. One power will subjugate all other powers, may be by uprooting them militarily or by subjugating them, making them tributary, submissive states or alliance states. But the ultimate hegemony is his goal. One ruler will ultimately become the hegemonic power in the sub-continental space' (EI Ranabir Chakravarti, New Delhi, 23 April 2012).
14. EI Ajit Doval, New Delhi, 2 May 2012.
15. 'Kautilya would suggest that when a victorious ruler has conquered an enemy state, he should not disrupt the existing practices, norms, cultural attitudes and social structures in the conquered country. Allow the old system to continue there, without meddling into it, because if you superimpose from a victor's point of view, it might lead to fissiparous tendencies. You allow autonomy in order to integrate. This is very, very significant!' (EI Ranabir Chakravarti, New Delhi, 23 April 2012)
16. However, Kautilya's secularism goes along with an 'instrumental' understanding of religion in politics. He appreciates the utility of religion as a factor of social and political stability. To that end, Kautilya knows no inhibitions to politically use religion (and magic, too).
17. 'Kautilya is a secular thinker [...]. If they [the rightwing Hindu nationalists] refer to anything, it is mostly to the Hindu classics, and not to his [Kautilya's] more secular handbook of statecraft' (EI Kanti Bajpai, political scientist, Frankfurt am Main, 25 September 2012).

18. EI Col. (ret.) P.K. Gautam, Research Fellow, IDSA, New Delhi, 15 April 2012.
19. 'Kautilya considers the shudras as the ideal cultivators, actually producing social wealth. This is an interesting departure from other texts of ancient India' (EI Ranabir Chakravarti, New Delhi, 23 April 2012).
20. 'I am very happy that Dr. Ambedkar has not criticized Chanakya. Dr. Ambedkar is the father of the Indian Constitution and was the son of a low-caste father serving in the Indian Army [...]. He said that he has no problem with Chanakya with respect to caste' (EI P.K. Gautam, New Delhi, April 15, 2012).
21. EI Ranabir Chakravarti, New Delhi, 23 April 2012.
22. EI Ranabir Chakravarti, New Delhi, 23 April 2012.
23. EI Sujit Dutta, New Delhi, April 11, 2012.
24. 'Kautilya's description as the "Indian Machiavelli" is anachronistic and inappropriate. Machiavelli could be better described as the "Italian Kautilya," except for the fact that his work nowhere approaches the intellectual breadth and vision of Kautilya's. I do not know if Kautilya has been compared to the Greek political philosophers, but I think he can and should be' (EI Upinder Singh, historian, New Delhi, 8 May 2012).
25. EI Srinath Raghavan, New Delhi, 15 May 2012.
26. 'Kautilya's importance for the Indian nationalists is obvious. They were truly excited when Shamashastry published the Arthashastra, because it gave them *a sense of delight that India does indeed have a tradition of political science and statecraft*. Up to that point, particularly the British had always maintained that the Indians were entirely spiritual and detached from the world and thus incapable of political thought. The British flatly denied that Indians ever developed an endogenous political theory. Initially, the Indians had even accepted that and said: Yes, we are a spiritual nation without a tradition of political theory. But then, this book of Kautilya turns up. And that has radically changed the Indian argument. *Now they said: Look, you Brits, we were political thinkers when you were still sitting on the trees. We have an ancient, highly elaborated tradition of political thought which is not matched by your Hobbes or Machiavelli*' (EI Dietmar Rothermund, Heidelberg, 9 January 2012, emphasis added).

Chapter 4

1. Kautilya writes in the *Arthashastra*: 'The object slips away from the foolish person, who continuously consults the stars' (KA, IX, 4, 26).
2. Arndt Michael notes: 'This passage reveals Nehru's admiration for Indian

classical traditions and Kautilya in particular. Considering that Nehru is mostly associated with having advocated a universal moralism in world politics, his words are hinting in the direction that the means advocated by Kautilya will eventually be employed to safeguard India's interests, rhetoric notwithstanding' (2008, 92).

3. This sentence—from Shamashastry's 1915 translation—cit. in *Glimpses of World History*.
4. The assessment of Kautilya's salience for Nehru's sense of India can be seen in these excerpts from expert interviews: 'Nehru was very engaged in the text. He obviously read the *Arthashastra*. There are copies of it in his own library collections [...]. I would say Kautilya is not episodic for Nehru. I think his interest in Kautilya as to intellectual figure is definitely deeper' (EI Srinath Raghavan, New Delhi, 15 May 2012).
'Nehru studied the Arthashastra very minutely and drew on every aspect in it that he considered interesting and progressive. For Nehru, Chanakya was a great scholar, statesman, visionary and administrator. And he saw him as an early representative of Indian nationalism' (EI P. Chandramohan, Curator—at the time of the interview—at the Nehru Memorial Museum and Library, New Delhi, 31 May 2012). 'I think there is a political project involved in *The Discovery of India*, of course, but there is an attempt to more systematically identify at least a few streams of thought which are critical to the making of modern India as well: statecraft, principles of statecraft, issues related to statecraft [...]. You can not do justice to every important thinker in India's past, but bringing Kautilya into the pantheon was important for Nehru' (EI Siddharth Mallavarapu, political scientist, New Delhi, 30 March 2012).
5. In *The Discovery of India*, Nehru situates the treatment of Kautilya in close textual proximity to that of Buddha and Ashoka. Some interviewees thought that he did so in order to avoid the impression of an unbridgeable gap between Kautilyan political realism and political idealism going back to Buddha and Ashoka. Moreover, presenting the traditions of Kautilyan realism and Ashokan idealism in opposition might have been interpreted as indicating an ideological conflict between Gandhi and Nehru. Therefore, Nehru expounded Kautilya and Ashoka next to each other.
6. EI Srinath Raghavan, New Delhi, 15 May 2012.
7. EI P. Chandramohan, New Delhi, 31 May 2012.
8. EI Srinath Raghavan, New Delhi, 15 May 2012.
9. Even though India is constituted as a federation, the central government has a very strong position in relation to the federal states (cf. Rothermund 1995, 389-93).

10. Replication of a wheel with twenty-four spokes.
11. EI Ranabir Chakravarti, New Delhi, 23 April 2012.
12. EI Namrata Goswami, New Delhi, 26 April 2012.
13. EI Srinath Raghavan, New Delhi, 15 May 2012. Raghavan referred to Nehru's speech in Parliament on 21 March 1956, in which he had said: 'What is the equation of defense [...]. Well, one thinks immediately about defense forces— army, navy, air force. Perfectly right. They are the spear points of defense. They have to bear the brunt of any attack. How do they exist? What are they based on? The more technical armies and navies and air forces get, the more important become the industrial and technological base of the country [...]. The equation of defense is your defense forces plus your industrial and technological background, plus, thirdly, the economy of the country and fourthly, the spirit of the people' (cit. in: Subrahmanayam/Malhotra 2005, 408).
14. The Hindustan Aeronautics *HF 24 Marut*. After the maiden flight in 1961, 129 *Maruts* were built until 1977. The superb aircraft suffered from inadequately powered jet engines. India depended on the import of high-powered jet engines, which were denied to her by Western governments. At last, India turned to the Soviet Union which provided her the *MiG 21* jet fighter for license production. Kurt Tank had been the chief designer at Focke-Wulf before and during WWII, where he developed the long-range, four-engine passenger aircraft *Fw 200* and the legendary fighter aircraft *Fw 190*. His 1945 design of the swept-wing, T-tail and nose-intake jet fighter *Ta 183* significantly influenced the later designs of the Soviet *MiG 15/17*, American *F 86* and Swedish *Saab J29*.
15. EI S. Kalyanaraman, political scientist, New Delhi, 26 April 2012.
16. EI Srinath Raghavan, New Delhi, 15 May 2012.
17. EI Srinath Raghavan, New Delhi, 15 May 2012.
18. The conceptual linkage between the *mandala* theory and non-alignment needs deeper research. Two of our interviewees point in that direction. 'Non-alignment was a very practical, realistic idea, but it got morally charged up' (EI Srinath Raghavan, New Delhi, 15 May 2012.). 'As a "kingly" person ruling India, Nehru said I have to maximize India's interest. How do I do it in this situation where there are two big powers? And he saw right away in Kautilyan terms that India could leverage, given the fact that India was very big in size and a potential great power, but at point in time impoverished, backward and underdeveloped. So how can I make use of the fact that these two warring blocs of nations are there for me to exploit?' (EI Bharat Karnad, New Delhi, 20 April 2012).
19. EI Kanti Bajpai, Frankfurt am Main, 25 September 2012.

20. In the Nehru years, India did not yet have a dedicated foreign intelligence service—the Research and Analysis Wing (R& AW) was only established in 1968. But the foreign intelligence provided by the Intelligence Bureau (IB) to the Indian government had been solid, the interviewees opined.
21. EI Srinath Raghavan, New Delhi, 15 May 2012.
22. EI Srinath Raghavan, New Delhi, 15 May 2012.
23. 'In his autobiography, Atish-e-Chinar, Sheikh Abdullah accuses Nehru of being Kautilyan. In his book, there is a chapter on Nehru. *Therein, he writes that Nehru would always keep a copy of Kautilya's Arthashastra on his bedside. And that book guided his political behavior*' (EI Noor Achmad Baba, political scientist, Srinagar, 24 May 2012, emphasis added). 'Sheikh Abdullah says that Nehru was a politician who quoted Marx and Lenin, but in the bedroom he consulted the *Arthashastra* [...]. *Sheikh Abdullah felt that Nehru was a person who had Kautilya deep in his mind* [...]. This does not mean, however, that I downgrade Kautilya' (EI B.A. Dabla, social scientist, Srinagar, 25 May 2012, emphasis added).
24. '*I do not think Nehru's policy was in any way Kautilyan.* There are people who argue that Nehru was a realist, but I disagree with the idea that Nehru was a realist' (EI Rajesh Rajagopalan, political scientist, New Delhi, 5 April 2012, emphasis added).
25. '*The Nehru period is deeply idealistic.* For he tries to follow the Ashokan model, without understanding the linkage between Ashoka and Kautilya, namely that the Ashokan state had a huge backup in terms of a national security doctrine based on a strong military. So nobody dared to invade the Mauryan Empire during Ashoka's times. Nehru took the peace strategy, he took the diplomatic strategy, but minus the hard power base [...]. *[It's] an idealism-built, socialdemocratic strategic culture that tries to replicate a world order that Ashoka tried to build* during the post-Kalinga years. Jawaharlal Nehru was deeply impressed, deeply influenced by the Ashokan international relations model. And his strategy laid huge emphasis on diplomacy to resolve inter-state disputes, the importance of the United Nations, global institutions, a cooperative world order—all that's typical of idealistic, liberal visions of the world' (EI Sujit Dutta, New Delhi, 11 April 2012, emphasis added).
26. EI Rana Banerji, former senior official at India's foreign intelligence service, R&AW, New Delhi, 24 April 2012.
27. EI Srinath Raghavan, New Delhi, 15 May 2012.
28. EI Krishnappa Venkatshamy, Research Fellow IDSA, New Delhi, 2 April 2012.

29. EI Krishnappa Venkatshamy, New Delhi, 2 April 2012.
30. Meanwhile, the term 'Nehruvianism' has become established in the political science literature. Kanti Bajpai defines the term as focusing on diplomacy, peaceful conflict resolution and socio-economic development, while firmly upholding national sovereignty and the pursuance of national interests (cf. Bajpai/Pant 2013).
31. EI Krishnappa Venkatshamy, Research Fellow IDSA, New Delhi, 2 April 2012.
32. EI Col. (ret.) P. K. Gautam, Research Fellow, IDSA, New Delhi, 15 April 2012.
33. Subhas Chandra Bose also belongs to the inner circle of top leaders of the Indian Independence movement. Examining his relation to Kautilyan thought is an obvious research desideratum.
34. The view that Gandhi can be characterized as a political realist in the Kautilyan tradition is also held by Rashed Uz Zaman in his essay *Kautilya: The Indian Strategic Thinker and Indian Strategic Culture*. 'Quite often people have compared Gandhi and Kautilya [...]. When it comes to realpolitik, how to negotiate, for example, Gandhi is a Chanakya' (EI Rakesh Batabyal, political scientist, New Delhi, 17 April 2012, emphasis added).
35. In World War I, more than one million Indians fought under British command in France, East Africa and the Near/Middle East. In World War II, more than two million Indian soldiers fought in North Africa against Nazi Germany and in Burma against Japan.
36. Cf. Gandhi, *Mohandas Karamcand: The Collected works of Mahatma Gandhi*, Delhi: Publ. Division, Ministry of Information and Broadcasting, Government of India, Index of Subjects (1988), Index of Persons (1992). We want to thank Annkatrin Kinzinger, South Asia Institute, Heidelberg University, for sharing this information with us.
37. EI Partha Ghosh, New Delhi, 15 May 2012.

Chapter 5

1. The latter company, a personnel service provider, explains its name on its website: 'Club Kautilya is the Personel Resource Planning arm of Microsec Group, a financial services provider [...]. Club Kautilya envelops in its sphere a wide range of knowledge-based services and solutions, tailored to match its members' needs and requirements. It is of paramount importance that we derive our name, philosophy and services from the fountain of knowledge which has come to us from our very own ethos and culture. The Great Kautilya (also known as Chanakya) who installed and ensured

prosperity in the Nation through his Principles (Niti's) based on Wisdom forms the cornerstone of our Resource Planning. Our Resource Planners are not only knowledgeable and well educated but are also certified as per Chanakya Niti to holistically ensure that our members benefit from ancient wisdom combined with modern principles and practices'.

2. 'Over the last ten years, we had two very important Kautilya-related TV programs; one is *Chanakya*, the other one is *Chandragupta Maurya*,... These TV series have been enormously popular' (EI Rakesh Batabyal, New Delhi, 17 April 2012). 'Kautilya has a strong legendary afterlife. And TV serials set in ancient times—also the *Mahabharata* and *Ramayana*—evidently excite a great interest among the viewing public' (EI Upinder Singh, New Delhi, 8 May 2012).

3. 'Concepts and words are symbols, just as visions, rituals, and images are, so too are the manners and customs of daily life. Through all of these a transcendent reality is mirrored [...]. Symbols hold the mind to truth but are not themselves the truth' (Zimmer 2011/1951, 1f).

4. In the expert interview, Dietmar Rothermund described this phenomenon with the term 'Kautilya metaphor'. The essential meaning of the metaphor is Kautilya is the cunning and unflinching statesman, who 'gets things done whatever it takes.' '*Kautilya is a name to conjure with—a metaphor without addressing his theories*' (EI Dietmar Rothermund, Heidelberg, 9 January 2012, emphasis added).

5. 'If you talk to "normal" people, young people, even to illiterate villagers, they will refer to someone who is very clever and giving clever advice, as giving advice like Chanakya. He is clever, he is very farsighted, and so he is supportive of a greater cause [...]. A learned man, a teacher who is fully committed to a big project, who is simple and austere [...]. So the very metaphor of Chanakya will become more comprehensive in spreading as a metaphor of understanding politics' (EI Rakesh Batabyal, New Delhi, 17 April 2012).

6. EI P.K. Gautam, New Delhi, 25 April 2012.

7. EI Noor Achmad Baba, Srinagar, 24 May 2012.

8. EI Rajesh Rajagopalan, New Delhi, 5 April 2012.

9. Later on, we shall examine the '*manifest absence*' of Kautilya in Indian social and political sciences during the past decades—and more recent indicators for a trend reversal.

10. It should be obvious that the 're-use' of Kautilyan thought in the political realm must not be mixed up with the 're-use' of the so-called 'Kautilyan wisdom' in daily life contexts like career promotion or business success.

11. The Indian newspaper *The Hindu* reported on Mukherjee's repeated references to Kautilya in parliamentary speeches. 'Delivering his budget speech for 2010-11, Mr. Mukherjee had said he has been *guided by the principles of sound tax administration as embodied in the words of Kautilya*, while formulating his own tax proposals. Earlier in July 2009 also, *Mr. Mukherjee had quoted Kautilya*: "In the interest of the prosperity of the country, a King shall be diligent in foreseeing the possibility of calamities, try to avert them before they arise, overcome those which happen, remove all obstructions to economic activity and prevent loss of revenue to the state." Way back in his budget speech for 1984-85, *Mr. Mukherjee had quoted a Sanskrit couplet of Kautilya*, while talking about his "endeavor to keep the budgetary deficit to a relatively low figure."' (*The Hindu*, 16 March 2012, emphasis added).

Chapter 6

1. EI Jawhar Sircar, New Delhi, 18 May 2012.
2. EI Vinod Anand, Senior Fellow, Vivekananda International Foundation, New Delhi, 16 May 2012.
3. Ajit Doval, New Delhi, 2 May 2012.
4. Maurice Halbwachs' theory of 'collective memory' could provide a promising research avenue for an in-depth analysis of the latent presence of historically distant ideational resources (cf. Halbwachs 1991).
5. A fruitful research approach for the phenomenon of 'unforgettable forgotten' is correlating Bourdieu's habitus concept with what modern neuro-biology defines as 'non-declaratory memory'; cf. Kastl (n.d.).
6. EI Bharat Karnad, New Delhi, 20 April 2012.
7. EI Bharat Karnad, New Delhi, 20 April 2012.
8. EI Satish Nambiar, Senior Fellow IDSA, New Delhi, 25 April 2012.
9. 'I think *my understanding of Kautilya comes more from interaction within the family and with friends, and reading books at home*. You know I come from a family which has got a tradition where we sit around and then talk—with cousins, brothers, uncles. We talk for hours on various things, about the ancient culture and civilization, or history, or politics, or global affairs' (EI Ajit Doval, New Delhi, 2 May 2012, emphasis added). '*Now Kautilya is coming back from my subconscious memory after 40 years, what I learned about him in early childhood*' (EI Rakesh Batabyal, New Delhi, 17 April 2012, emphasis added).
10. EI Namrata Goswami, New Delhi, 26 April 2012.
11. Admiral Alfred Thayer Mahan (1840-1914) was an American naval strategist and historian. He is the author of *The Influence of Sea Power*

Upon History (1890), which has exerted great influence on US naval strategy and geopolitical thinking up to the present.
12. EI Namrata Goswami, New Delhi, 26 April 2012.
13. Since September 2015, Jayant Prasad is the Director General of the Institute for Defence Studies and Analyses (IDSA) in New Delhi.
14. Its eight authors are: Sunil Khilnani, professor of politics and Director of King's College London India Institute, London; Rajiv Kumar, economist, senior fellow at the Center for Policy Research, New Delhi, and former member of the National Security Advisory Board; Pratap Bhanu Mehta, political scientist, and president and chief executive of the Centre for Policy Research, New Delhi; Lt. Gen. (Retired) Dr Prakash Menon, former commandant of the National Defence College; Nandan Nilekani, co-founder of IT company Infosys Technologies; Srinath Raghavan, historian and senior fellow at the Centre for Policy Research, New Delhi; Shyam Saran, diplomat, former Secretary in the Ministry of External Affairs; Siddharth Varadarajan, former Editor of *The Hindu* and now, founding editor of *The Wire*.
15. All page numbers of the document *NonAlignment 2.0—A Foreign and Strategic Policy for India in the Twenty First Century* (Centre for Policy Research 2012).
16. On India's internal security situation: cf. Lange (2009) and Behera/Sharma (2014).
17. EI Ajit Doval, New Delhi, 2 May 2012.
18. EI Namrata Goswami, New Delhi, 26 April 2012.
19. The ICBM 'Agni V' is named after the Sanskrit word 'agni' that denominates the Vedic God of Fire.

Chapter 7
1. The concept of strategic culture emerged in the context of the sub-disciplines of Political Science—International Relations and Security Studies.
2. To our best knowledge, so far, there are only very modest attempts to use Bourdieu's sociology for IR theory and Security Studies—but not with respect to strategic culture (cf. Adler-Nissen 2013; Jackson 2008).
3. EI Satish Nambiar, New Delhi, 25 April 2012.
4. K. P. S. Menon is the grandfather of Shivshankar Menon, whose multiple references to Kautilya are addressed in our study; cf. B 7.4; B 9.3.1–9.3.3.
5. EI Namrata Goswami, New Delhi, 26 April 2012
6. G.N. Curzon was the British Viceroy and Governor-General of India (1899–1905). He was the author of the geo-strategic study *The Place of India in the Empire*.

7. EI Sujit Dutta, New Delhi, 11 April 2012.
8. EI Namrata Goswami, New Delhi, 26 April 2012
9. EI Srinath Raghavan, New Delhi, 15 May 2012.

Chapter 8
1. I have always felt, having been instructor at our Defense Services Staff College in Wellington, that the Indian military establishment seemed to prefer referring to *Clausewitz and Sun Tzu rather than using our own resources like the Arthashastra* […]. This, I think, is a tragedy in many ways' (EI Satish Nambiar, New Delhi, 25 April 2012, emphasis added).
2. EI Partha Ghosh, New Delhi, 15 May 2012.
3. EI Satish Nambiar, New Delhi, 25 April 2012.
4. EI Kanti Bajpai, Frankfurt am Main, 25 September 2012.
5. In 2009, Pratap Bhanu Mehta (now president and chief executive of) from the renowned Centre for Policy Research in New Delhi, wrote a newspaper commentary entitled "Century of Forgetting." The occasion was the hundredth anniversary of Shamashastry's first edition of the complete text of Kautilya's *Arthashastra*. Mehta laments the disinterest of contemporary academia towards Kautilya, which he contrasts to the open-mindedness of and collaborative attitude among Indian intellectuals a century ago: '[T]*he gap between Sanskritists and a broader humanities culture was not as wide*. We are now in a university system where even historians of ancient India struggle with Sanskrit and *Sanskritists cannot think beyond their ossified paradigms* […]. [It's the] *Sanskrit pundits who are the worst obstacles to understanding the richness of the resources on which they sit*' (Mehta 2009, emphasis added).
6. On that, Gautam writes: 'The universal and blanket use of the term "Brahman" for Kautilya the *Strotiya* [Veda scribe] without care or qualification may also have offended the non-Brahmins and thus secular study of Kautilya. The artist's imagination in portraying a bare-chested, handsome and muscular Kautilya sporting a pony tail and *yanev* (holy thread across torso worn by the *dwija* or twice born) on a well-rounded shaven head with piercing eyes and his soap TV serialization with incessant lecturing may have done more harm than good. In sum, such attitude may seem to justify the Brahmanic Hinduism, varna and jati system and thus uttering of the word "Kautilya" may lead to mental blocks by an imagery of a stereotype of intellectual and religious arrogance' (Gautam 2013a, 86).
7. EI Romila Thapar, New Delhi, 27 March 2012.
8. Whether Marx knew the section on India in Hegel's *Lectures on the History of Philosophy* remains an open question (cf. Hegel 1971, Vol. 18).

9. EI Mohinder Singh, political scientist (and currently Assistant Professor, Centre for Comparative Politics & Political Theory, School of International Studies, Jawaharlal Nehru University), New Delhi, 2 May 2012.
10. EI Rajeev Bhargava, New Delhi, May 9, 2012.
11. Once again, exceptions confirm the rule. There are a few authors with postcolonial affinities who have called endogenous politico-cultural resources—like Kautilya, Buddha or the epic *Mahabharata*—for scholarly addressing without tangible consequences (cf. Acharya/Buzan 2007; Acharya, 2011).
12. The merits of postcolonial theory in exposing and deconstructing Eurocentric and Orientalist attitudes and values are undeniable. In particular, it is to the school's credit that the deep-seated and persistent effects of the epistemic and psychological 'colonization' of the 'Global South' have been thematized. However, the postcolonial theory's originality gets markedly relativized when one considers, for example, Helmuth Plessner's critique of epistemic Eurocentrism as early as 1931. In *Macht und menschliche Natur*, Plessner writes: 'Precisely the wide perspective that the Occident has gained necessitates the relativization of its own position vis-a-vis the positions of "others" […]. The deliberate relativization of one's own [European] position is crucial if the danger of uniformization of the "others" according to one's own standard is to be avoided when attempting to understand their "alien" positions […]. Relinquishing the supremacy of the European system of values and categories, the European spirit will gain the horizon of the original manifoldness of historically developed cultures and their world views—as an open, unrestricted manifoldness which is not orderly directed by some "world- spirit"' (Plessner 2003, 159, 185).
13. One wonders whether Gandhi saw the singularity of Indian culture represented by 'subaltern myths, cults and ideologies'. After all, he wrote a study on the *Bhagavad Gita*—certainly a prime example of 'Sanskritist high culture'. Nor can a summary repudiation of European philosophy and science be ascribed to Gandhi.

Chapter 9

1. In the Department of Political Science of the Faculty of Social Sciences, Kautilya was not part of the curriculum until 2011. Then, for the Master's degree in Political Science, the following module was introduced in the compulsory course 'International Relations': '*Realism, b) Indian Tradition: Kautilya's Real Politique*' (University of Delhi; MA Political Science, Rules, Regulations and Course Contents 2011–2012). It should be mentioned here

that Navnita Behera was, at the time of the interviews, the head of DU's Political Science department.
2. EI Mohinder Singh, New Delhi, 2 May 2012.
3. On April 6, 2016, Michael Liebig was invited by Professor Jayati Srivastava to give a lecture comparing Kautilya and Machiavelli at JNU's School of International Studies (SIS).
4. EI Siddharth Mallavarapu, New Delhi, 30 March 2012.
5. EI Mohinder Singh, New Delhi, 2 May 2012.
6. Awnanish Kumar submitted the PhD thesis titled *Kautilya's Thought and Administration: A Critical Analysis* in DU's Department of Political Science in 2012. The same year, another dissertation project at DU's Political Science Department was Tarun Kumar's PhD thesis, titled *Corruption in Administration: Evaluating the Kautilyan Antecedents*.
7. Professor Upinder Singh teaches and researches at DU's Department of History. In the expert interview, she stressed that Kautilya has long been part of the curriculum of her department. Kautilya is not only covered as a historical figure of the Maurya Empire, but the *Arthashastra* is treated as a source providing insights into the political, social and economic conditions of the Maurya Empire, and antecedent states of ancient India.
8. Before joining IDSA in 2012, Gupta had held a senior position in India's National Security Council to which he returned in 2014 as Deputy National Security Adviser. The current Director General of IDSA is Jayant Prasad who, among the many illustrious positions held, was formerly India's Ambassador to Afghanistan, Algeria, Nepal, and the UN Conference on Disarmament, Geneva.
9. This and subsequent remarks about the Kautilya discourse at IDSA, if not specifically referenced, are based on verbal and written communications with Col. Gautam that began in Summer 2011.
10. Cf. http://www.idsa.in/event/KautilyasArthashastraandIndiasStrategic Culture. Two years later, in the Spring of 2014, M. Liebig was invited for a three-month Visiting Fellowship at IDSA to conduct research on Kautilya's *Arthashastra*.
11. A good overview of the IDSA project *Indigenous Historical Knowledge* can be gained via the IDSA website: http://www.idsa.in/history/index.html. The website features speeches (in video and text format) at IDSA events on Kautilya as well as publications by IDSA relating to Kautilya and the *Arthashastra*.
12. All speeches delivered at the October 2012 'Kautilya conference' at IDSA are available as video files on the IDSA website (http://www.idsa.in/taxonomy/

term/1404?page=6).
13. State-subsidized (re-)publication of books was deemed valuable for the general public in cheap, high-volume editions.
14. The programme of the conference, available on IDSA website, shows the increasing reach and deepening of the Kautilya discourse at the IDSA.
15. All citations from Menon's 'Keynote Address' available at http://www.idsa.in/keyspeeches/ShivshankarMenonKautilya.
16. They were published 2015 and 2016 (Gautam/Mishra/Gupta 2015a, 2015b, 2016).

SECTION C
KAUTILYA REDUX?

1. For a trenchant presentation of this view, consider the following: Without access to the grassroots of the civilization one remains at the mercy of the hoes, the apprehensions and at times the self-deception of the vocal classes of educated Indians, whose lack of faith in themselves and fear of criticism or implied criticism from foreigners are, if understandable, depressing. Their addiction to academic works devoted to the description (usually uncritical and un-comparative) of the ancient Indian civilization is a symptom of the desperate belief that a rosy view of the past matters as much as, if not more than, an objective committal to the present (cf. Derrett 1968, 20). Derrett justifiably excoriates the tendency to condone the failings of the past by invoking the glories of an imagined past. This criticism has been a motivation behind our attempt to peg the resilience of Kautilya onto the discourse of elite informants.
2. Evolution is a concept used in biology to describe long-term developments that have a common point of origin in the past but are open-ended. An approach to apply this concept to Political Science is Evolutionary Institutionalism: Institutions are analysed analogous to living things from an evolutionary perspective. Institutions evolve, according to Evolutionary Institutionalism, influenced by ecological factors (exogenous change) or through re-interpretation and re-implementation in the course of daily routines (endogenous change) (cf. Gould 2002; Lewis/Steinmo 2012).

Chapter 1
1. The reference here is to Lloyd Rudolph's and Susanne Hoeber Rudolph's *The Modernity of Tradition* (1967), Ashis Nandy's *The Intimate Enemy* (1983) and Adda Bozeman's *Politics and Culture in International History* (1960).

Each of these three texts presents the pre-modern past as a vital reservoir of knowledge that the designers of modern India have re-used in order to create the institutional arrangement that has shown its resilience over the past six decades.

2. Cf. Douglas (1966) for a lucid and 'universal analysis of the rules of purity which applies equally to secular and religious life as to primitive and modern societies' (1).
3. In his *Chronicle of the French Revolution*, Schama writes: 'Suddenly, subjects were told they had become Citizens; an aggregate of subjects held in place by injustice and intimidation had become a Nation. From this new thing, this Nation of Citizens, justice, freedom and plenty could be not only expected but required. By the same token, should it not materialize, only those who had spurned their citizenship, or who were by their birth or unrepentant beliefs incapable of exercising it, could be held responsible. Before the promise of 1789 could be realized, it was necessary to root out Un-citizens' (1989, 859). The search for purity functions as the essence of legitimacy for totalitarian rulers, from Stalin to the Taliban.
4. The political development literature of the 1960s is replete with such developmental schemata which in turn draw on older categories such as *Gemeinschaft* and *Gesellschaft* (Ferdinand Toennies) that cast developing and developed societies in a model of developmental nexus. The responsibility to provide guidance to the developing societies was taken up by the institutions in charge of policing purity—experts, colonial masters or their postcolonial pupils to whom power was transferred at Independence—who were expected to detect, punish and eliminate impurity.

Chapter 4

1. 'Politics in classical India distinguished between *dharma*, a concept carrying the broad general meaning of righteousness and best rendered in legal literature as the divinely ordained norm of good conduct, and *artha*, which signifies utility and property. The sources of Indian political thought are thus essentially two-fold: the *dharmashastras*, or treatises on law and political theory, among which the *Code of Manu* is the most renowned, and the *Arthashastra* which deals with practical politics on the national and international level' (Bozeman 1960, 120).
2. North identifies two major factors that are responsible for incremental institutional change, namely 'the lock-in that come from the symbiotic relationship between institutions and the organizations that have evolved as a consequence of the incentive structure provided by those institutions,

and the feedback process by which human beings perceive and react to changes in the opportunity set' (1990, 7).
3. For an application of structural-functionalism to the transformation of a selection of states, both stable democracies and transitional societies, see Powell/Dalton/Strom (2012).
4. For an analysis of Indian tradition to the structural needs of Indian modernity, see the analysis of the Hindu Code Bill by Schöttli (2012).
5. One can imagine Nehru as the Kautilyan ruler, mindful of allies and foes within the Congress party, conflating norms and attentive to the significance of countervailing forces that he had to cope with constantly.
6. 'Bhabha himself has complicated the notion of hybridity even further by resorting to the Lacanian category of the imaginary, a move which hearkens back to Frantz Fanon's work. For Bhabha [*The Location of Culture*] the colonizer and the colonial subject both undergo a splitting of their identity positions, a splitting that occurs through their mutual imaginary identification (pictured in terms of mimicry). Bhabha's model also relies on Derrida and Bakhtin, bringing together a variety of poststructuralist concepts which are then catachrestically applied and juxtaposed in a variety of contexts and settings' (Fludernik 1998, 14).
7. What is to prevail in case there is a conflict between law, morality and custom? There is no clear, hard and fast rule in the classical tradition which gives the ruler considerable choice to make the most efficacious decision in a given context and take responsibility for it. 'Dharma overrides artha where the conflict is direct [...]. [However, in] politics the two are balanced, and if the loss of artha would be greater than the gain of dharma, artha is to be pursued and, if necessary, a penance performed for the breach of dharma' (Derrett 1968, 201, fn. 4, quoting Medhaththi o Manu, VII, 26).
8. 'The State in India from the time of Asoka, and perhaps earlier, to the days in which we live, has never been afraid to speak of Righteousness in terms of Law and Law in terms of Righteousness' (Derrett 1968, 29–30).

Chapter 5
1. For examples of re-use during the period of the decline of India's political autonomy, see Hegewald (2005, 2006).
2. Metcalf makes this point in his interpretation of the decorative role of past artefacts in the modern architecture of Lutyens (cf. Metcalf 1998).
3. Metcalf sums up the reciprocal relation of Orientalism and Empire in the following passage: 'Perhaps Curzon's lamp [which he got designed in Egypt and arranged to be placed on the grave of Mumtaz in the Taj Mahal]

might be taken to represent the colonial aesthetic. It is an aesthetic of difference, of distance, of substantiation, of control—an aesthetic in which the Taj Mahal, the mosque of Cairo, even the *Arabian Nights*, all merge and become indistinguishable, and hence are available for use however the colonial ruler chooses. It is an aesthetic in which the past, though ordered with scrupulous attention to detail, stays firmly in the past. It is an aesthetic Shah Jahan [the Mughal emperor who built the Taj Mahal as a memorium to Mumtaz Mahal, his deceased Queen] could never have comprehended' (Metcalf 1998, 24).

4. The signs of the lingering British presence—Sunday as the official holiday of the week, left-hand-drive of the Indian traffic and the ubiquitous Ambassador car, a hybrid British Austin Rover adapted to Indian roads which has become the sturdy emblem of Indian officialdom, are everywhere. The Dak Bungalows, outposts of the British Raj out in the country, temporary homes for the British civilian officers on tour, are tended with the same attention to details by the PWD—the Public Works Department, also of British vintage—just as are the post-Independence guest houses of the national and state governments.

Chapter 7

1. Cf. Coupland (1944, 128, 134, 151) for the evolution of statutory communalism.
2. Tillotson comments: 'The visual culture of the Mughals, so distinctive and instantly recognizable, was not conjured out of nothing. Its success was the product of the skillful blending together of the many different traditions that were available to the artists to draw on, including the Mughal's own central Asian heritage and the expertise and many long-established styles of India itself. The empire's greatest legacy is perhaps this composite culture; and that culture's most outstanding masterpiece is the building [Taj Mahal]' (2008, 44). The architectural designs 'drew inspiration from three related traditions: the architecture of the Mughals' central Asian homeland; the buildings erected by earlier Muslim rulers of India, especially in the Delhi region; and the much older architectural expertise of India itself' (ibid., 46).

Chapter 8

1. As George Sabine noted, Aristotle felt that 'too great a departure from common experience probably has a fallacy in it somewhere, even though it appears to be irreproachably logical' (1973, 99).
2. '[However] empirical evidence increasingly suggests that to a significant

extent the third wave of democratization could become less of a triumph of political liberalism and liberal democracy than a success story for "hybrid" or "ambiguous" regimes, "delegative", "defective", "semi-" or "illiberal" democracies, "competitive authoritarianism". These political systems include the "Potemkin democracies" where a democratic façade conceals an authoritarian leadership and those that are "ethnocratic", "plebiscite-populist", often even with sultanistic components, and which therefore may be identified as "false democracies"' (Croissant/Merkel 2004, 2).

3. See below for the concepts of trans-lingual and trans-cultural research. Students of comparative politics engaged in the classificatory analysis have much to learn from similar attempts in history, particularly the research on 'histoire croisée' (cf. Werner/Zimmermann 2006).

4. Diachronic data on legitimacy and efficacy in India show a steady rise from 1971 to 2004 for which we have evidence from survey data. Participation in free and fair elections has gone up steadily from 1951, when the first general election with universal adult franchise was held, and has reached levels that are respectable by the standards of liberal democracies (cf. Mitra/Singh 2009).

5. Conceptual stretching takes the shape of hybrid categories such as 'people's democracy', 'guided democracy', 'Islamic democracy', etc. 'When scholars extend their models and hypotheses to encompass additional cases, they commonly need to adapt their analytic categories to fit the next contexts. [...] [However] the overly strict application of a classical framework can lead to abandoning to category prematurely or to modifying it inappropriately' (Mahon Jr./Collier 1993, 845).

6. The motley crowd of resisters, united to fight the 'intrusive Other', come together under hybrid categories such as 'the Church' (see Charles Tilly's analysis of the counter-revolution in the Vendée) or 'Islam' in contemporary Afghanistan.

7. Purists like Jinnah and Bandaranaike, following their pure visions of Islam and Buddhism respectively, have run their states—Pakistan, the 'land of the pure', and Sri Lanka, the 'sacred land of Sirindip'—to political dead ends.

8. 'Two salient areas of Indian politics that call for critical attention and possible re-evaluation are the relations of the state and the market, and the attitudes of the state towards religion. The former has attracted some attention already. The Indian economy has belatedly come to terms with the necessity of taking painful decisions about restructuring and accepted the need for internal and international competition. But considerable confusion and outmoded assumptions still dominate the attitudes of the state towards

religion [...]. For its survival and growth, the state in India will need to go beyond simple accommodation and to transcend some contentious interests—religious, social, economic and political—when the occasion so demands' (Mitra 1990, 92, 93).

9. It is about time that the students of the modern state re-read Elias, Foucault, Nandy and Metcalf as well as the pre-modern political theorist Kautilya to decide for themselves how much there is to un-learn so that they might learn properly how the modern state in India has acquired its 'European' resilience without the benefit of European history.

10. 'When empiricists, structuralists or political economists look at what they consider the mere flimflam of the symbolic realm, they want to know where the real stuff is: the village, the irrigation network, the coalition between king and noble, the extractive mechanism. They ask, how many divisions does the pope have? [...] But as we address the state in Asia, we must treat the symbolic as a phenomenon. We must try to create theoretical frameworks that combine a demystified, rationalist worldview with an understanding of the phenomenology of the symbolic in societies where the gods have not yet died. And we must combine it with the understanding that we too construct and act within cosmologies and that we only deny the myths we live by because we cannot see or articulate them' (S. H. Rudolph 1987, 742).

11. Several articles point in the direction of the wider dimensions of this project. See Gallie (1956), Sartori (1970), Mahon Jr/Collier (1993), Collier/Levitsky (1997), Diamond (2002), Lindberg (2007) and Stepan (2008).

SECTION D
KAUTILYA, INDIA AND GLOBAL POLITICAL THEORY

1. Family resemblance (*Familienähnlichkeit* in German) is a philosophical idea made popular by Ludwig Wittgenstein with the best known exposition given in his posthumously published book *Philosophical Investigations* (2001/1953).

2. Lipset (1959, 69) refers to the symposium on the role of culture in democratization, published as "Cultural Prerequisites to a Successfully Functioning Democracy: A Symposium" by Griffith et al.. In contrast to the claims of 'culturists' who see the core of the democratic impulse in 'religion, particularly Christian ethics' (as argued by Lipset 1959, 70), he brings in modernization of the economic structure as the main driver of democratization.

Chapter 1

1. Indian democracy was certainly not on the radar screen of Lipset 1959. He talks instead of Japan, Israel, Lebanon, the Philippines and Turkey where, according to him, democracy appeared to have a fighting chance of survival.
2. The concept 'counter-factual' is used to refute existing theory on the basis of empirical exemplars. The expression is used to characterize India's democracy as a phenomenon whose existence could not be anticipated from within classical theories of democracy and democratization. For a theoretical exploration of this theme, see Stepan et al. (2011).

Chapter 2

1. Another factor for India's survival was the Partition of British India into India and Pakistan, which negated the Muslim League's objective of a weak centre and devolved periphery. This created the Congress wish of a strong 'Union', cooperative States and a strong commitment to prevent secessionism (Kumarasingham 2013, chapter 4).
2. North (1991, 94) describes a 'lock-in' as a solution which once reached 'is difficult to exit from'. In a two-person zero-sum game, a lock-in can be thought of as a Nash-equilibrium from which neither player has an incentive to withdraw unilaterally.

Chapter 4

1. The concept of 'Oriental despotism', most famously associated with Wittfogel (1957), actually has a deep root in European intellectual history, going back all the way to Greek thought in which the concept of despotism was used to indicate the superiority of Greek political organization over the Persian. The belief in the inability of non-Western cultures to sustain democracy runs as an undercurrent from Aristotle to Hegel and Marx.
2. The theoretical and methodological spirit of this volume can be seen in the following citation: 'If we believe that the ideal model is democracy of the western type, i.e., the European and American model of liberal democracy, then we will describe the global political process within the framework proposed by S. Huntington in his book *The Third Wave: Democratization at the End of the Twentieth Century*, and implicitly assume the correspondence, or lack thereof, of a particular specific model to the ideal one. Within the framework of this approach, the global political process will be described "simply" as a process of political modernization of the Western type and the evolution of "all nations and regions" in the direction of either the European

or the American modification of Western liberal democracy (the conception of "democratic transition", and the idiosyncrasies ignored, similar to the way that Karl Marx, due to his lack of knowledge of the East, "corrected" his famous formational theory with ad hoc explanations—with the conception of "Asian means of production" which for nearly one hundred years was subsequently debated within international and especially Russian Asian Studies until the discussants were convinced of the methodological limitations of such framing of the question). However, today, more and more researchers in both Western nations and in Russia express doubt that the simplistic theory of contemporary Western political modernization (Westernization) and democratic transition, defining democracy of the Western type as the sole and ideal model of democratic organization [...]. It is important to qualify that we are speaking here not of a rejection of the theories and conceptions of democracy and not of a rejection on the whole [...] but of the necessity of expanding the methodological base and "nomenclature" of the methodological approaches, particularly through utilizing the methodology of the regional and spatial-analytical approaches more adequately and in an unbiased way to explain the global political process' (Voskressenski 2017, op.cit.559).

3. Voskressenski writes: 'Our study, from the perspective of the political theory of the formation of the characteristics of the model of "non-Western democracy of the Asian type," i.e., national-constitutional democracy (Japan, Taiwan, Singapore, India, Malaysia, Sri Lanka) as well as the models of the evolutionary transformation of illiberal democracies (either authoritarian republics or constitutional monarchies, for example, Thailand) and "participatory democracies" (plebiscite democracies—China) into non-Western democracies will, perhaps, provide a code for deciphering the paths of the formation of such a model in other nations also (particularly, in Russia). The balance of factors comprising the essence of this model in other nations will, more than likely, be different from those observed in Japan, Singapore, India or Taiwan, in China and other nations, just as the correlation of these factors within these nations themselves, in comparison with each other, is naturally different' (2017, op.cit., 590).

4. By raising the viability of non-Western democracy as a model of rule that might obviate the imperative of rage-fueled violence, Voskressenski and his co-authors have responded to an urgent need for alternatives. By showing that one can compare apparently incomparable and how multiple paths might converge on a narrower range of 'democracies with national character', Alexei Voskressenski and his colleagues have rendered a great

service—both to comparative politics and to political man in need of knowledge of the Self and the Other and a space where both can share it with some semblance of dignity, equality and justice.

SECTION E
THE 'KAUTILYAN MOMENT', THE POWER-KNOWLEDGE MATRIX AND THE GENEALOGY OF GLOBAL POLITICAL THEORY

Conclusion

1. 'So it took painful adjustments [...]. India has over the last 65 years adjusted, adapted, learned through very difficult experiences what Kautilya had originally laid out for them. If Indian leaders had only paid more attention to Kautilya right from the beginning and understood the Kautilyan power basis of Ashoka's seemingly idealist policies—India would have fared much better' (EI Sujit Dutta, New Delhi, 11 April 2012).
2. These positive and negative experiences underpin India's strategic learning curve, which Namrata Goswami assessed as follows: 'I do not think that India anymore believes that you can just have a cooperative framework without being prepared for war simultaneously. So that change has come in India. The decision the country had to take is an enormous burden for the population because the amount of money that gets diverted for defense is really unbelievable for a country with 400 million people in poverty. I think politicians in India are handling this extremely difficult situation quite well. You could call it being practical, you could call it strategic, you could also call it Kautilyan' (EI Namrata Goswami, New Delhi, 26 April 2012).
3. EI Bharat Karnad, New Delhi, 20 April 2012.
4. EI Kanti Bajpai, Frankfurt am Main, 25 September 2012.
5. EI Rana Chhina, New Delhi, 25 September 2012.
6. It needs to be noted here that the British colonialists too attempted a 're-use of the past'. This 'colonial re-use', however, was meant to emasculate Indian tradition as a source and catalyst of authentic, potent modernity (cf. Nandy 1983; Inden 1990).
7. EI Rajeev Bhargava, New Delhi, 9 May 2012.
8. EI Rajeev Bhargava, New Delhi, 9 May 2012.

GLOSSARY OF SANSKRIT/HINDI TERMS

adivasis	Autochthonous tribal people, outside the caste system
ahimsa	Principle of non-violence
amatya	Minister and/or senior administrative official
ari	Adversary state
artha	Wealth, power, means to gain wealth and (political) power
asana	Wait and see (in foreign policy)
ashrama	The 'four stages of life': childhood and youth up to puberty; active working life and raising family; detachment from active life after the birth of grandchildren; contemplation and renunciation of worldly life
Bhagavad Gita	Epic poem within the *Mahabharata*
bheda	Divide et impera
brahmins	Caste with religious-ritual and intellectual assignment
chakra	Sanskrit word meaning wheel, circle and cycle
chakravartin	Ruler of the world—'world' meaning the Indian subcontinent
Chanakya-niti	Collection of aphorisms from Kautilya's *Arthashastra*
charkha	Spinning wheel, used by M.K. Gandhi as symbol for independence struggle
chatri	Umbrella; elevated, dome-shaped architectonic structure in India
dalits	'Untouchables', not belonging to one of four castes, but living on the fringes of the caste system
dana	Gift, making concessions
danda	Armed forces (plus police and secret service)
danda	Use of force
devaswam	Traditional worship of temple elephants in South India

dharma	(Ethical) prescription for right conduct (usually in a caste context)
dharmashastras	Ancient Indian treatises on duties, law and social conduct
durbar	Court or public reception (Persian origin)
durga	The 'fortress', i.e., the capital city
dvaidhibhava	Diplomatic double-game
gana	Flock, troop or class
harijans	Term for lowest social strata (dalits, adivasis), popularized by M.K. Gandhi
hartal	Political strike and mass action of civil disobedience during the Indian Independence struggle
janapada	The people (in the countryside)
jati	Sub-group within caste
kama	Sensual pleasure with or without sexual connotation
kapatika	Agent of the intelligence service
karman	Religious doctrine that good or bad deeds in this life have inescapable consequences in the next life
khadi	Indian, homespun, cotton cloth
khillat	Dress-of-honour
kosa	State treasury
kshatriyas	Caste with political and military assignment
kuta-yuddha	Irregular warfare
Lokayata	Atheistic, materialistic philosophy which sees the mind as an attribute of matter; similarities with philosophical materialism of the pre-Socratics in ancient Greece
madhyama	Neutral state
Mahabharata	Ancient Indian epic ascribed to the sage Vyasa
mandala (theory)	Configuration of friendly, adversary and neutral states
mantrin	Closest political adviser ('chancellor') of the ruler in ancient India
Manu-smriti	Ancient Indian treatise (*dharmashastra*) on duties, law and social conduct ascribed to the sage Manu
matsya-nyaya	'Law of the fishes': big fish devours small fish; anarchy

mitra (*mandala* theory)	Friendly state, no direct neighbour
mitra (*saptanga* theory)	Allied state
moksha	Individual salvation in this and/or the other world
Mudrarakshasa	Classical Indian play by Vishakhadatta featuring Kautilya
nazr	Offering or spiritual vow (Arabic origin)
neta	Political leader
Nitisara	Ancient Indian political treatise by Kamandaka (strongly influenced by Kautilya's *Arthashastra*)
Panchatantra	Ancient Indian collection of beast fables (is a text for political instruction; 'mirror for princes')
Panchsheel	'Five Principles of Peaceful Coexistence', formulated in a 1954 agreement between the Indian and Chinese governments
prakash-yuddha	Regular war
prakriti	The (seven) 'state factors'
purohita	Personal adviser of ancient Indian ruler in religious and life-world matters
Ramayana	Ancient Indian epic ascribed to the sage Valmiki
saman	Conciliation
samdhi	Peace
samkhya	Ancient Indian (atheistic) philosophy based on a dualistic ontology of spirit and matter, in which life is the mixture of both
samsara	Religious doctrine of the cyclicity of life (reincarnation)
samshraya	Alliance-building (offensive or defensive)
saptanga (theory)	The seven 'state factors' (*prakriti*): ruler, government, people, capital city, treasury, army, ally in foreign policy; they constitute the (patrimonial) state and its power potential
sattrin	Senior intelligence officer
satya	Truth

satyagraha	Hindi term coined by M.K. Gandhi ('insisting on truth') which stands for political actions of non-violent resistance
shadgunya (theory)	The 'six methods of foreign policy': peace, war, wait and see, coercive diplomacy, alliance-building, and diplomatic double-game
shanga	Association, assembly or community
shastra	Textbook, compendium
shudra	(Majority) caste whose function is physical labour
stupa	Mound-like architectonic structure in India and neighbouring Asian countries
swamin	The ruler or king
swaraj	M.K. Gandhi's concept of an independent, self-governing, decentralized and non-hierarchical political system in India
tusnim-yuddha	Covert actions
udasina	Distant powerful state
Upanishads	Ancient Indian collection of philosophical texts
upayas (cluster)	The four basic methods of political conduct: conciliation, gift, divide, and use of force
vaishyas	Caste with economic-entrepreneurial assignment
varna	Fourfold, hierarchical caste order
Vedas	Primordial Indian texts on religion, cosmology, philosophy and ethics
vigraha	War
vijigishu	Revisionist ruler intent to create a hegemonic state with sovereignty or suzerainty over neighbouring states
Yana	Pressure tactics (in foreign policy)
yoga	Contemplative and psycho-physical techniques to catalyze logical-rational or spiritual-mystical knowledge

BIBLIOGRAPHY

Acharya, Amitav. 2011. "Dialogue and Discovery: In Search of International Relation Theories Beyond the West." *Millennium* 39(3): 619–37.

Acharya, Amitav, and Barry Buzan. 2007. "Why is There No Non-Western International Relations Theory." *International Relations of the Asia-Pacific* 7(3): 341–68.

Adler-Nissen, Rebecca (ed.). 2013. *Bourdieu in International Relations: Rethinking Key Concepts in IR*. London: Routledge.

Aguirre Rojas, C.A. 1999. *Fernand Braudel und die moderne Sozialwissenschaft*. Leipzig: Leipziger Universitätsverlag.

Allert, Tilman. 1998. *Die Familie: Fallstudien zur Unverwüstlichkeit einer Lebensform*. Berlin/New York: de Gruyter.

Auboyer, Jeannine. 1965. *Daily Life in Ancient India from 200 BC to 700 AD*. London: Weidenfeld and Nicolson.

Badrinath, Chaturvedi. 1986. "Max Weber's Wrong Understanding of Indian Civilization." In *Recent Research on Max Weber's Studies of Hinduism*, ed. Detlef Kantowsky, 45–58. München: Weltforum Verlag.

Bajpai, Kanti P. 2003. "Indian Strategic Culture." In *South Asia in 2020: Future Strategic Balances and Alliances*, ed. Michael R. Chambers, 245–303. Carlisle, Pennsylvania: Strategic Studies Institute, U.S. Army War College.

Bajpai, Kanti P., and Amitabh Mattoo. 1996. *Securing India: Strategic Thought and Practice*. Delhi: Manohar Publishers.

Bajpai, Kanti P., and Siddharth Mallavarapu (eds). 2005a. *International Relations in India – Theorising the Region and Nation*. Delhi: Orient BlackSwan.

———. (2005b). *International Relations in India – Bringing Theory Back Home*. Delhi: Orient BlackSwan.

Bajpai, Kanti P., and Harsh V. Pant (eds). 2013. *India's Foreign Policy: A Reader*. Oxford: Oxford University Press.

Bajpai, Kanti, Saira Basit, and V. Krishnappa (eds). 2014. *India's Grand Strategy – History, Theory, Cases*. Delhi: Routledge India.

Balraj, Krishna. 2013. *Sardar Vallabhbhai Patel – India's Iron Man*. Delhi: Rupa Publications.

Barlösius, Eva. 2011. *Pierre Bourdieu*. Frankfurt am Main: Campus.

Behera, Navnita Chadha. 2007. "Re-imagining IR in India." *International Relations of the Asia-Pacific* 7(3): 341–68.
Behera, A., and S.K. Sharma. 2014. *Militant Groups in South Asia*. New Delhi: Pentagon Publishers/IDSA.
Behnke, Joachim, Nina Baur, and Natalie Behnke (eds). 2010. *Empirische Methoden der Sozialwissenschaft*. Paderborn: Schöningh.
Berg-Schlosser, Dirk. 2010. "Political Culture at a Crossroads." In *Political Sociology*, ed. Mitra et al., 31–50. Opladen: Budrich.
Berger, Peter, and Thomas Luckmann. 1966. *The Social Construction of Reality*. New York: Random House.
Boesche, Roger. 2002a. *The First Great Political Realist: Kautilya and His Arthashastra*. Lanham, USA: Lexington Books.
———. 2002b. "Moderate Machiavelli? Contrasting the Prince with the Arthashastra of Kautilya." *Critical Horizons* 3(2): 253–76.
Bogner, Alexander, Beate Littig and Wolfgang Menz (eds). 2009. *Experten interviews*. Wiesbaden: VS-Verlag.
Bond, G. C., and Angela Gilliam (eds). 1994. *Social Construction of the Past: Representation as Power*. London: Routledge.
Booth, Ken. 2005. "Strategic Culture: Validity and Validation." *Oxford Journal on Good Governance* 2(1): 25–8.
Booth, Ken and Russell Trood (eds). 1999. *Strategic Culture in the Asia-Pacific Region*. New York: St. Martin's Press.
Bourdieu, Pierre. 1992. *Rede und Antwort*. Frankfurt am Main: Suhrkamp.
———. 1990. *The Logic of Practice*. Cambridge, UK: Polity Press.
———. 1987. *Sozialer Sinn*. Frankfurt am Main: Suhrkamp.
———. 1982. *Die feinen Unterschiede. Kritik der gesellschaftlichen Urteilskraft*. Frankfurt am Main: Suhrkamp.
———. 1979. *Entwurf einer Theorie der Praxis*. Frankfurt am Main: Suhrkamp.
Bourdieu, Pierre, and Roger Chartier. 2011. *Der Soziologe und der Historiker*. Wien: Turia + Kant.
Bozeman, Adda B. 1960. *Politics and Culture in International History*. Princeton: Princeton University Press.
———. 1992. *Strategic Intelligence & Statecraft*. Washington, DC: Brassey's.
Bragta, Sanjay. 2012. "Will Pranab Prove to be the Kautilya in Rashtrapati Bhavan?" India TV, 2012. https://sanjaybragta.wordpress.com/2012/07/08/will-pranab-prove-to-be-the-kautilya-in-rashtrapati-bhavan/ (retrieved, Aug. 11, 2017)
Braudel, Fernand. 1993. *Schriften zur Geschichte II: Menschen und Zeitalter*. Stuttgart: Klett-Cotta.

———. 1992. *Schriften zur Geschichte I: Gesellschaften und Zeitstrukturen.* Stuttgart: Klett-Cotta.
Buciak, Sebastian and Rüdiger von Dehn. 2010. *Indien und Pakistan: Atommächte im Spannungsfeld regionaler und globaler Veränderungen.* Berlin: Köster.
Bühl, Walter L. (ed.). 1972. *Verstehende Soziologie: Grundzüge und Entwicklungstendenzen.* München: Nymphenburger.
Carr, Edward H. 1981/1939. *The Twenty-Years Crisis, 1919–1929 – An Introduction to the Study of International Relations.* London: Macmillan
Castro Verela, Maria do Mar, and Nikita Dhavan. 2005. *Postkoloniale Theorie: eine kritische Einführung.* Bielefeld: Transript.
Central Intelligence Agency. *The World Fact Book: Country Comparison (Purchasing Power Parity).* Available at https://www.cia.gov/library/publications/the-world-factbook/rankorder/2001rank.html?countryname=India&countrycode=in&regionCode=sas&rank=4#in (retrieved: Oct. 15, 2013)
Centre for Policy Research and National Defence College. 2012. *NonAlignment 2.0. A Foreign and Strategic Policy for India in the Twenty First Century.* Available at http://www.cprindia.org/research/reports/nonalignment-20-foreign-and-strategic-policy-india-twenty-first-century (retrieved: June 25, 2013)
Centre for the Study of Developing Societies. 2008. *State of Democracy in South Asia: A Report.* Delhi: Oxford University Press.
Chakravarty, Nilima. 1992. *Indian Philosophy: The Pathfinders and the System Builders (700 B.C. to 100 A.D.).* Delhi: Allied Publishers.
Chambers, Michael R. (ed.). 2003. *South Asia in 2020: Future Strategic Balances and Alliances.* Carlisle, Pennsylvania: Strategic Studies Institute, U.S. Army War College.
Chandra, B., M. Mukherjee, and A. Mukherjee. 2008. *India Since Independence.* Delhi: Penguin Books.
Chandrasekaran, Pravin. 2013. "Kautilya: Politics, Ethics and Statecraft." *The Indian Journal of Diplomacy* 14(3): 3–6.
Chakraborty, Gayatri. 1990. *Espionage in Ancient India (From the Earliest Time to the 12th Century A.D.* Calcutta: Minerva.
Chatterjee, Partha. 1986. *Nationalist Thought and the Colonial World: A Derivative Discourse.* London-Delhi: Zed Books.
Cohen, Stephen. 2002. *Emerging Power India.* Delhi: Oxford University Press India.
Collier, D., and J. Mahon. 1993. "Conceptual 'Stretching' Revisited: Adapting Categories in Comparative Analysis." *American Political Science Review* 97(4): 845–55.

Collier, D., and S. Levitsky. 1997. "Democracy with Adjectives: Conceptual Innovation in Comparative Research." *World Politics* 49(3): 430–51.

Coupland, Reginald. 1944. *The Indian Problem: Report on the Constitutional Problem in India*. Oxford: Oxford University Press.

Croissant, A., and W. Merkel. 2004. "From Transition to Defective Democracy? Mapping Asian Democratization." *Democratization* 11(5): 156–79.

Derrett, John Duncan Martin. 1968. *Religion, Law and the State in India*. Delhi: Oxford University Press.

Diamond, Larry. 2002. "Elections Without Democracy: Thinking About Hybrid Regimes." *Journal of Democracy* 13 (2): 22–35.

Dikshit, Sandeep. 2013. 'We would rather be called re-emerging powers, says NSA." *The Hindu* (February 3, 2013). http://www.thehindu.com/news/national/we-would-rather-be-called-reemerging-powers-says-nsa/article4373075.ece#! (retrieved: April 4, 2013)

Dixit, J.N. 2004. *Makers of India's Foreign Policy*. Delhi: HarperCollins India.

———. 2003. *India's Foreign Policy 1947–2003*. Delhi: Picus Books.

Douglas, Mary. 1966. *Purity and Danger: An Analysis of the Concepts of Pollution and Taboo*. London: Routledge.

Drekmeier, Charles. 1962. *Kingship and Community in Early India*. Stanford, CA: Stanford University Press.

Durkheim, Emile. 1977. *Die Entwicklung der Pädagogik*. Weinheim: Beltz.

Edwardes, Michael. 1965. *Everyday Life in Early India*. London: BT Batsford.

Eisenstadt, S. N. (ed.). 1992. *Kulturen der Achsenzeit II: Indien*. Frankfurt am Main: Suhrkamp.

Engelmeier, Tobias. 2009. *Nation-Building and Foreign Policy in India*. Delhi: Cambridge University Press.

Fetscher, Iring, and Herfried Münkler (eds). 1988. *Pipers Handbuch der Politischen Ideen I. Frühe Hochkulturen und europäische Antike*. München: Piper.

Fleck, Ludwik. 1980. *Entstehung und Entwicklung einer wissenschaftlichen Tatsache. Einführung in die Lehre vom Denkstil und Denkkollektiv*. Frankfurt am Main: Suhrkamp.

Fludernik, Monika (ed.). 1998. *Hybridity and Postcolonialism: Twentieth-Century Indian Literature*. Tuebingen: Stauffenburg-Verlag.

Frankel, Benjamin (ed.). 1996. *Roots of Realism*. London: Frank Cass.

Frei, Christoph. 1994. *Hans J. Morgenthau: Eine intellektuelle Biographie*. Bern: Haupt.

Fritze, Ludwig (ed.). 1886. *Mudrarakschasa oder des Kanzlers Siegelring. Ein indisches Drama von Visakhadatta*. Leipzig: Reclam.

Fürstenberg, Kai. 2015. *Panchayati Raj in India – The Evolution between 1947 and 1992.* Heidelberg University.
Gadamer, Hans-Georg. 2013. *Truth and Method.* London: Bloomsbury Academic.
———. 1986. *Hermeneutik I, Wahrheit undMethode.* Tuebingen: Mohr.
Gallie, W.B. 1956. "Essentially Contested Concepts." *Proceedings of the Aristotelian Society,* New Series 56: 167–98.
Garbe, Richard. 1917. *Die Samkhya-Philosophie.* Leipzig: Haessel.
Gautam, P. K. 2013a. "Relevance of Kautilya's Arthashastra." *Strategic Analysis* 37(1): 21–8.
———. 2013b. "Understanding Kautilya's Arthashastra: In Praise of Rote." *World Affairs: The Journal of International Issues* 17(1): 30–7.
———. 2013c. *One Hundred Years of Kautilya's Arthashastra.* Delhi: IDSA Monograph Series.
———. 2013d. *Shruti and Smriti: Some Issues in the Re-emergence of Indian Traditional Knowledge.* Delhi: IDSA Issue Brief.
———. 2013e. *Understanding Kautilya's Four Upayas.* Delhi: IDSA Comment.
———. 2015. *Kautilya's Arthashastra—Contemporary Issue and Comparison.* Delhi: IDSA Monograph Series.
Gautam, P. K., S. Mishra and A. Gupta (eds). 2015a. *Indigenous Historical Knowledge — Kautilya and his Vocabulary I.* Delhi: Institute for Defence Studies and Analyses/Pentagon Press.
———. 2015b. *Indigenous Historical Knowledge—Kautilya and his Vocabulary II.* Delhi: Institute for Defence Studies and Analyses/Pentagon Press.
———. 2016. *Indigenous Historical Knowledge—Kautilya and his Vocabulary III.* Delhi: Institute for Defence Studies and Analyses/Pentagon Press.
Gehrhardt, Uta. 2001. *Idealtypus – Zur methodischen Begründung der modernen Soziologie.* Frankfurt am Main: Suhrkamp.
Geiger, Theodor. 1932. *Die soziale Schichtung des deutschen Volkes.* Stuttgart: Enke.
Ghosh, Partha. 2007. *The Politics of Personal Law in South Asia: Identity, Nationalism and the Uniform Civil Code.* Delhi: Routledge.
Girtler, Roland. 2001. *Methoden der Feldforschung.* Köln: Böhlau.
Glasenapp, Helmuth von. 1974. *Die Philosophie der Inder. Eine Einführung in ihre Geschichte und ihre Lehren.* Stuttgart: Kröner.
———. (ed.). 1955. *Bhagavadgita.* Stuttgart: Reclam.
———. 1929. *Die Literaturen Indiens von ihren Anfängen bis zur Gegenwart.* Potsdam: Akademische Verlagsgesellschaft Athenaion.
Glenn, John, Darryl Howlett, and Stuart Poore (eds). 2004. *Neorealism vs. Strategic Culture.* Aldershot, UK: Ashgate.

Golzio, Karl-Heinz. 1984. "Zur Verwendung indologischer Literatur in Max Webers Studie über Hinduismus und Buddhismus." In *Max Webers Studie über Hinduismus und Buddhismus*, ed. Wolfgang Schluchter, 363–73. Frankfurt am Main: Suhrkamp.

Goswami, Namrata. 2013. "India's Strategic Culture is Plain to See." In *Asia Times* online. Available at http://www.atimes.com/atimes/South_Asia/SOU-01-050413.html. (retrieved: Sept. 28, 2013)

Gould, S. 2002. *The Structure of Evolutionary Theory*. Cambridge, MA: Harvard University Press.

Government of Tamil Nadu. 1971. "Report of the Centre-State Relations Inquiry Committee." Madras.

Griffith, Ernest S., John Plamenatz, and J. Roland Pencock. 1956. "Cultural Prerequisites to a Successfully Functioning Democracy: A Symposium." *American Political Science Review* 50 (1): 101–37.

Gupta, Arvind. 2015a. "Opening Remarks" by Dr. Arvind Gupta, DG, IDSA at Kautilya conference on Oct.18, 2012. In *Indigenous Historical Knowledge – Kautilya and his Vocabulary I*, Gautam et al.

———. 2015b. "Welcome Remarks" by Dr. Arvind Gupta, DG, IDSA at Kautilya conference on Oct. 8, 2013. In *Indigenous Historical Knowledge – Kautilya and his Vocabulary II*, Gautam et al.

Halbfass, Wilhelm. 1991. *Tradition and Reflection: Explorations in Indian Thought*. Albany, NY: State University of New York Press.

Halbwachs, Maurice. 1991. *Das kollektive Gedächtnis*. Frankfurt am Main: Fischer.

Hale, J. R. 1972. *Machiavelli and Renaissance Italy*. Harmondsworth, UK: Penguin Books.

Hali, S.M. 1999. "Raw at War – Genesis of Secret Agencies in Ancient India." In *Defence Journal* (Karachi) (February/March): 50–3.

Hardy, Adam (ed.). 2007. *The Temple in South Asia*. Volume 2, Proceedings of the 18th conference of the European Association of South Asian Archaeologists, London 2005. London: British Association for South Asian Studies and the British Academy.

Hees, Peter. 2003. "Shades of Orientalism: Paradoxes and Problems in Indian Historiography." In *History and Theory* 42(2): 169–95.

Hegel, G. F. W. 1971. "Vorlesungen über die Geschichte der Philosophie." In *Werke*, Vol. 18, Frankfurt am Main: Suhrkamp

Hegewald, Julia. 2013. "Building Citizenship: The Agency of Public Buildings and Urban Planning in the Making of the Indian Citizen." In *Citizenship as Cultural Flow: Structure, Agency and Power*, ed. S.K. Mitra, 229–64. Heidelberg: Springer.

——. 2006. "From Siva to Parshvanatha: The Appropriation of a Hindu Temple for Jaina Worship." In *South Asian Archaeology 2001*, ed. Catherine Jarrige and Vincent Lefèvre, 517–23.

——. 2005. "Domes, Tombs and Minarets: Islamic Influences on Jaina Architecture." In *The Temple in South Asia*, ed. Adam Hardy, 179–90.

Hegewald, Julia, and Subrata Mitra (eds). 2012. *Re-use: The Art and Politics of Integration and Anxiety*. Delhi: Sage.

Heimann, Betty. 1930. *Studien zur Eigenart indischen Denkens*. Tübingen: Mohr.

Henrich, Dieter. 1952. *Die Einheit der Wissenschaftslehre Max Webers*. Tübingen: Mohr.

Hillebrandt, Alfred. 1923. *Altindische Politik: eine Übersicht auf Grund der Quellen*. Jena: Fischer.

Howlett, Darryl. 2006. "The Future of Strategic Culture. Defense Threat Reduction Agency. Advanced Systems and Concepts Office." https://fas.org/irp/agency/dod/dtra/stratcult-future.pdf (retrieved: Sept. 9, 2013)

——. 2005. "Strategic Culture: Reviewing Recent Literature." *Strategic Insights* 4(10).

Huntington, Samuel P. 1968. *Political Order in Changing Societies*. New Haven and London: Yale University Press.

Husar, Jörg, Günther Maihold, and Stefan Mair (eds). 2009. *Neue Führungsmächte: Partner deutscher Außenpolitik?* Baden-Baden: Nomos.

Hwang, Karl. 2010. "Measuring Geopolitical Power in India: A Review of the National Security Index (NSI)." Working Papers, no. 136, 5–36. Hamburg: Leibniz-Institut für Globale und Regionale Studien (GIGA). http://www.giga-hamburg.de/dl/download.php?d=/content/publikationen/pdf/wp136_hwang.pdf (retrieved: Sept. 9, 2013)

Ihlau, Olaf. 2006. *Weltmacht Indien: Die neue Herausforderung des Westens*. München: Siedler/Random House (Bundeszentrale für politische Bildung, Schriftenreihe 558).

Inden, Ronald. 1990. *Imagining India*. Oxford: Basil Blackwell.

——. 1986. "Orientalist Constructions of India." *Modern Asian Studies* 20 (3): 401–46.

Jackson, Peter. 2008. "Pierre Bourdieu, the 'Cultural Turn' and the Practice of International History." *Review of International Studies* 34(1): 155–81.

Jalal, Ayesha. 1995. *Democracy and Authoritarianism in South Asia: A Comparative and Historical Perspective*. Cambridge: Cambridge University Press.

Jarrige, Catherine, and Vincent Lefèvre (eds). 2006. *South Asian Archaeology 2001*. 2 vols. Paris: Editions Recherches sur les Civilisations.

Jayaswal, K. P. 1943. *Hindu Polity: A Constitutional History of India in Hindu Times.* Bangalore: Banagalore Printing and Publishers.

Jepperson, R. I., A. Wendt and P. J. Katzenstein. 1996. "Norms, Identity and Culture in National Security." In Katzenstein: *The Culture of National Security: Norms and Identity in World Politics,* ed. Peter J. Katzenstein, 33–78. New York: Columbia University Press.

Jha, D.N. 1998. *Ancient India: A Historical Outline.* Delhi: Manohar.

Johnston, A. I. 1998. *Cultural Realism: Strategic Culture and Grand Strategy in Chinese History.* Princeton, NJ: Princeton University Press.

———. 1996. "Cultural Realism and Strategy in Maoist China." In *The Culture of National Security,* ed. P.J. Katzenstein, 216–68.

———. 1995. "Thinking about Strategic Culture." *International Security* 19(4): 32–64.

Jones, Rodney W. 2006. "India's Strategic Culture." Prepared for Defense Threat Reduction Agency; Advanced Systems and Concepts Office, 3–31. https://fas.org/irp/agency/dod/dtra/india.pdf (retrieved: Aug. 30, 2013)

Kalyanaraman, S. 2015. "Arthasastra, Diplomatic History and the Study of International Relations in India." In Gautam et al. *Indigenous Historical Knowledge – Kautilya and his Vocabulary I,* 1–4.

Kangle, R. P. (ed. and trans.). 2010a/1972. *The Kautilya Arthashastra Part II.* (English translation) Delhi: Motilal Banarsidass Publishers.

———. 2010b/1965. *The Kautilya Arthashastra Part III* (Commentary). Delhi: Motilal Banarsidass Publishers.

Kantowsky, Detlef (ed.). 1986. *Recent Research on Max Weber's Studies of Hinduism.* München: Weltforum Verlag.

Karnad, Bharat. 2002. *Nuclear Weapons and Indian Security.* Delhi: Macmillan India.

Kastl, Jörg Michael. 2004. "Habitus als non-deklaratives Gedächtnis: zur Relevanz der neuropsychologischen Amnesieforschung für die Soziologie." *Sozialer sinn* Jg. 5(2): 195–226.

Katzenstein, Peter J. (ed.). 1996. *The Culture of National Security: Norms and Identity in World Politics.* New York: Columbia University Press.

Kedourie, Eli (ed.). 1970. *Nationalism in Asia and Africa.* London: Weidenfeld & Nicolson.

Kelsen, Hans. 2008. *Reine Rechtslehre.* Tübingen: Mohr Siebeck.

Kennedy, Andrew, 2012. *The International Ambitions of Mao and Nehru: National Efficacy Beliefs and the Making of Foreign Policy.* New York: Cambridge University Press.

Khanna, V. N. 1997. *Foreign Policy of India.* Delhi: Vikas Publishing House.

Kiessling, Hein G. 2011. *ISI und RAW: Die Geheimdienste Pakistans und Indiens*. Berlin: Köster.
Kim, Marcus. 2004. "India." In *Neorealism vs. Strategic Culture*, ed. Glenn et al., 75–104.
Kissinger, Henry. 2014. *World Order: Reflections of the Character of Nations and the Course of History*. New York: Penguin.
Knoll, Manuel. 2015. "Max Webers Machiavelli-Rezeption – Die Konsequenzen des politischen Realismus für das Verhältnis von Ethik und Politik." In *Der Machtstaat*, ed. Reinhardt et al., 241–268.
Kohli, Atul (ed.). 2001. *The Success of India's Democracy*. Cambridge: Cambridge University Press.
Kosambi, D.D. 1975. *An Introduction to the Study of Indian History*. Bombay: Popular Prakashan.
Kothari, Rajni. 1970. *Politics in India*. Boston: Little Brown.
Kovac, Mitar, and Jan Marcek. 2013. "Konzepte und methodische Aspekte der Formulierung und Umsetzung der staatlichen Strategie." *Österreichische Militärische Zeitschrift* 51(1): 34–47.
Krieger, Wolfgang (ed.). 2009. *Geheimdienste in der Weltgeschichte*. München: Beck.
Kubálková, Vendulka (ed.). 2001. *Foreign Policy in a Constructed World*. Armonk, New York: Sharpe.
Kuckartz, Udo. 2009. *Einführtung in die computergestützte Analyse qualitativer Daten*. Wiesbaden: VS-Verlag.
Kühnhardt, Ludger. 1988. "Staatsordnung und Macht in indischer Perspektive– Kautilya Chanakya als Klassiker der politischen Ideengeschichte." *Historische Zeitschrift* 247: 333–55.
Kulke, Hermann. 2005. *Indische Geschichte bis 1750*. München: Oldenbourg.
———. 1992. "Ausgrenzung, Rezeption und kulturelles Selbstbewusstsein. Formen indischer Reaktion auf fremde Eroberungen inder frühen Geschichte." *Eisenstadt: Kulturen der Achsenzeit II*: 17–37.
———. 1984. "Orthodoxe Restoration und hinduistische Sektenreligiosität im Werk Max Webers." In *Max Webers Studie über Hinduismus und Buddhismus*, ed. Wolfgang Schluchter, 293–332.
Kulke, Hermann, and Dietmar Rothermund. 1998. *Geschichte Indiens*. München: Beck.
Kumar, Tarun. 2015. "Corruption in Administration: Evaluating the Kautilyan Antecedents." In Gautam et al., *Indigenous Historical Knowledge—Kautilya and his Vocabulary II*, 56–62.
Kumarasingham, Harshan. 2013. *A Political Legacy of the British Empire: Power*

and the Parliamentary System in Post-Colonial India and Sri Lanka. London: I.B. Tauris.

Lange, Klaus (ed.). 2009. "Security in South Asia: Conventional and Unconventional Factors of Destabilization." München: Hanns-Seidel-Stiftung.

Laping, Johannes. 1986. "Pragmatism and Transcendence: Aspects of Pragmatic Soteriology ('Heilspragmatik') in Indian Tradition." In *Recent Research on Max Weber's Studies of Hinduism*, ed. Detlef Kantowsky, 199–208.

Lerner, Max (ed.). 1950. *The Prince and the Discourses [of Machiavelli]*. New York: The Modern Library.

Lewis, O., and S. Steinmo. 2012. "How Institutions Evolve: Evolutionary Theory and Institutional Change." *Polity* 44: 314–39.

Liddell Hart, B.H. 1967. *Strategy*. Harmondsworth, UK: Penguin Books.

Lipset, Seymour Martin. 1959. "Some Social Requisites of Democracy: Economic Development and Political Legitimacy." *American Political Science Review* 53: 69–105.

Liebig, Michael, and Saurabh Mishra (eds.). 2017. *The Arthaśātra in a Transcultural Perspective: Comparing Kautilya with Sun-Zi, Nizam al-Mulk, Barani and Machiavelli*. New Delhi: IDSA/Pentagon Press.

Liebig, Michael. 2014a. "Kautilya's Arthasastra - A Classic Text of Statecraft and an Untapped Political Science Resource." *Heidelberg Papers in South Asian and Comparative Politics*, 74: 1–17. Heidelberg: Department of Political Science, South Asia Institute, Heidelberg University.

———. 2014b. *Endogene Politisch-Kulturelle Ressourcen: Die Relevanz des Kautilya-Arthashastra für das moderne Indien*. Baden-Baden: Nomos.

———. 2014c. "Statecraft and Intelligence Analysis in the Kautilya-Arthashastra." *Journal of Defence Studies* 8(4): 27–54.

———. 2013. "Kautilya's Relevance for India Today." *India Quarterly* 69(2): 99–116.

Lijphart, Arendt. 2009. "The Puzzle of India's Democracy." In *Politics of Modern South Asia, Critical Issues in Modern Politics*, Vol. 1, ed. S. K. Mitra. London: Routledge.

Lindberg, Steffan. 2007. "Institutionalization of Party Systems? Stability and Fluidity among Legislative Parties in Africa's Democracies." *Government and Opposition* 42: 215–41.

Loomba, Ania. 1998. *Colonialism/Postcolonialism*. London: Routledge.

Macaulay, Thomas Babbington: Minute on Indian Education. http://www.columbia.edu/itc/mealac/pritchett/00generallinks/macaulay/txt_minute_education_1835.html (retrieved: June 21, 2013).

Maddison, Angus. 2003. *The World Economy II: Historical Statistics*. Development

Centre Studies. OECD Publishing. http://www.theworldeconomy.org/MaddisonTables/MaddisontableB-18.pdf (retrieved: June 8, 2013)

Mahon Jr., James E., and David Collier. 1993. "Conceptual 'Stretching' Revisited: Adapting Categories in Comparative Analysis. *American Political Science Review* 87 (4): 845–55.

Mahoney, James. 2000. "Path Dependence in Historical Sociology. *Theory and Society* 29(4): 507–48.

Mannheim, Karl. 1965/1929. *Ideologie und Utopie*. Frankfurt am Main: Schulte-Bulmke.

Marx, Karl. 1969. "Der achtzehnte Brumaire des Louis Bonaparte." In *Marx-Engels-Werke*, Vol. 8, 115–207. Berlin: Dietz.

———. 1968. *Grundrisse der Kritik der politischen Ökonomie*. Frankfurt am Main: Europäische Verlagsanstalt.

———. 1960a. "Die britische Herrschaft in Indien." In *Marx-Engels-Werke*, Vol. 9, 127–33. Berlin: Dietz.

———. 1960b. "Die künftigen Ergebnisse der britischen Herrschaft in Indien." In *Marx-Engels-Werke*, Vol. 9, 220–26. Berlin: Dietz.

———. 1853. "Capital Punishment.— Mr. Cobden's Pamphlet.— Regulations of the Bank of England." *The New York Tribune*.

Mathur, B. P. 2008. "Kautilya: The Art of Governance." *Indian Journal of Public Administration* 54 (4): 785–802.

Maurer, Michael. 2007. *Eberhard Gothein: Leben und Werk zwischen Kulturgeschichte und Nationalökonomie*. Köln: Böhlau.

Mehta, Pratap Bhanu. 2009. "Century of Forgetting." *The Indian Express*. http://www.indianexpress.com/news/century-of-forgetting/476998/ (retrieved: May 9, 2013)

Mehta, V. R. 1992. *Foundations of Indian Political Thought*. Delhi: Manohar.

Meinecke, Friedrich. 1962a[1908]. *Weltbürgertum und Nationalstaat*. Stuttgart: Koehler.

———. 1962b[1924]. *Machiavellism: The Doctrine of Raison d'état and Its Place in Modern History*. New Haven: Yale University Press.

———. 1960/1924: *Die Idee der Staatsraison in der neueren Geschichte*. München: Oldenbourg.

Menon, Shivshankar. 2015a. "Keynote Address." At IDSA Kautilya Conference, Oct. 18, 2012. In *Indigenous Historical Knowledge – Kautilya and his Vocabulary I*, ed. Gautam et al.

———. 2015b. "Keynote Address." At IDSA Kautilya Conference, Oct. 8, 2013. In *Indigenous Historical Knowledge – Kautilya and his Vocabulary II*, ed. Gautam et al.

———. "Keynote Address." At IDSA Kautilya Conference, April 9, 2014. http://www.idsa.in/keyspeeches/ShivshankarMenonKautilya (retrieved: Dec. 27, 2015)

———. 2012. "K. Subrahmanyam and India's Strategic Culture." *Air Power Journal* 7(1): 1–11.

Metcalf, Thomas R. 1998. *Ideologies of the Raj*. Cambridge: Cambridge University Press.

Meyer, Johann Jakob (ed.). 1977/1926. *Das altindische Buch vom Welt-und Staatsleben – Das Arthacastra des Kautilya*. Graz: Akademische Druck- und Verlagsanstalt.

———. 1927. *Über das Wesen der altindischen Rechtsschriften und ihr Verhältnis zu Kautilya*. Leipzig: Harrassowitz.

Meyers Enzyklopädisches Lexikon. (1971–1979). 25 Vols. Mannheim: Bibliographisches Institut.

Michael, Arndt. 2008. *India's Foreign Policy and Panchsheel-Multilateralism: The Impact of Norm Sublimation, Norm Localization and Competing Regionalism on South Asian Regional Multilateralism*. Dissertation. Universität Freiburg, Freiburg im Breisgau.

Mitra, Subrata. 2017a. "Afterword: To Each His Own? Democratic Aspirations and Institutional Evolution in the Non-Western World." In *Is Non-Western Democracy Possible*, Alexei D. Voskressenski, 673–86.

———. 2017b. "Kautilya Redux? Re-use, Hybridity, Trans-cultural Flow and Resilience of the State in India." In *The Arthasastra in a Transcultural Perspective: Comparing Kautilya with Sun-Zi, Nizam al-Mulk, Barani and Machiavelli*, ed. Michael Liebig and Saurabh Mishra. Delhi: Pentagon Press (for Institute of Defense Studies and Analysis, IDSA).

———. 2012a. "From Comparative Politics to Cultural Flow: The Hybrid State and the Resilience of the Political System in India." In *Conceptualizing Cultural Hybridization*, P. W. Stockhammer, 107–132.

——— (ed.). 2012b. *Citizenship in the Era of Globalization: Culture, Power and the Flow of Ideas*. Delhi: Samskriti.

———. 2011a. *Politics in India: Structure, Process and Policy*. London: Routledge.

———. 2011b. "Democracy's Resilience: Tradition, Modernity and Hybridity in India." *Harvard International Review* XXXII(4): 46–52.

——— (ed.). 2009a. *Politics of Modern South Asia, Critical Issues in Modern Politics*. 5 volumes. London: Routledge.

———. 2005. *The Puzzle India's Governance: Culture, Context and Comparative Theory*. London: Routledge.

———. 2000. "The Nation, State and the Federal Process in India." In *Federalism*

and Political Performance, ed. U. Wachendorfer-Schmidt. London: Routledge.
———. 1999a. "Effects of Institutional Arrangements on Political Stability in South Asia." *Annual Review of Political Science* 2: 405–28.
———. 1999b. *Culture and Rationality – The Politics of Social Change in Post-Colonial India*. Delhi: Sage.
———. 1999c. "Caste and the Politics of Identity: Beyond the Orientalist Discourse." In *Culture and Rationality: The Politics of Social Change in Postcolonial India*, 112–30. Delhi: Sage.
——— (ed.). 1990a. *The Post-colonial State in Asia: Dialectics of Politics and Culture*. London: Harvester Wheatsheaf.
———. 1990b. "Between Transaction and Transcendence: The State and the Institutionalisation of Power in India." In *The Post-colonial State in Asia: Dialectics of Politics and Culture*, ed. S. Mitra, 73–99. London: Harvester Wheatsheaf.
———. 1988. "Paradoxes of Power: Political Science as Morality Play." *Journal of Commonwealth and Comparative Politics* 26(3): 318–37.
Mitra, S., M. Pehl, and C. Spiess. (eds). 2010. *Political Sociology*. Opladen: Budrich.
Mitra, Subrata, and V.B. Singh. 2009. *When Rebels become Stakeholders – Democracy and Social Change in India*. Delhi: Sage.
Mitra, Subrata, and Alexander Fischer. 2002. "Sacred Laws and the Secular State: An Analytical Narrative of the Controversy over Personal Laws in India." *India Review* 1(3): 99–130.
Modelski, George. 1964. "Kautilya: Foreign Policy and International System in the Ancient Hindu World." *The American Political Science Review* 58(3): 549–60.
Mohan, C. Raja. 2012. "Rising Power and Enduring Paradox—India's China Challenge." *USI Journal*: 21–9.
———. *Crossing the Rubicon: The Shaping of India's New Foreign Policy*. Delhi: Viking.
Morgenthau, Hans J. 2012. *The Concept of the Political*. Houndmills: Palgrave Macmillan.
———. 1978. *Politics Among Nations. The Struggle for Power and Peace*. New York: Alfred A. Knopf.
———. 1958. *Dilemmas of Politics*. Chicago: Chicago University Press.
Morris-Jones, W. H. 1964. *The Government and Politics of India*. London: Hutchinson University Library.
Müller, Harald. 2008. *Wie kann eine neue Weltordnung aussehen? Wege in eine nachhaltige Politik*. Frankfurt am Main: Fischer.

———. 2006. *Weltmacht Indien: wie uns der rasante Aufstieg herausfordert.* Frankfurt am Main: Fischer.
Mullik, B.N. 1971. *My Years With Nehru 1948-64.* Bombay: Allied Publishers.
Münkler, Herfried. 1987. *Im Namen des Staates: Die Begründung der Staatsraison in der Frühen Neuzeit.* Frankfurt am Main: Fischer.
Mylius, Klaus. 1983. *Geschichte der indischen Literatur.* Leipzig: Reclam.
Nanda, Meera. 2005. "Response to My Critics." *Social Epistemology* 19(1): 147-91.
Nanda, Meera. 2003. *Prophets Facing Backward: Postmodern Critiques of Science and Hindu Nationalism in India.* New Brunswick, NJ: Rutgers University Press.
Nandy, Ashis. 1983. *The Intimate Enemy.* New Delhi: Oxford University Press.
Narlikar, Amrita, and Aruna Narlikar. 2014. *Bargaining with Rising India – Lessons from the Mahabharata.* Oxford: Oxford University Press.
Nehru, Jawaharlal. 1972-1982. *Selected Works,* Vols 1-15. Delhi: J. Nehru Memorial Fund.
———. 1984-2015. *Selected Works, Second Series,* Vols 1-60. Delhi: J. Nehru Memorial Fund.
———. 1981. *The Discovery of India.* Delhi: Indian Council for Cultural Relations.
———. 1962. *Glimpses of World History.* Bombay: Asia Publishing House.
Niaz, Ilhan. 2008. "Cultures of Power, Continental Bureaucratic Empires, and South Asian History." *Pakistan Journal of History and Culture* 28(1): 41-74.
Niaz, Ilhan. "Kautilya's *Arthashastra* and Governance as an Element of State Power." Institute of Strategic Studies Islamabad (ISSI).
Niaz, Ilhan. 2008. "Kautilya's *Arthashastra* and Governance as an Element of State Power." *Strategic Studies,* Islamabad, XXVIII (2&3): 1-17 (retrieved: 11 August, 2017)
North, Douglass. 1990. *Institutions, Institutional Change and Economic Performance.* Cambridge: Cambridge University Press.
Oevermann, Ulrich. 1997. *Thesen zur Methodik der werkimmanenten Interpretation vom Standpunkt der objektiven Hermeneutik.* (Elektronische Ressource). Goethe-Universität, Frankfurt am Main. Universitätsbibliothek Johann Christian Senckenberg.
Olivelle, Patrick. (ed.) 2013. *King, Government and Law in Ancient India.* Oxford: Oxford University Press.
——— (ed.). 1997. *Pancatantra – The Book of India's Folk Wisdom.* Oxford: Oxford University Press.
Panikkar, K.M. 1963. *The Foundations of New India.* London: Allen & Unwin.
———. 1956. *The Principles and Practice of Diplomacy.* Bombay: Asia Publishing House.

Parekh, Bhikhu. 2010. "Some Reflections on the Hindu Tradition of Political Thought." In *Comparative Political Theory: An Introduction*, Fred R. Dallmayr, 107–116. New York: Palgrave Macmillan.

———. 1999. *Colonialism, Tradition and Reform: An Analysis of Gandhi's Political Discourse*. Delhi: Sage.

Parmar, Aradhana. 1987. *Techniques of Statecraft: A Study of Kautilya's Arthashastra*. Delhi: Atma Ram & Sons.

Patzig, Günther. 2002. *Über den Umgang mit Texten der philosophischen Tradition*. Münster: Aschendorff.

Pierson, Paul. 2000. "Increasing Returns, Path Dependence, and the Study of Politics." *American Political Science Review* 94(2): 251–67.

Pillai, R. 2011. *The Corporate Chanakya: Successful Management the Chanakya Way*. Mumbai: Jaico Publishing House.

Plessner, Helmuth. 2003. *Macht und menschliche Natur*. Frankfurt am Main: Suhrkamp.

Pollock, Sheldon. 2011. "Crisis in the Classics." *Social Research* 78 (1): 21–48.

Poore, Stuart. 2011. "Strategic Culture." In *Neorealism vs. Strategic Culture*, ed. Glenn et al., 45–71.

Powell, G. Bingham, Russel J. Dalton, and Kaare Strom (eds). 2012. *Comparative Politics Today: A World View*. Tenth edition. New York: Longman.

Prakash, Aseem. 1993. "State and Statecraft in Kautilya's Arthasastra." Working Paper. Indiana University, Bloomington, USA.

Prakash, Gyan. 1994. "Subaltern Studies as Postcolonial Criticism." *The American Historical Review* 99 (5): 1475–90.

Prasad, Jayant. 2010. Lecture at IISS Global Strategic Review Conference 2010, Geneva. http://www.iiss.org/conferences/global-strategic-review/global-strategic-review2010/plenary-sessions- and- speeches-2010/second-plenary-session/jayant-prasad/ (retrieved: 15 May 2013)

Puhle, Hans-Juergen. 2005. "Democratic Consolidation and 'Defective' Democracies." Working Paper 47 (Madrid). www.uam.es/centros/derechol/cpolitical/papers.htm (retrieved March 1, 2015)

Putnam, Robert D. 1993. *Making Democracy Work: Civic Traditions in Modern Italy*. Princeton: Princeton University Press.

Pye, Lucian. 1968. "Political Culture." In *Encyclopedia of Social Sciences*, ed. D. L. Sill, 218–24. New York: Macmillan.

Rajagopalan, Rajesh. 2012. "Nonalignment 2.0: A Realist Critique of an Establishmentarian Perspective." New Delhi. IDSA Comment. http://www.risingpowersinitiative.org/nonalignment-2-0-a-realist-critique-of-an-establishmentarian-perspective/ (retrieved 11 August, 2017)

Ramachandran, K.N. et al. (ed.). 1999. "Sun Zi and China's Strategic Culture." Delhi: Institute of Defence Studies and Analyses (IDSA Occasional Paper Series).

Ramachandran, K.N. 1999. "Sun Zi and Kautilya: Towards a Comparative Analysis." In *Sun Zi and China's Strategic Culture*, ed. K. N. Ramachandran et al. IDSA Occasional Paper Series, 46–78.

Rana, Kishan S. 2000. *Inside Diplomacy*. Delhi: Manas Publications.

Rangarajan, L.N. (ed.) 1992. *Kautilya: The Arthashastra*. Delhi: Penguin Books India.

Reichwein, Alexander. 2010. "Rethinking Morgenthau in the German Context." Paper presented at International Studies Association. Annual Convention, New Orleans.

Reinhardt, Volker, Stefano Saracino, and Rüdiger Voigt (eds). 2015. *Der Machtstaat – Niccolo Machiavelli als Theoretiker der Macht im Spiegel der Zeit*. Baden-Baden: Nomos.

Riencourt; Amaury de. 1986. *The Soul of India*. Delhi: Sterling Publishers.

Ritschl, Eva and Maria Schetelich. 1973. *Studien zum Kautilya Arthasastra*. Berlin: Akademie-Verlag.

Rohatgi, Manila. 2007. *Spy System in Ancient India*. Delhi: Kalpaz Publications.

Rösel, Jakob. 1982. *Die Hinduismusthese Max Webers*. München: Weltforum Verlag.

Rothermund, Dietmar. 2010. *Gandhi und Nehru. Zwei Gesichter Indiens*. Stuttgart: Kohlhammer.

———. 2008. *Indien: Aufstieg einer asiatischen Weltmacht*. München: Beck (Bundeszentrale für Politische Bildung, Schriftenreihe 731).

———. (ed.). 1995. *Indien: Ein Handbuch. Kultur, Geschichte, Politik, Wirtschaft, Umwelt*. München: Beck.

Roy, Gandhi Jee. 1981. *Diplomacy in Ancient India*. Patna: Janaki Prakashan.

Rudolph, Lloyd, and Susanne H. Rudolph. 1967. *The Modernity of Tradition*. Chicago: University of Chicago Press.

———. 1987. *In Pursuit of Lakshmi – The Political Economy of the Indian State*. Chicago: University of Chicago Press.

Rudolph, Susanne H. 1987. "Presidential Address: State Formation in Asia – Prolegomenon to a Comparative Study." *The Journal of Asian Studies* 46 (4): 731–46.

Ryder, Antony (ed.). 1925. *The Panchatantra*. Chicago: The University of Chicago Press.

Sabine, George. 1973. *A History of Political Theory*. New York: Hold, Rinehart and Winston.

Sachau, Edward C. (ed.). 1992. *Alberuni's India. An Account of the Religion, Philosophy, Literature, Geography, Chronology, Astronomy, Customs, Laws and Astrology of India About 1030 AD*. Delhi: Munshiram Manoharlal Publishers.

Said, Edward. 1979. *Orientalism*. New York: Vintage Books.

Sarkar, Benoy Kumar. 1919. "Hindu Theory of International Relations." *The American Political Science Review* 13(3): 400–14.

Sartori, Giovanni. 1970. "Concept Misformation in Comparative Politics." *The American Political Science Review* LXIV (4): 1033–53.

Schabinger, Karl Emil. (ed.). 1987. *Nizamulmulk: Das Buch der Staatskunst. Siyasatnama*. Zürich: Manesse.

Schama, Simon. 1989. *Citizens: A Chronicle of the French Revolution*. London: Penguin

Scharfe, Hartmut. 1968. *Untersuchungen zur Staatsrechtslehre des Kautalya*. Wiesbaden: Harrassowitz.

Scheuerman, William E. 2009. *Hans Morgenthau – Realism and Beyond*. Cambridge, UK: Polity Press.

Schieder, Siegfried, and Manuela Spindler (eds). 2006. *Theorien der Internationalen Beziehungen*. Opladen: Budrich/UTB.

Schlinghoff, Dieter. 1969. *Die altindische Stadt*. Wiesbaden: Franz Steiner.

Schluchter, Wolfgang (ed.) 1984. *Max Webers Studie über Hinduismus und Buddhismus*. Frankfurt am Main: Suhrkamp.

Schmidt-Glintzer, Helwig (ed.) 1996). "Max Weber, Die Wirtschaftsethik der Weltreligionen: Hinduismus und Buddhismus 1916 – 1920." In *Max Weber Gesamtausgabe*, Abt. 1, Bd. 20. Tübingen: Mohr.

Schnur, Roman (ed.). 1975. *Staatsräson: Studien zur Geschichte eines politischen Begriffs*. Berlin: Duncker & Humblot.

Schörnig, Niklas. 2006. "Neorealismus." In *Theorien der Internationalen Beziehungen*, ed. Schieder and Spindler, 65–92.

Schöttli, Jivanta (2012): *Vision and Strategy in Indian Politics: Jawaharlal Nehru's Policy Choices and the Designing of Political Institutions*. Milton Park/Abingdon: Routledge.

Schumpeter, Joseph. 2008/1939. *Konjunkturzyklen – Eine theoretische, historische und statistische Analyse des kapitalistischen Prozesses*. Göttingen: Vandenhoeck & Ruprecht.

Schwalm, Hansjörg. 1986. *Die Rolle des indischen Kriegswesens vor und während der Herrschaft Chandraguptas und seines Ministers Kautalya*. Osnabrück: Biblio-Verlag.

Shah, K.J. 2010. "Of Artha and the Arthashastra." In *Comparative Political Theory: An Introduction*, Fred R. Dallmayr, 117–28. New York: Palgrave Macmillan.

Shahi, Deepshika. 2015. "Arthashastra Beyond Realpolitik: The 'Eclectic' Face of Kautilya." In *Indigenous Historical Knowledge – Kautilya and his Vocabulary I*, ed. Gautam et al., 63–79.

Sharma, Ram Sharan. 1968. *Aspects of Political Ideas and Institutions in Ancient India*. Delhi: Motilal Banarsidass.

Shoham, Dany, and Michael Liebig. 2016. "The Intelligence Dimension of Kautilyan Statecraft and Its Implications for the Present." *Journal of Intelligence History (Taylor & Francis)* 15(2): 119–38.

Sidhu, W. P. Singh. 1996. "Of Oral Traditions and Ethnocentric Judgments." In *Securing India: Strategic Thought and Practice*, Kanti P. Bajpai and Amitabh Mattoo, 174–212.

Sil, Narasingha P. 1989. *Kautilya's Arthashastra: A Comparative Study*. New York: Peter Lang.

Sills, D. L. (ed.). 1968. *Encyclopedia of Social Sciences*. New York: Macmillan.

Singh, Jaswant. 1999. *Defending India*. Delhi: Macmillan India.

Singh, Upinder. 2010. "Politics, Violence and War in Kamadaka's Nitisara." *The Indian Economic and Social History Review* 47(1): 29–62.

Singh, Manjeet Pardesi. 2005. "Deducing India's Grand Strategy of Regional Hegemony from Historical and Conceptual Perspectives." (RSIS Working Paper, No. 76). Singapore: Nanyang Technological University.

Sinha, M.K. 2005. "Hinduism and International Humanitarian Law." *International Journal of the Red Cross* 37 (858): 285–94.

Spellman, John W. 1964. *Political Theory of Ancient India. A Study of Kingship from the Earliest Times to Circa A. D. 300*. Oxford: Clarendon Press.

Staatslexikon. *Recht, Wirtschaft, Gesellschaft*. (1957–1970). 11 volumes. Freiburg im Breisgau: Herder.

Stein, Otto. 1921. *Megasthenes und Kautilya*. Wien: Akademie der Wissenschaften in Wien. http://archive.org/stream/megasthenesundka00steiuoft#page/n3/mode/2up (retrieved: Sept. 2, 2013)

Stepan, Alfred. 2008. "Comparative Theory and Political Practice: Do We Need a 'State-nation' Model As Well As A 'Nation-State' Model?" *Government and Opposition* 43(1): 1–25.

Stepan, Alfred, Juan Linz, and Yogendra Yadav. 2011. *Crafting the State-nations— India and Other Multinational Democracies*. Baltimore: Johns Hopkins Press.

Stephens, David. 2009. *Qualitative Research in International Settings*. London: Routledge.

Stockhammer, P. W. (ed.). 2012. *Conceptualizing Cultural Hybridization: A Transdisciplinary Approach*. Heidelberg: Springer.

Subrahmanyam, K., and Inder Malhotra. 2005. *Shedding Shibboleths: India's*

Evolving Strategic Outlook. Delhi: Wordsmiths.
Tagore, Rabindranath. 2004/1917. *My Reminiscences.* Whitefish, USA: Kessinger.
Tanham, George K. 1992. *Indian Strategic Thought: An Interpretive Essay.* Santa Monica, CA: Rand Corporation. www.rand.org/pubs/reports/2007/R4207.pdf (retrieved: May 27, 2012)
Thapar, Romila. 2000. *History and Beyond.* Delhi: Oxford University Press India.
Tharoor, Shashi. 2006. *Die Erfindung Indiens. Das Leben des Pandit Nehru.* Frankfurt am Main-Leipzig: Insel.
———. 2005. *Eine kleine Geschichte Indiens.* Frankfurt am Main: Suhrkamp (Bundeszentrale für politische Bildung, Schriftenreihe 510).
Tillotson, Giles. 2008. *Taj Mahal.* London: Profile Books.
Tilly, Charles. 1964. *The Vendee.* Cambridge, MA: Harvard University Press.
The Hindu. 2012. "From Kautilya to Shakespeare: Budget Gets Modern on Quotes." *The Hindu* (March 12). http://www.thehindu.com/news/national/from-kautilya-to-shakespeare-budget-gets-modern-on-quotes/article3002355.ece (retrieved: July 20, 2013)
Trautmann, Thomas. 2012. *Arthashastra: The Science of Wealth.* Gurgaon: Penguin.
———. 1971. *Kautilya and the Arthasastra—A Statistical Investigation of the Authorship and Evolution of the Text.* Leiden: Brill.
Todorov, Tzvetan. 2010. *Die Angst vor den Barbaren. Kulturelle Vielfalt statt Kampf der Kulturen.* Hamburg: Verlag des Hamburger Instituts für Sozialforschung.
Tripathi, R. 1999/1942. *History of Ancient India.* Delhi: Motilal Banarsidass Publishers.
Trivedi, S. D. 1984. *Secret Services in Ancient India: Techniques and Operation.* Delhi: Allied Publishers.
Ulbert, Cornelia. 2006. "Sozialkonstruktivismus." In *Theorien der Internationalen Beziehungen,* ed. Schieder and Spindler, 409–49.
van Creveld, Martin. 1999. *The Rise and Decline of the State.* Cambridge, UK: Cambridge University Press.
Venkatshamy, Krishnappa and George Princy (eds). 2012. *Grand Strategy for India 2020 and Beyond.* Delhi: Institute of Defence Studies and Analyses. http://www.idsa.in/system/files/book_GrantStrategyIndia.pdf (retrieved: Sept. 2, 2013).
Vivekanandan, Jayashree. 2011. *Interrogating International Relations.* Delhi/London: Routledge.
Voegelin, Eric. 1990/1971. "Equivalences of Experience and Symbolization in

History." In *The Collected Works of Eric Voegelin*. Vol. 12, 115–33. Baton Rouge: Louisiana State University Press.

Voigt, Rüdiger, and Ulrich Weiß (eds). 2010. *Handbuch Staatsdenker*. Stuttgart: Steiner.

von Bülow, Andreas. 1998. *Im Namen des Staates. CIA, BND und die kriminellen Machenschaften der Geheimdienste*. München: Piper.

Voskressenski, Alexei D. 2017. *Is Non-Western Democracy Possible: A Russian Perspective*. Singapore: World Scientific.

Wachendorfer-Schmidt, Ute (ed.). 2010. *Federalism and Political Performance*. London: Routledge.

Wagner, Christian. 2009. "Führungsmacht Indien: Ein unbequemer Partner." In *Neue Führungsmächte: Partner deutscher Außenpolitik?*, ed. Husar et al., 68–82.

———. 2005. *Die „verhinderte" Großmacht? Die Auenpolitik der Indischen Union 1947-1998*. Baden-Baden: Nomos.

Watson, Adam. 1992. *The Evolution of International Society: A Comparative Historical Analysis*. London: Routledge.

Weber, Max. 2012. *Collected Methodological Writings*, trans. Hans Henrik Bruun. London: Routledge.

———. 2008a. *Religion und Gesellschaft. Gesammelte Aufsätze zur Religionssoziologie*. Frankfurt am Main: zweitausendeins.

———. 2008b. *Max Weber's Complete Writings on Academic and Political Vocation*. New York: Algora Publishing.

———. 2000. *The Religion of India – The Sociology of Hinduism and Buddhism*, trans. Hans H. Gerth and Don Martindale. Delhi: Munshiram Manoharlal Publishers.

———. 1994. *Political Writings*, ed. Peter Lassman. Cambridge: Cambridge University Press.

———. 1988a. *Gesammelte Aufsätze zur Wissenschaftslehre*. Tübingen: Mohr/UTB.

———. 1988b. *Gesammelte Politische Schriften*. Tübingen: Mohr/UTB.

———. 1972. *Basic Concepts of Sociology*. Secaucus NJ: Citatdel Press.

———. 1968. *Economy and Society—An Outline of Interpretive Sociology*, ed. Guenter Roth. Vol. I–III. New York: Bedminster Press.

———. 1956. *Wirtschaft und Gesellschaft*. 2 Volumes. Köln: Kiepenheuer & Witsch.

Wengraf, Tom. 2001. *Qualitative Research Interviewing*. Los Angeles-Delhi: Sage.

Werner, Michael, and Benedicte Zimmermann. 2006. "Beyond Comparison: Histoire Croisée and the Challenge of Reflexivity." *History and Theory* 45: 30–50.

Wilhelm, Friedrich. 2009. "Königsindisch – eine Variante im großen Spiel der

Geheimdienste." In *Geheimdienste in der Weltgeschichte*, ed. Krieger, 70–85.
Wittgenstein, L. 2001/1953. *Philosophical Investigations*. Oxford: Blackwell Publishing.
Wittfogel, Karl. 1957. *Oriental Despotism: A Comparative Study of Total Power*. New Haven: Yale University Press.
Witzel, Michael. 2010. *Das alte Indien*. München: Beck.
Witzens, Udo. 2002. "Kritik der Thesen Karl A. Wittvogels über den ‚hydraulischen Despotismus' mit besonderer Berücksichtung des historischen singhalesischen Theravada-Buddhismus." Dissertation. Universität Heidelberg, http://archiv.ub.uni-heidelberg.de/volltextserver/1937/ (retrieved: Sept. 29, .2013)
Zakaria, Fareed. 2009. *Der Aufstieg der Anderen: Das postamerikanische Zeitalter*. München: Siedler/Random House.
Zaman, Rashed Uz. 2009. "A 'Cultural' Understanding of War." *Comparative Strategy* 28(1): 68–88.
———. 2006. "Kautilya: The Indian Strategic Thinker and Indian Strategic Culture." *Comparative Strategy* 25 (3): 231–47.
Zimmer, Heinrich. 2011/1951. *Philosophies of India*. Delhi: Motilal Banarsidass
———. 1973. *Philosophie und Religion Indiens*. Frankfurt am Main: Suhrkamp.

INDEX OF NAMES

Abdullah, Sheikh, 225
Abu al Fazl (Abdul Fazal), 365
Adorno, Theodor W., 479
Akbar, 182, 186, 189, 197, 351, 355, 365, 469
Albiruni, 181
Alexander the Great, 6, 112, 180, 202
Allert, Tilman, 155
Almond, Gabriel, 296
Ambedkar, B. R., 192, 276, 287, 374
Anand, Vinod, 213, 252
Aquinas, Thomas, 347
Archarya, Amitav, 347, 367
Aristotle, 6, 20, 40, 195, 196, 389, 435
Ashoka, 6, 25, 28, 167, 168, 178, 179, 182, 185, 186, 189, 190, 197, 212, 216, 226, 228, 229, 230, 231, 253, 287, 295, 306, 309, 311, 321, 323, 327, 328, 350, 351, 425, 469
Asvaghosa, 11
Auboyer, Jeannine, 418
Aung San, 367
Azad, Maulana, 367, 383

Baba, Noor Achmad, 244
Badrinath, Chaturvedi, 475
Bajpai, Kanti, 223, 271, 314, 327, 333, 337, 364, 382, 465, 468
Balraj, Krishna, 233, 234, 235
Bandaranaike, S., 503
Banerji, Rana, 227
Barlösius, Eva, 258
Barni (Barani), 365
Batabyal, Rakesh, 491, 492, 494

Behera, Navnita Chadha, 346, 347, 366, 367, 378, 392
Behnke, Joachim, 154, 155
Berger, Peter L., 472
Berg-Schlosser, Dirk, 297
Bhabha, Homi, 218, 219, 220, 319
Bhargava, Rajeev, 168, 352, 468, 470
Bhishma, 327, 328
Bisht, Medha, 391
Bodin, Jean, 103, 195
Boesche, Roger, 17, 142, 147, 373, 391, 392
Bogner, Alexander, 154
Bond, G. C., 348
Booth, Ben, 299, 300
Bose, Subhas Chandra, 233
Botero, Giovanni, 117
Bourdieu, Pierre, 157, 243, 254, 255, 256, 257, 258, 259, 260, 261, 272, 273, 289, 290, 303, 348, 394, 410, 467
Bozeman, Adda B., 19, 20, 149, 184, 267, 397, 398, 409, 410, 412
Bragta, Sanjay, 251
Braudel, Fernand, 157, 158, 159, 160, 161, 173, 181, 254
Brihaspati, 45, 364
Buddha, 185, 186, 197, 226, 230, 231, 253, 287, 295, 311, 321, 323, 365, 366, 396
Bülow, Andreas von, 478
Bush, George, 274
Buzan, Barry, 336, 367, 368

Carr, E. H., 136, 146, 147, 148, 149
Castro Verela, Maria do Mar, 357
Chakravarti, Ranabir, 193, 194, 217
Chakravarty, N., 193
Chandragupta Maurya, 7, 35, 113, 178, 189, 198, 200, 202, 231, 240, 253, 269, 306, 309, 312, 321
Chandramohan, P., 215
Chandrasekaran, Pravin, 388, 389
Charles V, xxv, 476
Chatterjee, Partha, 358, 359, 361
Chhina, Rana, 164, 186, 466
Chiefale, N., 10
Chitra, Amar, 240
Churchill, Winston, 213
Clausewitz, Carl von, 94, 203, 273, 274, 303, 368, 386
Collier, David, 503–4
Confucius, 147, 367
Coupland, Reginald, 502
Creveld, Martin van, 5, 80
Cripps, Sir Stafford, 213, 214
Croissant, Aurel, 398
Curzon, G. N., 419

Dabla, B.A., 490
Dalton, Russell J., 500
Dandin, 11
Danton, Georges, 398
Derrett, J. Duncan M., 498, 501
Dhana Nanda, 232
Dhavan, Nikita, 357
Diamond, Larry, 399, 435
Dixit, J. N., 147, 196, 230, 253, 272, 320, 321, 322, 329, 410
Douglas, Mary, 499
Doval, Ajit, 169, 176, 183, 190, 253, 291, 292
Drekmeier, Charles, 4, 8, 19, 24, 25, 80, 112, 113, 119, 122, 124, 125, 134, 136, 137, 147, 148, 183, 193
Durkheim, Emile, 258
Dutta, Sujit, 194, 327

Edwardes, Michael, 418
Elias, Norbert, 503
Engelmeier, Tobias, 176, 294, 340, 349, 350, 351, 353
Erasmus of Rotterdam, 476

Fabian, K.P., 206, 226, 378
Firdausi, 198
Fischer, Alexander, 430
Fludernik, Monika, 414, 415
Foucault, Michel, 333, 357, 374
France, Anatole, 198
Frankel, Benjamin, xxv, 480
Frei, Christoph, 477, 478
Frey, Sandra, xxv
Fritze, Ludwig, 11, 268
Fürstenberg, Kai, 399

Gadamer, Georg, 14
Gallie, W.B., 504
Gandhi, Indira, 199, 228, 464
Gandhi, Mohandas K. (Mahatma Gandhi), 395, 396, 399, 414, 421, 422, 433, 434, 429
  ahimsa principle, 233
  political realism, 234
  strategy of non-violent resistance, 232
Gandhi, Rajiv, 431, 464
Garbe, Richard, 17, 47
Gautam, P. K., 132, 191, 231, 244, 252, 253, 331, 369, 377, 378, 383, 392
Geiger, Theodor, 289
Gerth, Hans H., 24
Ghose, Aurobindo, 360, 365
Ghosh, Partha, 234, 333
Ghosh, Ramachandra, 10
Gilliam Angela, 348
Giri, V. V., 234
Girtler, Roland, 154, 155, 156
Glaser, Barney, 481
Glassenapp, Helmuth von, 19, 21, 102, 139, 141, 264, 479, 496
Glenn, John, 309, 346

Goethe, Johann Wolfgang, 182, 392
Gorgias, 146, 348
Goswami, Namrata, 189, 218, 273, 274, 293, 308, 322, 329
Gould, Stephen J., 499
Gowalkar, M. S., 339
Gramsci, Antonio, 356, 357
Griffith, Ernest S., 504
Gupta, Arvind, 378, 379, 387

Halbfass, Wilhelm, 15, 20, 21
Halbwachs, Maurice, 410
Hartmann, Nicolai, 479
Haushofer, Karl, 209
Hees, Peter, 360
Hegel, G. F. W., 496, 505
Hegewald, Julia, 415, 433
Heimann, Betty, 44, 163, 265
Henrich, Dieter, 16
Hillebrandt, Alfred, 17, 74, 91, 126, 127, 132, 147, 264, 265, 267
Hobbes, Thomas, 103, 137, 195, 345, 347, 367, 374
Howlett, Darryl, 299, 300, 303
Humboldt, Wilhelm von, 171
Huntington, Samuel, 299
Husserl, Edmund, 479

Inden, Ronald, 357
Iqbal, Muhammad, 366

Jackson, Peter, 257
Jayaswal, K. P., 4, 79, 84
Jepperson, R. I., 297
Jeremiah, 103
Jinnah, M.A., 503
Johnson, Thomas J.
Johnson-Bagby, Laurie M., 480
Johnston, Alastair Iain, 157, 299
Jolly, J., 5, 17
Jones, Rodney W., 307, 308

Kalidasa, 11
Kalyanaraman, S., 219, 381, 391

Kamandaka, 11, 185
Kangle, R.P., 4, 5, 6, 7, 11, 17, 18, 19, 56, 58, 74, 133, 243, 382, 384, 388, 401, 403
Kant, Immanuel, 367, 374
Kantowsky, Detlef, 23
Karnad, Bharat, 147, 148, 149, 220, 221, 267, 317, 318, 319, 320, 465
Katzenstein, Peter J., 297, 353
Kedourie, Eli, 294
Keith, A.B., 5
Keyserling, Alexander Graf, 198
Khanna, V. N., 322, 323
Khilnani, Sunil, 494
Khrushchev, Nikita, 221
Kim, Marcus, 220, 309, 310, 311, 313, 317
Kinzinger, Annkatrin, 491
Kissinger, Henry, 463
Kosambi, D.D., 344
Kovac, Mitar, 270
Krishna, 172, 227, 234, 328, 421
Kubálková, Vendulka, 348
Kuckartz, Udo, 481
Kulke, Hermann, 6, 35, 167, 174
Kumar, Awnanish, 497
Kumar, Rajiv, 4194
Kumar, Tarun, 497
Kumarasingham, Harshan, 505

Lange, Klaus, 494
Langlois-Berthelot, Jean, 383
Levitsky, Steven, 504
Lewis, Orion, 499
Liddell Hart, B.H., 270
Liebig, Michael, 392
Lijphart, Arendt, 436
Lindberg, Steffan, 504
Lipset, Seymour Martin, 447, 504
Locke, John, 374
Lohia, R.M., 365
Loomba, Ania, 357
Luckmann, Thomas, 472

Macaulay, T.B., 183, 334
Machiavelli, Niccolo, 20, 33, 34, 100,
    101, 111, 113, 116, 117, 125, 132,
    134, 135, 141, 146, 147, 148, 149,
    195, 196, 203, 207, 244, 276, 286,
    287, 308, 317, 321, 322, 333, 345,
    347, 367, 368, 370, 371, 379, 389,
    469, 470
Mackinder, Halford, 209
Macmillan, Alan, 299
Maddison, Angus, xix
Mahan, Alfred Thayer, 273, 274
Mahavira, 364
Mahon, James E., 503–4
Malhotra, I., 177, 306, 307, 336
Mallavarapu, Siddharth, 271, 333, 336,
    337, 344, 364, 366, 371
Maneoseur, E., 10
Mannheim, Karl, 333
Manu, 12, 136, 137, 169, 185, 316,
    323, 364, 366, 371, 372, 403
Mao Tse-Tung, 302, 367
Marcek, Jan, 270
Martindale, Don, 24
Marx, Karl, 99, 341, 342, 343
Mattoo, Amitabh, 304
Mayawati, 453
Mazumdar, P.C., 169
Megasthenes, 7, 8, 88
Mehta, Pratap Bhanu, 494, 495
Mehta, V.R., 169, 334, 364
Meinecke, Friedrich, 116, 118, 119,
    120, 123, 124, 125, 126, 135, 175
Menon, K.P.S., 312, 495
Menon, Krishna, 227
Menon, Prakesh, 494
Menon, Shivshankar, 253, 276, 292,
    324, 327, 329, 379, 389, 466
Merkel, Wolfgang, 398
Metcalf, Thomas R., 419, 434
Meyer, Johann Jakob, 4, 5, 17, 18, 19,
    45, 56, 58, 71, 74, 133
Michael, Arndt, 24, 210, 212, 271, 323,
    324, 392

Mitra, Subrata, xiv, 467
    re-use of the past, xxv, 467
    hybridity: the Indian state, 399–400
    hybridity and comparative politics,
        398–9, 414, 416, 435, 437–8, 440,
        445
    hybridization as anti-colonial
        strategy, 224, 414
Modelski, George, 472
Modi, Narendra, 235, 464
Mohan, C. Raja, 220, 224, 325, 391
Morgenthau, Hans J., 101, 110, 111,
    115, 120, 126, 132, 135, 141, 143,
    149, 344
Morris-Jones, W. H., 415, 416, 427
Mukherjee, Pranab, 250, 251
Müller, Harald, 297
Müller, Max, 360
Mullik, B.N., 209
Mumtaz Mahal, 501
Münkler, Herfried, 116, 117
Mylius, Klaus, 41

Nair, Vijai, xv
Nambiar, Satish, 269, 305, 335
Nanda, Meera, 357, 359, 361
Nandy Ashis, 397, 420
Narlikar, Amrita, 368
Narlikar, Aruna, 368
Naroji, Dadabhai, 367
Nehru, Jawaharlal, 153, 162, 197, 224,
    270, 312, 326, 331, 359, 365, 371,
    411, 413, 426, 432
    as a 'crypto-communist, 221
    commitment to Panchsheel, 224
    economic policy, 217
    foreign policy, 221, 223
    intellectual engagement, 197–200
    'Nehruvianism', 228–31, 287, 315,
        324, 327
    non-alignment policy, 222, 267
    nuclear policy, 220
    perception as 'idealist', 225–8
    perception as 'realist', 228–31

political idealist, 225-8
references to Kautilya 1930-44,
    197-200
references to Kautilya 1947-64,
    215-220
references to Kautilya in *The
    Discovery of India*, 200-7
Nilekani, Nandan, 494
Nixon, Richard, 463
Nizam ul-Mulk, xxvii, 480
North, Douglass, 438

Olivelle, Patrick, 5, 18, 388

Panikkar, K.M., 179, 180, 201, 249,
    250, 409, 433
Panini, 41
Pant, Harsh V., 316
Pardesi, M.S., 223
Parekh, Bhikhu, 421
Parmar, Aradhana, 5, 332
Patel, Sardar V., 197, 231, 232, 234,
    235, 295, 367, 395, 414, 433
Pillai, R., 239, 239, 369
Plato, 20, 32, 103, 126, 146, 147, 195,
    196, 389, 435
Plessner, Helmuth, 19, 21, 102, 139,
    140, 141, 158
Pollock, Sheldon, 337
Poore, Stuart, 298
Powell, G. Bingham, 500
Pradhan, S.D., 238
Prakash, Gyan, 356, 359
Prasad, Jayant, 274, 275, 433
Protagoras, 146, 348
Putnam, Robert D., 452
Pye, Lucian, 296, 297
Pythagoras, 32

Radhakrishnan, S., 198
Raghavan, Srinath, 174, 196, 214, 216,
    218, 219, 220, 224, 229, 330
Rajagopalan, Rajesh, 244, 276
Ramachandran, K.N., 377

Ramesh, Jairam, 238
Rana, Krishnan S., 332
Rangarajan, R.N., 4, 7, 9, 18
Reichwein, Alexander, 479
Ritschl, Eva, 85
Rizal, Jose, 367
Robespierre, Maximilien de, 398
Rohatgi, Manila, 477
Rösel, Jakob, 361
Rothermund, Dietmar, 6, 35, 40, 41,
    165, 167, 174, 196, 197, 214, 242,
    334, 341
Roy, G.J., 115, 132
Roy, M.N., 169
Rudolph, Lloyd, 195, 295, 436, 499
Rudolph, Susanne Hoeber, 179, 295,
    436, 499

Sabine, George, 502
Sachau, Edward C., 181
Sahu, Balbhadra, 365
Said, Edward, 356
Salazar Antonio, 227
Saran, Shyam, 494
Sarkar, Benoy Kumar, 147, 344
Sartori, Giovanni, 504
Savarkar, V. D., 339
Schabinger, K.E., 480
Schaffer, Simon, 348
Schama, Simon, 499
Scharfe, Hartmut, 4, 5, 11, 58, 82, 407
Scheler, Max, 479
Scheuerman, William, 479
Schliemann, Heinrich, 9
Schlinghoff, Dieter, 88-9
Schoettli, Jivanta, xxi
Schörnig, Niklas, 346
Schumpeter, Joseph A., 482
Schwalm, Hansjörg, 93, 94
Seleucus Nicator, 7
Shah Jahan, 501
Shah, K.J., 431
Shahi, Deepshikha, 348, 372, 373, 374,
    375, 376, 383, 392

Shakespeare, William, 198
Shamashastry, R., 4, 9–10, 17, 244
Sharma, Ram Sharan, 74–5, 472
Sharma, S.K., 494
Sharma, Vishnu, 391
Shastri, Lal Bahadur, 228, 464
Shenzong, 302
Shoham, Dany, 57
Sidhu, W.P. Singh, 142, 305, 306
Sil, N.P., 17, 20, 134, 147
Simmel, Georg, 156
Singh, Jaswant, 177, 228, 324, 326
Singh, Mohinder, 343, 370, 371, 372
Singh, Upinder, 11
Sircar, Jawhar, 174, 252
Somadeva, 365
Spivak, Gayatri, 356
Spykman, N.J., 209
Srivastava, Jayati, 497
Stalin, Joseph V., 221
Stein, Otto, 7
Schliemann, Heinrich, 9
Steinmo, Sven, 499
Stepan, Alfred, 504
Strauss, Anselm, 481
Strom, Kaare, 500
Subrahmanyam, K., 177, 306, 307, 315, 327, 328, 329, 336, 377, 378
Sukarno, 367
Sun-Tzu, xxvii, 57, 143, 146, 147, 157, 196, 302, 379, 468, 480
Surya, 364

Tagore, Rabindranath, 186, 197, 270, 276, 287, 363, 365, 367, 374, 469
Tanham, George, 304, 305, 306, 307, 318, 327, 329, 378
Tank, Kurt, 218
Thapar, Romila, 11–12, 340, 473, 475, 496
Tharoor, S., 197
Thompson, Edward, 200
Thucydides, xxvii, 34, 146, 195, 303, 345, 347, 367, 472

Tilak, Bal Gangadhar, 363, 421
Tillotson, Giles, 502
Tilly, Charles, 503
Todorov, Tzvetan, 159
Toennies, Ferdinand, 499
Trautmann, T.R., 5, 403, 404
Trivedi, S.D., 477
Trotsky, Leon, 198
Trood, Russell, 299

Ulbert, Cornelia, 348

Vajpayee, Atal Bihari, 324, 464
Valmiki, 169, 170, 364, 366
Varadarajan, Siddharth, 494
Varma, V. P., 169
Vatsyayana, 11
Venkatshamy, Krishnappa, 229
Verba, Sidney, 296
Vishakhadatta, 11, 267, 268
Visvanathan, H.H.S., 391
Vivekanandan, Jayashree, 352, 353, 354, 355, 359, 373
Voegelin, Eric, 19, 103
Voskressenski, Alexei, 458, 460
Vyasa, 5, 169, 170, 364

Waltz, Kenneth, 274, 345, 346, 352
Watson, Adam, 17, 110, 111, 113, 147
Weber, Max, 13, 14, 15, 16, 17, 20, 23, 24, 25, 26, 27, 28, 29, 30, 31, 32, 33, 34, 35, 36, 37, 126, 127, 140, 141, 142, 144, 145, 147, 155, 156, 167, 170, 171, 172, 174, 255, 258, 264, 281, 297, 343, 401, 405
  cameralism, 29–30
  ideal-type, 24
  sociology of religion studies on Hinduism and Buddhism, 23–24
  political sociology, 25–27
  patrimonial state in India, 27–30
  'Machiavellianism' in ancient India, 33–37
Wendt, Alexander, 297, 374, 375

Wengraf, Tom, 154
Werner, Michael, 502
Wilhelm, Friedrich, 15, 21, 171
Windelband, Wilhelm, 479
Winternitz, M., 5
Wittgenstein, Ludwig, 102
Witzel, Michael, 24
Witzens, Udo, 485

Yadav, Laloo Prasad, 433

Zaman, Rashed uz, 207, 208, 297, 311, 312, 313, 410
Zimmer, Heinrich, 3, 4, 5, 17, 131, 138, 147
Zimmermann, Benedicte, 502

INDEX OF SUBJECTS

Absolutist monarchy, 77
Adivasis, 130, 407
Advisers and ministers, 54–55
Advisers and ministers, Qualification and deliberation, 55–56
Ahimsa, 189, 210, 233, 294, 310–11, 324
  doctrine of, 210
Amatya, 54, 74–75, 101–2, 106
Amoral political realist, 373
Amoral political realist, 373–4
Anarchy, 27
Anglo-American influence in Indian universities, 333–7
Anglo-French-Israeli attack, 222
Anti-colonial movements, 414
Arabic numerals, 149
Armed Forces Act, 436
Artha, 3, 46, 53, 133, 390, 412
Arthashastra,
  Ideal ruler in, 45–74
Asana, 104, 109, 319
Ashrama, 49
Asiatic despotism, 54, 188, 402
Asiatic mode of production, 78, 341, 343
Authoritarian emergency, 436

Balance of power, 114–15, 121, 132, 143, 209, 344–5, 403
Balkanization, 455
Bangladesh, 311–13, 328, 386, 389, 463
Bar-room politics, tradition of, 289
Basic orders of battle, 93
Bhagavad Gita, 171–2, 177, 247, 316, 418

Bharat, 148, 220, 247, 265, 267, 290, 317, 403, 425, 465
Bharatiya Janata Party, 324, 454
Bheda, 127, 129–30, 132, 234, 249–50, 307, 361, 390
Bipolar rivalry, 211
Bounded rationality, 440
Brahmanism, 31, 36
Brahmins, 31–2, 33, 51, 174, 181, 361, 407, 412
Breach of treaty, 96, 124
British Raj, 179, 183, 304–5, 409
Buddhism, 17, 23–24, 166–7, 230, 310–11, 317, 326, 391, 418
Bureaucratic modernity, 425

Cameralism, 29–30
Capital city, 60, 74–6, 81, 85, 87–9, 99, 101, 206, 402, 407–8
Capitalist free market, 345
Caste associations, 399
Caste order, 31–2, 48–9, 130, 407
Caste status, relativization of, 187, 190
Caste system, 30–2, 48, 130, 174, 188, 191, 405, 450
Centralization and autonomous spaces, 405–6
Centralized planning, 428
Chakravartin, 112–13, 311
Chanakya, 4, 7, 10, 29, 191, 196, 198–204, 207, 209, 215, 234–5, 237–41, 253, 270, 306–7, 321, 332, 377, 382, 384, 465
China's war of aggression, 463
China-India border war, 223, 294
Civil rights movements, 450

Civil war, 412
Classic warfare, sense of, 94
Coercive state power (Kautilya), 50, 53–4
Collective memory, 178, 180, 253, 260, 410–11, 440
Colonial program of education, 334
Colonialism (British), 211, 291, 336, 343
Combined arms, principle of, 93
Comparative Political Theory, 13
Comparative politics, 398–9, 414, 416, 435, 437–8, 440, 445
Concept of strategic culture
   academic discourse on Indian strategic culture, 308–24
   definitions of, 300
   empirical analysis, 300
   key features, 301
   political discourse, 324–30
Conceptual stretching, 438, 440
Congress (Indian National Congress), 199, 421–2, 426, 451, 456
Congress System, 426–7
Constitution of India, 216, 424, 455–56
Context-relevant modernity, 409
Contract theory, 137
Corporal punishment, 84, 90, 130, 406
Correlation of forces, 106–9, 120, 234
Corruption, 57, 83, 91, 130, 188–9, 205, 243, 285, 293, 406–7
Counter-factual democracy, 449
Countervailing forces, 454
Covariance (Helmut Plessner), 19–20, 103, 149, 474
Cuban Missile Crisis, 223
Cultural continuity, 11, 155–65, 170, 175, 180, 349, 352, 354–5
   in India, 161–4
Cultural nation (Meinecke), 175–6
Cultural revolution, 183
Cultural space, 178–80
Cultural/conceptual flow, 418, 421, 437, 440, 445

Dalits, 130, 192, 407, 453–4, 476
Dana, 127–30, 132, 234, 249, 390
Danda, 74–5, 98–9, 101–2, 106, 127, 130–2, 234, 249, 307, 390, 402
Defence Services Staff College, 332
Deliberation (strategic planning), 64–5, 92
Democracy, 216–17, 282, 328, 396, 398–9, 412, 417, 424, 435–7, 439, 444–54, 456, 458–60, 469
   Indian democracy, xxv, xviii, 282, 412, 448–9
Democratic governance, 413–14
Devaswam, 420
Dharma, 30–1, 33, 35–6, 46, 48–9, 53, 93, 124, 133, 172, 188, 310, 390, 402–3, 407, 412
Dharmashastras, 3, 51
Diplomacy, 3, 38–9, 66–7, 78, 102, 104, 109, 128, 130, 198, 222, 249–50, 268, 325, 353, 380, 389, 463
Directive Principles of state policy, 429
Discursive cognition, methodology of, 155
Discursive presence in contemporary India, 245–9
Diversity, 165–9, 173–4, 177, 189, 382, 396–7, 405, 429, 431, 435–7, 455
Divide and quit, policy, 462
Division of labour, 364, 468
Durbar, 419–20
Durga, 74–5, 101–2, 106, 407
Dvaidhibhava, 104, 109–10

Early feudalism, 344
Economic development, 283–5
Economic nationalism, policy of, 427
Economy, 3, 7, 20, 29, 49–50, 79, 90–91, 94, 187, 190, 193–4, 204–5, 217–18, 227, 243, 283–4, 344, 373, 396–7, 404–5, 418, 427–8, 432, 451, 453–5, 463, 465
Election Commission, 450, 452
Electoral democracy, 435–6

Electoral mobilization, 452–4
Emergency (1975–77), 450–451
Endogenous modernity, 414, 417
Endogenous politico-cultural
    resources, 154, 184–96, 248, 254,
    309, 337, 349, 356, 359, 363–70,
    373, 439, 467, 469
Enlightenment, 162, 190, 358
Entangled history, 440
Entertainment industry, 83, 88, 90, 404
Etatist dirigisme, 205, 217
Ethical nihilism, 126
European cultures, 162
European supremacy, 184, 397
Expansionism, 112, 402–3
Expert interviews, 154–6, 162, 165–6,
    168–70, 173, 176, 181, 185–90,
    192, 195, 197, 201, 212, 225,
    229, 253, 263, 265, 267–8, 270–1,
    286, 289, 307–8, 322, 327, 329,
    331–33, 335–6, 338–9, 343–4,
    352, 369, 462, 466, 469
Extra-judicial killings, 124

Fabian socialism, 206
Federal system (in India), 429
Federalism, 429–30, 459–60
Finance Commission, 456
Financial penalties, 90
First-past-the-post voting system, 426
Fiscal policy, 89
Fiscal resource, 88
Foreign Policy, 104, 253, 320, 322
  correlation of forces, 105–10
  instruments, 108–10
  mandala scheme, 113–15
  righteous, 190
  strategic goals of, 110–13
  understanding of 'idealism', 210
  subversion of, 63–4
Foucauldian knowledge-power paradigm, 374
Freedom Movement, 428, 451

Gana, 403
Gandhism, 358
Geo-cultural space, 112, 172–8, 180, 402
  Indian subcontinent, 172–8
German Institute for International and Security Affairs (SWP), 376
Global North, 467–8
Global South, 184, 299, 357, 468–70
Good governance, policy of, 78
Government of India Act, 1935, 424–5
Greco-Persian states, 403
Gram panchayats, 399
Grand strategy, 187, 270, 273, 276–9, 287, 314–15, 319
Gupta Empire, 179, 411

Habitus figure, idea-contents, 261
Hard realism, 276–9
Hard realpolitik, 188, 302
Harijans, 429
Hartal, 422
Hindu nationalism, 450
Hindu nationalism, ascendency of, 451
Hinduism, 17, 23–4, 27, 31, 166, 317, 325, 418
Hindu-Muslim riots, 448
Hindu-Muslim unity, 422
Hiroshima and Nagasaki, America's nuclear bombing, 233
Hyperrealism, 315, 327

Ideal-type, 7, 15–16, 24, 39–41, 71–2, 74, 77, 79, 87, 113, 148, 153, 204, 401, 407–8
  advantages, 16
  cultural homogeneity, 165
  intellectual construction of relations, 16
  concept, political science-based interpretation, 15
Idea-migration, 103
Ideological homogenization, 416
Ideological movements, 453

Imperialism, 112, 190, 221-2, 359
Inclusive pluralism, durability of, 170
Indian culture, 12, 155-6, 158,
    161-71, 173, 175, 178-83, 214,
    229, 247, 268, 313, 325, 336, 341,
    343, 349, 351-2, 356, 358, 416,
    422, 448, 459, 467
Indian IR theory, 345-7, 352, 364,
    366, 374, 386
Indian Military Academy, 332
Indian Personal Law, 430-31, 441
India's nuclear policy, 219-20, 228,
    396
India's role in world affairs, 224
Indigenous Historical Knowledge
    (IDSA project), 368, 378-9,
    381-4, 386
Indology (Sanskrit philology), xx,
    xxviii-ix, 10, 24, 153, 181, 331,
    359-60
Indo-Pakistani War, 463
Industrial revolution, 29
Institute for Defence Studies and
    Analyses (IDSA), 154, 253-4,
    306, 363, 369, 372, 376-2
  concept of security, 376
  Kautilya discourse 2012 at, 378-82
  Kautilya discourse 2013 at, 382-9
  Kautilya discourse 2014 at, 389-92
  objectives of the conference, 379
Institutional arrangement, 454
Intellectual evolution of Political
    Realism, 146
Intellectual gestalt, 245
Intellectual history of Political
    Realism, 145-6
Intellectual revolutions, 163
Intelligence, 3, 38-9, 56-64, 66-8, 70,
    77, 82, 87, 95, 106-7, 110, 118,
    209, 216, 219, 223-4, 228, 268,
    270, 286-7, 300, 322, 377, 382,
    384, 433
Inter-community riots, 396
Inter-community conflict, 439

Internal economic development, 78,
    284
Internal security, 61-2, 63, 204, 276,
    285-7, 293, 314, 325, 382, 384,
    403
  importance of, 285-7
International Relations theory, 13, 95,
    338, 365, 369
Inter-personal communication, 440
Inter-state relations, 35, 41, 97, 106,
    109-11, 114-15, 131, 138-9,
    143-4, 189, 224, 298, 321, 353,
    374, 380, 382
Inter-state relations, theory of, 106,
    390

Jainism, 310, 317, 418
Jamia Millia University, 237, 332, 383
Janapada, 74-5, 84, 101-2
Jati, 130
Jawaharlal Nehru University (JNU),
    270, 322, 331, 371
Journalism, 154
Journalistic time, 159
Justice system, 83-4, 406

Kapatika, 58
Kargil conflict, 293
Karman, 32-3
Kashmir, 210, 219, 225, 234, 423, 450,
    453
Kautilya in Indian life-world, 237-45
Kautilya metaphor, 242-5, 262-3, 305
Kautilyan penal code, 84
Kautilya's latent presence, 252-95
Khadi, 421
Khillat, 419
Kosa, 74-75, 101-2, 106
Kshatriya, 30-1, 33, 48, 87, 93, 172,
    405-7
Kuta-yuddha, 94

Land reclamation policy, 85
Language movements, 455

Legal system, 80, 82, 84, 404, 406, 431
Liberation movement, 176
Licence Raj
  quasi-socialist system of the, 284
  reforms of, 463
Linguistic and religious diversity, 165–8, 174
Linguistic association, 243
Lock-in (between Indian society and state), 413, 438, 450–51
Lokayata, 47, 202
Longue durée, 157–63, 248, 300, 348

Machiavellianism, 34, 36, 244
Madhyama, 114
Magadha, 6–7, 34, 232, 268, 402
Mahabharata, 5, 12, 34, 36, 48, 52, 91, 164, 169–71, 176, 185–6, 248, 263–5, 268–9, 309, 316, 321, 323, 327–8, 338, 364, 368, 379, 469
Mandala concept, 113–14, 207, 274–5, 305–6, 312, 374
Mantrin, 54, 58, 60–1, 77, 80–1, 90, 130, 407
Manu-smriti, 12, 323, 371–2
Marxist social science, 340–44
Matsya-nyaya, 50, 53, 98, 123, 136–8, 311, 324, 412
Maurya Empire, 6–8, 35, 39, 88, 178–80, 201–4, 206, 214, 216, 230, 240, 244, 268, 309, 311, 401–2, 411, 433
Media objectifications, 263
Mercantilism, 29, 195, 405
Methodological individualism, 413, 431, 450–51
Militarist adventurism, 189
Military strategy
  conceptual importance for, 94
  theoretical treatment of, 94
Mirror of Kings, 79
Mitra, 74–75, 95–97, 101–2, 114, 118
Mixed economy, 194, 284–5, 404, 425, 427–8

Modern state, quintessence of the, 401–3
Modernity of tradition, 295, 398, 436–7, 470
Modernization theory, 413
Moksha, 31, 48
Monarchy, 53–4
Montagu-Chelmsford scheme, 430
Moralpolitik, 221, 317, 465
Morley-Minto reforms, 430
Mudrarakshasa, 11, 200, 202, 208, 267–8
Multiparty system, 460
Multipolar world, 380, 464, 469–70
Muslim League, 422
Muslim women Protection of Rights on Divorce bill, 431

National Defence College, 332
National power (Morgenthau), 101–3, 121, 132,
National security, 218, 221, 227, 282–5, 314
Nationalist independence movement, 176, 294–5
Nazr, 419
Neo-institutionalism, 415, 437
Neoliberalism, 315, 327
Neorealism, 345–6
Neta, 432
Nitisara, 11, 185, 355
NonAlignment 2.0 (document), 276–88
Nonalignment policy, 313
Non-weaponized deterrence, 220
Nuclear doctrine, Ambiguity of the, 396
Nuclear tests, 320, 464

Occidental cultural space, 299
One-dominant-party system, 426, 451, 456
Ontology of the state, 424–6
Oral tradition, 9, 310
Oriental despotism, 79, 341, 458

Orientalist imagination of Eastern authority, 403

Pakistan, 166, 194, 207–8, 218–19, 221, 278–9, 293–4, 312–13, 328, 413–14, 422, 430–2, 454, 458, 462–3
Palimpsest, 162, 253, 317, 410
Palm-leaf manuscripts, discovery of, 10
Panchatantra, 12, 164, 185–6, 265–8, 319, 377, 379, 391, 469
Panchsheel, 224, 350, 462
Paradigmatic ruptures, 163
Parliamentary democracy, British-style, 217
Pataliputra, 6–8, 88–9, 206
Path dependency, 448
Patriarchalism, 27
Patrimonial state in India (Max Weber), 27–30
  Machiavellianism, 33–37
Patrimonialism, 27
Personal Law (India), 430–1, 457
Political anthropology of power, 53–4
Political anthropology, 52–3, 102, 133–41, 144–45
  basic assumptions, 138–9
  basic features, 135–6
  character traits, 133
  of Kautilya, 133–41
  of Plessner, 140
  principle of bodily boundaries, 139
  resolution of conflicts of interest, 136
Political capital, 446, 448, 451–2, 459
Political classics, 187, 195–6
Political culture, 286, 296–7, 300, 351, 412, 426, 446, 459
Political economy, 3, 187, 193–5, 344, 373, 404–5, 427–8
Political grammar (D. Rothermund), 40–41
Political habitus, 411, 462

Political idealism, 217, 225–6, 228, 326–7
Political normativity, 122–4, 126
Political realism, 101, 142–6, 149, 168, 212–13, 216, 221, 225, 227–9, 234, 250, 267, 274, 281, 292, 294–5, 317, 327–8, 344–7, 374
  early representative of, 146
  history of, 145–6
  Kautilyan idea of, 142
  Morgenthau's theory of, 101, 144, 345
Political Science, evolution of, 21, 100
Political sociology (Max Weber), 25–7
Political space, 178–80, 298, 444
Political unification of the Indian subcontinent, 111–12, 131, 190, 209, 402
Politico-administrative offices, three categories of, 81
Politico-strategic traditions, 340, 354
Politics as a Vocation (Max Weber), 17, 34, 142
Polycentric state system, 380
Popular politicizing, 288–95
Positivist social science, 339–40
Postcolonial hybridization, 417
Postcolonial theory, 356–62, 373
Postmodernism, 372–76
Post-structuralism, 373
Poverty line, 453
Power of the state, 29, 33, 35, 41, 49, 74, 76, 78, 99–100, 119, 121–24, 221, 283, 293, 402
Power politics, 34–6, 98, 115, 121–2, 132, 141, 144, 188, 209–10, 225–7, 230, 232, 293, 317–18, 344, 373, 391, 402–3, 422, 463
Power-knowledge matrix, 333, 468
Prakriti, 38, 41, 74–6, 95, 99, 101; 104–9, 112, 118–19, 123, 324, 382, 402–3
Presidential democracy, American-style, 217

Program of recovery (of endogenous resources), 363-70
Program of recovery, 363-70
Public buildings, 433-4
Purohita, 60, 71, 77, 80, 82
Purposive political rationality, duality of, 124

Quality of a state factor, 87
Quit India campaign, 214

Raison d'état, 14, 19, 116-26, 132, 142, 226, 293, 402-4
  as optimization of the state factors, 117-21
  Kautilyan idea of, 116-26, 401-3
  Meinecke's definition of raison d'état, 118
  Meinecke's theory of raison d'état, 120
  normative dimension, 121-6
  operationalization of, 118
  strategic directionality for statecraft, 120
Raj (British), 179, 183, 304-5, 409
Ramayana, 12, 34, 36, 48, 164, 170-71, 185, 248, 263, 265, 268-70, 316, 328, 338, 355, 364, 469
RAND Corporation, 304
Rational bureaucracy, 407, 432-3
Rational choice neo-institutional model of state, 437
Rational-logical design process of the ideal type, 16
Realpolitik, 94, 108, 188-89, 220-21, 227, 232, 234, 292, 302, 308, 318, 321, 346, 350, 403, 465
Resilience (of the modern Indian state), 248, 394-5, 400, 421, 437
Re-use of the past, with respect to Kautilya, 245-51, 409-11,
Royal Institute of International Affairs (RIIA), 376

Royal succession of ruler, 67-9
Ruler (king), 27, 33, 45-73, 75-80, 98, 100, 111, 122, 199, 204, 264, 310, 390, 403-4, 412
  character formation of, 52-3
  personal security of, 72-3
  scientific education, 51-2
  commitment to the material welfare of the people, 79
  first servant of the state and the people, 70-2

Saman, 127-30, 234
Sandhi, 104, 108
Samkhya, 47
Samsara, 32
Samshraya, 104
Sanskrit, Atrophy of language skills, 337-9,
Sanskritism, 338-9
Saptanga theory, 22, 38, 41, 74, 98-107, 117, 119-20, 211
Sassanid Empire, xxv
Sattrin, 59-61, 67-8
Satya, 310
Satyagraha, 232, 399, 421-2
School of International Studies (SIS), 331, 371
Science of politics, 3, 50, 66, 77-8, 147
Secession movements, 439
Secret service (Kautilyan), 57-61, 107
Secularism, 187, 190, 325, 328, 361, 436, 459-60
Self-rule and shared rule, 429-30
Sepoy Mutiny, 419
Sex industry, 90
Shadgunya (theory), 22, 38, 41, 104, 375
Shah Bano case, 431
Shastra, 3-4, 7, 41, 43
Shudra, 30, 32-3, 48, 85-86, 88, 93, 192
Sino-Indian war, 219, 223
Skillful diplomacy, 78

KAUTILYA'S *ARTHASHASTRA* • 547

Social capital theory, 452
Social constructivism, 347–57, 362, 373
Social hierarchy, 407, 432–3
Social science schools, 339–62
    International Relations (IR) theory in India, 344–7
    Marxism and Indian social sciences, 340–44
    positivist approach, 339–40
    Postcolonial theory, 356–62
    Social constructivism, 347–56
Social space, 258
Socially marginal, electoral mobilization of, 453
Sociology of religion (Max Weber), xxvii, 17, 23, 474
Soft power, 469–70
Sovereign freedom of state, 281
State abdication, 285
State and state capacity, 282–3
State bureaucracy, 29, 38, 57, 74, 76, 80–3, 85–6, 91, 99, 106, 117, 130, 188, 204–5, 216, 302, 401–2, 407–8, 433
State capacity, 20, 50, 79, 86, 100, 193, 205, 217, 226, 282–4, 404
State crimes, 57, 84, 406
State factor, 22, 38–9, 74–9, 85, 87–8, 95–102, 105–6, 108, 111, 117–21, 123, 402
    amatya (the minister), 80–4
    danda (coercive power), 92–5
    durga (the fortress), 87–9
    janapada (the people of the land), 84–7
    kosa (the Treasury), 89–92
    mitra (the ally in foreign policy), 95–7
State power (aggregate of seven *prakriti*), 98–103, 119
State reorganization in 1953 and 1956, 429
State's coercive power, right use of the, 49–50

State-of-the-art weapon systems, 218
Strategic autonomy, 277, 279–81, 328, 380, 462
Strategic culture, 153, 157, 249, 282, 296–305, 307–11, 313–20, 322, 324–30, 346, 349–52, 354–6, 376–7, 379–80, 387, 410, 471
    concept of, 296–303
    Kautilya's influence on, 308–24
    of India, 304–8
Structural deficit, 167
Structural functionalism, 440
Structural-functional approach, 413
Stupa, 433
Subversion, 29, 63, 66–7, 95, 109, 121, 189
Suicide terrorists, 460
Supreme Court of India, 413, 450
Supreme functionary, 402
Swamin, 74–5, 77, 101–2
Swaraj, 310
Syncretism, 409

Tax collection, 82, 130, 407
Tax rate, 90
Tax/fiscal policy, 89
Telengana movement, 456
(The) pure, 291, 398–9, 431, 435, 437–8
The Seven Military Classics, 302
Theories of statecraft, 168
Third space, 414, 416, 425
Third world, 396
Three-language formula, 431–32, 455
Tibet, 227, 279, 378
Time structures (Braudel), 159–61
Totalitarian dictatorships, 204
Traditional Authority, 27
Transfer of Power, 434, 450
Transposition concept, 19
Transposition, methodological concept of, 15
Tusnim-yuddha, 94, 131, 219
Two level games, 440

Udasina, 114, 275
UN Security Council, 222, 463
Uncritical nativism, 366
United Nations, 222, 281
United Service Institution of India (USI), 154
Unity in diversity, principle of, 455
University of Delhi (DU), 270, 322, 332–63, 367, 369–70, 378, 383, 392
Upanishads, 24, 316, 391
Upayas (cluster), 127–32, 211

Vaishyas, 32, 407
Value ideas of the epics (*Mahabharata, Ramayana*), 169–72
Varna, 30–2, 48, 130, 405–6
  Kautilya's exposition of, 48
  Weber's analysis of, 30–1

Vedas, 32, 47–49, 51, 187, 310, 316, 323, 364
Vedic-Brahmanical religion, 166
Vetting advisers and ministers, 56–7
Vigraha, 104, 108
Vijigishu, 40, 105, 111–15, 138, 311
Vivekananda International Foundation (VIF), 154

Welfare of the people, 33, 35, 41–2, 49, 76, 78–79, 122–4, 188, 284, 310, 403
Welfare policies, 205–6
Western model of parliamentary democracy, 216
World International Studies Committee (WISC), 392

Yana, 104, 109, 223
Yoga, 47